Summary of Contents

Active Server Pages

Professional
Active Server
Pages

Alex Homer
Andrew Enfield
Christian Gross
Stephen Jakab
Bruce Hartwell
Darren Gill
Brian Francis
Richard Harrison

Wrox Press Ltd.®

Professional Active Server Pages

© 1997 Wrox Press

Published by Wrox Press Ltd. 30 Lincoln Road, Olton, Birmingham, B27 6PA
Printed in USA

ISBN 1-861000-72-3

Trademark Acknowledgements

Credits

Authors
Alex Homer
Andrew Enfield
Christian Gross
Stephen Jakab
Bruce Hartwell
Darren Gill
Brian Francis
Richard Harrison

Technical Editors
Chris Ullman
Tim Briggs

Technical Reviewers
Andrew Enfield
Richard Harrison
Brian Francis

Technical Reviewers
Alex Homer
Bob Beauchemin
Luigi Ghirardi
Mark Ross
Zor Gorelov
Ron Miller

Development Editors
David Maclean
Gina Mance

Cover/Design/Layout
Andrew Guillaume
Graham Butler

Copy Edit/Index
Wrox Team

Cover photo supplied by Robert Harding: Creative Resource

About the Authors

Alex Homer

Alex Homer is a software consultant and developer, who lives and works in the idyllic rural surroundings of Derbyshire UK. His company, Stonebroom Software, specializes in office integration and Internet-related development, and produces a range of vertical application software. He has worked with Wrox Press on several projects.

Andrew Enfield

Andrew Enfield is currently finishing his computer engineering undergraduate degree at the University of Washington. He enjoys living in beautiful, green, wet, Seattle in a big house with seven roommates and a pool table. When he's not in the lab engraving circuit diagrams on his arm, he might be found reading (all kinds of things), bicycling, hiking, watching a baseball game, drinking beer, or taking a long walk in one of many parks. He recently returned from a whirlwind 2 month tour of Europe and would like to return soon, or travel to other parts of the world outside of Washington state.

Christian Gross

Christian Gross is an Internet expert who has the ability to share his technical visions with management and IT professionals. He regularly speaks at professional developers' conferences such as the Borland Developers' Conference and Client Server 95 conference. He also writes articles for technical magazines. As an IT consultant, Christian has advised companies such as National Westminster Bank (UK), NCR, Standard Life and Union Bank (Switzerland).

Stephen Jakab

Stephen Jakab has experience in writing custom solutions for corporate companies. He worked on the Consort II car fleet management system written in CA Clipper and the Bandit report writer. As a consultant and contractor, he has worked on various Visual Basic projects including Price Decision Support Systems, and he specialises in database programming. While he's not working, he enjoys many sports, reading and travelling. He's recently come back from a two month visit to America, and a holiday in Hungary.
Thanks Valérie Gonzales for your friendship and support over the years.

Bruce Hartwell

Bruce Hartwell has eight years of experience in the development, designand implementation of distributed systems. From programming Clipper DOS applications he has progressed to the development of large scale, multi-tiered, client/server systems. *To Carmen for her love.*

Darren Gill

From the humble beginnings of college Pascal, Darren quickly discovered Visual Basic to help with office automation and multimedia solutions. He has since evolved from that beginning and now builds web-based intranet applications.

Brian Francis

Brian is a Senior Developer with NCR's Human Interface Technology Center in Atlanta, Georgia. At the HITC, Brian is responsible for prototyping and developing advanced applications that apply superior human interfaces as developed at the Center. His tools of choice include Visual Basic, Visual C++, Java, and all of the Microsoft Internet products. Brian has developed and deployed Multimedia Kiosk applications, Computer-based Training applications, and other advanced user interface prototypes for the past three years.
All my love and thanks go to my wife Kristi, without whom my life would not be complete. Thank you for always being there for me, and for supporting me in the first of my writing adventures.

Richard Harrison

Richard is a Microsoft Certified Product Specialist and a senior consultant for a major global IT services company. He has recently been specialising in Microsoft Internet architectures and helping organisations to use these technologies to build mission critical Web solutions.

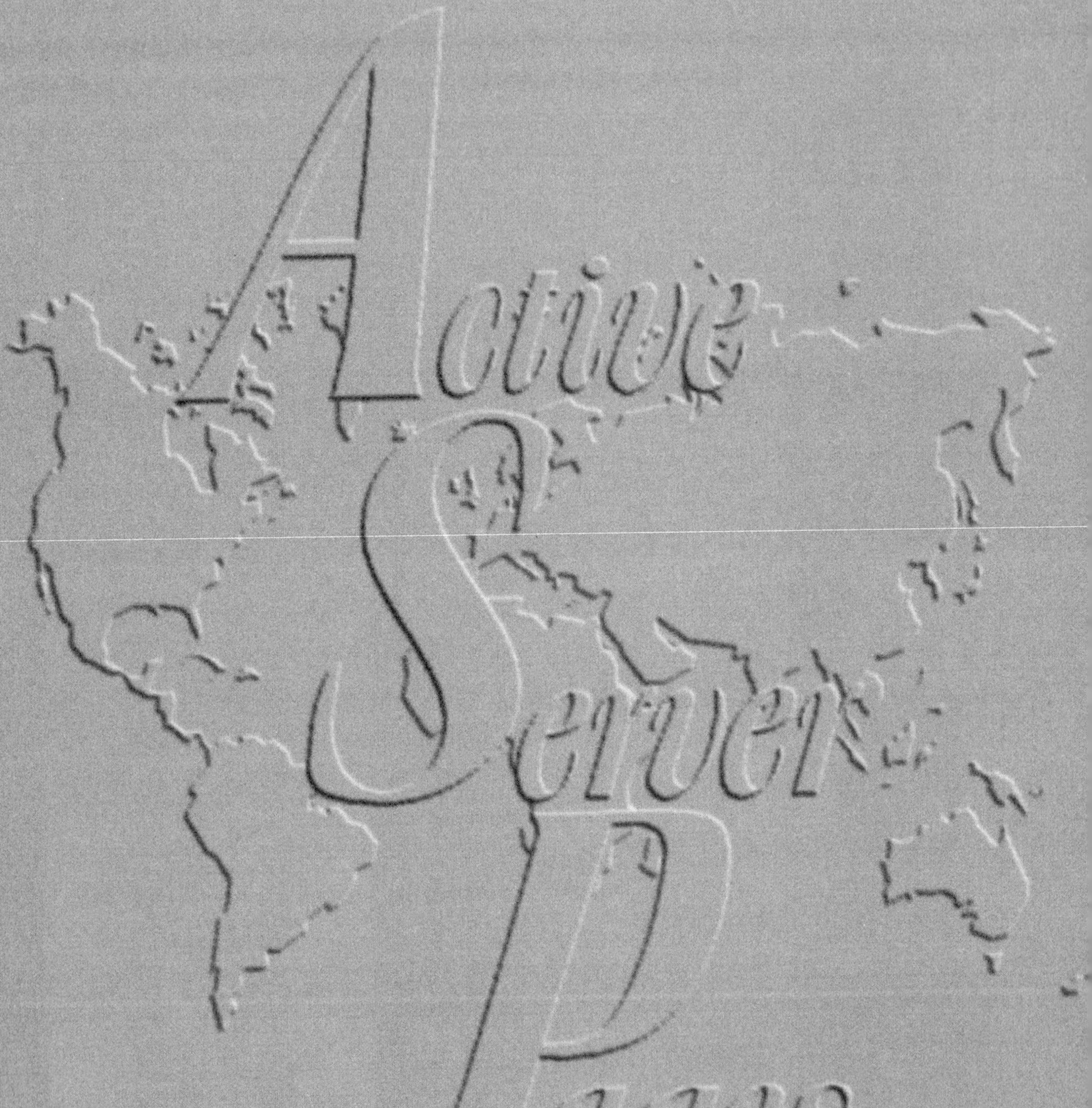
Active Server Pages

Table of Contents

Chapter 9: Implementing Server Security 309

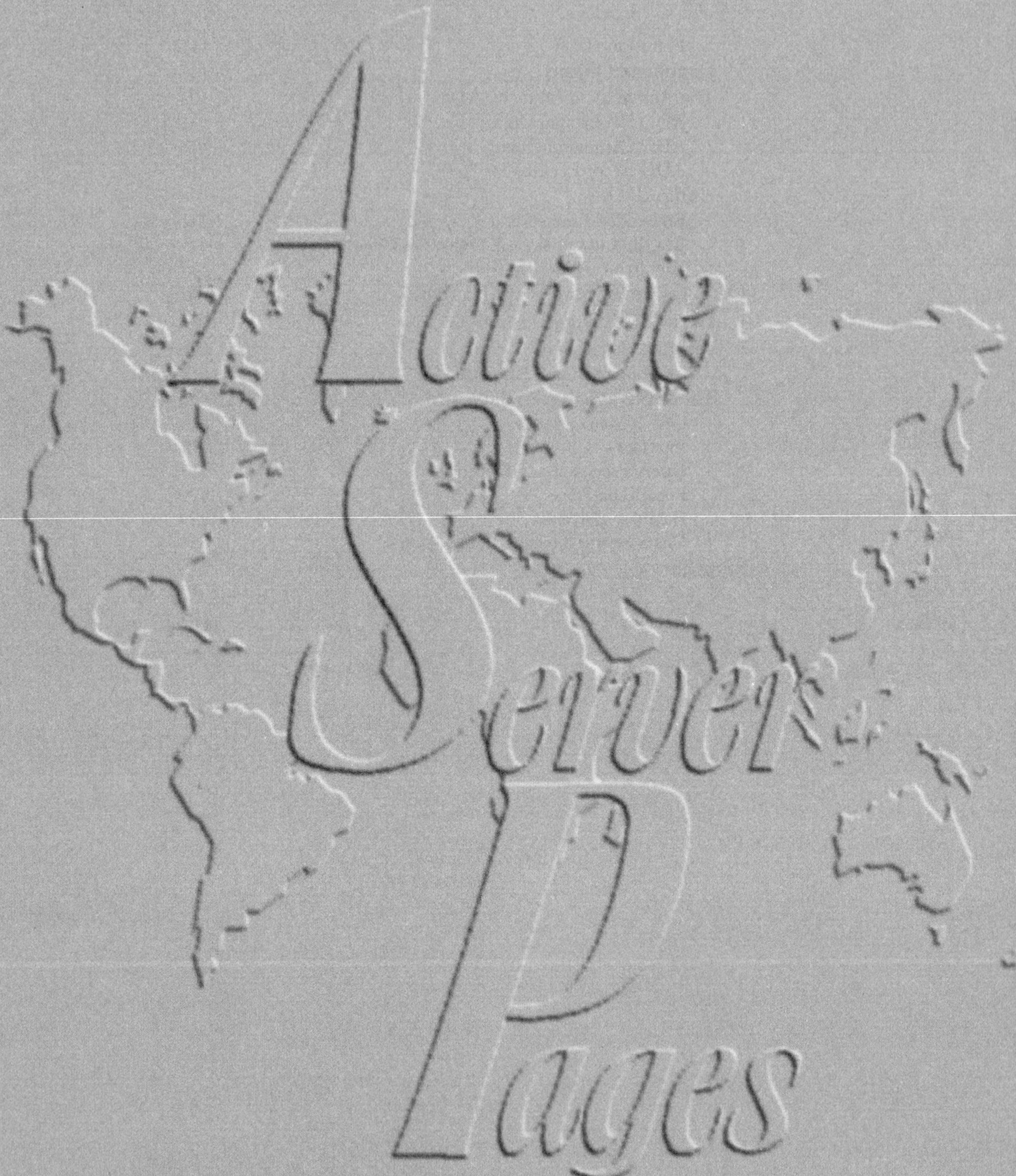
Active
Server
Pages

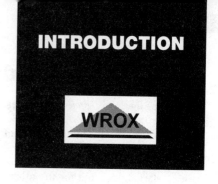
What Is This Book About?

Active Server Pages is the latest server-based technology from Microsoft, designed to create dynamic HTML pages for an Internet World Wide Web site, or corporate Intranet. It is just part of an all-encompassing concept called the **Active Server** environment, which has been developed along with Microsoft Windows NT Server, and Microsoft Internet Information Server (IIS). In this book, we start by focusing on how you can get started using Active Server Pages, showing just how easy it is to create truly dynamic pages–and how it adds a whole new dimension to Web site design. Then we'll show you how Active Server Pages fits into the grand scheme of things, and how you can use it to build really great Web sites and Intranet applications.

Who Is This Book For?

Anybody and everybody who has the responsibility of planning, building, or maintaining a Web site, on the Internet or a company Intranet, will find this book invaluable. It covers everything you need to know to move from traditional static HTML programming, to creating attractive and interactive pages that will make your site more productive–and more fun.

However, we need to assume that you already have some background knowledge. In particular, we expect that you understand the basic principles of the World Wide Web, and the underlying language **Hypertext Markup Language** (HTML) which creates the static pages we are used to seeing.

We're also going to be using existing script languages. Active Server Pages uses an extended dialect of **VBScript**, which you may already have used in the browser. It also allows us to include **JavaScript**–or, to be more precise, Microsoft's implementations of this called **JScript**. However, JScript does not offer the same range of facilities in this sphere as VBScript, so in the main we will be concentrating on this. If you have used any of the Microsoft versions of Basic, such as Visual Basic or Visual Basic for Applications (VBA) before, you'll have no problems with VBScript.

If you want to learn more about VBScript and HTML, look out for other Wrox Press publications, such as Instant VBScript and Instant HTML Reference.

What Isn't Covered In This Book

Like all of the Wrox *Professional* series of books, this is designed to give in depth information that will be useful for the developer. As Active Server Pages is a new technology, we'll be wasting no time in getting you up to speed with the new technology quickly. We won't start by telling you what the Internet is, or how you install NT Server. We assume that if you have already been through the tribulations of setting up your Web site, you won't want to read about it again. And if you are just planning your first site, or just getting started, look out for the other Wrox Press books that can get you up and working quickly.

What does this Book Cover?

This book is broken up into four self-contained sections:

In **Part 1** we start with a look behind Active Server Pages, at what the overall Active Server environment brings to the party. For example, we'll show you how to get started creating your own pages, and introduce you to the pre-built **Active Server Components** that are part of the Active Server Pages installation. Of these components, the most important by far is the **Active Database Object**, which allows easy yet powerful connections to be made to almost any database system. Publishing and collecting data on the Web are now a great deal easier than ever before.

In **Part 2**, we move on to look at **client/server programming** with Active Server Pages, and how to go about building your own Internet or Intranet based applications with it. We'll also talk about security issues, show you ways of interfacing with enterprise systems, and how easy it is to build your own server components.

In **Part 3**, we look at some **real-world scenarios**, where Active Server Pages has been used to build different kinds of applications. You can download these applications from our own Web site, and modify and use them yourself. They also demonstrate some of the other Active Server Pages programming techniques, which you are sure to find useful.

Finally, **Part 4** is the **reference section**, which contains all kinds of information that you'll find useful as you work with Active Server Pages. This is one book that you'll want to have open on your desk all the time!

What You'll Need to Use This Book?

To get the most from this book, you'll need to be running **Windows NT Server** version 4, with **Internet Information Server** version 2 or 3 installed. You'll also need the **Active Server Pages** files, which can be downloaded from Microsoft's site at `http://www.microsoft.com`. You can create and run your pages from another machine on the network connected to your server.

Active Server Pages will also run on Microsoft's **Personal Web Server** (PWS), which provides an ideal environment to develop and test your pages. However, you'll need a machine with plenty of horsepower, and at least 32MB of memory, for this to be a practical consideration.

Where You'll Find the Sample Code

Most of the **Server Components** you'll see in this book are included in the Active Server Pages package, however others are available. For example, you can download the **Microsoft Personalization System** components, and others, from: `http://www.ms-normandy.com`

Finally, if you want to try out the examples in this book, you can download them as well. We've provided them all as compresses files on our Web site. The index page can be found at:
`http://www.rapid.wrox.com/books/0723/`

If you're located in Europe or the United Kingdom then you may prefer to use our mirror site which can be found at: `http://www.rapid.wrox.co.uk/books/0723/`

Conventions

We have used a number of different styles of text and layout in the book to help differentiate between the different kinds of information. Here are examples of the styles we use and an explanation of what they mean:

> **Advice, hints, or background information comes in boxes like this.**

Important Words are in a bold type font.

- ▲ Words that appear on the screen in menus like the File or Window menu are in a similar font to what you see on screen.

- ▲ Keys that you press on the keyboard, like *Ctrl* and *Enter*, are in italics.

- ▲ Code has several fonts. If it's a word that we're talking about in the text, for example, when discussing the **For...Next** loop, it's in a bold font. If it's a block of code that you can type in as a program and run, then it's also in a gray box:

```
Private Sub cmdQuit_Click()
    End
End Sub
```

- ▲ Sometimes you'll see code in a mixture of styles, like this:

```
Private Sub cmdQuit_Click()
    End
End Sub
```

- ▲ The code with a white background is either code we've already looked at and that we don't wish to examine further, or when you're typing code in, this is code that Visual Basic automatically generates and doesn't need typing in.

These formats are designed to make sure that you know what it is you're looking at. I hope they make life easier.

Tell Us What You Think

We've worked hard on this book to make it useful. We've tried to understand what you're willing to exchange your hard-earned money for, and we've tried to make the book live up to your expectations.

Please let us know what you think about this book. Tell us what we did wrong, and what we did right. This isn't just marketing flannel: we really do huddle around the email to find out what you think. If you don't believe it, then send us a note. We'll answer, and we'll take whatever you say on board for future editions. The easiest way is to use email:

`feedback@wrox.com`

You can also find more details about Wrox Press on our web site. There, you'll find the code from our latest books, sneak previews of forthcoming titles, and information about the authors and editors. You can order Wrox titles directly from the site, or find out where your nearest local bookstore with Wrox titles is located. The address of our site is:

`http://www.wrox.com`

Customer Support

If you find a mistake, please have a look at the errata page for this book on our web site first. The full URL for the errata page is:

`http://www.wrox.com/Scripts/Errata.idc?Code=0723`

If you can't find an answer there, tell us about the problem and we'll do everything we can to answer promptly!

Just send us an email to `support@wrox.com`.

or fill in the form on our web site: `http://www.wrox.com/Contact.htm`

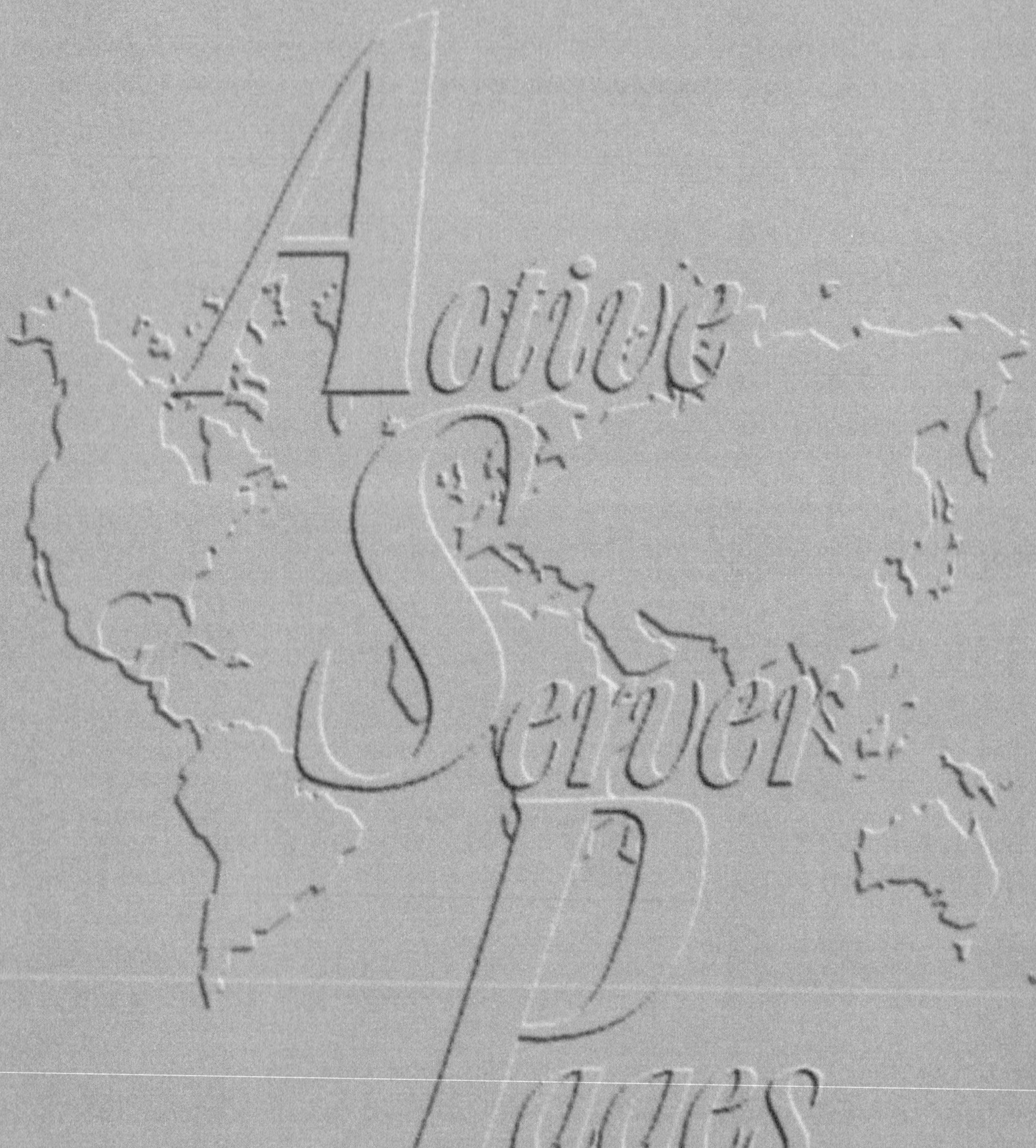
Active
Server
Pages

Understanding Active Server Pages

Welcome to the party. At least, it will seem like a party if you've been building dynamic Web sites the 'old-fashioned' way—with Perl scripts, custom applications written in normal programming languages, or even the newer technologies like the Internet Database Connector. On the Web or on Intranet sites powered by Windows NT Server operating systems, Active Sever Pages is set to sweep all of these techniques away.

In this opening part of the book, we'll start by introducing you to the background of Active Server Pages, so you'll get a feel for where they sit in the ever-changing world of Web server technology. You'll feel at home with it quickly, because once you start to use it, it just seems like the natural way to program dynamic sites—and you won't want to go back to the old ways.

The first two chapters in Part 1 are aimed at showing you the basics of writing Active Server Pages—understanding how the server allows us to gather information being sent from the visitor's browser, and how we can send information back to it. Chapter 3 describes some of the pre-built objects and components that we can use to add more power to our pages, while reducing development time.

The two final chapters in this part of the book look at how we can work with databases in Active Server Pages. First, we describe the standard methods available by using the special Active Data Object component. Then we move on to consider some of the more advanced techniques available, and see how we can work with other types of databases.

So sit back, relax, and get ready for the ride. You never know—Active Server Pages may just change your whole outlook on building dynamic Web sites!

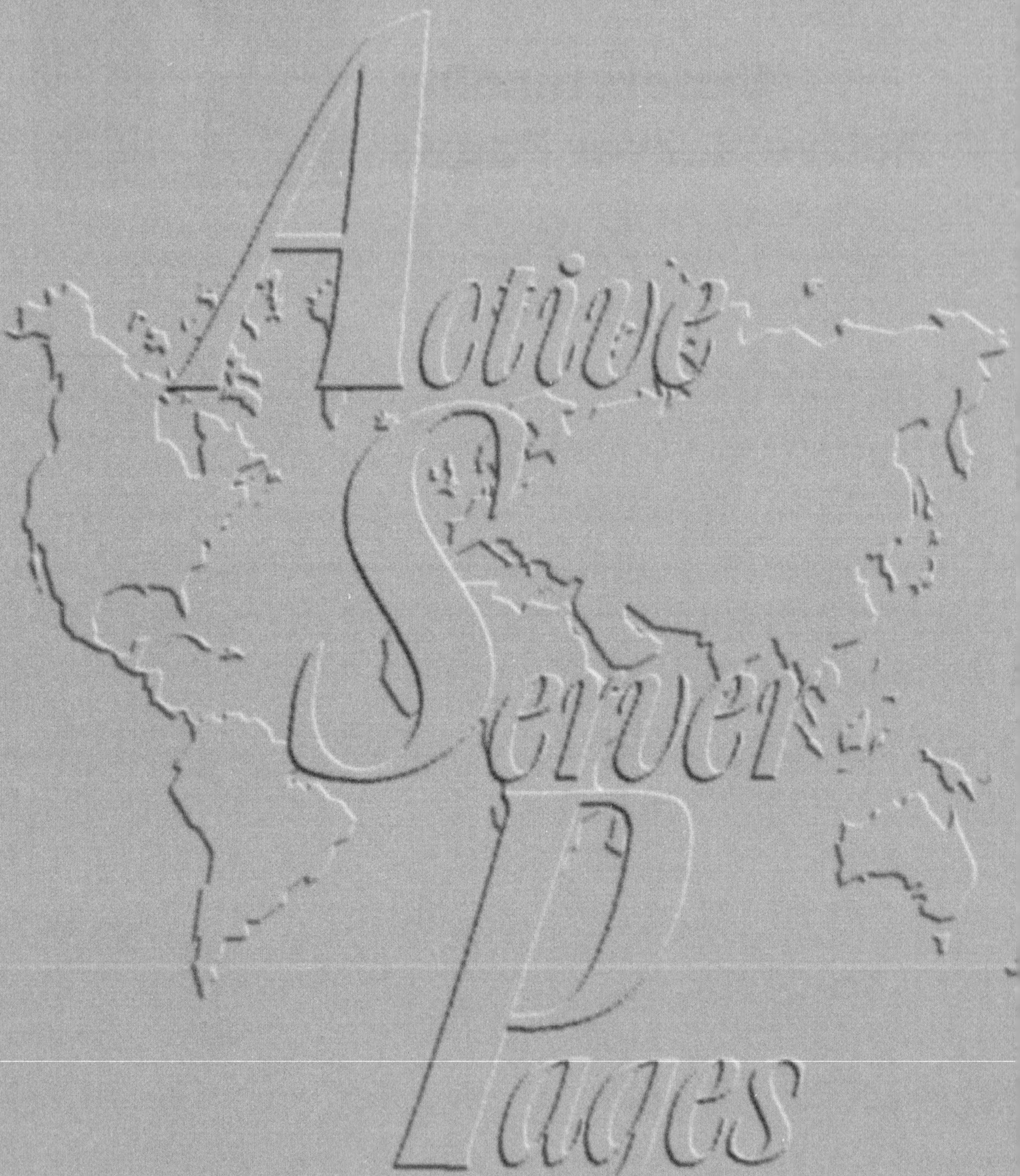
Active
Server
Pages

Introducing Active Server Pages

Active Server Pages is Microsoft's newest server-based technology for building dynamic and interactive web pages for your World Wide Web site, or your company's intranet. In this book, you'll see just how powerful it is-even though it's much easier to implement than traditional methods. All in all, it's a very compelling technology, and one that will make many of the older methods obsolete.

There are a great many different kinds of web site and intranet installation. You may be building sites that advertise your company's products or promote its services. Alternatively, it may be an information-related site where the whole purpose is to provide up-to-the-minute news of events, technologies, or achievements. You might even be using it for conferencing, reducing travel times and costs by allowing people on the other side of the world to take part in meetings directly from their desks.

If you're based in an educational or scientific establishment, you may be involved in publishing discussion documents, while commercial sites might be oriented towards carrying out surveys of some kind. With Active Server Pages, collecting information from visitors is also a prime activity, so you'll need to be able to access various databases. And on your company intranet, you could be doing any or all of these things.

In this chapter, we'll start with a look at exactly what Active Server Pages is (or *are*, if you prefer to think of the rather odd name with which Microsoft has christened it as being plural). We'll also take a look at how it's implemented conceptually within the server and client environments. Active Server Pages, when used in conjunction with a browser-based scripting language, is able to turn web browsing into a true client-server system, by distributing processing at both sides of the network connection. This is something you'll see more of later in the book.

So, to start with, in this chapter we'll be considering:

- What the Active Server Pages technology actually is, and how it works
- How we create the pages, and where and how they are executed
- Some examples of the different ways that we can use Active Server Pages
- How we can work with the HTTP connection information

The first step is to take a look at what Active Server Pages is all about....

What Are Active Server Pages?

With any new technology, the first questions you tend to ask are the obvious ones. You know the sort of thing–What is it? What can it do? Will it do what I want it to? Whose turn is it to make the coffee? Is Active Server Pages (ASP) designed for the guy who runs a web site, or the poor IT manager who's trying to make an intranet do something (but he's not sure what)? Here are a few ideas we found floating around in the developer community:

- ▲ ASP is the latest application from Microsoft that allows web site developers and service providers to make their pages even more pretty, dynamic, and interactive. It's exactly what's needed to attract the visitor's and advertiser's attention. It's particularly useful because it means they don't have to abandon their CGI apps, IDC scripts, and custom components straight away (as long as they'll run on IIS, of course). Providing it all hangs together reasonably well, it's OK.

- ▲ ASP is aimed at the people who already have a network, and need to implement an intranet over it. They've got an IBM in one corner, an ICL in the other, and 200 different makes and models of PCs to connect together. This means a separate HTTP server with links to other systems and applications, and ASP is great because it can handle all kinds of things that would be very difficult any other way. They're interested mainly in databases, and the rest of the time they're interested in database processing, with the occasional foray into data management. They couldn't care if the browser is green text on black only, as long as the whole system works by itself. To them, custom components are things you buy to restore your 1965 Ford Mustang at weekends.

- ▲ ASP is a way of building secure transaction, server-based applications and web sites, to allow people to buy easily and with no risk. It's aimed at the big boys in the game who want to build shopping centers on the Net. They need 10 million transactions a second, even though nobody is really buying very much over the Net at the moment.

- ▲ ASP is aimed at the geek community who are only interested in stuff that no one else uses, knows about, or even cares about. Once it's popular, they'll move on. However, they'll want to stretch it to the limits, and generally 'the means' is more important than 'the end'. As long as it works, it doesn't matter what it does.

- ▲ ASP isn't an application. It's a 'quick-fix' glue technology that might just manage to stick all the variably useful bits that are falling out of Microsoft together, in a way that's convincing enough to make people buy Window NT4 Server.

So, which is true? Well, the great thing is that, to a large extent, they all are. Perhaps we were a little cruel to Microsoft with the last one (sorry, guys) but in fact there's a lot of truth in this as well. The basis of Active Server Pages, and many other Microsoft technologies, is their **Internet Information Server** (IIS) software. Because this is now almost completely subsumed into the Windows NT4 Server operating system, it's about as efficient a combination as is possible. This means that other 'bits' can be dropped in as required to add extra features, while maintaining efficiency and a clean interface.

So, if you've got NT4 Server, you've got Active Server Pages (after a bit of a wait if you need to download the files off the Net, of course). It is also included in the NT Service Pack 2 CDs, if you don't fancy downloading it. Active Server Pages is basically a VBScript and JScript interpreter that's integrated with Internet Information Server, together with an interface for other custom components. Maybe it doesn't sound like much of a technology after all....

So What Can Active Server Pages Do?

Of course, a technology doesn't have to be of gargantuan proportions to be good—the software industry doesn't measure the quality of a product by the number of megabytes of disk space it consumes, although it may sometimes seem like it. As far as interactive web server technologies go, Active Server Pages is probably the hottest product ever for building multitier Internet and intranet applications. As an example, here's an application you'll be seeing more of later in the book. It's one of the case studies, which show some of the ways that you can use Active Server Pages to build powerful and dynamic web applications. In this case, it's an online error and bug reporting application.

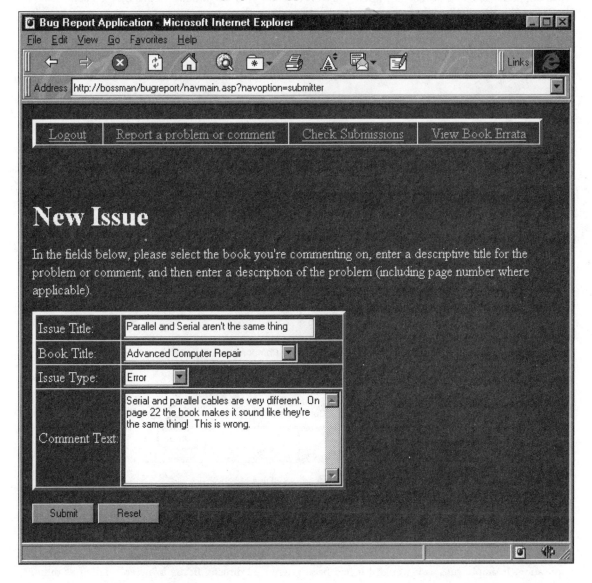

If you consider Active Server Pages as just a set of interfaces and language interpreters then understanding what it can do is a lot easier. And of all the ways of looking at Active Server Pages, probably the best at the moment is to consider it as a 'glue' technology. In this section, we'll outline the way that Active Server Pages fits in with all the other parts of your web server system, starting with an overview.

An Active Server Pages Overview

This next diagram is a stylized view of how the different parts of the system, and any existing web server-based applications, could fit together when you start to build your site around Active Server Pages. It's clear from this that ASP really is the glue that holds it all together.

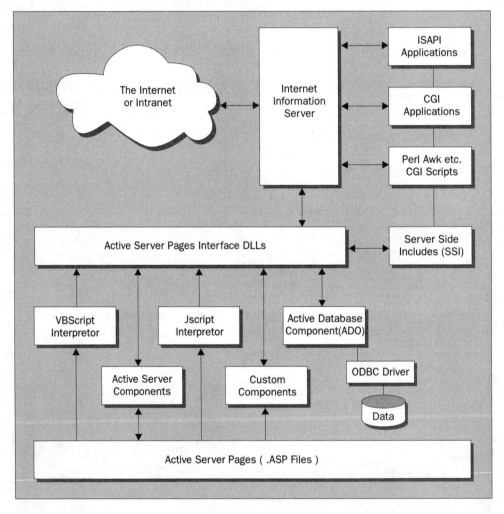

You can see how an Active Server Page can interact with almost any existing dynamic web page technology. For example, we can include instructions in an ASP file that will execute an existing CGI application. It simply runs as it would if it had been referenced directly in the browser, sending its output to the web server and, from there, out on to the network.

Using Your Existing Web Applications

Of course, there's no reason why a CGI application can't still be referenced in the usual way from the browser, as well as through a `.ASP` file–that's part of the flexibility Active Server Pages offers. If you've already created dynamic pages using existing CGI or ISAPI applications, or scripts written in the more traditional languages such as Perl, Python, and Awk, you can still use them until you get round to replacing them with a new Active Server Page. This high degree of backward compatibility is an immense advantage in a busy site, as you move to ASP.

If you're new to server-side web programming, then don't worry about the things in the top right of our diagram, i.e. **CGI**, **ISAPI**, and **CGI scripts**. Now that you've taken up with Active Server Pages, you aren't likely to need these.

> *CGI stands for **Common Gateway Interface**, and **ISAPI** refers to the **Internet Server Application Programming Interface**. Both of these interfaces are (relatively) standard across different web servers, and are methods of invoking executable logic on the web server, typically to dynamically create HTML pages. We won't be considering either of these in depth in this book.*

What Are Server-side Includes?

Server-side Includes (SSI) is a generic term used to describe the way that other elements can be inserted into a web page. For example, we can create a text file that contains some regularly used code, and then insert it into any of our web pages with an SSI instruction.

We can also use SSI to retrieve the size and last modification date of a file, define how variables and commands are displayed, print characters direct to the HTML stream sent back to the browser, and execute other programs or scripts. This last option is how we can execute our existing CGI and ISAPI programs from an ASP page.

What Are Dynamic Web Pages?

The big attraction with Active Server Pages, of course, is the ability to include script directly in the file that's referenced by the browser, and thereby create **dynamic pages**. It's important to recognize how ASP differs from existing methods such as referencing a static page, executing CGI and ISAPI applications, or running traditional scripts.

Static Web Pages

When the user enters a URL into their browser's address box, or clicks a hyperlink on another page, a request for that page is sent to the server. This is just a file on the server's disk, and the web server software starts by loading it into memory. If it's a normal **static** HTML page, the server adds a few transmission protocol requirements such as the document type, encodes it so that it can be transmitted over HTTP, and sends the whole thing to the browser. The user sees the contents as a rendered HTML page, but the source is the same as the file that is stored on the server's disk.

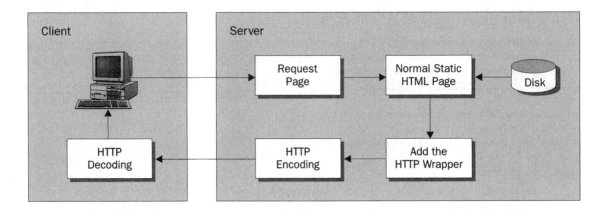

Dynamic Pages with CGI and ISAPI

To create a **dynamic** page using traditional methods, the server has to do more than just package up and send a file from disk. If the request from the browser is for a CGI or ISAPI application file, the server loads the application and executes it. The application itself creates a stream of text and HTML code, just like it was sending it to a printer. This is assembled into a temporary page on the server, packaged up for HTTP transmission, and sent to the browser. To the user, it looks just like a normal static page, because it's still just HTML code. However, the actual page is no longer just a copy of the file on the server's disk. It is created 'on the fly', and the page can be different each time the application that creates it is referenced.

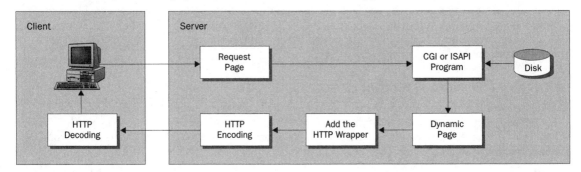

Dynamic Pages with CGI Scripts and IDC

Traditional scripting languages, and technologies such as the Internet Database Connector (IDC), create dynamic pages in a similar way. However, now there is an extra step required. First the script itself, a file of commands and statements stored as text on the server's disk, is loaded. In the case of a scripting language such as Perl or Awk, this script is then passed to an appropriate interpreter on the server. This interpreter acts on the instructions in the script, producing a stream of text and HTML code–in a similar way to a CGI or ISAPI application.

If you've used IDC or Microsoft's Index Server, you'll appreciate that there's a third step involved. These technologies use a template, which contains the main body of the page that is to be returned to the user. However, unlike a static page, it isn't sent back as it stands–it's used as a guide to what the finished page will look like. First the interpreter loads and executes the script file that's referenced by the browser. This contains instructions that the interpreter uses to build up a set of values dynamically, often from a database.

The script also contains the name of the template file to use, and the interpreter reads this file from disk and replaces special markers or placeholders within it with the values it generated by following the instructions in the script. Only then does the page exist in memory, where it is packaged up and sent back to the browser. Using a separate template like this has several advantages, particularly when it comes to modifying the text and code that creates the fixed parts of the page. Instead of having to rewrite the parts of the application or CGI script that create the output text and HTML, you just modify it directly in the template file.

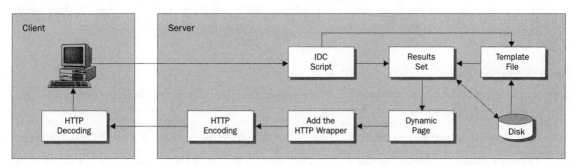

With the template methods, the browser references the script file, which in turn references the template file. Remember, however, that neither of these is actually returned to the browser. It's a combination of the two, as a dynamically created page, that the user sees.

Why Are Active Server Pages Different?

IDC, and other methods that use a template as the pattern for the returned page, offer an immediate boost in productivity. Updates to the page's text or general layout only require the template to be changed–unlike an ISAPI application where the code has to be changed, and then recompiled each time. However, they also have two disadvantages: first the script has to produce a 'result set', and only then can the template be turned into a web page; second, the template often has a fixed structure, and limits the way that the information in the 'results set' can be manipulated. In general, it's only possible to list the values that are returned, and make simple decisions on what to include in the page, based on these values.

Active Server Pages does away with the need for a separate script and template combination. The browser actually references the page that it wants, and this page is read into memory like a normal static page. However, before it's transmitted back to the browser, the server examines it for any script that it should be handling, and executes it. This script can calculate and insert values into the page, or create extra text and HTML code, as required. And, because it's working directly on the page while it's loaded, rather than creating a 'results set' first, it offers far more control over how the finished page will appear.

Once the server has finishing modifying the loaded page, it packages it up in the HTTP wrapper, and sends it off to the browser. When it arrives there, it's just text and HTML code like a normal static page. So in this case, the browser actually *does* reference the file that is returned, but it's a modified copy of this file, containing the results of executing any script in it, that the user sees.

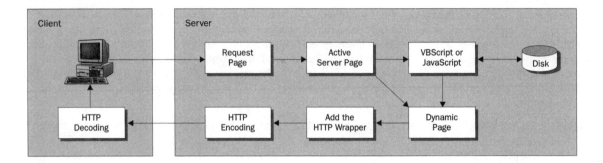

Is It Script or Code?

Notice that we've talked about two distinct kinds of **script** here. The difference isn't important, just terminology. To avoid confusion later, however, here's how we define the two words in this book.

The traditional use of the word script describes a file on the server that contains a series of instructions or statements that create the returned page. In Active Server Pages, the script refers to the individual commands and statements written in the page, which also contains text and HTML code. This terminology comes from the fact that the first uses of programming code in the browser adopted the names JavaScript and VBScript—even though the code isn't actually a script in the true sense of the word. The code we use on the server is basically just specially adapted versions of JavaScript and VBScript

VBScript and JScript on the Server

So having seen how Active Server Pages is different from traditional methods, we should look at how JavaScript (or JScript) and VBScript are used within it. We also need to consider the situation where we want to create pages that, within the client's browser, are themselves dynamic. We've so far ignored the fact that many modern browsers themselves support script languages such as VBScript and JavaScript, which means that we have to be able to include more than just text and HTML code in the pages that we return to it.

ActiveX Controls and Java Applets

There's no reason why our dynamic pages can't also contain script that is returned to the browser, as well script that is executed on the server. In fact, to create real client-server applications, we need to take advantage of this—by being able to include not only script, but also ActiveX Controls and Java applets in the returned pages. As far as the applets and controls are concerned, this isn't a problem. They are inserted into the HTML page using special tags—either `<APPLET>...</APPLET>` for Java applets, or `<OBJECT>...</OBJECT>` for ActiveX controls and other objects. As long as the Active Server Page contains the tags, these will be passed on to the browser like all the other normal HTML tags.

Where is the Script Actually Executed?

Including script is more complicated, however. It means that the server has to be able to differentiate between script that is to be executed while the dynamic page is being created, and script that is to be sent back to the browser as it is. In fact, this isn't difficult because, in general, Active Server Pages uses the `<%...%>` tags to enclose script for execution on the server, while the browser expects script to be encapsulated in the HTML `<SCRIPT>...</SCRIPT>` tags.

The only problem arises when we come to use another feature of server-side ASP scripts. Code inside <%...%> tags is executed as the page is being interpreted on the server, in the same way that code in <SCRIPT>...</SCRIPT> tags is executed on the browser as the page is loading there.

For example, if we want to write code that is executed by an event in the **browser**, we have to put it inside a subroutine or function. We could use code like this:

```
<SCRIPT LANGUAGE=VBScript>              'for execution in the browser

Sub cmdShow_onClick ()                  'executed when a button is clicked
   Call ShowTheMeaning                  'calls the ShowTheMeaning routine
End Sub

Sub ShowTheMeaning()                    'executed only when called
   MsgBox gstrMyValue, 64, gintMyValue  'displays the values
End Sub

gstrMyText = "The Meaning of Life"      'executed as the page loads
gintMyValue = 42                        'sets the variable values

</SCRIPT>
```

However, we have a problem if we want to use a subroutine or function in our ASP file. Active Server Pages won't allow us to place subroutines or functions inside the <%...%> tags: they can only be used to enclose code that is executed as the page is being interpreted. To include a subroutine or function, we have to enclose it in the normal <SCRIPT>...</SCRIPT> tags like code destined for the browser. To solve the problem of confusing the two, and to prevent the script being sent to the browser, ASP introduces a new attribute–**RUNAT**. So, to include a subroutine that is executed on the **server**, we could use:

```
<SCRIPT LANGUAGE=VBScript RUNAT=Server>     'for execution on the server

Function GetTheMeaning()
   'returns a new string, executed only when called from elsewhere in code
   GetTheMeaning = gstrMyText & " is " & gintMyValue
End Sub
</SCRIPT>

<% gstrMyText = "The Meaning of Life" %>    'executed as the page loads
<% gintMyValue = 42 %>                      'set variable values
```

This next figure demonstrates these rules in a graphical way. It shows an outline of an ASP page, with the various kinds of tags you can use and the results they produce. Later in this chapter, you'll see examples of pages that use these different types of script tags, and the **#include** Server-side Include statement.

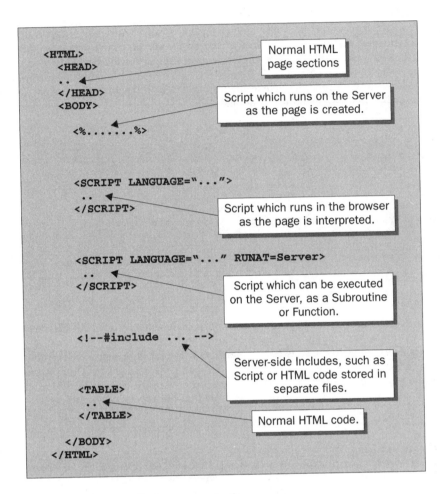

What Are Active Server Components?

So we can now create pages that contain script, and there is almost no limit to what we can achieve. The process is more like writing an application than creating an HTML page, and so it will become more and more complex as we find exciting new effects we decide to include. This has its own dangers, and—as you'll see later in the book—the pages soon grow to quite an amazing size and mixture of text, HTML, and code.

But let's be realistic here. The code we're using is only interpreted VBScript or JScript. Once we start to create really complex routines, we'll see the effects as a slowing down of server response, while it processes our code. And remember that we'll hit the same limitations using script on the server as you did when you started writing code for execution in the browser. Both VBScript and JScript are limited-functionality languages. They can't, for example, access files or other applications directly.

Using Objects on the Server

The answer to these performance limitations, server-side, is in one new statement that's available in VBScript–CreateObject. Using this, we can create instances of other objects on the server, and access their methods and events directly. Suddenly, we're freed from the limitations imposed by the scripting language. If we can't do it in script, or it's going to take too long to execute, we just use an object written in almost any other language to do the job instead.

Specially created objects, designed for use in this way, are generally referred to as **Active Server Components**. There's a range of these already available, and many more on the way. In later chapters, we'll be taking a close look at the ones that are supplied with Active Server Pages or available from Microsoft directly. However, they are all really only OLE Automation Servers (or ActiveX Controls), supplied as DLLs. If there isn't one available to do what we want, we can create our own. Again, you'll see more of this later in the book.

The Active Database Object Component

One of the main reasons for using dynamic pages in a web site, and particularly on the corporate intranet, is to provide **database access**. This may just be retrieving values to display, such as a list of the currently available products and the up-to-date prices. Alternatively, we may also want to collect information from the user, and store this back in a database.

One of the standard Server Components that is supplied with Active Server Pages is specially designed to do just that. The **Active Database Object** (ADO) can provide full access to almost any database system for which an Open Database Connectivity (ODBC) driver is available. ODBC allows you to use this single component with different database systems, simplifying the process of creating and maintaining your web site.

ADO is probably the most important of all the standard components, and is itself quite complex. We'll be devoting a couple of chapters to using it, and seeing how we can link to some of the popular database systems around today. It's also at the heart of one of the other new developments from Microsoft. The latest version of their popular office suite, Office™ 97, adds the ability to create web pages to all the applications. And, in one particular case, these are more than just simple static web pages... as you'll see next.

Active Server Pages and Microsoft Access

In later chapters, you'll see how we use the Active Database component to create dynamic pages that are linked to various kinds of database system. In one particular case, that of Microsoft Access™, the task has been partially automated by a **wizard** within Access itself. This allows us to create Active Server Pages files directly from an existing database–with almost no effort at all.

It's as easy as selecting Save As HTML from the File menu. As an example, we've used it here with a simple customer database. The database contains several tables, and we're going to be publishing the software table on our web site, so that prospective customers can see what is currently available.

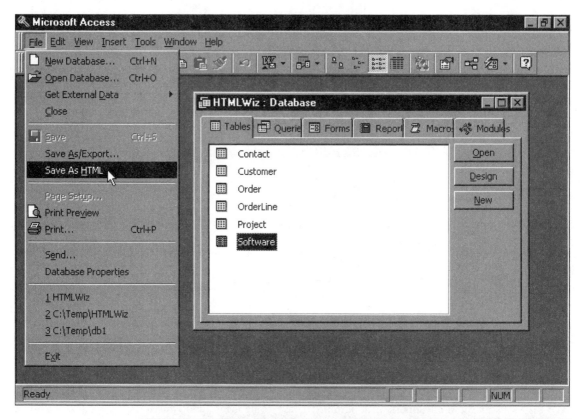

The Save As HTML command starts the Publish to the Web wizard. The first couple of dialogs that it produces explain the process, and allow us to select which tables (or other objects in the database, such as forms and queries) we want to publish. Then, the third dialog allows us to select what type of pages we want to create. We've chosen the Dynamic ASP option, to create an Active Server Pages file.

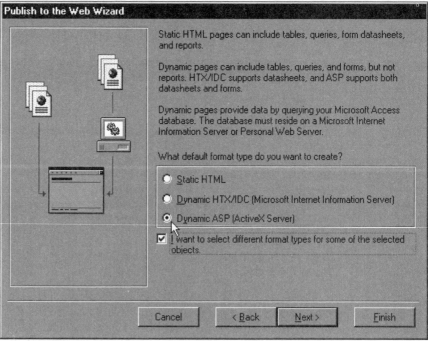

A couple more steps allow us to identify the data source name and the URL of the server, and the final location of the page. We can even get the wizard to create a 'Home Page' to link several of our dynamic pages together. In our case, we've chosen to publish just the single table, and—once the wizard has finished—we end up with a file named **Software_1.asp** on the disk. Here's what it looks like in Internet Explorer:

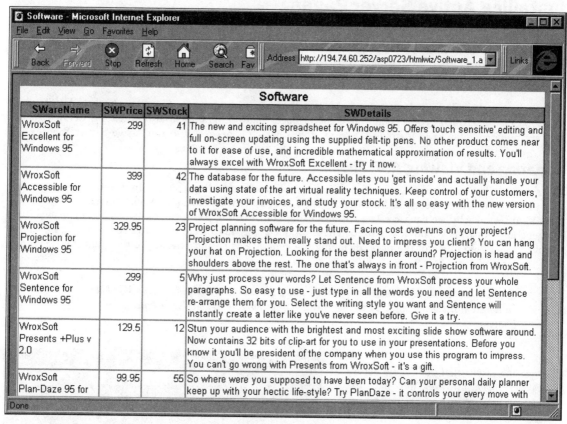

While it looks just like a static copy of the data in the table, it's actually a dynamic page that will change as the data in the underlying table changes. Each time a visitor to our site requests this page, they'll see the latest information. Of course, it would benefit from some tidying up, but it does show just what Active Server Pages can easily achieve.

You'll see a lot more about publishing information from databases later in the book, and we'll also cover the things you need to know about the various database drivers that are required, and how you go about setting up data source names, etc. For now, though, we'll get started using Active Server Pages, and see just what kinds of things it can achieve.

Getting Started with Active Server Pages

In the remainder of this chapter, we'll show you how to get started using Active Server Pages. The first step is to install the files, and set up any directories you want to use for the pages. We'll briefly show you how this is done, assuming that you're reasonably familiar with the workings of NT4 Server and Internet

Information Server. All in all, it's reasonably simple, but if you need more help you'll find the Wrox companion books, such as *Professional NT Internet Information Server Admin. (ISBN 1-861000-48-0)*, very useful.

Installing Active Server Pages

*Active Server Pages is part of Microsoft **Internet Information Server** (IIS), and thereby part of the Windows NT 4 Server operating system. However, depending on which version of NT4 and IIS you've installed, you'll probably need to install Active Server Pages as an add-in, on top of your existing installation. It also runs under **Peer Web Services** and the Windows 95 **Personal Web Server**.*

This add-in is available from Microsoft's web site at `http://www.microsoft.com`, or the FTP site at `ftp://ftp.microsoft.com`. The Active Server Pages setup program will also install any Service Packs that are required. These will upgrade IIS to version 3, which is necessary to run Active Server Pages.

Creating and Viewing ASP Files

Once the installation is complete, we can start to use Active Server Pages simply by creating the pages in a text editor, or with a tool such as Microsoft's **Visual Studio 97**, which includes **Visual InterDev**. Of course, there's no reason why we can't create ASP files using your existing web page design software, or even (as we generally do) with Windows NotePad. These products may not create the script sections, but we can use it to build the outline of the page, including the general layout and formatting, then add the ASP code later in a text editor.

> *Remember to save the file as **plain text**, with the **.asp** file extension. Some editors, like Windows NotePad, insist on adding the **.txt** file extension if you forget to set the Files of type option to All Files.*

To view the results that our Active Server Pages files create, however, they have to *executed* on the server, and not just sent to the browser like a normal HTML page. If we simply create a page on the server, and save it with the **.asp** file extension, the server will just download it to the browser when we reference it. This is the default action for any kind of file that it doesn't recognise.

If you're wondering why the browser doesn't recognise Active Server Pages files, remember that the ASP file itself isn't what we aim to send to the browser–it's the result, as plain HTML, after the page has been interpreted on the server by the Active Server Pages system. To force the server to execute our pages, we have to place them in a suitable existing directory, or set up a new virtual directory for them.

Server Script Directories

When IIS is installed, it creates a series of standard directories on the server. These include the **wwwroot** directory, which is the effective 'Home' of your web site. This is identified in HTTP as just '/'–rather like the root of a hard disk. There's also a directory named **scripts**, which is the default for any executable programs or scripts that you want to be executed when referenced, rather than being downloaded.

We can place our ASP files within the **scripts** folder if required, and they will automatically be executed when the browser references them. However, this can soon clog up with all kinds of current, half-working, and leftover pages, as we develop our dynamic web site. A far better solution is to create new directories for each separate group of pages, and for testing and developing new pages. However, these new directories have to be set up so that the ASP files are executed when referenced, rather than being downloaded.

Directory Read and Execute Permissions

By default, directories within the **wwwroot** home directory have **Read** permission set, so that the pages stored there can be downloaded to the browser. This means that any files there, such as zip files or images, will also be downloaded when referenced, and it's then up to the browser to decide what to do with them.

However, the default **scripts** directory, and any directories that IIS has created within this directory, have **Read** permission turned off so that the contents can never be returned to the browser. Trying to access this directory simply creates an error message in the browser.

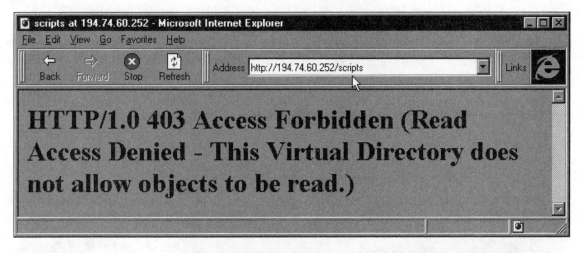

But, these directories do have the **Execute** permission set, so that referencing an executable file or a script (such as an ASP file) stored there executes it—and the results are returned to the browser as HTML. This is exactly what we want for the Active Server Pages we create. We can specify the **Read** and **Execute** permissions for a directory using the NT Internet Service Manager.

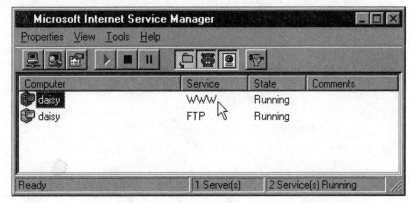

Internet Service Manager shows the currently available services provided by IIS, and double-clicking the WWW service displays its Properties dialog. In the Directories tab is a list of the virtual directories that are already set up.

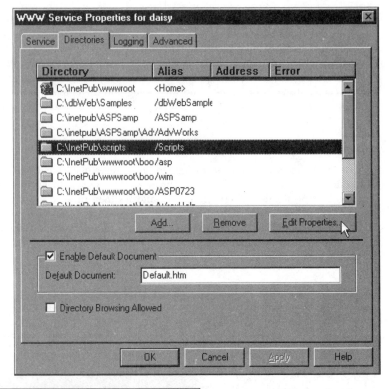

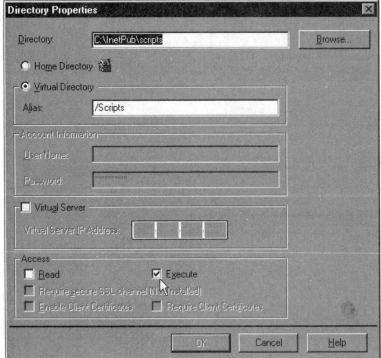

The Edit Properties button opens another dialog, where we can set the properties for just that directory. Here, you can see that the **scripts** directory is actually the physical directory **C:\InetPub\scripts** on the server, and that the virtual directory name, or **alias**, is **/Scripts**. This is why we can reference files in it just by using the server URL and the virtual directory name.

At the bottom of the dialog are the checkboxes where we set the permissions for the directory. As expected, the /Scripts directory has only Execute permission. If we turn on **both** options, however, IIS will make a decision based on the file type. Any files which have an extension that is recognised by IIS as an executable, or for which it has an interpreter available, will be executed. All other files will be downloaded to the browser instead. We can use this behaviour to our advantage....

Creating a Virtual Directory

For most of our web site developments, we'll need to provide normal HTML files, and other downloadable files, together with our ASP scripts. If we place all these in the same folder, and set both **Read** and **Execute** permission, IIS will automatically execute the scripts and download the rest. This makes it easy to develop tidy sites on the server, where all the pages for a particular section of the site are in the same physical directory on the server.

Once we create a new physical directory within the wwwroot directory, however, we have to provide a way for visitors to navigate to it. The easiest way is to set up an alias to it, so that we have a virtual directory name. This is also done using Internet Service Manager. In the Directories tab of the WWW service Properties dialog, we click the Add... button to add a new virtual directory name.

This displays the Directory Properties dialog, and we can select the directory and enter the alias we want to use. At the bottom of the dialog, remember to set the Execute permission as well as the default Read permission.

Script Security

The process of creating virtual directory aliases like this allows us to control our visitors' access to the web server. Because the wwwroot directory is the virtual root directory, visitors can't navigate below this to the real physical root of the server's disk. The default scripts directory is separate from the wwwroot directory, which keeps visitors out of this directory except where a script or application within it is directly referenced.

Be warned, however, that using a directory that contains both scripts and downloadable files can reduce the security of your site. Visitors will be able to see the scripts, if you have left the Directory Browsing Allowed option (in the main WWW Service Properties dialog) turned on.

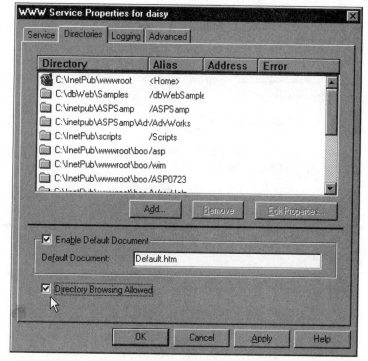

It's generally not a good idea to allow indiscriminate access to your scripts, except under controlled conditions, and so you may prefer to place your ASP files in a directory created under the default **scripts** directory, and reference them using a new alias which points to this directory. We'll be looking at this, and other web server security issues, in more detail later in the book. We'll also be building a server component that will allow you to provide directory browsing for individual directories under IIS, something that isn't normally possible.

Adding Script to our Pages

So, now that we've got somewhere to store them, let's get down and create some pages. Earlier in this chapter, we saw briefly how we can include script in an Active Server Page, using the `<%...%>` and `<SCRIPT>...</SCRIPT>` tags. In this section, we'll look at this in more detail, and create a few simple pages to show you how it works. In the next chapter, you'll see a lot more ways of using scripts.

Watching Our Language

Active Server Pages is designed to be flexible and expandable. Like most modern browsers, it can support a whole range of scripting languages either directly, or through various add-ins. The two languages that are supported automatically are **VBScript** and **JScript** (Microsoft's version of JavaScript).

Defining Which Language We Are Using

Most browsers assume a default script language of JavaScript. If we write code in VBScript, and don't tell the browser otherwise, it will pass it to its JavaScript interpreter and we'll get an error message because the syntax requirements of the two languages are different. To use VBScript in a browser, we have to add a **LANGUAGE** attribute to the `<SCRIPT>` tag, which identifies the language we are using:

```
<SCRIPT LANGUAGE=VBScript>
```

Active Server Pages, however, works in a different way. It assumes a default language of VBScript, by setting a value in the Windows registry, and we need to tell it if we are using a different one. When we use server-side `<SCRIPT>` tags, which include the **RUNAT** attribute, we can add a language attribute in the same way, like this:

```
<SCRIPT LANGUAGE=JScript RUNAT=Server>
```

> *Remember that the **RUNAT** attribute is the only way that ASP can identify which sections of script are designed to be executed on the server, and which are destined for the browser.*

The problem arises when we use normal script, which is designed to be executed on the server as the page is interpreted. Unlike script destined for the browser, ASP uses the special tags `<%...%>` (often referred to as **delimiters**) which define the sections of the page that should be executed on the server. We can't include a **LANGUAGE** attribute here as we can in the browser, and so the server will assume that the code is VBScript.

Setting the Default Language

To get round this, we can identify which language we're using in our `<%...%>` tags by specifying the **default language** for the whole page. This is done using a special statement:

```
<%@ LANGUAGE = JScript%>
```

We can specify any language for which interpreters have been installed, as long as it supports the requirements of ASP correctly. It's also possible to use scripting languages that aren't fully ASP-compliant, though we won't be going into that in this book. It's done by adding new entries to the Windows Registry, and the documentation supplied with ASP describes the process in detail.

Statements That We Cannot Use

ASP code is executed on the server, so there are some things that we can't do. There's not much point displaying a message box, for example, because the viewer could be on the other side of the world. They probably won't be very keen on popping over to your server room just to click the OK button. So, some of the standard statements and functions available in VBScript (and JScript) aren't supported in ASP. The obvious ones are, of course, **MsgBox** and **InputBox**.

Creating Our First Page

No, it isn't 'Hello World'. We're assuming that you're reasonably familiar with VBScript already, so we'll dive straight in and create something a bit more intellectually challenging. Here's an example that shows how your site can offer different greetings to each visitor. Much of the page is normal HTML code, but we need to examine the whole program to understand which parts are executed by the server and how they're laid out.

```
<HTML>
<HEAD>
<Title>Lazy Web Server</Title>
<STYLE>  {Font-Family="Arial"} </STYLE>
<BASEFONT SIZE=2>
</HEAD>
<BODY BGCOLOR=#FFFFC0>
<FONT COLOR=Teal SIZE=3><B>
The Lazy Web Server, at <% = Time %> on <% = Date %>
</B></FONT><P><B>
<% If Hour(Now) < 8 Then %>
    Don't you know what time it is? I was still in bed!
<% Else
    Randomize
    intChoice = Int(Rnd * 4)
    Select Case intChoice
      Case 0 %>
        So, where do you want me to go today?
      <% Case 1 %>
        Well, look whose back visiting us again...
      <% Case 2 %>
        Hi there, and welcome to our site.
      <% Case 3 %>
        It's raining here, what's the weather at your end like?
    <% End Select
  End If %>
</B><HR>
<CITE>&copy;1997 - <A HREF="http://www.wrox.com">Wrox Press Limited</A></CITE>
</BODY>
</HTML>
```

The first thing that you'll notice is it actually looks a lot like a normal HTML page. Here's one of the results it produces in Internet Explorer (the file is called **Random.asp**). Of course, it could be different when *you* try it–but that's the whole point!

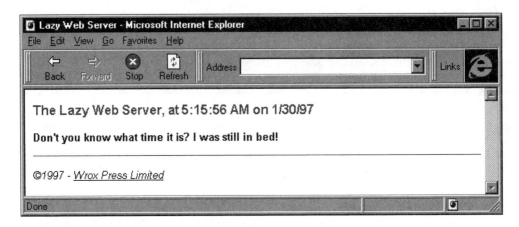

This example, together with all the other sample files for this book, is available from our web site at:
http://www.rapid.wrox.com/books/0723/

How It Works

The code in the previous example shows two of the ways that we can use VBScript in our Active Server Pages. The page heading is created with the line:

```
The Lazy Web Server, at <% = Time %> on <% = Date %>
```

This is the most basic format of VBScript. We're using an equals sign and the name of a variable or an expression inside the script delimiters to display information. When the page is interpreted on the server, the variable or expression is evaluated, and its value at that point replaces the entire **<%...%>** tag. In our example, the two expressions are actually built-in VBScript functions, which just return strings equivalent to the current time and date from the server's operating system.

The second section of code is just a little more complex. Again, it uses the **<%...%>** delimiters to identify the sections that are VBScript code. We're using a standard **If...Then...Else** construct and a nested **Select Case** construct, to determine which text to include in the returned page. The VBScript function **Now** returns the current time and date, and the **Hour** function simply retrieves the hour from this as a number between **0** and **23**.

```
<% If Hour(Now) < 8 Then %>
    Don't you know what time it is? I was still in bed!
<% Else
    Randomize
    intChoice = Int(Rnd * 4)
    Select Case intChoice
      Case 0 %>
        So, where do you want me to go today?
      <% Case 1 %>
        Well, look whose back visiting us again...
      <% Case 2 %>
        Hi there, and welcome to our site.
      <% Case 3 %>
        It's raining here, what's the weather at your end like?
```

```
    <% End Select
  End If %>
```

If it's eight o'clock in the morning or later, we seed the random number generator using the **Randomize** statement, then create a random number between **0** and **3**. We can then use this to decide which text to include in the page. Notice in this case how we've used the **<%...%>** delimiters around the code, and left the text that will form part of the page outside them.

> *Of course, the time that's shown in the page will be the time on the server's clock. It won't be correct in a different time zone.*

Building a Calendar with Active Server Pages

Well, the previous example was fairly simple. Here's a more complicated one, which creates a calendar for the current month, and highlights the current day. This exercise demonstrates how we can use a loop to place repeated sections of HTML or text in the returned page, and how we can include separate subroutines or functions in our pages.

Creating a calendar is really only awkward when it comes to deciding on what actual day the first and last of the month fall. Our calendar will be laid out from Sunday through to Saturday, so we need to place day 1 in the correct column. And we need to find out how many days there are in the current month, to know when to stop. Before we look at the code, here's how the completed page, **WhatDay.asp**, looks in Internet Explorer:

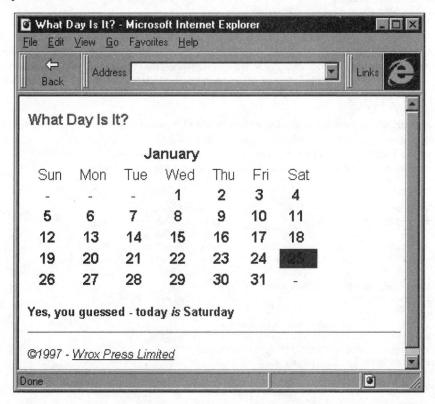

This example, together with all the other sample files for this book, is available from our web site at:
http://www.rapid.wrox.com/books/0723/

How It Works

The first part of the code is a separate `<SCRIPT>...</SCRIPT>` section, containing a function which we've written to provide the number of the last day of any month. It's pretty easy to do. We just create a series of dates using the month and year supplied in the **datTheDate** parameter, with the days from **28** to **31**. Where we have, for example, **Year = 97**, **Month = 4** and **Day = 31**, the **DateSerial** function will automatically produce the date **1st May 1997**. All we do here is see when it 'overflows' into the next month, and use the previous value.

```
<SCRIPT LANGUAGE=VBScript RUNAT=Server>
  Function GetLastDay(datTheDate)
    intMonthNum = Month(datTheDate)          'find the month number
    intYearNum = Year(datTheDate)            'and the year number
    intResult = 28                           'start from the 28th
    For intLastDay = intResult To 31         'up to the 31st
      'create the date and see if its still in the same month
      datTestDay = DateSerial(intYearNum, intMonthNum, intLastDay)
      If Month(datTestDay) = intMonthNum Then
        intResult = intLastDay
      End If
    Next
    GetLastDay = intResult                   'return the result
  End Function
</SCRIPT>
```

This function will not be executed until we call it from elsewhere in our code, because it's enclosed in `<SCRIPT>` tags rather than the normal `<%...%>` delimiters. Notice the **RUNAT** attribute, which prevents the script being sent to the browser. The placing of `<SCRIPT>` sections within the page is arbitrary—we just chose to put it at the beginning.

The code that *does* run when the page is loaded comes next. This gets the current date using the **Date()** function, and stores it in a variable named **datToday**. From this, it calculates the current year, month, and day numbers and the month name. Then, we can get the name of the current day—specifying Sunday as the first day of our week in line with the column layout we want for our calendar.

```
<%
datToday = Date()                            'today's date
intThisYear = Year(datToday)                 'the current year
intThisMonth = Month(datToday)               'the current month
intThisDay = Day(datToday)                   'the current day
strMonthName = MonthName(intThisMonth)       'the name of the current month

'now get the name of the current day
strWeekDayName = WeekDayName(WeekDay(datToday), False, vbSunday)

'find the first and last days of this month
datFirstDay = DateSerial(intThisYear, intThisMonth, 1)
intFirstWeekDay = WeekDay(datFirstDay, vbSunday)
intLastDay = GetLastDay(datToday)

intPrintDay = 1    'the value of the day number to print in the page
%>
```

Next, we get the date of the first day of the month, again using the **DateSerial** function but this time with the value **1** for the **Day** argument. Then the **WeekDay** function will tell us what day this date represents, where 1 is Sunday and 7 is Saturday because we've again used the VBScript built-in constant **vbSunday** as an argument to the function. We get the number of the last day by calling our own **GetLastDay** function with today's date, then finally set a day counter variable to **1**–the first of the month–ready to start building the calendar.

The most obvious way to format a calendar is to use HTML tables. The next section of code creates the output we see on the browser, by using VBScript to build up the rows and columns of the table inside two nested loops.

```
<TABLE>
  <TR><TH COLSPAN=7><% = strMonthName %></TH></TR>
  <TR>
    <TD>  Sun  </TD> <TD>  Mon  </TD>
    <TD>  Tue  </TD> <TD>  Wed  </TD>
    <TD>  Thu  </TD> <TD>  Fri  </TD>
    <TD>  Sat  </TD>
  </TR>
  <% For intLoopWeek = 1 To 5 %>
    <TR>
      <% For intLoopDay = 1 To 7 %>
        <% If intPrintDay = intThisDay Then %>
        <TD ALIGN=CENTER BGCOLOR=Red>
        <% Else %>
        <TD ALIGN=CENTER>
        <% End If %>
          <% If intFirstWeekDay > 1 Then %>
            -
            <% intFirstWeekDay = intFirstWeekDay - 1 %>
          <% Else %>
            <% If intPrintDay > intLastDay Then %>
              -
            <% Else %>
              <B><% = intPrintDay %></B>
            <% End If %>
            <% intPrintDay = intPrintDay + 1 %>
          <% End If %>
        </TD>
      <% Next %>
    </TR>
  <% Next %>
</TABLE>
```

The first part of the code creates the headings for the month name, and the names of the days. Then we use the statement **For intLoopWeek = 1 To 5**, with the **<TR>** and **</TR>** tags inside it, to create the five rows we'll need. Each time round this loop, we use another loop, **For intLoopDay = 1 To 7**, to create the seven columns for the days. Inside this second loop, we first check the value of **intPrintDay** to see if it's actually today, and if so we change the table cell's background color to red.

Now for the fiddly bit. Because the calendar starts at Sunday (**WeekDay = 1**), we have to skip columns until we get to the correct one if the first day of the month isn't Sunday. We do this by checking the value of **intFirstWeekDay**, which holds the **WeekDay** number of the first day. If it's greater than **1**, we print a hyphen and decrement its value. Eventually, somewhere within the first row, we'll get to a point where **intFirstWeekDay** is equal to **1**.

Then we check to see if the value of **intPrintDay** is greater that the last day of the month. If it is, we're printing hyphens again to complete the last row. If not, we can print the day number, and increment it ready for the next column. After both loops are complete, we finish up by adding the **</TABLE>** tag, and the code to print the last line using the name of the current day:

```
<B>Yes, you guessed - today <I>is</I> <% = strWeekDayName %></B>
```

Again, we're using the date from the server's clock, and it might be different in another time zone.

> *You may also have realized that our calendar will not be correct for the month of February, when the first of the month falls on a Sunday. In this case, we only really need four rows, and we'll get an extra blank row. However, it isn't likely to be a regular occurrence and adding code to prevent this would only make our example harder to understand.*

Coping with Script Errors

While it's easy enough to download a working page (as we saw in our last example), what happens if you've typed in all of the code for a page, only to find when you run it that it doesn't work? On all but the simplest pages, like us, you'll spend a lot of time looking at error messages or wondering why you've got a page that bears no resemblance to what you expected.

Runtime Errors

Active Server Pages currently provides almost no support for debugging and error checking, although this is planned for future versions. If you've used VBScript to program the browser before, you'll no doubt be familiar with this situation. All we can do is rely on the error messages that it produces when something goes wrong. For example, here's a page, **esle_err.asp**, which doesn't work in the way we might expect, followed by the result in Internet Explorer:

```
<HTML>
<HEAD>
<Title>Got An Error</Title>
<STYLE>  {Font-Family="Arial"} </STYLE>
<BASEFONT SIZE=2>
</HEAD>
<BODY BGCOLOR=#FFFFC0>
<FONT COLOR=Teal SIZE=3><B>Got An Error</B></FONT>
<P>
<CITE>This page demonstrates what happens when an error occurs.</CITE><P>
<% If MyVariable = YourVariable Then %>
    <B>We'll put this text in the page</B>
<% Esle %>                                '<- whoops - bad spelling!
    <B>We'll put something else in the page</B>
<% End If %>
</BODY>
</HTML>
```

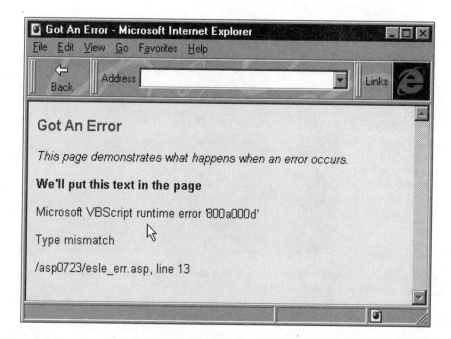

Notice how we still get part of the page returned. It's only when ASP tries to interpret the **Esle** statement that things go wrong. **Esle** isn't a known keyword, and it can't be an attempt to place a variable's value in the page because it isn't preceded by an equals sign. It's unfortunate, though, that ASP only guesses that we have a **Type Mismatch** error—not a great deal of help, but at least we do get a line number where the error was found.

ASP will return as much as it can of the page, followed by an error message. This makes sense, because it can't produce an error dialog, except on the server's screen where it wouldn't be very useful because we're likely to be working from a computer elsewhere on the network.

Compilation Errors

Sometimes, ASP can't even get that far. If the interpreter can make no sense of the page at all, it returns just an error message. Here's a program, **endif_err.asp**, which produces this kind of behavior, again followed by the result in Internet Explorer:

```
<% If MyVariable = YourVariable Then %>
    <B>We'll put this text in the page</B>
<% Else %>
    We'll put something else in the page
<% EndIf %>                              '<- should be 'End If'
```

If you're used to Visual Basic, you'll probably encounter this error regularly. VB, though, is clever enough to recognize that when we type **EndIf**, we actually mean **End If**—and it will change it for us. VBScript, unfortunately, ranks lower in the intelligence stakes. The misspelling throws the whole thing out and the interpreter just gives up, but this time it returns a rather more helpful error page.

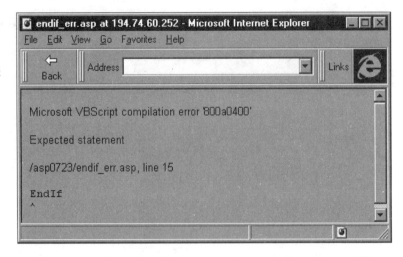

Notice here that the error is a **compilation error**, while the previous example was a **runtime error**. ASP generally makes some attempt to identify exactly where the fault lies for a compilation error, and displays the offending line. These types of error are usually the easiest to cure. In the case of the runtime error we saw previously, the problem code can be more difficult to find.

Of course, just because we don't get an error, doesn't mean that the code is correct. An error in the program logic, or a simple misspelling, can give interesting, and obviously incorrect results. Here, we've misspelled the variable name in one line of our calendar page code:

```
<% intPrintDay = intPritDay + 1 %>
```

As you can see, we get a very interesting result. The variable that holds the current day number is no longer incremented as we would expect. The question is how would we actually track down an error like this from scratch?

This page is in the samples, and is called **whatday_err.asp**

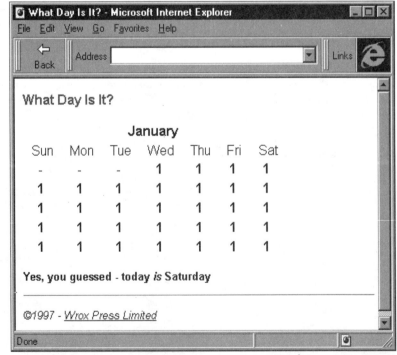

Some Tips for Finding Errors

Finding errors in code is a thankless task, though it often provides an interesting challenge. Everyone tackles debugging in a different way, but here are a few tips that you may find useful.

Add **indenting, spaces**, and **blank lines** to your code to make the layout as tidy and readable as possible. Never put more than one statement on a line, as you may be used to doing with Visual Basic. **Good layout** of the code makes understanding what's going on, and finding errors, a lot easier.

Print out the page as text, from your editor. Reading **hard copy**, where you can see the whole of the page, often seems to show errors up more readily.

Add code that places the **values of variables in the page** at various points. For example, if we were debugging our recalcitrant calendar, we could add code that showed the value of the day number after we had incremented it:

```
<% = intPrintDay %>
```

It would still be 1, because we failed to increment it properly. So it would be obvious that the fault lay in one of the lines before this. By adding several of these statements, we can narrow down the location of the fault.

An error message only tells us the point at which the error in our code actually stopped the interpreter. The **real cause of the error** could be before that. For example, we may have misspelled the name of a variable in an assignment, as in our previous calendar example. The code still runs, however, until we come to use the value in the denominator of a division. It's only at this point that the **Divide by zero** error message appears.

When coding in **JScript**, rather than VBScript, there are a couple of other issues that often cause errors. JScript keywords are case-sensitive, so incorrect capitalization will cause an error. Also, make sure that the syntax requirements for semicolons, brackets, parentheses, and single and double quotation marks are met, especially by checking for correct pairing and nesting.

If you get fed up counting the lines to find out where an error occurred, try using an editor that displays line numbers. Many proper code-editing programs can do this, and so can (for example) Microsoft Word. Just be sure that you save the files in plain text format!

When we come to use the various types of components that are available, you'll see a lot more ways in which errors can arise. We'll look in more detail at this as we go along.

Some Tips for Preventing Errors

Again, the **layout** of your code makes understanding what's going on easier, and helps to prevent obvious errors creeping into it. Consider adding **comments** to the code as well, so that you can still understand it in three months time.

Write complicated code in **separate subroutines and functions**. You can test these more easily as discreet entities and this helps you to isolate the errors. If they are generally useful routines, they can be fully tested and debugged, then stored in separate text files and dynamically included in any page as a **Server-side Include**. You'll see more of this later.

We strongly advise you to use a **variable naming convention**, like we've done in the examples. Although it doesn't stop you from assigning the wrong type of value to a variable, it is a useful reminder of the type of value it's supposed to contain. For example, `strMyValue` will hold a string, and `datToday` will hold a date. The conventions we use are listed in appendix B.

Handling Errors That You Can't Prevent

VBScript contains only one error-handling statement, `On Error Resume Next`. This is useful if we're performing some operation that may possibly fail, and cause an error. For example, we could be using values returned in a form from the browser, and applying some mathematical calculations to them. Though it's easy to test for and prevent **divide by zero errors**, it's a lot harder to prevent **overflow errors** when two large values are multiplied together.

All we do is include the `On Error Resume Next` statement in our code, and from that point the interpreter will ignore any errors that occur, and simply move on to the next line of our code. Of course, the chances of producing the correct answer at the end of all this are fairly slim, but at least we keep control of the page, and we can issue an error message of our own, or send a different page to the browser instead. VBScript maintains an object called the `Err` object, which holds a range of information about the last error that occurred. We can use this to find out if our code ran correctly, or if not, what kind of error we met.

> *This is intentionally a brief description of VBScript's error handling methods. We'll be looking in a lot more detail at the `Err` object, and how we can use it in our code, later in the book.*

Server-side Includes

We mentioned Server-side Includes (SSI) earlier in this chapter. They are a very useful way of making your site easier to manage, and providing extra information. We'll have a brief look at the possibilities here, and you'll see them used throughout this book. One important point to note is that the 'including' is done **before** the Active Server Pages interpreter gets to see the page. So it isn't possible to use code to decide **which** SSI `#include` directives we want to put into action. They will all be all included automatically.

There are five basic types of SSI we can use. We can:

- Include text files in our pages, as they are loaded
- Retrieve the size and last modification date of a file
- Define how variables and error messages are displayed
- Insert the values of HTTP variables in the page sent back to the browser
- Execute other programs or scripts, such as CGI and ISAPI applications

Only the first of these is directly applicable to Active Server Pages, but we'll cover the others briefly as well. They are normally used in a separate file, which can be referenced and loaded from an ASP file.

Including Text Files in a Page with #include

One of the most useful techniques with SSI is to insert pre-built blocks of text into a page. As an example, we created a function for our calendar page that calculated the last day of any month. We can save this as a text file called, say, `GetLastDay.txt`. Then, anytime that we want to use the function, we just add an include statement to the page, and call the function:

```
<!-- #include file="GetLastDay.txt" -->
...
intLastDayAugust = GetLastDay(datAugust)    'call our included function
...
```

The only point to watch out for is that if you want to include script from another file, this file must contain complete script sections. In other words, it has to have opening and closing `<SCRIPT>` or `<%...%>` tags—we can't place part of the code section in an included file, and the rest in the main page. However, we could include half of, say, an `If...Then` construct in the file, and the rest in the main page, as long as each part was enclosed in the `<%...%>` tags. This isn't likely to produce code that is easy to read or debug later, though!

Of course, the text we include doesn't have to be VBScript or JScript code. We can quite easily use it to include HTML or just plain text. If your site uses pages with standard footers for your copyright notice, or a standard `<STYLE>` tag to set up the text and page styles, these can equally well be stored as a separate file, and referenced with a `#include` statement.

Virtual and Physical File Addresses

The `#include` directive allows us to specify a file using either its **physical** or **virtual** path. For example, the file `MyFile.txt` could be in the directory `C:\TextFiles`. If this directory also had an alias (virtual path) of `/Texts` set up as we saw earlier in this chapter, we could then reference it using either method:

```
<!-- #include file="C:\TextFiles\MyFile.txt" -->    'physical path
<!-- #include virtual="/Texts/MyFile.txt"    -->    'virtual path
```

We can also, as you've already seen, use relative paths. If the file is in the same folder, we just use the file name. If it's in the `Projects` subdirectory, we can use:

```
<!-- #include file="Projects\MyFile.txt" -->    'physical path
```

> One point to note is that if you place the included file *outside* a virtual root directory on the server, then make changes to the file, these changes are *not* available to Active Server Pages until the web server is next restarted.

Retrieving File Details—#flastmod and #fsize

The `#flastmod` and `#fsize` directives insert the last modification date, and the size of a file respectively, into the page. For example:

```
'insert the last modification date
<!-- #flastmod file="C:\TextFiles\MyFile.txt" -->    'using physical path
<!-- #flastmod virtual="/Texts/MyFile.txt"    -->    'using virtual path

'insert the file size in KBytes
<!-- #fsize file="C:\TextFiles\MyFile.txt" -->    'using physical path
<!-- #fsize virtual="/Texts/MyFile.txt"    -->    'using virtual path
```

The same rules about relative paths apply, and the default for the values returned are as a 'long' format date (such as Friday January 24 1997), and the file size in kilobytes. Generally the **#flastmod** and **#fsize** directives will only be used in a separate file, with the **.stm** file extension. They will **not** be automatically processed in an Active Server Pages file.

Configuring Variable Formatting—#config

The **#config** directive is useful for changing the way SSI variables are formatted. For example, we can change the date/time and file size formats for the **#flastmod** and **#fsize** directives we met in the previous section. There are three possible **#config** options:

```
'change the default date/time format
<!-- #config timefmt="tokens" -->   'set format using tokens

'change the default file size format
<!-- #config sizefmt="bytes"   -->   'display as number of bytes
<!-- #config sizefmt="abbrev"  -->   'default - display as kilobytes

'change the default error message
<!-- #config errmsg="New SSI Error Message" -->
```

Using Date/Time Format Tokens

To change the way that SSI variables are formatted, with the **#config timefmt** directive, we use tokens to represent the parts of the date and time we want to include. The default is **%A %B %d %Y**, where **%A** represents the name of the day in full, **%B** is the name of the month in full, **%d** is the day number, and **%Y** is the year including the century. So we get Friday January 24 1997 for instance. However, we can change the default to (for example) 01/24/97 11:25:46 by using:

```
<!-- #config timefmt="%m/%d/%y %H:%M:%S" -->
```

Generally, the **#config** directive will only be used in a separate file, with the **.stm** file extension. It will **not** be automatically processed in an Active Server Pages file. There's a full list of **timefmt** tokens in Appendix H.

Inserting HTTP/CGI Variable Values with #echo

Active Server Pages only works if the reference to the page on the server is made through **HyperText Transfer Protocol** (HTTP). You can't load a page as though it was a file on the network, by double-clicking on it in *Explorer* or *My Computer*. This isn't a technical discussion of how HTTP works, but we will show you how we can retrieve the values that are sent from the browser, stored within the request's HTTP wrapper. In the next chapter, we'll be looking at other ways of accessing these, and how we can control (to some extent) what goes into the HTTP wrapper sent back to the browser.

We can place the value of an HTTP variable into the page using a **#echo** directive. Here's an example, **echohttp.stm**, which uses these, plus some of the directives we looked at earlier, followed by the result as it appears in the browser:

```
<HTML><STYLE> {Font-Family="Arial"} </STYLE><BASEFONT SIZE=2>
<BODY BGCOLOR=#FFFFC0>
   <FONT COLOR=Teal SIZE=3><B>SSI and HTTP/CGI Variables</B></FONT><P>
   Remote Address: <B> <!-- #echo var="REMOTE_ADDR" -->      </B><BR>
   Script Name: <B>      <!-- #echo var="SCRIPT_NAME" -->      </B><BR>
```

```
Server Software: <B> <!-- #echo var="SERVER_SOFTWARE" --> </B><BR>
Last Modified: <B>   <!-- #echo var="LAST_MODIFIED" -->   </B><P>
<!-- #config sizefmt="bytes" -->
File 'WhatDay.asp' - Size: <B>
<!-- #fsize virtual="/ASP0723/WhatDay.asp" --> bytes</B><BR>
Last Modified: <B><!-- #flastmod virtual="/ASP0723/WhatDay.asp" --></B>
</BODY>
</HTML>
```

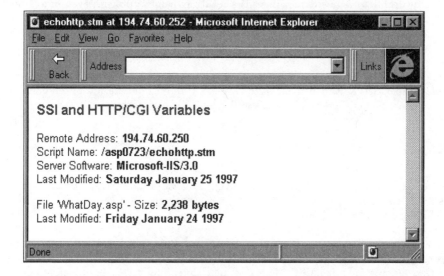

> Please note that Server-side Includes aren't supported on Windows 95 Personal
> Web Server and therefore this example will only work with Peer Web Server and
> IIS.

Generally, the `#echo` directive will only be used in a separate file, with the `.stm` file extension. It will **not** be automatically processed in an Active Server Pages file. There's a full list of HTTP variable names in Appendix H.

Executing CGI Scripts and Applications—#exec

The final SSI directive we'll consider is `#exec`. This is used to run a separate application or script. There are three possibilities:

```
<!-- #exec cmd="physical path to the application" -->
<!-- #exec cgi="/virtual path of a cgi script" -->
<!-- #exec isa="/virtual path of an ISAPI DLL" -->
```

In all three cases, we can append command line or URL parameters to the path and name of the application. For example:

```
<!-- #exec cmd="C:\Apps\MyApp.exe /sAUTO /a" -->
<!-- #exec cgi="/Scripts/FormHandler.pl" -->
<!-- #exec isa="/DLL/ProjectA/Act.dll?StartAction" -->
```

Normally, the `#exec` directive will only be used in a separate file, with the `.stm` file extension. It will **not** be automatically processed in an Active Server Pages file. To run an existing application or script, however, we can load the `.stm` file from within our ASP file.

Integrating Existing Applications

Of course, many people will be using existing techniques, such as CGI, ISAPI and IDC on their Internet and intranet sites. Switching to Active Server Pages is a relatively painless process, even in this case. Instead of using Server-side Includes, we can take advantage of a Server Component which allows our page to execute any existing scripts and applications, and then return the page they generate to the browser in the usual way.

In the case studies section of this book, in Chapter 13, you'll see an example of this technique used to integrate Microsoft Index Server with Active Server Pages. And throughout the rest of the book, we'll provide pointers to help you convert your site to use this exciting new technology.

Summary

In this chapter, we've looked at the background to Active Server Pages, and taken a broad overview of what they can do. There's a lot of ground to cover yet, but we've now got a good idea of where we'll be going through the remainder of this book.

We also looked at the basic rules for using script in our Active Server Pages, and saw some examples of dynamic pages created with VBScript. This led us on to look at ways that we can cope with errors that occur once we start to 'program our pages'. We ended the chapter with a very brief look at how Active Server Pages can interface with existing sites, and use the Server-side Include directives that are supported by Internet Information Server and Windows NT4.

The main points of this chapter are:

- Active Server Pages acts like a 'glue' technology, which can bind together various other server-based systems to help us build dynamic web sites. It runs on Internet Information Server 3 with Windows NT4 Server, or Microsoft Personal Web Server software.

- Once we've set it up, our visitors can reference the pages to execute the scripts they contain. This can produce far more interactive pages than most other technologies, while being simple to use and maintain.

- We can include script in the page that is executed on the server, as well as script that is sent to the browser for execution there. Together with ActiveX Controls and Java applets, this means that the returned pages can themselves be dynamic instead of just static HTML.

- We can also use components that execute on the server to add extra functionality to our pages. These are special ActiveX Controls, and one that's particularly useful is the Active Data Object.

- Active Server Pages' error handling and debugging features are minimal. We have no control over the way that the code is executed, and we can't 'single-step' through it as in many other languages. We have to insert the values of variables into the page, and manage with the rudimentary error pages it creates, to debug our script.

▲ We can still use traditional methods like Server-side Includes, and access them from an ASP file. One of the most useful of the SSI commands is **`#include`**, which lets us build libraries of reusable code or HTML.

Early in this chapter, we talked about how we can plug components into ASP to get more functionality from our pages. This is the main thrust of Chapter 3, but in the meantime we need to look more closely at how we can use script in our pages.

To be able to access and manipulate the various parts of the client-server process where the browser and server exchange information, we have to understand the **object model** that Active Server Pages is built around. This is the main subject of the next chapter.

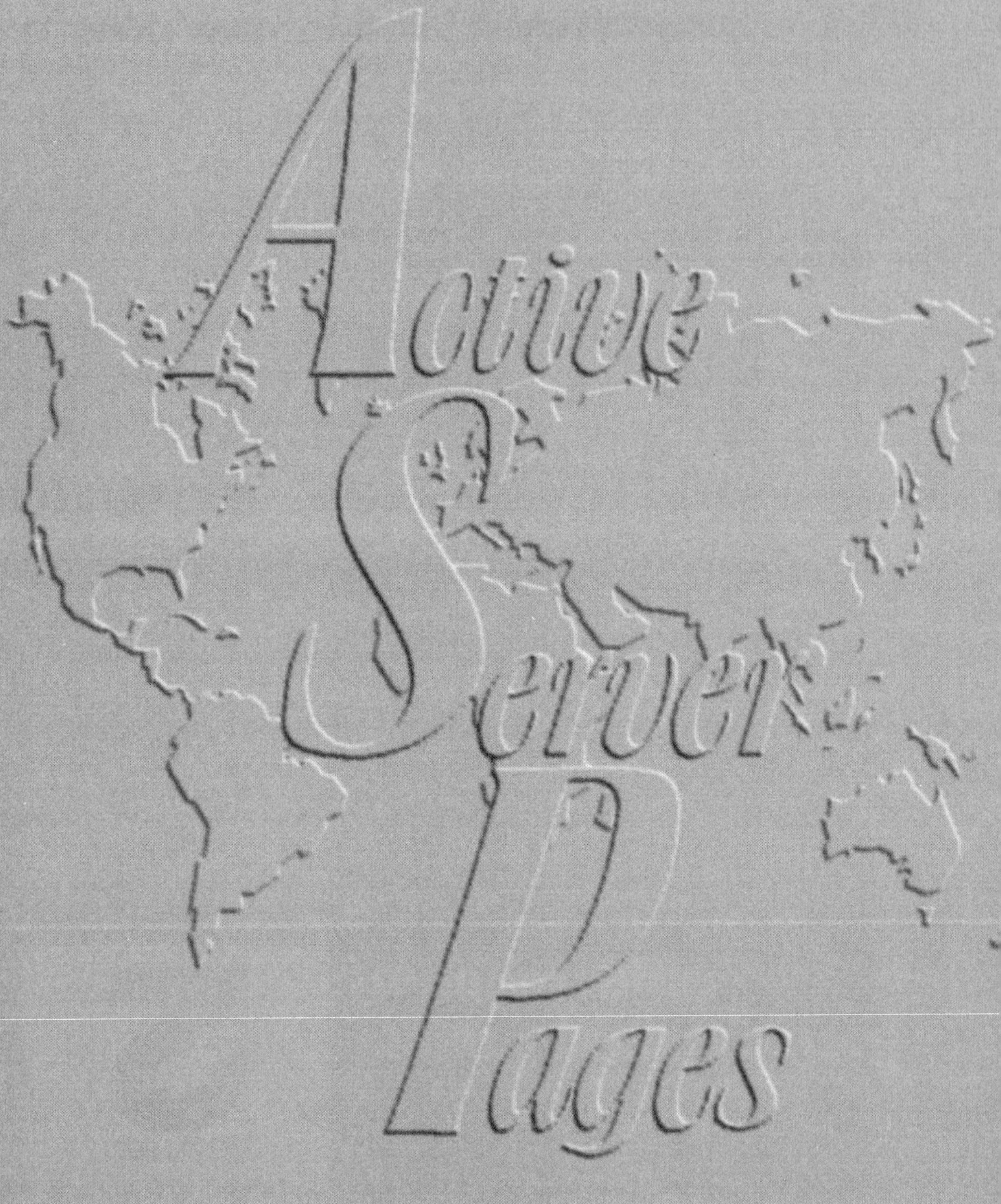
Active
Server
Pages

Active Server Pages Object Model

In the previous chapter, we looked at the background to the development of **Active Server Pages**, and Microsoft's **Active Server** technology in general. We saw how it allows us to include VBScript or JScript code in our pages, which is executed on the server. This is in contrast to being sent to the browser, which receives just normal text and HTML code. Server execution provides us with all kinds of extra facilities when we come to build interactive and dynamic web sites. For example, we don't have to worry about whether the browser can support the programming languages that we choose to use—we can tailor our pages on the fly to suit different browsers. Active Server Pages also provides us with all kinds of other possibilities for providing customized pages to our visitors, as you'll see in the coming chapters.

In fact, we've only just scratched the surface so far. The version of VBScript that's supported by Active Server Pages contains statements that aren't used in the VBScript code we send to the browser. It allows us to extend the server's capabilities, by plugging in other modules and components. In this chapter, you'll see how we can introduce server-executed components into our pages in this way, and we'll be looking at many of the available components in the next chapter.

To be able to do all these things, we have to understand how Active Server Pages interfaces with the rest of the system. The introduction of programming languages that execute in the browser moves us into the realms of client-server technologies. We must consider *where* we actually execute our code, as well as how. To tie the whole lot together, we need to be able to access both the server and the client, and of course the data that passes between them. Active Server Pages does this by implementing an **object model**, in much the same way as the browser does. This gives us a means of integrating our code with the requests sent from the browser (the client), and the web pages, or responses, sent back from the server.

In this chapter, we're going to examine that object model in detail. You'll see:

- The overall object structure that Active Server Pages provides
- How we can access and decipher the client requests
- How we provide our own responses, as customized web pages
- What we can achieve through the other parts of the object model
- How we can manipulate cookies, and use the concept of an application

But first, let's see why we need an object model at all....

Communicating with a Web Site

So far in this book, we've shown you how we can use VBScript on the server to modify the content that is seen in the web browser. This allowed us to collect and display values such as the current date and time, and the values of various HTTP variables. Using this information we could make decisions about what to send the client browser, based on known quantities—such as in the calendar where we highlight the current date.

This may well be *dynamic*, but it is not *active*. The visitor to our site is a passive receptor of information. Their only input to the information path they follow is defined by which links they click in our pages. What we need to consider now is how to actually communicate with the user using Active Server Pages.

The traditional method for a web browser to communicate with the server was through **forms**, where information was sent to a server CGI program. The program could then examine this information, and produce a new HTML document on the fly to be sent back to the requesting client.

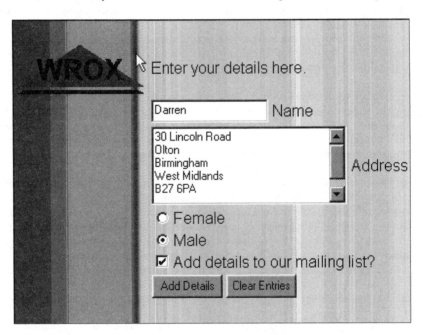

Alternatively, in some situations, the page may contain hyperlinks that include information about the user's selections. This is often seen in Web Search pages, where clicking on a link in the page sends one or more values back to the browser, by appending them to the URL to form a **query string**. This is visible in the status bar and Address box in the browser.

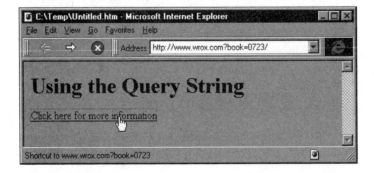

In both these cases, the Active Server Pages object model allows us to collect this information, and more, so that we can use it in our scripts.

The Active Server Pages Object Model

Although we can use script in an Active Server Page, this alone still exerts constraints on what we can actually achieve–the scripting languages we're using have very limited functionality. However, they have one star quality, which we can use to bring our web site to new levels of interactivity. They can act upon objects that are part of the Active Server Pages environment, by calling their methods and setting their properties. Active Server Pages provides a distinctive set of objects that we can manipulate using scripting languages.

The Overall Object Model Structure

There are five main built-in objects provided automatically by Active Server Pages, which we can use in the interactions between the clients' browsers and our server. These objects form a hierarchy. At the top of the pile is the **Server** object. The methods and properties of this object offer general utility functions that we can use throughout our scripts. The **Server** object represents the environment in which our pages run, and the remaining four objects fit together to make up an **Active Server application**. These objects are: **Application**, **Session**, **Request** and **Response**. The diagram below shows how these objects fit together.

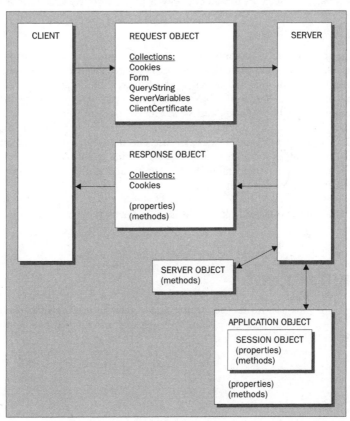

The diagram illustrates several important concepts. First of all, there can be multiple applications running on a single server. An application is simply defined as all of the script files, HTML documents, images, etc. that are stored in a single **virtual directory** or **virtual mapping**. This mapping points to a physical directory in our server's file system, where we store all the files that make up our application. We saw how to create a virtual directory, and provide an **alias** to access it with, in the previous chapter.

Applications and Sessions

Each **Application** object can have many **Sessions**. A **Session** object is maintained for each person who requests a document from the application. **Session** objects are maintained (by default) for 20 minutes after the last request for a page by that particular client. Using a time-out mechanism in a session is the only method by which an interaction can be handled. This is because the HTTP protocol over which HTML documents are transported is essentially anonymous—without sessions the server would have no indication if this was the first, second, or twenty-first page that this particular client had requested.

In more traditional client-server based computing environments, like a local area network, the client connects to the server and remains connected until all the necessary work is done (assuming, of course, that no one accidentally pulls the network plug). In our HTTP-based applications, without the **Session** object, we wouldn't know whether that visitor had just entered our site, or whether they were so entranced with it that they'd been exploring it nonstop for the last two days.

This concept of an application, and the sessions within it, is at the heart of Active Server Pages programming, and we'll be coming back to it again later in the chapter. You'll also see it come up in most other chapters, as we take advantage of the unique way it binds all our pages and visitors together.

Requests and Responses

To be able to manage the way HTTP communication methods work, Active Server Pages has to be able to capture all the information from each individual request made by the client, and store it so that it can be accessed in our application. To do this, the details of the browser, the request itself and a whole host of other information are placed in a **Request** object. Our scripts can then use the methods and properties of this object to determine what action to take, and what kind of page to return.

To get the information back to the client browser, we use another object. The **Response** object effectively stores all the information required for the server's response to the client. Again it provides methods and properties that can be used to create and modify what is returned to the client browser, and perform other tasks such as redirecting a request to another page.

Now that you have a feel for the overall plan, we'll look in detail at each of the objects and see how we can work with them.

The Request Object

The **Request** object provides us with all the information about the user's request to our site, or application. The following diagram and table show the interface provided by the **Request** object. This takes the form of five **collections** of variables.

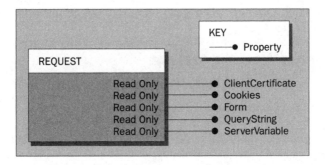

Collection	Description
QueryString collection	Values of variables in the HTTP query string.
Form collection	Values of form elements sent from the browser.
ServerVariables collection	Values of the HTTP and environment variables.
Cookies collection	Values of cookies sent from the browser.
ClientCertificate collection	Client certificate values sent from the browser.

*A **collection** is a data structure, rather like an array, which can store values by linking each one to a unique **key**. If we know the key, we can retrieve and set values in the collection. However, in many ways it is more powerful than an array, as you'll see in a while. And in case if you haven't heard the term **interface** before, it simply describes the way that the values in the object can be accessed, through that object's methods and properties.*

The Request Collections

As you can see, the **Request** object simply provides us with information that we can use in our scripts to make decisions. Each of the properties is a **collection** of values of the same type. You'll be familiar with these if you've used Visual Basic or VBA before, or even if you've only used VBScript to program in the browser. As an example, we can access the **QueryString** collection to see if there was a value sent from the browser with the key **Answer**, like this:

```
strAnswer = Request.QueryString("Answer")
```

If we wanted to add a value to, or change an existing value in a collection, we just assign a new value using the key we want to attach it to. We can't actually do this in the **Request** object, because all the values are read-only—it doesn't make sense to be able to change the information, because it's just a copy of the request made by the browser. However, you'll see how we do it with the **Response** object later in this chapter.

*So for now, we can treat these collections as just being like arrays of variable names and value pairs, although the different collections are actually implemented in subtly different ways—sometimes as a **dictionary** as well. A dictionary is actually a built-in VBScript object, which we'll be discussing in a lot more detail in the next chapter.*

Before we look at how to utilize the information in the **Request** object, we should consider just how that information gets there in the first place.

Accepting Information from the Browser

The information that is represented by the **Request** object originates from the client, and is passed to the server as part of the HTTP document request. The server decodes all this information, and makes it available to us through the **Request** object's interface.

Apart from the normal information contained in the HTTP header parts of the request, there are basically two ways that the browser can send specific information to the server. The information can come from a **<FORM>** section on the page, or be appended directly to the end of the URL as a query string.

Getting the Information We Want

As an example of the way the information can be sent to the server, the following HTML creates a page containing two text boxes and a Submit button:

```
<FORM NAME="frmDetails" ACTION="GetDetails.asp" METHOD=GET>
   Name: <INPUT TYPE=TEXT NAME="txtName">
   Age: <INPUT TYPE=TEXT NAME="txtAddress">
   <INPUT TYPE=SUBMIT>
</FORM>
```

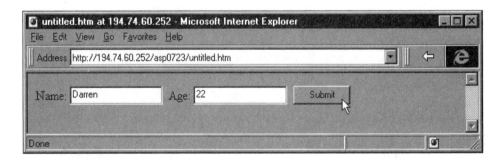

When the page is submitted, the values in the text boxes are put into a query string–together with the names of the text boxes–and appended to the URL after a question mark. The complete URL, which will be visible in the browser's Address box, looks like this:

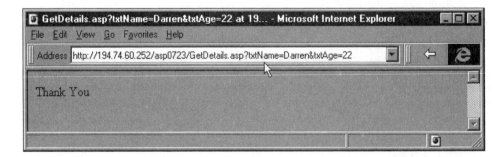

We could get the same effect by inserting an **<A>** tag in the page, and appending the query string to the URL we specify for the **HREF** attribute, like this:

```
<A HREF="GetDetails.asp?txtName=Darren&txtAge=22"> Click here </A>
```

The Limitations of GET

The query string appended to the end of the URL isn't the only way we can receive data from the browser. In fact, this often isn't the best way to send information at all. For a start, the values of the controls are clearly visible in the browser's address box, and could very easily be intercepted while the request is in transit over the Net.

The query string method also suffers another severe limitation. The amount of data that can be sent on the URL is limited to around 1000 characters, as part of the HTTP protocol specification. So if we want to collect a lot of information from a form, we're likely to find that some of it is truncated in transit. Thankfully, there's a better way....

Having the Information Posted To Us

The reason that our example form sends its data as a query string, which is appended to the URL, is because its **METHOD** attribute is set to **GET**. There is, however, a second way of sending data from the **<FORM>** section of a page to the server. Instead of using **GET** for the **METHOD** attribute, we use **POST**. This buries the information inside the HTTP header, rather than adding it to the URL as a query string:

```
<FORM NAME="frmDetails" ACTION="GetDetails.asp" METHOD=POST>
    Name: <INPUT TYPE=TEXT NAME="txtName">
    Age: <INPUT TYPE=TEXT NAME="txtAddress">
    <INPUT TYPE=SUBMIT>
</FORM>
```

When this page is submitted, the names and values of the text boxes are encoded into the request header, and there is no sign of them in the browser's **Address** box:

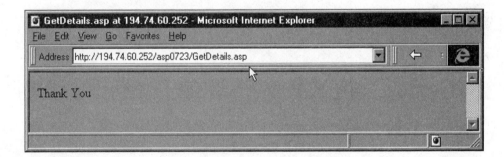

This time, the values can't be accessed from the **QueryString** collection. Instead, Active Server Pages implements a **Form** collection, which contains the information sent from forms that use the **POST** method. We'll look in detail at the **QueryString** and **Form** collections next, and it should now be obvious why we have these two separate collections.

So, don't be fooled into thinking that, just because we've received input from a **<FORM>**, that we'll actually have any values in the **Form** collection—it's all down to that **METHOD** attribute in the declaration of the form.

The QueryString Collection

To see how we can use the **QueryString** collection, let's go back to that form we saw at the beginning of the chapter. Here's the form itself, followed by the HTML code that creates it:

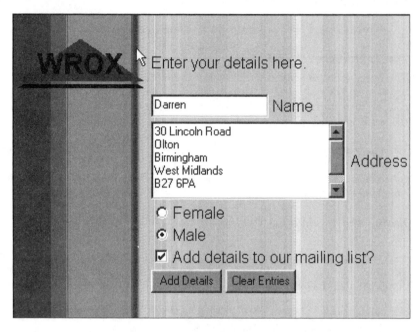

```
<FORM NAME="frmDetails" ACTION="GetDetails.asp" METHOD=GET>
  <TR>
    <TD><INPUT TYPE=TEXT NAME="txtName">Name</TD>
  </TR>
  <TR>
    <TD><TEXTAREA SIZE="25,7" NAME=txtAddress ></TEXTAREA> Address </TD>
  </TR>
  <TR>
    <TD><INPUT TYPE=RADIO NAME=optGender VALUE="Female"> Female </TD>
  </TR>
  <TR>
    <TD><INPUT TYPE=RADIO NAME=optGender VALUE="Male"> Male </TD>
  </TR>
  <TR>
    <TD><INPUT TYPE=CHECKBOX VALUE="True"> Add to our mailing list? </TD>
  </TR>
  <TR>
    <TD>
      <INPUT TYPE=SUBMIT VALUE="Add Details">
      <INPUT TYPE=RESET VALUE="Clear Entries">
    </TD>
  </TR>
  </TR>
</FORM>
```

What We Actually Get From Our Form

When this form is submitted, we'll expect to get all of the data about the contents back in the query string, appended to the URL, like this:

```
txtName=Darren&txtAddress=30+Lincoln+Road%0D%0AOlton%0D%0A
Birmingham%0D%0AWest+Midlands%0D%0AB27+6PA&optGender=Male&=True
```

Notice that every ampersand (**&**) delimits a single piece of data in the query string, and that the spaces have been translated into 'plus' signs. Other characters are referenced by their ANSI code in hexadecimal, and preceded by a **%** character–so **%0D%0A** is just the two return and line feed characters, **Chr(13)** and **Chr(10)**. This is an example of **URL-encoding**, and you'll come across it in more detail later in this and the next chapters.

So, from looking at the query string, it would seem to be a difficult task to actually find out what the values in the form were. This, as you've probably guessed, is where our **QueryString** collection comes in. We can retrieve the value of the **txtName** control just by referring to it in the **QueryString** collection:

```
strName = Request.QueryString("txtName")
```

Looping Through a Collection

Collections implement a very useful feature that makes it easy to get all the values from them. Each value is accessed using a unique string key, such as **txtName**, and–unlike an array–there is no concept of a numeric index to each value. So it's difficult to loop (or **iterate**) through all the values in a collection using the traditional **For...Next** loop with a numeric counter variable.

Instead collections support the **For...Each** construct, where we don't need to know the names of the keys up front. We just iterate through the whole collection, retrieving the keys and values as we go:

```
For Each member in collection
   ...
   ...
Next
```

So, if all we wanted to do was display the data sent from our form, we could use code like this to iterate through the **QueryString** collection:

```
<% For Each Item in Request.QueryString %>
    Control name '<% = Item %>'
    has the value '<% = Request.QueryString(Item) %>' <BR>
<% Next %>
```

However, we have a problem. Using this code with our example form above produces an error message:

```
Request object error 'ASP 0101'
Unexpected error
GetDetails.asp, line 2
The function returned I.
```

What went wrong? Well, this is a useful lesson in how debugging often needs to start somewhere other than the line in the code that produced the error. There's nothing wrong with our **For...Each** code, it's actually due to a fault in the HTML that creates the **<FORM>** which is sending us the data! Look at the query string again:

```
txtName=Darren&txtAddress=30+Lincoln+Road%0D%0AOlton%0D%0A
Birmingham%0D%0AWest+Midlands%0D%0AB27+6PA&optGender=Male&=True
```

The value after the last **&** separator has no key, only the value **True**. The reason is that we forgot to give the control on the form a name, when we created it:

```
<TD><INPUT TYPE=CHECKBOX VALUE="True"> Add to our mailing list? </TD>
```

We just need to add a **NAME** attribute to the **INPUT** tag:

```
<TD><INPUT TYPE=CHECKBOX NAME="chkAddToList" VALUE="True"> ... </TD>
```

Now, our query string is correct, and the **For...Each** loop no longer causes an error:

```
txtName=Darren&txtAddress=30+Lincoln+Road%0D%0AOlton%0D%0A
Birmingham%0D%0AWest+Midlands%0D%0AB27+6PA&optGender=Male&chkAddToList=True
```

> Control name 'txtName' has the value 'Darren'
> Control name 'txtAddress' has the value '30 Lincoln Road Olton ... etc.'
> Control name 'optGender' has the value 'Male'
> Control name 'chkAddToList' has the value 'True'

Of course, the reason we didn't get an error when we just accessed an individual value earlier, using **strName = Request.QueryString("txtName")**, is that this particular member of the collection does exist, and has a proper key name stored in the collection. It was only the checkbox that had no name, and this caused a **Null** value to appear in the key, which the **For...Each** loop simply couldn't cope with.

The Form Collection

You'll recall we discovered earlier that data is only sent to the server as a query string when the **METHOD** attribute of a form is **GET**, or when it's directly added to the URL in the **HREF** attribute of an **<A>** tag on the page. When the **METHOD** attribute of a form is **POST**, the data comes to us wrapped up in the HTTP headers instead. In this case, the **QueryString** collection is empty, and the values from the controls are placed in the **Request** object's **Form** collection.

Because it's a collection, like **QueryString**, we can retrieve values from it, and iterate through it, in the same way:

```
strName = Request.Form("txtName")
```

```
<% For Each Item in Request.Form %>
      Control name '<% = Item %>'
      has the value '<% = Request.Form(Item) %>' <BR>
<% Next %>
```

To iterate through the data like this also requires that all the form elements be named, just as with the query string.

Working with Control Groups

Often, we need to create forms that contain multiple groups of related information. In the example earlier we used two radio buttons to enable us to choose between genders. So that we could identify them, when we come to access the **Form** collection, we gave them unique values:

```
<INPUT TYPE=RADIO NAME=optGender VALUE="Female"> Female
<INPUT TYPE=RADIO NAME=optGender VALUE="Male"> Male
```

When the browser submits the page, it only includes the values of radio button and check box controls which are actually set, or selected. That's why we only received the name/value pair **optGender=Male** in the query string.

Radio buttons have the property of belonging to a **group**, where the user can only select one of them in that group. Clicking on one of the buttons clears the others in the same group. To tell the browser that they belong to a group, all we have to do is give them the same **NAME** attribute, but different **VALUE** attributes, like we did in the previous code.

> *This is very different from traditional programming languages, where we would put all the related controls into some type of container control, such as an option frame. In this case, the value of the option frame would be the index of the selected button.*

Collections Items with Multiple Values

To get several different groups of radio buttons to behave correctly on a single page, we have to give the buttons in each group the same name, but use different names for each of the groups. For example, if we wanted to produce a questionnaire like this:

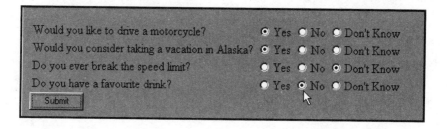

we would have to give each radio button in the row the same name, but use a different name for the other rows:

```
<TR>
  <TD>Would you like to drive a motorcycle?</TD>
  <TD>
    <INPUT TYPE=RADIO NAME="OPTQMOTORCYCLE" VALUE="Yes"> Yes
    <INPUT TYPE=RADIO NAME="OPTQMOTORCYCLE" VALUE="No"> No
    <INPUT TYPE=RADIO NAME="OPTQMOTORCYCLE" VALUE="Unknown"> Don't Know
  </TD>
</TR>
<TR>
  <TD>Would you consider taking a vacation in Alaska?</TD>
  <TD>
```

```
        <INPUT TYPE=RADIO NAME="OPTQALASKA" VALUE="Yes"> Yes
        <INPUT TYPE=RADIO NAME="OPTQALASKA" VALUE="No"> No
        <INPUT TYPE=RADIO NAME="OPTQALASKA" VALUE="Unknown"> Don't Know
     </TD>
   <TR>
     ...
     ...
   </TR>
```

Previously, we just retrieved the name and value of the form element. However, each **NAME** now has three possible values. We can do what we did earlier, and just retrieve the **VALUE** of the selected one:

```
   strMotorcycle = Request.Form("OPTQMOTORCYCLE")
```

This will give us the result **Yes** from the selections we made in the form. However, in some cases, the **Form** object may have to hold several values for one **member**–i.e. one control name. These values *are* available using their index, like an array, and we can retrieve them using:

```
   strTheValue = Request.Form("ControlName")(Index)
```

The only problem now, is figuring out how many values there are for each collection member. To do this, we use another useful property of a collection.

Using a Collection's Count Property

A collection's **Count** property returns the number of items in the collection. This lets us decide if there are multiple values, and provides a way to iterate through them. Again using our questionnaire, we can retrieve all the values from all the option groups, like this:

```
<% For Each Item in Request.Form
     If Request.Form(Item).Count Then
        For intLoop = 1 to Request.Form(Item).Count %>
           <% = Item & ": Index = " & intLoop & " Value = " _
                      & Request.Form(Item)(intLoop) %> <BR>
     <% Next
     Else %>
        <% = Request.Form(Item) %>
   <% End If
   Next %>
```

We're using a **For...Each** loop to iterate through all the members of the **Form** collection. Because some of the members (all in our example) may be named groups, we first check the **Count** property of that member. If it's not zero, i.e. **True**, we have a collection of values that we need to iterate through. If it's zero, then we just have a single value. For the questionnaire, we get a result like this:

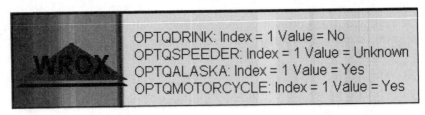

```
OPTQDRINK: Index = 1 Value = No
OPTQSPEEDER: Index = 1 Value = Unknown
OPTQALASKA: Index = 1 Value = Yes
OPTQMOTORCYCLE: Index = 1 Value = Yes
```

It may seem that we've gone to a lot of effort to retrieve little extra information. We still only receive one value for each collection member, because the user can only select one option for each question. In effect, what we're seeing here is just the first value in each collection member:

```
Request.Form("OPTQDRINK")(1)
Request.Form("OPTQSPEEDER")(1)
Request.Form("OPTQALASKA")(1)
Request.Form("OPTQMOTORCYCLE")(1)
```

Notice also, that the results don't necessarily appear in the same order as on the page in the browser.

Collections of Checkbox Values

The situation with multiple-value collection members is rather different when we have a group of **check boxes** or **text boxes** on a form. Look at this group of check boxes.

☐ ACE
☐ TWO
☐ THREE
☑ FOUR
☐ FIVE
☐ SIX
☐ SEVEN
☐ EIGHT
☐ NINE
☐ TEN
☑ JACK
☐ QUEEN
☑ KING
Submit

 These are all part of the same group–they have the same **NAME** attribute, **CHKDATA**, but different **VALUE** attributes. When we send this form to the code we used with our questionnaire, we get a multiple-value member in our **Form** collection, with these three values:

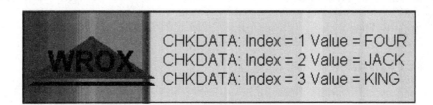

CHKDATA: Index = 1 Value = FOUR
CHKDATA: Index = 2 Value = JACK
CHKDATA: Index = 3 Value = KING

This is, of course, because three of the check boxes were ticked, and they come back with index values of 1, 2, and 3. Remember, however, that these are *not* the indexes of the original check boxes–just the indexes of the three values within the collection member.

Because of the browser's habit of selectively supplying data from a form, we can never make any assumptions about the number or order of elements in the collections. However, we can use this feature to our advantage. If we want to produce an address entry form, we could give all the individual address-line text boxes the same **NAME** attribute. Then, the only data that will appear in the **Form** collection will be from text boxes where the user actually entered some text. No more blank lines in our database's **Address** table!

Searching in All the Collections

When we've used the `Request` object's collections so far, we've always specified the collection name. In fact, this isn't actually required. If we omit the collection name, ASP will search through the collections in a pre-defined order, and return the first value it finds with a matching key. The search order is:

- ▲ `QueryString`
- ▲ `Form`
- ▲ `Cookies`
- ▲ `ClientCertificate`
- ▲ `ServerVariables`

However, this might not be what we actually want to happen. If the `QueryString` and `Cookies` collections both contain a value which has the key `ImportantValue`, and we want the cookie's value, we'll end up getting the wrong `ImportantValue`. For example:

```
strResult = Request.Cookies("ImportantValue")
```

returns the value of the cookie with the key (or name) `ImportantValue`, while:

```
strResult = Request.("ImportantValue")
```

will look in the `QueryString` and `Form` collections for a key `ImportantValue` first, and return the matching value from that collection if it finds one. It might never get as far as the `Cookies` collection.

Of course, the shorthand method ought to be faster. The actual statement is shorter, and so requires less processing by the script interpreter. However, unless the item we want is actually in the `QueryString` collection, it will probably be slower because it has to search through other collections as it goes.

Besides that, the risk of finding a value in the wrong collection means that you really ought to avoid this technique. It's one way of producing really erratic behavior in your pages, the source of which could take weeks of debugging to find!

The ServerVariables Collection

The next collection provided by the `Request` object is `ServerVariables`. Although this sounds as though it has little to do with the client request, much of the information that we've looked at with the other collections actually originates here in the server variables collection. Any HTTP header that is sent by a client browser is available in this collection, through code like this:

```
strTheValue = Request.ServerVariables("HeaderType")
```

The standard HTTP headers are automatically defined as members of the `ServerVariables` collection. For example, when form data is sent to the server, the method by which it was sent can be determined from:

```
<% = Request.ServerVariables("REQUEST_METHOD") %>
```

This will return **GET**, **POST**, **HEAD**, etc., depending on how the data was sent from the browser.

We can also use the **QUERY_STRING** header to obtain the original unadulterated query string that was passed to the server from the browser. There are a great many headers available in this collection, and some have been processed for us, and presented in collections such as **QueryString**, while others have not. We've included a list of the HTTP header types in Appendix H, so we'll just show you a few examples here.

```
User's IP Address: <% = Request.ServerVariables("REMOTE_ADDR") %>
User's Logon Account: <% = Request.ServerVariables("LOGON_USER") %>
The whole HTTP string: <% = Request.ServerVariables("ALL_HTTP") %>
```

The Cookies Collection

The **QueryString** and **Form** collections that we examined earlier are only ever available in a single browser request. Each time the user requests any file from our server, the **Request** object's collections are updated with just the information from that request. Occasionally we find that there's a need for more persistent data storage. To achieve this, the concept of cookies was introduced into the HTTP 1.1 protocol specification, and quickly adopted by Netscape in their Navigator 2.0 browser.

A **cookie** is a packet of information that is sent by the browser to the server with each request. Data items within each cookie are available in the **Cookies** collection, and it is accessed in a similar manner to the **QueryString** and **Form** collections we've just been looking at. The cookie may also be stored as a file on the client machine, which means that it can be used to store information that is available the next time the browser starts. However, unless this is done specifically by the server, the cookie will disappear when the browser is closed down.

When accessed through the **Request** object, the cookies are read-only–since the information they represent is actually held on the client browser, and not the server. We *can* change cookie information, but only by using with the **Response** object. We'll come to this shortly.

In their simplest form, we access cookies as we did form data. You can use the following code to get a listing of all the members of the **Cookies** collection:

```
<% For Each Item in Request.Cookies %>
    <% = "Cookie: " & Item & "=" &Request.Cookies(Item) %> <BR>
<% Next %>
```

And as with the **Form** collection, each member of the **Cookies** collection can hold multiple values for that cookie name. In other words, one cookie name can have many items of data stored within it. However, cookies don't have a **Count** property. Instead, each multiple value member is said to contain **keys** to the information in that member

> *This is because the* Cookies *collection is implemented in the same way as the* Dictionary *object that we'll be meeting at the beginning of the next chapter. Just bear with us for now, and it will all become clear.*

To determine if a particular cookie is a dictionary type we need to look at its **HasKeys** property:

```
blnMultiValue = Request.Cookies("myCookie").HasKeys
```

This code will set our `blnMultiValue` variable to `True` for a cookie that is a dictionary, i.e. has multiple values for this member. To use the values stored in cookie dictionaries, we have to specify the key by name, in a way similar to specifying a number for the numeric index of the `Form` collection. Again, we can iterate through the keys collection of the cookie dictionary with a `For...Each` loop. So, to display all the cookie information that is supplied by the browser we can use something like this:

```
<% 'Get all cookie data
   For Each Item in Request.Cookies
      If Request.Cookies(Item).HasKeys Then
         'use another For...Each to iterate all keys of dictionary
         For Each ItemKey in Request.Cookies(Item) %>
            Sub Item: <%= Item %> (<%= ItemKey %>)
                     = <%= Request.Cookies(Item)(ItemKey)%>
      <% Next
      Else
         'Print out the cookie string as normal %>
         <%= Item %> = <%= Request.Cookies(Item)%> <BR>
   <% End If
   Next %>
```

Notice that `Item` in the outer `For...Each` loop isn't actually an object variable. It's just a string used to reference the required object in the `Cookies` collection, so code such as:

```
If Item.HasKeys
```

would produce an error. Instead, we have to use:

```
If Request.Cookies(Item).HasKeys
```

If this is true, the inner `For...Each` loop will retrieve the values of each of the sub-keys.

A cookie can also have attributes that describe its lifetime and availability, but we'll leave this discussion to the `Response` object, where we can actually set these values using script, rather than just being able to read them

The ClientCertificate Collection

Security is currently a big issue on the Net. If you're concerned about security in your electronic transactions, then some thought and planning needs to be applied to your web site. One feature that is becoming increasingly available in browsers is access to the **secure sockets layer** (**SSL**). When a browser is using the SSL protocol, the requested URLs are prefixed by `https://` instead of the more usual `http://` protocol.

When SSL is in use, the browser sends the server **certificates** that identify the client. If we want to make use of this information in our web pages, to assure ourselves that we're sending out information to only those users who are authorized to receive it, we can use the `ClientCertificate` collection of the `Request` object. We also need to include the `cervbs.inc` file in our scripts to declare the appropriate constants used with client certificates. There are actually only two constants defined in this particular file:

```
Const ceCertPresent = 1
Const ceUnrecognizedIssuer = 2
```

We could, of course, just declare these ourselves, but it makes things clearer if we use the appropriate server-side include in our ASP files for this:

```
<!--#include file="cervbs.inc" -->
```

The `cervbs.inc` file can be found in the `ASPSamp` directory that contains the Adventure Works sample site supplied with Active Server Pages.

Accessing the information in the `ClientCertificate` collection follows a similar pattern to the one we saw with the other `Request` object collections. We reference the collection, then a `key` to the item of information we require. Two of the keys, `Subject` and `Issuer`, have sub-fields for which we can specify more specific information, although this is accessed a little differently to the way we have previously seen. The following table summarizes the available keys.

Key	Meaning
Certificate	A string containing the entire certificate content.
Flags	Flags that provide additional certificate information. The following are available: `ceCertPresent` and `ceUnrecognizedIssuer`.
Issuer	A string containing a list of sub-field values which hold information about the certificate issuer. If requested without specifying a sub-field it returns a comma-separated list such as `"C=US, O=Verisign, ..."`.
ValidFrom	A date specifying when the certificate becomes valid. This date follows scripting formats, and varies with the international settings. For example, in the U.K. it could be `31/1/97 11:59:59 PM`.
ValidUntil	A date specifying when the certificate expires.
SerialNumber	A string containing the certification serial number as ASCII representations of hexadecimal bytes separated by hyphens (-). For example, `"04-67-F3-02"`.
Subject	A string containing a list of sub-field values which hold information about the owner of the certificate. If specified without a sub-field, it returns a comma-separated list of sub-fields, in a similar way to `Issuer`.

If we intend to verify that our users are who they say they are, we first have to check for the presence (or absence) of a **certificate**. If a certificate is present, the length of the string returned when we retrieve the `Subject` key will be greater that zero:

```
<% If Len(Request.ClientCertificate("Subject")) = 0 %>
     You did not present a client certificate.
<% End if %>
```

Once we've determined the presence of a certificate, we can check various aspects of it before finally letting the client have the information they requested. For example, we may want to check the organisation that the user belongs to. In this case we refer to the `SubjectO` key. No, this isn't a spelling error! Where there's sub-field information available in the certificate, we just append the sub-field identifier character(s) to the key to get the specific information, rather than a comma-separated list. The following table lists all the sub-field identifiers we have access to.

Identifier	Meaning
C	Specifies the name of the **country** of origin.
O	Specifies the company or **organization** name.
OU	Specifies the name of the **organizational unit**.
CN	Specifies the **common name** of the user. Used with the **Subject** key.
L	Specifies a **locality**.
S	Specifies a **state** or province.
T	Specifies the **title** of the person or organization.
GN	Specifies a **given name**.
I	Specifies a set of **initials**.

One of the benefits of this level of information becomes apparent when we think about commerce on the Internet. Assuming that certification is available, we could provide the user with an accurate price for their request based on the State they are registered in—this code assumes that we have declared a constant **CALIF_SALES_TAX** for the sales tax rate in California:

```
<% If Request.ClientCertificate("SubjectS") = "CA" Then
      Cost = Cost * (1 + CALIF_SALES_TAX)
   End If %>
```

In case you're wondering just why we have had to bother with the include file, it's all to do with the **Flags** key. We can use the value of **Flags** combined logically with the constants defined by the included file to make decisions about the requesting client. For example, the following code could be used to determine whether the issuer of the certificate is known:

```
<% If Request.ClientCertificate("Flags") and ceUnrecognizedIssuer Then
        Your certificate is not form a recognized issuer.
<% End If %>
```

These simple examples of using the **ClientCertificate** collection will give you some idea of how we can add security features to our web site. In Chapter 9, we'll see a lot more details about how SSL and other security methods can be implemented using Active Server Pages.

Debugging Your Forms and Pages

The technique we've seen for displaying all the members of a collection, including the values of multiple-value collection members, is a handy way of debugging our forms or pages when we come to work with the data that they return to our server.

Microsoft have an Active Server Pages debugging script that you can download from their web site, but in effect we can easily create our own to achieve the same result. To examine all the data coming from the browser, we just need to look at the five collections maintained by the **Request** object:

```
<H3> QueryString Collection </H3>
<% For Each Item in Request.QueryString
      For intLoop = 1 to Request.QueryString(Item).Count %>
         <% = Item & " = " & Request.QueryString(Item)(intLoop) %> <BR>
   <% Next
   Next %>
<H3> Form Collection </H3>
<% For Each Item in Request.Form
      For intLoop = 1 to Request.Form(Item).Count %>
         <% = Item & " = " & Request.Form(Item)(intLoop) %> <BR>
   <% Next
   Next %>
<H3> Cookies Collection </H3>
<% For Each Item in Request.Cookies
      If Request.Cookies(Item).HasKeys Then
         For Each ItemKey in Request.Cookies(Item) %>
            Sub Item: <%= Item %> (<%= ItemKey %>)
                      = <%= Request.Cookies(Item)(ItemKey)%>
      <% Next
      Else
         <%= Item %> = <%= Request.Cookies(Item)%> <BR>
   <% End If
   Next %>
<H3> ClientCertificate Collection </H3>
<% For Each Item in Request.ClientCertificate
      For intLoop = 1 to Request.ClientCertificate(Item).Count %>
         <% = Item & " = " & Request.ClientCertificate(Item)(intLoop) %> <BR>
   <% Next
   Next %>
<H3> ServerVariables Collection </H3>
<% For Each Item in Request.ServerVariables
      For intLoop = 1 to Request.ServerVariables(Item).Count %>
         <% = Item & " = " & Request.ServerVariables(Item)(intLoop) %> <BR>
   <% Next
   Next %>
```

Here's part of the results we get when we submit the form we've been using earlier to it. If you scroll down the page you'll see it displays a huge amount of information from the **ServerVariables** collection.

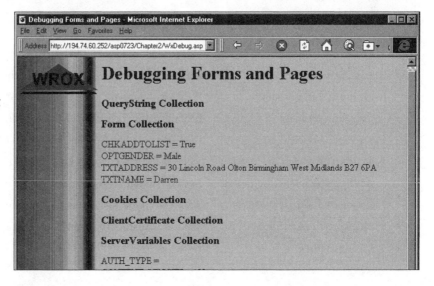

61

We've included this page in the samples that you can download from our site at
`http://www.rapid.wrox.com/books/0723`*. The form is called*`TestForm.htm`*, and
the debugging page is* `WxDebug.asp`*.*

The Response Object

We've spent half a chapter so far looking at just one of the five objects in the Active Server Pages object model, and you're probably wondering if we'll ever get to the end of it all. Don't panic, we covered a lot of groundwork there, and this means that the other objects will seem quite familiar as you meet them.

The second main object in the hierarchy is the **Response** object. Whereas the **Request** object is totally concerned with what is coming to our server from the browser, the **Response** object, not surprisingly, handles all the stuff we want to send back to it. This is what its interface looks like:

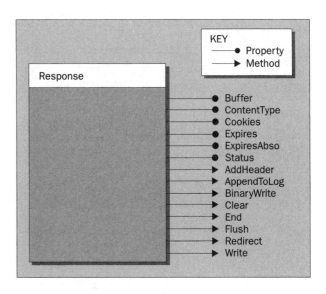

Interface Item	Description
Cookies collection	Values of all the cookies to send to the browser.
Buffer property	Indicates whether to buffer the page until complete.
ContentType property	HTTP content type (i.e. **"Text/HTML"**) for the response.
Expires property	Length of time before a page cached on a browser expires.
ExpiresAbsolute property	Date and time when a page cached on a browser expires.
Status property	Value of the HTTP status line returned by the server.
AddHeader method	Adds or changes a value in the HTML header.
AppendToLog method	Adds text to the web server log entry for this request.
BinaryWrite method	Sends text to the browser without character-set conversion.
Clear method	Erases any buffered HTML output.

Interface Item	Description
End method	Stops processing the page and returns the current result.
Flush method	Sends buffered output immediately.
Redirect method	Instructs the browser to connect to a different URL.
Write method	Writes a variable to the current page as a string.

As you can see, the **Response** object implements a single collection, **Cookies**, five properties, and eight methods. The **AppendToLog** method adds a text string to the web server's log file, if logging is enabled. The string can be up to 80 characters long, but must not contain any commas:

```
Response.AppendToLog "Adding this additional information to the log file"
```

The remaining **Response** interface elements can be divided into groups, like this:

Description	Response Items
Inserting information into a page.	**Write, BinaryWrite**
Sending cookies to the browser.	**Cookies**
Redirecting the browser.	**Redirect**
Buffering the page as it is created.	**Buffer, Flush, Clear, End**
Setting the properties of a page.	**Expires, ExpiresAbsolute, ContentType, AddHeader, Status**

Inserting Information into Pages

The most obvious requirement for the **Response** object is for it to be able to send back a page containing text, graphics and other interesting 'content' that our visitors would expect. As we've seen in earlier chapters, we can insert the values of variables or the results of calculated expressions into our returned pages using this syntax:

```
This is the value: <% = strSomeValue %>
```

Sometimes, however, this becomes unwieldy. Instead of having to bracket each block of code separately, and use the **<% = ... %>** syntax to insert values, we can take advantage of the **Response** object's **Write** method instead. All it does is insert a string into the HTML output that the browser receives. For example:

```
Response.Write("This is the value: " & strSomeValue)
```

This is just like real programming. We can construct strings in code and **Write** them to the page. It also makes our code look tidier in some situations, especially when we have a loop or conditional test to perform. The following two examples produce exactly the same output:

```
<!-- Example 1 -->
<% For intLoop = 1 to 6 %>
     The number is: <% = intLoop %> <P>
<% Next %>

<!-- Example 2 -->
<% For intLoop = 1 to 6
     strOutput = "The number is: " & intLoop & "<P>"
     Response.Write(strOutput)
   Next %>
```

As we create more complex scripts, we find that the ratio of script to HTML increases—and using the **Write** method helps make our code a lot more readable.

The **Write** method automatically converts the text to an appropriate character set when it is sent. If we need to prevent this conversion, we can use the complementary **BinaryWrite** method instead.

Sending Cookies to the Browser

Earlier on, when we looked at the **Request** object, we saw how cookies can be accessed on the server when a request is received from the browser. Cookies store information on the client machine, and are sent to the server with each request for information. The server can set or change the cookie's values, and the **Response** object provides an interface for just this purpose. Like the **Request** object, it holds a **Cookies** collection—but this time we *can* use it to write values to the cookies that are sent back with our page.

This code adds a cookie to a the client's cookie set, or changes the value of this cookie if it already exists:

```
<% Response.Cookies("IndependentCookie") = "4th of July" %>
```

All modifications to cookies with the **Response** object cause HTTP headers to be sent to the client, and so they must be done *before* any text or HTML is written to the client. An attempt to modify them in an ASP file after any text or HTML code will cause an error.

Cookie Lifetime and Availability

Cookies can also have properties relating to their lifetime and availability. If we don't set these explicitly, any information stored in them will be lost when the user shuts down their browser. If we want to store some information about the user that is still available weeks later, we can set an expiry date for it. Our **IndependentCookie** can be set to expire after the fourth of July quite simply:

```
Response.Cookies("IndepedentCookie").Expires = #7/5/1997 00:00:00#
```

We can also set various other properties of a cookie, to restrict which servers can gain access to information stored in it. In other words, we can prevent other web sites gaining access to the information we store in our cookies. These properties are the **Domain**, **Path** and **Secure**.

Setting the **Domain** to **/www.rapid.wrox.com/** would mean that only pages existing on that particular network would receive the cookie from the browser. We can also be more specific by setting the path to, say, **/Books0723**. The final attribute, **Secure**, indicates that the cookie should only be transmitted to the server over a Secure Sockets Layer connection.

```
Response.Cookies("IndepedentCookie").Expires = #7/5/1997#
Response.Cookies("IndepedentCookie").Domain = "/www.rapid.wrox.com/"
Response.Cookies("IndepedentCookie").Path = "/Books0723"
Response.Cookies("IndepedentCookie").Secure = True
```

Multiple Value Cookies

If we needed to produce a cookie dictionary, where a cookie has several values, we just have to specify a key along with the cookie name. As an example, we can create a **CleaningNeeds** cookie dictionary like this:

```
<% Response.Cookies("CleaningNeeds")("item1") = "Soap"
   Response.Cookies("CleaningNeeds")("item2") = "Water"
   etc.
   ...  %>
```

When dealing with cookies, we have to take some care that we don't overwrite existing information. Whenever we set a cookie value, any previous information is lost–there are no warnings that a cookie dictionary is about to be replaced by a single value, for example. So if we made a mistake in the code above, and wrote the second line as:

```
Response.Cookies("CleaningNeeds") = "Water"
```

we would replace the entire dictionary of values with a single value **Water**. To prevent errors, it's wise to check the **HasKeys** property of that cookie, like we did with the **Request** object, to determine whether we're dealing with a dictionary of several values or a single value.

Why Use Cookies?

Of course, one question remains with cookies. Why use them at all? We could store the same information in a database, or file of some other type, on the server's disk. In fact, it would be more flexible using a database, since it can handle data other than text.

However, there will always be an overhead associated with accessing an external data source on the server, as we'll see later in this book. Using a cookie is a very fast and convenient way of storing small amounts of information. There are limits of course–we shouldn't store more than twenty cookies for any one domain–but with a little thought this resource can be put to great use in our web sites.

Redirecting the Browser

A particularly useful method of the **Response** object is **Redirect**. This can be used to refer users to alternative web pages. When they load a page that specifies a redirection, their browser loads the new page, which we specify in the **Redirect** method, immediately.

Consider a multinational corporation, *BigCorps*, which has web servers based in France, Australia, and the United States. The corporation runs a global Internet marketing campaign, where a single URL is plastered over hundreds of advertisements on sites all over the world. So when a potential customer clicks on an advertisement, we could be sending the response to anywhere around the globe. What we want to do is automatically redirect them to our nearest server, optimizing the use of resources both on our servers, and the Net as a whole.

Redirection Headers

The first thing to note about redirection: it's bound up with the HTTP protocol. When the client makes an HTTP **GET** request, they expect to get back headers informing the browser what is actually coming from the server. One of the things that they can receive is a **redirection header**, which tells the browser to go and get the information elsewhere. If we use this header, we can't also send other headers. What this essentially means is that, like the **Cookies** collection, our Active Server Page must carry out the task before we supply any other headers, i.e. any text or HTML for a page.

The following code will allow **BigCorps** to redirect their visitors to the nearest server. All it does is take a look at the **REMOTE_HOST** HTTP variable, using the **Request** object's **ServerVariables** collection. This provides the visitor's text URL, and an examination of the final two characters will reveal a country code if they are outside the United States:

```
<% 'Determine where in the world client originates and redirect
   Dim strRemHost   'The human readable address of the client computer
   Dim strCountryCode
   strRemHost = Request.ServerVariables("REMOTE_HOST")
   strCountryCode = UCase(Right(strRemHost, 2)) ' CCITT country code
   Select Case strCountryCode
      Case "AU", "JP": 'Australia and Japan
        Response.Redirect("http://BigCorps.co.au/MirrorSite/MyApp.asp")
      Case "FR", "DE", "IT", "UK", "IL": 'Some Europeans
        Response.Redirect("http://BigCorps.co.fr/MirrorSite/MyApp.asp")
      Case Else:  'The rest of the world
        Response.Redirect("http://BigCorps.com/MirrorSite/MyApp.asp")
   End Select %>
```

Buffering the Page

Another useful feature that we can take advantage of with the **Response** object is **buffering**. Buffering allows us an extra degree of control over *when* a client receives information, as well as *what* they receive. The **Buffer** property can be set **True** to indicate to the server that all of a page's script must be executed before any data is sent back to the requesting client. When it is **False**, the default, the server streams the page to the client as it is created.

Setting the **Buffer** property alone gives us no advantage. However, by setting it to **True**, we then have access to the auxiliary methods of **Clear**, **Flush** and **End**—attempting to use these methods when the **Buffer** property is **False** gives an error.

Now the page is created as before, but held on the server until we issue a **Flush** or **End** command in our code. This means we get to select which parts of the page are sent while it's being created. It also means that we can change our mind halfway through, and issue a **Clear** command that empties the buffer without sending the page to the client.

To use buffering, we need to set the **Buffer** property before the opening **<HTML>** tag in our source ASP files:

```
<%@ LANGUAGE="VBScript" %>
<% Response.Buffer = True %>
<HTML>
```

Why Use Buffering?

Here's a couple of examples of when buffering might be useful. In our first example, imagine there's a quiz, where the questions and answers are stored in a text file or database on the server's disk. Accessing the file each time can produce a sluggish response. To make the application appear faster we can use buffering to send parts of the results early.

For example, our page may have to do three things–display the score so far, display the next question, and display a list of answers to choose from. Stages two and three will require the access to the file, and can be expected to take longer than stage one. So we could send just the results of stage one early, by including a `Flush` command to send the current contents of the output buffer to the client browser:

```
<% 'Display current score
   ...
   Response.Flush
   'Continue with stage 2
   ... %>
```

We would then do a similar `Flush` at the end of stage two. Stage three would not require a call to the `Flush` method, since when we reach the end of the page the remaining contents of the buffer are sent automatically.

Trapping Errors by Buffering

A second possible use of buffering is the potential to handle data access or other errors in our pages. In the script that accesses the database to retrieve the question information, we can check for errors and modify the output of the page as appropriate. For example:

```
<%  ... 'If an error has occurred
Response.Clear 'Clear the current buffered output without sending it
Response.Write("<H1> There has been an error please try again </H1>")
Response.End  'Stop processing the page and send the new buffer contents
 ...  %>
```

Buffering can also be utilized in our general quest for dynamic content. For instance, if some large report were being created from a database or other external source, we may want to `Flush` the contents to the browser at regular intervals. That way the client can at least start to digest the information, while our script continues to produce the rest.

Setting the Page's Properties

Each page we send to the client's browser has a set of properties, which we can specify values for in our scripts. In most cases, there's no real need to do this, but it does come in handy now and then. For example, we've seen how we can redirect a browser to a different page, by sending a redirection header. There are a lot of other kinds of headers that we can specify, and change the default values of.

Headers and Status

The `Response` object gives us access to the **headers** that are sent as part of the HTTP stream that makes up the page on the client's browser. They are used to determine how the browser should translate the information that follows in the main body of the page. Each header has a unique number; for example, our `Redirect` method sent a header of value `303` to the browser. The value of the header is also known as the **status code**, and is available through the `Status` property of the `Response` object.

There are too many different headers and status codes to discuss individually here. A full list can be obtained from the World Wide Web Consortium's site at: `http://www.w3.org/pub/WWW/Protocols/rfc2068/rfc2068.txt`.

However, you'll have seen many of them before, no doubt **404** (*Document not found*) will at least be familiar. All codes consist of three digits and a phrase explaining the status. For a normal document response this will be **200 OK** . The first digit of the code represents the type of response:

First Digit	Type of response
1	Information
2	Success
3	Redirection
4	Client Error
5	Server Error

Creating Headers

We can add our own header information using the Response object's **AddHeader** method, supplying two string parameters, one for the **name** of the header and one for its **contents**. As an example, we can instruct the client to modify the contents of its cookies using the **Set-Cookie** header. This code produces a cookie dictionary containing the same **CleaningNeeds** items we previously used in the **Cookies** collection to create:

```
Response.AddHeader "Set-Cookie","CleaningNeeds=item1=Soap&item2=Water"
```

We can create some headers using the other properties of the **Response** object, rather than with the **AddHeader** method. For example, we can set the **ContentType**, to tell the browser what type of information to expect. For normal HTML pages, this is **"text/HTML"**, and for pictures it could be **"image/GIF"**.

```
Response.ContentType="text/HTML"
```

The browser will generally cache our pages locally when it loads them. The **Expires** and **ExpiresAbsolute** properties control when the page cached on the browser will expire, and the browser will then load a fresh copy from our server.

```
Response.Expires=180      'in minutes, i.e. in 3 hours time
Response.ExpiresAbsolute=#7/5/1997 00:00:00# 'after the 4th of July
```

As with the **Cookies** collection, redirection, and buffering, we must add headers before the server parses the `<HTML>` tag in our Active Sever Pages.

The Server Object

We now come to the important **Server** object, which is at the roof of the object model hierarchy. It provides some basic properties and methods that are used in almost every Active Server Page that we create. First, we'll take a look at its interface:

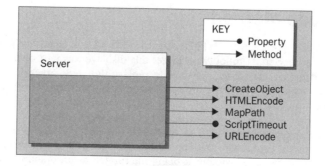

Property / Method	Description
`ScriptTimeout` property	Amount of time a script can run before an error occurs.
`CreateObject` method	Creates an instance of an object or server component.
`HTMLEncode` method	Applies HTML encoding to the specified string.
`MapPath` method	Converts a virtual path into a physical path.
`URLEncode` method	Applies URL encoding including escape chars to a string.

We'll start with a look at the single property, then move on to the methods available for use in our code.

The ScriptTimeout Property

Active Server Pages allows us to create HTML dynamically, using scripting language code. This means we can now produce pages that, just like a real programming language, have bugs. If our script enters an infinite loop, the server will eventually terminate the script to protect itself from being overloaded by running processes. The delay before all scripts are terminated (including ones with no errors) is defined in this property, which is set by default to 90 seconds—a long time for the user to be staring at the screen waiting for something to happen.

We can read and change the timeout period ourselves, using the `ScriptTimeout` property. For example, this code just inserts the current value into an HTML page:

```
ScriptTimeout = <%=Server.ScriptTimeout%>
```

ScriptTimeout is the length of time the server will allow a piece of script to run before the script is terminated. The value returned is in seconds.

ScriptTimeout = 90

This was produced by inline script
<%=Server.ScriptTimeout%>

The HTMLEncode Method

Have you ever had to write a document in HTML about HTML? Look again at the previous screenshot. It contains the text <%=Server.ScriptTimeout%>. To get this displayed as part of the page on the browser, rather than having it executed on the server, we have to replace the angle-brackets (and other special characters) with an **escape** sequence which the browser can understand. An example escape sequence would be < (*less than*).

Fortunately, the server object can help us out. The **HTMLEncode** method takes a string of text, and converts any illegal characters it contains to the appropriate HTML escape sequence. For example, to produce the text <TABLE> in our page, without it being interpreted as an opening table tag, we could use:

```
<% = Server.HTMLEncode("<TABLE>") %>
```

In the HTML page, the result is <TABLE> and this produces what we actually want to see. You might quite reasonably think that this is how we created the page above, but unfortunately it isn't that easy. The following produces an error message, because the server recognizes and translates the closing **%>** within the string as ASP code, and then it can't find the closing quotation mark:

```
<% = Server.HTMLEncode("<%=Server.ScriptTimout%>")%>
```

To make this work, we have to cheat a little, and escape the closing angle-bracket by preceding it with a backslash character:

```
<% = Server.HTMLEncode("<%=Server.ScriptTimout %\>")%>
```

The URLEncode Method

The **Server** object's **URLEncode** method is similar to **HTMLEncode**, but takes a string of information and converts it into URL-encoded form rather than HTML. All the spaces are replaced by plus signs (+), and certain other characters are replaced by a percent sign and their ANSI equivalent in hexadecimal. We saw this earlier in the chapter, when we looked at the query string returned from a form.

So **URLEncode** can translate a string into the correct format for use in a query string, but why would we want to do that? Well, it could be that we want our Active Server Page to have hyperlinks to other script pages, or even some old CGI programs. These can, in turn, take information from the query string. If we're creating hyperlinks in our code, we can use **URLEncode** to ensure that they are correctly formatted:

```
<H1> What is half expressed as a percentage? </H1>
Is it: <BR>
<A HREF="Checkit.asp?Answer=<%=Server.URLEncode("33%")%>"> 33% </A> <BR>
<A HREF="Checkit.asp?Answer=<%=Server.URLEncode("50%")%>"> 50% </A> <BR>
<A HREF="Checkit.asp?Answer=<%=Server.URLEncode("75%")%>"> 75% </A> <P>
```

This produces the following HTML code ready to send to the browser:

```
<H1> What is half expressed as a percentage? </H1>
Is it: <BR>
<A HREF="Checkit.asp?Answer=33%25"> 33% </A></BR>
<A HREF="Checkit.asp?Answer=50%25"> 50% </A></BR>
<A HREF="Checkit.asp?Answer=75%25"> 75% </A><P>
```

To see why, you only need to understand that the percent (%) sign itself can't be sent as text within a query string, because this character is used to indicate URL-encoded characters. In other words, **33%** has to be sent as **33** followed by something that represents a percent sign. Using the rules we discovered earlier, we need the ANSI code of the percent character, which is **25**, preceded by a percent sign–in other words the complete string is **33%25**. This is used within the query string, as **?Answer=33%25**.

The MapPath Method

We can use the **Server** object's **MapPath** method to provide file location information for use in our scripts. Its purpose is to translate the logical path information that might be used by a client browser, into a physical path on the server. For example, if a script needs to know the actual physical location on disk of the application's virtual root, in order to create a new document, we could get the information with this code:

```
<% 'Application virtual directory has the alias '/ObjModel'
   Dim strAppRoot
   strAppRoot = Server.MapPath("/ObjModel")
   ... %>
```

The result in **strAppPath** could be something like **C:\InetPub\Demo\ObjModel**. We could then go on to use this information to create or modify documents on the fly–perhaps using the **FileSystemObject** and **TextStream** objects, which we'll come across in the next chapter.

MapPath will accept either relative or absolute virtual paths. In the example above, we used the absolute path **/ObjModel**, which is a **virtual directory** (or **alias**) on our server. If we omit the leading '**/**' or '****', the path will be treated as a **relative** path from the page that is currently being executed.

The CreateObject Method

The last of the **Server** object's methods is certainly the most useful for creating interesting applications. The Active Server Pages environment can be extended by the use of **server components**. Some of these components are supplied 'out of the box' with ASP, and we shall be looking at them in detail in the next couple of chapters.

To actually use the components in our scripts, we need to be able to instantiate them–in other words create instances of the objects they contain, so that we can use their methods and access their properties. This is where the **Server** object's **CreateObject** method comes in. Every component that is correctly installed on our server has a programmatic identifier (**ProgID**) to reference it by. We pass this to the **CreateObject** method, and it creates an object of the appropriate type for us to use in our script.

Since the number of available components will only increase with time, **CreateObject** is potentially the most useful method that you'll ever use. For example, one of the components supplied with Active Server Pages is the **Browser Capabilities** component. This code shows how we could create and use it in our pages:

```
<% Dim objBrowser      'define an object variable
   Set objBrowser = Server.CreateObject("MSWC.BrowserType") %>
The <%=objBrowser.Browser%> <%=objBrowser.Version%> browser supports? <P>
<UL>
```

```
<LI>Tables = <%=objBrowser.tables%>
<LI>Frames = <%=objBrowser.frames%>
...
```

Here, we've created an instance of the Browser Capabilities object, using its **ProgID** of **MSWC.BrowserType**. Notice the use of the **Set** keyword to assign it to an object variable. We can then use this new object's methods–viewed in Internet Explorer this code produces the results you can see here. Don't worry too much about what it's actually doing, that's coming in the next chapter.

The IE3.01 browser supports?

- Tables = -1
- Frames = -1

As you'll see in more detail through later chapters, we need to be sure that we can actually create the object, and that there were no errors encountered doing so. One obvious way is to 'turn off' the built-in error handling in the code, then use the **IsObject()** function to check that we did manage to create the object successfully:

```
<% Dim objBrowser                    'define an object variable
   On Error Resume Next              'ignore any errors that occur
   Set objBrowser = Server.CreateObject("MSWC.BrowserType")
   If IsObject(objBrowser) Then      'check that we've got an object
   ...
   'use the object
   ...
Else
   Response.Write ("Error creating the object.")
End If %>
```

The Application Object

Now that we've taken a look at the other objects in the overall Active Server Pages object model, we need to consider how an application built with ASP fits together. As we saw at the beginning of this chapter, each server can have many applications running on it. An application comprises all the files that can be referenced through a single virtual mapping, or aliased directory, on your web server.

In coming chapters, especially Chapter 6 where we take a look at building applications with Active Server Pages, we'll be exploring in depth how we can use both the **Application** and the **Session** objects. In the meantime, though, we'll look briefly at what they offer. The **Application** object can store information for use by script files, process requests, and even respond to **events**. This is the interface of the **Application** object:

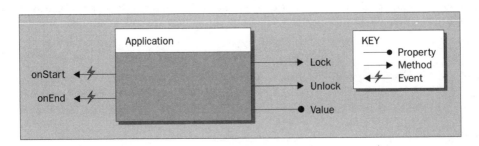

Method / Event	Description
`Lock` method	Prevents other clients from modifying application properties.
`Unlock` method	Allows other clients to modify application properties.
`onStart` event	Occurs when a page in the application is first referenced.
`onEnd` event	Occurs when the application ends, i.e. when the web server is stopped.

The first thing to note is that an Active Server Pages application has a lifetime, just like any other program that might be run on a computer. When the application starts the `onStart` event occurs, and when an application finishes the `onEnd` event occurs.

Application Event Handlers

If we need to write code to be run when the application either starts or finishes, we need to put it into an appropriate **event handler**. In VBScript, an event handler takes the form:

```
Sub <ObjectName>_<EventName>(<ParameterList>)
 ...
End Sub
```

Since this sort of script requires a home, we place it in a particular file in the root directory of the virtual mapping, called `global.asa`. As its name suggests, this file contains information, routines and variables that are globally available to all of the pages in the application. So, if we need to do some processing at the beginning or end of an application, we can put some code in the `global.asa` file:

```
<SCRIPT LANGUAGE="VBScript" RUNAT="Server">
Sub Application_OnStart
   'Insert script to be executed when the application starts
End Sub

Sub Application_OnEnd
   'Insert script to be executed when the application ends
End Sub
</SCRIPT>
```

How Long Do Applications Live?

What isn't obvious about an application in ASP is just when it starts, and when it terminates. For a regular program running on your computer this is easy to answer—the program starts when you ask the operating system to run it, and it ends when you close the window or click an Exit button.

For an Active Server Pages application, the timing is a little different. Because what we are doing is creating dynamic and interactive web content, our application has to be based around the client machines' requests for pages from our server. Since our application is defined as all the documents contained in a single virtual mapping on the server, the application starts the first time any client requests a document from that virtual mapping.

Now that we know how an application *starts*, all we need to consider now is how it *ends*. Web servers are supposed to give continuous access to information all the time, so generally speaking we don't want our application to end while there are people out there who might want to use it. Only when the web server is stopped by the operating system does our application stop, and the script in the **onEnd** event handler runs. If the server actually crashes for some reason, however, the application still ends–but the **onEnd** script won't run in this case!

> *Future revisions to Active Server Pages are expected to change this behavior. It's likely that the application will actually terminate after a pre-defined period of no activity, saving various values connected with it to disk so that it can restart where it left off.*

Application Variables

When creating event handlers for **Application_onStart** and **Application_onEnd**, the important question is 'What information are we going to manipulate?' The answer is absolutely anything that we might want to use in our scripts in other parts of the application, and hence needs to be **Global** or **Public**. One obvious value is the time that the application started.

Storing Global Information

To store global information in the **Application** object, we just dream up a name for it and assign it to that name. The name becomes the key by which we access that value in future. You can think of it as being a custom property of the object. To store the time that the application started, we can add code to the **Application_onStart** event:

```
Sub Application_OnStart
    Application.Value("dtmStartTime") = Now()
End Sub
```

Here's part of an example page, **ApplicationObj.asp**, which uses this stored time value, and also creates a global value of its own. You can find this among the samples available from our web site:

```
<H1>Application Started at: <%=Application("dtmStartTime")%> </H1>
The <B>Foo</B> property does not really exist until the button
below is clicked.<BR>
Trying to get its value gives us: <%=Application("Foo")%> <P>
<FORM ACTION="MakeFoo.asp" METHOD=GET>
  <INPUT TYPE=HIDDEN NAME=Foo Value="5">
  <INPUT TYPE=SUBMIT>
</FORM>
```

Here are the results it produces. The time value that's displayed is the one we set in the application's **onStart** event:

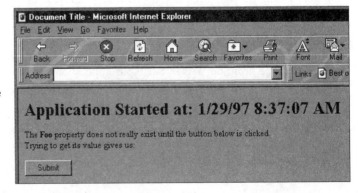

This page also makes a second use of the **Application** object, to access a variable named **Foo** and retrieve its value:

```
Trying to get its value gives us: <%=Application("Foo")%>
```

The first time the **ApplicationObj.asp** page is requested after the application starts, **Foo** will not have been saved and so nothing is returned, as in the previous screenshot. Notice that referencing a nonexistent property doesn't cause an error. It just returns an empty value—which can have an important impact on debugging your application, since spelling errors in variable names will not be easy to find.

When we click the Submit button, we reference another ASP file, called **MakeFoo.asp**. This contains the following code:

```
<% 'Stop other clients modifying Application properties
    Application.Lock
    Application("Foo") = Request.QueryString("Foo")
    Application.Unlock
    Response.Redirect("./ApplicationObj.asp") %>
```

This takes the information from the **<FORM>**, where the **HIDDEN** control named **Foo** has the value **5**. This is stored as a global value in the **Application** object, and the browser is redirected to the original **ApplicationObj.asp** page. This time **Foo** will be a valid variable containing the value **5**. So we get the same page displayed, but this time **Foo** has a value:

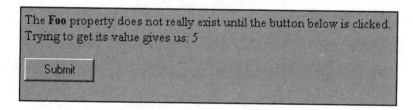

Using the Lock and Unlock Methods

You'll have noticed that the previous example used the **Lock** and **Unlock** methods of the **Application** object. Since the **Application** object is global to all the clients that may be visiting our site, it's possible that two clients could try to access the same data at the same time. To prevent the value being corrupted in this situation we can **Lock** and **UnLock** access to the object. When the **Lock** method is invoked, no other scripts can change the information stored in the **Application** object until the **UnLock** method is called.

The **Application** object will be the main topic of discussion in Chapter 6, so we'll leave it there for now. However, like all the other objects in the ASP object model, you'll be meeting it regularly throughout this book. To finish off the object model, we just need to consider the **Session** object.

The Session Object

Before we look at the Session object, we need to introduce the concept of **scope,** which is where data is either made available to all pages of an application, or just localized to certain pages. This is actually demonstrated by the **Application** object. You can use the **Application** object to store both simple data values, and—as you'll see later in this book—references to objects such as database connections. These become **Global** to the whole application, and are available in any of its pages.

However, when we have data that needs to be shared between different pages, but not necessarily between different *clients*, we can make use of the **Session** object. Each client that requests a page from our application is assigned a **Session** object. A **Session** is created when the client first makes a document request and destroyed, by default, twenty minutes after their last request was received.

The interface to the **Session** object is shown here:

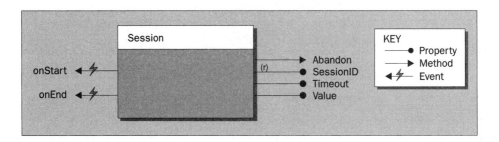

Interface Element	Description
SessionID property	Returns the session identification for this user.
Timeout property	The timeout period (minutes) for sessions in this application.
Abandon method	Destroys a **Session** object and releases its resources.
onStart event	Occurs when a user first requests a page in the application.
onEnd event	Occurs when the session ends, i.e. when no requests have been received for the timeout period (default 20 minutes).

Session Event Handlers

The two **Session** object events, **onStart** and **onEnd**, are similar to those of the **Application** object. **onStart** occurs when a client browser first requests a document from the application's virtual directory. Since these events occur outside of any particular script, we need to create the event handler routines within the **global.asa** file, along with those for the **Application** object:

```
Sub Session_OnStart
    'Insert script to be executed when a session starts
End Sub

Sub Session_OnEnd
    'Insert script to be executed when a session ends
End Sub
```

Session Variables

As in the **Application** object, these can store values in the session object. Again, these are like custom properties, and can be used to store information for a session. However, unlike the **Application**, this information is maintained on an individual client basis. It becomes **Global** to that client, but is not available to other clients who are using our application concurrently.

When we store information in the **Session** object, the client that owns that session is assigned a **SessionID**, which can be used in our pages to identify them while they are browsing our site. The **SessionID** is assigned by the server, and is only available to us as a read-only property.

> *The actual* **SessionID** *information is stored as a cookie with no expiry date set, so that it expires when the client browser is closed down. If the browser doesn't support cookies, Active Server Pages can't create a session for that user.*

Storing Local Information

To see how we can use local values stored in the **Session** object, here's a simple script. It retrieves the current user's **SessionID**, and the current setting of the session **Timeout**, and displays them in the page. Then it retrieves the value of a session-wide variable **intSessionObjVisit** and displays this. Finally, it increments the stored value, so the page shows the number of times it has been opened from the server during the current session:

```
<H3>SessionID = <%=Session.SessionID%></H3>
<H3>Timeout = <%=Session.Timeout%></H3>
<P>You have visited this page
<%=Session("intSessionObjVisit")%> times this <B>Session</B>.</P>
<% Session("intSessionObjVisit") = Session("intSessionObjVisit") +1 %>
```

SessionID = 13477

Timeout = 20

You have visited this page 6 times this **Session**.

When Do Sessions Start and End?

Although we generally consider that a session starts when a client's browser first requests a document from the application's virtual directory, this isn't the whole story. Active Server Pages will only start a session for that client automatically if there is a **Session_onStart** routine in the **global.asa** file. This means that you can build applications that don't implement individual sessions for each client–saving resources if this feature isn't actually required.

However, the code in a page can store values in the **Session** object–even if it hasn't already been established when the user requested the page. At this point a session is automatically created. There will also be a session created if the `global.asa` file contains an `<OBJECT>` tag which creates an instance of an object with **session-level scope**, i.e. by including the `SCOPE=Session` attribute:

```
<OBJECT RUNAT=Server SCOPE=Session ID=objAdRot ProgID="MSWC.Adrorator">
```

> *You'll see how we create objects using an `<OBJECT>` tag like this in the next chapter, when we come to look at Active Server Components in detail.*

There are two ways in which a session can end. The most direct is by use of the `Session` object's `Abandon` method. This ends the session immediately, and frees the resources it uses. Any code in the `Session_onEnd` event handler runs when the session ends.

Alternatively, looking at the previous sample, you'll notice that we're referencing the `Timeout` property. If the client that owns the `Session` doesn't make a request from the application within this time period (in minutes), the server will destroy that `Session` object and release its resources. The default value is twenty minutes, but we can alter this on a per-session basis by changing the value of the `Session.Timeout` property in our code, or for all sessions by changing the registry parameter setting. The key that contains the information is:

```
HKEY_LOCAL_MACHINE\System\CurrentControlSet\Services\W3Svc\ASP\Parameters
\SessionTimeout
```

If we were expecting a lot of hits on our site, and needed to conserve resources, we could reduce this value so that clients will be 'logged off' more quickly. In an environment where the application has less users, and very sporadic document requests, we could consider increasing this value. At the end of the day, the needs of the application must be balanced against server resources to get the best results.

An Active Server Application Example

We've skipped quite quickly through the concepts and objects that define the `Application` and its `Sessions`. There's a lot more to come in this area in part two of the book, but if you would like to see a real working example now, download the sample Fun Math Quiz (`FunMath.htm`). This is included with all the samples for this book at:

`http://www.rapid.wrox.com/books/0723/`

It's designed to be easy for a youngster just getting into mathematics to grasp, and simply displays a set of questions—one by one—with a graphical indication of their score so far:

Score so far

1 Out of 2

What is the sum of all the angles in a triangle

- 180
- 270
- 360

It uses two Active Server Pages, though one of these is just used to check the answers and redirect the browser back to the first one again, like we did with our **AppliationObj.asp** example earlier:

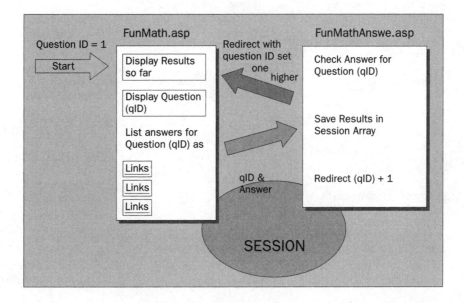

One interesting aspect is that the application has to maintain an array of correct answers, but the **Application** object won't allow us to store an array as a global custom property or value. Instead, we store the array inside a **Variant** variable, and store this in the **Application** object with the key **gResult**. We set it up in the **Session_onStart** event, so that it's available when the quiz is loaded:

```
Sub Session_onStart
    Dim arrScores(4)
    Session("qResult") = arrScores
End Sub
```

Now we can display our quiz page, **FunMath.asp**. The first time round **qID**, the question number, will be **1**, so the **For...Next** loop will not be entered because **Request("qID")-1** will be zero. The code just displays the question and a series of possible answers. Each of these is a hyperlink to the **FunMathAnswer.asp** file, and includes the answer number and the current question number as a query string. Once we get back here for question 2, however, the **For...Next** loop at the top of the page will be entered, and it will place the score so far in the page:

```
...
<H2> Score so far </H2>
<% Dim intLoop                    'this is in FunMath.asp
    Dim intScore
    Dim arrScore
    arrScore = Session("qResult")      'retrieve Score array
    For intLoop = 1 To Request("qID") - 1
        If arrScore(intLoop) = 1 Then
            Response.Write("<IMG SRC='../images/wxTIC.gif' ALT='Yes'>")
        Else
            Response.Write("<IMG SRC='../images/wxCROSS.gif' ALT='Yes'>")
```

```
              End If
              intScore = intScore + Session("qResult")(intLoop)
          Next
          Response.Write( intScore & " out of " & Request("qID") -1) %>
<!-- The Question -->
<IMG SRC="../images/wxQ.gif" ALT="Question." ALIGN=TOP>
<% 'Get question - ideally would come from a database or text file !
    Select Case Request("qID")
        Case 1:
            Response.Write("What is one half expressed as a percentage?")
        Case 2:
            ...
            ...
        Case Else:
            Response.Write("No More questions")
    End Select
<!-- Possible Answers -->
<UL>
<% Select Case Request("qID")
        Case 1: %>
<LI><A HREF='./FunMathAnswer.asp?qID=1&answer=25%25'> 25% </A>
<LI><A HREF='./FunMathAnswer.asp?qID=1&answer=50%25'> 50% </A>
<LI><A HREF='./FunMathAnswer.asp?qID=1&answer=75%25'> 75% </A>"
<%    Case 2:
        ...
        ...
    End Select %>
</UL>
...
```

The processing of the answer is done in **FunMathAnswer.asp**, part of which is shown below. The value **qID** is the question number, which is delivered to the script as part of the query string. When you start the quiz it's set to **1**, and then incremented each time you answer a question. The score so far is added to the array each time:

```
...                                      'this is FunMathAnswer.asp
arrScore = Session("qResult")            'get the Application variable
Redim Preserve arrScore(Request("qID"))  'dimension it to hold qID values
Select Case Request("qID")               'check answer for this question
    Case 1:
        If Request("Answer") = 180 Then
            Correct = 1
        Else
            Correct = 0
        End If
    Case 2:
        ...
        ...
End Select
arrScore(CInt(Request("qID"))) = Correct  'set result in the array
Session("qResult") = arrScore             'save array back in session
...
```

We'll leave you to experiment with it, and find better ways of storing the questions and answers.

Summary

In this chapter we've taken a tour around the object model exposed by Active Server Pages. We've seen how to write script that can access the objects and their collections, methods, events, and properties–both to store and retrieve information. We've taken a close look at how information is passed from the client's browser to our application, and we've used this and the server's own methods and properties to create dynamic content.

We've also looked at some of the ways we can control document retrieval using the redirection capabilities of the **Response** object, as well as some of the other HTTP header-based manipulations that can be achieved. And we've seen how to use cookies to give our sites access to persistent data from day to day.

We finished up with a quick tour of the **Application** and **Session** objects. These are fundamental to building real applications with Active Server Pages, so we've left a lot of the detail to later chapters, where you'll see them in use in more realistic situations. The main points of this chapter are:

▲ Active Server provides an **object model** that we can manipulate using scripting languages. This gives us a structured way of accessing all kinds of information, and producing dynamic content for our site.

▲ The main communication between the client's browser and our server is through two objects. The **Request** object contains all the information about the client's request for a file, and the **Response** object contains the details and content of the page we're sending back from the server.

▲ We can control **which** documents the client receives, or even buffer output and control which **sections** of the document are sent. We can also add **headers** to the documents, which can change the document itself, how long it is cached, or even **redirect** the browser to a different document or site.

▲ We can store information locally, using the **Application** and **Session** objects, or remotely on the client's machine using **cookies**. We can use either method to exchange information between different active documents.

The Active Server Pages object model can also be extended by using add-in **server components**. In fact, this is the subject that we'll be covering in detail in the next chapter.

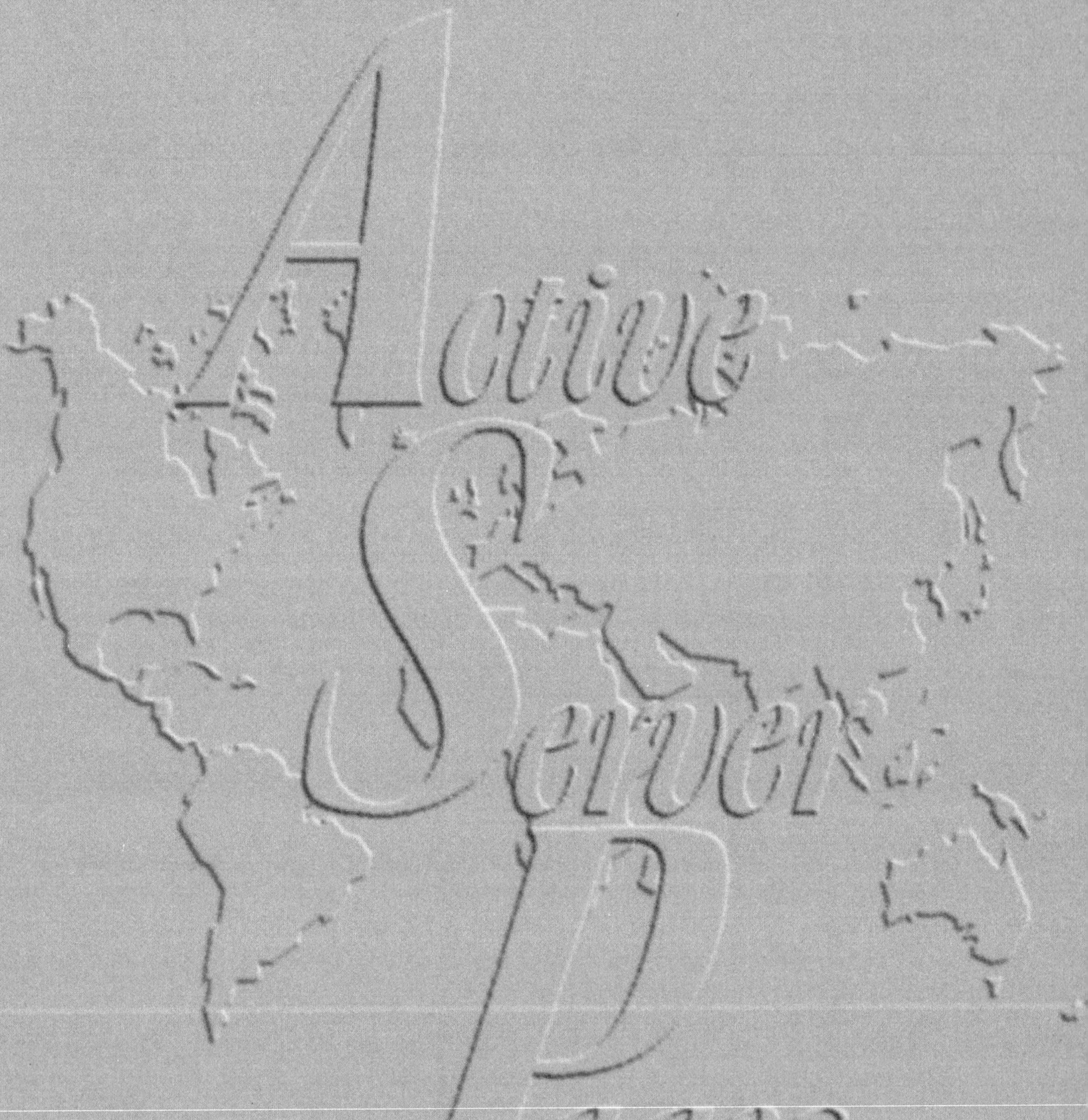
Active
Server
Pages

Scripting Objects and Server Components

In the previous chapter, we saw how **Active Server Pages** can create instances of objects on the server, and take advantage of the methods and properties that they provide. These components are generally referred to as **Active Server Components**. In many ways, they are like ActiveX Controls, but are designed for execution on the server rather than being sent as an object to the browser. This has many advantages, as you'll see in this chapter.

The obvious question is, then, where do these components come from? Some are provided as part of the Active Server Pages installation, while others are available free or as a bought-in product. In this chapter, we'll show you just how useful the various components available from Microsoft are. Once you're familiar with using components, you'll have no trouble slotting other supplier's products into your pages. We'll even show you how to build your own components later in the book.

There's one standard component that we won't be covering in this chapter, however. One of the principal uses of dynamic web site technologies is to publish information direct from some type of database management system. This, and the need to collect data and store it in a database, led to the original development of server-side programming. To achieve these tasks using Active Server Pages, we take advantage of a special, but general-purpose component, called the **Active Data Object**. This is too large a subject to fit in a chapter with all the other components, so we'll give it a whole chapter of its own later in the book.

Several of the standard components rely on objects that are part of the scripting language itself (rather than being part of the ASP object model we looked at in the previous chapter). We also need to be able to use the VBScript **Err** object to control how our pages react to the inevitable errors that they'll encounter once we start to incorporate components into our pages. And there's one other very useful object we can use to store values as we work with components, and in our code generally.

In this chapter, then, we'll see:

- How we can use the VBScript built-in Text, Error and Dictionary objects
- How we use the standard components supplied with Active Server Pages
- Other Microsoft components that are being developed, and how they are used

We'll start off with a look at the VBScript built-in objects that we can use with components.

Built-in VB Scripting Objects

Active Server Pages introduces an updated version of the original VBScript language that was incorporated into Internet Explorer 3. This is generally referred to as **VBScript2**, though we use the generic term VBScript in this book. It adds several new functions, and develops on existing system objects, or **scripting objects**, which we use in our code.

What Are Scripting Objects?

In the previous chapter, we introduced the **object model** for Active Server Pages. This is basically a way of understanding how the various parts of the system are related together, and provides us with a structure that we can use to manipulate the different elements in the HTTP requests and responses, and the whole ASP environment. For example, we saw how we can find out the values of any cookies sent from the browser by looking in the **Cookies** collection–which is part of the **Request** object.

The scripting languages we use also have an object model, but for the objects that they provide, as opposed to the objects provided directly by the Active Server Pages system. In this part of book we're working mainly with VBScript, and it provides some objects that we can use to manipulate elements of the language. Among these are the **Dictionary** object, the **FileSystemObject** object, the **TextStream** object, and the **Err** object.

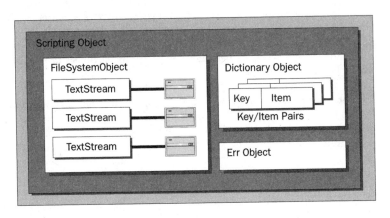

The diagram shows how the scripting objects are related. While the **Dictionary** and **Err** objects are separate, the **TextStream** object is part of the **FileSystemObject** object. In the next few sections, we'll look at each of these objects in turn, and see how they can be used.

The Dictionary Object

In many other languages, including Visual Basic, we can use a feature called a **collection**. This is an object-oriented way of storing data, using a key with which it can be retrieved. We can think of a collection as being like an **array**, but with its own built-in intelligence which looks after the basic tasks of storing and manipulating the data. We don't have to worry about which row or column the data is in, we just access it using a unique key.

VBScript offers a similar object called the **scripting dictionary**, or just the **Dictionary** object. It acts like a two-dimensional array, and holds the key and the related item of data together. However, in true object-oriented fashion, we can't just access the data items directly. We have to use the methods and properties supported by the **Dictionary** object instead. As an example, we can create an instance of the **Dictionary** object like this:

```
Set objMyData = CreateObject("Scripting.Dictionary")
```

*Notice that we're using the VBScript **CreateObject** function directly here, rather than the **Server** object's **CreateObject** method we used in the previous chapter. This makes sense, because we're creating an object that is part of the scripting language. However, the **Server** object is the default object in Active Server Pages anyway, so we don't actually need to specify it. When we're working with server components, however, we will do so.*

Once we've got a new (empty) dictionary, we can add items to it:

```
objMyData.Add "MyKey", "MyItem"          'add items to the dictionary
objMyData.Add "YourKey", "YourItem"
```

And we can retrieve and remove them again:

```
blnIsThere = objMyData.Exists("MyKey")   'True because the item exists
strItem = objMyData.Item("YourKey")      'retrieve an item from dictionary
strItem = objMyData.Remove("MyKey")      'retrieve and remove an item
objMyData.RemoveAll                       'remove all the items
```

Here's the full list of methods and properties for the `Dictionary` object.

Method / Property	Description
Add *key, item* method	Adds the key/item pair to the `Dictionary`.
Exists(*key*) method	`True` if the specified key exists, `False` if not.
Items method	Returns an array containing all the items in a `Dictionary` object.
Keys method	Returns an array containing all the keys in a `Dictionary` object.
Remove(*key*) method	Removes a single key/item pair.
RemoveAll method	Removes all the key/item pairs.
CompareMode property	Sets or returns the string comparison mode for the keys.
Count property	Read-only. Returns the number of key/item pairs in the `Dictionary`.
Item(*key*) property	Sets or returns the value of the item for the specified key.
Key(*key*) property	Sets or returns the value of a key.

An error will occur if we try to add a key/item pair when that key already exists, remove a key/item pair that doesn't exist, or change the comparison mode of a `Dictionary` object that already contains data.

Changing the Value of a Key or Item

We can change the data stored in a `Dictionary`, by either changing the value of the key or the item of data associated with it. To change the value of the item with the key **MyKey**, we could use:

```
objMyData.Item("MyKey") = "NewValue"
```

If the key we specify (**MyKey**) isn't found in the `Dictionary`, a new key/item pair is created with the key as **MyKey** and the item value as **NewValue**. One interesting aspect is that, if we try to retrieve an item using a key that doesn't exist we not only get an empty string as the result (as we'd expect) but also a new key/item pair that is actually added to the `Dictionary`. This has the key we specified (**MyKey**), but with the item left empty.

To change the value of a key, without changing the value of the corresponding item, we use the **Key** property. So, to change the value of an existing key **MyKey** to **MyNewKey**, we could use:

```
objMyData.Key("MyKey") = "MyNewKey"
```

If the specified key (**MyKey**) isn't found, a new key/item pair is created with the key **MyNewKey** and the item left empty.

Setting the Comparison Mode

The **CompareMode** property of a dictionary allows us to define how the comparison is made when comparing string keys. The usual values are:

VB Constant	Value	Description
vbBinaryCompare	0	Binary comparison–i.e. matching is *not* case sensitive.
vbTextCompare	1	Text comparison–i.e. matching *is* case sensitive.
vbDatabaseCompare	2	Comparison is based upon information contained in the string. Values greater than 2 can be a Locale ID (**LCID**).

Iterating Through a Dictionary

There are two methods and a property that are of particular interest when dealing with a **Dictionary**. These allow us to iterate, or loop, through all the key/item pairs stored in it. The **Items** method returns all the items in a **Dictionary** as a one-dimensional array, while the **Keys** method returns all the existing key values as a one-dimensional array. To find out how many keys or items there are, we can use the **Count** property.

For example, we can retrieve all the keys and values from a **Dictionary** called **objMyData** using the following code. Notice that although the **Count** property holds the number of key/item pairs in the **Dictionary**, a VBScript array always starts at index zero. Therefore we have to iterate through the array using the values **0** to **Count - 1**:

```
...
  strKeysArray = objMyData.Keys            'get all the keys into an array
  strItemsArray = objMyData.Items          'get all the items into an array
  For intLoop = 0 To objMyData.Count -1    'iterate through the array
    strThisKey = strKeysArray(intLoop)     'this is the key value
    strThisItem = strItemsArray(intLoop)   'this is the item (data) value
  Next
...
```

A Real Use for the Dictionary Object

In the previous chapter, where we looked at the object model of Active Server Pages, we found that we can retrieve the values of fields on a form submitted from the client's browser. However, we had to know the names of the fields (the controls on the form) for this to be possible. In theory we'll know these names, because we create the forms as well as the Active Server Pages that process them. However, a **generic form handler**, which will accept *any* form, is a popular application with web site developers. We can quite easily create a page to do this, using VBScript and Active Server Pages together.

The point is that we don't know the names of the fields, or how many there will be. This makes the **Dictionary** object an ideal tool for storing the values, rather than creating a dynamic array, or counting the number of fields first. The first question, then, is how do we actually get the values from the fields on the form?

Using the Request Object's Form Collection

In the previous chapter, you saw how we use the individual elements of the **Form** collection to get a list of their contents. Even when we don't know how many controls there are on a **<FORM>**, or their names, we can still retrieve them using the collections with the **For Each...Next** construct. There's another way we can work with the Form object—the statement **Request.Form** with no arguments returns the complete query string, sent back from the form, in **URL-encoded** format. For example, if our form has two controls, **txtName** and **txtEmail**, we could get a result that looked like this:

```
txtName=Alex+Homer&txtEmail=alex@stonebroom.com
```

Notice that the controls and their values form the standard name/value pairs, with the control name and its value separated by an equals sign. You'll have seen this format before if you've used other languages to create server-based form handling applications. Each name/value pair is separated from the next by an ampersand (**&**). You can also see that spaces have been replaced by plus signs, and so plus signs would then need to be replaced by something else—certain non-alphanumeric characters are encoded with a percent sign followed by their ANSI character number.

Coping with URL Encoding

So before we can do anything with the string of values, we have to be able to decode them. Though Active Server Pages helpfully provides a function to encode strings, it doesn't provide one to decode them. Here's one we've written ourselves, and we've stored it in a separate text file named **URLDecode.txt**. We can make it available in any of our pages by using a Server-side Include tag, which simply inserts the text into the page as the server loads it into memory.

```
<SCRIPT LANGUAGE=VBScript RUNAT=Server>
Function URLDecode(strToDecode)
  strIn = strToDecode
  strOut = ""                   'the result string
  intPos = Instr(strIn, "+")    'look for + and replace with space
  Do While intPos
    strLeft = ""
    strRight = ""
    If intPos > 1 Then strLeft = Left(strIn, intPos - 1)
    If intPos < Len(strIn) Then strRight = Mid(strIn, intPos + 1)
    strIn = strLeft & " " & strRight
    intPos = Instr(strIn, "+") 'and then look for next one
    intLoop = intLoop + 1
  Loop
  intPos = Instr(strIn, "%")    'look for ASCII coded characters
  Do While intPos
    If intPos > 1 Then strOut = strOut & Left(strIn, intPos - 1)
    strOut = strOut & Chr(CInt("&H" & Mid(strIn, intPos + 1, 2)))
    If intPos > (Len(strIn) - 3) Then
      strIn = ""
    Else
      strIn = Mid(strIn, intPos + 3)
    End If
```

```
        intPos = Instr(strIn, "%") 'and then look for next one
    Loop
    URLDecode = strOut & strIn
End Function
</SCRIPT>
```

The Generic Form Handler Code

Now we have a way of decoding the string of values sent from the browser, so we need to split them up, and add them to a **Dictionary** object. Here's the complete code for the page. It first creates the **Dictionary**, and then reads the **Request** object's **Form** property to get the string of name/value pairs. Then it parses the string, looking for the ampersands that divide the name/value pairs from each other and the equals signs that separate the name from the value within the pair. Each pair is decoded and added to the **Dictionary** with its **Add** method, using the name as the **Key** and the value as the **Item**. Lastly, it iterates through the values stored in the **Dictionary** object just as we saw earlier, and puts them into the page with a **Response.Write** statement.

```
<!--#include file=URLDecode.txt-->

<%
'First we create a Dictionary object to hold the results
Set objResult = CreateObject("Scripting.Dictionary")

'Then we get the complete query string for the FORM
strQuery = Request.Form

'Now we can parse the query string and fill the Dictionary
intSep = Instr(strQuery, "&")
Do While intSep                            'split the string into
    strKey = ""                            'remove the last key we found
    strValue = ""                          'remove the last value we found
    strNVPair = Left(strQuery, intSep - 1) 'name/value pairs.
    strQuery = Mid(strQuery, intSep + 1)
    intEqu = Instr(strNVPair, "=")         'separate the name and value.
    If intEqu > 1 Then strKey = URLDecode(Left(strNVPair, intEqu-1))
    If intEqu < Len(strNVPair) Then strValue = URLDecode(Mid(strNVPair, intEqu+1))
    objResult.Add strKey, strValue         'and add to the dictionary.
    intSep = Instr(strQuery, "&")
Loop
strKey = ""                                'lastly, we have to handle
strValue = ""                              'the remaining name/value pair.
intEqu = Instr(strQuery, "=")
If intEqu > 1 Then strKey = URLDecode(Left(strQuery, intEqu-1))
If intEqu < Len(strQuery) Then strValue = URLDecode(Mid(strQuery, intEqu+1))
objResult.Add strKey, strValue

'Now we can loop through the Dictionary and output the results
strKeysArray = objResult.Keys              'get the keys into an array
strItemsArray = objResult.Items            'get the items into an array
For intLoop = 0 To objResult.Count -1      'iterate through the array
    strThisKey = strKeysArray(intLoop)     'this is the key value
    strThisItem = strItemsArray(intLoop)   'this is the item (data) value
    Response.Write strThisKey & " = " & strThisItem & "<BR>"
Next
%>
```

We've supplied a sample of this code that you can try. The file **GenForm.htm** contains a simple **<FORM>**, whose **ACTION** attribute is the ASP file **GenForm.asp**. You'll find them on our web site at **http://www.rapid.wrox.com/books/0723/** or you can use the code we've shown above with any of your own pages that contain a **<FORM>** section.

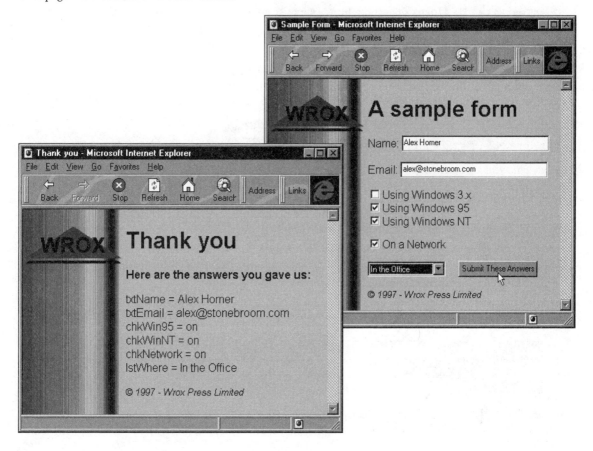

The FileSystemObject Object

The **FileSystemObject** object provides access to the computer's file system, allowing us to manipulate text files from within our code. It's part of the **Scripting** object, and we can create an instance of the **FileSystemObject** using:

```
Set objFSO = CreateObject("Scripting.FileSystemObject")
```

Once we've got a **FileSystemObject** object, we create **TextStream** objects using its methods:

Method	Description
`CreateTextFile`	**Creates** a file and returns a `TextStream` object used to access the file.
`OpenTextFile`	**Opens** a file and returns a `TextStream` object used to access the file.

The CreateTextFile Method

The `CreateTextFile` method creates a new text file, or overwrites an existing one. It returns a `TextStream` object that we can use to read from or write to the file. We first create a `FileSystemObject` object, as we saw above, then use it to create a `TextStream` object, like this:

```
Set objFSO = CreateObject("Scripting.FileSystemObject")
Set objNewFile = objFSO.CreateTextFile("C:\TextFiles\MyFile.txt")
```

The full syntax of `CreateTextFile` is:

[*object.*]`CreateTextFile`(*filename*[, *overwrite*[, *unicode*]])   where:

object   Name of a `FileSystemObject`. Optional argument.

filename   Full physical path and filename for the file we want to create or overwrite.

overwrite   `True` to indicate we can overwrite an existing file or `False` if it can't be overwritten. Optional argument—if omitted existing files will be overwritten.

unicode   `True` to indicate that the file should be created as a Unicode file, `False` as an ASCII file. Optional argument—if omitted an ASCII file is created.

> If the overwrite argument is `False`, and a file with the same filename already exists in the specified directory, an error occurs.

Unicode files *use two bytes to identify each character, removing the ASCII limitation of 256 available characters. VBScript includes special functions to work with Unicode files—see Appendix A for more details.*

The OpenTextFile Method

The `OpenTextFile` method opens an existing text file. It returns a `TextStream` object that we can use to read from or append data to the file. Again, we first create a `FileSystemObject` object, then use it to create a `TextStream` object, like this:

```
Set objFSO = CreateObject("Scripting.FileSystemObject")
Set objNewFile = objFSO.OpenTextFile("C:\TextFiles\MyFile.txt")
```

The full syntax of `OpenTextFile` is:

[*object.*]`OpenTextFile`(*filename*[, *iomode*[, *create*[, *format*]]])   where:

object   Name of a `FileSystemObject`. Optional argument.

filename   Full path and filename for the file we want to open.

iomode	Either `ForReading` or `ForAppending`. Optional argument–default `ForReading`.
create	`True` to indicate we can create a new file or `False` if it must already exist. Optional argument–if omitted a new empty file is not created if it doesn't already exist.
format	Format for the file. Optional argument–if omitted the file is opened as ASCII.
	A value of `TristateTrue` (-1) opens the file in Unicode format.
	A value of `TristateFalse` (0) opens the file in ASCII format.
	A value of `TristateUseDefault` (-2) opens the file using the system default.

> If the *create* argument is `False` or not provided, and a file with the same filename *does not* already exist in the specified directory, an error occurs.

The TextStream Object

So we can create a new text file, or open an existing one. Once we've done this, we have a `TextStream` object reference to it, and we can manipulate the file using the methods and properties of the `TextStream` object. For example, once we've created the file using a `CreateTextFile` or `OpenTextFile` method, we can write to it and close it with:

```
objNewFile.WriteLine("At last I can create files with VBScript!")
objNewFile.Close
```

Here's a full list of the properties and methods available for the `TextStream` object. We'll look at the important ones in detail shortly. Notice that all the **properties** are **Read-only**:

Method / Property	Description
`Close` method	Closes an open file.
`Read(`*numchars*`)` method	Reads *numchars* characters from a file.
`ReadAll` method	Reads an entire file as a single string.
`ReadLine` method	Reads a line from a file as a string.
`Skip(`*numchars*`)` method	Skips and discards *numchars* characters when reading a file.
`SkipLine` method	Skips and discards the next line when reading a file.
`Write(`*string*`)` method	Writes *string* to a file.
`WriteLine([`*string*`])` method	Writes *string* (optional) and a newline character to a file.
`WriteBlankLines(`*n*`)` method	Writes *n* newline characters to a file.
`AtEndOfLine` property	`True` if the file pointer is at the end of a line in a file.
`AtEndOfStream` property	`True` if the file pointer is at the end of a file.
`Column` property	Returns the column number of the current character in a file, starting from 1.
`Line` property	Returns the current line number in a file, starting from 1.

> The `AtEndOfLine` and `AtEndOfStream` properties are only available for a file that is opened with *iomode* of `ForReading`. Referring to them otherwise causes an error to occur.

A Real Use for the TextStream Object

When we looked at the Dictionary object, earlier in the chapter, we saw how we can use it to store name/value pairs being sent from a `<FORM>` section in a page on the client's browser. The next question is, then, what do we do with them once we've got them? Well, the combination of the `FileSystemObject` and the `TextStream` object means that we can easily store the values in a file on disk.

As an example, we'll add the values to a log file called `MyLog.txt`, which is stored in the `C:\Logfiles\` directory on our server. If you want to try this example yourself, you'll have to create this directory on your server and use NotePad, or another text editor, to create an empty file named `MyLog.txt` first. The actual opening, writing to, and closing of the file is done by a separate function `WriteToLogFile`, which accepts the string to write and returns `True` on success, or `False` otherwise. We've also included the `On Error Resume Next` statement so that it will not halt our code if something goes wrong:

```
<SCRIPT RUNAT=SERVER LANGUAGE="VBScript">
  Function WriteToLogFile(strLogMessage)
    On Error Resume Next    'prevent the code from halting on an error
    WriteToLogFile = False  'default return value of function
    Set objFSO = CreateObject("Scripting.FileSystemObject")
    Set objLogFile = objFSO.OpenTextFile("C:\Logfiles\MyLog.txt", 8)
    objLogFile.WriteLine(strLogMessage)
    objLogFile.Close
    WriteToLogFile = True
  End Function
</SCRIPT>
```

> *Notice that we've used the explicit value 8, instead of the `ForAppending` constant in our code. We found that the constant may not be recognized implicitly by some releases of VBScript.*

This function is stored as a separate text file `WriteLog.txt` on the server, and we use another `#include` statement to insert it into our page:

```
<!--#include file=WriteLog.txt-->
```

The other changes to the `GenForm.asp` page we used earlier just create a string `strToLog` containing the control names and values, including the `vbCRLF` constant that adds carriage returns in the appropriate places. Once we've got this string, we can send it to our `WriteToLogFile` function and check the result. If it fails, by returning `False`, we place an error message in our page:

```
'Now we can loop through the Dictionary and output the results
strToLog = "Results received from FORM on " & Now() & vbCRLF
strKeysArray = objResult.Keys              'get the keys into an array
strItemsArray = objResult.Items            'get the items into an array
For intLoop = 0 To objResult.Count -1      'iterate through the array
```

```
    strThisKey = strKeysArray(intLoop)       'this is the key value
    strThisItem = strItemsArray(intLoop)     'this is the item (data) value
    Response.Write strThisKey & " = " & strThisItem & "<BR>"
    strToLog = strToLog & strThisKey & " = " & strThisItem & vbCRLF
  Next
  strToLog = strToLog & "---------------------------- " & vbCRLF

  'Lastly, we write the results to the file, and put a message in the page
  If WriteToLogFile(strToLog) Then
    Response.Write "Results successfully logged."
  Else
    Response.write "Error in " & Err.Source
    Response.write "<BR>" & Err.description & "<P>"
  End If
```

If you try this code yourself, without creating the log file first, you'll get an error. This is because we've used the `OpenTextFile` method in the `WriteToLogFile` function without setting the *create* argument to `True`. The reason is that it better demonstrates how we have to consider errors that can arise, and find ways of handling them gracefully. This is the subject of the next section.

The Err Object

In several of the earlier sections, we've noted occasions where an error will occur if certain conditions arise when using the built-in scripting objects. OK, so we should always try to make sure that errors can't occur, by checking values entered by the user or resident in the operating system. However, as you've just seen, there will be times when it's very hard to predict exactly the state of the environment in which our code is running.

For example, the `FileSystemObject` and `TextStream` objects can create an error if we try to open a file that doesn't exist, or create a new file with the same name as one that already exists. VBScript doesn't include advanced file manipulation commands like `Dir`, which you can use in Visual Basic to see if a file exists. To prevent an unceremonious collapse of the script in our page, and the rather embarrassing error page being returned to the user, we can trap errors in our code and recover gracefully from them. To do this, we use the `On Error Resume Next` statement we first met in Chapter 1.

Using an On Error Statement

In Visual Basic, there are several different ways of using the `On Error` statement to control how our code should react to any errors it encounters. Unfortunately, VBScript–even in its latest incarnation–only contains one of these. By placing the statement `On Error Resume Next` at the beginning of our code routines, we instruct the script interpreter to ignore any errors it encounters, and carry on chugging through our code.

Then, once we've completed the processing we need to do, we can check to see if an error actually did occur. While there's not much we can do to change the result, we can at least provide a custom message to the user or load a different page. If they are submitting values from a form, we might even decide to give them a chance to try again with different values.

Using On Error Resume Next

The `On Error Resume Next` statement causes execution to continue with the statement immediately after the one that caused a runtime error. If the error is in a subroutine or function that we have called from elsewhere in our code, however, this subroutine or function is terminated immediately and execution continues with the line in the main body of the code after the one that called it. Of course, if the subroutine or function has its own `On Error Resume Next` statement, execution of *its* code continues after an error. Once execution leaves a subroutine or function, the `On Error Resume Next` statement within that routine is deactivated. You can think of it as being local to the routine.

This corresponds to a system referred to as the **call chain**. When our code calls another procedure (subroutine or function), this can itself call other procedures, creating a call chain. As each one completes, control passes back down the call chain to the procedure that called it. When an error occurs in a procedure which doesn't have an `On Error Resume Next` statement, control passes back down the call chain to the first one that does.

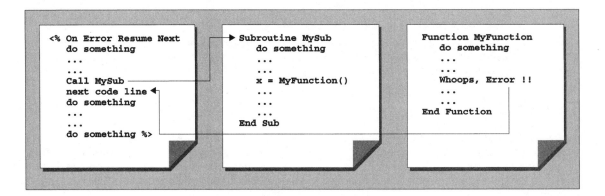

However, if none of the routines have an `On Error Resume Next` statement, the default error page is created and sent back to the user–and our code stops altogether. At this point, we've lost control. Therefore, we should always consider using `On Error Resume Next` at least in the main body of our code, so that we can trap an error that occurs in any of the other procedures we call.

Checking for an Error

Right, we've now trapped any errors that might have left our pages in a heap on the server-room floor. The problem is that our code might still be executing, even if an error did occur. Before we tell the user that they've got 4 million dollars in their checking account, we should make sure that there wasn't an error in the calculation. This is where the `Err` object comes in.

The `Err` object stores information about runtime errors, and we can use it to create an error. Why would we want to do this? Well, there are times when we might want to pass a custom error message back to the user. We can set the properties of the `Err` object to any value we please, then call its **Raise** method to raise this error. This stops execution of the code, and passes the error back to the Active Server Pages system. Here's a list of the available methods and properties:

Method / Property	Description
`Clear` method	Clears all current settings of the `Err` object.
`Raise` method	Generates a runtime error.
`Description` property	Sets or returns a string describing an error.
`Number` property	(Default) Sets or returns a numeric value specifying an error.
`Source` property	Sets or returns the name of the object that generated the error.

If a runtime error occurs, the properties of the **Err** object are set to values that uniquely identify the error. When an **On Error Resume Next** statement is executed, or when control passes back to a routine from a procedure it called, the properties are reset to zero or empty strings again. We can also reset the values on the **Err** object ourselves, using the **Clear** method.

So, to check for an error, we only need to examine the value of the **Err.Number** property after our call to **On Error Resume Next**, and before we exit from the routine. If it's zero, we know that an error hasn't occurred *in that routine*. However, remember that it is reset when we leave a subroutine or function, so we also need to check it here if we want to protect ourselves from incorrect information being returned. One of the easiest ways to use the object is to make sure that functions only return a value if they successfully run to completion. Remember, if an error occurs and we haven't used an **On Error Resume Next** statement in the function, execution immediately passes back to the code that called it.

Raising Our Own Errors

There are times when something goes wrong, and we need to pass custom details back to the routine that called our code. For example, we may be trying to open a text file that has been deleted. Normally, the VBScript interpreter will set the values of the **Err** object to the standard error code and description when this happens. By using **On Error Resume Next**, and examining the **Err** object, we can decide what kind of error occurred, and raise an appropriate message.

Here are some more modifications we've made to the code that was used in the generic form handler example, which has gradually been assembled throughout the previous sections of this chapter. Notice how we use the constant **vbObjectError** to make sure that the error number we select doesn't conflict with an existing error number. By adding our own randomly selected number to the constant, we can be more certain that we will not affect existing error numbers.

```
Function WriteToLogFile(strLogMessage)
  WriteToLogFile = False  'default return value of function
  On Error Resume Next
  Set objFSO = CreateObject("Scripting.FileSystemObject")
  Set objLogFile = objFSO.OpenTextFile("C:\Logfiles\MyLog.txt", 8)
  Select Case Err.Number
    Case 0            'OK, do nothing
    Case 50, 53       'standard file or path not found errors
      'create custom error values and raise error back to the system
      intErrNumber = vbObjectError + 1073       'custom error number
      strErrDescription = "Log file has been deleted or moved."
      strErrSource = "WriteToLogFile function"
      Err.Raise intErrNumber, strErrSource, strErrDescription
      Exit Function
    Case Else       'some other error
```

```
        'raise the standard error back to the system
        Err.Raise Err.Number, Err.Source, Err.Description
        Exit Function
    End Select
    objLogFile.WriteLine(strLogMessage)
    objLogFile.Close
    WriteToLogFile = True
End Function
```

We've assumed that if we can successfully find and open the file, we'll be able to write our string to it and close it again. Obviously, we could extend the error handling to cover these actions in the same way. You can download the complete example, **LogForm.htm** and **LogForm.asp**, from our web site to try yourself. Here are the results, both when the file exists and when it doesn't:

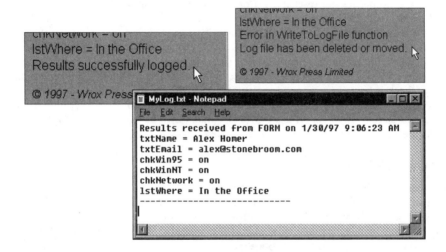

> For the data to be successfully logged, there must already be a text file by the name of **Mylog.txt** present under the path **C:\LogFiles**.

Scripting Objects vs. Server Components

Having seen the various VBScript scripting objects at work, we'll move on to look at how these are used with other components. It's important not to confuse the issue here when referring to server components, and built-in script objects. The **VBScript scripting objects**, like **TextStream** and **Err**, are part of the VBScript system itself, which is implemented by a DLL as part of the Active Server Pages system. In Chapter 1, we saw how we can use different scripting languages with Active Server Pages if we wish. These other languages, and their associated scripting objects, are implemented in a similar way, using a different DLL.

Server components are separate from the scripting language DLLs. They are implemented within their own DLL–for example, the Content Linking component you'll see later in this chapter is implemented within the file **Nextlink.dll**. Once this is installed and registered on the server, the object is available within any scripting language that Active Server Pages is set up to support.

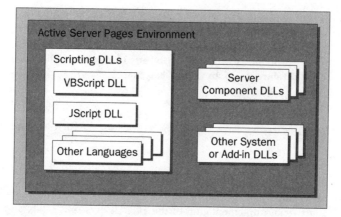

As you'll see, some of the server components use the capabilities of the built-in scripting objects we've already looked at. Before we look at individual ones, however, we'll take an overview of the way we use server components in general.

An Overview of Server Components

In the previous chapter, we briefly saw one way of making use of the components that are supplied with the Active Server Pages package. We created an instance of the **Browser Capabilities** component using one of the methods of the **Server** object:

```
Set objBCaps = Server.CreateObject("MSWC.BrowserType")
```

This creates a reference to the object in the variable **objBCaps**, and we can then work with the object in our script. In other words, we can manipulate its properties, and call its methods from code as required. In this section we'll be looking more closely at the ways we can create instances of components like this, the different components that are available, and the functions they offer.

Most of the standard components are aimed at specific kinds of tasks you need to accomplish in your web site or company intranet. As we saw in Chapter 1, there are a great many different *kinds* of web site and intranet installation. What you want to achieve with Active Server Pages will, obviously, depend on the kinds of information you want to publish, and the overall aims of your site. However, using pre-built components can, as you'll see, provide a headstart when you come to getting the show on the road.

Creating Instances of Components

There are two ways to create an instance of a component using VBScript. We can make use of the **Server** object's **CreateObject** method, as you saw earlier, to assign a reference to the object directly to a variable for use later in our code. Alternatively we can use an **<OBJECT>** tag–as you'll see in a while.

Reacting to CreateObject Errors

One common source of errors is attempting to create an instance of an object that isn't properly installed, or using the wrong identifier for the object. Active Server Pages will create an error page, and return this to the browser in the usual way. However, if we're using an **On Error Resume Next** statement in our page, we won't pick up this error automatically, and often the first we see of the error is when we try to use one of the object's methods, or refer to one of its properties.

An easy way to guard against this problem is with the `IsObject()` function. This returns `True` only if the parameter we supply is a valid reference to an object. For example:

```
On Error Resume Next
Set objMyObject = Server.CreateObject("MSWC.NotInstalled")
If IsObject(objMyObject) = False Then ...   'CreateObject method failed
```

Using an <OBJECT> Tag

Alternatively, we can use a normal `<OBJECT>` tag to create an instance of an object in our Active Server Pages, in the same way as we would when creating an object instance in a web page on the browser. Active Server Pages supports a special implementation of the HTML `<OBJECT>` tag, and we can use this to place an object in our pages. To define an instance of a component or scripting object in a normal `.asp` file, we use the syntax:

```
<OBJECT RUNAT=Server ID=ObjectReference PROGID="ObjectIdentifier">
</OBJECT>
```

`ObjectReference` is the name, such as `objMyObject`, by which we'll refer to the object in our code when we come to work with it. `ObjectIdentifier` is the name of the object or component in the Windows Registry; for example, `MSWC.Adrotator`. So we can declare an Ad Rotator object with the code:

```
<OBJECT RUNAT=Server ID=objAdRot PROGID="MSWC.Adrotator">
</OBJECT>
```

Notice the `RUNAT` attribute, which must be set to `Server`. The `PROGID` is a text string which uniquely defines the component or object, in the form `[Vendor.]Component[.Version]`.

Alternatively, we can use the `CLASSID` of the object instead of the 'friendly name' `PROGID`:

```
<OBJECT RUNAT=Server ID=objAdRot
  CLASSID="Clsid:00000293-0000-0010-8000-00AA006D2EA4">
</OBJECT>
```

Setting an Object's Scope

When used in a normal `.asp` file, there will generally be no difference in the performance of the page between using `CreateObject` or an `<OBJECT>` tag. The real difference is the point at which the object is actually instantiated, or created. The `CreateObject` method creates the instance of the object as soon as it is called. However, an object defined within an `<OBJECT>` tag isn't actually created until it is first referenced. This can allow us to minimize resource use or increase performance on the server, where the object isn't actually defined in the `.asp` page but in the `global.asa` file.

We met `global.asa`, and the notion of `Session` and `Application` objects, in the previous chapter, and we'll be coming back to it in a lot more detail later in the book. In the meantime, we only need to appreciate that we can create instances of objects in this file, and they then have a scope that is defined by the `Session` or `Application`, rather than just the lifetime of the reference variable in the `.asp` page. We do this by including the `SCOPE` attribute within the `<OBJECT>` tag:

```
<OBJECT RUNAT=Server SCOPE=Session ID=objAdRot PROGID="MSWC.Adrotator">
</OBJECT>
```

The valid values for **SCOPE** are **Session**, **Application**, or **Page**. If we use an **<OBJECT>** tag in a normal **.asp** file, we have to use **Page**, or omit the **SCOPE** attribute altogether. However, if we place the **<OBJECT>** tag in **global.asa**, we create an object that is available throughout the current session, or globally throughout the application. This has particular performance implications when we come to use the database component, as you'll see in later chapters.

Component Methods and Properties

The whole reason for using components in our Active Server Pages is to benefit from the extra functionality they provide, which is either unavailable, or inefficient or difficult to achieve, using just a scripting language. Once the object instance is available, and we have a reference to it, we can call its **methods** and manipulate its **properties** to achieve the effects we require.

Each component has its own particular methods and properties, so we need to know what these are, and (in the case of methods) the exact syntax and arguments each one supports. For example, the **Content Linking** component has a method called **GetNextURL**, while the **Advertisement Rotator** component has a **GetAdvertisement** method. In the next section, we'll look in detail at the standard components, then a few of the others that are available as well.

Many component methods return a value. In most cases this will be something that we want to actually work with, such as the URL returned by the Content Linking component **GetNextURL** method. Others just accept a value, such as the **Append** method of the User Properties component. However, many of these methods also return **True** or **False** values that we can use to make sure that the operation was successful. For example:

```
If objProp("shirts").Append("Hawaiian") = TRUE Then ...   'it worked OK
```

The Standard Components

Active Server Pages includes four standard server components. We'll be covering the Active Database Object (ADO) component in the next chapter. In the remainder of this chapter, we'll see how we can gain extra functionality for our web site or intranet using the other three. You'll see:

- ▲ The **Content Linking** component
- ▲ The **Browser Capabilities** component
- ▲ The **Ad Rotator** component

The Content Linking Component

The **Content Linking** component is a very useful tool for sites that provide contents pages, or pages that contain a list of links to other pages on the same site. It automatically matches the URL of the currently displayed page to a list of pages stored in a text file on the server, and can allow users to browse through the list of pages in forward or reverse order. In other words, even after the visitor has clicked on a link in the contents page, and is viewing one of the pages in the list, the component can still tell whereabouts that page is within the list.

And because all the details are stored in a text file, maintaining the site—and the links between the pages—becomes a matter of just editing the text file. For example, we can change the order that the pages are displayed in just by rearranging them in the content linking list file.

The Content Linking List File

The **Content Linking List file** contains a simple list of page URLs, in the order they are to be displayed. We also supply matching descriptions, which are displayed in the contents page, and we can add comments to each one if required. These help identify the links later, and aren't visible to visitors. The file contains one line of text for each page. Each line consists of the URL, description and comment, separated by *Tab* characters and ending with a carriage return. For example:

```
newline.htm      New additions to our site      we update this weekly
offers.htm       Special Offers for this week    we only update this monthly
register.htm     Registration for new users
main.htm         The main forum and chat area    must be registered first
index.htm        Back to the contents page
```

> *URLs must be specified as a virtual or relative path, such as* `forum\enter.htm`. *URLs that start with* `http:`, `//`, *or* `\\` *can't be used.*

Using the Content Linking Component

Once we've created our content linking file, we can add the component to our pages. We can use the standard `CreateObject` syntax, or an `<OBJECT>` tag. In the examples in this chapter, you'll mostly see `CreateObject` being used:

```
Set objNextLink = Server.CreateObject("MSWC.Nextlink")
```

Then, we can use the methods it provides to manipulate the list, and create our pages:

Method	Description
`GetListCount(list)`	Number of items in the file *list*.
`GetListIndex(list)`	Index of the current page in the file *list*.
`GetNextURL(list)`	URL of the next page in the file *list*.
`GetNextDescription(list)`	Description of the next page in file *list*.
`GetPreviousURL(list)`	URL of the previous page in the file *list*.
`GetPreviousDescription(list)`	Description of previous page in file *list*.
`GetNthURL(list, n)`	URL of the nth page in the file *list*.
`GetNthDescription(list, n)`	Description of the nth page in the file *list*.

> The index number of the first item is 1. If the current page isn't in the Content
> Linking List file, GetListIndex returns 0, GetNextURL and
> GetNextDescription return the URL and description of the last page in the list,
> GetPreviousURL and GetPreviousDescription return the URL and
> description of the first page in the list.

Creating a Contents Page

We've created a simple example that uses pages describing some of our other books. You can download it
from http://www.rapid.wrox.com/books/0723/ and try it out yourself. It creates a table of
contents, using a Content Linking List file named contlink.txt. This code is in the main page,
content.asp:

```
<UL>
  <% Set objNextLink = Server.CreateObject("MSWC.NextLink")
  intCount = objNextLink.GetListCount("contlink.txt")
  For intLoop = 1 To intCount %>
    <LI>
      <A HREF="<%= objNextLink.GetNthURL("contlink.txt", intLoop) %>">
        <%= objNextLink.GetNthDescription("contlink.txt", intLoop) %>
      </A>
  <% Next %>
</UL>
```

Inside the normal <UL> and </UL> tags, the code creates a Content Linking object .The correct reference
for this, as stored in the Window's Registry, is MSWC.NextLink. Then it uses the object's GetListCount
method to find out how many links there are in the Content Linking List, and loops through them. For
each one, it places an <LI> tag in the page, followed by an <A> tag. The HREF is retrieved from the list
file using the GetNthURL method, and the description with GetNthDescription. The Content Linking
List file contlink.txt, and the results it produces, look like this:

```
wh20.asp    Beginners C++ Programming
wh21.asp    Visual C++ Masterclass
wh30.asp    Beginners Guide to VB
wh40.asp    Instant VBScript
wh50.asp    Beginner's Guide to Access
```

Here our content list file is in the same folder as the ASP page. If it wasn't, we could provide either a
relative physical path, or a full virtual path, to it:

```
intCount = objNextLink.GetListCount("links\contlink.txt") 'physical path
intCount = objNextLink.GetListCount("/demo/contlink.txt") 'virtual path
```

Each item on the page is a hyperlink. Selecting View Source in the browser shows that we've just created an unordered list. Each list item is the **Description** from the content linking file, enclosed in an **<A>** tag that uses the URL as the **HREF**.

```
<UL>
  <LI>
    <A HREF="wh20.asp">
        Beginners C++ Programming
    </A>
    ...
    ...
</UL>
```

All pretty standard stuff, but we can do better than this....

Browsing Through the Pages

When we create an instance of the Content Linking component, and access one of its methods, it matches the *current* page's URL with the entries in the Content Linking List file we specify in that method call. We can use it not only to create a contents list (as we've just seen), but also to navigate between pages in the list while we've got one of them open in the browser.

This means that we can use hot links or buttons to move to another page, from one of the listed pages. For example, we can add Back and Next buttons to a page, because we can tell which is the next or previous item in the list by using the **GetNextURL** and **GetPreviousURL** methods. Alternatively, we can jump to any other page in the list, using the **GetNthURL** method. And, of course, we can tell where we are in the list at the moment using the **GetListIndex** method.

Here's the code that adds Next and Previous buttons to our pages. All we have to do is place it in each of the pages listed in the Content Linking file:

```
<% Set objNextLink = Server.CreateObject("MSWC.NextLink")
strListFile = "contlink.txt"
intThisPage = objNextLink.GetListIndex(strListFile)
If intThisPage > 1 Then %>
  <INPUT TYPE=BUTTON VALUE="< Back"
  ONCLICK="location.href='<% = objNextLink.GetPreviousURL(strListFile) %>';">
<% End If %>
<INPUT TYPE=BUTTON VALUE=" Home " ONCLICK="location.href='content.asp';">
<% If intThisPage < objNextLink.GetListCount(strListFile) Then %>
  <INPUT TYPE=BUTTON VALUE="Next >"
  ONCLICK="location.href='<%= objNextLink.GetNextURL(strListFile)  %>';">
<% End If %>
```

The first step is to create the Content Linking component, and then put the name of the list file into a variable. We need to do this if we want to use it in the JScript code later in the page. Besides, it makes the page easier to maintain, because we only have to change it in one place if we want to use a different filename.

Now we can see where we are within the Content Linking list. The **GetListIndex** method provides the line number, starting from **1**. If the current page has an index greater than **1**, we know we can go back—so we include the HTML to create the Back button in the page. Similarly, if the current page's index is less that the number of items in the list, we can include a Next button. We always include a Home button, so that the visitor can get back to the contents page easily at any time.

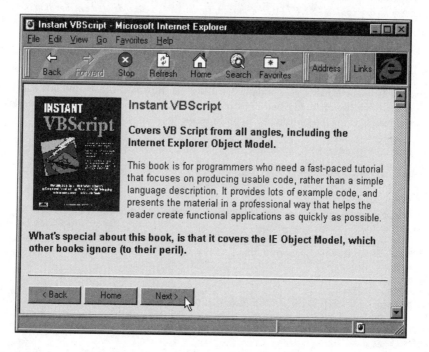

The screen shot above shows the three buttons, on a page in the middle of our list. If we browse to the end of the list, however, the index of the current page **intThisPage** is no longer less than the number of lines in the file **objNextLink.GetListCount(strListFile)**.

In this page, we don't get a Next button:

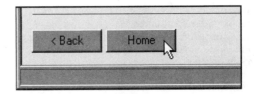

Jumping with JScript

You'll see that our navigation buttons use JScript (rather than VBScript) statements to load the new page. For example, the Back button contains the attribute:

```
ONCLICK="location.href='<% = objNextLink.GetPreviousURL(strListFile) %>';"
```

When the HTML version of the page is created by ASP, the expression inside the **<%...%>** tags is replaced with its value, so the page sent to the browser could look like this:

```
ONCLICK="location.href='wh21.htm';"
```

You can also see why we chose to use a variable to hold the name of the Content Linking List file–it's cumbersome to have to try to include a third level of nested quotes inside a single statement.

> *Remember, the default language in the browser is JavaScript or JScript, not VBScript. By using JScript, we avoid having to provide a LANGUAGE argument in the OnClick code, and anyway it makes a change.*

Going to Usability Extremes

Before we leave the Content Linking component, we'll just see how two other methods can be used to go to the extreme in usability. By changing two lines of our code, we can actually display the description of the next and previous pages in the buttons or hyperlinks on the current page:

```
<% Set objNextLink = Server.CreateObject ("MSWC.NextLink")
strListFile = "contlink.txt"
intThisPage = objNextLink.GetListIndex (strListFile)
If (intThisPage > 1) Then %>
  <INPUT TYPE=BUTTON
  VALUE="< Back to <%= objNextLink.GetPreviousDescription(strListFile) %>"
  ONCLICK="location.href='<%= objNextLink.GetPreviousURL (strListFile)  %>';">
<% End If %>
  <INPUT TYPE=BUTTON VALUE=" Home "
  ONCLICK="location.href='content.asp';">
<% If (intThisPage < objNextLink.GetListCount(strListFile)) Then %>
  <INPUT TYPE=BUTTON
  VALUE="Forward to <%= objNextLink.GetNextDescription(strListFile) %> >"
  ONCLICK="location.href='<%= objNextLink.GetNextURL (strListFile)  %>';">
<% End If %>
```

This uses the **GetPreviousDescription** and **GetNextDescription** methods in the same way as we used **GetPreviousURL** and **GetNextURL**. Of course, this time we get the description from the Content

Linking List file, rather than the URL. And remember—all these links are dynamically created just from the Content Linking List. Simply changing the list automatically changes which buttons or hyperlinks appear, and sets the correct captions. This has got to be a hot choice for many intranet-related tasks, where you need to provide regularly changing pages of information for your users.

The Browser Capabilities Component

One of the problems we face when creating all kinds of web pages, not just dynamic ones that use Active Server Pages, is deciding which of the increasing range of tags and techniques we should take advantage of. While it's great to be able to use all the latest features, such as Java applets, ActiveX controls, and the most recent HTML tags, we need to be aware that some visitors will be using browsers that don't support these. All they might see of our carefully crafted pages is a jumble of text, images, and—even worse—the code that makes them work.

This isn't a discussion on how you should design pages to support different browsers. To make the whole job easier, though, we can use a special server component called the **Browser Capabilities** component. This allows us to determine which of a whole range of features a browser supports, at the point when it actually references one of our pages.

When a user requests a page from the server, the HTTP header includes details of the browser they are using. In HTTP-speak it's called the **user agent**, and is a string defining the browser software name and version. This is effectively mapped to the Browser Capabilities component, which then adopts a range of properties equivalent to the user's browser features. Hence, at any time while the page is being executed, the Browser Capabilities component can provide details of which individual features are or are not supported.

The Browscap.ini File

The Browser Capabilities component consists of a single DLL **Browscap.dll**, plus a text file **Browscap.ini** that must be in the same directory as the DLL. **Browscap.ini** contains the information about each known browser, and there's also a default section of the file, which is used when the browser details don't match any of the ones more fully specified in the file. So adding new information about browsers, or updating the existing information, is as easy as editing the **Browscap.ini** file.

We'll look at the format of this file first. All of the entries in **Browscap.ini** are optional, however it's important that we always include the default section. If the browser in use doesn't match any in the **Browscap.ini** file, and no default browser settings have been specified, all the properties are set to **"UNKNOWN"**.

```
; we can add comments anywhere, prefaced by a semicolon like this

; entry for a specific browser
[HTTPUserAgentHeader]
```

105

```
parent = browserDefinition
property1 = value1
property2 = value2
...

[Default Browser Capability Settings]
defaultProperty1 = defaultValue1
defaultProperty1 = defaultValue1
...
```

The [`HTTPUserAgentHeader`] line defines the start of a section for a particular browser, and the `parent` line indicates that another definition contains more information for that browser as well. Then, each line defines a property that we want to make available through the Browser Capabilities component, and its value for this particular browser. The `Default` section lists the properties and values that are used if the particular browser in use isn't listed in its own section, or if it is listed but not all the properties are supplied.

For example, we may have a section for Internet Explorer 3.0. This has no `parent` line, and so the only properties it will have (other than those defined in the default section) are those we explicitly define:

```
[IE 3.0]
browser=IE
Version=3.0
majorver=#3
minorver=#0
frames=TRUE
tables=TRUE
cookies=TRUE
vbscript=TRUE
javascript=TRUE
ActiveXControls=TRUE
...
```

Now, we can add the definition for another browser. For example:

```
[Mozilla/2.0 (compatible; MSIE 3.01; Windows 95)]
parent=IE 3.0
version=3.01
minorver=01
platform=Win95
```

Here, we've specified `IE 3.0` as the `parent` for this browser. The properties we've explicitly provided replace, or add to, those values in its parent's definition–but it will also assume any other property values there, which aren't explicitly listed in its own section. Then, lastly, we add the default browser section:

```
[Default Browser Capability Settings]
browser=Default
frames=FALSE
tables=FALSE
cookies=FALSE
backgroundsounds=FALSE
vbscript=FALSE
javascript=FALSE
...
```

This assumes a 'worse case scenario', where the browser supports almost nothing at all. However, it's up to us to define the actual values we want to use as this base. But we need to appreciate that if we've defined some of the default properties as **TRUE**, and we *do* get a visit from someone running a green-on-black, text-only browser on a Unix terminal, they might not see our page to full effect.

Maintaining Browscap.ini

Keeping `Browscap.ini` up to date with new browsers as they are released, and adding older or specialist ones that we may have to contend with, is obviously important. To make life easier, a reasonably comprehensive version of `Browscap.ini` is supplied with Active Server Pages and updated ones can be downloaded from Microsoft's web site at `http://www.microsoft.com`.

To help with recognizing very similar versions of a browser, we can use the asterisk (*) wildcard in the `HTTPUserAgentHeader` line. Then:

```
[Mozilla/2.0 (compatible; MSIE 3.0;* Windows 95)]
```

will match:

```
[Mozilla/2.0 (compatible; MSIE 3.0; Windows 95)]
[Mozilla/2.0 (compatible; MSIE 3.0; AOL; Windows 95)]
  ... etc.
```

However, wildcard matches are only used if the user agent string sent by the browser doesn't fully match an `HTTPUserAgentHeader` which does *not* include an asterisk. Only if this test fails will it attempt to match with wildcard `HTTPUserAgentHeader` values, and it will use the first one it finds in the file that does match.

Using the Browser Capabilities Component

Having grasped how the `Browscap.ini` file can provide customizable properties containing information about a particular browser, it's time to actually see the Browser Capabilities component in use. This is relatively simple—we just create an instance of it, and refer to its properties. Notice that to avoid having the `Browscap.ini` file accessed every time, which makes our code more efficient, we read the value once and assign it to a variable:

```
Set objBCap = Server.CreateObject("MSWC.BrowserType")
blnTablesOK = objBCap.tables  'save the value in a variable
If blnTablesOK Then Response.Write "<TABLE><TR><TD>"
Response.Write "This is some text."
If blnTablesOK Then
  Response.Write "</TD><TD>"
Else
  Response.Write "   "
End If
Response.Write "This is some more text."
If blnTablesOK Then
  Response.Write "</TD></TR></TABLE>"
Else
  Response.Write "<P>"
End If
```

This will create a table if the browser supports them, or just place the two items of text next to each other, separated by non-breaking spaces, if not. Modern browsers will receive:

```
<TABLE><TR><TD>
This is some text.
</TD><TD>
This is some more text.
</TD></TR></TABLE>
```

while non-tables browsers will receive:

```
This is some text.
   
This is some more text.
<P>
```

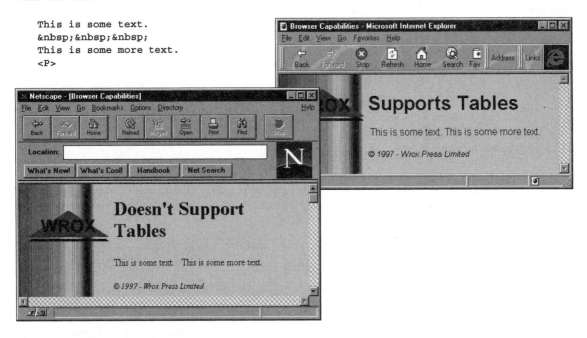

Of course, we can use the properties to do other things. One of the favorite techniques is to load a different index page for a site, depending on what features the browser supports. If our site has a set of pages using frames, and a different set using only simple text, we can check the browser's ability to display frames when it first hits our site, and redirect it to the appropriate index page.

Ad Rotator Component

The **Ad Rotator** component allows us to display a different graphic on our pages, each time the page is referenced from a browser. Hence the first time you access the site you may see a graphic advertising holidays, the next time you return to the page it might be for pizzas. In fact, this technique is often used in sites that display advertisements, hence the component name. Every time the page is opened or re-loaded, Active Server Pages uses the information in a **Rotator Schedule File** to select a graphic, and insert it into the page. However, the Ad Rotator component can do more than this. We can arrange for the image to be a hyperlink rather than a static picture, and even record how many users click each one of the advertisements.

Of all the components we're looking at in this chapter, the Ad Rotator is probably the most complicated to use because it involves several different files. Before we start to look at each file in detail, an overview of the process might help you to see how it all fits together. The visitor sees an advertisement on the page, usually a graphic that is also a hyperlink. Each time they load our page, however, a different one may be displayed from a fixed selection. Clicking on the graphic loads a redirection file, which itself sends the user off to the advertiser's site.

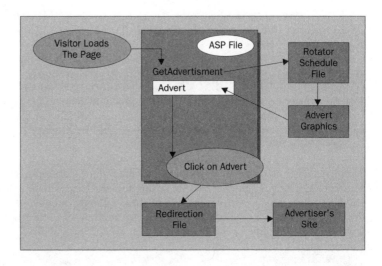

Creating the Component Object

To create an instance of the Ad Rotator component, we've used the **Server** object's **CreateObject** method:

```
Set objAdRot = Server.CreateObject("MSWC.AdRotator")
```

Once we've got our **objAdRot** object, we can work with its properties, and the single method it provides. The first step is to decide on the width of the image border, the frame where we want the graphic to be displayed, and whether it accepts mouse clicks from the user. Notice how this particular component requires us to set its *properties* in the same way as we would if we were actually calling a *method*:

```
objAdRot.Border (0)                 'no border
objAdRot.Clickable (TRUE)           'is a hyperlink
objAdRot.TargetFrame ("fraAdFrame") 'load into frame named fraAdFrame
```

Then, we need to insert the HTML for the graphic into the page that will be returned to the user. The **GetAdvertisement** method creates this, by getting details of the next advertisement to display from the rotator schedule file. We then have to place the HTML code into the page:

```
StrHTML = objAdRot.GetAdvertisement("AdFiles\MyAdFile.txt")
Response.Write(strHTML)     'put the HTML into the page
```

The argument for the method is the location of the rotator schedule file relative to the current directory. For example, if this file is stored in the **AdFiles** directory within the current directory, we use **AdFiles\MyAdFile.txt**. Here are the methods and properties that the Ad Rotator component supports:

Method / Property	Description
GetAdvertisement method	Gets details of the next advertisement and formats it as HTML.
Border property	Size of the border around the advertisement.
Clickable property	Defines whether the advertisement is a hyperlink.
TargetFrame property	Name of the frame in which to display the advertisement.

The `TargetFrame` *can also be set to one of the standard HTML frame identifiers such as* `_top`, `_new`, `_child`, `_self`, `_parent`, *or* `_blank`.

The Rotator Schedule File

The Ad Rotator component depends on the rotator schedule file to specify the advertisements, or graphics, which are to be displayed. This includes the name of the image files, the size they are to be displayed at, and the relative percentage of times each one should be displayed. It's divided into two sections, which are separated by a line containing only an asterisk (*).

The first section is optional, and sets the default values that apply to all the advertisements in the schedule. This provides us with another way of setting these values, without using the object's parameters directly as we did earlier. If we omit one or more of these optional parameters, and don't set the properties explicitly, the object will use its own default values. If we omit all of these parameters, we still have to include the asterisk as the first line of the file.

```
REDIRECT URL
WIDTH width
HEIGHT height
BORDER border
*
adURL
adHomeURL
text
impressions
```

URL	Virtual path and name of the program or ASP file that implements the redirection.
width	Width in pixels of the advertisement on the page. Default is **440**.
height	Height in pixels of the advertisement on the page. Default is **60**.
border	Border width around the advertisement, in pixels. Default is **1**, use **0** for no border.

The second section, after the asterisk, must exist in the file. It provides details of the individual advertisements, and is repeated for each one:

adURL	Virtual path and filename of the advertisement image file.
adHomeURL	Advertiser's home page URL. A hyphen indicates there is no link for this ad.
text	Text for display if the browser doesn't support graphics.
impressions	A number indicating the relative display time for the advertisement.

If the file contains three advertisements, with their **impressions** *set to 2, 3, and 5, the first is included in 20 percent of the returned pages, the second in 30 percent, and the third in 50 percent. It doesn't indicate the actual time that the advertisement will be displayed in the browser.*

An Example Rotator Schedule File

So, let's see what a rotator schedule file looks like in practice. Here's a simple one containing only two advertisements, which will be displayed an equal number of times. It depends on the virtual directory path `/ASP0723`, which we've created on the server, to be able to find the files it lists:

```
REDIRECT /ASP0723/AdRot/AdFiles/AdRedirect.asp
*
/ASP0723/AdRot/AdFiles/AdPics/wrox.gif
http://www.wrox.com
Better books from Wrox Press
10
/ASP0723/AdRot/AdFiles/AdPics/lunar.gif
http://www.wrox.com
Acme Lunar Boost Supplies
10
```

When we call the **GetAdvertisement** method, it returns HTML code that we can insert into our page to create the advertisement. For the first advertisement in our file, we'll get this:

```
...
<A HREF="/ASP0723/AdRot/AdFiles/AdRedirect.asp?url=http://www.wrox.com&image=/ASP0723/
AdRot/AdFiles/AdPics/wrox.gif">
<IMG SRC="/ASP0723/AdRot/AdFiles/AdPics/wrox.gif" ALT="Better books from Wrox Press"
WIDTH=440 HEIGHT=60 BORDER=0>
</A>
...
```

You can see that it has placed the image inside a normal **<A>** tag. The **HREF** attribute is set to the name of our **Redirection File**, **AdRedirect.asp**, with the advertiser's home page URL and the image we used appended to it with a question mark. Therefore, our redirection file will be loaded and executed on the server when the user clicks on the advertisement. Here's what our example looks like:

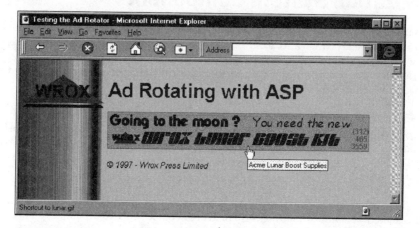

The Redirection File

The redirection file can be an ASP page, an ISAPI DLL, or a CGI application, which accepts the advertiser's home page URL and the image name parameters sent to it. It can examine these and decide what to do next–for example, it will usually redirect the user to the URL associated with the advertisement. This is easy to do, using the VBScript code:

```
Response.Redirect(Request.QueryString("url"))
```

However, the redirection file provides us with the opportunity to do more than this. For example, we can count the number of users that have clicked on each advertisement—which is particularly useful if we're getting paid according to the number of redirections we achieve. We could do this with the `WriteToLogFile` function we used earlier:

```
...
If Instr(Request.QueryString("url"), "wrox.com") Then
  'this is a jump to the Wrox Press site
  strToLog = "Wrox Press on " & Now() & vbCRLF
End If
...
...
blnOK = WriteToLogFile(strToLog)
Response.Redirect(Request.QueryString("url"))
```

As the query string contains the name of the image file, we can also refer to this in our script. If the same advertiser had three images in the rotator file, we could combine the number of responses for all three:

```
...
If Instr(Request.QueryString("image"), "wrox") Then
  'this is an image with 'wrox' in the name, so it must be a jump to them
End If
...
```

Personalization System Components

Just posting your beautifully crafted pages on the Web isn't enough any more. To succeed in today's competitive business climate you have to stand out from the rest, and the Internet is no different. One way to offer that 'bit extra' on your site is to make it appear as though it's tailored specially for each visitor. For example, you can alert them to new pages dealing with particular subjects they are interested in, or email specific information to them.

Most modern applications allow the user to specify the settings for various options they want to use. There's no reason why this can't be extended to web pages as well. We can allow users to select a background color or font, for example, then use this in all the pages we send them. And, of course, we need to remember these settings not only between the pages they view during one visit, but when they come back again in a week's time.

Microsoft provides a set of server components designed to help us manage these kinds of tasks, in what's euphemistically called a **community-building system**. Three components come under the heading of the Microsoft Personalization System, previously code-named 'Normandy'—the **User Property Database Component**, the **Voting Component**, and the **SendMail Component**. The components are not directly part of Active Server Pages, but beta versions are currently available from Microsoft's web site at: `http://www.ms-normandy.com`. No doubt, they'll be a chargeable item in time. In the final part of this chapter we'll look very briefly at each of these, plus a couple of other Microsoft components.

The User Property Database Component

When a user references and loads a page in our web site, their browser sends an HTTP header telling our web server various details about itself, such as the machine's IP address and the username. However, Active Server Pages also uses a cookie exchange system to allow a 'persistent connection' to be established. The first time the user references a page in our application, ASP sends them a cookie containing a unique user code. This is included in the HTTP header each time they connect to our site to load a different page.

Time for a Cookie

So by examining the cookie sent from the browser, we can not only tell that the user has been here before, but also who they are (at least in relation to his or her last visit–technology hasn't managed to provide more intimate details automatically yet). This is how Active Server Pages manages the concept of a **session**, using cookies that expire after 20 minutes.

The **User Property Database Component** builds on this technique by adding cookies that don't expire. This cookie contains an **ID** by which the user will be recognized within the user properties database, and to which their user preferences will be attached. When we create an instance of the User Property Database object, it automatically connects the user to the matching ID in the database. The object instance is created in the normal way:

```
Set objProp = Server.CreateObject("MPS.PropertyDatabase")
```

Then we can examine the user's ID, or connect the page to a different ID if required. Note that we don't need to do either if we want to work with the current user's properties–the connection is made automatically using the cookie sent from the browser. It's only when the browser doesn't support cookies that this fails, and we may need to do it ourselves:

```
strUserID = objProp.ID     'read the current user ID
objProp.ID = NewUserID     'change it to a new ID
```

Here's a list of all the methods and properties we can use with our **PropertyDatabase** object:

Method/Property	Description
ID property	Sets or returns the user's **ID** in the database.
Item method	(Default) Reads or writes user properties to the database.
Defaults property	Sets default user properties in the database.
LoadFromString method	Writes properties direct from the browser's query string.
Append method	Adds items to multivalue user properties.
Remove method	Removes items from multivalue properties in the database.
Count property	The number of items in a multivalue user property.
PropertyString property	Returns all the user properties as a complete query string.
ReadOnly property	Sets the database to read-only mode for the page.

Problems with Proxy Servers

When we use the `PropertyDatabase` object, or any other technique that sends customized content to a user, we need to consider what happens if they are accessing our pages through a proxy server. This sits between our web server and their internal network, and is usually there to provide security by only allowing certain users to access the network the other side of the proxy server. It takes their request and passes it on to our web server, then collects the page we send back and hands it on to the user. Hence, it stops us from being able to directly identify the user who referenced the page–we only get the details of the proxy server.

The problem is that the proxy server is also likely to cache pages we send to users, so if another user on the network the other side of it requests our page, they'll get the copy in the proxy's cache instead of a personally tailored one from us. To get round this, we must prevent the proxy from caching our page by including an instruction in the HTTP header. To do this, we set the **Expires** property of the **Response** object:

```
Response.Expires = 0
```

This actually prevents any caching, forcing a full reload of the page from our site even when the Back button is clicked on the browser. Some proxy servers support the Cache-Control header variable, which prevents the proxy caching the page, but allows the browser to cache it. If we can be sure that all the proxy servers which might reference our page will support this, we can use **Response.AddHeader("Cache-Control", "private")** *instead.*

Reading and Writing Property Values

Once we've got our component up and running, we can use it to query the property database. To set a user's property, we specify the name of the property and the value for it:

```
objProp("PropertyName") = "PropertyValue"
```

To get a value back into a string variable **strPropValue**, we just have to specify the name of the property:

```
strPropValue = objProp("PropertyName")
```

This is actually a shorthand form of the command. Like the ASP object model, the full syntax is **objProp.Item("**PropertyName**")**, *but* **.Item** *is optional.*

So, to set a user's **bgcolor** property in the database to red, and find out what color text they chose last time, we can use the following code:

```
Set objProp = Server.CreateObject("MPS.PropertyDatabase")
objProp("bgcolor") = "red"
strTextColor = objProp("textcolor")
```

Of course, this doesn't automatically set the text or background colors. We have to do this in the HTML code as usual, but it does supply the values we need. Note, however, that all values stored in the user property database are **strings**. If we want to store a **number**, we have to convert it to a string using the

`CStr()` function before we store it, and convert it back to a number using the `CInt()` function after each retrieval. It's also a good idea when setting properties in response to values sent from a form to first check that the user actually entered a value. We can use the built-in constant `Empty` to see if there was a value sent in the request:

```
If Request("txtTextColorField") = Empty Then ...   'no value submitted
```

Default Property Values

If we decide to use the properties to set, for example, the color of the text on a page, we can retrieve it and use it inside the page's `<BODY>` tag, like this:

```
<% Set objProp = Server.CreateObject("MPS.PropertyDatabase") %>
<BODY TEXT=<% = objProp("textcolor")%> >
```

This is great as long as we have a value in the database for this user's text color preference. If not, we get an empty string returned for the property `objProp("textcolor")`, and the HTML will contain just `<BODY TEXT= >`. To avoid this, we set a default value for the property first. This is a default for just this page, and the value isn't actually stored anywhere. It's only used if a request for a particular property is made, and a value for that property isn't already stored in the user properties database. For example:

```
<% Set objProp = Server.CreateObject("MPS.PropertyDatabase") %>
<% objProp.Defaults = ("textcolor=#2E2E00") %>
<BODY TEXT=<% = objProp("textcolor")%> >
```

Multiple-value Properties

The properties we've considered so far only hold one value. If we set them to a new value, the original one is, as you'd expect, lost forever. However, we can use the `Append` method to add more than one value to a property:

```
objProp("shirts").Append("Hawaiian")
objProp("shirts").Append("Blanket")
objProp("shirts").Append("White")
```

This code produces a `shirts` property value of `Hawaiian, Blanket, White`. To read these multiple-value properties we can then use:

```
strMultiProp = objProp("shirts")        'returns: Hawaiian, Blanket, White
strFirstProp = objProp("shirts")(1)     'returns the first item only
```

To find the number of values available, we can use the `Count` property, to loop through them all, like this:

```
For intLoop = 1 to objProp("shirts").Count
  strThisProp = objProp("shirts")(intLoop)
Next
```

And to remove a value from a multiple-value property, we can use the `Remove` method:

```
objProp("shirts").Remove(2)                'removes the second value
```

Handling a Query String

Lastly, we can set and retrieve a whole heap of values in one go, using a query string of the same format as the browser sends from a `<FORM>` section. We can also use this method if we specify the query string as part of the request directly; for example, if the referring page contains the link:

```
<A HREF="http://mypage.asp?shirts=Hawaiian&color=BrightRed">
```

The `LoadFromString` method takes the query string, parses it into separate property name and value pairs, and updates all the properties in one go. The `PropertyString` is the reverse of this. It returns all the stored properties for the current user and their values, as a single URL-encoded string of property/ value pairs. This is useful for sending them to another `.asp` page, for example:

```
objProp.LoadFromString(Request.Form)    'put the values into the database
strAllPropsURL = objProp.PropertyString  'get all the values out again
```

Read-only Database Access

The final property we need to consider is the `ReadOnly` property. We can set this to `TRUE` as soon as we create the `PropertyDatabase` object, and before we reference any of the properties stored in it, to improve the performance of our page. It informs the object that we won't be updating any properties, just reading existing values.

The Voting Component

If we want to use our web site to collect opinions, or allow users to vote on particular subjects, we can use the **Voting Component**. Unlike the User Properties component (which stores its values in special-format flat files on the server's disk), this requires a 'real' database to operate. We can easily use Microsoft SQL Server or Microsoft Access straight away, because databases in the correct format for both of these are supplied with the Personalization System.

However, because the link to the database is through ODBC, we can create our own database in any system, and link the Voting Component to it. The help files supplied with the component detail the database format required. We also have to set up a **System Data Source Name** in the ODBC Administrator to point to our database. Details of how we do this are in the Appendix G, and the process is discussed in more detail in later chapters.

Registering Votes in a Ballot

Using the Voting Component is relatively simple. The Active Server Pages file can be referenced from a `<FORM>` section that contains controls (text boxes, list boxes, etc.) where the user enters their vote or opinion. Each subject or question they vote on is part of a **ballot**, which can hold more than one question. The database holds the results of all users' votes on each question in each ballot. The results can be a single numeric value, where we just want to count the number of votes, or a series of values where we want to know the relative score of each answer.

First, we create our instance of the `MPS.Vote` object, and then open the vote database by supplying the correct System Data Source Name, user ID, and password if required. The setup program automatically creates a System DSN named **vote** pointing to the supplied Access database, which doesn't require a user name or password:

```
Set objVote = Server.CreateObject("MPS.Vote")
If objVote.Open("vote", "", "") Then
  If objVote.SetBallotName("Shirts") Then
    If objVote.Submit("Colors", "Bright Red") Then
      'everything worked OK, and the vote was accepted
    End If
  End If
End If
```

Second, we tell the component which ballot we want to work with, using the **SetBallotName** method. The name we supply is used as an identifier for that ballot, both to store votes and to display the results. Lastly, we can register the vote using the **Submit** method–in our example here, we're voting for **Bright Red** on the question named **Colors**, which is part of the **Shirts** ballot. Notice how we check the return value at each stage, with an **If...Then** construct, to make sure all the steps are completed successfully.

Showing the Results

As well as collecting votes, the component can also return the results as HTML pages to a browser. First, at the top of the **.asp** file, we set the expiry of the page to zero so that users get a new copy, rather than one that's been cached and contains out-of-date results:

```
Response.Expires = 0
```

Next, we create the object, open the database, and set the ballot name we want to use. Then we can do one of two things–we can get numeric values for the number of votes, or an HTML string that defines a table holding the results.

The GetVoteCount Method

To get the number of votes, we use the **GetVoteCount** method. We can get the number for each value submitted against a particular question, or a total for all votes on that question. This allows us to calculate percentages of the total for each value. Here's part of the example page named **Vote.asp** that we've included in the rest of the samples:

```
intNumberOfVotes = CInt(objVote.GetVoteCount("Colors"))
intChoseBrightRed = CInt(objVote.GetVoteCount("Colors", "Bright Red"))
sngPercentChoseBrightRed = Cint(intChoseBrightRed * 100 / intNumberOfVotes)
```

The GetVote Method

The **GetVote** method works in a similar way, but returns a string that is an HTML table ready to inset into the returned page. It can provide the results for all the questions in a ballot, all the values for just one question, or the results for one particular value for one question:

```
strTableOfAllShirtQuestionResults = objVote.GetVote
strTableOfAllColorVotes = objVote.GetVote("Colors")
strTableOfAllBrightRedVotes = objVote.GetVote("Colors", "Bright Red")
```

Doing It All In One Page

Generally, when we use the Voting Component, we'll want to show the current results when we accept a vote. We can actually do both together, in the same page. All we have to do is check the **Request** object's **Content_Length** (the length of the string following the question mark in the request string) to see if this is a submission from a **<FORM>**–that is, the control's values are appended to the query string after the URL. If it is, we process the vote in the query string, then display the new results and add the controls to allow the user to place another vote. If it wasn't a vote submission (i.e. the page is being loaded normally), we just display the current results of the vote and the controls for the user to vote for the first time.

Here's the code we use in **Vote.asp** to do this. We first create the component, then check the **Content_Length**. If it's greater than zero, we process the user's vote. This will be a color that they entered into the **txtColor** text box on the **<FORM>** section of this page:

```
<%
Set objVote = Server.CreateObject("MPS.Vote")

If Request("Content_Length") > 0 Then        'this is a FORM submission
  If objVote.Open("vote", "", "") Then       'so we process the vote
    If objVote.SetBallotName("Shirts") Then
      If objVote.Submit("Colors", Request("txtShirtColor")) Then %>
        Your vote was accepted <P>
  <% End If
    End If
  End If
End If %>
```

Now we can display the results. We put them into a series of variables for inserting into the page afterwards. Notice how we use the **GetVote** method with no parameters to get the totals for all the results as an HTML table:

```
The results so far: <BR>
<% 'we always display the results, even if they didn't vote
If objVote.Open("vote", "", "") Then
  If objVote.SetBallotName("Shirts") Then
    intNumberOfVotes = CInt(objVote.GetVoteCount("Colors"))
    intChoseBrightRed = CInt(objVote.GetVoteCount("Colors", "Bright Red"))
    sngPercentChoseBrightRed = intChoseBrightRed * 100 / intNumberOfVotes
    strTableAllShirts = objVote.GetVote
  End If
End If %>
```

Lastly, we can place the results into the page, and add the **<FORM>** section that allows the user to register a vote. You'll see that the **ACTION** attribute which specifies as URL is actually set to this page–the **Submit** button just reloads the same page, which processes the vote and displays the new result:

```
There were <% = intNumberOfVotes %> votes in all of which
<% = intChoseBrightRed %>, or <% = CInt(sngPercentChoseBrightRed) %>% were
for Bright Red.<P>

<% = strTableAllShirts %>  <!--this is the table-->

<FORM ACTION="Vote.asp" METHOD="POST">
  <INPUT TYPE=TEXT NAME="txtShirtColor" VALUE="Bright Red"> <P>
  <INPUT TYPE=SUBMIT VALUE="Register My Vote">
</FORM>
```

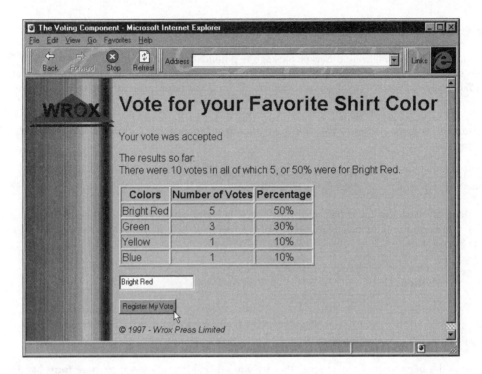

Here's a summary of all the methods available with the Voting Component:

Method	Description
Open method	Opens a connection to the vote database.
SetBallotName method	Specifies the ballot on which the vote should be counted.
Submit method	Processes the user's vote.
GetVote method	Returns the results of the votes as an HTML table.
GetVoteCount method	Returns a count of the numbers of votes.

It's possible to prevent user's voting twice on a question if you wish. In fact, there's a lot more functionality available from the Voting Component, which we haven't had room to cover here. The help files provide more information on these topics.

The SendMail Component

The third part of the Personalization Server package is potentially the most useful, and (once you've got it set up) the simplest to use. It allows us to send simple text email to anyone, as long as we have an SMTP (Simple Mail Transfer Protocol) mail server available. During the setup program for Personalization Server, you are prompted to enter the name or IP address of this server, so messages can be posted to it.

Using **SendMail** is just a matter of creating the component instance and calling its single **SendMail** method, like this:

```
Set objMail = Server.CreateObject("MPS.SendMail")
blnWorked = objMail.SendMail("from", "to", "subject", "body")
```

The only thing to watch out for is that you must supply a 'valid' email address for the **from** parameter, as well as the **to** parameter. This means one that has the user and host name parts separated by **@**, such as **feedback@wrox.com**.

Method	Description
SendMail (*from, to, subject, body*)	Sends a message using an SMTP mail server

A Real Use for the SendMail Component

You'll recall at the beginning of this chapter that we started building a general-purpose form handler using Active Server Pages. We got to the point where we could create the results string, and send it back to the browser or write it to a log file.

However, it's often far more useful to mail the results of a form submission to someone. This may just be the Webmaster's postbox—or, if you rent out web server space to others, it could be their email address. And there's no reason why we can't allow the user to enter an email address, even their own, and post the results to whoever they specify when they submit the form.

Our code already collects the user's email address, so we can create a message containing the results of the form submission and send it to them by email as a confirmation. Here's the changes required to our previous code:

```
'Now we can loop through the Dictionary and output the results
strToMail = "Results received from FORM on " & Now() & vbCRLF
strKeysArray = objResult.Keys              'get the keys into an array
strItemsArray = objResult.Items            'get the items into an array
For intLoop = 0 To objResult.Count -1      'iterate through the array
  strThisKey = strKeysArray(intLoop)       'this is the key value
  strThisItem = strItemsArray(intLoop)     'this is the item (data) value
  Response.Write strThisKey & " = " & strThisItem & "<BR>"
  strToMail = strToMail & strThisKey & " = " & strThisItem & vbCRLF
Next
strToMail = strToMail & "--------------------------- " & vbCRLF

'Now create the SendMail object and the other message strings
Set objMail = Server.CreateObject("MPS.SendMail")
strFrom = "The Webmaster"
```

```
strTo = objResult.Items("txtEmail")
strSubject = "Results from the form submission.

'Finally send the mail, and put a results message in the page
If objMail.SendMail(strFrom, strTo, strSubject, strToMail) Then
  Response.Write "Results successfully mailed."
Else
  Response.write "Error in " & Err.Source
  Response.write "<BR>" & Err.description & "<P>"
End If
```

Some Other Components

Microsoft's 'Normandy' project takes in more than just the three Personalization System components we've looked at in this chapter. There are two other areas of development that you may want to consider for your site. We won't be looking at how these work, though you can get more details about them from the Microsoft web site at **http://www.ms-normandy.com**.

We'll also take a very brief glimpse at a couple of other components that are available from Microsoft. Notice that these are **samples**, not commercial components, which are designed to show you how you can create your own server components in a range of different languages.

Replication Server

As Web technology spreads through a company intranet, the sites it supports often have to encompass more than one server. While content can be segregated so that each server handles a fixed subset of the information, life is reasonably simple. However, when a large slab of geography such as a continent or ocean physically separates the servers, it makes sense to start mirroring content. This provides faster access to users in all locations, and minimizes network traffic between the sites.

However, this brings new problems such as how do we ensure that information is up-to-date on all the servers? One answer is Microsoft Replication Server, which consists of a series of components that transfer content continuously between the servers keeping them all in synchronization. We can use it in a range of configurations, and it will operate in a secure mode to prevent security risks and protect the servers.

Internet Chat Server

Another up-and-coming use of the Internet is as a chat system. In the past, over the Web, this has tended to be classed more as a leisure activity. However, it can be used in similar ways to video conferencing, although it requires a little more imagination—you have to work with words rather than moving images—at least for the moment!

Microsoft Chat Server components are broadening the capabilities of the Web in this area by allowing active content to be passed from one point to another. While bandwidth will always be a limitation in this kind of exercise, unless you're working on your own intranet-based system, it looks likely to provide a great deal of extra functionality as it continues to be developed.

Transaction Server

If your site needs to be high-performance, scalable, and robust, you should consider deploying your Active Server components in the environment provided by Microsoft's **Transaction Server**, and the forthcoming clustering products. These technologies provide an infrastructure for deploying and managing distributed component-based transaction processing solutions.

Transaction Server insulates the designer of ASP components from the many complex issues of developing scaleable server objects allowing them to simply concentrate on the business logic of the function. It transparently provides for ASP:

- ▲ **Object re-pooling**–objects that are continually created and destroyed by ASP scripting are in fact persistent, and are reused across ASP sessions which greatly increases the efficiency of the system.

- ▲ **Location transparency**–aided by a deployment manager facility, allows distribution of ASP components to be easily controlled.

- ▲ **Shared resources**–for example, allowing ODBC connections to be shared across multiple ASP sessions.

- ▲ **Transaction coordination**–allows distributed ASP components to simply state whether a transaction has succeeded or failed, and allows Transaction Server to handle the atomicity and consistency of the transaction.

- ▲ **Transaction context**–information about the state of the transaction.

At the time of writing, these clustering technologies (codenamed *Wolfpack*) are still in beta and development stages. Phase 1 will provide fail-over facilities whereby two NT systems are interconnected, with one machine designated the primary node and the other the standby node. Any failure of the primary machine will cause the standby machine to automatically takeover the primary roles. An IP address is assigned to the cluster, and HTTP requests are routed to whichever node is active. Phase 2 will support the clustering of multiple machines and the eventual goal is for the Transaction Server components to be load-balanced over all the available resources.

Microsoft Sample Components

Microsoft's Internet Information Server site contains a selection of sample components that you can download and use directly, or as a basis for developing your own components. Each one has the source code included, and they are written in a variety of languages such as C++, Java, and Visual Basic. We'll be covering how you can create your own components later in the book. To download these samples from Microsoft, go to `http://www.microsoft.com/iis/usingiis/developing`.

The Content Rotator Component

The **Content Rotator Component** is like a simplified version of the **Ad Rotator** component we looked at earlier in this chapter. We provide a **Content Schedule File**, which is just a text file containing different sections of text and HTML code. The Content Rotator component automatically displays one of them in our pages. We can include almost any number of text content entries in the schedule file, and specify the weighting that will control how often each one is included in the returned page.

To create the component instance in the page, we use:

```
Set objMyContent = Server.CreateObject("IISSample.ContentRotator")
```

Then we can get a specific section of text and HTML from the schedule file using the object's **ChooseContent** method. It simply retrieves an entry, and inserts it into the page at that position:

```
objMyContent.ChooseContent("mycontent.txt")
```

This uses a schedule file in the same directory as the page. If it's stored elsewhere, we have to supply the path of the schedule file, which can either be a relative physical path or a full virtual path, for example:

```
objMyContent.ChooseContent("\content\mycontent.txt")   'relative path
objMyContent.ChooseContent("/demo/ mycontent.txt")     'full virtual path
```

The Content Schedule File

The **Content Schedule File** for the Content Rotator component is much simpler than the equivalent Ad Rotator's schedule file in structure. We just supply a list of the individual text strings we want to use, separated by a line that starts with two percent signs (**%%**). To set the relative weighting of each, which determines how often each will appear in the return page, we add a number to this line, and we can also append comments to it using a pair of forward slash characters:

```
%% 3 // This is the first line of the schedule text file
For more information, mail us at <A HREF="mailto:feedback@wrox.com">Wrox Press</A>

%% 4 // This is  a multi-line text string
<H2>Wrox Press</H2>
  <UL>
    <LI> Language Primers
    <LI> Advanced Programming
    <LI> Systems and Databases
  </UL>
<HR>

%% 2
Visit us on the <A HREF="http://www.wrox.com">World Wide Web</A>
```

This example shows three different text strings, one of which will be used in our page. The weightings are 3, 4 and 2, so the strings will be shown in three out of nine, four out of nine, and two out of nine pages overall.

Notice, however, that (like the Ad Rotator component) the actual occurrence of each individual string is determined at random, then modified to achieve the weighting. If you load the page nine times, you may not get exactly these results. When we come to look at creating applications, in Chapter 6, we'll see ways of using these components in an application-wide scope. This improves the accuracy of the weightings.

The Text Formatter Component

This is a very simple component, but one that may be useful if you use a lot of forms or tables in your pages. Its sole purpose is to format a single string of text into fixed-length lines. This is handy where you want to display the text in a **TEXTAREA** control, or when you want to control the width of individual columns in a table.

There are different language versions of the control supplied, and each is defined by a subtype to the `ProgID`, when it's created in the page. The three versions are:

```
Set objTextFormat = Server.CreateObject("IISSample.TextFmt.VB")
Set objTextFormat = Server.CreateObject("IISSample.TextFmt.C++")
Set objTextFormat = Server.CreateObject("IISSample.TextFmt.Java")
```

Once we've created an instance of the appropriate component, we can use its **WrapTextFromFile** method to insert the text into the page. The text itself is stored in a text file on the server, and we specify the full physical path to it. The second parameter is just the maximum number of characters for each line:

```
objTextFormat.WrapTextFromFile("C:\Demo\TxtFiles\ThisFile.txt", 35)
```

Don't forget that we can use the **FileSystemObject** and **TextStream** objects to dynamically create the text file if required, either from the same or another ASP file.

Other Sample Components

You'll see some other samples from the Microsoft IIS site used through out this book. For example, in Chapter 4 we'll see how the **HTML Table Formatter Component** can be used to save us having to create tables in HTML ourselves, when we want to display the contents of records from a database.

In Chapter 6, we'll look at a way of counting and displaying the number of visitors (hits) that your pages receive, using the **Page Counter Component**.

Summary

In this chapter, we've looked at how Active Server Pages can take advantage of objects from outside its own environment, to increase the performance our pages or offer extra features that aren't otherwise available. We saw how:

- ▲ The scripting language we choose can provide objects to help us work with files, store values in a collection-like dictionary, and provide information on errors that occur.

- ▲ Extra components can be added to the Active Server Pages environment. Instances of these components can exist in just a single page, for a whole session, or permanently as part of the application.

- ▲ We can protect our pages from returning errors to our visitors, and react to them ourselves instead. We also saw how we can help to prevent errors arising.

The one component we haven't mentioned so far, however, is probably the most important. It's likely that the major requirement for dynamic pages on your site is the need to interface with data in existing systems—especially in a company intranet, rather than global Internet, situation. We've devoted the next couple of chapters just to this topic. You'll first see the basic ways of using the ADO (Active Data Object) component, then we'll move on to some real-world situations.

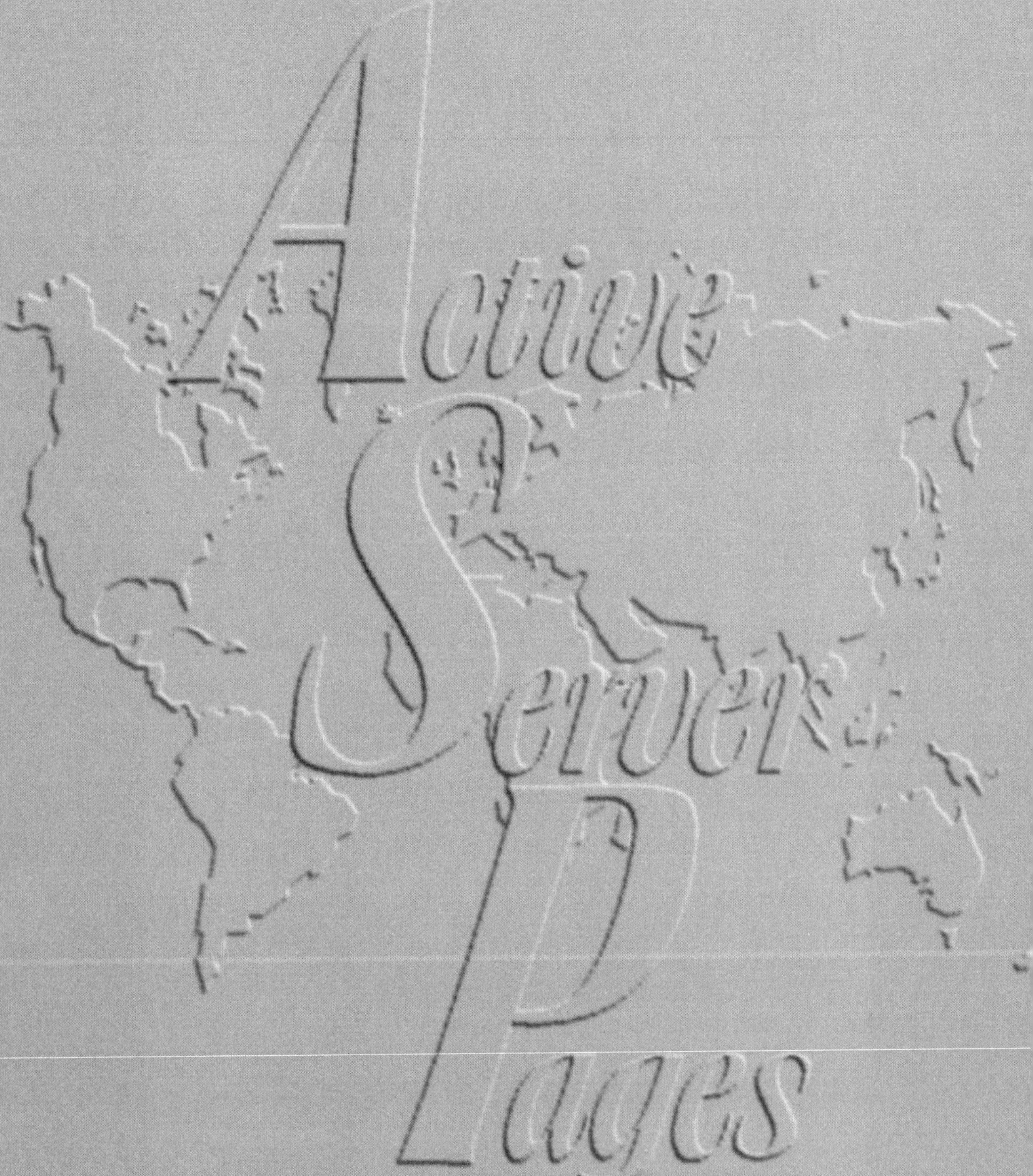
Active
Server
Pages

The Active Database Component

In previous chapters, we've learned how we can use **Active Server Pages**, and the overall **Active Server** technology, to make our web pages more dynamic–and more useful in today's increasingly competitive environment. On the Internet, or your own company's intranet, ASP gives you new ways of making sure that the content is always up to date, while reducing the costs involved in maintaining the site as a whole.

We looked at the basic ways of using Active Server Pages, and then moved on to incorporate some of the standard Server Components into our pages. However, the topics we've covered so far have really only been the icing on the cake. In the real world, the driving force behind the development of dynamic web sites is to link the pages with a database of some kind.

Under Windows NT and Internet Information Server (IIS), this has generally been accomplished with an existing technology called the **Internet Database Connector** (IDC), but this always had some limitations. Even though it gained more features in each release of IIS, there was always something you wanted to do that was difficult, or even impossible, using just IDC. The result was that often you had to go back to a 'real' programming language of some kind, and work with the **Common Gateway Interface** (CGI) or **Internet Server Application Programming Interface** (ISAPI) directly.

So you'll be pleased to know that Active Server Pages ends all that. It's supplied with a component called the **Active Database Component**. This provides us with a whole hierarchy of objects, collectively known as the **Active Data Object** (ADO)–which is the 'missing link' between your web pages and almost any kind of stored data. In this and the next chapter, we'll be showing you how this important component can be used to bring all the benefits of a truly dynamic web site.

In this chapter you'll see:

- What the **Active Data Object (ADO)** is, and what it allows us to achieve
- The structure or **object model** of the ADO Server Component
- How we use ADO methods to manipulate databases, and build dynamic pages
- Some useful techniques for writing your own dynamic ADO pages

In this chapter, we're aiming to build an understanding of the Active Data Object in general, and give you a background in using it with the Active Database Component that is supplied with Active Server Pages. Then, in the next chapter, we'll be putting our knowledge into practice with some real-world examples. So let's start with an overview of the Active Data Object.

Active Data Object Overview

The Active Data Object (ADO) is really a connection mechanism that provides access to data of all types. The most common use is with data stored in a relational database, accessed from a client application. In the context of Active Server Pages, this allows us to write code in a scripting language such as VBScript or JScript that can interact with a database. With the flexibility already available in the form of ASP, ADO allows us to create client-server applications that run over the Internet, and are not specific to any make of client browser.

In this chapter, you'll see how ADO is powerful enough to achieve excellent results with a minimum amount of work. We'll be extending the basic use of ADO in the next chapter, and seeing how you can use it when building industry strength applications. For now though, let's have a look at ADO in general.

The ADO Data Interface

ADO is designed, in its simplest form, to interface with databases through **Open Database Connectivity** (**ODBC**) methods. You can use it with any data source for which an ODBC driver is available. This means not only 'proper' database applications, like SQL Server, Oracle, Access, etc., but spreadsheet files like Microsoft Excel and text, or other, plain format data files.

However, ADO is actually built on top of another technology called **OLE-DB**. This provides a uniform data interface through the methods and properties it maintains internally. ODBC data is one kind of data that ADO and Active Server Pages can access, but it isn't the *only* kind. For example, it can also access Windows NT Directory data—at present this technology is called OLE-DS.

The Data Provider

Because ADO is built upon another layer, OLE-DB, we also need to be able to specify another layer of connectivity in our links to a data source. In other words, it's no longer sufficient to think of just the **driver** software (such as ODBC), we need to consider what the actual **provider** of the data is. ODBC is just the most popular of the OLE-DB providers.

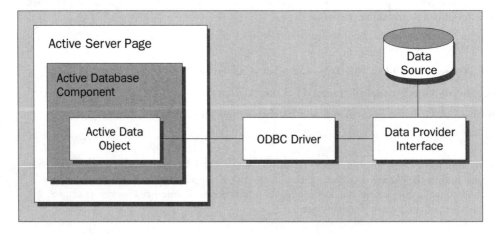

ADO capabilities vary widely based on the capabilities of the OLE-DB provider. Some objects may work differently, properties may be missing, or certain objects may not exist or be usable.

ADO capabilities when using the ODBC provider vary widely also, based on the capability of the ODBC driver. Most ODBC drivers don't provide all the cursor types, for example. And SQL Server and Access ODBC provide the `AbsolutePage` property, while most other ODBC database drivers do not.

Our Provider/Driver Combination

So you can see that what's actually going on 'under the hood' with ADO is less than simple to grasp. Fortunately, although it's good to appreciate what's under there, we don't need to be a mechanic to drive the car. In most cases, you'll be using a supplied ODBC driver for your database system, which will support almost all of the standard techniques we'll be seeing in this chapter.

In fact, for this chapter, we'll specifically be using Microsoft Access for the examples. In some areas, especially stored procedures, Access ODBC allows us to use a syntax that will not work with many other relational database ODBC drivers. However, it is compact, simple to set up, and more universally available for you to experiment with as you learn the basics of ADO. In the next chapter, we'll move on to see how you can use SQL Server and other database systems with ADO. For now, though, we'll start with a look at how you use the main objects in the ADO hierarchy.

The ADO Object Model

ADO is an altogether simpler and clearer mechanism for providing database access than those included in Microsoft Access, and other object-based applications. For instance, the hierarchy has only three main objects, `Connection`, `Recordset`, and `Command`, and several collections of subsidiary objects, `Parameters`, `Properties`, and `Errors`.

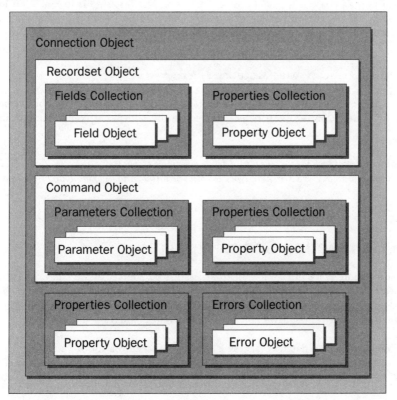

Using the `Connection` object, we can establish an active connection that allows us to gain access to data stored elsewhere–generally in a database. To obtain records from this data source, execute SQL queries, or manipulate the data directly, we can use the `Command` object. The `Recordset` object gives us access to the data that is returned from executing an SQL query, a stored procedure, or by opening a table.

The `Connection`, `Command`, and `Recordset` objects each have a collection of `Properties`, just like many of the objects we've looked at in earlier chapters. The `Connection` object also maintains a collection of `Error` objects, detailing the errors that occur as we use the objects. Finally, the `Recordset` object contains a `Fields` collection. Each member of this collection is, as you might expect, a `Field` object–which contains information about the individual fields in the recordset. Don't worry about exactly what all these terms mean for now, we'll discuss each one as we come to use them in our examples.

As well as a much simpler object hierarchy, ADO provides greater flexibility for developers than most other mainstream database applications. So even though the `Connection` object appears at the top of the diagram, we aren't forced to use it when creating a recordset. In fact, we can use the objects on their own without having to follow the hierarchy. We'll show you how this is done a little later in the chapter.

First, however, let's look at how we go about connecting to a data source and manipulating the data. We'll begin with a look at the three main objects that ADO provides.

The Connection Object

Defining a connection to a database is a straightforward process. The first step is to create an instance of the `Connection` object. This is just one of the objects implemented by the Active Database Component, whose ProgID is `ADODB`. Here's how we set up a `Connection` object that is capable of referencing a data source:

```
Set oConn = Server.CreateObject("ADODB.Connection")
```

By using the `CreateObject` method of the `Server` object, we can instantiate a variable to hold a reference to the newly created `Connection` object, just as we did with other components in the previous chapter.

> *Notice that this is different from the way we would define a variable of type* `Database` *in Visual Basic. Because VBScript deals with* `Variant` *data types, we can't declare a variable of the appropriate type directly.*

Setting the Connection Scope

We can create this connection every time we want to access a data source, or we can create it once in the page and use it repeatedly. Alternatively, we can create it with `Session`- or `Application`-wide scope, and use it in several pages. When we're performing several operations with the database, it is usual to maintain active connections, even though we could use a different connection for each one.

By maintaining one connection, the database access is improved because a lot of validation occurs during the connection phase. We can do this by placing the `Server.CreateObject` statement in either the `Session_onStart` or `Application_onStart` routines in `global.asa`, or by using an `<OBJECT>` tag.

To create an **Application**-wide instance of the connection, we can use:

```
Sub Application_onStart()
    Set oConn = Server.CreateObject("ADODB.Connection")
End Sub
```

or:

```
<OBJECT RUNAT=Server Scope=Application ID=oConn ProgID="ADODB.Connection">
</OBJECT>
```

To create a **Session**-wide instance of the connection, we can use:

```
Sub Session_onStart()
    Set oConn = Server.CreateObject("ADODB.Connection")
End Sub
```

or:

```
<OBJECT RUNAT=Server Scope=Session ID=oConn ProgID="ADODB.Connection">
</OBJECT>
```

However, ODBC version 3.0 includes a feature called **connection pooling**, which manages connections across multiple users. When using connection pooling it's best to open and close the database connection in each page that uses it, which allows ODBC to manage the connections most efficiently. In the next and subsequent chapters, we'll look into this subject in more depth. For the purposes of this chapter, because we're using ODBC 3.0 with Microsoft Access 97, we'll create each connection once at the start of a page, and use it throughout that page.

Connection Object Methods and Properties

The **Connection** object provides methods and properties that allow us to work with it. These fall into three groups: opening and closing a connection, executing a command on the data source specified by the connection, and controlling transactions. We'll look at each group and what it does in turn, but first here's a list of all the methods and properties:

Method	Description
Open	Opens a new connection to a data source.
Close	Closes an existing open connection.
Execute	Executes a query, SQL statement or stored procedure.
BeginTrans	Begins a new transaction.
CommitTrans	Saves any changes made and ends the transaction. May also start a new transaction.
RollbackTrans	Cancels any changes made and ends the transaction. May also start a new transaction.

Property	Description
Attributes	Controls whether to begin a new transaction when an existing one ends.
CommandTimeout	Number of seconds to wait when executing a command before terminating the attempt and returning an error.
ConnectionString	The information used to create a connection to a data source.
ConnectionTimeout	Number of seconds to wait when creating a connection before terminating the attempt and returning an error.
DefaultDatabase	Sets or returns the default database to use for this connection.
IsolationLevel	Sets or returns the level of isolation within transactions.
Mode	Sets or returns the provider's access permissions.
Provider	Sets or returns the name of the provider.
Version	Returns the ADO version number.

Opening a Connection

Once we've created an instance of the **Connection** object, using the **Server** object's **CreateObject** method, we're ready to start using it. However, it doesn't actually refer to anything yet. The next step is to use the connection to open our data source, so that we can access and manipulate the data in it. This is achieved using the **Open** method that the **Connection** object provides. The general form of the **Open** method for the connection object is:

connection.**Open** *ConnectionString, User, Password*

The *ConnectionString* parameter is a string that specifies a data source either as a **data source name** (**DSN**), or by specifying a detailed connection string made up of individual *parameter=value* arguments separated by semicolons.

> *It's generally easiest to create a **System Data Source Name**, using the ODBC Administrator program on your server, and this is what we've done for this chapter. Full details are included in Appendix G— refer to this if you haven't done it before.*

If we provide a detailed connection string, instead of a System DSN, ADO recognizes five standard parameter names. Any *ConnectionString* containing an equals sign is interpreted as a detailed connection string.

Parameter	Description
Provider	Name of the provider to use for the connection.
File Name	Name of a file containing provider-specific preset connection details.
Data Source	The source name or filename of the data source, that is, an SQL Server database register with ODBC, or the filename of an Access database.
User	User name to apply when opening a connection.
Password	Password to apply when opening a connection.

Any additional parameters we include aren't interpreted by ADO, and are just passed through to the provider. Note also that we can specify either the *Provider* or the *File Name* parameters, but not both. Once we open the connection, the *ConnectionString* is available as a read-only property.

For extra security, you can specify a *UserName* and *Password* as parameters, along with the *ConnectionString*. If we're using a System DSN as the *ConnectionString*, this is the only way that we can specify them on a per-connection basis.

Here's a simple example of opening a connection, using a System DSN called `Contacts`:

```
Set oConn = Server.CreateObject("ADODB.Connection")
oConn.Open "Contacts"
```

Alternatively, we can use the detailed form of the *ConnectionString*, like this:

```
Set oConn = Server.CreateObject("ADODB.Connection")
oConn.Open  "DATABASE=pubs;DSN=Publishers;UID=sa;Password=;"
```

We can set the `ConnectionTimeout` property of the `Connection` object to determine how long to wait (in seconds) for a connection to be opened. By default the value is `30`. If the value is set to `0`, ADO will wait indefinitely until the operation has completed.

Executing Commands with the Connection

Having created and opened a connection to our data source, we can begin to use it. Later in the chapter, you'll see how we can return information as a recordset. For now, we'll just confine ourselves to executing commands that *change*, but don't actually *return*, any data.

To carry out commands that change the data in our data source, we use the `Connection` object's `Execute` method. This can accept a string containing an SQL statement, the name of a stored procedure, or the name of a table in the data source. The last of these, a table name, simply returns a recordset containing all the data in that table, and you'll see how this is used when we come to look at recordsets in detail later on.

A **stored procedure** is a command or procedure that already exists in the source database system, such as an Access query. These often consist of one or more SQL statements, and provide efficient ways of updating the data because only the instruction to run the procedure needs to pass across the network. Stored procedures can return information, or just update existing data. In this case, we're going to assume that they don't return any data.

> *To use ADO successfully, you really need to be reasonably conversant with **Structured Query Language** (**SQL**). To learn more about it, look out for Joe Celko's book* Instant SQL Programming *(ISBN 1-874416-50-8), from Wrox Press of course. You can also use the Query Builder in Microsoft Access to help you create SQL strings.*

Here's an example that uses an SQL string directly:

```
Set oConn = Server.CreateObject("ADODB.Connection")
oConn.Open "Contacts"
oConn.Execute "DELETE * FROM Contact WHERE State = 'LA'"
```

If we have a stored procedure in the database, such as an Access query named `DeleteAllLA`, we can execute it using:

```
Set oConn = Server.CreateObject("ADODB.Connection")
oConn.Open "Contacts"
oConn.Execute "DeleteAllLA"
```

If we were using SQL Server, or most other databases, the string for the `Execute` argument could well be different—remember it will have to match the syntax requirements of the provider not ADO, because ADO just passes it directly back to the provider to execute. For example, in SQL Server, we would need to use:

```
Set oConn = Server.CreateObject("ADODB.Connection")
oConn.Open "Contacts"
oConn.Execute "[call DeleteAllLA]"
```

Being able to use stored procedures (or queries) gives us flexibility—we don't need to recreate the SQL queries for our ASP scripts. However, even though this method is fine for simpler cases, we can optimize database operation by providing extra information.

Specifying the Command Type

We've used the simplest form of the `Execute` statement so far, by just specifying the query or procedure we want to execute. We can improve the efficiency of the operation by using other, optional parameters:

*Connection.***Execute** *CommandText, RecordsAffected, Options*

What we've been using up to now is the mandatory *CommandText* parameter. We can also specify a value for the *Options* parameter, which tells ADO what *type* of instruction we actually want it to carry out.

Because the *CommandText* parameter can be one of three different types of command, ADO has to query the data source to find out what to do with it, slowing down the whole process. If we supply one of the following values for the *Options* parameter, ADO will use the *CommandText* option as that type of command. This technique makes the whole thing more efficient, and you'll see it used in several places with ADO.

Constant	Value	Description
`adCmdUnknown`	0	Unknown. This is the default if not specified.
`adCmdText`	1	A text definition of a command, such as an SQL statement.
`adCmdTable`	2	The name of a table from which to create a recordset.
`adCmdStoredProc`	4	A stored procedure, or query, within the data source.

To use the constant names in your code, instead of specifying the actual values, you need to include a constants definition file in the page using a Server-side Include (SSI). These files are supplied with ASP, and installed by default in the `ASPSamp/Samples` directory on the server. For VBScript you use `Adovbs.inc`. For JScript, use `Adojavas.inc`. For example, using VBScript:

```
<!-- #include virtual="/Aspsamp/Samples/Adovbs.inc" -->
```

You can copy the file into the application directory instead, and include it using:

```
<!-- #include file="Adovbs.inc" -->
```

See Chapter 1 for more information about using #include SSI statements.

The other parameter in the **Execute** method is *RecordsAffected*. We can provide the name of a variable for this parameter, and ADO will attempt to set it to the number of records that were affected by the query or stored procedure.

Here's the two examples we used earlier, but now optimized by specifying the type of command being used, and supplying a variable, **lngRecs**, to hold the number of records that are affected by the query or stored procedure:

```
'Using a text SQL query definition directly
oConn.Execute "DELETE * FROM Contact WHERE State = 'LA'", lngRecs, adCmdText
```

```
'executing a stored procedure
oConn.Execute "DeleteAllLA", lngRecs, adCmdStoredProc
```

We can set the **CommandTimeout** property of the **Connection** object to determine how long to wait (in seconds) for execution of the query to finish. By default the value is **30**. If the value is set to **0**, ADO will wait indefinitely until the operation has completed. Notice this is different from the **ConnectionTimeout** property, which defines how long to wait while the data source connection is opened.

Closing the Connection

Once we're done using the database, we can close the active connection. This doesn't actually free the resources that the object is using. To do this, we have to set the object variable to **Nothing** as well:

```
oConn.Close
Set oConn = Nothing
```

We don't have to explicitly do any of this. Active Server Pages will do it automatically once the reference variable (in our case **oConn**) goes out of scope. Our example **Connection** object was created in the page that is executing, so it will be destroyed once that page has been completed and sent to the browser. Of course, if we create the connection object in **global.asa**, it will only be destroyed when the appropriate **Session**, or the entire **Application**, ends.

Using Connection Transactions

The final subject we need to look at before we leave the **Connection** object is how we use **transactions**. You may be familiar with this subject from other databases you've worked with. The principle is that when we need to perform a series of updates on a data source, we can improve efficiency by getting the system to store up all the changes, and then commit them in one go—rather than writing each change individually to the records.

This generally has another advantage: because the changes are not committed until we've completed them all, and we've informed ADO that we're done, we can always change our mind up to that point—before we actually commit the changes. This is called rolling back the changes, and is used most often where an error occurs. Rather than having an undetermined number of changes to the data, we know that we can roll back all of them so that the data isn't changed at all. Only if all the operations complete successfully do we actually commit the changes to the database.

We'll be looking in detail at how transactions are used in later chapters. For now, here's some code that shows how it all fits together:

```
Set oConn = Server.CreateObject("ADODB.Connection")
oConn.Open "Contacts"
oConn.BeginTrans                         'start the transaction

oConn.Execute "DELETE * FROM Contact WHERE State = 'LA'"
sngErrorFound = oConn.Errors.Count       'number of errors for this query

oConn.Execute "DELETE * FROM Names WHERE State = 'LA'"
sngErrorFound = sngErrorFound + oConn.Errors.Count

oConn.Execute "DELETE * FROM Phones WHERE State = 'LA'"
sngErrorFound = sngErrorFound + oConn.Errors.Count

If sngErrorFound = 0 Then
   oConn.CommitTrans          'everything worked, keep the changes
Else
   oConn.RollbackTrans        'something went wrong, abandon the changes
End If
oConn.Close
Set oConn = Nothing
```

You can see that we only commit the changes to the database with **CommitTrans** if all the queries execute without an error. If any one fails, we abandon all the changes with **RollbackTrans**.

> *The* **Connection** *object's* **Attributes** *property can be set so that either* **CommitTrans** *or* **RollbackTrans** *automatically starts a new transaction.*

The Command Object

So far, to query or update a data source, we've used the **Connection** object to execute commands which run a stored procedure or an SQL query. Instead, however, we can use the **Command** object directly, providing that we specify a connection string for its **ActiveConnection** property.

In this case a connection is still established, but no intermediate connection variable is maintained, as it was when we created a **Connection** explicitly in the last section. This is really only efficient if we need the data from all the operations at the same time. If we're using the same connection for several operations, then we should really create a separate **Connection** object, and perform successive operations with it.

Command Object Methods and Properties

We create a **Command** object and define its scope as we did with the **Connection** object, by using the **Server.CreateObject** method or with an **<OBJECT>** tag. The **Command** object provides methods and properties we use to manipulate individual commands. These are:

Method	Description
CreateParameter	Creates a new **Parameter** object in the **Parameters** collection.
Execute	Executes the SQL statement or stored procedure specified in the **CommandText** property.

Property	Description
ActiveConnection	The **Connection** object to be used with this **Command** object.
CommandText	The text of a command to be executed.
CommandTimeout	Number of seconds to wait when executing a command before terminating the attempt and returning an error.
CommandType	Type of query specified in the **CommandText** property.
Prepared	Whether to create a prepared statement before execution.

Creating an Active Connection

The first step in using the **Command** object is to specify the **ActiveConnection** we want to use it against. If we've previously created a **Connection** object we can use that, or we can supply a *ConnectionString* as we did in the **Connection** object's **Open** method:

```
Set oCmd = Server.CreateObject("ADODB.Command")
oCmd.ActiveConnection = "Contacts"
```

or:

```
Set oCmd = Server.CreateObject("ADODB.Command")
oCmd.ActiveConnection = "DATABASE=pubs;DSN=Publishers;UID=sa;Password=;"
```

Executing a Query

Once we've established the active connection, we can use the **Command** object in a similar way to the **Connection** object. And we don't need to explicitly open the data source, or close it afterwards–we just use the **Execute** method directly.

However, the different properties of the **Command** object mean that we can specify some parameters outside the **Execute** method, and get more control over the operation. For example, we can set the **CommandText** and **CommandType** first, instead of specifying them in the **Execute** statement. We can also tell the data provider to create a temporary stored representation of the query. This may be slow for the first execution, but the compiled form of the query is then used in subsequent executions, which speeds up command processing significantly:

```
Set oCmd = Server.CreateObject("ADODB.Command")
oCmd.ActiveConnection = "Contacts"      'the system DSN for the data source
oCmd.CommandText = "DELETE * FROM Contact WHERE State = 'LA'"
```

```
oCmd.CommandType = 1                    'an SQL query.
oCmd.Prepared = True                    'compile the statement...
oCmd.Execute                            '...and then execute it
Set oCmd.ActiveConnection = Nothing     'release the resources used
```

Again, we can set the **CommandTimeout** property first, to determine how long to wait for the command to execute. By default the value is **30**. If the value is set to **0**, ADO will wait indefinitely until the operation has completed.

Using Parameters

If our query requires parameters, then we can either supply them by adding them to the **Command** object's **Parameters** collection first, or by creating them 'on the fly' as we execute the query. The syntax of the **Command** object's **Execute** method is subtly different from that of the **Connection** object, because it contains an argument for the parameters to be used in the query:

command.**Execute**   [*RecordsAffected*] *Parameters, Options*

The *RecordsAffected* and *Options* parts are the same as those of the **Connection** object, but we use the *Parameters* part this time to specify an array of parameters that are to be used while executing the query. The individual parameters in this array correspond by position to the values in the **Parameters** collection (which we'll come to next) and to the parameters required by the query. To specify three parameters, we could use:

```
oCmd.Execute Array(Parameter1, Parameter2, Parameter3)
```

If we don't specify a value for any of the parameters, the existing values in the **Parameters** collection are used instead:

```
oCmd.Execute Array(Parameter1, , Parameter3)
```

For example, our earlier stored procedure example, which deletes records for the State of LA could be replaced by a stored parameter query–where the table name and the State are parameters:

```
Set oCmd = Server.CreateObject("ADODB.Command")
oCmd.ActiveConnection = "Contacts"
oCmd.CommandText = "DeleteStateQuery"    'name of the stored procedure
oCmd.CommandType = 4                     'a stored procedure
oCmd.Execute Array("Contact", "NY")
Set oCmd.ActiveConnection = Nothing
```

The Parameters Collection

The **Parameters** collection holds all of the parameters for a query executed by a **Command** object. Instead of specifying parameters to a query 'on the fly', in the call to the **Command** object's **Execute** method, we can add them to the **Command** object's **Parameters** collection first. Here are the methods and properties of the **Parameters** collection:

Method	Description
Append	Adds a parameter to the collection.

Table Continued on Following Page

Method	Description
Delete	Deletes a parameter from the collection.
Refresh	Updates the collection to reflect changes to the parameters.

Property	Description
Count	Returns the number of parameters in the collection.
Item	Used to retrieve the contents of a parameter from the collection.

Creating and Adding Parameters to a Collection

Each member of the **Parameters** collection is itself a **Parameter** object, and has a set of properties of its own:

Property	Description
Attributes	The type of data that the parameter accepts.
Direction	Whether the parameter is for input, output or both, or if it is the return value from a stored procedure. Refer to the **ParameterDirectionEnum** in Appendix E for a complete list.
Name	The name of the parameter.
NumericScale	The number of decimal places in a numeric parameter.
Precision	The number of digits in a numeric parameter.
Size	The maximum size, in bytes, of the parameter value.
Type	The data type of the parameter. Refer to the **DataTypeEnum** values in Appendix E for a complete list.
Value	The value assigned to the parameter.

To add a new parameter to the **Parameters** collection, we must first create an instance of a **Parameter** object, then set its property values, and finally use the **Append** method of the **Command** object. To create a new parameter object, we use **Command** object's **CreateParameter** method:

Set *parameter* = *command*.**CreateParameter**(*Name, Type, Direction, Size, Value*)

For example, we can create a new parameter and append it to the **Parameters** collection like this:

```
...
Set oParam = oCmd.CreateParameter("State", 129, 1, 2, "NY")
oCmd.Parameters.Append oParam
...
```

This uses the specific numeric values for the *Type, Direction,* and *Size* arguments, and creates the parameter in one go. Alternatively, we can set each argument separately, and use the pre-defined constants. In this example, we're taking the parameter value from a text box on a form, submitted to our ASP page in the **Request** object's **Form** collection:

```
Set oCmd = Server.CreateObject("ADODB.Command")
oCmd.ActiveConnection = "Contacts"
oCmd.CommandText = "DeleteStateQuery"
oCmd.CommandType = 4
strValue = Request.Form("txtState")          'as submitted from a form
Set oParam = oCmd.CreateParameter("State")   'the parameter name only
oParam.Type = adChar                         'a string value
oParam.Direction = adParamInput              'a query input parameter
oParam.Size = Len(strValue)                  'the size of the string
oParam.Value = strValue                      'the string value
oCmd.Parameters.Append oParam                'add it to the collection
oCmd.Execute
Set oCmd.ActiveConnection = Nothing
```

Of course, we're not just limited to using parameters in stored procedures. We can also use them in SQL statements in Access, where parameters are indicated by being placed in square brackets within the statement. This provides an alternative method for building up SQL statements with the appropriate **WHERE** clause dynamically.

Referencing Collection Objects

Once we've got our parameters into the collection, we can refer to them either by using the **Item** property, or directly because **Item** is the default property for the collection. We can also use the index within the collection, or the parameter name:

```
oCmd.Parameters.Item(0)          'all these refer to the same parameter
oCmd.Parameters(0)
oCmd.Parameters.Item("State")
oCmd.Parameters("State")
```

The **Parameters** collection is also the default collection for the **Command** object, so we can even omit the collection name. However, this makes understanding the code more difficult, and should generally be avoided:

```
oCmd(0)
oCmd("State")
```

Setting the Parameter Size and Type

One thing to note is that if we want to specify a parameter that stores a variable length value such as a **string** (as defined by the *Type* argument), we must also specify the *Size* argument—otherwise an error will be generated.

The same applies to **numeric** values, but this time we specify values for the **Precision** and **NumericScale** properties of the **Parameter** object instead. **Precision** determines the number of digits that are to be stored, and **NumericScale** indicates the position of the decimal place. To store a number like **173.25**, we would need to set **Precision** to **5** and **NumericScale** to **2**.

Reading, Refreshing and Deleting Parameters

As you've seen in earlier chapters, we can use a **For...Each** loop to iterate through all the members of a collection. We can do this with the **Parameters** collection, but first we need to make sure that all the parameters are up to date. The **Refresh** method of the **Parameter** object instructs the provider to fill the parameters collection with parameters from the query specified in the **CommandText** property of the **Command** object.

Here's an example of how we can use these concepts to output the names and values of all the parameters in the **Parameters** collection. It places them in the current page using **Response.Write**:

```
...
For Each oParam In oCmd.Parameters
    Response.Write "Parameter name = " & oParam.Name & "<P>"
    Response.Write "Parameter value = " & oParam.Value
Next
...
```

If the need arises, we can also **delete** a parameter from the **Parameters** collection. To delete the parameter named **State** from our collection, we can use the parameter name or its index:

```
oCmd.Parameters.Delete "State"
oCmd.Parameters.Delete 0
```

The Recordset Object

Up to now, we've only looked at queries which add, update or delete existing records in our data source. Of course, in many cases we'll actually want to return some records via ADO, so that we can put some values into our page. For queries that return values, we must assign the results to a **Recordset** object. This is like a table in memory, holding records (or rows of data) that are subdivided into individual fields (or columns).

Both of the methods we've looked at for executing a query, that is, those of the **Connection** object and the **Command** object, can create recordsets containing the data returned from that query. We can even create a recordset directly, without having to open a connection or execute a command first.

Recordset Object Methods and Properties

To begin with, here's a table of the more common methods and properties of the **Recordset** object. There are many more than this, but we won't be using them all in this chapter. You'll find a full list in Appendix E:

Method	Description
AddNew	Creates a new record in an updateable recordset.
CancelBatch	Cancels a pending batch update.
CancelUpdate	Cancels any changes made to the current or a new record.
Close	Closes an open recordset and any dependent objects.
Delete	Deletes the current record in an open recordset.
Move	Moves the position of the current record.
MoveFirst, MoveLast, MoveNext, MovePrevious	Moves to the first, last, next or previous record in the recordset, and makes that the current record.

Table Continued on Following Page

Method	Description
Open	Opens a cursor on a recordset.
Requery	Updates the data by re-executing the original query.
Supports	Determines whether the recordset supports certain functions.
Update	Saves any changes made to the current record.
UpdateBatch	Writes all pending batch updates to disk.

Property	Description
AbsolutePosition	The ordinal position of the current record.
BOF	True if the current record position is before the first record.
Bookmark	Returns a bookmark that uniquely identifies the current record, or sets the current record to the record identified by a valid bookmark.
CursorType	The type of cursor used in the recordset.
EditMode	The editing status of the current record.
EOF	True if the current record position is after the last record.
LockType	The type of locks placed on records during editing.
RecordCount	The number of records currently in the recordset.
Source	The source for the data in the recordset, that is **Command** object, SQL statement, table name, or stored procedure.

Getting Back a Recordset

We can create a recordset as the result of executing a query, either an SQL statement, a stored procedure, or by just specifying the name of a table in the data source. This can be from either the **Command** or the **Connection** object. You'll recognize these as being similar to the way we execute a query that doesn't return any records. The only difference is that we **Set** the result to refer to a recordset object, and we enclose the parameters in brackets:

Set *recordset* = *connection*.**Execute**(*CommandText*, *RecordsAffected*, *Options*)

Set *recordset* = *command*.**Execute**(*RecordsAffected*, *Parameters*, *Options*)

Creating Recordsets with a Query

As an example, here we're using the **Connection** object, and just specifying the *CommandText* argument. This time the SQL query is a **SELECT** query which should return records from the data source:

```
Set oConn = Server.CreateObject("ADODB.Connection")
oConn.Open "Contacts"
Set oRs = oConn.Execute("SELECT * FROM Contact WHERE State = 'LA'")
```

If we want to know more about the results, and be more specific when supplying the *CommandText*, we can supply a variable for the *RecordsAffected* argument and set the *CommandType* for query in the *Options* argument:

```
Set oConn = Server.CreateObject("ADODB.Connection")
oConn.Open "Contacts"
strSQL = "SELECT * FROM Contact WHERE State = 'LA'"
Set oRs = oConn.Execute(strSQL, lngRecs, adCmdText)
```

Alternatively, we can use the **Command** object to create our recordset:

```
Set oCmd = Server.CreateObject("ADODB.Command")
oCmd.ActiveConnection = "Contacts"
oCmd.CommandText = "SELECT * FROM Contact WHERE State = 'LA'"
oCmd.CommandType = adCmdText
Set oRS = oCmd.Execute
```

And, of course, we can still supply a variable for the *RecordsAffected* argument and a list of *Parameters*. This time we've put the *CommandType* in the **Execute** method call as well:

```
Set oCmd = Server.CreateObject("ADODB.Command")
oCmd.ActiveConnection = "Contacts"
oCmd.CommandText = "SELECT * FROM Contact WHERE State = 'LA'"
Set oRS = oCmd.Execute(lngRecs, Array("Contact", "LA"), adCmdText)
```

Creating Recordsets from a Table

One way of using the **Execute** method that we haven't seen so far, because it can only return data and not update it directly, is to specify a table name. This works for either the **Connection** or the **Command** object. For the **Connection** object:

```
Set oConn = Server.CreateObject("ADODB.Connection")
oConn.Open "Contacts"
Set oRs = oConn.Execute("Contact")     'the name of the table
```

Of course, we can supply the *CommandType* argument to improve processing efficiency:

```
Set oConn = Server.CreateObject("ADODB.Connection")
oConn.Open "Contacts"
Set oRs = oConn.Execute("Contact", , adCmdTable)
```

And, finally, we can use the **Command** object in a similar way:

```
Set oCmd = Server.CreateObject("ADODB.Command")
oCmd.ActiveConnection = "Contacts"
oCmd.CommandText = "Contact"           'the name of the table
oCmd.CommandType = adCmdTable
Set oRS = oCmd.Execute
```

Creating Recordsets Directly

For a single access to our data source, where we don't need to maintain a connection for several operations, it's possible to create a recordset directly, without going through the **Connection** or **Command** objects. The **Connection** is still created in the background automatically, just as it was when we used the **Command** object without specifically creating a **Connection** object first.

To create a recordset directly, we first have to create an instance of a recordset object, using the `Server.CreateObject` method or with an `<OBJECT>` tag. Then we can use the `Open` method of the `Recordset` object to fill the new recordset with values from the data source. The syntax of the `Open` method is:

recordset.`Open` Source, ActiveConnection, CursorType, LockType, Options

Argument	Description
Source	A `Command` object, SQL statement, table name or stored procedure.
ActiveConnection	An existing `Connection` object.
CursorType	The type of **cursor** to use when opening the recordset: `adOpenForwardOnly` (0– *the default*), `adOpenKeyset` (1), `adOpenDynamic` (2), or `adOpenStatic` (3)
LockType	The type of **locking** to use when opening the recordset. See Appendix E for a full list.
Options	The type of query or table represented by *Source*.

Remember that, to use the constant names in your code, instead of specifying the actual values, you need to include a constants definition file in the page using a Server-side Include (SSI). For example, using VBScript:

```
<!-- #include virtual="/Aspsamp/Samples/Adovbs.inc" -->
```

See Chapter 1 for more information about using `#include` SSI statements.

The *Source* argument indicates where the data will come from. If we already have an active connection string, we can use this as the *ActiveConnection* property, and supply a table name for the *Source* argument:

```
Set oRs = Server.CreateObject("ADODB.Recordset")
oRs.Open "Contact", "Contacts", , , adCmdTable
```

Alternatively, we can follow the same principles as with the `Command` object, by setting the properties first and then calling the `Open` method:

```
Set oRs = Server.CreateObject("ADODB.Recordset")
oRs.Source = "Contact"              'the name of the table
oRs.ActiveConnection = "Contacts"   'the DSN to use for the connection
oRs.Options = adCmdTable            'the type of query/table to assume
oRs.Open                            'and open the recordset
```

Recordset Cursor Types

There are four **cursor types** available when opening a `Recordset` object. The different cursor types have their own merits, and each one lends itself to particular uses. In our examples, we've assumed the default cursor type of `adOpenForwardOnly`. Here's a summary of the different types:

▲ **Dynamic cursor**–provides a fully updateable recordset where all additions, changes and deletions made by other users while the recordset is open are visible. Allows all types of movement through the recordset. This is the type created by specifying the value **adOpenDynamic** for the *CursorType* argument of the **Recordset** object's **Open** method.

▲ **Keyset cursor**–provides an updateable recordset, like a dynamic cursor, except that it prevents access to records that other users add after it was created. Allows all types of movement through the recordset. Created by specifying **adOpenKeyset** for the *CursorType* argument.

▲ **Static cursor**–provides a static non-updateable copy of a set of records, useful for retrieving data. Changes to the records made by other users while the recordset is open are not visible. Allows all types of movement through the recordset. Created by specifying **adOpenStatic** for the *CursorType* argument.

▲ **Forward-only cursor**–(*the default*) provides a non-updateable recordset identical to a static cursor except that it only allows us to scroll forward through the records. This improves performance in situations where we need to make only a single pass through the recordset. This is the type of recordset created either by specifying **adOpenForwardOnly** for the *CursorType* argument, or by omitting this argument from the Open method.

You can see that we'll get a forward-only cursor from our earlier examples of the **Open** method, because we didn't specify a *CursorType* value. If we want to be able to edit the records, or even move around the recordset at will, we need to specify a different, more appropriate, type. You'll see more of this in a while.

The reason for using different cursor types is that it provides ways of making the access to the data source more efficient. ADO and the data provider have to do a lot more work to maintain dynamic and updateable recordsets. Even static recordsets that allow full movement require several accesses to the database to allow the user to scroll up as well as down. It's far more efficient if ADO knows which records it has to send next, so that it can cache them successfully.

Closing a Recordset

Once we're finished using a recordset, we can close it with the **Close** method, then release any resources it was using by setting its variable reference to **Nothing**:

```
oRS.Close
Set oRS = Nothing
```

Again, ADO will do this automatically when the variable referencing the recordset goes out of scope.

Using Recordsets in ADO

When we create a **Recordset** object and fill it with data, we'll generally want to use it for something. We may want to move around from one record to another, edit existing records and add new ones to it, and extract data from the records. In order to do this, we need to consider several aspects of how recordsets work, and look at the **Fields** collection which it implements.

It's likely that your main use of Active Server Pages, at least to start with, will be to display the contents of a data source, such as an Access, SQL Server, Oracle or other database system. So the first step is to look at how we get the information from the recordset onto the web page.

Moving Around within a Recordset

After all the esoteric descriptions of creating objects, connections, and commands, you'll find this section easy going—especially if you've programmed using Microsoft Access or the Visual Basic Jet database methods before. We're now at the point where we've got a recordset, and we can actually start to do something with it.

It's often convenient to regard the **Recordset** object as having the same structure as a table; in other words it consists of rows (each of which is a complete record) and columns (each of which represents a field). We can move from one record to another, making it the **current record**, and access the individual fields within this current record. There are two main methods we can use to move around a recordset, and we'll look at these now.

The Move Method

The **Move** method moves a number of records in either direction, relative to the current record, and makes the record to which it moves the new current record. We can specify positive or negative numbers for the argument, to move forward or backward.

Bear in mind the limitations imposed by the type of the recordset—the **cursor type**. In a recordset opened with the default cursor type of **adOpenForwardOnly**, we can only move forward. If we want to be able to move around in a recordset, we need to open it with a cursor type of **adOpenStatic** (or a dynamic cursor type of **adOpenDynamic** or **adOpenKeyset**) instead. The **adOpenStatic** type is still very efficient, because it's only a 'snapshot' of the contents of the data source at the point it was created.

> *ADO caches records as it creates the recordset. Even in a recordset created with the* **adOpenForwardOnly** *cursor type, we can still move backwards within the cached records; however this isn't really good practice.*

Here are some examples of the **Move** method:

```
oRs.Move 7        'move forward seven records
oRs.Move -4       'move backward four records
```

There are a couple of other things that we can do to move around a recordset in a random manner like this. We can establish the number, or position, of the current record within a recordset using the **AbsolutePosition** property of the **Recordset** object. This returns either the ordinal position of the current record within the recordset, or one of these values:

Constant Name	Value	Description
adPosUnknown	-1	No current record
adPosBOF	-2	Before the first record
adPosEOF	-3	After the last record

So if we know we are on the ninth record, and we want the seventeenth, we just:

```
oRs.Move 8
```

Using a Bookmark

In Access we can also use a **bookmark** to identify a record in a recordset, although other database systems may not support them. A bookmark does what it says–it marks a record so that we can come back to it later. We can use a *StartBookmark* argument with the **Move** method to move relative to that bookmark, instead of relative to the current record:

```
varMyBookmark = oRs.Bookmark        'save the bookmark of the current record
oRs.Move 3                          'move around the recordset
oRs.Move -7
oRs.Move 1, varMyBookmark           'move to the record after the bookmarked one
```

Other Ways of Moving

ADO provides four other related **Move** methods. Each one moves to another record and makes it the current record. The four methods are **MoveFirst**, **MoveLast**, **MoveNext**, and **MovePrevious**. As you'll no doubt have guessed, these move to the first or last record in the recordset, or the next or previous one. The most useful of them is **MoveNext**, which we can use to move through a recordset examining records one at a time, and putting the contents into our page–after all, that's often the whole purpose of the exercise.

The only other consideration when we use the **Move** methods is how do we know when we get to the end of the recordset? If the current record is the last one in the recordset, calling **MoveNext** will generate an error. While we could trap the error and stop moving, there's a far better way.

The Beginning and End of a Recordset

Although it seems a strange concept, the current record pointer in a recordset doesn't actually have to point to a 'real' record. It can indicate a point before the first record, or after the last one. In some cases, it can even point to a record within the body of the recordset that doesn't exist. This can happen if we have a dynamic recordset, which reflects the actual contents of a table in the data source. If another user deletes the record that is the current one in our recordset, our pointer is pointing to a deleted record. This is one reason why there is an 'unknown' value **adPosUnknown** that can be returned by the **AbsolutePosition** property.

However, the situation we're most likely to come across is when we use the **MoveNext** or **MovePrevious** methods, and we need to know when we get to the end or the beginning of the recordset. The **Recordset** object provides two properties, **BOF** and **EOF**, which represent 'Beginning Of File' and 'End Of File'. This goes back to the days when we used to think of recordsets as being individual files on a disk that, together, made up a database–in fact some databases still work in this way.

> *You have to speculate whether, if we were naming the properties afresh now, they'd be called BOR and EOR instead!*

The BOF and EOF Properties

The **BOF** property of a recordset is True when the current record pointer is positioned before the first record in the recordset, and the **EOF** property is True when the current record pointer is beyond the last record. If there are no records in the recordset, then both **BOF** and **EOF** are True.

When **BOF** is True, any attempt to move backward in the recordset will produce an error. Similarly, when **EOF** is True any attempt to move forward in the recordset will generate an error. It's always a good idea, therefore, to inspect the **BOF** and **EOF** properties when we first open a recordset, to ensure that there is at least one record in it before any operations are attempted.

Checking for an Empty Recordset

When we first open a recordset as a forward-only cursor type, the current record position is always set to the first record (if there is one). For the other types of recordset, the **MoveFirst** method should be used explicitly as soon as we open it. In fact, it doesn't do any harm to get used to using it every time we open a recordset.

The other **Move** methods will create an error if the recordset is empty, so it's a good idea to check the **BOF** and **EOF** properties are **False** first, to ensure that we aren't trying to move to a nonexistent record.

Checking How Many Records We've Got

We can find out the number of records in a recordset using the **RecordCount** property. However, before we do this, we must use the **MoveLast** method to get an accurate value. This is because the provider itself doesn't know how many records there are in the recordset until the last one is reached.

You may decide to use this property to iterate through a recordset, using a **For...Next** loop. This is a bad habit to get into–if the recordset is a dynamic one, the number might change while you're looping through the records, and you'll get an error. A better way, is to use the **EOF** property, or the **BOF** property if (for some reason) you decide to iterate through the records in reverse.

Iterating Through a Recordset

To iterate through the records in a recordset, we generally use the **MoveNext** method. Combining this with a **Do While** loop, and examining the **EOF** property each time, means we will access every record in turn:

```
Set oConn = Server.CreateObject("ADODB.Connection")
oConn.Open "Contacts"
Set oRs = oConn.Execute("Contact", , adCmdTable)
oRs.MoveFirst            'not actually required, but good practice
Do While Not oRS.EOF     'while not at end of file
   ...                   'do something with the record
   oRS.MoveNext          'and move to the next one
Loop
```

When we have no more records to read, the **EOF** property returns **True**. In this case, our **CurrentRecord** reference is actually *beyond* the last record, and so attempting to read data would cause an error. We've used a **Do While** loop because there may not be any records in the recordset when it's opened, and in this case we'll never want to perform the **MoveNext** method or access any records.

Working with the Fields Collection

While this proves a useful way of getting at each record in the recordset in turn, it doesn't do much towards extracting the data from it. That's the job of the **Fields** collection. Every **Recordset** object has a **Fields** collection, which contains the data and other information about each field in the current record.

Method	Description
Refresh	Updates the collection to reflect changes to the field values.

Property	Description
Count	Returns the number of fields in the collection.
Item	Used to retrieve the contents of the fields in the collection.

This is a relatively simple collection, containing the single method, **Refresh**, and the two properties **Count** and **Item**. We saw how to use the **Item** property to reference members of the collection when we looked at the **Parameters** collection earlier in the chapter:

```
oRs.Fields.Item("State")    'all these refer to the same field
oRs.Fields.Item(0)
oRs.Fields("State")
oRs.Fields(0)
```

The **Fields** collection is also the default collection for the **Recordset** object, so again we can omit the collection name. In this case (unlike the **Command** object, where this was true of the **Parameters** collection) it *does* make sense now. In fact, there's another way of referencing a member of the default collection which is even more 'readable':

```
oRs("State")                'all these refer to the same field
oRs(0)
oRs!State                   'and this is often a useful syntax
```

The Field Object

Each member of the **Fields** collection is itself a **Field** object, and has a set of properties of its own:

Property	Description
ActualSize	The actual length of the field's current value.
Attributes	The kinds of data that the field can hold.
DefinedSize	The size or length of the field as defined in the data source.
Name	The name of the field.
NumericScale	The number of decimal places in a numeric field.
OriginalValue	The value of the field before any unsaved changes are made.
Precision	The number of digits in a numeric field.
Type	The data type of the field.
UnderlyingValue	The field's current value within the database.
Value	The value currently assigned to the field, even if unsaved.

So now, we have a way of referencing each field in the current record. Let's use it in a real example.

A Simple Contact Tracking System

Here's a simple example that demonstrates how we can use ADO to view data from a data source. The example collects together many of the techniques we've seen so far in this chapter.

The Active Server Page `RecordsetMethods.asp` displays a list of all the contacts from our database, nicely formatted into a table.

> *There are two versions of our example, `RecordsetMethods.asp` and `SQLMethods.asp`, described in the text. The first makes use of the `Recordset`'s `Field` collection, while the second uses SQL statements.*

Here's what the page looks like:

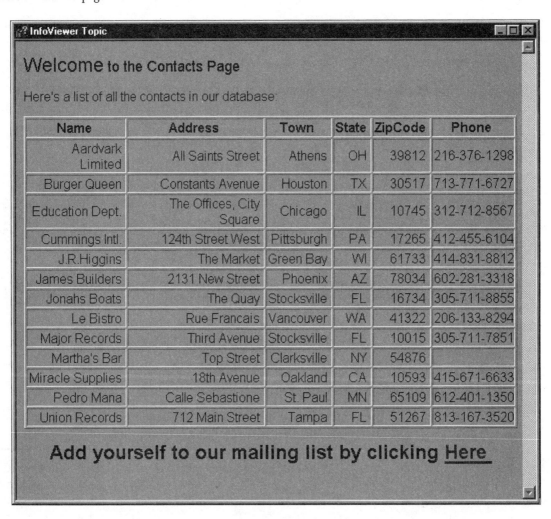

InfoViewer Topic

Welcome to the Contacts Page

Here's a list of all the contacts in our database:

Name	Address	Town	State	ZipCode	Phone
Aardvark Limited	All Saints Street	Athens	OH	39812	216-376-1298
Burger Queen	Constants Avenue	Houston	TX	30517	713-771-6727
Education Dept.	The Offices, City Square	Chicago	IL	10745	312-712-8567
Cummings Intl.	124th Street West	Pittsburgh	PA	17265	412-455-6104
J.R.Higgins	The Market	Green Bay	WI	61733	414-831-8812
James Builders	2131 New Street	Phoenix	AZ	78034	602-281-3318
Jonahs Boats	The Quay	Stocksville	FL	16734	305-711-8855
Le Bistro	Rue Francais	Vancouver	WA	41322	206-133-8294
Major Records	Third Avenue	Stocksville	FL	10015	305-711-7851
Martha's Bar	Top Street	Clarksville	NY	54876	
Miracle Supplies	18th Avenue	Oakland	CA	10593	415-671-6633
Pedro Mana	Calle Sebastione	St. Paul	MN	65109	612-401-1350
Union Records	712 Main Street	Tampa	FL	51267	813-167-3520

Add yourself to our mailing list by clicking Here

You'll find this example among the samples available from our web site at:
`http://www.rapid.wrox.com/books/0723`

How It Works

The code in the page is quite simple. It opens a recordset on the **Contact** table in our data source, for which we've previously defined a System DSN named **Contacts**. Then it uses the **Count** property of the **Fields** collection to find out how many fields there are in the recordset, and creates a table with that number of columns.

This same value is then used in a **For...Next** loop to create the **<TH>** heading cells for the table. Into each cell is placed the field name, retrieved by referring to the field in the **Fields** collection by its ordinal position–and specifying its **Name** property.

```
...
<% Set oRs = Server.CreateObject("ADODB.Recordset")
   oRs.Open "Contact", "Contacts", , , adCmdTable
   oRs.MoveFirst %>
   <TABLE BORDER=1 COLS=<% = oRS.Fields.Count%>>
      <TR>
         <% For Each oField In oRS.Fields %>
            <TH> <% = oField.Name %> </TH>
         <% Next %>
      </TR>
      ...
```

Note that we must include the **Adovbs.inc** *file to provide the constant* **adCmdTable** *as we mentioned earlier.*

Now we've created the headings for the table, we can retrieve the values from the records. We use a **Do...While** loop to iterate through all the records, and for each one we include a **<TR>** tag in the page to define the start of a row. Within the main loop, we have a second loop–this time a **For...Each** loop which iterates through all the **Fields**. This achieves the same result as using a **For..Next** loop with the **Count** property, as we did earlier, and just demonstrates a different technique.

```
       ...
      <% Do While Not oRS.EOF %>
         <TR>
            <% For Each oField In oRS.Fields %>
               <TD ALIGN=RIGHT>
                  <% If IsNull(oField) Then
                       Response.Write " "
                  Else
                       Response.Write oField.Value
                  End If %>
               </TD>
            <% Next
               oRS.MoveNext %>
         </TR>
      <% Loop %>
   </TABLE>
<% oRs.Close
   Set oRs = Nothing %>
   ...
```

For each field in the recordset, we include an opening `<TD>` tag, then we need to get the value. Recordsets based on a database table, and some other data sources, can include the special value `Null`, which indicates that there's no data for that field. We can't include a `Null` in our page, so we use the `IsNull` function to check for this first. If the field does contain `Null`, we include the non-breaking space character instead. This provides the nice beveled edge to the cell, which would otherwise appear flat.

If the value of the field is not `Null`, we retrieve it and place it in the page, followed by a closing `</TD>` tag. Once we've done all the fields in the `oRs.Fields` collection, we `MoveNext`, add a closing `</TR>` tag, and go back to the `Do...While` condition. Once all the records are listed, we close the table with a `</TABLE>` tag, `Close` the recordset and set the recordset variable we were using to `Nothing`.

> *If the scripting language that we're using doesn't support iteration through collections with* `For...Each`, *we can still access the members of the collection using their ordinal number in a* `For...Next` *loop, as in this example.*

Adding a User's Details

At the end of the page, we've provided a hyperlink so users can jump to a page where they can add their own details to the table:

```
<H2>
    Add yourself to our mailing list by clicking
    <A HREF="Getdetails.htm">Here</A>
</H2>
```

Here's the Posting Page, `GetDetailsRS.htm`, where the user enters their details. It's created with a single form and normal HTML `TEXT` controls, plus a `Submit` button labeled Finished:

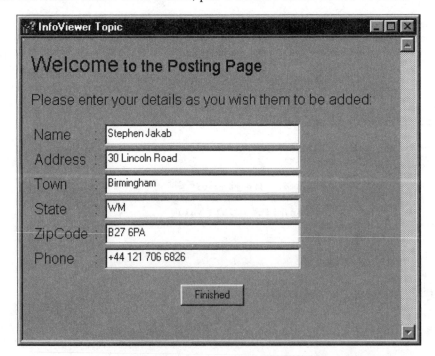

Once the user has entered their details, so that every field has some entry, and clicked the Finished button, the form is submitted to the Active Server Pages **ProcessUserRS.asp** (or **ProcessUserSQL.asp** in the second version). This is responsible for updating the database, and returning a 'thank you' message with a hyperlink back to the contacts list page (which may need refreshing to show the changes that you've made to the database):

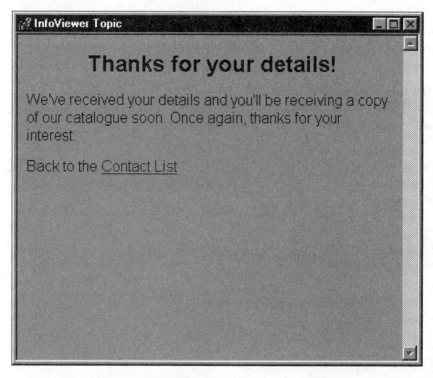

So, from the **<FORM>** section of the Posting Page, we can get the values entered by the user for their contact details. Notice the **#include** statement that allows us to use the named constant values in our code. We also explicitly convert the values into strings with the **CStr()** function, because that's the data type we need for our database:

```
<!-- #include file="Adovbs.inc" -->
    ...
<% strName = CStr(Request.Form("txtName"))
    strAddress = CStr(Request.Form("txtAddress"))
    strTown = CStr(Request.Form("txtTown"))
    strState = CStr(Request.Form("txtState"))
    strZipCode = CStr(Request.Form("txtZipCode"))
    strPhone = CStr(Request.Form("txtPhone"))
    ...
```

The next step is to add them to our database. It's time to consider how we can update records in a recordset, and add new ones.

Updating the Source Data with a Recordset

We can only achieve so much by dynamically creating HTML, based on data taken from a recordset. What we really want to do is capture data that is sent from users of our applications, and submit this to the database.

There are two main ways of updating a database using ADO. We can run SQL statements against the data using the **Execute** method of the **Recordset**, **Command** or **Connection** objects, and we can manipulate the individual records within a recordset directly. We'll now have a look at both of these techniques.

Using SQL to Update Records

We saw early on in this chapter how the **Execute** methods of the **Command** and **Connection** objects accept SQL statements that can delete records in our data source. We can also use this method to run **INSERT** and **UPDATE** queries as well.

In our Contact Tracking application we've got the details of a new contact stored in string variables. We can use an SQL **INSERT** statement to get them into our **Contact** table, as you can see in **ProcessUserSQL.asp**:

```
...
<% Set oConn = Server.CreateObject("ADODB.Connection")
    oConn.Open "Contacts"          'the database's System DSN
    strSQLStatement = "INSERT INTO Contact " _
                    & "(Name, Address, Town, State, ZipCode, Phone) " _
                    & "SELECT '" & strName & "' AS Name, '" _
                    & strAddress & "' AS Address, '" _
                    & strTown & "' AS Town, '" _
                    & strState & "' AS State, '" _
                    & strZipCode & "' AS ZipCode, '" _
                    & strPhone & "' AS Phone;"
    oConn.Execute(strSQLStatement) %>
    oConn.Close
    Set oConn = Nothing %>
...
```

This is a quick and easy way to add or update records in a database. If you're using Microsoft Access, you can create the queries using the graphical Query Builder tool then copy the SQL statement into your ASP code.

Using Recordset Methods to Update and Delete Records

Using SQL statements to update the database is very convenient, but it's often not the optimal way of performing multiple individual updates. Using **recordset methods**, we can modify the data in individual fields in individual records. To do this, we use the **AddNew** and **Update** methods of the **Recordset** object.

We also have to open the recordset with a dynamic cursor type of **adOpenDynamic** or **adOpenKeyset**, so that the changes we make are actually passed back to the data source. Remember that the default static forward-only recordset is not updateable. Here's how we handle the recordset in outline:

```
Set oRs = Server.CreateObject("ADODB.Recordset")
oRs.Open "Contact", "Contacts", adOpenKeyset, adLockPessimistic, adCmdTable
...
'do something with the records
...
oRS.Update      'save the changes to the records
oRS.Close
Set oRS = Nothing
```

Once we **Open** the recordset, we automatically have read/write access to all the relevant fields in the current record. Using the **Fields** collection we met earlier, we can get at the contents of the individual fields. The example **ProcessUserRS.asp** page updates the contents of the current record to the values submitted from the Posting Page form we looked at earlier:

```
Set oRs = Server.CreateObject("ADODB.Recordset")
oRs.Open "Contact", "Contacts", adOpenKeyset, adLockPessimistic,  adCmdTable
oRS.Fields("Name") = strName
oRS.Fields("Address") = strAddress
oRS.Fields("Town") = strTown
oRS.Fields("State") = strState
oRS.Fields("ZipCode") = strZipCode
oRS.Fields("Phone") = strPhone
oRS.Update
oRS.Close
Set oRS = Nothing
```

> *Remember that the* **Fields** *collection is the default collection of the* **Recordset** *object, so you can use* **oRS("Name")** *or* **oRS!Name** *instead of the full syntax of* **oRS.Fields("Name")** *if you wish.*

Once we've finished editing the records, we use the **Update** method to save the changes to that record. If we move to another record or close the recordset before calling **Update**, we lose the changes. We can also choose to abandon any changes explicitly by calling the **Recordset** object's **CancelUpdate** method.

We can always tell if there are any changes waiting to be saved by examining the **EditMode** property of the **Recordset** object. It will be **adEditInProgress** when there are, and **adEditNone** when they've been saved. Finally, we can delete the current record using the **Recordset** object's **Delete** method.

Adding New Records

Of course, when we collect a new contact's details, we don't want to overwrite an existing record with them—we want to add a new record to the database containing them. To add a new record, we use the **Recordset** object's **AddNew** method:

```
Set oRs = Server.CreateObject("ADODB.Recordset")
oRs.Open "Contact", "Contacts", adOpenKeyset, adLockPessimistic, adCmdTable
oRs.AddNew
oRS.Fields("Name") = strName
oRS.Fields("Address") = strAddress
oRS.Fields("Town") = strTown
```

```
oRS.Fields("State") = strState
oRS.Fields("ZipCode") = strZipCode
oRS.Fields("Phone") = strPhone
oRS.Update    'save the changes to the records
oRS.Close
Set oRS = Nothing
```

Once a new record has been added with **AddNew**, the **EditMode** property of the recordset is **adEditAdd**. Again, we can choose to abandon any changes with the **CancelUpdate** method, where the record that was current prior to the **AddNew** call becomes the current record again. Once the **Update** method has been executed, **EditMode** goes back to **adEditNone**.

We can also use the **AddNew** method to set the values of the fields in the new record, instead of specifying them individually afterwards. For example, this code sets the value of the **Name** field as we add the new record:

```
varName = "Stephen Jakab"
oRs.AddNew "Name", varName
```

We also create a **Variant** array of field names, and another **Variant** array of values, and specify these in the **AddNew** method:

```
varFields = Array("Name", "Address", "Town", "State")
varValues = Array("Stephen Jakab", "Wrox Press Ltd.", "Chicago", "IL")
oRs.AddNew varFields, varValues
```

In this case, we don't have to use the **Update** method to save the changes, as ADO does it automatically. When the **AddNew** parameters are arrays like this, they must have the same number of members, otherwise an error occurs. The order of field names in the first array must also match the order of field values in the second one.

Updating Records in Batch Mode

We can add or update records in two different operating modes–**immediate mode** and **batch mode**. In the previous examples, we've specified **adLockPessimistic** for the *LockType* property in the **Open** method call. This means that the data provider will lock the records so that they can't be changed by another user while we have them open for editing. As soon as we call the **Update** method for each record, while it is the current record, the changes are passed back to the data source. This is **immediate mode** updating.

Rather than writing changes to individual records back to the data source separately, we can add and update data in **batch mode**. This means that we can make multiple changes to different records, then flush these to the database in one go when we're finished. The changes to all of the records in the recordset are saved up until we call the **UpdateBatch** method, or cancel the update using the **CancelBatch** method.

To tell ADO that we want to use this mode, we open the recordset with the value **adLockBatchOptimistic** for the **LockType** parameter:

```
Set oRS = Server.CreateObject("ADODB.Recordset")
oRs.Open "Contact", "Contacts", adOpenKeyset, adLockBatchOptimistic, adCmdTable
...
'update several records here
...
```

```
oRS.UpdateBatch
oRS.Close
Set oRS = Nothing
```

Some Tips on Updating Recordsets

You need to remember that all these methods of updating data, whether with an SQL statement or by using recordset methods, will only succeed if the provider allows the update to take place. The data integrity rules of the database, or the properties of the fields in the tables, may prevent certain updates and generate an error. For example, a field marked as **Required** may not have been given a value, or a related record in another table may be required before a new record can be added.

When the **Update** method is called, the new data items are kept in the ADO cache. We can call the **UpdateBatch** method of the **Recordset** object, which propagates all changes back to the underlying data source. This update can also be canceled by using the **CancelBatch** method.

Changes to the original tables may not always be visible in the recordset. For this reason, ADO provides us with the **Requery** method. Calling this updates the data in the **Recordset** object by re-executing the query on which the recordset is based.

That about covers the **Recordset** object—the last main object in the ADO hierarchy. However, there are a couple of collections that we need to look at briefly before we move on to the next chapter. These are the **Properties** and the **Errors** collections.

The Properties Collection

All three of the main objects in ADO, the **Connection**, **Command**, and **Recordset**, implement their own **Properties** collection. These collections house a set of **Property** objects, but the actual member objects are different for each parent object.

Method	Description
Refresh	Updates the collection to reflect changes to the property values.

Property	Description
Count	Returns the number of properties in the collection.
Item	Used to retrieve the values of the properties in the collection.

The Property Object

Within the **Properties** collection, as you will by now have come to expect, the members are **Property** objects. And again, the **Property** objects have their own properties:

Property	Description
Attributes	Indicates when and how the value of the property can be set. See the **PropertyAttributesEnum** values in Appendix E for a list.
Name	The name of the property.
Type	The data type of the property.
Value	The value of the property.

One of the most difficult concepts to grasp is the difference between the ADO **built-in properties** and the **dynamic properties** which come from the data provider.

Built-in properties are automatically defined by ADO for objects as they are created. These properties are available directly from the parent object, such as the **CommandType** property of a **Command** object. The values of these properties are retrieved and set (where they are not read-only) by referring to that object directly–that is, oCmd.CommandType. Because built-in properties are provided in this way, they don't appear as **Property** objects in an object's **Properties** collection, and they are always available–independent of the provider being used.

In addition to these built-in properties, many data providers expose additional object properties to the ADO, known as **dynamic properties**. These properties are generally specific to the provider, and are used to indicate additional functionality that is available. For instance, a property specific to the provider may indicate if a **Recordset** object supports transactions. Any additional properties of this nature will appear in the **Properties** collection of the relevant object.

How to Determine Dynamic Properties

It's easy to find out which provider-specific properties are available from a particular object. If we want to find the dynamic properties available for a standard **Recordset** object for a specific provider, we can iterate through the **Properties** collection. This is what we'll do next. In **PropertyObjects.asp**, we'll create two different types of recordset, and pick out the **Property** object's **Name** and **Value**:

```
Set oConn = Server.CreateObject("ADODB.Connection")
oConn.Open "Contacts"                   'the database's System DSN
Set oRS = oConn.Execute("Contact")      'the name of a table

'first the default recordset type
Response.Write "<I> Default recordset: </I><BR>"
For Each oProp In oRS.Properties
  Response.Write "Name = " & oProp.Name & " : "
  Response.Write "Value = " & oProp.Value & "<BR>"
Next
oRS.Close

'now using a different recordset type
oRs.Open "Contact", "Contacts", adOpenKeyset, adLockBatchOptimistic, adCmdTable
Response.Write "<I> Keyset recordset with optimistic batch locking: </I><BR>"
For Each oProp In oRS.Properties
  Response.Write "Name = " & oProp.Name & " : "
  Response.Write "Value = " & oProp.Value & "<BR>"
Next
```

You'll find this page among the samples available for this book. When we run it, we get around twenty-five lines of properties for each recordset type. Here we've picked out part of the results, and you can see that the values of two of the properties have changed:

```
Default recordset:
Name = ODBC Concurrency Type : Value = 14
Name = BLOB accessibility on Forward-Only cursor : Value = True

Keyset recordset with optimistic batch locking:
Name = ODBC Concurrency Type : Value = 11
Name = BLOB accessibility on Forward-Only cursor : Value = False
```

Handling Runtime Errors

Even with the most careful coding, we can be sure that runtime errors are bound to occur, especially in a multiuser environment. Even with the most stringent testing, errors can occur in any application that we create. When they do, we need to be able to detect them, and recover in as graceful a way as possible.

Detecting and Handling Errors

There are mechanisms available in ADO to help us detect and handle errors. We can use the VBScript **On Error Resume Next** statement, or the equivalent in other scripting languages. In addition, we can inspect either the **Connection** object's **Errors** collection, or the built-in scripting object **Err**. Often, a combination of the methods is used—we use **On Error Resume Next** to ensure that our code continues to execute when an error occurs, rather than throwing up an error message and stopping, then we inspect the **Errors** collection or the **Err** object to see what went wrong.

When we build applications that will include error handling, it's important to create an explicit **Connection** object, so that its **Error** objects can be inspected. If we use an implicit **Connection** object (that is, allow a **Command** or **Recordset** object to create it automatically), we won't be able to access the **Error** objects. In this case, we have to rely on the **Err** object provided by VBScript, or the equivalent in other scripting languages. OK, we'll get a description and error number, but this isn't nearly as informative as several **Error** objects in the **Errors** collection.

Consider this simple example, from **Error_1.asp**:

```
Set oConn = Server.CreateObject("ADODB.Connection")
oConn.Open "Contacts"
Set oRS = oConn.Execute("Contact")   'a table in the database
oRS.AddNew
Response.Write "Won't reach this far"
oRS.Fields("Name") = "Valerie Gonzales"
oRS.Update
```

You'll notice that we're attempting to add a new record to a non-updateable recordset. This produces an error, and the script terminates. We must stop this because, even if we can't complete the update, we still want the script to run to completion. By simply adding **On Error Resume Next**, the script will run to completion, as is shown by the output message in this example:

```
On Error Resume Next
Set oConn = Server.CreateObject("ADODB.Connection")
```

```
oConn.Open "Contacts"
Set oRS = oConn.Execute("Contact")  'a table in the database
oRS.AddNew
oRS.Fields("Name") = "Valerie Gonzales"
oRS.Update
Response.Write "Will reach this far now"
```

Of course, the only problem now is that we have no way of knowing if the update actually succeeded. To remedy this, we have to use the **Errors** collection or the **Err** object.

The Errors Collection

The **Errors** collection holds all the **Error** objects for a specific **Connection**. It has one method, and the usual two collection properties:

Method	Description
Clear	Removes all of the errors in the collection.

Property	Description
Count	Returns the number of error objects in the collection.
Item	Used to retrieve the contents of the error objects in the collection.

Generally, if an operation being performed by ADO encounters an error, one or more new **Error** objects are automatically created and added to the **Errors** collection. These are the result of just *one* operation not completing successfully—a single database operation can create several errors.

Detecting Errors and Warnings

By examining the **Error** objects that were created, our code can determine more precisely what went wrong, rather than just relying on vague error codes generated by the scripting language. However, some method calls and property accesses don't create **Error** objects in the **Errors** collection when they fail. An example of this is the **AddNew** method, which will raise an error in VBScript, but can't be detected by inspecting the **Count** property of the **Errors** collection. In this case, we have to examine the **Err** object.

In addition to critical errors, which stop script execution, some properties and methods return warnings that appear as **Error** objects within the **Errors** collection. Warnings do not stop execution of the script, but may indicate a subtle problem such as implicit data conversion, which can compromise the accuracy of results stored. For this reason, in larger applications, it's a very good idea to explicitly test the **Count** property after any ADO operation:

```
On Error Resume Next
Set oConn = Server.CreateObject("ADODB.Connection")
oConn.Open "Contacts"                  'the database's Systm DSN
Set oRS = oConn.Execute("Contact")     'the table in the database
oRS.Fields("Name") = "Valerie Gonzales"  'update the 'Name' field
If oConn.Errors.Count > 0 Then         'errors or warnings occurred
   Response.Write "<B> Cannot update the 'Name' field </B><P>"
```

```
...
    'code to display and handle the errors
    ...
Else
    oRS.Update
End If
```

The `Errors` collection can contain warnings that didn't halt the code, and so may be left from a previous operation. We can remove these by calling the `Errors` collection's `Clear` method before executing the operation.

The Error Object

Each `Error` object within the `Errors` collection is itself an object, with its own properties:

Property	Description
Description	A description of the error.
HelpContextID	Context ID, as a **Long** value, for the matching help file topic.
HelpFile	The path to the help file for this topic.
NativeError	The provider-specific error code number.
Number	The ADO error code number. Refer to Appendix E for a list.
Source	Name of the object or application that generated the error.
SQLState	The SQL execution state for this error.

After an ADO operation fails and adds one or more `Error` objects to the `Errors` collection, we can use these to get a better idea of what went wrong. You'll find this code, `ErrorHandling.asp`, among the samples for this book available from our web site:

```
On Error Resume Next
Set oConn = Server.CreateObject("ADODB.Connection")
oConn.Open "Contacts"
Set oRS = oConn.Execute("Contact")
oRS.Fields("Name") = "Valerie Gonzales"
If oConn.Errors.Count > 0 Then
    Response.Write "<B> Cannot update the 'Name' field </B><P>"
    For intLoop = 0 To oConn.Errors.Count
        Response.Write "Error Number: " & oConn.Errors(intLoop).Number
        Response.Write " - " & oConn.Errors(intLoop).Description & "<P>"
    Next
Else
    oRS.Update
End If
```

The **Errors** *collection in the current version of ADO is not fully implemented—as the above code shows, by not returning any errors. If, however, you comment out the* **On Error Resume Next** *line, an error is flagged up.*

The Err Object

We looked at the **Err** object in detail in Chapter 3, so we won't go over it all again. However, you'll recall that an error in your code will set the **Number**, **Source** and **Description** properties of the **Err** object, and we can use these in the sample **Error_2.asp** code–in a similar way to the **Errors** collection:

```
On Error Resume Next
Set oConn = Server.CreateObject("ADODB.Connection")
oConn.Open "Contacts"
Set oRS = oConn.Execute("Contact")
oRS.Fields("Name") = "Valerie Gonzales"
If Err.Number > 0 Then    'an error occurred
    Response.Write "<B> Cannot update the 'Name' field </B><P>"
    Response.Write "Error Number: " & Err.Number
    Response.Write " - Source: " & Err.Source
    Response.Write " - " & Err.Description & "<P>"
Else
    oRS.Update
End If
```

Preventing Errors

Of course, the best way to deal with errors is to make sure that they don't arise in the first place! There's no way to prevent *all* runtime errors; for example when the database is unavailable for some reason, or the network between web server and database has gone down. Often, however, we can avoid having to use specific error handling by pre-empting the causes of errors. One example would be when we try to perform an illegal operation on an object.

Imagine that we've already got a **Recordset** object available, created from an existing **Command** object. We may want to move to the previous record using the **MovePrevious** method. This will generally cause an error if the recordset was opened with a forward-only cursor. We can check what kinds of operations are supported by the recordset using its **Supports** method:

```
...
If oRS.Supports(adMovePrevious) Then oRS.MovePrevious
...
```

The **Supports** method of the **Recordset** object can provide a range of information about that recordset and the functions it supports, such as whether **AddNew**, **Delete**, and **UpdateBatch** are available, if **Bookmarks** can be used, and whether **AbsolutePosition** is supported. Look for the **CursorOptionsEnum** values in Appendix E for a full list.

Summary

In this chapter, we've introduced the Active Data Object and talked about the individual objects that make up its hierarchy. We've shown you the most widely used methods and properties of those objects, and how you can use them to fulfill your data processing needs.

Of course, there are many more ways that you can use ADO, and you'll see some of these in the next chapter, and throughout the remainder of the book. In particular, two of the case studies in Part 4 of the book use ADO to great effect. In the meantime, the most important points of this chapter are:

▲ ADO is the data connection mechanism provided with ASP that allows interaction with a data provider, generally a database of some kind. Using the `CreateObject` method, ADO allows us to create objects of type `Connection`, `Command` and `Recordset`, and use them to manipulate our data source.

▲ The `Connection` object is used to provide an active link to the data source through a Data Source Name (DSN), or with a connection string. By explicitly creating a `Connection` object, we can use it to perform multiple database operations on the same set of data.

▲ The `Command` object is used to perform execution of SQL queries and statements, table record resolution, and stored procedures. We need to create an explicit `Command` object if we want to access the `Parameters` collection.

▲ The `Recordset` and `Field` objects give us access to the rows of data contained within the database. We can manipulate the underlying tables at the record level using `Recordset` methods.

▲ In larger applications, we must provide error handling so that our scripts run to completion, and never leave the database in an unstable state.

In the next chapter, we continue to look at the ADO—but in a wider context. Now that you've got a good grounding in the ways ADO can be used, you'll see ways that we can extend this and perform more complicated types of operations. We'll also be looking at using a data source other than Microsoft Access—in particular, how the data can be moved into more enterprise-oriented systems such as SQL Server.

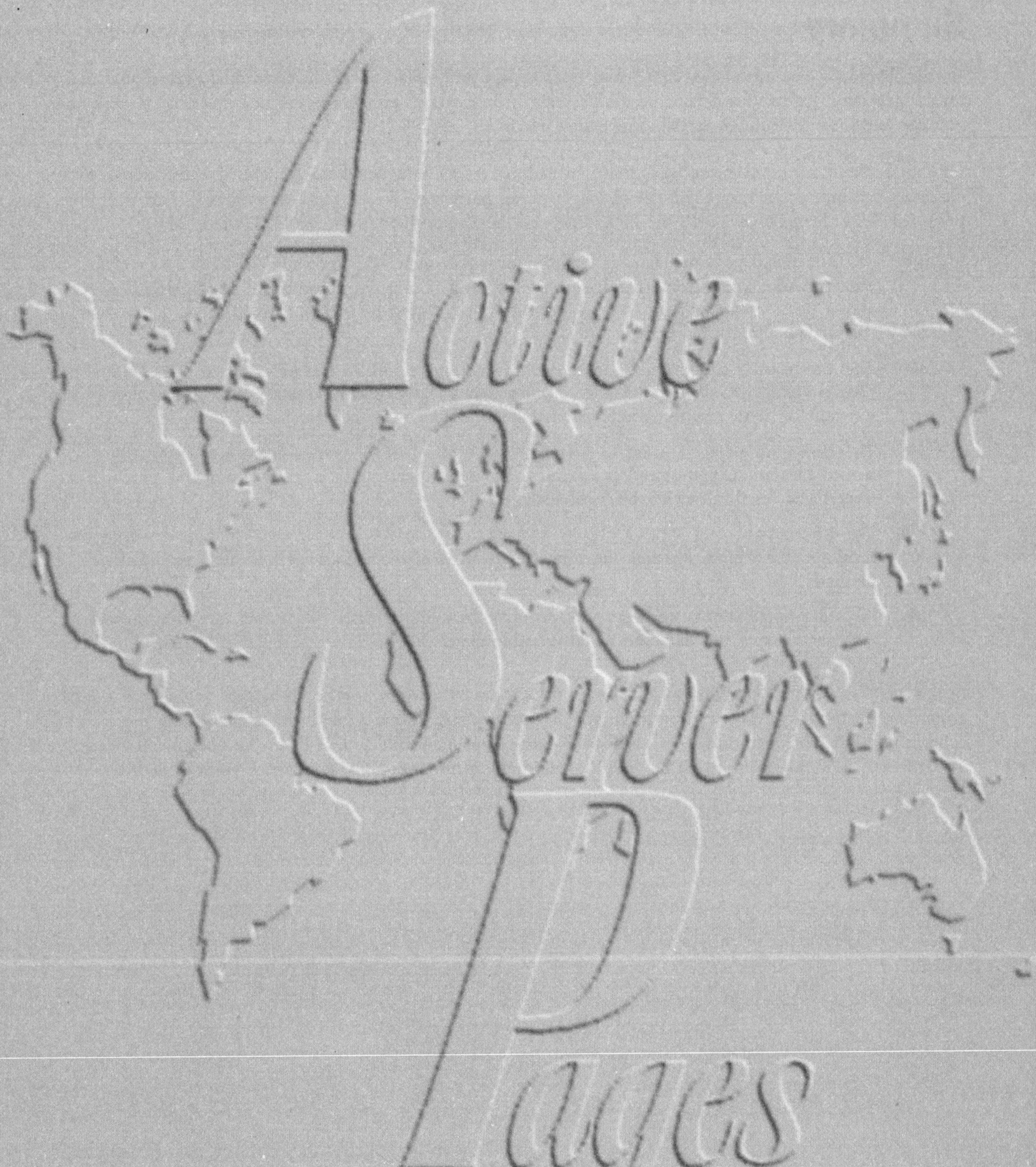
Active
Server
Pages

Advanced Database Techniques

In the last chapter, we spent a lot of time looking at the basic structure of the **Active Database Component**. This was intentional because, while it isn't as complex as many other Microsoft database engines, it's important that you are comfortable with the way that it's used before we go on to look at more complicated techniques. As you've seen, ADO follows the example of earlier database systems in being built around a defined object structure. This means that working with it requires a structured approach, but it brings many benefits.

For example, we've see that there are several different ways of creating a `Recordset`, and directly updating the database. The ADO is very flexible, and a great deal more complicated that any of the other Server Components we looked at in earlier chapters. However, while the techniques we used in the previous chapter are fine for databases such as Microsoft Access, in the real world we often have to connect our Web site to one of the more commercially-oriented systems. This might be Microsoft's SQL Server, Oracle, Sybase, DB2 or any of the other enterprise-based systems.

We also need to investigate some of the more advanced ways that the Active Database Component can be used. Rather than the simple examples you saw in the previous chapter, you'll now see how some real-world problems can be solved. For example, we need to consider how our pages might affect the security of our data, and take steps to protect our database systems. We'll be putting all the techniques you saw in the previous chapter to good use, and combining them to produce examples that more closely resemble the kinds of situation that you are going to meet.

So, in this chapter, we'll be looking at:

- How the Active Data Object links to different databases
- Techniques for manipulating enterprise-oriented databases
- Real-world problem-solving techniques with the Active Data Object
- How we can maintain security when linking a database to the Web

To begin, then, we'll examine how the connection to a database works. You'll also find some useful reference material in Appendix J, which goes deeper into the background of this exciting new technology.

Manipulating Enterprise Data

So far we have assumed that the data source used to supply data to our Web page was an Access database. However, Access is not designed to handle really large volumes of data, or high transaction rates from multiple users. As we begin to look at developing an Internet or Intranet site, we need to consider the potential number of simultaneous visitors we might have to cater for. Hundreds of users might visit a typical Internet site in any given day, potentially dozens at the same time. In this environment, Microsoft Access would quickly overheat. So let's take a step beyond Access, and look at how the ADO can be used with other sources of data, including enterprise database systems such as Microsoft SQL Server.

Expanded Data Access

The ADO is a collection of objects that expose a standard set of properties and methods that our applications can use when accessing data. Like many of its predecessors, such as DAO and RDO, ADO relies on an underlying layer of software to actually interact with a given data source. As we saw in the last chapter, **OLE DB** is this underlying layer.

OLE DB technology is being positioned as the cornerstone to Microsoft's component database architecture. It is a set of OLE interfaces that provide applications with a standard means of accessing data stored in various information sources. These standard interfaces support specific elements of the Database Management System's (DBMS) functionality that are appropriate to the data source, enabling it to share its data.

The benefits of component DBMS's can be seen in the success of the **Open Database Connectivity** (ODBC) database access interface. ODBC is provided as a means of accessing data from a diverse set of sources, using a standard series of functions and commands, the idea being that the programmer is shielded from having to code to each specific data source's requirements, thus vastly increasing productivity.

OLE DB takes ODBC a step further, towards a truly standard means of accessing data from diverse sources. Whereas ODBC is designed around accessing relational data sources using Structured Query Language (SQL), OLE DB is focused on providing access to *any* data, anywhere. For example, an ODBC provider has just been released that provides access to NT 4, Novell version 3, and NDS directory services, all through OLE DB. And there are more to come.

In addition to simplifying the programmer's job, the OLE DB interface layer provides the developer with a means of accessing data which may not be stored in a traditional DBMS format. As we all know, there is a large amount of mission-critical data stored in systems that are not classified as a DBMS. One of the most significant limitations of the ODBC approach to data access is that it is difficult for non-relational database vendors to support. Building a data provider layer means exposing the data via SQL. For a non-SQL data provider, such as an Excel file or a Mail system, this requires the equivalent of a SQL engine within the ODBC driver.

OLE DB simplifies the development of access methods for simple tabular data providers by only requiring them to implement the functionality native to their data source. At a minimum, an access provider must implement the interfaces necessary to expose data in a tabular form. This requirement allows for the development of query processor components, such as SQL query processors, that can work with tabular information from any provider that exposes its data through OLE DB. In essence then, OLE DB provides an interface layer that is consistent despite its having an underlying data structure that may be very diverse.

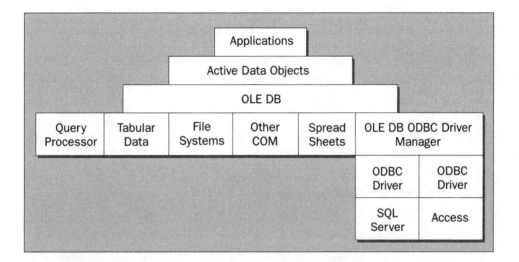

OLE DB and the ADO

As we have seen, OLE DB is a collection of components that work together to provide data access capabilities to an application. These components are loosely grouped into two classes, **consumers** and **providers**. Consumers are the components that submit requests for data. Providers service these requests by accessing the data sources, and retrieving the information requested. In these terms, ADO is an OLE DB consumer. In other words, it makes requests to a provider. The name of the provider that will service a request is supplied either as a part of a **connection string**, or as the **Provider** property of the **Connection** object.

In this example, we supply the name of the Microsoft ODBC provider for OLE DB and the ADO, **MSDASQL**, as a parameter to the **Provider** method of the **Connection** object.

```
Set DBConn = Server.CreateObject("ADODB.Connection")
DBConn.Provider ="MSDASQL"
DBConn.Open "DSN=SQLForum;UID=sa;PWD=;"
Set Session("DBConn") = DBConn
```

> *Be careful not to include a **Provider Name** as both a part of the connection string, and as the **Provider** property of the **Connection** object. If you do, the result is unpredictable.*

Providers, like any other OLE object, must be defined in the registry before the OLE DB layer can use them. They are identified by the **OLE DB Provider** sub-key, under the class ID of the provider. Within the **HKEY_CLASSES_ROOT** key, providers must have the following sub-keys and values for the programmatic identifier (**ProgID**):

```
ProviderProgID = FriendlyDisplayName
ProviderProgID\CLSID = ProviderCLSID
```

The entries for the **MSDASQL** ODBC provider are show here–the **CLSID** value is a unique key that identifies the provider installed:

```
MSDASQL = Microsoft OLE DB Provider for ODBC Drivers
MSDASQL\CLSID = {c8b522cb-5cf3-11ce-ade5-00aa0044773d}
```

Under the **HKEY_CLASSES_ROOT\CLSID** sub-key, providers must have the following sub-keys and values:

```
ProviderCLSID = FriendlyDisplayName
ProviderCLSID\ProgID = ProviderProgID
ProviderCLSID\VersionIndependentProgID = VersionIndependentProgID
ProviderCLSID\InprocServer32 = ProviderDLLFilename
ProviderCLSID\InprocServer32\ThreadingModel = Apartment | Free | Both
ProviderCLSID\OLE DB Provider = Description
```

Again, the entries for the **MSDASQL** ODBC provider are:

```
{c8b522cb-5cf3-11ce-ade5-00aa0044773d} = MSDASQL
{c8b522cb-5cf3-11ce-ade5-00aa0044773d}\VersionIndependentProgID = MSDASQL
{c8b522cb-5cf3-11ce-ade5-00aa0044773d}\InprocServer32 = MSDASQL.DLL
{c8b522cb-5cf3-11ce-ade5-00aa0044773d}\InprocServer32\ThreadingModel = Both
{c8b522cb-5cf3-11ce-ade5-00aa0044773d}\OLE DB Provider = Microsoft OLE DB
                                       ↳ Provider for ODBC Drivers
```

In addition, the ODBC provider entry references a second key that points to another OLE object, which is used for error processing. Other providers are identified in the registry in this same way. Thankfully, the installation of ADO provides all the registry entries required, but you'll find the information here useful if you need to delve into the registry yourself.

Connecting to a Data Source

Let's take a moment to look at how we connect to various data sources. The ADO provides a number of ways of actually establishing a connection to a data source. Each has its advantages and disadvantages but, underneath the covers, each is limited by the ability of the provider to service the connection. As we walk through various examples, keep in mind that some of the features discussed may only be appropriate for the provider being used in that example.

The Connection Object

In the previous chapter, we reviewed how the **Connection** object is used to create a connection between an ASP page and a data source. Now let's look in more detail at the **Connection** object and at some of the more advanced options we can take use when connecting to and working with various data sources, including SQL Server.

The **Connection** object is the parent object in a hierarchy of several other objects including the **Errors** object, **Command** object and **Recordset** object. The **Connection** object can be used to create a new connection to a data source, by providing it with a connection string or connection information. This connection can then be referenced by each of the other objects in the hierarchy to interact with the described data source.

```
Set DBConn = Server.CreateObject("ADODB.Connection")
DBConn.Provider="MSDASQL"
DBConn.Open "DSN=SQLForum; UID=sa; PWD=; APP=Forum; WSID=MAINFRAME; Database=Forum"
Set Session("DBConn") = DBConn
```

However, unlike the DAO and RDO libraries, the ADO doesn't require you to work your way down a hierarchy of objects in order to instantiate the one you actually require. The **Command** and **Recordset** objects can be called independently of any **Connection** object, allowing these objects to create a new **Connection** directly and interact with the database through it:

```
Set oRS = Server.CreateObject("ADODB.RecordSet")
oRS.Open "Select * from Message", "DSN=SQLForum;UID=sa;PW="
Response.Write "<B> Records Found: </B><P>"
Do While Not oRS.EOF
    For intCount = 0 to oRS.Fields.Count -1
        Response.Write oRS.Fields(intCount).Value & " - "
    Next
    Response.Write "<BR>"
    oRS.MoveNext
Loop
```

In this example, we create a simple listing of each record in the **Message** table. You will notice that no **Connection** object is explicitly created, we simply create a **Recordset** with the **Open** method of the **Recordset**, using an SQL query and a connection string. Behind the scenes, ADO creates a **Connection** object and associates it with the **Recordset** we just created. When the **Recordset** goes out of scope or is set to **Nothing**, the **Connection** object is released.

Let's take another example. Here we need to call an SQL Server Stored Procedure only once per session. Rather then opening a **Connection** object, and passing a reference to it to a **Command** object, we can take advantage of the **Command** object's ability to create a **Connection** object for us automatically in the background:

```
Set oCmd = Server.CreateObject("ADODB.Command")
oCmd.ActiveConnection = "dsn=SQLForum;database=Forum;uid=sa;pwd=;"
oCmd.CommandText = "{call myproc}"
oCmd.Execute
```

In the above example, we supply a connection string to the **Open** method of the object. The connection string is passed directly to the underlying ODBC driver, which in turn uses it to attach to the specified data source. Here a connection object is created for temporary use and destroyed when the **oCmd** object variable goes out of scope, or is set to **Nothing**.

Connection Tips

When defining connections, here are a few simple guidelines that are useful to follow:

▲ Generally you will want to use a connection *variable* instead of a connection *string* as the **ActiveConnection** for commands. By using a connection variable, you're calling an existing connection. If you use a string, as we saw above, you are creating a new connection.

▲ Make sure you explicitly close a connection when it's no longer needed. Although a connection is closed when it goes out of scope, it's better to make sure it is closed when you think it is. You can proactively call **Close** and set the variable to **Nothing** when you know that you will no longer need a connection. This frees up resources before it actually goes out of scope.

When working with a SQL Server data source, consider these points:

- ▲ With forward-scrolling, read-only cursors (also known as **firehose** cursors) against SQL Server, you will not be able to start a new transaction on that connection. This is because the connection is dealing with the cursor and needs to complete what it's doing (i.e. get to the end of the cursor and close it) before continuing.

- ▲ In addition, it is a good idea to separate your forward-scrolling cursor code from your command execution code. You could get into a situation where the same SQL pages are used concurrently, for example a query such as **SELECT * FROM TableX** and an update to **TableX**. Without setting the **CommandTimeout** property, your could hang your system due to locking contention.

Connection Pooling

In each of the examples we've discussed, we've created a new **Connection** object for each session, and then done something with it. However, consider a site where the number of simultaneous users is in the hundreds. In this environment, creating a new **Connection** object for each and every user can be very resource intensive. To help alleviate this problem, ADO can take advantage of a new feature provided with ODBC 3.0 and ASP known as **connection pooling**. This is a resource manager for connections, maintaining the open state on frequently used connections, and thereby avoiding the need to continuously create new connections.

Enabling Connection Pooling

By default ASP does not take advantage of this ability. To turn this feature on you will have to update the Registry and manually adjust the appropriate key. This can seem a daunting task. However, it is really very straightforward and the performance benefits can be well worth the effort.

> ***Note for IIS users****: Unless you install Microsoft Windows NT Service Pack 2 (SP2) or later, using Microsoft Access with connection pooling enabled may cause system failures when shutting down IIS.*

To edit the Registry, run the **REGEDIT** utility. You will need to modify the following registry entry:

```
HKEY_LOCAL_MACHINE\System\CurrentControlSet\Services\W3SVC\ASP\Parameters
```

Find the **StartConnectionPool** entry and change the value from **0** to **1**. For example:

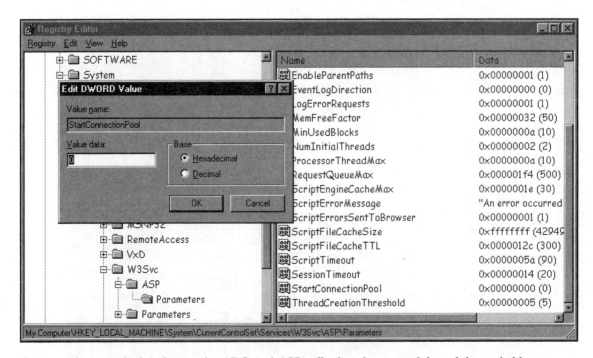

Once you have made this change, the ADO and ASP will take advantage of their ability to hold open frequently-used connections between sessions. However, we now need to consider whether, and to what extent, the data source we are attaching to can support connection pooling. If your data server is Microsoft SQL Server, you'll want to take into account which underlying network library is being used to support a connection. Let's take a look at the changes that we should made to the SQL Server environment to support connection pooling with ADO.

SQL Server Performance and Stability with Connection Pooling

In order to take advantage of connection pooling when using SQL Server, the TCP/IP or Multi-Protocol network library must be used. In most cases, as we are developing an Internet or Intranet based solution, TCP/IP will be the default underlying network library in use at our site. However, to verify the library in use, use the **SQL Server Client Configuration** utility. Remember that even if the Web Server and SQL Server are running on the same physical system, the Web Server (and thus our ASP pages) is still a client of SQL Server.

The **SQL Server Client Configuration** utility is an easy-to-use GUI tool that displays the **DB Library** and **NET Library** defined for use on the machine, along with any DB LIB-defined names tied to a specific library. (DB LIB is the native database library supplied with SQL Server and Sybase). As ASP interacts with ODBC and its underlying SQL Server driver, no changes are required to the DB LIB settings. However, both DB LIB and ODBC communicate with SQL Server using an underlying Net Library driver.

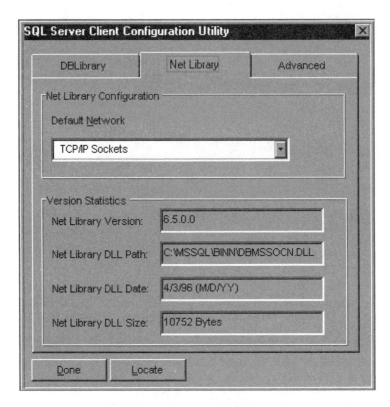

To configure a client system (in our case the Web server) to use the TCP/IP Net Library when communicating with SQL Server, we click on the Net Library tab, and under **Default Network** select TCP/IP Sockets.

Creating a DSN 'on the Fly'

So far, each of our connections has assumed that we have previously defined a **Data Source Name** (DSN). The DSN describes a data source, and the standard settings to be used when attaching to it. However, this can be limiting in some circumstances—especially when attaching to data sources that are dynamic in nature.

For example, let's take a situation where the user connects to several servers, depending on the information they need. We could setup an ODBC Data Source Name definition for each server and selectively attach to it. A better way is to create the connection 'on the fly', without using a DSN:

```
ServerName = Request.QueryString("ServerName")    'from the submitted page
DBConn.Open  "Driver={SQL Server};Server=" & ServerName & _
             ";UID=sa;PWD=;WSID=MAINFRAME;Language=us_english;Database=Forum;DSN=;"
...
```

In this example we create a definition on the fly, using the server name from a form submitted by the user to determine which SQL Server to attach to.

Expanding the Connection Object

The **Connection** object is responsible for more than just the initialization of communication between the server and the application. It is also used to manage transactions, submit SQL statements directly to a provider, and set provider-specific attributes.

Let's look at an example of using several of the advanced features of the **Connection** object to update our database. Typically, when working with the ADO, you might assume that to update a record in a table we would open a **Recordset**, use **AddNew** to add a new record, update the fields in the **Recordset** and then **Update** the **Recordset**. This is how we did it in the previous chapter:

```
...
Set rsAddMessage = Server.CreateObject("ADODB.Recordset")
rsAddMessage.Open "Message", Conn, adOpenKeyset, adLockBatchOptimistic
rsAddMessage.AddNew
rsAddMessage.Fields("FromMsg") = strFrom
rsAddMessage.Fields("Email") = strEmail
rsAddMessage.Fields("Subject") = strSubject
rsAddMessage.Fields("Body") = strBody
rsAddMessage.Fields("WhenMsg") = CStr(Now())
rsAddMessage.Fields("MsgLevel") = intNewMsgLevel
rsAddMessage.Fields("PrevRef") = lngPrevRef
rsAddMessage.Fields("ThreadPos") = intNewThreadPos
rsAddMessage.UpdateBatch
rsAddMessage.Close
Set rsAddMessage = Nothing
...
```

However, consider the number of steps involved, as well as the potential server traffic issues that could arise, if the **UpdateBatch** method were not supported. In our example, we applied all of the required changes as a single transaction, using the **UpdateBatch** parameter, and thus reduced the amount of interaction that had to occur between the server and the application. However, your ADO access provider must support this facility in order for it to be of value.

Now, let's take a look at a piece of code that does the same thing, using a different tactic:

```
...
SQLQuery = "INSERT INTO Forum.dbo.Message " _
         & "( FromMsg, Email, Subject, Body, WhenMsg, MsgLevel, PrevRef, TopRef ) " _
         & " VALUES ( '" & strFrom & cDlm & strEmail & cDlm & strSubject _
         & cDlm & strBody & cDlm & CStr(Now()) & "', " & intNewMsgLevel _
         & ", " & lngPrevRef & ", " & intNewThreadPos & " )"
oConn.Execute SQLQuery, lRecs
...
```

Here we build an **INSERT** statement to apply the data stored in a number of variables to the records. The SQL Statement is syntactically compatible with **Transact-SQL** (TSQL), the native SQL language of SQL Server.

The SQL statement is then submitted to the provider using the **Execute** method of the **Connection** object. Notice that an **lRecs** variable is supplied as a parameter to the **Execute** method call. This variable will contain a count of the number of records affected by this statement after it is submitted. It can be used to test for the successful completion of the statement.

One of the advantages of this approach is that it simply requires fewer steps. More importantly, it provides us with the ability to supply **batches** of SQL to the Server. In the above example, we use a single **INSERT** statement. However, the need for multiple inserts or updates–or perhaps additional data validation that might occur during, or as a part of, the submission–means that this isn't always the best answer.

Batch and Transaction Management

Perhaps the most compelling reason to use a batch SQL approach is the need for a finer level of transaction control. When using an Access database with a single user, transaction management is a minor concern at best. However, when multiple users are accessing a data source, with the potential of simultaneous updates, transaction management can have a huge impact on the performance and reliability of SQL Server.

In the previous example, the transaction is committed to the server–i.e. the changes are actually applied to the data–as soon as it is executed. In many cases this is perfectly acceptable. However, if we need a finer level of control over when a transaction is committed, either for performance reasons or due to dependencies between records, we can choose to define the beginning and the end of each transaction.

We looked briefly at transactions in the previous chapter. To define the beginning and end of transaction, we use the **BeginTrans** and **CommitTrans** methods of the **Connection** object:

```
Conn.BeginTrans
Conn.Execute SQLQuery, lRecs
Conn.CommitTrans
```

Here we explicitly define the beginning of a transaction. By doing so, the underlying ODBC provider will no longer automatically commit a transaction. To apply changes to a database, the **Connection** object's **CommitTrans** method is called. If an error occurs, the **RollbackTrans** method is available. **RollbackTrans** will 'undo' any changes made as a result of the SQL that has been submitted since the last **CommitTrans** was called.

Things to Consider when Using Transactions

To get the maximum performance when using transaction statements to process database records, we need to structure them well. The following is a list of guidelines that may be helpful as you experiment with transactions:

▲ Keep the transaction processing blocks as short as possible. Remember that as long as a transaction is open on a series of records (especially in the case of an update), other people cannot access or change them. For example:

```
Conn.BeginTrans
    Statement1...
    Statement2...
    Statement3...
```

```
        Statement4...       '*** If you have a number of statements,
                            '*** you could slow processing and increase
                            '*** the chance of errors occurring.
    Conn.CommitTrans  (or RollbackTrans)
```

▲ When working with transaction statements, don't create a new connection or perform further database processing until the transaction is complete. Jumping out of an open transaction can lead to contention and lockout conditions:

```
Conn.BeginTrans
    Statement1...
    Statement2...

    '*** Don't create a new transaction within an open tranaction

    Set RS = Server.CreateObject("ADODB.RecordSet")
    RS.Open "select * from Message", DBConn, 3, 1, 2
    If NOT RS.EOF Then
        Statement3...
        Statement4...
    End if
Conn.CommitTrans  (or RollbackTrans)
```

▲ When working with a `Recordset` object, don't refresh the object in the middle of a series of transactions. Doing so will create the "Attempt to Commit or Rollback without BeginTrans" error:

```
Conn.BeginTrans
    Statement1...
    If UserReset Then
        Rs.Refresh  '*** Can cause an error
    End If
    Statement2...
    Statement3...
Conn.CommitTrans  (or Rollback)
```

▲ When using transactions to control server updates, don't execute a `Close` in the middle of a transaction. This can lead to problems when attempting to commit the transaction:

```
Conn.BeginTrans
    Statement1
    If Error Then
        db.Close  '*** Commit will fail after this
    End If
    Statement2...
    Statement3...
Conn.CommitTrans  (or Rollback)
```

As you can see, we can now specify when and under what conditions data is applied to our data server. In addition, and perhaps more importantly, we can undo these changes at any point in the process.

Connection Attributes

Depending on the **Connection** object's **Attributes** property, calling either the **CommitTrans** or **RollbackTrans** methods may automatically start a new transaction. If the **Attributes** property is set to **adXactCommitRetaining**, ADO automatically starts a new transaction after a **CommitTrans** call. If **Attributes** is set to **adXactAbortRetaining**, ADO automatically starts a new transaction after a **RollbackTrans** call.

Take care to note what state the driver is in. The ODBC provider for ADO does not support multiple simultaneous transactions within a single connection. As such, if we attempt a **BeginTrans** and the previous **CommitTrans** automatically created a new transaction, an error will result.

> *Note that once you start a transaction yourself, rather than having it started automatically, you will have to manually manage transactions until the connection is closed and reopened.*

The Command Object

The Command object is used to obtain records and create **Recordset** objects, as well as to execute bulk operations or manipulate the structure of a database. Depending on the functionality the provider exposes; some collections, methods, and properties of a **Command** object may not be available. Refer to your provider's documentation to verify a command feature is available before attempting to use one.

In previous chapters we have taken a look at how we use the **Command** object. Now let's take a closer look at one of its most appealing capabilities, especially when working with SQL Server.

Using Stored Procedures

Stored procedures provide an alternative to executing batches of SQL statements in ADO. We looked briefly at how we can call a stored procedure earlier. Let's take a look at how to get values back out of one procedure. Here's a simple code sample showing how to call a stored procedure with a single output parameter.

```
Set cmd = Server.CreateObject("ADODB.Command")
oCmd.ActiveConnection = "dsn=SQLForum;database=pubs;uid=sa;pwd=;"
oCmd.CommandText = "{call recordcount(?)}"
'now specify parameter info
oCmd.Parameters.Append oCmd.CreateParameter("cnt", adInteger, adParamOutput)
oCmd.Execute
Response.Write "RecordCount = " & oCmd(0)
```

In this example, we have a stored procedure called **recordcount**, which accepts one integer parameter and returns the number of records in our table. Alternately we can use this approach with the same stored procedure:

```
Set oCon = Server.CreateObject("ADODB.Connection")
Set oCmd = Server.CreateObject("ADODB.Command")
oCon.Open "SQLForum", "sa", ""
Set oCmd.ActiveConnection = oCon
```

```
oCmd.CommandText = "{? = call recordcount}"
'now specify parameter info
oCmd(0).Direction = adParamReturnValue
oCmd.Execute
Response.Write "RecordCount = " & oCmd(0)
```

The Recordset Object

The **Recordset** object is the real heart of the ADO. It's the primary mechanism we use to interact with a database. In previous chapters we've introduced the **Recordset**, and seen what it has to offer. In this section, we'll consider some of the things we must take into account when creating **Recordsets**. Then we'll look at how we go about retrieving **Binary Large Object** (BLOB) data using a **Recordset**.

A **Recordset** is in essence a **cursor**. A cursor is a subset of a database, organized and sorted in accordance with an SQL query. Cursors are powerful tools within a relational database engine. They allows developers to retrieve a subset of data, position that data in tables and columns, and then navigate the result set–both forward and backward–updating and changing the data as required. The following are some things to consider when creating and working with **Recordsets**.

Tips for Working with Cursors

Some providers, such as SQL Server, implement a forward-scrolling, read-only (or 'firehose') cursor mode, meaning that they can efficiently retrieve data by keeping a connection open. When working with such providers, the connection could be blocked by another user's transaction. The following examples demonstrate scenarios that result in errors.

```
dbConn.Open "DSN=SQLForum;UID=sa;PWD=;"          'Example 1
dbConn.BeginTrans
RS.Open "SELECT * FROM Message", dbConn
Set dbCmd.ActiveConnection = dbConn
```

▲ **Example 1**: The problem is that the command object's **ActiveConnection** is being set to a connection that is forward-scrolling and in 'firehose' mode. This is the same connection involved in the batch mode. The error from the provider will only appear in the **Err** object, and it will return as unspecified. For example, with the ODBC Provider, you will get "Unspecified error".

```
dbConn.Open "DSN=SQLForum;UID=sa;PWD=;"          'Example 2
RS.Open "SELECT * FROM Message", dbConn
dbConn.BeginTrans
```

▲ **Example 2**: The problem here is that the connection is forward-scrolling and in firehose mode, so it cannot be put into transaction mode. The error returned in the **Errors** collection from the provider will indicate that it is operating in firehose mode, and can't work in transaction mode. For example, with the ODBC Provider against Microsoft SQL Server, you will get the error "Cannot start transaction while in firehose mode".

```
dbConn.Open "DSN=SQLForum;UID=sa;PWD=;"          'Example 3
```

```
RS.Open "SELECT * FROM Message", dbConn
Set dbCmd.ActiveConnection = dbConn
dbConn.BeginTrans
```

▲ **Example 3**: The problem here is that the connection is in forward-scrolling firehose mode, so it cannot also be involved in a batch mode. The error returned in the **Errors** collection from the provider will indicate that the transaction could not be started. For example, with the ODBC Provider against Microsoft SQL Server, you will get the error "Cannot start transaction because more than one hdbc is in use".

Working with the CacheSize Property

When dealing with **Cursors**, especially those created by ODBC, it is important to control how much data is cached by ODBC in client memory. ASP assists in this area considerably, as the actual ADO processes are executed on the Web server. As such, cached data is stored in the server's memory, as opposed to the actual end-user or client machine. However, this can also have a downside as we scale up our server. If our default **Recordset** cache is large, and our server incurs a large volume of traffic, we can fast run into resource issues.

The **CacheSize** property is used to control how many records our underlying ODBC driver keeps in its memory buffer, and how many to retrieve at one time into local memory. For example if the **CacheSize** is set to **10**, the ODBC driver retrieves the first ten records into a local cache as soon as a **Recordset** object is opened. As we navigate through the **Recordset** object, the ODBC driver then retrieves data from the data source and puts it into the cache as required, for example as soon as we move past the last record in the cache, it retrieves the next ten records from the data source.

Typically, for a read-only forward-scrolling **Recordset**, we only want to cache one record at a time, and **CacheSize** is set to **1**. Because we don't need to move backward, and we're not changing the data, caching records on the client isn't efficient. Bringing them into memory as they are read is all that is needed.

However, when data is being updated, or we create a **Recordset** that supports forward and backward navigation, a larger **CacheSize** may be appropriate. In the case of updates, when the cache size is **1**, the recordset will need to go back to the server for each changed record. With a recordset that allows backward as well as forward navigation, it has to go back to the server to retrieve the same data many times, especially as we move upwards (**MovePrevious**) in the recordset.

The value of the **CacheSize** property can be adjusted during the life of the **Recordset** object, but changing this value only affects the number of records in the cache after subsequent retrievals from the data source. To force the cache size to be adjusted immediately, we can **Resync** the **Recordset**. However, we cannot set the cache size to **0**—if we do an error will result.

Binary Data

The **Recordset** is an extremely flexible object. In addition to working with data of various types, it supports the retrieval and manipulation of raw binary data stored in a database. This can be especially valuable if our database contains items such as graphical or sound data.

It's important to note that although BLOB (Binary Large Object) data can be retrieved from a database, it is not wise to store all of the graphical images on the Web site in the database. SQL Server, or Access for that matter, was not designed to process and work with this type of data. Typically it's far more efficient to store BLOB information as normally, as `.gif` or `.wav` files, along with our Web pages.

BLOB data manipulation comes in handy when we have graphics that are supplied from other sources, and are typically dynamic in nature. For example, a workflow imaging system may track document images across various users, and we may need to display some of these images within a dynamic Web page. To do this, the `GetChunk` method of the `Field` object is used. Let's take a look at an example:

```
ID = Request.QueryString("ID")
BlockSize = 4096
Response.ContentType = "image/JPEG"
strQuery = "SELECT * FROM Blob WHERE Blob_ID = " & ID
Set oRS = oConn.Execute(Query)        'oConn is a Session level object
oRS.MoveFirst
Set Field = oRS("Blob")
FileLength = Field.ActualSize
NumBlocks = FileLength \ BlockSize
LeftOver = FileLength Mod BlockSize
Response.BinaryWrite Field.GetChunk(LeftOver)
For intLoop = 1 To NumBlocks
  Response.BinaryWrite Field.GetChunk(BlockSize)
Next
oRS.Close
```

Make sure the BLOBs are the last things in your **SELECT** *statement. Currently they don't work if they are not the last field(s).*

In this example, a **jpeg** image has been stored in an **Image** field within our SQL Server database. We're retrieving it from the database, and displaying it on our Web page. SQL Server supports several binary data types. Two of these, **Binary** and **VarBinary** are limited to a maximum of **255** characters. In addition, SQL Server supports an **Image** type that stores data as **2KB** increments of binary information. This type meets our need for this example.

Our first step is to obtain a key that references the binary object in which we are interested. Here, we will use an **ID** that is selected by the user on a previous page. In a real world scenario, the previous page would include a number of "thumb nail" pictures, that when selected would call this page and pass the appropriate **ID** for the image required.

A **BlockSize** value is used to determine how much data will be read from the data source at one time. Take care when setting this value. It is best to use a value that is a multiple of the field increment size to avoid an excessively large or small leftover chunk. It may seem logical to read the whole image as a single chunk, but keep in mind that we need to move this data from our server to our Web site in a single transaction, a process that can be very resource intensive with large files.

The next step is to define the type of data that will be displayed on the page. This is done using the **ContentType** property of the **Response** object. Then, with our initial values set, we can define a query to retrieve the data. Using the **Execute** method of the **Connection** object, we submit the query and return a **Recordset** containing the query results. To verify that the data set is populated, we call the **MoveFirst** method of the **Recordset** object.

Now we are ready to actually read the data from our **Recordset**. To do this we define an object variable representing the **BLOB** field. In this example we use:

```
Set Field = RS("BLOB")
```

The object variable **Field** now has a reference to the actual binary data. Our next step is to calculate how much data we need to retrieve in terms of the block size defined earlier. We do this by retrieving the actual size of the object (using the **ActualSize** property as you might guess), and then dividing that value by our block size variable to determine the number of chunks our data can retrieved in. As our block size may not be evenly devisable by the size of the image, a **LeftOver** value is calculated to determine any partial chunk of data that needs to be retrieved:

```
FileLength = Field.ActualSize
NumBlocks = FileLength \ BlockSize
LeftOver = FileLength Mod BlockSize
```

Using the **BinaryWrite** method of the **Response** object, we can output a chunk of the data read from the data source with the **GetChunk** method. **GetChunk** is design to read an unstructured binary data stream from an object of a given size. Here, we initially retrieve the extra bytes (if any), and then read blocks of data of the size defined, and write them to the Web page:

```
Response.BinaryWrite Field.GetChunk(LeftOver)
For i = 1 To NumBlocks
   Response.BinaryWrite Field.GetChunk(BlockSize)
Next
```

Using Recordset Filters

At the risk of sounding repetitive, a **Recordset** object works with a result set of data. We can think of a result set as a table that is a subset of the original table from which the **Recordset** retrieved its data. Consider the need to retrieve further subsets of this result data. We have two options—either create a new **Recordset** with the additional filtering criteria, or apply the filtering criteria to the existing record set.

Creating a new **Recordset** introduces a great deal of overhead and processing time, as well as the need to cache data that may be duplicated. To avoid this the **Recordset** object supplies a filtering method: **Filter**.

A **Filter** can be a string that provides filtering information to the **Recordset**, or an array of bookmarks on specific records in the record set. Keep in mind however, that the ADO must do the filtering work itself, and incur the processing overhead it entails. With a large recordset, this overhead can exceed the effort of simply creating a new recordset.

Let's take a look at how a string of filtering criteria might be applied. A **criteria string** is made up of values in the form *FieldName Operator Value* (for example, **"LastName = 'Smith'"**). We can create compound clauses by joining individual clauses with **AND** (for example, **"LastName = 'Smith' AND FirstName = 'John'"**). The following lists some guidelines for creating filter strings:

FieldName must be a valid field name from the **Recordset**. If the field name contains spaces, we must enclose the name in square brackets. *Operator* must be one of the following: <, >, <=, >=, <>, =, **LIKE**. *Value* is the value with which we will compare the field's values (for example, '**Smith**', **#8/24/95#**, **12.345** or **$50.00**). Use single quotes with strings and hash signs (#) with dates. For numbers, we can use decimal points, dollar signs, and scientific notation. If *Operator* is **LIKE**, *Value* can include wildcards. Only the asterisk (*) and percent sign (%) wild cards are allowed, and they must be the last character in the string. *Value* may not be **Null**.

The filter property also allows us to supply a number of constants that effect the way in which the filter is applied to the data, and the results it produces. The constants that can be applied are:

Constant	Value	Description
adFilterNone	0	Removes the current filter and restores all records to view.
adFilterPendingRecords	1	Allows you to view only records that have changed but have not yet been sent to the server. Only applicable for the batch update mode.
adFilterAffectedRecords	2	Allows you to view only records affected by the last **Delete**, **Resync**, **UpdateBatch**, or **CancelBatch** call.
adFilterFetchedRecords	3	Allows you to view records in the current cache, that is, the results of the last fetch from the database.

Beyond Microsoft Access

In the previous sections, we've looked at the workings of OLE DB and the ADO in detail. It's time to put some of it into practice. We'll take an example database, and move it from Access to the SQL Server platform. This is a surprisingly straightforward process. With some thought as to the differences between the two platforms, and some good up-front design work, we can create and develop an ASP application using Access, then **upsize** it to SQL Server for use in an enterprise-oriented, high volume environment.

Upsizing to SQL Server

Since release 2.0 of MS Access, an add-on tool has been available from Microsoft that can greatly simplify moving an Access database into the SQL Server environment. This tool is called the **Upsizing Wizard**. It is available from a variety of sources, including Microsoft Office 97 Professional and the Microsoft Developer Network. In this example, we'll use the version supplied with Office 97.

Upsizing Wizard consists of two tools. The first is the wizard itself, which takes a Microsoft Access database and creates an equivalent database on SQL Server—with the same table structure, data and most (but not all) of the attributes of the original Microsoft Access database.

The second tool supplied is the **SQL Server Browser**. This allows the developer to view, create, and edit SQL Server objects, including tables, views, defaults, rules, stored procedures and triggers. SQL Server Browser can be used to manage both a SQL Server database created by the Upsizing Wizard, and any existing SQL Server objects.

Upsizing Design Issues

Before we can upsize an Access database to SQL Server, there are several important design issues we need to consider. Ideally, we would design our database from the very beginning with Web deployment in mind. As we'll see, the design of a database optimized for access from the Internet, or on an intranet, is very different to that of a typical single-user database. If you have an existing database that was not built with Web access in mind, you're likely to have to redesign certain aspects of it to take advantage of the upsizing process. We'll look at these aspects first.

Design Tips from the Client Side

Throughout this book, we're looking at how to build Active Server Pages. Let's take a moment to recap on some of the things we should take into account when designing a Web page that accesses data using ADO. These can have an enormous impact on the performance of our site.

- ▲ Use `Recordset` objects of the **static cursor** type if the result set contains relatively few columns, doesn't contain `OLE Object` or large `Memo` fields and when you don't need to update the server tables. If you are simply presenting data, and multi-directional strolling is not required, use the `adOpenForwardOnly` cursor type. This makes a single pass through the request table to present the results, incurring a minimum overhead.

- ▲ Minimize the number of items in server-populated combo boxes, list boxes and other selection controls. Use **static cursor** type `Recordset` objects to populate these controls wherever possible. Don't let the selection lists get too big–keep in mind that you have to pump all this data across to the user's Web browser. Anyway, from a design perspective, a selection list with too many items quickly becomes unwieldy.

- ▲ Adhere to server-based naming restrictions from the beginning. Upsizing Wizard can correct many common errors in this regard, but not all of them. It's best to adhere to SQL Server restrictions from the beginning, in order to assure a painless migration. SQL Server field names must be 30 characters or less. The first character must be a letter or the symbol @. The remaining characters may be numbers, letters, or the symbols, $, # and _. No spaces are allowed.

- ▲ Make sure you have an ODBC data source defined *before* you start the upsizing process. Upsizing Wizard requires you to log into an SQL Server database. If you are creating a new database, you should make sure you have an ODBC data source for the Master database for the SQL Server to which you want to upsize. If you are upsizing to an existing database, make sure you have an ODBC data source name for it set up first. You can create an ODBC data source name by running the ODBC Administrator–see Appendix G for details.

Design Tips from the Server Side

On SQL Server, we also need to take into account some basic design issues. Addressing these before we start the process can save us the difficulties associated with having to start again.

▲ To make upsizing go as smoothly as possible, you should make sure that you have sufficient access permissions on the SQL Server you want to upsize to. The permissions you need will vary according to what you want to accomplish. At minimum, you must have `CREATE TABLE` permission. If you want to build a new database from scratch, you must have `CREATE DATABASE` permissions. Finally, if you want to create new devices, you must be a member of the Admin group.

▲ Calculate how much disk space upsizing will require, by multiplying the size of your Microsoft Access database by two, and make sure you have enough free. This will ensure that Upsizing Wizard has enough space to upsize your database and leave it some room to grow as well. If you expect a lot of data to be added to the database, you should allow more space.

▲ If your server has more than one physical hard disk, you may want to place your database on one disk, and the log for the database on a different disk. In the event of a disk failure, the likelihood of recovering will be much greater.

Upsizing the Sample 'Forum' Database

In the case studies in Part 3 of this book, we discuss a Forum application that allows you to create a discussion group on your Web site. The original was developed in Microsoft Access, with no regard for the problems that would arise from upsizing it to SQL Server. In this case, it's an ideal example of how we go about the process.

Upsizing Wizard allows us to create a new SQL Server database or, if we have previously upsized our Access database (or just want to add Microsoft Access tables to an existing SQL Server database), we can upsize to an existing database. Typically, we will have created a database beforehand, as opposed to having the wizard create it. By creating the database up front, we are assured that it is created with the attributes and permissions required.

The first step is to install and start Upsizing wizard from the Access Tools | Add_Ins menu.

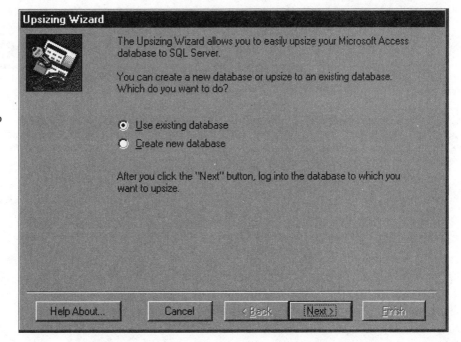

Here we will be using a database that has already been created. Clicking Next brings up a Data Source dialog requesting the name of the data source to upsize to. This list reflects the ODBC data sources defined on our system–in our case we select a Data Source Name (DSN) which we previously defined using the ODBC Administrator for the SQL Server we are upsizing to. If we hadn't already created the DSN, we can define it at this point.

Using the DSN we selected, the wizard will attempt to connect to the SQL Server specified. Once connected, it presents a list of the tables stored in the Access database. We simply select the tables we want to be upsized.

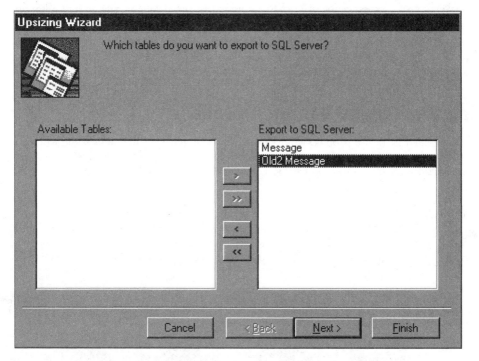

Now things get a bit more interesting. Although Access and SQL Server have many common characteristics, there are several significant differences in the way data is structured, and the indexes maintained. The wizard goes a long way in trying to simplify the conversion from Access to SQL Server, but we need to give it a bit of guidance. First, we need to decide what attributes that we want to upsize. The wizard can convert **indexes**, **validation rules**, **Access defaults** and **relationships** to SQL Server.

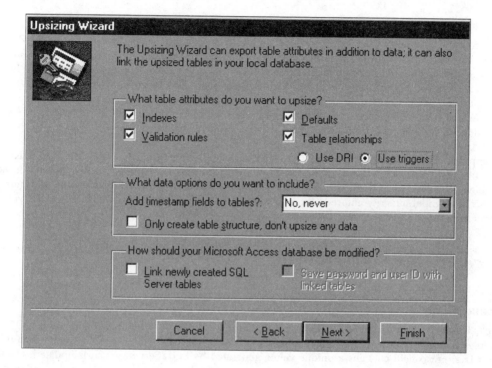

Indexes

Indexes in SQL Server and Microsoft Access are very similar. If we choose to have the Access indexes upsized, the wizard will convert primary keys to SQL Server clustered, unique indexes named `aaaaa_PrimaryKey`. In an Access database, a primary key does not have a user-assigned name. However, SQL Server requires a name for all objects, including the unique index created to represent the Access primary key.

All other indexes retain their names, except where they contain illegal characters–which are replaced with an underscore. Unique and non-unique Access indexes become unique and non-unique SQL Server indexes. SQL Server doesn't support ascending or descending indexes, and so this attribute is ignored.

Default Attributes and Validation Rules

Default attributes are directly supported by the SQL Server catalog, and as such are ported directly between the two platforms. However, **validation rules** are by necessity treated differently. Validation rules and referential integrity, in Access, are part of the data dictionary and are enforced at the engine level. SQL Server validation rules and referential integrity are not part of the data dictionary, and are enforced through code bound to a table (stored procedures and triggers). This can lead to difficulties if a validation rule cannot be implemented as a stored procedure. The wizard is very good at making this conversion, but it is always a good idea to check the procedures generated for accuracy.

*A **data dictionary** is a repository of information concerning the structures in the database.*

Relationships

When we create a **relationship** between two Access tables, a new index on the foreign key in the relationship is created automatically. These system-generated indexes do not appear in the Access index editor. Access names these relationship-indexes Reference and, if the index name is not unique within a database, adds a suffix. Because an index named Reference could also be created by a user, Upsizing Wizard exports all indexes, and does not distinguish between system-generated and user-created ones. System-generated relationship indexes improve performance when tables are joined. However, if we end up with two identical indexes, one user-created and the other system-generated, we can drop one of them.

Relationships can also be enforced in SQL Server 6.5 through **Declarative Referential Integrity** (DRI) as opposed to triggers. Upsizing Wizard for Access 97 allows us to enforce the relationships defined in our Access tables using DRI in SQL Server. DRI can be easier to administer, better performing, and more flexible then referential integrity enforced through triggers. If you are upsizing to SQL Server 6.5 you, may want to consider this option.

> *For more information on SQL Server 6.5 and DRI see Professional SQL Server 6.5 Admin (ISBN 1-874416-49-4), published by Wrox Press.*

Timestamp Fields

By default, Upsizing Wizard creates additional new columns, with the `timestamp` datatype, in SQL Server tables generated from Access tables that contain floating-point (single or double), memo or OLE fields. A `timestamp` field contains a unique value, generated by SQL Server, which is updated whenever that record is updated. Access uses the value in `timestamp` fields to see if a record has been changed before updating it.

Allowing Upsizing Wizard to create `timestamp` columns is most often used when Access Tables will be attached to the corresponding SQL Server. In this instance, Access will use these `timestamp` columns to determine if data in a table has changed, without having to scan the whole table. Upsizing Wizard can also attach the upsized tables to an Access database. This can be of value in a system where Access databases will provide local storage. In our case, this would not be practical.

When we reach the final screen of the Upsizing Wizard, it offers to create an Upsizing Report. This documents the objects that the wizard has created in SQL Server. It includes information about any databases that were created, as well as a complete explanation of how each Access object that was upsized maps to an SQL Server object. After upsizing is complete, we can view this report on screen, or print it for future reference.

Differences between Access and SQL Server

As we mentioned earlier, Access and SQL Server are not 100% compatible. These differences, as well as design decisions made by Upsizing Wizard, mean that much of the Microsoft Access data dictionary cannot be mapped directly to SQL Server constructs. The following table summarizes how objects are mapped from Microsoft Access objects to SQL Server:

Microsoft Access object	SQL Server object
Database	Database

Table Continued on Following Page

Microsoft Access object	SQL Server object
Table	Table
Indexes	Indexes
Field	Field
Default	Default
Table validation rule	Update and Insert triggers
Field validation rule	Update and Insert triggers
Field Required property	Update and Insert triggers
Relations	Update, Insert and Delete triggers

Database and Table Objects

An Access **mdb** file maps directly to an SQL Server database. A Microsoft Access table, excluding much of its data dictionary, maps to an SQL Server table. Access maintains this information as a part of the **mdb** database. Upsizing Wizard replaces illegal characters with the _ symbol. Any names that are SQL Server keywords, for example **FROM** and **GROUP**, have the _ symbol appended to them, resulting in the names **FROM_** and **GROUP_**.

However, this does not always avoid problems. For example, the Access Forum database has two column names that SQL Server cannot work with. Here's our Access table in design view:

	Field Name	Data Type
🔑	ID	AutoNumber
	Subject	Text
	From	Text
	Email	Text
	Body	Memo
🔑	When	Text
	MsgLevel	Number
	PrevRef	Number
🔑	TopRef	Number

Notice that one column has been named **When** and another **From**. These are both keywords in SQL Server. As such, the wizard attempts to create a table using:

```
CREATE TABLE TemporaryUpsizedTable
(
    ID int IDENTITY(1,1),
    Subject varchar (50),
    From_ varchar (50)   ,
    Email varchar (40)   ,
    Body text            ,
    When varchar (30)    ,
    MsgLevel smallint    ,
    PrevRef int          ,
    TopRef int           ,
    CONSTRAINT aaaaaOld2_Message_PK
       PRIMARY KEY NONCLUSTERED
       (When ,TopRef ,ID)
)
```

SQL Server rejects this syntax as invalid, and fails to create the table. To correct the problem, we will need to rename these tables to something that SQL Server can work with. For expediency sake, we can simply rename the columns `FromMsg` and `WhenMsg`. Of course, we then need to make sure that any dependent queries reflect the changes that we make.

Also, we need to keep in mind that the data types supported by SQL Server differ from those supported by Access. Upsizing Wizard will convert our Access data types to the nearest matching SQL Server types. The conversions are made as follows:

Access Data Type	SQL Server Data Type
Yes/No	Bit
Number (Byte)	Smallint
Number (Integer)	Smallint
Number (Long Integer)	Int
Number (Single)	Real
Number (Double)	Float
Currency	Money
Date/Time	Datetime
Counter	Int
Text(n)	varchar(n)
Memo	Text
OLE Object	Image

The Upsizing Report indicates whether the Upsizing Wizard was successful in converting all the field names and creating the new tables.

Using the SQL Server Browser

The second of the Upsizing Wizard's two tools is the **SQL Server Browser**. It's essentially a database container integrated into the Access development environment. It allows us to view, edit and modify SQL Server objects, including **Tables**, **Views**, **Rules**, **Defaults** and **Stored Procedures**. This allows the developer to take advantage of their understanding of Access when developing against a back-end database.

Just like Upsizing Wizard, the SQL Browser requires an ODBC definition to create the connection to SQL Server. It provides an "Access-like" view of SQL Server:

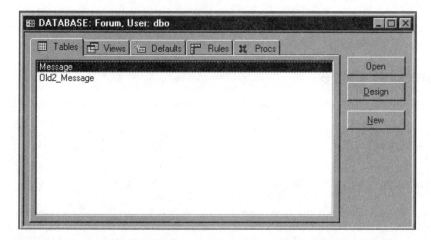

A developer familiar with Access should have no difficulty interacting with the SQL Server database using this utility. By using Upsizing Wizard and the SQL Server Browser, moving from an Access data source to a SQL Server data source can be relatively painless.

Database MAP Example

With our database now in SQL Server, let's take a look at some techniques we can use to access it. In this example we'll use many of the techniques we've already discussed to pull catalog data from our new data source. So far, we have seen how to get data from a data source using various objects. In this example we'll take a look at retrieving information concerning the data source itself.

The **MAP** Example is designed to present us with a listing of all the tables it finds in a SQL Server database we specify. We then have the option of selecting a table, and seeing its structure. The source code for this example is available for download with the other samples, from our Web site at:
http://www.rapid.wrox.com/books/0723/.

The Login Page

To start things off, we are presented with a screen where we enter the information that will connect us to our SQL Server. This is **SQLServerMAP.htm**, and is created with a single form containing normal HTML **TEXT** controls and a **SUBMIT** button:

The Server name, along with a Database Name, Login ID and Password, are used to locate and attach to a SQL Server database. A straightforward HTML page produces this screen. When we click the Login button an ASP page `List.asp` is executed, which will actually attempt the connection.

The Table List Page

To start things off, we define a number of variables that will be used throughout this page:

```
Dim oServer
Dim sServerName
Dim sUid
Dim sDatabase
Dim sPassword
```

Of interest, as you will soon see, is the **oServer** variable. It will be used to hold a reference to the SQL Server OLE Object–in this first part of our sample, we have to take a step beyond ADO. Why? Well, we want catalog information concerning what structures are actually maintained by the SQL Server, and typically this information would be gathered from the ODBC provider.

However, at the time of this writing, the ODBC/ADO provider supplied for SQL Server does not include catalog level functionality. As such, we need to find an alternative method. The alternative is to create a reference to the SQL Server OLE Object directly. SQL Server 6.5 client utilities provide a number of OLE Objects that can be used to access SQL Server services. These OLE objects take advantage of the underlying SQL Server network libraries in order to communicate with the server.

First off, we use the same **CreateObject** method to create an instance of the SQL Server Object, **sqlole.sqlserver**, within ADO:

```
Set OServer = Server.CreateObject("sqlole.sqlserver")
```

With this reference created, we now have an access mechanism we can use to talk to a SQL Server. Before we can establish a connection, we will need the information supplied by the user on the main page. To do this we use:

```
sServerName = Trim(Request.Form("ServerName"))
sDatabase   = Trim(Request.Form("DatabaseName"))
sUid        = Trim(Request.Form("Login"))
sPassword   = Trim(Request.Form("Password"))
```

Then, with this information, we call the OLE Object's **Connect** method to establish a link to the server specified by the user:

```
OServer.Connect sServerName,sUid,sPassword
```

An important point to note here is that, because we are accessing the SQL Server via its OLE Object libraries, we are bypassing ODBC completely. Any previous ODBC definitions have no impact on this connection.

With a connection established, we are ready to retrieve the catalog data needed. In this case, we want a list of all the tables that exist for the selected database. This can be done using the catalog functions that are provided via the SQL OLE interface. First we display a confirmation of the login details, then retrieve the information we want by querying the **Database** object's **Tables** object. The name of each table found is used to populate a drop down list box:

```
<SELECT NAME="TableNames" SIZE="1">
<% Set oSQLdb = oServer.Databases(sDatabase)
   For Each oSQLTable In oSQLdb.Tables
      Response.Write "<option value=""" & oSQLTable.Name & """ > " _
                     & oSQLTable.Name & "</option>"
   Next %>
</SELECT>
```

And here's the result:

Please Select A Table Name from the List Below:

Given the following data, I will display a map of the Table you select.

Server Name	Database Name	Login ID	Password
Borg	Forum	sa	

Table Name

Message

Submitt

Now we can select a table on which to gather additional information, and click the Submit button to bring up our final ASP page **Map.asp**. This will display all of the fields in the selected table, along with their type, size, precision etc..

To do this, ADO does provide the functionality we need. To begin, we create a read-only, forward-scrolling **Recordset**:

```
Set oRS = Server.CreateObject("ADODB.recordset")
oRS.Open "SELECT * FROM " & sDatabase & ".dbo." _
         & Request.Form("TableNames"), "Driver={SQL Server};Server=" _
         & sServerName & ";uid=" & sUid & ";pwd=" & sPassword _
         & ";Database=" & sDatabase & ";DSN=;"
```

Note that in this instance, the use of a forward-scrolling **Recordset** is very important. If you remember earlier, we indicated that the default **CacheSize** setting for this type of cursor is one. As such, even though we are doing a **SELECT *** SQL command, only a single record will actually be retrieved. You may also notice that this recordset is created without using a DSN. This is because we do not know what the connection will be defined as until the user of the application provides us with a server name. We define the connection 'on the fly'.

With a cursor in place, we are ready to retrieve information about the fields in our table:

```
iRow = RS.Fields.Count
For iCount = 0 to (iRow - 1)
   Set Fld = RS.Fields(iCount)
   response.write "<TR>"
```

```
   response.write "<TD> " & Fld.Name & "</TD>"
   response.write "<TD> " & Fld.Type & "</TD>"
   response.write "<TD> " & Fld.ActualSize & "</TD>"
   If Int(Fld.Precision) >= 255 Then
      response.write "<TD> 0 </TD>"
   Else
      response.write "<TD> " & Int(Fld.Precision) & "</TD>"
   End If
   If Int(Fld.NumericScale) >= 255 Then
      response.write "<TD> 0 </TD>"
   Else
      response.write "<TD> " & Int(Fld.NumericScale) & "</TD>"
   End If
   response.write "</TR>"
Next
```

Here we use the number of **Field** objects in the data source's **Fields** collection to control how many cells are created in the output table. We then populate each cell with data from each **Field** object. The end result is a presentation of each **Field**, along with its attributes:

Here is your Table

Table Name: Message

Field Name	Type	Length	Precision	Scale
ID	3	4	10	0
Subject	200	20	0	0
FromMsg	200	12	0	0
Email	200	1	0	0
Body	201	2	0	0
WhenMsg	200	16	0	0
MsgLevel	2	2	5	0
PrevRef	3	4	10	0
TopRef	3	4	10	0

Some Components, Tips and Methods

Once you come to use ADO regularly, you'll find that there are lots of ways to achieve the same thing, and all kind of things that you can't easily achieve with other dynamic Web page technologies. Here are a few useful tips, which may help to expand your outlook, and make different kinds of task that bit easier. It's a mixed bag of components, add-ins, and methods.

The HTML Table Formatter Component

In our previous example, and in examples you saw in the last chapter, we've come up against the need to display data from a table in our Web pages. This is a regular requirement and is, of course, the main reason that HTML sports the **<TABLE>** tag and the wide range of formatting options it offers.

However, we still have to manually create the `<TR></TR>` and `<TD></TD>` tags to get the layout right. There are tools that help to do this, but a sample component that is now available from Microsoft can do it all automatically. You can get the component from: `http://www.microsoft.com/iis/usingiis/developing/samples`

It's written in Java, so you'll also need to install the latest Java Virtual Machine (VM) from Microsoft, as well as the component. Because it's a sample, rather than part of ASP, you need to install it separately, but full instructions are included in the distribution file.

So what can it do? Well, it has four properties, and one method. The best way to learn about it is to see how we use it:

```
' Create a connection, and open it using the System DSN 'MyDatabase'
Set oConn = Server.CreateObject("ADODB.Connection")
oConn.Open "MyDatabase"

' Create a recordset containing the records from the table 'MyTable'
Set oRs = oConn.Execute("MyTable")

' Create an instance of the HTML Table Formatter Component
Set oTblfmt = Server.CreateObject("IISSample.HTMLTable")

' Now set its properties for the borders, caption, style and headings
oTblFmt.Borders = False
oTblFmt.Caption = "Displaying my data"
oTblFmt.CaptionStyle = "ALIGN=CENTER VALIGN=BOTTOM"
oTblFmt.HeadingRow = True

' And insert the formatted table into the page
oTblFmt.AutoFormat(oRs)
```

If you are into creating components, you'll find the download worth it just to see how it's done—all the source code is included. And it certainly saves a lot of coding, and keeps the actual size of the page down as well!

Converting from IDC to ASP - IDC2ASP

If you've already got a Web site or corporate Intranet bulging with data that is supplied via the Internet Data Connector (IDC) there is help available. IDC is an interface supplied with IIS that allows quite complex data retrieval from ODBC data sources, for use in a Web page. We discussed it briefly in Chapter 1, and we have no intention of covering it in depth. ASP is not only more powerful and efficient, but is also a lot easier to work with as well.

However, that doesn't help you to convert existing IDC scripts and templates into ASP format. What does help, is the IDC2ASP tool that is available free of charge from Microsoft. It can be downloaded from `http://www.microsoft.com/iis/usingiis/developing/samples`, and comes in two versions:

`IDC2ASP.EXE` is a command-line utility that will convert IDC files into ASP form automatically. There are a series of command-line switches available that control all kinds of aspects of the conversion, and it leaves the original files intact so that you can test the new ones before committing yourself fully to the new technology.

Alternatively, there is an active server component version of IDC2ASP, which can be instantiated within an ASP page, just like any other component. All that's needed then is to set its properties and call the `Convert` method.

IDC2ASP carries the IntraActive name, and is not supported by Microsoft. However its potential usefulness makes it worth a try if you have a lot of IDC files to convert.

Using Arrays and the GetRows Method

We'll often find ourselves wanting to repetitively scan through a recordset searching for different sets of data. This can easily be achieved using dynamic cursor recordsets or multiple SQL queries, but both are less that ideal in the efficiency stakes. There is a far more efficient method at our disposal. ADO provides us with a method that enables us to easily convert a `Recordset` object into an array—which can then be scanned efficiently using ordinary code. This is the syntax:

variantarray = *recordset*.`GetRows` (*NumberOfRows*)

The `GetRows` method takes a `Recordset` object and converts it into the equivalent multi-dimensioned array. Just as we'd expect, a recordset consisting of three fields and ten records is converted to a 3 x 10 array—think of the first dimension being horizontal and the second vertical, just like a normal table is displayed in Access or SQL Server. The *NumberOfRows* argument is optional, and specifies the number of records to retrieve. This argument is frequently used on ordered recordsets, where the record ordering has been set by a defined table index, or an `ORDER BY` clause in the SQL query. You'll see the `GetRows` method used in the Forum case study chapter later in the book.

Using Multiple Recordsets

One other nice method available for the `Recordset` object is `NextRecordset`. So far, we've only talked about a `CommandText` property as containing one SQL query. We can provide multiple SQL queries as long as they are separated by semicolons, in the form `SELECT * FROM Table1; SELECT * FROM Table2;` etc.. Normally, when we open a recordset from a query like this, it's only the first set of results that are available. To retrieve the next set of records we just call the `NextRecordset` method. We can also supply the name of a variable that will be set to the number of records affected by the query, though this is optional:

`Set` *recordset* = *recordset*.`NextRecordset` (*RecordsAffected*)

When we use the `NextRecordset` method, we're provided with a new `Recordset` variable that is one of the following:

- If a row-returning command returns no records, the `Recordset` object referenced by the variable will be empty. We can test for this case by inspecting the `BOF` and `EOF` properties, which will both be `True`.

- If a non row-returning command completes successfully, the `Recordset` referenced by the variable will be closed. We can test for this case by ensuring that the `Recordset` object variable is not equal to `Nothing`. In this case, inspecting the `EOF` property will generate an error.

- When there are no more statements, the `Recordset` variable returned will be set to `Nothing`.

Note that the `NextRecordset` method will continue to return `Recordset` objects as long as there are additional SQL statements in our `CommandText` parameter.

ADO and OLE-DB in the Real World

In response to the increased capacity of personal computer software tools, and their extended accessibility to external and remote data, businesses have a growing need to provide solutions that span desktop, midrange, mainframe, and Internet technologies. The expanding diversity in structure and complexity of business data creates the need for a universal data access middleware that enables a new class of solutions to be easily built and managed.

ADO can bridge the gap. As we've discussed in these two chapters, ADO is a higher level interface to OLE-DB. It provides the programmer with a very usable interface both for client server, Internet and intranet applications–allowing standardized access to almost any data provider. This doesn't just mean Active Server Pages programming. ADO can provide a translation layer for use with other tools and applications as well.

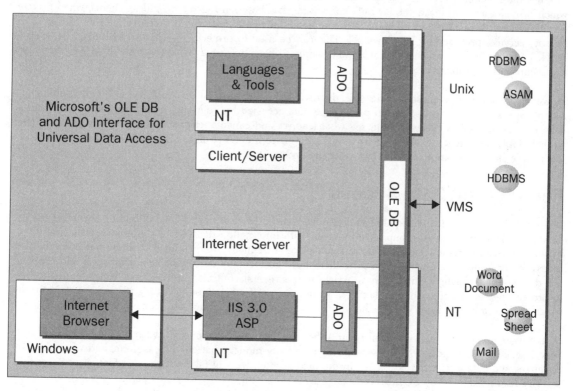

We haven't covered the real core of OLE-DB in these two chapters because, as an ASP programmer, you really don't need to know what's happening 'over the fence'. However, we have included an Appendix in the reference section that describes OLE-DB in more depth, and discusses a middleware tool from ISG called **Navigator**. This can accomplish the real-world requirements of connecting your Active Server Pages code to a range of database systems and other data providers, including legacy systems. Check out Appendix J for more information.

ADO and SQL Server Security

Security is a growing concern in the Internet/intranet development community. It is a constant trade off between access to services and data, and protection of those services and data. This is really the heart of the security dilemma–if your site is *too* secure it could lose its value. On the other hand, without appropriate security measures, you might find someone corrupting your database for you, or selling your company's secrets to your competitors.

Security issues can be addressed at three different levels–the features offered by the Web server, those offered by the operating system, and those offered by the data source being accessed. In the Microsoft world, the operating system and the Web server are tightly coupled, as are the security features they offer.

Internet Information Server (IIS) supports advanced security facilities, such as a Secure Sockets Layer (SSL) which provides a security scheme for bulk-encrypting data between the server and its clients, when private communication is required. In addition, IIS completely integrates with the object-level and user-level security services provided by Windows NT. This can be used to protect a specific area of your site, such as DSN definition files, to which you don't want people to have access. In Chapter 9, we'll be looking at Web site security in a lot more detail.

However, as powerful as these facilities are, they will generally need to be supplemented with additional security measures that can be used to protect the data accessed by your site. In this section we will take a brief look at SQL Server security, and see what features and capabilities are available in this product. Then we will apply these features to accessing a SQL Server from an ASP page. Finally, we will take a look at a few simple steps you can take to protect your site and its data.

Security and Data Access

The level of security actually required is dependent on the level of access needed by our clients. If our database is servicing a small group of individuals, with information that requires minimal protection, then a very open security framework could be put into place. Essentially, we just need to allow our users to access the data they need, while protecting them from accidentally destroying or damaging it. However, if our database is servicing a public forum, much more stringent controls must be built. Not only do we need to protect the data from accidental damage, we need to verify that those accessing it have the right to do so, as well as protect it against those that do not–or who might intentionally damage it.

SQL Server supports several powerful security features that can be applied to each of these scenarios. SQL Server security options determine a server's login security mode, what auditing is done, and what objects, resources and data a user has access to. In the next section, we will take a high-level look at some of the security features offered by SQL Server.

Login Security

SQL Server 6.5 offers three login security modes. The mode we choose will significantly effect how the server handles security. Let's take a look at each of the options available, and how these options affect our environment:

▲ **Standard Security Mode**: This is the default security mode. In standard mode, SQL Server manages its own login validation process for all connections (except client applications that explicitly request integrated security over trusted connections).

▲   **Windows NT Integrated Security Mode:** This mode uses Windows NT authentication mechanisms for all connections. Only trusted connections are allowed into SQL Server. SQL Server always ignores the login name and SQL Server password submitted in the login request from an Open Database Connectivity (ODBC) client application. Network users, who were assigned user-level privileges to SQL Server, log in using their network username or the default login ID (if their network username is not found in `syslogins`).

▲   **Mixed Security Mode:** This mode allows both trusted and non-trusted connections, and is a combination of integrated and standard modes. For trusted connections, SQL Server examines the requested login name as specified by the client ODBC application. If this login name matches the user's network username, or if the login name is null or spaces, SQL Server first tries the Windows NT integrated login rules as described above. If this fails, SQL Server uses the standard rules. If the requested login name is any other value, the user must supply the correct SQL Server password, and SQL Server handles the login using the standard rules described above. All login requests from non-trusted connections are handled using the standard rules.

Integrated and mixed security modes are best utilized in an intranet environment. In this environment, user IDs and privileges are defined in the Windows NT domain, and subject to domain security. The user ID can be retrieved from the client system directly, and authenticated against the domain master list. Here, the user is never required to provide authentication information.

In the big wide world of the Internet, a domain-based authentication model would not be realistic. Here, security must be tightly controlled and access provided only as is necessary.

User Groups

Creating a Login is just the first level of security associated with SQL Server. A Login ID does not permit the user to access any of the objects in a database. Access to a database and the objects within it are granted to individual users or groups of users.

SQL Server security is based on a detailed hierarchy of **groups**, which include **users**. Both groups and users are defined as having specific access to, and control over, services and data. In SQL Server, permissions for services and data can be controlled at a very granular level. For example, access to an individual object can be controlled, and then the actions that are possible on that object can also be regulated.

A group is simply a means of organizing the users of a database. Permissions are assigned to the group, as opposed to individual users. Users in the group have access to any resources available to the group as a whole. This simplifies the administration of users and objects in an SQL Server environment.

There is a built-in group, public, in every database. Each user automatically belongs to public and can be added to only one other group. A user cannot be remove from the public group. If a group is deleted (or 'dropped'), all users in that group are automatically removed from the group. However, dropping a group does not drop its users. Users who were members of the dropped group are still valid users in the database and members of the public group.

Database and Object Owners

SQL Server is organized around databases. Each one contains **objects**, such as tables, stored procedures, rules etc.. Each object has an **owner**, who has full authority over that object. SQL Server recognizes two types of owner—the database owner (DBO) and database object owner.

The **database owner** is the creator of a database, and has full privileges over it. However, beyond simply having the ability to manipulate the object itself, the DBO has the option of granting access to the database to other users or groups. In summary, the DBO can:

- Allow users access to the database.

- Grant users permission to create objects and execute commands within the database.

- Set up groups

- Assign users to groups and add guest accounts, which give users limited access to a database.

Just like any other user, the database owner logs into SQL Server by using an assigned login ID and password. In their own database, the user is recognized as DBO; in databases which they haven't created, the user is just known by their database username.

As we said earlier, a database contains objects. The user who creates a database object is the **database object owner** for that object. In order for a user to create an object within a database, the database owner must first grant that user permission to create that particular type of object. Just as the database owner can grant permissions for their database to other users, the object owner can grant permissions for their object.

Database object owners have no special login IDs or passwords. The creator of an object is automatically granted all permissions to it. An object owner must explicitly grant permissions to other users before they can access the object. Even the database owner cannot use an object unless the object owner has granted the appropriate permission.

As you can see, database and database object privileges are assigned at a very detailed level. Let's take a look at what privileges (referred to as **permissions**) can be granted to users and groups.

Security Permissions

SQL Server has two categories of permissions: object and statement. Some statement permissions (for the `SELECT`, `UPDATE`, `INSERT`, `DELETE` and `EXECUTE` statements) are handled as object permissions because these statements always apply to database objects that are in the current database.

Object permissions regulate the use of certain statements on certain database objects. They are granted and revoked by the owner of the object. Object permissions apply to the following statements and objects:

Statement	Object
SELECT	Table, view, columns
UPDATE	Table, view, columns
INSERT	Table, view
DELETE	Table, view
REFERENCE	Table
EXECUTE	Stored procedure

Statement permissions are not object-specific. They can be granted only by the system administrator (often referred to as the **sa**) or the database owner. Statement permissions allow the user to create new objects within a database. The following are examples of these statements:

CREATE DATABASE (can be granted only by **sa**, and only to users in the master database)

CREATE DEFAULT

CREATE PROCEDURE

CREATE RULE

CREATE TABLE

CREATE VIEW

Each database has its own independent permissions system. In other words, being granted permission to perform a given task in one database has no effect in other databases.

Now that we have had a chance to take a brief look at SQL Server Security, let's look at a few tips that will help us design our next database.

Security Tips

When designing a database in the SQL Server environment, which will be accessed by public sources, here are a few guidelines to keep in mind:

- ▲ Take advantage of the Guest default login. The Guest login is a special login defined by default in SQL Server. Guest has no rights to any object in the server aside from the ability to login. The Guest login can be granted **read** access to the specific views, tables, or objects needed for your Web site. The Web site can then use this account when attaching to SQL Server objects, minimizing your site's exposure.

- ▲ Use stored procedures where possible for updates and insertions. Coding static SQL in your ASP page is perhaps the most straightforward way to provide dynamic data content. However, keep in mind that not only can your Web site see this code, but so might a really clever hacker. To minimize this exposure it is often better to call a stored procedure, which in turn performs the required updates or inserts. A stored procedure can be granted permissions to access and modify objects and data that the ID calling the stored procedure cannot. This provides a shield between your site and the actual data being changed.

- ▲ When tables are scanned for data, views can serve as security mechanisms. Through a view, users can query only the data provided by the view. The rest of the database is neither visible nor accessible. Permission to access the subset of data in a view must be granted or revoked, regardless of the set of permissions in force on the view's underlying tables. Data in an underlying table that is not included in the view is hidden from users who are authorized to access the view but not the underlying table.

Don't expose more then you have to. In most cases, you will want to retain the majority of your data behind the 'firewall', and supply a mechanism to access this data. Always keep in mind that the any security can be compromised and, as such, preventative measures must be in place that assume that this will occur. One recommendation is to store only high-volume transactional data on the SQL Server that is directly accessed from a Web site. Supportive information can be maintained on a separate secured system, and retrieved as needed using Remote Stored Procedures, or other similar technologies.

Summary

In this chapter we have had the opportunity to review a wide variety of techniques and technologies that we can bring to bear when developing Active Server Web sites. ASP is a very powerful tool. Its ability to access data via ADO only scratches the surface of the many features that are made available by this exiting new product. The issues that we have addressed here provide you with a good introduction into the many features and capabilities of ASP and the ADO.

The main points of this chapter are:

- Connecting to a data source: In this section we examined the hows and whys of connecting to a data source, and then went beyond the basics to take a look at the flexibility built into the **Connection** object.

- With an understanding of the **Connection** object under our belts, we dug into the workings of ADO, looking at expanding the **Recordset** object and accessing binary data.

- With the fundamentals behind us, we took a look at moving our Access database into the SQL Server environment using the upsizing tools available for Access.

- With a lot of information behind us, we took a look at a 'real' example of how to make some of this stuff to work for us. The **MAP** example goes outside ADO, and walks through pulling more then just data from the database.

- In the end, we had to consider the nature of things on the wild and woolly Internet. A brief introduction to SQL Server security provided some insight as to how we can protect our data.

With this chapter, we've reached the end of Part 1, and the introduction to the basics of Active Server Pages, Active Server Components and, in particular, the ActiveX Data Object. We've come a long way in these five chapters, but by now we have all the information we need to put ASP to work on our Web sites.

ASP isn't, however, just a Web site tool for creating dynamic pages. As you've seen in some of the examples, it allows us to start building real client/server applications in an environment (i.e. HTTP and TCP/IP) which was never really designed with this task in mind. This is the subject for Part 2 of this book.

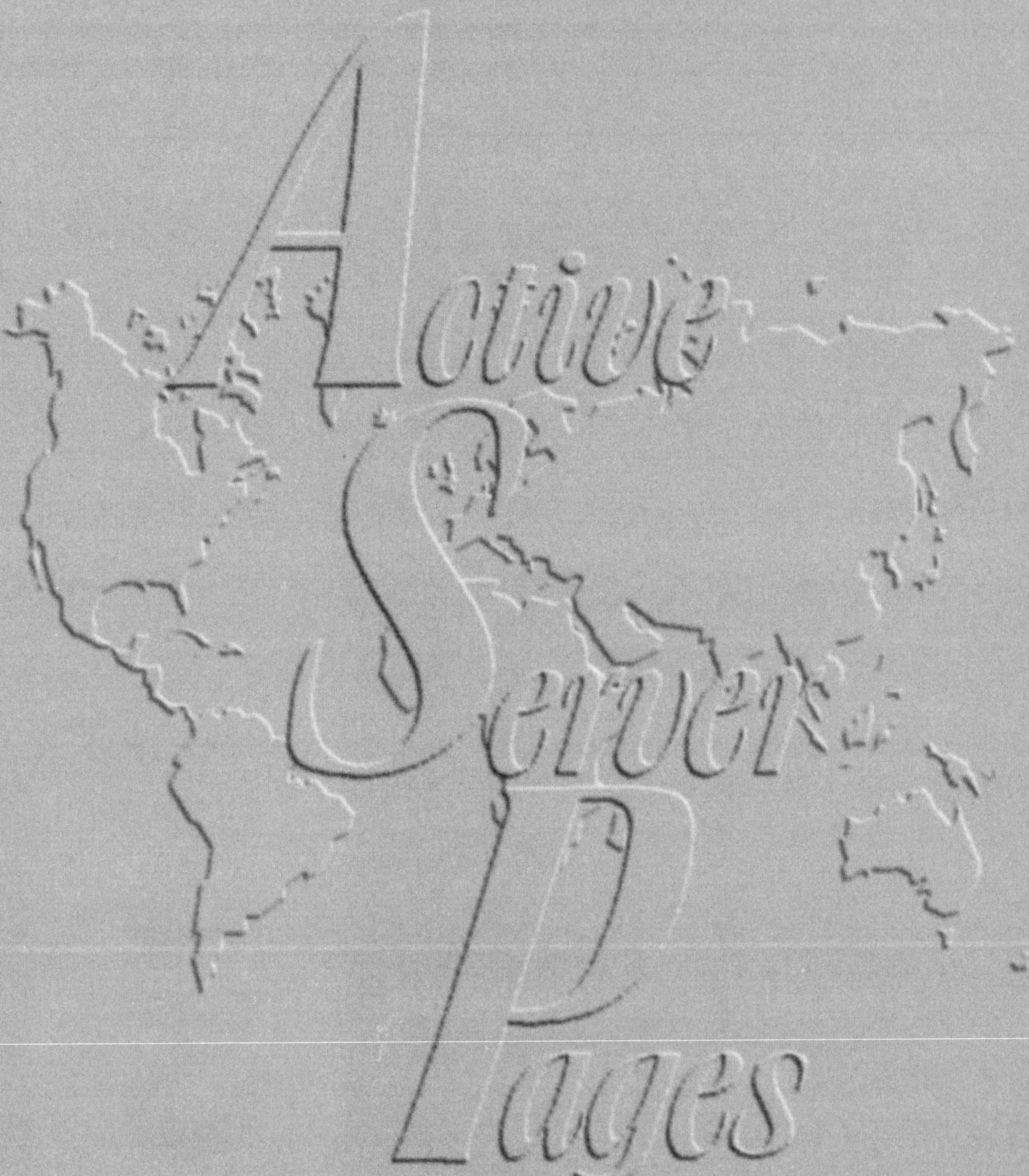
Active
Server
Pages

Building Active Server Applications

In the first part of this book, we've been learning about Active Server Pages almost as though it was a technology on its own. Though we discovered that it could achieve some very clever effects with our web pages, and do a lot of server-based information processing, we only ever sent what were effectively static pages back to the client's browser. In other words, all we were really doing was churning out text and HTML code–to the browser, it seemed like it was talking to a traditional web site full of normal, static pages.

Of course, this is a good thing in many ways. It means that we minimize any compatibility concerns at the client's end, because we can produce pages to a lowest common denominator standard. Almost any browser can understand them. For a site that is in the business of supplying static information, this is an ideal scenario.

But today, we generally need to do a lot more than that. Our visitors expect 'cool', dynamic, exciting pages–especially if they're just surfing rather than seeking particular nuggets of information. This means we need to use other techniques, not just Active Server Pages. Once the page has been sent to the client, ASP on its own can do nothing to influence the content.

The other topic that we must consider is how we can combine all our pages into a working application. Again, on a site that just needs to supply static information, this may not be a priority, though it can make a visitor's experience more rewarding. However, in many cases, and especially on the corporate intranet, this is an absolute necessity.

In this part of the book, we move on from focusing solely on Active Server Pages to consider how we can combine it with other techniques to create these interactive applications. We're into the client-server world now, so stand up and feel proud–you're no longer just a Webmaster, you're a client-server developer!

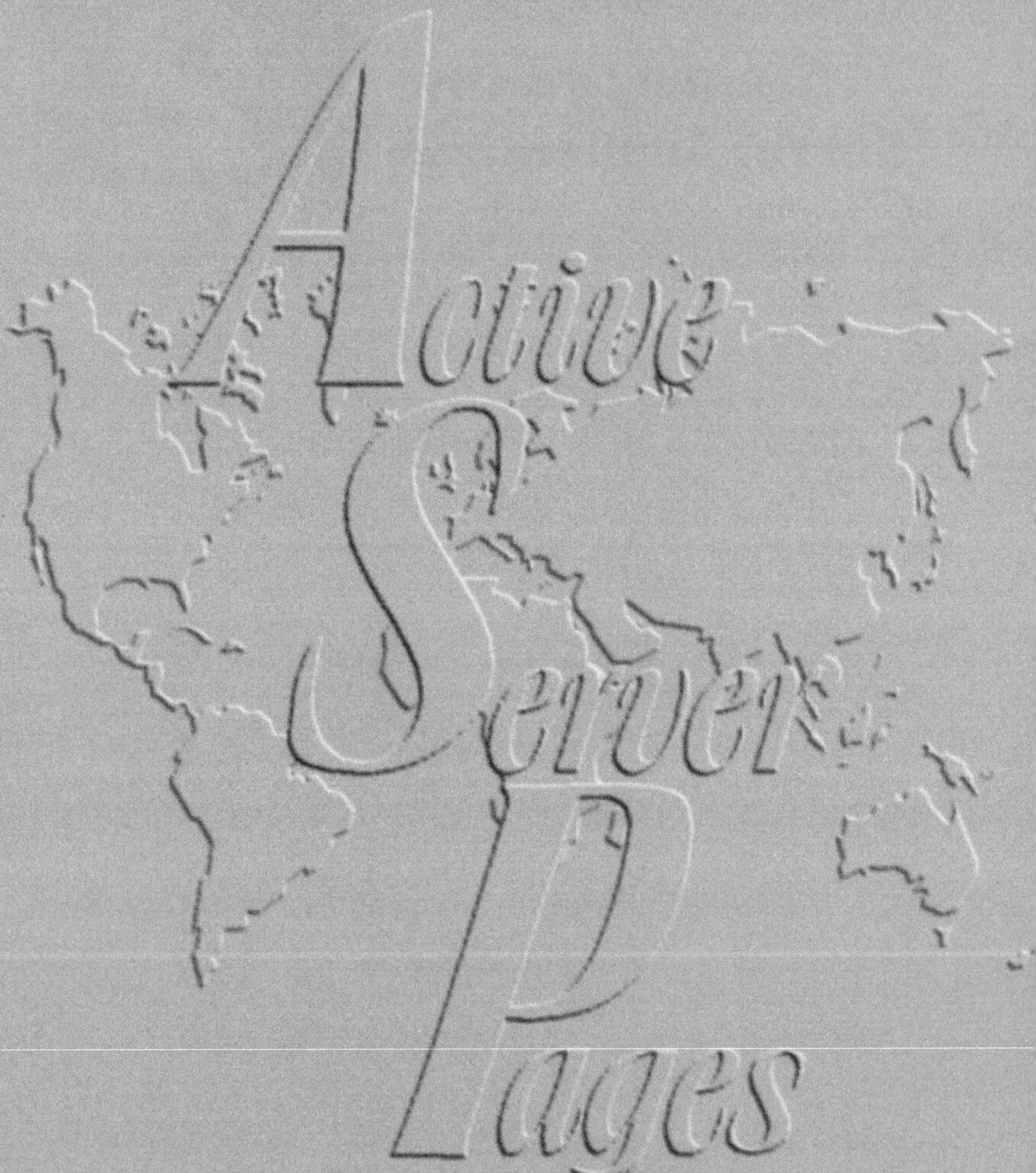
Active
Server
Pages

Getting Into Client-Server

Up to now, our discussion of Active Server Pages has centered on the application of the specific technologies within the Active Server framework. In Chapters 1 and 2 we discussed what Active Server Pages is, and learned about its object model and the ways we can program our pages in this context. In Chapter 3, we discovered Server Components, which can make our life easier by providing plug-in objects that will perform specific tasks. Then, in Chapters 4 and 5, we discussed how we can integrate databases with our pages using the Active Database Component.

This chapter begins a broader exploration of Active Server Pages. Now that you are familiar with the individual techniques, we'll move on to look at how they can be combined with existing technologies available on the client's browser—and implemented from a client-server point of view.

Developing a client-sever application is never a simple task. The key benefits of the Web and the Active Server platform in designing such applications are universal access, richer content and easier creation. Active Server Pages doesn't trivialize the process, but it does simplify the distribution of server code and client code. In this part of the book, we'll learn how to start building client-server applications that can be used in mission critical situations.

But first we need to understand the background to client-server as a whole. If you're coming to ASP from a web site developer's point of view, the term client-server may well carry threatening overtones. So we'll use this chapter to explain what client-server actually is, where it comes from, and how you can easily get into it using Active Server Pages.

Specifically, we'll be looking at:

- Where client-server came from, and where it's going
- How client-server can be applied to Active Server Pages
- How we go about designing a client-server application
- How we integrate server-side components and database connections

So, to start the ball rolling, just what are client-server applications?

What Is Client-Server?

In previous chapters, we've used the term **client** regularly enough, and it's pretty reasonable to assume you wouldn't have got this far if you didn't know what a **server** was. However, as any good cook will tell you, you can't always define the results of something in terms of its constituents. Just because my mother can take some flour, water, and a few other ingredients and turn out a wonderful sponge cake, it doesn't mean that my desperate attempts at stirring them together and incinerating them in an oven will produce anything remotely edible.

So, it's all about the subtler ways that we combine the ingredients of our applications, that make them greater than the sum of their parts—the cream buns in the World Wide Web delicatessen. Our ingredients may be just lumps of hi-tech electronic equipment, and some files full of text, HTML, and code—but the combination can produce remarkably smooth and dynamic **client-server applications**. By the end of this book, you'll be in a position to receive your own web site 'chef of the year' award.

The Background to Client-Server

So where did client-server come from? To answer this, and give you some background that will help you to understand the design principles we'll be discussing later in this chapter, we need to go back to the beginnings of computer networks.

Even the earliest computers were network based, in that the user sat at a terminal in the corner of the room, and the computer filled the other four floors of the building. In effect, the control of the machine was from a terminal—a remote keyboard, card reader, printer, or screen.

Dumb Terminal Networks

If this sounds a little far-fetched, consider the modern PC. The DOS interpreter still understands the kind of commands that were used then; for example, the keyword **CON** refers to the **console**—what the operating system understands as the keyboard and the screen. In a DOS Command Window, **COPY C:\MYFILE.TXT CON** produces a listing of the file's contents, and **COPY CON NEWFILE.TXT** creates a new file containing the character you type. (If you decide to try this, don't forget that you have to press *Ctrl-Z* to close the file and get control of the system again).

The advent of graphical interfaces has blurred this distinction somewhat, but in effect you're still sitting at a machine where the keyboard and screen form a 'dumb terminal', which talks to the rest of the system behind the scenes. This is a similar scenario to the first kinds of distributed computing. All you needed to do was allow the central processing unit to support several sets of screens and keyboards—or terminals—and scatter them around the building.

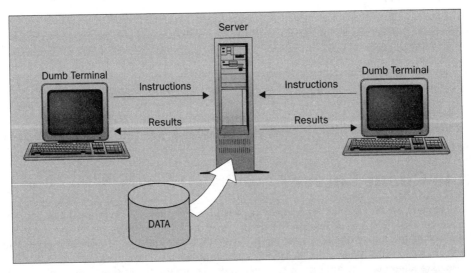

In a dumb terminal network, the server stores all the data and carries out all the processing

This was the traditional central processing system model. 'Dumb terminals' carried no processing power of their own, other than that required to collect keystrokes and send them back to the main processing unit, and display information coming from it.

This is still a common model for modern-day computing, where a mainframe or minicomputer drives the network. It stores all the data, and carries out all the processing. All the terminal sees is the results of the commands it sends–and this concept has even been extended to provide graphical user interfaces on the client terminal.

The Advantages of Dumb Terminal Networks

The traditional dumb terminal network is the administrator's dream come true. All of the configuration and (most important of all) the power of the system, is contained inside that air-conditioned room. As long as the physical network connections are intact, and the simple terminals aren't belching smoke, it all works. Central control means that the entire network can be managed, monitored, and maintained from one place. It also means that network traffic is minimized. All that has to travel the wires are the instructions coming from the terminals, and the results being sent back.

And if you think that the dumb terminal network is dead, then just take a look at Java. Right now there is a huge development effort going into the Java Station, the Network Computer, and even 'TV set-top box' web terminals. All these, by and large, are terminals with limited processing power, zero configuration requirements, and no local storage.

The Internet as a Dumb Terminal Network

So how does the Internet, and especially the World Wide Web, fit in? It's easy to see that the concept of a dumb terminal network almost exactly matches the way in which we use the Net. Although the machine on our desk has huge reserves of processing power, and (in theory anyway) plenty of local storage space, all we are doing with a browser is acting as a dumb terminal.

We send a request off to the web server, and it sends back the processed information as a static page that the browser just has to display. Up until the advent of client-side technologies like Java, ActiveX and scripting languages, the browser was literally a dumb terminal.

The physical structure of the Internet also matches this model very well. Bandwidth is at a premium, so the minimization of network traffic is a major bonus. And the remote geographical nature of the terminals makes visits by the network technician impossible.

Putting PCs on the Network

Of course, with the arrival of the personal computer, users wanted more than just a dumb terminal on their desk. Seeing what was possible with their own 'real' computer meant that static information coming from a server, over which they had little or no control, was obviously severely limiting when the technology beckoned with ever-increasing capabilities. Soon, PCs were strung together to form **local area networks**. Users could share files and resources, like printers, between the machines.

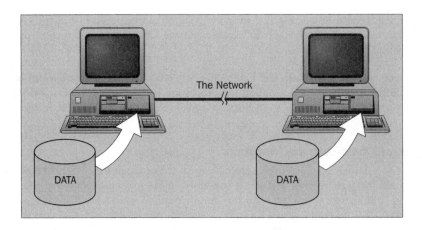

*On a peer-to-peer network, each machine holds its own data
and carries out its own processing on that data*

This is great, except for three things. First, there's no real central management, so everyone ends up using different applications, styles, and formats–documents stray from the standard corporate design, and everyone can do their own thing. Second, because each machine has its own local storage, files are duplicated across the network. Each user keeps their own copy of the corporate data, and so backing up–and even just getting an overall picture of the information available–becomes impossible.

Finally, the PC is a rather more complex beast than a dumb terminal. Configuration and maintenance now involve the technician rushing around the building, installing and upgrading each machine separately. Even strict management of the users, and new technologies which allow remote configuration of machines and replication of data across them, generally fail to achieve real solutions to these problems.

Peer-to-Peer vs. Central File Storage

Linking individual PCs together, as we've just been discussing, is generally referred to a **peer-to-peer networking**, because everyone has equal rights on the network. And, as we've seen, one of the major problems is that data becomes duplicated across the various machines. One simple way to cure this problem is to place a single copy of each file on a nominated machine, and let every user access that copy.

Now, the junior accountant keeps the customer database on his hard disk, and remembers to back it up daily. However, the constant accesses from all the other users are going to limit the responsiveness of his machine. It could well slow to a crawl when the sales desk is busy. The solution is to dedicate one machine on the network as a **central file server**, provide it with oodles of disk space, and put all the files there. It becomes a lot easier to do proper backing up, and duplication of the data is prevented.

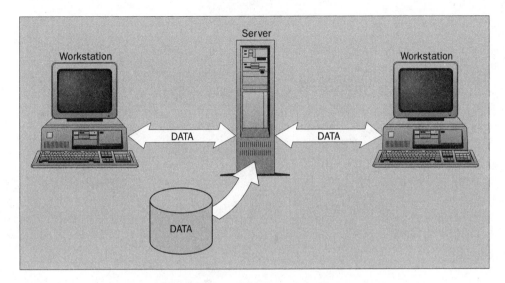

*Using a central file server means that all the data has to pass
across the network each time it is queried or updated*

While this network model solves the file duplication problem, and to some extent aids network management, it does little to solve the concerns of configuring and maintaining the rest of the machines on the network. It also, unfortunately, adds another problem. Every file has to travel across the network from the server to the end user, then back again to be saved. If the junior accountant needs to update the customer database, the complete file has to be fetched from the server, processed, and saved back there again. Network bandwidth requirements go through the roof.

Intelligence at Both Ends of the Network

In recent years, technologies have been developed which were aimed solely at solving the mixture of problems we've seen so far in the various networking models. An example of this is Microsoft Access, which can work either as a stand-alone application, or in a kind of client-server mode.

When we create a new database on our hard disk, Access works as a single-user local processing application. All the data storage and manipulation is done on our machine. However, we can use Access as a 'front end' to a set of database tables, by linking them to it. These tables can then be placed on another part of the network, say the central file server. Now, everyone can have an Access front-end (and not necessarily all the *same* one), while working with a single set of data.

But this alone isn't client-server computing, and it does little to limit bandwidth requirements. What completes the picture is that the central server can carry its own copy of the database engine, minus the 'front end'. Now, instead of the client machines fetching a whole table of data across the network each time, they can issue an instruction to the central database engine, which extracts the results they need from the tables and sends just that back across the network.

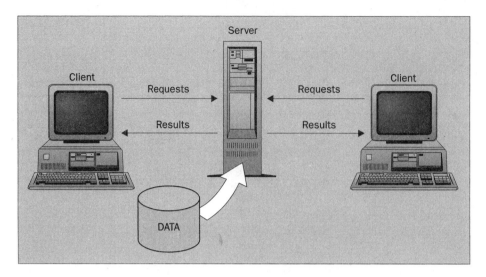

Client-server systems minimize network traffic by distributing the processing between the server and the client machines

In Microsoft Access terms, the database engine is executing **stored procedures**, something we came across back in Chapters 4 and 5 when we looked at the Active Data Object. This itself is just a way of connecting to, among other things, different database engines.

So client-server, at least in theory, gives us the best of all the worlds. We get minimized network traffic, central data storage, and easier systems management because the 'important' processing can be done at the server end if required. The only real downside, and the one that is currently the biggest cause for concern in the corporate world, is the continued difficulty of individual client machine maintenance, upgrades and configuration.

The Internet as a Client-Server System

As you'll have already guessed from our earlier discussions of Active Server Pages, one thing it aims to achieve is to allow easy development of client-server applications on the Internet, and more particularly in the environment of the World Wide Web. In many ways, this is the only way to go, because the prospect of any real increases in the bandwidth available in the near future is unlikely. While a modern corporate network will run at 10Mbps, and even up to 100Mbps, many users are usually limited to 28.8Kbps or 56Kbps. Even an ISDN connection can only manage somewhere up to 128Kbps.

As for the client end of the network, almost without exception, the user has a modern PC with plenty of local storage space, and spare horsepower available, so the browser can afford to do more and more of the processing at its end. Even the downside of system maintenance, upgrades and configuration is less of a problem. At least, on the Internet as a whole, it's the user's problem now, and not the network administrator's. In a corporate intranet environment this isn't the case, but standardization on one browser does tend to make the job a great deal easier.

So, having seen some of the background to client-server development, let's move on to look at what it offers in the environment of the Web. Client-server on the Web is exciting, because it solves many problems that are making traditional client-server projects expensive, overdue, and hard to maintain. More specifically, Web-based client-server solves the problems of:

▲ **Distribution**: Distribution is automatic, because new copies of the pages (the components of our application) are downloaded to the client machine whenever the local client cache says they need updating. No more walking round the building installing software, or expecting your web site visitors to download and install it themselves.

▲ **Flexibility**: The automatic distribution and installation means that applications can be updated much more easily. This is a huge benefit if the environment requires quick turn around on changes to the specifications or just bug fixes. Even 'Interface du jour' could be implemented, where different interfaces and content are deployed daily—of great interest to marketing departments when selling products.

▲ **Central Control**: With the deployment of PCs and local installations, the system administrators lost control, and help desk costs for maintaining non-standard desktops increased. Being able to control the applications at the server end is highly cost effective.

The Theory of Client-Server

So having justified the case for client-server, we need to investigate further what this enticing new technology actually is. This is a question that has many different interpretations. The reason is that client-server has become a buzzword that every new product must contain. In its simplest form, we can use this definition:

> **Client-server computing is the splitting of a computing task between client and server processes.**

Getting More Specific

This literal definition is very vague; however, there are more concrete definitions. For example, the following diagram is more specific. It states that there are four layers to a client-server system.

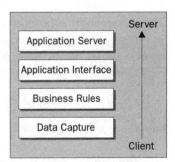

These four layers are from the classic model of client-server design, and can show up in various different forms. But to be able to develop a client-server system you must be able to understand the four layers.

The Data Capture Layer

The first layer is called **Data Capture**. This means that the data is captured and converted from a human representation to a computer representation. The previous sentence could be more easily termed as punching in the data. However, using that type of definition implies that the user has something that they can actually punch—such as a keyboard. The more precise definition is better, because it sums up all possibilities. For example, in the future, input devices could use voice, gesture, or neural transmitters. Coming back to reality, current input devices may be a mouse, keyboard or virtual reality interface device. The only limit is human imagination.

The reverse of input is output, and the statement also applies in this context. Examples of output devices are monitors, printers, or tape drives. Programming operations that are acceptable in this layer would be filling or reading the contents of a list box or a combo box, and then packing the data into a pre-defined structure.

However, it's important to note that this layer is only responsible for the translation of the data from one form to another, human to computer or vice-versa. The actual contents of the data aren't verified for correctness or accuracy here.

The Business Rule Layer

This layer is responsible for applying the **Business Rules** to the data captured in the first layer. It is responsible for converting the data to a business context, and adding information about the business rules. The user doesn't interact with the software in this layer at all, however this layer is critical because it validates the data to make sure that it is in the correct form—and is applied to the data that is both coming from or going to the server. The business rules must only be *rules*, they must not process the data.

Consider, for example, the implementation of a mortgage loan application. The business rule layer would filter the input first for completeness, then apply any other validation. A valid rule would be granting loans only to people who are at least 18 years old. However, a rule that denied a mortgage application just because the applicant did not earn enough for the property at a specific price would not be a valid business rule. In reality, denial of a mortgage is more complicated than a simple rule could cover. And while rules like this could be expressed in computer terms, they tend to contain too many ands, ifs, and buts.

A business rule should nest within other business rules, otherwise this layer becomes too fat, and requires too much processing. And it shouldn't depend on any data coming from higher layers—it needs to be self-supporting in all cases. In programming terms, the rules should be able to be stored in a small local file or, even better, coded within the program.

The Application Interface Layer

The third layer is called the **Application Interface** layer. This is responsible for converting the data from a business context to a technology context. The technology context is whatever the final layer, the **Application Server** layer, requires.

Going back to the mortgage example, the application interface might convert the request and associated data into an SQL statement, and then pass that to the final layer. By convention you would not to put any business logic into this layer, to allow for future expandability.

The Application Server Layer

The final layer is called the **Application Server** layer. This layer has the task of processing the data, which is now in a technology context, and the process is not dependent on the actions of the user interface. The processing doesn't need to be logical in human terms either. This layer is all about the storing of data and calculation of results.

For example, the equation $y = x\ /\ b$ is a mathematical reality, and can be computed for all values where b isn't zero. However, when b is zero, the results are undefined in mathematical terms and an overflow error occurs. Yet in our own human terms, the result still has sense of reality—it's just a very big number. The point is that in this layer the data is manipulated as something only mathematics, science or computers can fully understand. Our conceptions of the result will often be wrong.

As another example, take an SQL statement that we generated in the previous layer. While we would understand the plain English definition of the query, and probably have a good idea of what the SQL statement actually meant, we would have no conception of what actually went on inside the database while the query was being processed. It is considered to be a 'black box'.

These four layers form a definition of client-server computing in a nutshell, and are of interest to anyone who needs to develop corporate solutions. But they prompt the questions 'Why do we really care about these layers at all?' and 'Why don't we just create programs and let the layers sort themselves out?'.

Partitioning a Client-Server System

In fact, the whole purpose of the layer definitions is to help us understand how we divide up, or **partition**, our client-server applications. We ultimately have to define the split between the client and the server, in other words decide which layers will be on either side of the network connection. This is the subject of a great deal of industry debate. Typically, what has happened in the past is that the layers one, two and three were on the client, and the fourth layer was on the server. This is the infamous **fat client**, plagued with problems of poor performance, complex maintenance, and high costs.

Client-Server Middleware

A second problem with corporate client-server architecture, running on the company network, has always been how the client and server communicate with each other. The technical term for this is **middleware**– the software that makes it simple to abstract the communication. Every vendor has a solution, and they aren't always compatible with each other. This causes many network headaches, and solving it would make client-server development that much easier.

However, we won't be delving into the details of which other architectures are acceptable and workable in this book, but instead we'll focus on the single architecture that interests us–web client-server. The Web solves the communication layer problem because the HTTP protocol it uses provides a common base for all applications. What we do need to do is decide how we're going to partition our applications in this environment.

Partitioning a Web Based Application

To end our look at the theory of client-server computing, we'll go through how a typical application would be partitioned under the web client-server architecture. Layer one is the human-to-computer interface, and it would typically be a HTML based browser. There may be some client-side controls or scripts to add richness to the user interface, but this is purely optional.

Layer two is the business rule layer, and is generally handled on the client by the scripts and controls in the HTML page. However, no parts of the rules are hard-coded into the browser, they only exist in the pages themselves. There's an argument that this can pose a security risk because the rules then need to pass across the network. The risks involved here though can be reduced by the use of Secure Sockets Layers (or Secure Channel Services). We'll be discussing all these topics in Chapter 9. So in some cases, either to enhance security or because a rule requires features that aren't available on the client, all or part of the business rules layer may reside on the server.

Layer three, the conversion from a business context to a technological context, occurs on the server. It could be that an HTTP request triggers a routine that creates a structure of data, or that ASP converts it to a new representation ready for the final layer.

Layer four, the application server layer, is again located on the server, and is the 'back end' that actually does the processing and produces the results. This may be a database or other business object, and the result might be retrieval of information for return to the client, or just storage of data sent from it.

So in our Web based model, layers one and two are on the client machine, and the server contains layers three and four. We have a more balanced and better performing system, with one exception–the middleware.

Middleware on the Web

At the time of writing there was no standard middleware based on the HTTP protocol. There is new software that is showing some promise of being accepted, however for it to become reality, a standard method of **tunneling protocol** needs to become freely available.

> Tunneling is the process of securely embedding one protocol within another, so that information can be sent directly from one client-server layer to another across the Net, within the HTTP packets.

This ends our theoretical, and perhaps rather dry look, at client-server. However, it should have indicated that there is more to the subject than just script and components. We need to think seriously about how we design our applications to conform to the accepted standards, and to get the best performance–in terms of processing, usability, and security. The remainder of this chapter looks at different aspects of designing an application that will combine Active Server Pages and some of the other technologies that are relevant. At the same time, we'll be setting the scenes for the remainder of this part of the book and the case studies that follow.

Applications, Sessions and State

Traditional network based applications have always had one major advantage–the automatic maintenance of **state** by the network itself. The previous lack of this feature within HTTP has tended to limit the development of true Web based applications. What do we mean by state? In a traditional local or wide area network, the software (such as Novell, Banyan, or Microsoft's own protocols) combined with features of the operating system in such a way that once a user logged into the network, they could be automatically recognized by all the applications on it.

Bringing State to HTTP

On the Web, with previous applications based on technologies such as CGI, the problem has always been that, when a client submits a request, the server just produces a response and returns it. When another request is received from that user, the server has no idea if there was a previous request. This is because the HTTP protocol is **stateless**. Building client-server programs with a stateless protocol can become very complicated.

Why Do We Need State?

To understand why, imagine building a traditional application in, say, Visual Basic. You design a form with a dozen or so command buttons, and write a piece of code that runs when each button is clicked. VB itself knows which button was clicked, and so runs the correct code routine for that button. Now imagine that

VB was designed like HTTP. Instead of running individual routines for each button, you would have only a single block of code. VB would run this code when any of the buttons is clicked, without telling you which one it was. You can see how this would, to say the least, make building applications difficult.

To get around this problem Netscape developed the concept of a **cookie**. A cookie is purely a small informational text string that is stored on the user's hard disk—we looked at them in some depth back in Chapter 2.

> *Many people worry that cookies can be dangerous. While they can be used in all kinds of ways by server-based applications, they pose no risk to you as a user. Cookies, as they are documented, will not format your disk, send back information about your system, or put you on a mailing list. Unfortunately, they don't make the coffee either.*

Creating State with Cookies

Typically, when the client makes a request for a document from a specific virtual directory on a server (which can include the `wwwroot` directory), the server returns a cookie—or token of information. When the user returns to the same virtual directory, or one of its subdirectories the browser sends that cookie back, as part of the HTTP request.

If we were building CGI-based applications, we would use the cookie information to check who the user was and collect other information regarding their interaction with our application. Working with cookies directly can be fun and interesting for about 30 seconds. As we saw in Chapter 2, ASP does make the task a lot easier through the `Cookies` collections of the `Request` and `Response` objects.

However, the big advantage that the Active Server Pages framework provides, is an automatic mechanism for maintaining state in our applications, without having to directly manipulate cookies ourselves—although ASP requires the browser to support and accept cookies in order to function properly. If the user refuses to accept cookies through settings in their browser's security options, or if their browser doesn't support cookies, this automated mechanism will fail.

Using Applications and Sessions

We looked briefly at what the `Application` and `Session` object are in Part 1 of this book, and had a brief glimpse of the way they could be used. When we come to build Web based client-server applications, these two objects assume a far greater importance that we've previously credited them with. They allow us to connect together all the parts of our application.

For example, we can tell where on our site our visitor has already been, where they need to go next, and what they've decided to buy as they go along. In other words, we can store and maintain the values of variables for each user, as well as globally for all users. In this section, we'll explore some of the possibilities in detail.

Understanding Global.asa

To make `Application` and `Session` work in ASP, we use a single file named `global.asa` for each 'application'. This file resides in the directory on the server that is the root of that application—i.e. where the files that make up the application are located. Any subdirectories of the main application directory are also part of the application, and the `global.asa` file applies to their contents as well. This means that you need to be aware of the possibility of overlap between applications, and should generally create separate directories for each one. For example:

Physical directory	Virtual directory	Application
`C:\InetPub\WWWRoot\`	`/`	
`C:\InetPub\WWWRoot\Demo\`	`/DemoApp`	`Demo`
`C:\InetPub\WWWRoot\Demo\Images\`		`Demo`
`C:\InetPub\WWWRoot\Apps\Main\`	`/MainApp`	`MainApp`
`C:\InetPub\WWWRoot\Apps\Main\Test\`	`/TestApp`	`TestApp` *and* `MainApp`

So, when we talk about an **application** in ASP, we are actually talking about all the files included in the same directory as `global.asa`, and any of its subdirectories.

Application and Session Events

We talked about the events that `Application` and `Session` implement back in Chapter 2. However, we'll summarize these briefly in the context of state, and then quickly move on to look at how we can use them in our applications.

The Application_onStart and Session_onStart Events

Both of these events are to be used to initialize state, by setting up variables that are global either for the application or a specific user. When the first user accesses a file in our application, the `Application_onStart` event is triggered. This is used to initialize any application-wide global variables. When the user begins a session for the first time, the `Session_onStart` event is triggered. This is used to initialize user-specific information.

The power of the `Session` object comes from the fact that it can store variables that are global to just that specific user, and so each user can have their own individual value for that variable. `Session` objects aren't always created automatically for every user when they enter our application. However, storing or accessing a variable in the `Session` object will create it, and fire the `Session_onStart` event. We can force new sessions to always be created as soon as a visitor enters our application by writing code in `global.asa` to respond to this event.

When responding to the `Application_onStart` event, we must not under any circumstances use code specific to any one particular user. In this event, we would typically create global objects, such as a server side component that needs to be shared and available to every visitor.

> *Session* and *Application* events only happen when a client retrieves an *ASP* page—they are not triggered when an *HTML* page in the application is requested. Therefore, if you have additional server-side applications such as *ISAPI* or *CGI* scripts, make sure that they don't depend on specific events having occurred within an *ASP* page. Otherwise the *ISAPI* or *CGI* script may crash and cause the web server to hang.

The Session_onEnd and Application_onEnd Events

The `Session_OnEnd` event occurs either when a current `Session` is abandoned by using the `Session.Abandon` method, or when it times out. By default this is 20 minutes after the last request for a page from the application, though this can be changed either by setting the `Session.Timeout` property or by editing the registry. See Chapter 2 for more details.

Something we need to consider is if we have objects that themselves contain timeouts. If, for example, we create a database connection in a `Session`, and the connection timeout is less than the `Session` timeout, it's possible for corruption of the object to occur. If the database connection times out after ten minutes, and the `Session` times out after twenty minutes, the database connection will not be valid, even though the object in the `Session` still is.

The `Application_onEnd` event can be used to clean up all of the global objects and variables. There's a problem at the present time, however, in that this event may not actually be triggered until the web server is stopped. Revisions of ASP seem likely to specify that the `Application_onEnd` event be triggered, once the last `Session_onEnd` event occurred, that is when the last session ends and there are no current application users.

Application and Session Variables

The `Application` and `Session` objects can be used to store values that are global either to a particular user (the `Session`) or to all users (the `Application`). Within the `onStart` events, we can initialize these variables. We can also store new variables, or change existing values, in the code inside any other ASP page.

Initializing variables is very important, especially with a language like VBScript that uses `Variants`. Imagine the following code in a page:

```
Response.Write("The current value is: " & Session("MyValue"))
```

This places the contents of the `Session` variable `MyValue` in the page. The only problem with this code is if the variable hasn't been initialized. What we get is:

```
The current value is:
```

Any `Variant` (the only data type available in VBScript) that hasn't been assigned a value is said to be `Empty`. Because we're dumping the variable as its default type, we get nothing. The best way to solve this type of problem is either assign a default value to it, or examine the variable using the `IsEmpty()` function. Here's how we could use `IsEmpty()`:

```
varTheValue = Session("MyValue")
If IsEmpty(varTheValue) Then varTheValue = "* Undefined *"
Response.Write("The current value is: " & varTheValue)
```

Alternatively, we can set any default value we like in the `Session_onStart` event, so that we have a value ready for access in that session:

```
Sub Session_OnStart
  Session("MyValue") = 42
End Sub
```

Counting Sessions

An immediately obvious use of this technique is to count how many sessions have occurred during the current application. All we do is use a variable stored in the **Application** object, which is then available to all sessions:

```
Sub Application_OnStart
  Application("NumVisitors") = 0
End Sub
```

Now, in **Session_onStart**, we can increment the value for each new session:

```
Sub Session_OnStart
  Application.Lock
  Application("NumVisitors") = Application("NumVisitors") + 1
  Application.Unlock
End Sub
```

Then we can drop it into the 'welcome' page with a few lines of code:

```
<% Application.Lock %>
<H3> Your are visitor number <% = Application("NumVisitors") %> </H3>
<% Application.Unlock %>
```

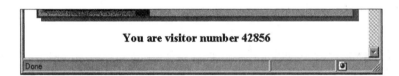

Storing Array Variables

As we briefly mentioned in Chapter 2, we have a problem when storing arrays in a **Session** or **Application** object, which maintain all values as **Variants**. The following example shows how we can get round this limitation:

```
'Create and initializing the array
Dim MyArray()
ReDim MyArray(5)
MyArray(0) = "hello"
MyArray(1) = "some other string"

'Store the array in the Session object
Session("StoredArray") = MyArray

'Now retrieve the array from the Session object
LocalArray = Session("StoredArray")
LocalArray(1) = "there"
...
'and then store the updated one back again
Session("StoredArray") = LocalArray
...
```

We create the array **MyArray()** and **ReDim** it to hold five elements. Then we assign strings to the elements **0** and **1**, and simply assign the array directly to a variable **StoredArray** in the **Session** object. We've effectively converted our array of strings into a **variant array**, and stored it in a single **Variant** in the **Session**.

Later in the same script, or in another request in the same session, we can retrieve the array using **LocalArray = Session("StoredArray")**, then access it as normal using the indexes. You might be tempted to believe that instead of assigning the array to a single **Session** variable, we could access it using **Session("StoredArray")(1) = "there"**, but this is *not* the correct method. It will result in loss of data.

> *The **Application** and **Session** objects' variables are implemented as collections, however we should not actually access them in this way—it is not documented or recommended. Neither is it possible to store references to any of the Active Server Pages built-in objects—for example, the statement **Set Session("MyRequest") = Request** is not legal.*

Reference Counting with the Application Object

You'll recall we suggested earlier that the **Application_onEnd** event might not be fired until the web server is stopped. So what happens to the global objects that are stored within the active **Application** object? They are kept alive and available all of the time. If you have a resource that you don't want to be kept in memory for days on end, when the application isn't in use, the following code solves the problem. It demonstrates some of the ways of using the **Application** and **Session** objects:

```
Sub Session_OnStart
  Application.Lock
  If IsEmpty(Application("Object")) Then
    Set Application("Object") = Server.CreateObject("global.connection")
    Application("ObjectCount") = 0
  End If
  Application("ObjectCount") = Application("ObjectCount") + 1
  Application.Unlock
End Sub
```

```
Sub Session_OnEnd
  Application.Lock
  Application("ObjectCount") = Application("ObjectCount") - 1
  If Application("ObjectCount") = 0 Then
    Set Application("Object") = Nothing
  End If
  Application.Unlock
End Sub
```

The technique we use in this code is called **reference counting**. Notice that the **Application** *events* aren't used, but the **Application** *object* is. All the events are those that occur for each **Session**. The technique, however, is simple enough. At the start of each **Session**, we only create an instance of the object we want (in this case a fictitious **"global.connection"**) if it doesn't already exist. At the end of each **Session**, we destroy the object if no one else is using it. If you like, it's the old 'last one out turn off the lights' trick.

How It Works

This code works by keeping a count of the number of users that are using the application at any one time, storing this count in a global variable called **ObjectCount**. If this is zero, or doesn't exist, the **Session_onStart** code creates the object and stores the reference to it in the **Application** object as a variable called **Object**, and it's then available to all users. At the same time, it sets the value of **ObjectCount** to zero, in case it didn't actually exist–in other words if this was the first ever session to use the application.

The next step is to increment the value of **ObjectCount**, so that it reflects the number of current sessions. If the object already exists when a **Session** starts, and the **Object** variable does reference an object when this session begins (i.e. it's not **Empty**), the code will just increment **ObjectCount** without creating a new instance of the object.

The **Session_onEnd** code, which runs for each **Session** as it ends, just has to decrement the value of **ObjectCount**, and it can then tell how many other sessions are still active. If this is zero it can destroy the object by setting its reference variable to **Nothing**.

Notice that we've again used the **Application** object's **Lock** and **Unlock** methods before changing the values of any of its variables. Failing to do this can cause all kinds of problems by allowing more than one session to access the values at the same time. This concept is called **concurrency**, and we'll look at the implications that arise from it next.

Application Concurrency Issues

As we've already seen, the purpose of the **Application** object is to be able to store information that is globally used among all application users. These could be object reference variables or other values that all application users require access to. However, the problem is that, because they are shared, we can come up against concurrency problems. Consider the following example:

```
Application("NumberOfSales") = Application("NumberOfSales") + 1
```

This line of code in an ASP file could be used to count the number of users who had ordered goods from our site. It maintains the count in the **Application** variable **NumberOfSales**. However, if two users access this variable at the same time corruption is likely occur, because the single **Application** object has global scope and is visible to all. User **A** reads the value of **NumberOfSales** at the same time as user **B**. Both instances of the ASP page get the same value, they both increment it, and they both store it back in the **Application** object. The result is that it only gets incremented once. It might even corrupt it altogether if both writes occurred at the same moment.

Locking the Application Object

To solve the problem, we just change the code to read:

```
Application.Lock
Application("NumberOfSales") = Application("NumberOfSales") + 1
Application.Unlock
```

> *You don't need to use* **Lock** *and* **Unlock** *in the* **Application_onStart** *event, because this event can only be called once–by the single session that starts the application. The* **Application_onStart** *event is called before the first* **Session_onStart** *event, which is called before the ASP page is actually processed.*

Read-Only Session and Application Variables

You may think that with a simple assignment like the one we've just looked at, the chances of corruption are remote. That may be true for a single-processor computer, but with multiprocessor machines becoming popular this assumption isn't safe under all circumstances. One useful trick, where appropriate, is to make variables read-only for all sessions by checking the value first—as shown here:

```
Sub Session_OnStart
  Application.Lock
  If IsEmpty(Application("myData")) Then
     Application("myData") = strTheValue
  End if
  Application.Unlock
End Sub
```

This code only sets the value of the variable if it hasn't been set before, giving it—in effect—a default value. Once the variable has been assigned a value, and isn't **Empty**, it can't be changed. However, any other code can read the value as required, and with no fear of corruption:

```
Application.Lock
MyVar = Application("myData")
Application.Unlock
```

Using Global Values and Object References

While the previous example solves the concurrency problem, it brings with it new ones. In a very busy site, the code to read the value could be called thousands of times a day. Locking the application just to read a value could drastically hit server performance. The situation is even worse when we come to store references to objects, which could be required by all users.

If we only need to read the value of a variable as it stood at the start of a session, we could copy it from the **Application** object into that user's **Session** object. Then, each ASP page could reference the **Session** version. This has the downside, however, in that the value will not keep up with changes to the value in the **Application** object automatically—but it all comes down to what we actually use the values for.

Connection Pooling with ADO

When we come to use objects like the Active Data Object, we often need to access a single instance of it several times in a page, and across our application. For example, we use the **ADODB.Connection** object to create a database connection. Instead of doing it on every page, we might consider just opening a single database connection once (in **Session_onStart**, or even in the **Application_onStart**) and then using that connection throughout the entire session or application.

Database applications designed for a multi-user audience will generally run on something like SQL Server, or another high-end database. While reusing a connection stored in the **Session** or **Application** object might be an efficient way to work with low transaction volume databases like Microsoft Access, this method loses its attractiveness as the number of users of our application increases.

You might recall from Chapter 4 that ODBC 3.0 includes a feature called **connection pooling**, which manages connections across multiple users. When using connection pooling it's best to open and close the database connection on each page that uses it—this allows ODBC to manage the connections most efficiently. Without it, there could be ten users logged onto our application, but who weren't actually doing anything, and this could cause ten idle connections that decrease performance and consume server and database resources.

So, with Access, you should consider a **Session_onStart** instantiation of connections—while for other databases it may well be wiser to use local connections in each page. The Roadmap help file that ships with ASP has more information on connection pooling.

Global Object Reference Problems

When we come to create global references to objects, however, we can't just shuffle the values around between the **Application** and **Session** objects, because we run the risk of creating problems as the object's own internal state changes. Instead, we need to make the decision as to where we actually want to use the object. We saw ways of creating and destroying an object at global **Application** level earlier. We can, of course, create **Session** level objects in **Session_onStart**, and destroy them in **Session_onEnd**. In this case, we don't have to worry about concurrency, and we know they will not hang around in memory on the server when the session ends.

Creating objects at **Session** level is generally the best solution. If we do need a global object for the whole application, like the Card Game case study you'll see in Part 3, we have to take some extra care when using it. Have a look at these two extracts of code:

```
Sub Application_OnStart
    Application("myObject") = Server.CreateObject("game500.player")
End Sub
```

This is in **global.asa**, and it creates the global instance of the object that will manage the whole game. In one of the ASP files that are used as part of the game, we call the **SetData** method of this object to change the game state at that point—when a card is played.

```
Application("myObject").SetData(Request.QueryString("txtUser"))
```

The problem here is that we run the risk of corruption again. Two users could call this method at the same time, leaving the results undefined. This time, the concurrency problem isn't at the *script* level, but at the *object* level. It needs to be handled by the object itself, and is concerned with the threading model it uses, and the way that the COM interface is implemented. These topics are beyond the scope of this chapter, but we'll investigate them in some depth in the case study in Chapter 14.

When State Doesn't Look After Itself

The whole concept of **Applications** and **Sessions** requires the browser to accept and implement cookies. If it doesn't, then ASP is unable to maintain state information of any kind. We have to resort to the older methods of CGI programming.

How State Works in ASP

As we said earlier, the HTTP protocol is inherently stateless, and relies on cookies to be able to manage and recognize requests, and match them to the users. When ASP wants to establish a session, it sends the **Set-Cookie** HTTP header to the browser, to establish a unique user session ID and the path of the application it corresponds to—i.e. where the appropriate **global.asa** file resides:

```
Set-Cookie: ASPSESSIONID=LRUSDYXQMWRTNWEB; path=/TestApp
```

From our discussions of cookies in Chapter 2, you'll realize that this one doesn't expire until the browser is shut down. In theory, if the browser was to be left running for weeks on end, the cookie will remain current. But the **Session** object has a default **Timeout** of twenty minutes, and that point the **Session** is marked as having ended and any variables in it are destroyed.

The Un-expired Cookie Problem

The fact that a user's **Session ID** cookie may not have expired, while the matching **Session** on the server has already expired, raises an interesting question. What happens if that user comes back to our site again? The server will check the session ID in their cookie against the currently active sessions, and if it doesn't match will just create and initialize a new **Session**. The user then effectively 'goes back to the start'.

Of course, this assumes that the session ID will be unique for every user. If this isn't the case, the application might find itself with two users sharing a **Session**. We have to assume that Microsoft has thought of this, and that the session ID generator is sufficiently random to prevent it happening!

When the Cookie Jar is Empty

One problem that Microsoft can't prevent is the situation where the session ID cookie our server sends isn't supported by the browser, or accepted by the user. Or more critically, it's possible for the server administrator to turn off the ability to maintain sessions altogether by editing the registry. Now, the automatic state mechanism isn't going to work, so we need an alternative plan.

We could use a system originally implemented in ASP, but then removed again, which added parameters to all the hyperlinks in the pages so as to pass on the session ID. We could emulate this, or just shunt the user off to a separate version of our site that worked without requiring state information. We could even throw them out altogether, though this may tend to discourage future visits....

Checking for Cookie Acceptance

But before we can do any of this, we need a way of determining whether the browser can support cookies, without causing havoc. Easy enough. We just use a default opening page that gets sent to *every* user, when they first enter the application. We could include a 'Welcome' graphic, like a real application's splash screen, or possibly some introduction to the site:

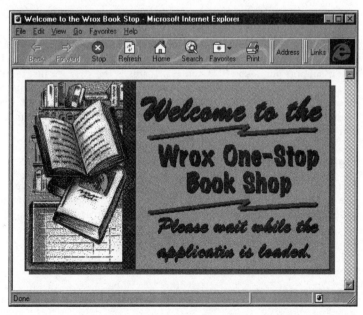

Here's the code that creates this page, with the important lines highlighted:

```
<HTML>
<HEAD>
<META HTTP-EQUIV="REFRESH" CONTENT="5; URL=hellotest.asp">
<TITLE>Document Title</TITLE>
</HEAD>
<BODY>
<CENTER><IMG SRC="Welcome.gif"></CENTER>
<% On Error Resume Next
   Session("TestBrowser")="Hello" %>
</BODY>
</HTML>
```

The ASP code first turns off error checking, then stores a value in a **Session** level variable named **TestBrowser**. If the browser doesn't support cookies, or if they're turned off, there will be no **Session** object and the code will fail–however, there won't be an error message because of the **On Error Resume Next**. The real key to this page is the first highlighted line:

```
<META HTTP-EQUIV="REFRESH" CONTENT="5; URL=hellotest.asp">
```

Once the page has finished loading, the browser waits five seconds and then loads the page **hellotest.asp**–which contains this code, placed before the **<HEAD>** section:

```
<% On Error Resume Next
   If IsEmpty(Session("TestBrowser")) Then
     Response.Redirect "NoCookie.asp"
   Else
     Response.Redirect "AllowCookie.asp"
   End If %>
<HTML>
<HEAD>
   . . .
```

All it does is check the value of the **TestBrowser** variable. If it's **Empty** we know that the browser, for one reason or another, doesn't have the ability to use a **Session**–which is likely to be because it can't (or won't) support our session ID cookies. If this is the case we just redirect the visitor to a page that is intended for non-session ASP users. Otherwise it's business as usual, and we redirect them to the main menu of our application. Notice that it's necessary to wrap the **If** statement in another **On Error Resume Next**, in case the **IsEmpty** test fails. If it does, the next statement to be executed still sends them to the non-session area of the site.

Using Document Redirection

The code we've seen in the previous section is an excellent example of the way that we can redirect users to a different page at will. We can often take advantage of this method to route users through an application, depending on the current state for that user, or the application as a whole.

For example, we might allow them to choose goods they want to purchase, in a kind of virtual shopping trolley. Each time they click the Yes, I Want One button, we add the details to our **Session** object, using an array as we saw earlier:

```
Sub cmdYesIWantOne_onClick
  'Retrieve the array and current item count from the Session object ...
  LocalArray = Session("BoughtItems")
  intNumberOfItems = CInt(Session("ItemCount")) + 1
  LocalArray(intNumberOfItems) = strItemCodeNumber
  'then store the updated values back again.
  Session("BoughtItems") = LocalArray
  Session("ItemCount") = CStr(intNumberOfItems)
End Sub
```

When they've finished shopping, and click the All Done Now button, we only need to route them to the virtual checkout if they've actually bought anything. It's easy using document redirection:

```
If CInt(Session("ItemCount")) > 0 Then
  Response.Redirect "cashdesk.asp"
Else
  Response.Redirect "thankyou.asp"
End If
```

Redirecting From Within a Page

Doing a redirection like the last example is only possible from the header of a document, before any content has been sent to the browser. If we attempt it after that, we get a Buffer not empty error. Remember from Chapter 2 that if we want to provide an opportunity for redirection to occur part way through a page, we need to turn on **buffering**, and clear the buffer, first:

```
<%@ LANGUAGE="VBSCRIPT" %>
<% Response.Buffer = True %>
<HTML>
<HEAD><TITLE> Document Title </TITLE></HEAD>
<BODY>
<H1>Welcome to our site</H1><P>
<% If Session("TestCondition") = True Then
     Response.Clear
     Response.Redirect "anotherpage.asp"
   End If %>
   ...
   rest of page
   ...
</BODY>
</HTML>
```

Making Use of State Information

We've now established the ways that Active Server Pages can provide us with the state information we need to create working client-server applications. We have a unique **Session** object for each user, and we can store values and object references in it, which will remain valid while that user is working with the application. In this section, we'll look at ways that we can use this information, then move on to consider how it might influence the design of our site, and the pages it contains.

Logging Users into an Application

One of the primary reasons that we use the state information is to identify each user. They are already identified within ASP by a session ID, but this tends not to be very useful. What we will generally want to do is change the behavior of our application based on the user's absolute identity, i.e. a **UserID** or **nickname**. This follows a similar practice to a normal, non-Web-based client-server application.

It's possible to identify users through advanced communication methods, when using Secure Channels or Challenge/Response Authentication–subjects that we cover in Chapter 9. However, often we'll need to implement a standard log-on type of dialog, and then use the information the user provides within our application.

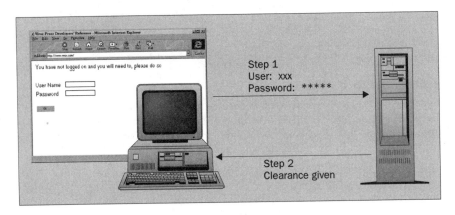

The user supplies a user name and a password, and clicks the Submit button. All we need to do is respond to the request by checking these details. It makes sense to use the **POST** method for the form so that the information isn't sent attached to the URL in the query string, but at least partly concealed within the HTTP header. Of course, we should really use some type of secure transmission as well, to ensure maximum privacy.

Using the User's Information

However, having got the request at the server, we can examine the values the user entered:

```
txtUserName = Request.Form("txtUserName")
txtPassWord = Request.Form("txtPassWord")
```

The question now is what do we do with it? We can use it in our code in minimalist ways, like:

```
Welcome <% = txtUserName %> to our site
```

and even to redirect users, or control access to the pages:

```
If txtUserName = "Admin" And txtPassWord = "secret" Then
    Response.Redirect "AdminPage.asp"
ElseIf txtUserName = "Manager" And txtPassWord = "reports" Then
    Response.Redirect "SalesReports.asp"
Else
    Response.Redirect "UserMenu.asp"
End If
```

Even so, this doesn't really provide a foundation for 'proper' application design. We need to be able to log users in, verify their passwords against a central list, and decide what further action to take. For example, we might want to deny access to users who don't have an existing user name (i.e. not accept new users), or we might want to automatically add them to our user list and give them certain default access permission. And if they have been here before, do we have any user preferences we need to set, like the background and foreground colors of their pages?

Verifying the User

Generally, the first step will be to verify who the user is, and decide if we already know them. Then, if we do know them, we can check to see if they've supplied the correct password. This process involves three basic steps, and we'll normally be taking the information from a database of some kind. In the following example we'll work through the steps, which are:

- See if the user name exists in the database
- If it does, check that the password is correct
- If it doesn't, add the user to the database if appropriate

Does the User Already Exist?

To see if the user already exists in our database, we just need to search for their user name in the appropriate table. Assuming we have a table **UserDetails** with **UserName** and **UserPword** fields, we can use an SQL query to extract the details. However, we may need to ensure that the length of the database fields and the validation are identical, depending on how the database actually stores text fields.

The database system may offer two types of text field–**varChar** and **char**. If the field is of type **char** and length **10**, we would need to pad out the string to **10** characters first, to ensure that we get a match. Using **varchar**, or a normal **Text** field in Access, avoids this problem.

So, we can use the normal ADO object methods in our page to find out if the user exists. Here, we're using a **connection string** that we previously stored in the **Session** object, so that we can retrieve it as required:

```
'create SQL string using the value in the txtUserName control on the form
strSQL = "SELECT UserName, UserPword FROM UserDetails WHERE UserName = '" _
      & Request.Form("txtUserName") & "')"

'create the database connection and open a recordset with the results
Set oConn = Server.CreateObject("ADODB.Connection")
oConn.Open Session("Logon_ConnectionString"),
Set oUsers = Server.CreateObject("ADODB.Recordset")
oUserRs = oConn.Execute(strSQL)

'now check if there is a record
If oUserRs.BOF AND oUserRs.EOF Then               'we didn't get any records
   Response.Write("User name does not exist")
   ...
```

Once we've got the recordset, we just need to see if there was a record in it–there will only be one at most, because the user name would need to be unique, and defined this way in the database tables. We might try using the **RecordCount** property, but this requires a move to the last record first (see Chapter 4 for more about how this works). And if we do this with an empty recordset, it causes an error anyway. The easier way is to do what we do here, and check the values of **BOF** and **EOF**. Only if the recordset is empty will they both be **True**.

Does the Password Check Out?

If this first check discovers a record, then the user exists in the database, so we can now compare the password. The recordset we retrieved contains the password field as well, so it's just a matter of a straight comparison:

```
...
Else
    If Request.Form("txtPassword") <> oUserRs.Fields("UserPword") Then
        Response.Write("You did not enter the correct password")
        ...
```

The usual option here would be to allow them another attempt, by displaying the login form again. It's quite possible to do this in the same page, and in the next few chapters you'll see how we can achieve this.

Adding New Users to the Database

If the user name check fails, in other words the user doesn't already exist, we need to decide if we want to add them to the database as a new user. Again, an SQL statement can do this. We know that the username they have supplied is unique compared to the existing ones, because we didn't get a record returned. All we need is an appropriate SQL **INSERT** statement:

```
...
'add the user to the database
strSQL = "INSERT INTO UserDetails (UserName, UserPword) VALUES ('" _
        & Request.Form("txtUsername") & "','" _
        & Request.Form("txtPassword") & "')"
oConn.Execute(strSQL)
...
```

Ensuring Concurrency during Log-on

There's just one problem. If we're going to add records to a globally accessible database, we need to make sure that we don't upset any other logons that are being performed concurrently. For small sites this risk is marginal, but consider what would happen if two new users specified the same user name. The recordset we retrieved would be out of date by the time we came to add the new record, and the original could by now already contain the user name we're trying to add.

We could get round this in several ways, such as by making sure the database table design specified unique values—and then trapping the error that would arise. However, this approach isn't ASP-centric, so instead we'll try one that makes use of the features available in ASP. What we need is a concurrency model that controls access to an item during the process, preventing two sessions accessing it at the same time.

Locking the Connection

Here's one possibility. Having decided to add the user, we do another database search for this user name in case it has been added meanwhile, by another visitor. However, we first lock the **Application** object while we read the connection string, and keep it locked until we've finished the whole process. Now, no other session can create a connection, and upset our code. Notice also that we only need to extract the user name and not the password as well. And the result we want is to *not* find a record this time

```
'create SQL string using the value in the txtUserName control on the form
strSQL = "SELECT UserName FROM UserDetails WHERE UserName = '" _
        & Request.Form("txtUserName") & "')"

'create the database connection and open a recordset with the results
Application.Lock
Set oConn = Server.CreateObject("ADODB.Connection")
oConn.Open Session("Logon_ConnectionString"),
Set oUsers = Server.CreateObject("ADODB.Recordset")
oUserRs = oConn.Execute(strSQL)

'now check if there is a record
If oUserRs.BOF AND oUserRs.EOF Then        'we didn't get any records
   strSQL = "INSERT INTO UserDetails (UserName, UserPword) VALUES ('" _
           & Request.Form("txtUsername") & "','" _
           & Request.Form("txtPassword") & "')"
   oConn.Execute(strSQL)
Else
   Response.Write("Error accessing database, please try again")
End If
Application.Unlock
```

We could, of course, have just locked the **Application** originally, and this would have saved the second search through. It all depends on whether you expect to get more existing users than new visitors, or vice-versa.

Making Use of the Logon Information

Having identified our users as they log onto the application, what are we actually going to do with the information? This is open to the design of your applications, and it's not possible to lay down criteria, methods, or examples that are going to be specific to any individual's needs. However, there are a few obvious details that we should consider.

Setting User Preferences

Recall that when we logged an existing user into our application, we extracted the single record from the **UserDetail** table in our database that contained their user name and password. This record could just as easily contain a great deal more about the user, such as their department, workgroup, page color preferences, or even the name of their dog. All we need to do is change the SQL query to include all the fields in the recordset, and then capture the other details in **Session** level variables ready for use while the user is touring our site:

```
strSQL = "SELECT * FROM UserDetails WHERE UserName = '" _
        & Request.Form("txtUserName") & "')"
...
...
Session("BackColor") = oUserRs.Fields("BackColor")
Session("FontColor") = oUserRs.Fields("FontColor")
Session("DogsName") = oUserRs.Fields("DogsName")
...
```

Now, we can really make them feel at home:

```
<HTML>
<HEAD>
<TITLE> Welcome to the Wrox Pets Supermarket </TITLE>
</HEAD>
<BODY BGCOLOR=<% = Session("BackColor") %>>
 <FONT FACE=Arial COLOR=<% = Session("FontColor") %>>
  <CENTER><IMG SRC="welcome.gif"><CENTER><P>
  <H3> Great News... </H3> We now have a new variety of Scrummy<BR>
  <I><B>the dog food for champions</B></I><BR>
  available from the new products page.<P>
  Why not take some home for<B> <% = Session("DogsName")%> </B>- we
   <I>guarantee</I> it will be a hit!
</BODY>
</HTML>
```

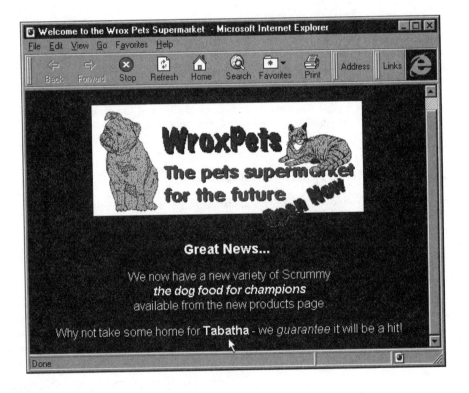

Checking the Success of Object Creation

One thing we regularly do in the **Application_onStart** and **Session_onStart** events is create instances of objects that we need to use throughout the application. In our logon example, we're also creating objects to check the user's identity–database connections and recordsets. If any of these processes fail, the state of our application is invalid. In this case, with the login page for example, we must be sure to set the 'logged on' status to **False**.

The easiest way is to examine the object variable that is now supposed to be referencing the object instance. We can use either **IsEmpty()** or **IsObject()** for this, or compare it to the standard value **Nothing**. It depends on whether we're referring to the object itself or a variable that holds a reference to it. In both cases, for it to work, we have turn off error checking with an **On Error Resume Next** statement first:

```
On Error Resume Next
Set oConn = Server.CreateObject("ADODB.Connection")
If IsObject(oConn) Then
   '... success, OK to continue
Else
   '... error, could not create object
End If
```

```
On Error Resume Next
Set Session("MyConnection") = Server.CreateObject("ADODB.Connection")

'now check if it failed
If Session("MyConnection") Is Nothing Then
   '... got an error

'or use this method
If IsEmpty(Session("MyConnection")) Then
   '... got an error
```

Designing for Client-Server

We spent some time early in this chapter looking at what client-server really is, and how we need to build applications to a structure that makes sense for the environment where they are used. In our case, whether on the Internet or an intranet, we're looking to share processing as evenly as possible between the client and the server. This involves moving the business rules, wherever appropriate, to the client–and leaving the server to do the actual processing work.

The browser (our client) can no longer be just the dumb terminal that we've been assuming all the way through this book so far. It has to do its share of the work where appropriate, and to achieve this we need to extend our application's processing across the network. We need to be able to program the client. Much of the rest of this book details how we can do this, and how we integrate the processing at both ends of the wire into a seamless application.

To finish off this chapter, we'll look briefly at the methods available to do this, and consider how this affects the design of our applications. We'll be considering three main areas:

▲ Designing to match the Business Rules

▲ Different ways to use a browser

▲ Client-side scripting and components

Designing to the Business Rules

The key to developing successful client-server applications is to develop the objects within it using the business rules. Allowing a programmer to create their objects as they go along, without understanding the ultimate needs of the application and the business it must support, leads to long term maintenance and expansion problems. Any team developing client-server applications, or any other programs, needs to talk to the business team, so that they are aware of the problems they face, and the solutions they need.

As an example, imagine building a house. If it was built according to the *builder's* needs, i.e. speed, ease of construction, and minimum cost, the house would be functional and not overly complex. However, the people who actually live in the building may find it confining, unsuitable for their domestic requirements, and when it comes time to redecorate they may find it too expensive to realize their wishes.

But didn't the team leader at your last project meeting say that the current main aims of the project were speed, ease of construction, and minimum cost?

Use Good Design Techniques

This is an absolute requirement. You must begin by designing your application and not launch straight away into building parts of it to see what happens. Grab a book on client-server systems design (Grady Booch's work is the 'bible'), read and analyze the examples, and then develop your design for the final application. Good design, which matches the needs of the business, will ensure that the application will be maintainable and expandable, and as a by-product the debugging requirements will fall dramatically.

The key to good design is developing the application as components, be they individual pages, HTML files, or compiled standard or custom components. Active Server Pages allows even script code to be built into modules and used as required. Remember the Server-side Include command `#include`? We can use this to insert any file into an ASP file, and it's an ideal way of storing functions and subroutines as text files that are used by several other pages:

```
<!-- #INCLUDE FILE="MyFunction.inc" -->
```

By defining and maintaining the same interface, (i.e. names and parameters of the routines it contains) we can update them as required, without affecting the pages that use them.

Use Small and Efficient Components

Active Server Pages aren't supported by a very efficient debugging environment, and they are still interpreted at run-time. So it makes sense to move much of the standard functionality into components where possible. Using small well-defined components can speed up the entire development process, and the execution speed of the application. It has other advantages as well, as we'll discuss in Chapter 10. For example, we can update the component, and all the pages that use it will automatically take advantage of the changes. It also gives us the opportunity to encapsulate secret business rules inside the component, rather than as script in a page.

The question is, how do we define a small component? In reality, what we want is the minimum code and the optimum functionality–based on a business rule or business object. Remember, we may have many instances running at a time if they are created at page or session level.

A Sample Page Counter Component

We saw how we can use the `Application` object and VBScript code to maintain a count of visitors to our site, by counting new sessions. There is, however, a problem with this. The contents of the `Application` object are lost when it is destroyed, i.e. when the application ends. This may be when the Web server is stopped, or in future when all active sessions have ended. So we need to consider some more solid way of saving the data.

The Microsoft IIS web site contains a sample **page counter component** that neatly demonstrates the principles of component design. It's written in C++, and is reasonably compact in code terms. It also has added functionality in that it can maintain a count of accesses to almost as many different pages as we like. The details of the 'hits' to each page are stored in a text file on the server's disk. Before the server shuts down, and at undetermined intervals while it is running, the component updates this file from a memory-based cache of hit counts.

The component is instantiated on any page for which a count is required—it can't be created at session or application level like most other components because it uses the URL of the current page (where it is running) to identify the page:

```
Set MyCount = Server.CreateObject("IISSample.PageCounter")
```

This is all that's required to maintain the hit count. Each time the page is accessed by the server, the count is incremented. To get the count for the current page, we just use the **Hits** method:

```
Response.Write("You are visitor number " & MyCount.Hits)
```

To reset the counter for the current page, we just call its **Reset** method. So this is a simple but highly efficient component, packaged up and available to be dropped into a page easily. You can get a copy from:

```
http://www.microsoft.com/iis/usingiis/developing/samples
```

Different Ways to Use a Browser

In a client-server situation, the browser is going to become a lot more than just a way of viewing static pages. It actually becomes part of the application, and so we need to be aware of some of the other ways it can be used. For example, we can embed the browser inside another application, or use a special control called the **Web Browser Control** that comes as part of the Internet Explorer controls installation.

Alternatively, we can embed other applications within the web browser, although this gives us only limited opportunity for adding extra features to our applications. We can even use a control called the **Internet Transfer Control**, that allows us to retrieve pages from the server without actually displaying them—but we can then get at the information in the HTTP stream, the HTML code, and the text contents. You'll see an example of this control's use, and embedding a browser in a Visual Basic application, in the case studies in Chapters 13 and 14.

Embedding a Browser within an Application

Typical web browsing involves either surfing from one site to another, or searching for specific information. In many situations, the user simply types in a URL, or clicks on previously defined bookmarks. While this is simple enough, it isn't the most user-friendly method. And if you have a set of predefined sites that the users go to regularly—such as the technical catalogue menu on your intranet or a shares value monitor on the Net as a whole—how do you keep the lists up to date?

Microsoft's Internet Explorer is actually an object, and the program `IExplore.exe` that we run to start it is just a shell. We can create our own instances of the `InternetExplorer` object in code in Visual Basic, or most other languages. By embedding the browser within another application like this we have the ability to create a lightweight shell, and maintain dynamic content within that shell.

This has many advantages. For example, it can give us a standard corporate interface with pop-up forms, and extra features. The regularly used sites can be catalogued and controlled by the application, even allowing the server administrator to shift all of the users from one site to another, without the clients even realizing that it is happening. Selecting certain sites could be entirely automatic, and the server can control the whole process. Of course, all these techniques are really intranet-bound, where you can specify the client software directly.

Using the InternetExplorer.Application Object

Creating and controlling the browser in code is easy, and can be done from any application that supports Visual Basic for Applications, or most other programming languages. Here's an example that uses VBA:

```
Set TheBrowser = CreateObject("InternetExplorer,Application")
TheBrowser.Visible = True
```

Once we've got the browser instance, and made it visible, we just use its methods and properties like any other object. Appendix F contains a list of the common ones, but here are a few examples:

```
TheBrowser.Navigate URL:= "http://www.wrox.com
TheBrowser.Top = 100                  'set the browser in the top
TheBrowser.Left = 100                 'left of the user's screen
TheBrowser.StatusBar = True           'display the status bar
TheBrowser.GoSearch                   'open the default Search page
TheBrowser.GoHome                     'open the default Home page
TheBrowser.Refresh                    'refresh the current page
TheBrowser.Quit                       'close the browser
```

Running an Application within the Browser

The browser will quite happily download and display different kinds of documents, as well as the usual defaults of `.htm` pages, `.txt` files, and `.jpg` or `.gif` images. However, Internet Explorer will also handle standard office documents, like Word `.doc` files and Excel `.xls` spreadsheets. It hosts a copy of the office application within its own window, and displays it just like the original application would.

Here, we've used Word 97 to create a document, and saved it in Word's standard `.doc` format. The template contains custom macros that manipulate the Office Assistant character, and produce a user guide.

> *You can learn about programming Office Assistant, and other technologies that can be used to guide users - such as HTML Help and Microsoft Agent - from the book 'Instant HTML Help Programming' by Wrox Press*

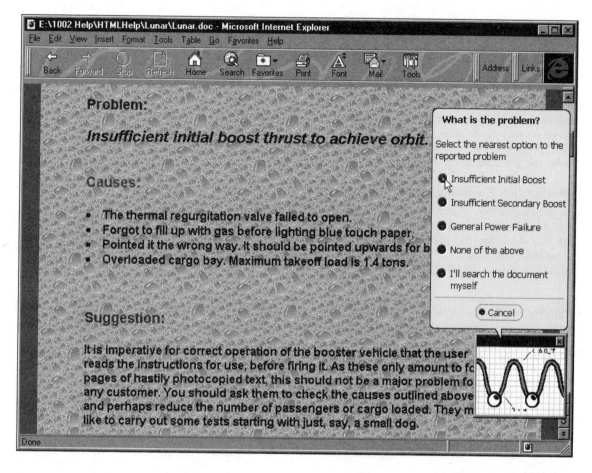

This is really only useful in an intranet environment, because of the size of the documents. And the user can't normally edit the original, only the copy that is downloaded to their own browser. However, by maintaining local copies of templates, and loading files directly over the network (using the syntax `HREF="file://C:\Documents\Lunar.doc"`, for example) we can achieve a great deal this way.

Client-side Scripting and Components

Before Active Server Pages came along, there were web browsers that could interpret script code embedded in the HTML, and host Java or ActiveX components. ASP is a very powerful environment that enables quick and easy creation of a huge variety of web pages. However, there are times when the fact that ASP can only execute script and use objects on the web server creates limitations, such as we've discovered with client-server applications. Quite often, these limitations can be overcome by using client-side code and a range of special objects, in tandem with pages generated by ASP.

Why use Client-side Features?

In the next two chapters, we'll be covering the ways that we can program the client in detail. As just a simple example of the power this provides, think back to the task of performing validation of data entered on a form like our earlier logon code. If the user is supposed to supply a six character user name, and they enter only four characters, verification is bound to fail–but it still involves a trip across the network to the web server and back again, just to inform them that they didn't enter enough characters. Client-side code can do this validation, and inform the user of their mistake, before the form is actually submitted to the server.

But we know that it's generally much easier to perform complicated computations and tasks on the server and send back a completed page consisting solely of HTML, than it is to send a page and attempt to perform many of the same tasks via HTTP (especially with today's technology). And since we know the kind of browser our page will be viewed on, we can modify our page so that it suits that browser well. So there are two sides to the argument.

Sharing the Processing Load

To decide how you split the processing in your applications, keep in mind the different layers of the client-server model, and the arguments for and against client-side programming in your particular environment. We saw earlier that the business rules should exist on the client-side where possible, and the length of an acceptable user name is a valid business rule. However, as we've seen earlier, actually processing the user name is a server-side job–to maintain security, concurrency and efficiency.

There are also the concerns of browser compatibility. However, next-generation browsers like Internet Explorer and Netscape Navigator have capabilities that are reasonably standardized, and make client-side interactivity a reality. For example:

- We may need to display data in a format more robust and interactive than allowed by HTML? Just add an object to your page and let it do the work.

- We may need to provide immediate feedback to someone entering text on a form without requiring that they send another request to your server? Use client-side code to validate their input.

- We may want to show some snazzy animation or graphics, but don't know how to do it in HTML? Insert a Java applet or ActiveX control and control it with code in the web page.

The MSN Investor page at `http://investor.msn.com` shows an excellent example of how client- and server-side code can be combined to produce a really interactive web page. It uses an ActiveX control to track your portfolio and provide current information on stocks.

New Things to Learn Client-side

Based on all we've seen up to now, you might be wondering exactly how we can accomplish these wonderful new tricks. How does the browser know what to execute as script code? How exactly does the script code interact with the browser, and with objects on the page? How do objects get from the server to the client in the first place? These are the subjects we'll be talking about for much of the next chapter, and we'll be putting the techniques to use with ASP in the rest of this book.

Fortunately, there are a lot of similarities between client-side and server-side scripting, and experience working with Active Server Pages code makes it easy to pick up the new topics that we'll be introducing. In many cases, the script language you're using with ASP at the moment can be used inside a browser. And because you're used to using objects with ASP, you won't have to learn a completely new way to use objects within HTML.

The Undefined Programming Platform

The major change is the platform or computer system our code will be running on. If we're using ASP, we know a lot about our system: it has certain software packages (like database management systems) installed, it's running a Microsoft operating system, and so on. In other words, it's a relatively constant environment that we have some measure of control over. The client system is a completely different ballgame.

People viewing our pages may be doing so from a variety of operating systems, with many different browsers, and with different software installed. If you've used the Browser Capabilities component we introduced in Chapter 3, you've had some experience with the differences in browsers. Some support Java applets, others support Java applets and ActiveX controls, and others support no objects at all.

The same thing occurs for scripting languages: the browser may be able to interpret VBScript and/or JavaScript, or it might not even know what a script is. In fact, it's possible that our pages may be accessed by browsers that understand different dialects of these languages. For example, the version of JavaScript in Navigator 3.0 differs from both the versions in Internet Explorer and Navigator 2.0. With ASP, we've been using VBScript version 2.0, but many of our Internet Explorer users may only have version 1.0. While the difference between these languages is often minor, it illustrates how different browsers can be, and how this must be a consideration when we design pages with client-side functionality.

In fact, it's a bit like writing a program in Fortran and then giving it to someone else, who may know nothing about programming, to compile. And just for fun, not telling them what language it actually is, but letting them see what happens with the compiler they use for all their other daily jobs.

The Undefined Software Platform

Another important difference in platforms is the software that is installed or available on each system. We know that we can always use the Browser Capabilities component when writing ASP code, because we know that it's installed on our server. When we use objects in our HTML pages, we don't have any sort of assurance that this is the case. Just because I have a cool ActiveX control on my machine doesn't mean that you do too. We need to make sure that the code gets sent to the client machine so that it can be executed.

Both browsers that support objects, Navigator and Internet Explorer, have mechanisms to make sure that this happens, and we'll cover this in Chapter 8. Of course, if you're developing for the corporate intranet, you can control your whole environment. Selecting the correct browser software solves the problem as far as both the scripting language and object support are concerned. And you can also more closely control what software is installed on each client.

> *If you're an old client-side scripting master—as if those really exist in a field as new as this one—you might want to skip ahead to the 'examples' section of Chapter 8. These hands-on examples show the code you'd need to write to perform some common tasks that aren't possible with ASP alone, as well as showing you how you can use ASP to enhance previous client-side only web pages.*

Choosing Your Applets and Controls

Before we embark on our client-side excursion, we'll finish up this chapter with a look at some of the object terminology you'll be seeing throughout the rest of the book. This will also help you to understand some of the pressures that web developers are under when designing applications that use client-side objects. Again, on the corporate intranet, you can control your environment and make more free choices about the technologies you decide to run with.

The two most common external objects used in client-side programming today are Java Applets and ActiveX Controls. Both of these technologies provide the same end-result: a portion of the page dedicated to whatever visual representation the object provides for itself, and a portion of the browser's processing time for whatever computations the object needs to execute. Objects can range from a simple button to a complete word-processor or spreadsheet in a window.

Looking at Java Applets

Web browsers first supported applets. Created with the Java programming language (similar to C++), these small lumps of code run on any system that can interpret the 'bytecodes' that a Java compiler produces. Because Java-enabled web browsers run on Windows, Macintosh, and Unix operating systems, Java applets can be viewed on any of these platforms. Although some vendors are developing full-blown applications with Java, the primary use of the language today is in creating applets that only run inside web pages.

Currently Java applets don't have any standard way to communicate between each other, though Sun has proposed a standard called **Java Beans** that achieves this. Microsoft already supports applet interaction through the same component object model (COM) that it uses for communication between ActiveX controls and other OLE/COM components. Java applets in today's web browsers run inside of a 'sandbox', which limits their functionality to operations that can't hurt the computer they're running on. Both Netscape Navigator and Internet Explorer support Java applets, although their methods of connecting script code to applets differ greatly.

Looking at ActiveX Controls

Browsers that can host ActiveX controls provide an alternative way to add objects to a web page. ActiveX controls are components that can plug into any ActiveX control host. Controls have been around for a long time and there are literally thousands of pre-written ones implementing every function under the sun available for purchase or download. In addition to Internet Explorer and the next version of Navigator, a wide range of other applications, including Visual Basic, all Office 97 applications, Visual C++, and Visual J++ can also use these ActiveX controls.

While Java applets are *platform* independent, ActiveX controls are *language* independent–they can be created with a wide variety of languages, including C, C++, Java, and Visual Basic. Microsoft has announced their intention to support ActiveX controls on other platforms. Currently, controls only run on Windows operating systems, though COM has been ported to both the Mac OS and Solaris, and we'll soon be able to create controls for use on these operating systems.

ActiveX controls in a web page have full access to the computer and can control all of its parts. This is useful because it doesn't limit developers in what they can do with a control although, without proper safety measures, a malicious control could possibly harm the computer it's running on. Controls achieve safety through a method known as **code signing**. We'll cover this topic in more detail in the following chapters, when we talk about security and code download.

So what does all this mean for us? If we're creating a page with an object that needs to be viewable on many platforms, Java is the way to go. If we're developing with Windows and our clients are going to be running a Windows operating system, we might want to use an ActiveX control (or group of controls) instead. This way we can take advantage of the huge base of previously written controls, and the easy development of custom controls offered by Visual Basic 5.0.

Summary

In this chapter, we've wandered across a lot of topics concerned with client-server applications, their design, and implementation. We've also talked about using the processing capabilities of modern browsers to spread the processing load, and minimize the network bandwidth our applications require.

In this part of the book, you're going to be seeing a lot more on these and other related topics. Our aim is to change your way of thinking from being *server*-centric to *application*-centric. After all, if you look at all the best sites out there on the Web at the moment, it soon becomes obvious that they are very cleverly designed and constructed client-server applications. And for the internal office network, as you develop your own intranet, this is the kind of technique that will offer you the fastest payback, and the optimum efficiency.

The main points of this chapter are:

▲   Developing applications with Active Server Pages is a very different task to the traditional static web sites we are used to seeing. We need to understand how **client-server theory and practice** are applied to our design and development efforts.

▲   By using **client-side programming techniques**, we can spread the processing load between the client and the server. We aim to place the **data capture** and **business rules** layers of the traditional client-server application model on the client wherever possible.

▲   To make client-server programming work on the Web, using HTTP, we take advantage of the **Application** and **Session** objects provided by ASP to preserve **state**. Unlike a traditional LAN-based application, this is the only way we can provide consistency over the network.

▲   Once we can maintain state in our application, we have ways of linking each phase of our application's environment to the appropriate client. The whole process is no longer **anonymous** like a traditional web site.

▲   We need to understand the importance of **good application design** before we can create professional and efficient client-server applications. To help us in our development goals we can take advantage of the many prewritten **components** available, or even create our own as required.

So now, we're ready to look in more detail at the specifics of creating client-server applications. The next two chapters are dedicated to learning how we implement and integrate client-side processing with our server-based Active Server Pages.

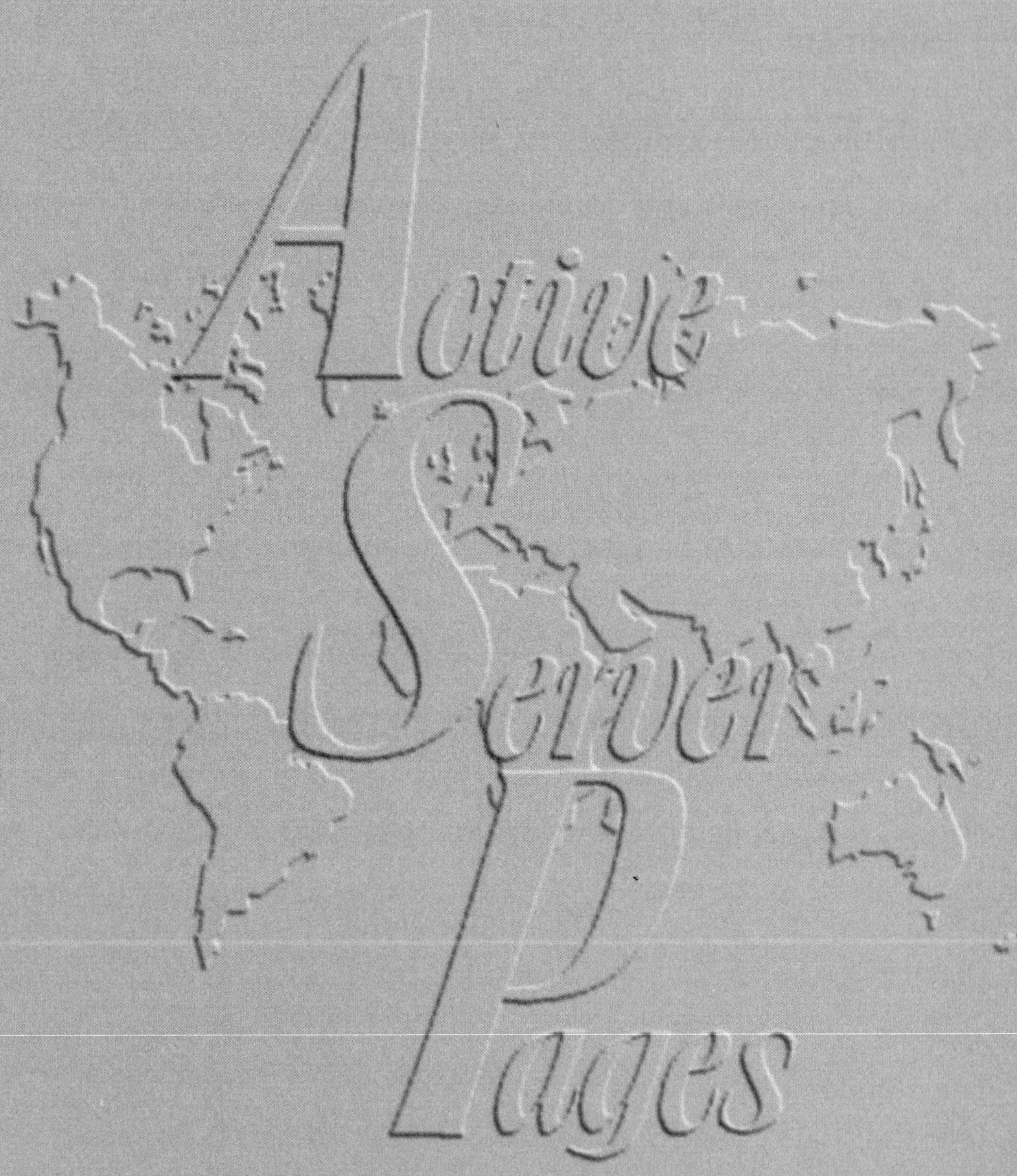
Active
Server
Pages

Client/Server - Programming the Client

In the previous chapter, we looked at how to go about building client/server applications using Active Server Pages. We discovered that, in order to achieve the kind of flexibility and efficiency we want, we have to look at how we can spread the processing load between the client and the server. To do this, we have to understand two main topics: how we can program the browser (the client), and how we can link the processing to that going on in ASP on the server.

These two topics are the subject of this chapter and the next. We won't be providing detailed coverage of every possible client-side topic, since this isn't a book on programming Internet Explorer or Netscape Navigator. However, we want to introduce the concepts and tools, so we can determine when a particular task might be better accomplished with some addition of client-side functionality. To make this decision we need to know what technologies are available on the client, and how they're used.

This chapter shows how code can be added to an HTML page, and how the browser object model is used. The next chapter talks about using objects on the client, and shows some real-world examples of how combining these techniques with Active Server Pages can be helpful.

So, specifically, in this chapter, we'll cover:

- ▲ The mechanics of writing scripting code on the client browser.
- ▲ How to connect the script to the browser's objects and events.
- ▲ The browser object model, and how we use it in our programs.

So let's get right on and look at how script code fits in on client-side.

Scripting on the Client

So how exactly do we write code that runs on the client and uses objects? We'll start by looking at the HTML page itself and we'll examine where the code goes and how it's connected to objects, both to respond to events and to manipulate the objects themselves. After this we'll cover the details of the browser including the sorts of objects that are available for use in our scripts. Later we'll talk briefly about the capabilities of the two browsers we're most likely be targeting while writing client-side code: Netscape Navigator and Internet Explorer.

While we'll some examples are in JavaScript, we'll tend to stick to VBScript as our primary scripting language, as it is our first choice language in the rest of the book. However nearly everything should remain applicable to both languages–it's just a matter of making the translation between one syntax and the other. Netscape Navigator supports the same scripting object model that is used by Internet Explorer. In fact, Netscape invented this object model with Navigator 2.0–the first browser to support client-side scripting.

Scripting and HTML

If you're a developer, you've probably seen plenty of "Hello World" examples in your lifetime, but we're going to ask that you put up with just one more. It sets the stage well for the rest of this chapter. If you haven't, then consider this just one more privilege of learning how to program for the client-side of the Web.

Our "Hello, World" sample is going to be simple. The code we'll write displays a page with some text and a button. Clicking on the button displays a plain message box with the text Hello, World in it. As it turns out, there a number of different ways that we can do this, and we'll cover them all in this section by writing different code that performs the same end function.

If you have access to your computer, fire up a copy of NotePad (or whichever HTML editor you prefer) and enter the following text:

```
<HTML>
<HEAD>
<TITLE> Hello Client-Side World </TITLE>
</HEAD>

<BODY>
<CENTER>
<H1> Our First Client-Side Code </H1>

<INPUT TYPE="BUTTON" NAME="btnHello" VALUE="Say Hello">

<SCRIPT LANGUAGE="VBScript">
Sub btnHello_onClick
  Alert "Hello World!"
End Sub
</SCRIPT>

</CENTER>
</BODY>
</HTML>
```

Save the file as something descriptive, like **Hello World.htm**, and start up a copy of Internet Explorer. Load up the page we just saved, and click the Say Hello button. If you've entered everything OK, you'll see a message box proclaiming to everyone that you've entered the client-side world:

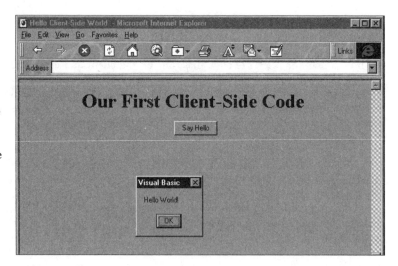

Connecting Code to the Page

So how does this work? Outside of the `<SCRIPT>` and `</SCRIPT>` tags (and the code between them), everything on this page probably looks familiar, because it's just a standard Web page. Our HTML code is specifying a page with a title, a heading, and one button. The button is created with a single line of HTML code:

```
<INPUT TYPE="BUTTON" NAME="btnHello" VALUE="Say Hello">
```

If we're using a button simply to submit a form, there isn't any point in giving it a name. However, when using a button with server-side *or* client-side scripting, we need a way to refer to the button, so we give it a name – `btnHello`. Using prefixes like `btn` (signifying a normal button) with our form elements and objects makes it easy to determine what element we're talking about when writing code. There's a list of the common prefixes in Appendix B.

But what about the `<SCRIPT>` block? Let's go over the different parts of this HTML.

```
<SCRIPT LANGUAGE="VBScript">
```

All browsers that support scripting in HTML recognize the `<SCRIPT>` tag. This tag tells the browser that all the text between itself and the closing `</SCRIPT>` tag is code that should be interpreted and executed. The optional **LANGUAGE** attribute can be used to specify a scripting language. Internet Explorer supports both VBScript and JScript (Microsoft's implementation of JavaScript) while Navigator currently only natively supports JavaScript. Both browsers by default treat the code inside a `<SCRIPT>` tag without a **LANGUAGE** attribute as JavaScript.

The next three lines might look familiar – they're very similar to a subroutine we'd write on the server in ASP code, with two exceptions. Let's consider these differences in detail.

```
Sub btnHello_onClick
   Alert "Hello World!"
End Sub
```

Triggering an Event

The first difference is in the declaration itself. Instead of a name we choose ourselves, we have the name of the button, an underscore, and the word `onClick`. This is an **event declaration**. Like most objects, the button has properties and methods, but it also has a third feature associated with it, namely **events**. Methods and properties are a way for the programmer to look at the object's state, or tell it to do something. Events, in contrast, are a way for the object to tell the programmer that something has happened to it.

When an event occurs, the programmer has the option to do something about it. Different objects have different events, depending on what the object does. Buttons have an event named `onClick` that is fired when the button is clicked. As we'll see later, other objects may not have an `onClick` event, but they will most likely have other events that signify different things have occurred.

In our code, the first part of the event handler, `btnHello`, is just the name of the object that the event is coming from, and the `onClick` part is the name of the event we're handling.

Displaying Message Boxes

The only remaining part of this subroutine is the line:

```
Alert "Hello World!"
```

We haven't seen this while writing ASP code for sure. It pops up a message box that suspends processing–not something we'd want to happen on a server! The code here just displays a message box on the screen with the text Hello World!. The **Alert** keyword is actually a method of the **Window** object, but we'll look at that a little bit later.

This example is simple, but it illustrates the principles of client-side scripting. Any code to be executed by the browser needs to be placed inside both the **<SCRIPT>** tag, and generally include an appropriate event handler that will executed.

However, there is a way to cause code outside of an event handler to be executed as the page is interpreted, although this isn't used as commonly as the event handler syntax. This is by cobbling together a pale imitation what ASP can do on the server. We'll talk about this technique briefly later in the chapter.

Other Ways to Connect up our Code

The previous example required us to name our event handlers rigidly–in the form **ObjectName_EventName**. There are a few other ways to connect code to an event, and we'll explore them here.

Specifying Scripts as HTML Attributes

First off, we can specify the routine that should be called, when we write the HTML that creates the object. If you still have the above example open in NotePad, replace the **<INPUT>** and **<SCRIPT>** lines with the code below:

```
...
<BODY>
<CENTER>
<H1> Our First Client-Side Code </H1>
```

```
<INPUT TYPE="BUTTON" NAME="btnHello" VALUE="Say Hello" ONCLICK="Pressed"
LANGUAGE="VBScript">

<SCRIPT LANGUAGE="VBScript">
  Sub Pressed
   Alert "Hello World!"
  End Sub
</SCRIPT>
```

```
</CENTER>
</BODY>
</HTML>
```

Reload the page, and press the button and you get the same result. Even though we've changed the code a bit, we're still seeing the message box displayed by our subroutine. The code is different, but not by much. All we've done is change the name of the subroutine in the **<SCRIPT>** block, and add the **ONCLICK** and **LANGUAGE** attributes to the **<INPUT>** tag:

```
<INPUT TYPE="BUTTON" NAME="btnHello" VALUE="Say Hello" ONCLICK="Pressed"
LANGUAGE="VBScript">
```

When the browser sees this, it knows to look for and run the code in the routine called **Pressed** when the button is clicked. The routine can be named anything we like, because the linkage is made explicitly in the **<INPUT>** tag, not implicitly by the name of the routine. The **<INPUT>**, **<A>** (anchor), **<FORM>**, and **<BODY>** tags all support this syntax, but with different events. Keep in mind that this method only works for these specific tags, and not for other objects.

This is fine until we start inserting our own objects that we want to script. For that we'll need an alternative method to hook up script code for all objects. But first we'll look at how JavaScript can be used interchangeably with VBScript.

Using JavaScript Code

Code can be hooked up with events in both VBScript and JavaScript, but JavaScript doesn't support the syntax we showed you. To see it in action, you'll need to replace the code we've been using so far with this JavaScript code:

```
...
<FORM>
<INPUT TYPE="BUTTON" NAME="btnHello" VALUE="Say Hello" ONCLICK="Pressed()"
LANGUAGE="JavaScript">
</FORM>

<SCRIPT LANGUAGE="Javascript">
  function Pressed()
  {
   alert("Hello World");
  }
</SCRIPT>
...
```

The only real differences here are the addition of parentheses to the function name in the **<INPUT>** tag and the actual change from VBScript to JavaScript code in the **<SCRIPT>** block. Notice, though, that we need to use **Pressed()**, instead of just **Pressed**, in the **<INPUT>** tag's **ONCLICK** argument, because JavaScript uses only functions and not subroutines.

Other Ways to Specify Scripts in HTML Attributes

As mentioned previously, the method of adding an attribute to the HTML tag to specify the name of the routine to execute only works for certain HTML elements. Once we go beyond the integral parts of HTML to use objects in our pages, we'll need a more robust way to connect code with these objects. The **ObjectName_EventName** method we used in our first example will work correctly, or we can use the following alternative.

This method creates separate script blocks for each event we'll handle, naming the event and the object in the opening **<SCRIPT>** tag. Here's the code:

```
...
<BODY>
<CENTER>
<H1> Our First Client-Side Code </H1>
```

```
<INPUT TYPE="BUTTON" NAME="btnHello" VALUE="Say Hello">

<SCRIPT FOR="btnHello" EVENT="onClick" LANGUAGE="VBScript">
   Alert "Hello World!"
</SCRIPT>
```

```
</CENTER>
</BODY>
</HTML>
```

The above code says to the browser: when the object called **btnHello** (**FOR="btnHello"**) fires an event called **onClick** (**EVENT="onClick"**), then execute the following code using the VBScript interpreter (**LANGUAGE="VBScript"**).

Using this method we do away completely with a separate named subroutine or function, and instead we keep the code in a script block of its own. In effect, the **<SCRIPT>** tag together with the **FOR** and **EVENT** attributes is our subroutine declaration, because this is what tells the browser when to fire the code inside the **<SCRIPT>** block. This style will work with events from any form element, or from any arbitrary object that we might insert using the methods we'll talk about in the next chapter.

There is an even more compact method, though it's generally only suitable for simple, one line routines like our "Hello World" example. This is called **inline scripting**. We just put the actual code we want to execute in the **<INPUT>** tag, as the **ONCLICK** argument:

```
...
<BODY>
<CENTER>
<H1> Our First Client-Side Code </H1>
```

```
<INPUT TYPE="BUTTON" VALUE="Say Hello" LANGUAGE="VBScript" ONCLICK="Alert 'Hello
World!'">
```

```
</CENTER>
</BODY>
</HTML>
```

Reading Properties and Executing Methods

In the last few pages, we've concentrated on the different methods that we can use to connect code with events fired by objects on a page. However we've deliberately kept it simple. The only code we've been executing is a simple routine that displays a message box on the screen. If that's all you ever want to do, then you can get by with skipping the rest of this chapter. If, however, like the rest of us, you need to do more ambitious things with your code, then you'll be interested in this next section. Here we'll look at how to code the methods of different objects, and how you can read and modify an object's properties.

Switch to or open up NotePad again, and enter this new code:

```
<HTML>
<HEAD>
<TITLE> Methods And Properties </TITLE>
</HEAD>
```

```
<BODY>
<CENTER>
<H1> Using Methods and Properties </H1>

<FORM NAME="frmTest">
New URL:
<INPUT TYPE="TEXT"   NAME="txtURL"><p>
<INPUT TYPE="BUTTON" NAME="btnURL" VALUE="Change URL">
</FORM>

<SCRIPT LANGUAGE="VBScript">
Sub btnURL_onClick
    Dim newURL
    newURL = Window.Document.frmTest.txtURL.Value
    Window.Alert "The current URL is " & Window.Location
    Window.Alert "The new URL will be " & newURL
    Window.Navigate newURL
End Sub
</SCRIPT>

</CENTER>
</BODY>
</HTML>
```

Next load the page into Internet Explorer:

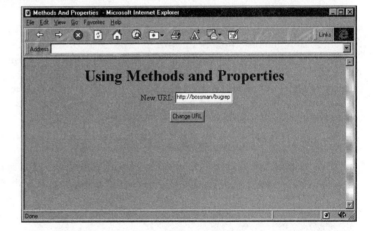

If you enter a valid URL into the text box and press the Change URL button, then you'll get a message box displaying the current URL. If you click OK to dismiss this first message box, another message box appears which displays the URL entered in the text box. After clicking OK a second time, the browser loads the page specified by the URL we entered, and displays it.

The code that does this looks a little more complicated than last time, but it's quite logical–and it shows many things we're interested in learning about. Specifically, the code on this page reads properties and calls a method, and–as a bonus–it even uses a variable to do some of its work.

How It Works

Since we've already covered how to hook up code to events, we're now free to focus just on the code inside the `<SCRIPT>` block. We'll talk about each section in turn.

```
Dim newURL
```

The `Dim newURL` line declares a variable named `newURL`, which will be valid for the duration of this subroutine execution. This line isn't absolutely necessary, because VBScript doesn't require variable declaration. However, it's always good practice and makes the code we write easier to read and understand.

It's the next line that's more interesting. The horrendously long string starting with `Window` is actually just a way to access the property we're interested in, which in this case is the value inside the text box on the form:

```
newURL = Window.Document.frmTest.txtURL.Value
```

Generally, you access properties to read or write to by using this syntax:

Assigning to a variable	`VariableName = ObjectName.PropertyName`
Setting a property	`ObjectName.PropertyName = VariableName`

In our case, we actually have to access three additional properties in succession, before we get to `Value`, the one we're interested in. `Document` is a property of the default `Window` object, `frmTest` is a property of the `Document` object (because in our HTML we created a form in the document called `frmTest`), and `txtURL` is a property of the `frmTest` object. Finally, after this long string, we get to what we want. Don't worry about understanding why exactly we needed to use `Document`, `frmTest`, or `txtURL` here, it's more important to understand how we set and retrieve properties in general. It shouldn't be too hard – it's identical to how it's done in server-side code.

Specifying the Default Window Object

In this example, we always enter the `Window` object wherever it applies. This isn't strictly necessary, because the `Window` object is the default object when we write client-side code. Look at the two lines of code below:

```
Alert "Hello World!"
Window.Alert "Hello World!"
```

Both of these lines accomplish the same thing, but the first line doesn't bother to say `Window`. This is fine, because `Window` is always assumed if it's not entered.

The next two lines call our old friend the `Alert` method, displaying a message box with the current location and then a message box with the location we're jumping to.

```
Window.Alert "The current URL is " & Window.Location
Window.Alert "The new URL will be " & newURL
```

The current location comes from the **Location** property of the **Window** object, and our new location is stored in the **newURL** variable we set earlier. We just concatenate these two values into strings with some descriptive text, and display them in their own message boxes.

Navigating to a New URL

Navigate is a method of the **Window** object. It takes a URL as a parameter, and changes the current location to that URL:

```
Window.Navigate newURL
```

This example just shows how we can call a method of an object using VBScript. It's simple: use the same **ObjectName.MethodName** syntax like we would in ASP on the server.

So we've covered how our scripts are located in HTML, how they're connected to events, and how methods and properties are accessed. We're now ready to get into the second major part of this chapter and talk about how to control the browser itself.

The Browser Object Model

As you've learned and worked with ASP, you've come to depend on the server object model documentation to answer many queries. When do we need the properties of the **Server** object? Where is that **Cookies** collection? Is it the **Response** object, the **Request** object, or both? The object model provided by ASP is how we interface with the server, and it's of utmost importance.

As you might expect, on the client-side, the **browser object model** is just as important. All of the interactions between our code and the browser take place via the object model, and without a good knowledge of how it is set up, our code either won't work as well as it could, or it won't work at all!

For the rest of this chapter, we'll be covering the different objects in the browser object model, explaining how they relate to each other, and showing you some more examples. We need to understand exactly why we have to say things like **Document.frmTest.txtURL.Value**.

An Overview of the Browser

In the ASP object model, there are five main objects: **Server**, **Response**, **Request**, **Session**, and **Application**. These top-level objects have properties, methods, and subordinate objects where appropriate. Although it's set up a bit differently, the browser object model follows the same principle of providing access to the features of the browser. Instead of five separate objects, the browser has one top level object called **Window**. The rest of the browser's objects are located beneath the **Window** object in a logical hierarchy of functionality.

The **Window** object represents the browser itself. It has a number of self-contained properties, like **status** (the current text of the status bar at the bottom of the browser) that reflect and provide access to the browser. Its methods perform operations that make sense for the browser window, like opening another window and navigating to a new page. And, last but not least, it fires events every time it finishes loading a page, or completes the unloading of a page in preparation to move to a new URL, or to shut down.

To a script programmer, the **Window** subordinate objects are just as interesting as its immediate properties, methods, and events.

▲ The **Document** object: represents the document currently displayed

▲ The **Frames** collection: represents the frames in the current window

▲ The **History** object: represents the history list of the browser

▲ The **Location** object: represents the current URL that the browser is displaying

▲ The **Navigator** object: represents information about the browser itself, like the version number

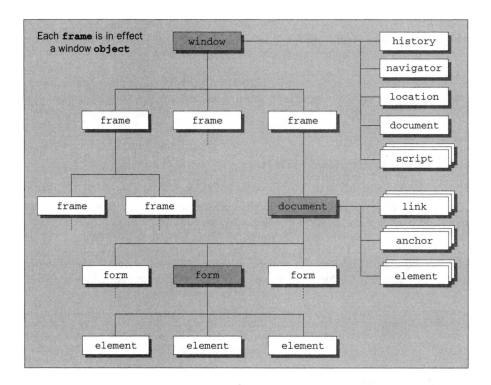

Of these objects, the **Document** object is by far the most utilized by the average script developer. It provides access to objects in the page currently displayed in the browser with the **Link**, **Anchor**, and **Form** collections. If we think back to our previous series of Hello World examples, we'll realize that we've been using the **Forms** collection of the **Document** object from the beginning of this chapter.

The rest of this section covers each of these elements in a bit more detail, focusing especially on the **Window** and **Document** objects.

> *Covering every last aspect of the scripting object model would occupy many chapters (and indeed does in many books about client-side scripting). In this chapter we'll give an overview and cover the most important elements. For more information, please check out the Wrox Press book Instant VBScript on* `http://www.wrox.com`, *and the Scripting Object Model document available from Microsoft's Web site at* `http://www.microsoft.com` *(search for* `scriptom`*).*

Since the **Window** object is the root of many useful objects in the object model, we'll start by looking at it first.

The Window Object

In the previous code in this chapter we've already used many parts of the `Window` object. The `Alert` method, the `Location` object, and the `Document` object and its descendants are all subordinate to the grand-daddy of them all, the `Window` object.

The table below shows the properties, methods, and events supported by the `Window` object. The entries in the *Properties* column that include the string (object) are objects in themselves, accessible through the `Window` object.

Properties	Methods	Events
name	alert	onLoad
parent	confirm	onUnload
opener	prompt	
self	open	
top	close	
location (object)	setTimeout	
defaultStatus	clearTimeout	
status	navigate	
frames (object)		
history (object)		
navigator (object)		
document (object)		

We'll leave the descendant objects for now, and concentrate on the rest of the `Window` object–don't worry, there's plenty to keep us occupied for a while. In the following examples, we'll explicitly use the current `Window` object for the sake of clarity. Don't forget that, since `Window` is the default object on the page, most code will work identically without a qualifying `Window` prefix (note that we **always** have to use it when declaring an event handler like `Window_onLoad`).

The onLoad and onUnload Events

We'll often want to perform some action immediately after a page is loaded, or before someone viewing our page jumps to another link. The `Window` object provides the `onLoad` and `onUnload` events to tell our code when these things happen. Fire up NotePad again and enter the following few lines of HTML and code:

```
<HTML>
<HEAD>
<TITLE> Window Events </TITLE>
</HEAD>
```

```
<BODY>
<CENTER>
<H1> Events of Window </H1>

Go to the <A HREF="file:c:\">root directory</A> of the C: drive.

<SCRIPT LANGUAGE="VBScript">
Sub Window_onLoad
  Alert "onLoad fired"
End Sub

Sub Window_onUnload
  Alert "onUnload fired"
End Sub
</SCRIPT>

</CENTER>
</BODY>
</HTML>
```

Now load this file into Internet Explorer. As soon as the page has loaded and is displayed, we hear a beep and see a message box displayed. This action is caused by the code we've connected to the **Window**'s **onLoad** event.

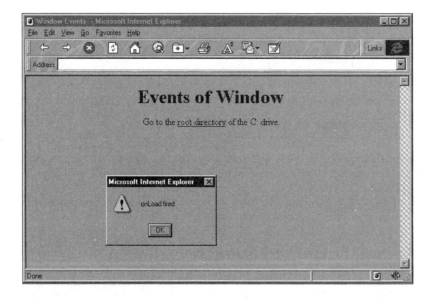

Now dismiss the message box and click on the single link on the page. Before we see the contents of the root directory of our **C:** drive, we get another message box, this time from the **onUnload** event.

Placing message boxes in the **onLoad** and **onUnload** events isn't very useful– there aren't many cases where we'd want to do this in real life. However, our example shows how simple it is to execute code when our page is loaded or unloaded.

Note that any action that causes the page to be unloaded, not just clicking to another link, will fire the **onUnload** event. If the current page has a code in an **onUnload** handler and we refresh it, or even shut down the browser, the code will be executed.

Window Object Properties

The **Window** object has a number of non-object properties, which we'll look at briefly in this section. In addition we'll take a look at the **Location** object, since it reoccurs in other parts of the object model hierarchy. We'll leave the other object properties until later in this chapter.

The Name Property

This property returns the name of the **Window** object, and is read-only. If the current **Window** object doesn't have a name, it returns an empty string.

Parent, Opener, Self and Top

These properties return references to a given **Window** object. In this sense, they aren't used directly, any more than the **Window** object itself is used directly. Instead, they're only used as references to access other properties or methods. For example, the following code will give a syntax error:

```
Alert "Window.Parent is " & Window.Parent
```

But this code will work fine, returning the **Name** of the **Parent** window:

```
Alert "Window.Parent.Name is " & Window.Parent.Name
```

If the current **Window** object has a parent (like it would if it was part of a frameset), then **Parent** returns the **Window** object of the current window's parent. If the current window doesn't have a parent, i.e. it occupies the whole browser window, **Parent** returns the current window's **Window** object.

Top is a bit like **Parent**, and they sometimes return a reference to the same object. However, there is one major difference. **Top** always returns a reference to the top-level frame in a frameset, while **Parent** only returns the **Window** object of the frame immediately above it.

Opener returns a reference to the **Window** object of the window that opened the current window, or returns nothing if the current window wasn't opened in code (i.e. by a **Window.Open** statement). Finally, **Self** just returns a reference to the current **Window** object. **Window** and **Window.Self** both return the same reference.

In a simple page without frames, these properties aren't very useful. However, as soon as we start experimenting with frames or multiple browser windows, we'll find that these properties come in handy.

Status and defaultStatus

Both **Status** and **defaultStatus** can be used to set the text displayed in the status bar at the bottom of the browser. The code is as simple as:

```
Window.Status = "Display me"
```

and

```
Window.defaultStatus = "Display me"
```

In the current implementation of the Internet Explorer object model these properties do the same thing, and are both write-only if you're using VBScript. This means we can set the text of the status bar, but we can't read what's there already, or what we've set it to.

Window Object Methods

The last major portion of the **Window** object's programmability is embodied in its methods. The methods allow us to tell the browser to do a certain job, or perform some task that it knows how to accomplish.

The Window's Dialogs

The **Window** object contains three methods that display basic dialogs. We've already seen the **Alert** dialog in our examples. It's about the simplest dialog we could experience–it just displays one text string and an OK button, but it's exactly what we need in a lot of cases.

The other two dialog methods are **Prompt** and **Confirm**. The **Confirm** method displays a message box with the string specified in the method call, but instead of providing an OK button, it displays both OK and Cancel buttons, allowing the user to choose to confirm or abort an action. The method returns **True** value if the user presses OK, or **False** if the user presses Cancel.

Prompt is another way to request user input. This method displays yet another message box, with whatever string is passed as a parameter, but this time instead of OK or Cancel buttons, it displays a text box allowing the user to enter an arbitrary string. The code below uses all three of these methods, and shows the correct calling syntax for each method:

```
<HTML>
<HEAD>
<TITLE> Window Dialogs </TITLE>
</HEAD>

<BODY>
<CENTER>
<H1> Window Dialogs </H1>

<INPUT TYPE="BUTTON" NAME="btnTest" VALUE="Click Me">

<SCRIPT LANGUAGE="VBScript">
Sub btnTest_onClick
    Dim retValue
    retValue = Confirm("Press OK or Cancel")
    Alert "Confirm returned " & retValue
    retValue = Prompt("Enter a string", "Default String")
    Alert "Confirm returned '" & retValue & "'"
End Sub
</SCRIPT>
```

```
</CENTER>
</BODY>
</HTML>
```

Pressing the single button on the page brings about a series of dialog boxes, first a **Confirm** dialog, then an **Alert** displaying the results of the previous **Confirm**. After these two dialogs, a **Prompt** dialog is displayed, and another **Alert** then shows the result. The second parameter to the **Prompt** method is the default string that will be displayed in the user entry text box.

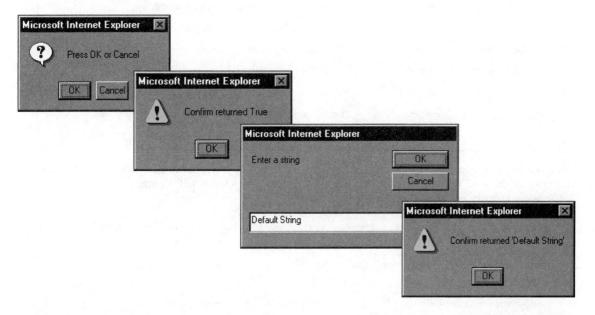

If we're using VBScript, we can get increased functionality with the **MsgBox** and **InputBox** statements and functions. Some languages, like JavaScript, don't have the built in dialog functions of VBScript, and so these functions of the **Window** object can come in handy.

The Open Method

As is fitting for the object representing the browser window itself, the **Window** object provides methods to open new browser windows, close a window, and navigate to a new location. We'll cover the **Open** method first.

Open is a simple method with many options that increase its complexity. In its simplest form, it just creates a new browser window, pointing to a given URL. For example, the following code creates a window named **myWindow**, which displays the Wrox Web page:

```
Window.Open "http://www.wrox.com", "myWindow"
```

The complexity comes from **Open**'s optional third parameter, which we're not using in this line of code. The extra parameter provides a fine level of control over the way the new window is displayed.

The following aspects of the window can be controlled by specifying values in the third parameter of our call to the **Open** method.

Parameter Text	Variable Type	Function
`toolbar`	boolean	display a toolbar
`location`	boolean	display the location text box
`directories`	boolean	display the special link buttons
`status`	boolean	display a status bar
`menubar`	boolean	display the menus at the top of the window
`scrollbars`	boolean	display scrollbars if the document is larger than the window
`resizeable`	boolean	allow the window to be resized
`width`	integer	the width of the window (in pixels)
`height`	integer	the height of the window (in pixels)
`top`	integer	the top position of the window (in pixels)
`left`	integer	the left position of the window (in pixels)

Using this list of optional parameters, we can create a huge variety of windows with different properties. The next few lines of VBScript code create some interesting new windows. Try pasting them into a page and running them to see what you get.

```
Window.Open "http://www.wrox.com/", "myWindowOne", "toolbar=no, menubar=no,
location=no, directories=no"

Window.Open "http://www.wrox.com/", "myWindowTwo", "width=100, height=100,
resizeable=no"

Window.Open "http://www.wrox.com/", "myWindowThree", "menubar=no, toolbar=yes,
location=yes"
```

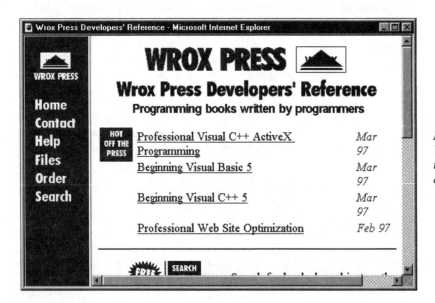

Browser created by Window.Open: with no toolbar, menubar, location or directories

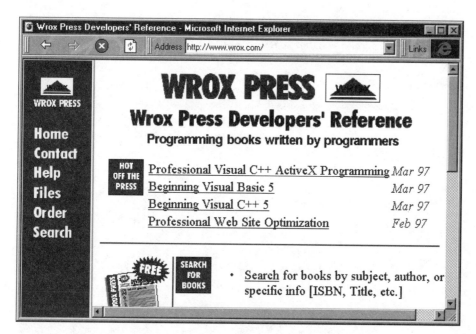

Browser created by Window.Open: has location and toolbar, but no menubar

The value of each parameter that we don't define is unpredictable, so be sure to explicitly turn on or off each feature you do or don't want to appear in your new window.

> In the `Window.Open` code we're ignoring the return value of the `Open` call. This is fine if we don't care about what happens to the window we're creating. However, if we want to manipulate it after the `Open` call, we need to save a reference to the window. Fortunately, `Open`'s return value is just this reference. We'll show you an example of this in the next section.

The Close Method

The **Close** method doesn't have the variety that the **Open** method does, but it's still powerful. For example it can end a user's session, and shut down their browser! Admittedly, in most cases, this would be rather rude—but it does have its uses. In addition to closing the current browser window, it can be used to close other windows that we've opened with a call to the **Open** method. We just need be sure to save a reference to the windows when we open them.

Enter the following code into a new file and save it:

```
<HTML>
<HEAD>
<TITLE> Window Open And Close Tester </TITLE>
</HEAD>

<BODY>
<CENTER>
<H1> Window.Open And Window.Close </H1>
```

```
<INPUT TYPE="BUTTON" NAME="btnOne" VALUE="Open One">
<INPUT TYPE="BUTTON" NAME="btnDOne" VALUE="Close One"><p>
<INPUT TYPE="BUTTON" NAME="btnCloseMe" VALUE="Close Me">

<SCRIPT LANGUAGE="VBScript">
Dim objNewWindow

Sub btnOne_onClick
  Set objNewWindow = Window.Open("http://www.wrox.com/", "myWindowOne", "toolbar=no,
menubar=no, location=no, directories=no")
End Sub

Sub btnDOne_onClick
  objNewWindow.Close
End Sub

Sub btnCloseMe_onClick
  Window.Close
End Sub
</SCRIPT>

</CENTER>
</BODY>
</HTML>
```

Next load it into your browser:

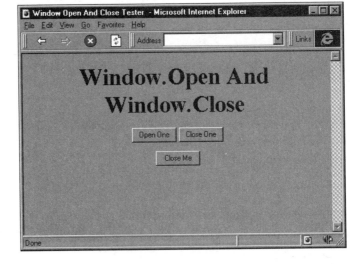

When this page loads, we see three buttons. Try clicking the Open One button. After a moment, we see a new browser window (incidentally, without a menubar, toolbar, location text box, or extra link buttons) appear on our screen. Now press the Close One button, and our new window disappears. Don't press the third Close Me button just yet! We don't want to shut down this browser until we're done experimenting with the code.

The explanation for this behavior is in a few lines of code. First, we declare a variable called `objNewWindow` to store the reference to the window we're going to create. Then our `Window.Open` method actually creates the window, returning a reference to be stored in `objNewWindow`:

```
Dim ObjNewWindow

Sub btnOne_onClick
  Set objNewWindow = Window.Open("http://www.wrox.com/", "myWindowOne", "toolbar=no,
menubar=no, location=no, directories=no")
End Sub
```

After this our code to close the window is simple, we just use the **objNewWindow** variable and the **Close** method:

```
Sub btnDOne_onClick
  objNewWindow.Close
End Sub
```

The code for the third button just shows how **Close** can be used with the **Window** object to terminate the current browser instance.

Timers: setTimeout and clearTimeout

These methods of the **Window** object can be used to execute a function after a certain amount of time. Their use is relatively simple. **SetTimeout** takes the name of a function, and a time value in milliseconds. After the time value has passed, the function is called automatically.

For example, the following code calls a routine named **TimerFunc** after **5000** milliseconds (5 seconds):

```
ID = Window.setTimeout("TimerFunc",5000)
```

Once we've started a timer with **setTimout**, we may find that we want to cancel it so that the function specified in the **setTimeout** call isn't executed. This is where the **clearTimeout** function comes into play, assuming we've saved the return value of the **setTimeout** function. In the line of code above we've saved our return value in a variable called **ID**, and it's this variable that we'll use in our call to clear the timer:

```
Window.clearTimeout ID
```

If we call **clearTimeout** with an **ID** value that doesn't exist, then nothing will happen and any timers we have active will continue to work.

> Note that the **setTimeout** call only executes the function that it is passed once. If we want to have a routine called repeatedly, we need to reset the timer with another **setTimeout** call within the function that's called by it.

The Navigate Method

The very useful **Navigate** method brings us to the end of our **Window** object odyssey, at least where the non-object properties are concerned. **Navigate** takes a string parameter and jumps to the URL in that string. We saw **Navigate** in action way back, when we were still talking about connecting code to events. The line of code below simply redirects the current browser to the URL of the Wrox Press home page:

```
Window.Navigate "http://www.wrox.com/"
```

Note that we're not limited to using `Navigate` with just the current `Window` object. We can also use it in combination with the `top`, `parent`, and `opener` properties to act on other windows or parts of the window – all `Navigate` requires is that it be called from a valid reference to a `Window` object.

The Window's Location Object

An alternative to using `Navigate` is to change the `HRef` property of the `Window` object's `Location` object. The effect is the same. The browser window always shows the page at some URL–so it makes sense to have some way to represent the various properties of this spot on the World Wide Web or on an Intranet. The `Location` object is the way we do it.

Paying attention to this object now will save us some time later– the properties of the `Location` object are reused more than once in the rest of the browser object model. You'll find that the `Document` object has its own `Location` property, *and* that all of the links on a page are represented by a set of properties that mimic the properties of `Window`'s `Location` object.

The mother of all `Location` properties is `HRef`. Out of the eight total properties that are a part of `Location`, seven are derived from the `HRef` property–and the eighth property is `HRef` itself. `HRef` returns the current URL for the page in the browser. If the page is the top level page of a frameset, it returns this top level URL.

In addition to reading the current location, we can change it simply by setting this property. For example, the following line of code redirects the browser to the Wrox Press home page. *Window*, in this instance, is optional:

```
Window.Location.href = "http://www.wrox.com"
```

The remainder of `Location`'s properties are born from the `HRef` property. To illustrate what we mean, suppose we were viewing a page with the URL:

> `http://www.wrox.com:80/asp/book.htm?abc`.

The following table shows how each of the properties would be set (a hash mark in this context is a `#` in the page's HTML):

Property	Value	Description
href	http://www.wrox.com:80/asp/book.htm?abc	complete URL
protocol	http:	URL's protocol
host	www.wrox.com:80	hostname and port number
hostname	www.wrox.com	name of host
port	80	port number (default is 80)
pathname	/asp/book.htm	path after host
search	?abc	any query string
hash	(nothing – would contain any hash specified with #)	any hash value

The Document Object

The **Document** object represents the HTML document currently displayed by the browser. Its properties reflect the characteristics of the page, and allow script code to manipulate and react to different conditions. Among the most interesting properties are the **anchors**, **links**, and **forms** collections, which represent all of the anchors, links, and forms respectively, on the page. The **Document** object also supports some methods that can be used to change the HTML displayed by the browser. These methods duplicate much of the functionality that ASP provides, but differ in that the HTML manipulation is done after the document is transmitted from the server instead of before. When these methods are used, the server sends an HTML document with embedded script code, and the browser interprets it and displays the resulting HTML. The **Document** object has no events.

This section covers the **Document** object and it's descendants, with one exception. One of the most used parts of the **Document** object is the **Elements** collection of the **Document's Form** object. This part of the object model is used when interacting with the elements of an HTML form, like buttons, text boxes, radio buttons, and so on, and is important enough to warrant its own section. We'll cover the **Elements** collection and the **Element** object as soon as we're through with the **Document** object. Finally, when we cover the **anchors**, **links**, and **forms** collections, we'll also talk about the objects that make up these collections: **Anchor**, **Link**, and **Form**.

So, without further ado, lets get right into it by talking about the methods that are part of the **Document** object.

Methods of the Document Object

Like we've said before, the methods of the **Document** object are all concerned with modifying the HTML of the document. As usual, a quick example is often the easiest way to explain what we mean. Fire up NotePad once again, and enter the following code:

```
<HTML>
<HEAD>
<TITLE> Document Methods </TITLE>
</HEAD>

<BODY>
<H1> Document Object Methods </H1>

<SCRIPT LANGUAGE="VBScript">
Document.Write "The current time is " & Now & "."
</SCRIPT>

</BODY>
</HTML>
```

Load up the page and look at the results. It's displaying the current date and time—even though we didn't enter it in our HTML or have the file processed on the server before it was sent to the client. The language interpreter on the client machine is still interpreting our code—it's just generating HTML instead of responding to an event and doing things like popping up message boxes or navigating to a new page. If we view the source for this page we'll still see our script code and not the results, unlike if the script was executing on the server where it would just send us HTML.

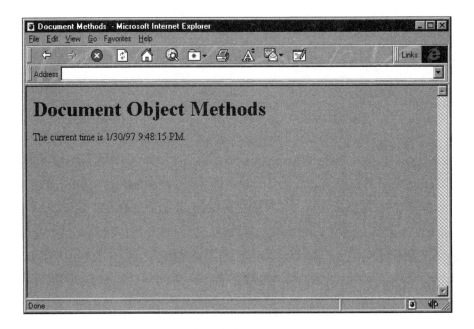

All of the **Document** object's methods work this way – they modify the HTML as they're interpreted. If you're curious you could try a little experiment to show that ASP code is indeed executed earlier than client-side code. Add a few lines of ASP code to the example above to read the current time on the server and output it to the page. When the browser finally finishes rendering the page, you'll see two time values that differ by a second or two—even if the browser and server are running on the same machine.

The Write and WriteLn Methods

Lets take a look at the **Write** method in a little more detail. This method simply takes a string, and outputs it as part of the HTML stream. Because the text is actually interpreted by a script engine, it can include variable references and function calls, in addition to plain text. The interpreter executes all of the calls and resolves all variables, before sending a final string to the browser.

Since the string is going to the browser, it can (and should) include whatever HTML markup tags are needed. For example, the following **Document.Write** line displays the current date and time in the **Header 1** font of the current browser:

```
Document.Write "<H1>" & Now & "</H1>"
```

Calls to the **Document.Write** method can be interspersed with standard HTML, just as calls to the **Response.Write** method can be intertwined with HTML on the server.

WriteLn is nearly identical to **Write**, with one difference that may be important to us depending exactly upon the point at which we need to use the **Write** methods. **WriteLn** writes a string to the document just like **Write**, however it appends a new-line character to the end of each string. Since the HTML specification ignores white space and new-line characters when interpreting standard text, the browser output may look the same, independent of which **Write** method is used. The only place we'll see a difference is when the output we're writing is inside a formatting tag that pays attention to line-feeds. For example, when **WriteLn** is used inside of a **<PRE>...</PRE>** block, separate **WriteLn** statements will result in text that is displayed on separate lines.

One last question you might have regards what happens if **Write** or **WriteLn** are used after a page is already loaded—as part of an event handler, for example. We're going to postpone the answer to this question until we've covered the **Document's** **Open**, **Close**, and **Clear** methods in the next section. You'll see why afterwards.

The Open, Close and Clear Methods

As we've seen in the example above, it's possible to use the **Write** or **WriteLn** methods by themselves. Sandwiching our calls to **Write** and **WriteLn** between a call to the **Document** object's **Open** and **Close** methods gives us more control over when the strings are outputted to the page. In effect, using these methods is like using the buffering ability ASP provides with the **Response** object.

> *Although the documentation claims that calling* **Open** *after the output stream already has data will clear the output stream, we haven't been able to see this behavior with* Internet Explorer 3.01. *Our recommendation is to experiment with these methods on the latest version of your browser, and determine how close your browser, and the browsers your customers may have, come to the original specifications. This omission on the part of the browser isn't catastrophic—in many cases this functionality isn't necessary. Perfect software is great, but certainly not a reality in an imperfect world.*

Non-Object Document Properties

Besides the object-based properties, i.e. the **Location** object and the **Anchor**, **Link**, and **Form** collections (which will be covered in a moment), the **Document** object has a number of other properties that we might find useful in our client-side programming. We'll briefly outline these properties next.

The Color Properties

As is fitting for an object that represents the current HTML page, there are a number of **Document** object properties that represent the color scheme of the current page. All of these properties return a seven character string when queried, in this form: **#RRGGBB**, where the **R**, **G**, and **B** values represent the current color setting for red, green, and blue, in hexadecimal.

Property	Description
linkColor	Color of non-visited links in the current document
vLinkColor	Color of visited links in the current document
aLinkColor	Color of active (clicked on but not visited) links.
fgColor	The current foreground color
bgColor	The current background color

You can also set the colors in script within the page, by assigning a new value to the properties.

The Title Property

The `Title` property simply returns the current title of the document. The value of this property is whatever the HTML author placed between the `<TITLE>` and `</TITLE>` tags. This property is set to read-only after the page has loaded.

The Cookie Property

`Cookie` is a very useful read and write property, and can be used in conjunction with ASP's `Response.Cookies` collection. This property returns or sets the cookie associated with the current page. Reading the `Document.Cookie` property returns the keys and values of the current page's cookie, but doesn't give other information. While this information isn't returned when querying the property, we can set such things as expiration date and path when setting a cookie using client-side code.

To read the cookie into a variable named `MyVar`, we use the following code:

```
MyVar = Document.Cookie
```

After reading the value we can use the string-manipulation capabilities of our scripting language to find the part of the cookie we're interested in.

To set the value of a key named `MyKey` to `MyValue`, we use this code. If `MyKey` already exists, its value will be replaced with the contents of `MyValue`:

```
Document.Cookie = "MyKey=MyValue"
```

Finally, if we'd like to set the path or other properties, like the expiration date, we just append them to the end of the key/value string, like this:

```
Document.Cookie = "MyKey=MyValue;expires=Monday, 01-Jan-98 12:00:00 GMT"
```

Cookies can also be used solely on the client-side to exchange information between pages. On the server we're used to using the `Session` object to remember information from page to page, and script to script. There isn't a handy object like this on the client, but simply by setting the cookie property of the document with a key/value pair that holds our variable name and its value, we can remember the contents of variables across pages. This method doesn't work with object references, only with text and numerical values, but it can still be very useful. Microsoft's VBScript site has a sample that shows the code needed to add this functionality to our pages.

The LastModified Property

This read-only property returns the date that the current document was last modified. Note that this property is only up to date as far as the most recently retrieved copy of the document–which may be older than the last modified version if our browser caches any pages (as most do).

The Referrer Property

On paper, the `Referrer` property returns the URL of the document that contained the link to the current page. In the real world, this is less than true. Internet Explorer 3.0's `Referrer` property always returns the URL of the current page.

The Subordinate Objects of the Document Object

OK, we've covered a lot of **Document**'s functionality in the last few pages, but we're not finished yet. We still have some of the most useful things to talk about. Not surprisingly, these are actually objects in themselves. We'll be talking about the **Anchor**, **Link**, and **Form** objects (as well as their respective collections) and the **Location** object (which, all by its lonesome self, doesn't have a collection). All of these objects are generated when the page is parsed, and they reflect the properties of the page currently in the browser.

Like we've said, three of the four objects we'll be talking about here are actually stored in **collections**. Objects inside collections can't be referenced in code without the collection being named first in some manner. After covering the objects themselves, we'll talk about some special cases that can arise when programming with collections. You've already had experience with many ASP collections, like **Request.Cookies**, and **Request.Form**, and you can rest assured that using collections on the client is nearly identical—only the names of the collections, the objects, and their properties and methods, are different.

The Link Object

The **Link** object represents something you're very familiar with if you've ever browsed the web—a hypertext link on a page. The **Links** collection is made up of **Link** objects, one for each anchor tag containing an **HREF** attribute (**<A HREF="..."**>) on the page. We can't change the links on the current page when browsing and so, not surprisingly, all the elements of this collection and their properties are read-only. The link object has nine properties and two events, but no methods.

Link Object Properties

Guess what? The properties of the **Link** object (with one addition) are identical to the properties of the **Location** object we covered earlier. We won't repeat them here, but if you need to you can refresh your memory a few pages back.

In addition to the eight properties that it shares with **Location**, a **Link** object also possesses an additional property called **Target**. This property is blank unless the link has a **TARGET** attribute used to refer to a new browser window or frame. For example, the **Target** property of the following URL is **MainFrame**:

```
<A HREF="http://www.mysite.com" TARGET="MainFrame">
```

Link Object Events

Viewers of our page can do things to links: they can click them or move their mouse over them. The events supported by **Link** allow us to respond appropriately to these actions.

The **Link** object has an **onMouseOver** event that is fired when the user moves the mouse over a link. We can do some cool tricks with links by hooking up code to this event. Since links really don't have a **name** per se, it's easiest to specify the desired behavior in the anchor tag itself:

```
...
<A HREF="http://bossman" onMouseOver="MyFunc">Bossman<A>
...
...
<SCRIPT LANGUAGE="VBScript">
```

```
Sub MyFunc
  Alert "Moved"
End Sub
</SCRIPT>
...
```

In this example, the combination of the anchor tag's **onMouseOver** attribute and the **MyFunc** subroutine causes an alert message box to be displayed whenever the mouse is moved over the link. Use this for demonstration purposes only. Doing something exactly like this could be annoying to the viewer of our page– they'll have a hard time clicking on the link if they're always trying to dismiss a message box first!

Link objects also have an **onClick** event that works the same as the **onMouseOver** event, except that it is only fired when the link is actually clicked on. To hook up code to this event we just add an **onClick** attribute to the HTML for our link, like this:

```
<A HREF="http://bossman" onClick="MyFunc">Bossman</A>
```

If we're not going to do much in the function, we might find it easier to just include our code within the anchor tag, as in-line script. We outlined how to do this in the 'hooking up the code' section at the beginning of this chapter.

The Anchor Object

The **Anchor** object is one of the simplest objects we'll see in any object model, and it isn't very useful in most client-side programming. In HTML an anchor is simply an **<A>** tag. In the object model, we have access to a collection of these tags via the **Document** object's **Anchors** property. Anchor objects have one property, **Name**, which is set to the **NAME** attribute of the given tag.

Internet Explorer 3.01's **Anchors** collection only includes HTML elements with a **NAME** property and without an **HRef** property.

The Form Object

In contrast to the **Anchor** object, the **Form** object is supremely useful to client-side programmers. Its properties encompass such information as the current **ACTION** address, the **METHOD**, and the encoding for the form. Its sole method and event encapsulate form submission. In addition to the normal properties, each **Form** object has an **Elements** collection that provides access to each HTML element (the text boxes, buttons, etc.) on a given form. We'll cover this very important collection as soon as we finish talking about the **Form** object itself.

The Form Object Properties

The five properties of **Form** are **Action**, **Encoding**, **Method**, **Target**, and **Elements**. This section talks about the first four properties. These are derived from the opening **<FORM>** tag. So, like we did with the **Location** object, we'll invent a tag and then show the resulting property values. Our tag for this demonstration will be:

```
<FORM NAME="myForm" ACTION="http://www.mysite.com/search" METHOD="GET"
TARGET="NewWindow" ENCTYPE="text/html">
```

Property	Value	Description
Action	http://www.mysite.com/search	Action for form processing (usually a URL)
Method	GET	Form data submission to server (GET or POST)
Target	NewWindow	Name of target window to display results in
Encoding	text/html	Encoding for the form

These properties can be read or set to determine the current form settings, or possibly to change the behavior of the form before it is submitted.

The Form Submit Method and onSubmit Event

The **Form** object's single method (**Submit**) and event (**onSubmit**) handle form submission. Calling **Submit** submits the form, with the same result as a viewer clicking on a Submit button in the form.

As you'll see in the simple code in this section, and in a detailed example in the next chapter, client-side code can be very useful in performing validation of data entered on a form before the form is submitted. By doing this, we save a trip to the web server and back just to inform a user that they entered invalid data. Keep in mind that this only guarantees that information coming from *our* page is properly validated and acceptable. It *doesn't* actually mean that *any* data received is OK.

For example, there's nothing stopping someone from writing an application that sends data to our Web server, and in this case the data will never have seen the validation code in our Web page. The moral of the story: if it's extremely important that only certain data ends up in your database, then you'd better check it at the server end too. However, most applications don't require this depth of protection.

The page below submits the form when the Submit button is clicked, unless the user has entered "no" in the text box—in which case the form is not submitted:

```
<HTML>
<HEAD>
<TITLE> Form Submit </TITLE>
</HEAD>

<BODY>
<H1> Form Submit </H1>

<FORM NAME="myForm" ACTION="http://mysite.com/" METHOD="GET">
   <INPUT TYPE="TEXT" NAME="txtOne">
   <INPUT TYPE="SUBMIT" NAME="sbmTest">
</FORM>

<SCRIPT LANGUAGE="VBScript">
Function myForm_onSubmit
   If Document.myForm.txtOne.Value = "no" then
      myForm_onSubmit = False
   Else
      myForm_onSubmit = True
   End if
```

```
    End Function
    </SCRIPT>
    </BODY>
    </HTML>
```

Looking closely at the code on this page, you might notice something odd: the handler for the `onSubmit` event is a **function**, not just a normal **subroutine**. Every other event handler we've written has always been a subroutine, so why the change now? The answer is in the way Internet Explorer and Navigator are set up to process the `onSubmit` event. In this one single case, they look for a return value and act accordingly. If this event returns `False`, the form isn't submitted. If it returns anything else, the form is submitted normally.

An alternative to this method is to create a normal (i.e., non-submit) button with an `<INPUT TYPE="BUTTON">` tag. In the handler for the `onClick` event of this button, we perform our validation. We only submit the form, using the `FormName.Submit` method, when the data meets our requirements. The next chapter includes a more in-depth example of client-side validation.

The Elements Collection

Each `Form` object has an `Elements` collection, which represents the HTML form elements inside a pair of `<FORM>...</FORM>` tags. Any element that can be created with HTML (including objects created with the `<OBJECT>` tag) can be represented in the `Elements` collection.

As we'll see in the next section, it's important to correctly name the form where the object we're interested in resides (both in script code and in HTML). If this information is incorrect, the browser won't be able to find the object we're talking about, and will give us a rude error message saying that the object doesn't exist! If we don't identify the object correctly, as far as the browser is concerned, it doesn't exist.

Once we have access to the elements of a form, we might want to know how they act. We'll cover the HTML form elements next.

HTML Form Elements and the Element Object

HTML form elements can be very different. We can create text boxes, buttons, check boxes, and more with HTML. Accordingly it will probably come as no surprise to you, having worked with these elements before, that the properties, methods, and events for these elements are also different. Fortunately, however, similar objects usually have the same properties, methods, and events, making our job of understanding them easier.

Rather than cover how to use each and every one of these elements, and duplicate a lot of code and text in the process, we'll instead provide a table showing the properties, methods, and events for each object, and some general comments about these characteristics.

> *For a much more detailed coverage of this topic, check out the Wrox Press book* Instant VBScript.

If you're interested in actual code (and who isn't?), be sure to take a look at the in-depth examples in the next chapter, and at the code samples throughout this chapter.

Element	Properties	Methods	Events
`button, reset, submit`	form, name, value	click	onClick
`checkbox`	form, name, value, checked, defaultChecked	click	onClick
`radio`	form, name, value, checked	click, focus	onClick
`password`	form, name, value, defaultValue	focus, blur, select	None
`text, textarea`	form, name, value, defaultValue	focus, blur, select	onFocus, onBlur, onChange, onSelect
`select`	name, length, options, selectedIndex	focus, blur	onFocus, onBlur, onChange
`hidden`	name, value	None	None

Many of these properties will be familiar to you from prior reading and work, but we'll review them briefly below.

The Element Object's Properties

Fortunately for us, each object has a **Name** property. If it didn't, we'd have a hard time referring to the object in code, and the object model wouldn't be much use to us. Other useful properties include **Form** and **Value**. Here **Form** returns a reference to the element's form object, while **Value** gets or sets the value of the element. While all the elements have a **Value** property, the actual contents of this property vary depending on the object itself. For example, the **Value** of a **text** element is the string in the text box, while the **Value** of a **button** is the button's caption.

The Element Object's Methods

Some combination of the click and focus methods is common to all elements except for the **hidden** element (which has no methods or events). The **click** method causes the same result as a user clicking on the object. Calling the **focus** method of an object moves the current input location, or focus, to the object. For example, the code:

```
txtOne.Focus
```

moves the input cursor to the text box object named **txtOne**. The **blur** method is the converse of **focus**; it removes the focus from the current object. Finally, the **select** method, a feature of the **password**, **text**, and **textarea** input elements, selects the current contents of the object. This has the same effect as if the viewer of the page had clicked and dragged the mouse across the text in the input element.

The Element Object's Events

We've already seen one input element event many times: **onClick**. Each object that has a **click** method also has an **onClick** event, where code is placed ready to be executed when the object is clicked. Other interesting events that can be used in a similar way are **onFocus** (called when the element receives the focus), **onBlur** (called when the element loses focus), and **onChange** (called when the **Value** property of the object changes).

Referencing Objects in Collections

Now that we've covered the most important collections in the **Document** object, it's a good time to refresh our memory on how collection objects need to be referenced in code. Just like with ASP collections, items in the collections of the browser object model can be referenced one of two ways: by name or by index.

The choice of these collections has a practical aspect: whenever we refer to an object in a form (a very common client-side task) we need to make sure we reference the object correctly. Remember that the browser creates a **Form** object in the **Forms** collection for each **<FORM>** tag on the HTML page, and an item in the **Form**'s **Elements** collection for each element in the form. All collections have the additional property **Count**, which returns the number of objects that are currently held in the collection.

To illustrate this concept, we'll use the **Form** and **Elements** collection. Suppose a page with a single HTML form laid out like this:

```
<FORM NAME="myForm">
    <INPUT TYPE="BUTTON" NAME="btnOne" VALUE="Click Me"><BR>
    <INPUT TYPE="TEXT" NAME="txtElement">
</FORM>
```

After the page is parsed and displayed the **Count** property of the page's **Forms** collection would hold the value one, as the page boasts a single form, named **myForm**. The **Count** property of the **myForm.Elements** collection would be two, because there are two input elements inside **myForm**.

Why does this matter, outside of knowing how many objects are in a collection? When referring to objects in code, the index numbers of the collections can be used instead of, or in tandem with, the names of the objects. For example, the **Action** property of **myForm** could be referred to with this code, which uses the name of the form:

```
Document.myForm.Action
```

or with this code, which uses the index:

```
Document.Forms(0).Action
```

Note that, while **Count** returns **1**, the collection is indexed from **0** to **Count – 1**.

Similarly, the form's elements could be named in code like this:

```
Document.Forms(0).btnOne.Value
Document.Forms(0).txtElement.Value
```

or by index, like this:

```
Document.Forms(0).Elements(0).Value
Document.Forms(0).Elements(1).Value
```

It's important to remember that we need to include this relatively long qualifier when referring to input elements (or **OBJECT**s) inside a form. If we don't do this, the browser will think we're trying to refer to a control that's not on a form, i.e. that we're talking about a control that's on the page itself. Using simply **btnOne.Value** instead of one of the longer lines of code above will cause an Object required error (unless of course an element named `btnOne` exists outside the form). Without specifying the form that the object resides in, the browser can't tell what form element we're talking about.

Form elements or objects created with the `<OBJECT>` tag that are placed outside of a `<FORM>` tag should be named without a preceding object reference–they don't belong to any form, and so they aren't a part of any form's `Elements` collection. And because objects are only created when an `<OBJECT>` tag is encountered while parsing the page, we need to make sure that any `<OBJECT>` tags come before script code that references them.

Wrapping up the Document Object

Having finally got the end of our discussion of the `Document` object, it should be clear why we spent so much time on it. It's one of the most useful objects in the browser object model. Understanding how `Document` is organized will make your client-side programming quicker and more painless.

Wrapping up the `Document` object also leaves us with just a few more objects to cover before we've seen the entire object model.

History, Navigator and Frames

The last part of the object model that we still need to discuss is the remainder of `Window`'s properties: the ones that are actually objects in themselves. These objects are much simpler than `Window` and `Document`, and they aren't used as commonly as these objects either. However, they can be very useful in certain situations, and warrant a few pages of explanation. Here's the object model again, so you can see how they're related to the rest of the hierarchy.

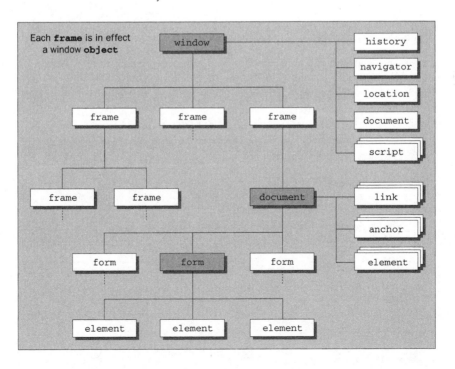

The **History** object, **Navigator** object, and **Frames** collection all lie immediately off of the **Window** object in the browser hierarchy. These objects, in the order listed, provide information about the browser's history list, the browser version, and the frames in the current document (if any).

Using the History Object

Using the **History** object we can navigate through the current user's history list. It's important to note that this object doesn't provide the exact text of each stop the user has made on the World Wide Web, so we can't loop through each location and snoop out where the user has been before they hit our page (well... at least not directly). We can, however, use **History**'s methods to go backward and forward any number of links.

The three methods of **History** are **forward**, **back**, and **go**. **Forward** and **back** are, not surprisingly, the opposite of each other. These methods simply take a positive integer and move forward or back in the history list that specified number of locations. The location is relative, in contrast to the **go** method, where the location is absolute. So, to implement a function that returned the user to the last page they visited, we'd just need to add the following code to a routine and provide a way for the user to execute this code (we'll show an example of this in the next chapter):

```
History.back 1
```

The **go** method is also interesting, although it's hamstrung by problems in current versions of Internet Explorer. Theoretically (according to the documentation) the **go** method should take an integer and move to that absolute position in the history list. Calling **go** with the number 1 should cause the browser to display the first page in the history list. Internet Explorer doesn't implement this behavior exactly, but if you have the time or inclination you might like to play around with this method to see exactly how it behaves in your browser.

The Navigator Object

This object provides detailed information about the current browser, including its name and possibly the build number and even operating system. The sample output we got from our copies of the Windows NT 4.0 version of Internet Explorer 3.01 and Netscape Navigator 3.01 are outlined in the table below:

Navigator Object Results with Internet Explorer 3.01

Property	Value
appCodeName	Mozilla
appName	Microsoft Internet Explorer
appVersion	2.0 (compatible; MSIE 3.01; Windows NT)
userAgent	Mozilla/2.0 (compatible; MSIE 3.01; Windows NT)

Navigator Object Results with Netscape Navigator 3.01

Property	Value
appCodeName	Mozilla
appName	Netscape
appVersion	3.01 (WinNT; I)
userAgent	Mozilla/3.01 (WinNT; I)

You'll probably notice a few things about these results. Firstly, the **userAgent** property is the same as if we'd examined **Request.ServerVariables(HTTP_USER_AGENT)** on the server with ASP code. Secondly, the **userAgent** property is the concatenation of the **appCodeName** and **appVersion** properties. Thirdly, the odd names and divisions for these properties. Don't spend too much time thinking about it– it's what Netscape came up with when they wrote Navigator 2.0. Some of the original developers of Navigator also worked on Mosaic–the browser that started it all. They wanted Navigator to be a gorilla that would stomp all over Mosaic, hence the name.

So, if we'd like to take some action on the client depending on the exact browser version that someone viewing our pages is using, the **Navigator** object is the way to go. To do the same thing on the server with ASP, we can use either the **HTTP_USER_AGENT** header, or the more capable and powerful **Browser Capabilities** component.

Manipulating Frames in Script

The **Frames** object is a collection of all of the frame windows in the current frameset. Each frame is a **Window** object in itself, and has its own **Document** object to represent the HTML in the frame. This really isn't as confusing as it might sound–it mimics the organization of frames without an object model. The top-level frame subdivides the browser window and loads separate HTML pages for each frame.

It can be confusing to use this property though. By default the **Window** and **Document** object that a script refers to are the **Window** and **Document** objects of the current frame. This means that, if we execute a script in the left-hand frame of a two-frame window, the **Document**, **Window**, and **Frames** objects the script uses will be those of the left-hand frame. Since the left-hand frame has no sub-frames, examining the **Count** property of the **Frames** collection will return **0**.

However, if we use the **Top** (or, in this case, **Parent**) property of the left-hand frame's **Window** object, we can gain access to the top-level frameset that loaded both the frames. Examining the **Count** property of this **Frames** collection will show the expected value of **2**, because this top-level page has loaded two frames.

We're giving this brief coverage here because it's both a simple and complex topic. In the sense that the **Frames** collection has only one property, **Count**, and that it just provides access to other objects that we've covered before, like **Window** and **Document**, it is a simple object. However, the relationships between the different frames in a frameset can be complex, and to best understand how it works, we should really see some code. A more in-depth example of using frames with the object model is part of the next chapter.

Summary

So that's it! We've worked through a tremendous amount of material in this chapter, but at least we've covered the object model thoroughly. You should now have a deep enough understanding to understand the detailed examples in the next chapter, and to know when and how to use the object model in your own client-side programming.

The main points of the chapter are:

- All modern Web browsers support a standardized object model, for which we can write script using any of the available scripting languages such as VBScript and JavaScript.

- The object model gives us a way to link our script to the browser itself, and to the pages it is displaying. We can emulate and automate most of the tasks that are possible on the browser.

- The concept of attaching script to events means that we can react to things that happen in the browser. This is not something that we are used to with server-side scripting.

In the next chapter, you'll stop thinking about the browser as something separate from the server. Instead, as in a true client/server situation, you'll start to think about the actual combination of the ability to create dynamic web pages on the server, while executing code on the client as well. For this, you need to be comfortable with how the browser can handle script that is sent from our Active Server Pages on the server in the first place. We'll show you how this works out in practice. We'll talk about using new objects, and show you many real-world examples of how client-side code can help to share the processing load.

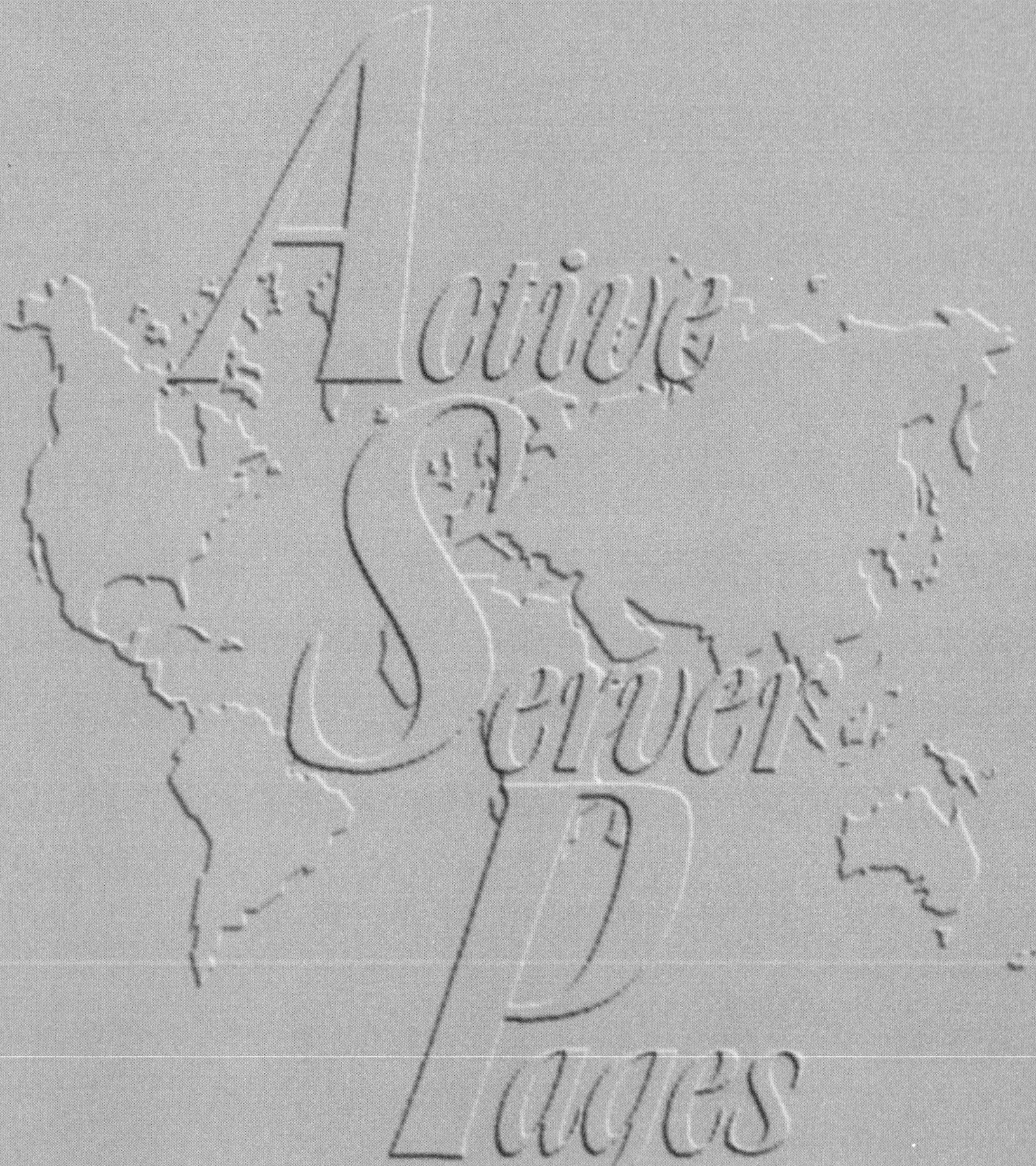
Active
Server
Pages

Client/Server Integration

We're now midway through our jaunt into client-side territory. We spent the last chapter learning about how script code looks in HTML, and how the browser object model provides programmatic access to the functionality of the browser. In this chapter, we'll continue our look at client-side programming. First, we'll talk a little more about how we can use objects outside of those that the browser provides. Then, we'll move on to the main part of this chapter: real-world examples that demonstrate how we can add client-side functionality to our pages. We'll see how this client-side functionality can help us overcome many programming difficulties and actually improve upon what ASP allows us to accomplish.

Along the way, we'll see four separate examples. The first, and simplest, shows how we can make our page more 'usable', by simply changing the default focus on an input form. From there, we'll move on to look at how we can use client-side code to validate the entries on a form before we submit it to our server. We'll also have a closer look at using frames in a Web page, with an example that uses ASP to make them responsive to user input. Finally, we'll see how we can improve the user interface by using objects that are not part of the browser itself.

All these examples are aimed at demonstrating some of the ways in which the combination of Active Server Pages, client-side scripting and objects can be used to create client/server applications. These, after all, are what real-world use of the browser, especially on a closed network like a corporate Intranet, is all about.

The main points we're covering in this chapter are:

- A comparison between objects on the client to those on the server
- How we create objects in HTML with the **<APPLET>** and **<OBJECT>** tags
- How we can manipulate these client-side objects in code
- How we can create client-side code dynamically on the server

So, without further ado, let's talk about new objects...

Creating Objects on the Client

You'll probably have noticed that whether we're interacting with browser objects on the client, or server-side objects with ASP, the code we write is very similar. The last chapter showed how we could connect client-side code to objects, how we could respond to events fired by objects, and how we could call methods and access the properties of objects. We also talked about a number of the objects provided by the browser itself. What we haven't covered is how we create instances of *additional* objects.

On the server, we'd use the **<OBJECT>** tag with **RUNAT=SERVER** or the **CreateObject** method of the **Server** object, like this:

```
<OBJECT RUNAT="Server" ID=MyObject ProgID="MyProjectName.MyClassName">
</OBJECT>
```

or:

```
MyObject = Server.CreateObject "MyProjectName.MyClassName"
```

On the client, things work a bit differently, and the objects themselves are quite different from those we've used on the server. However, the great thing is that our code will generally stay the same, in the same way that the syntax doesn't change much when we move from the server to the client. We create objects and hook up code differently, but the code itself is the same. This greatly simplifies our task.

Object Creation in HTML

Client-side objects, like those we discussed briefly in Chapter 6, are created with a variety of HTML tags. The two most common are the **<OBJECT>** tag and the **<APPLET>** tag. **APPLET** is generally only used to specify Java applets; **OBJECT**, on the other hand, can be used to specify any arbitrary object of any type (depending on the browser).

Using Java Applets

The use of the **<APPLET>** tag is relatively simple. Here's a sample example:

```
<APPLET CODE="MyClass.class" WIDTH=10 HEIGHT=10>
</APPLET>
```

The **CODE** attribute's value is the name of the Java **.class** file that implements the applet. With this name, the browser can request that the server send the **.class** file. When it arrives, it can interpret it and display the results within the browser, or in a separate window if the applet has been so designed. **APPLET** also supports the **WIDTH** and **HEIGHT** attributes that tell the browser how wide and how tall the space it devotes to the applet should be.

Hooking up script code to a Java applet is not so straightforward. How we do this depends upon whether we're using Internet Explorer or Navigator, and sometimes (as with Navigator) it even requires a complete recompile of our Java applet. We're used to using Active Scripting languages with ASP. However, Navigator and Internet Explorer enable script code to be connected to Java applets in very different ways. Since we're not going to be covering these dissimilar methods, we won't spend too much time talking about them here. These browsers don't actually ship with any Java applets that we can use for a demonstration anyway. If you do have the **.class** file for a Java applet on your machine (perhaps from experimentation with Java development), feel free to load up a page and compare the HTML with that used for ActiveX controls–which we'll look at next.

Using ActiveX Controls

The programming model for ActiveX Controls is simple, and that model will be very familiar to anyone with ASP experience. ActiveX Controls are created in HTML with the **<OBJECT>** tag. This tag, developed and endorsed by the World Wide Web Consortium (W3C), is extendable and can be used to insert any arbitrary object (including Java applets). Currently, its most common use is with ActiveX Controls.

The Client-side <OBJECT> Tag

This is what a client-side <OBJECT> tag might look like in HTML:

```
<OBJECT CLASSID="clsid:79176FB0-B7F2-11CE-97EF-00AA006D2776" ID="spnTest"
  CODEBASE="http://activex.microsoft.com/controls/mspert10.cab"></OBJECT>
</OBJECT>
```

A lot different from the **Server.CreateObject** method we're used to. It is, of course, the same basic format as the other way of creating objects on the server, which is by using an <OBJECT> tag. Although it doesn't look identical, it is doing the same thing. The string used with a call to **CreateObject** on the server is called a **Programmatic ID** or **ProgID**. This syntax isn't supported on the browser (yet), so the long ugly string making up the **CLASSID** attribute has to do the same job. It's known as a **Class ID** or **CLSID**. You may recall from Chapter 3, however, that we can also use the **CLASSID** method on the server if we're feeling particularly obtuse.

The second part of the tag, the **ID="spnTest"** attribute, is simply telling the browser that this object will be referred to in our code by the name **spnTest**. Finally, the **CODEBASE** attribute specifies a URL from where the control can be downloaded if it isn't already present on our machine. This last attribute isn't supported in the server-side version of the <OBJECT> tag.

ProgIDs, CLSIDs, and Versions

On the server, **ProgIDs** and **CLSIDs** are complementary: each **ProgID** has an associated **CLSID**, and vice-versa. **ProgIDs** are generally easier for a human to read and understand, so they're commonly used when an ActiveX object needs to be identified. They have one problem, though; especially in the Internet world. Suppose I create an object for a card game and give it the **ProgID "CardServer.Hand"**. You visit my page, download the control, create the object, and play my card game. Everything is fine and dandy until you happen to visit someone else's page—for sake of argument, let's say they live in Australia (mainly because I'd like to visit Australia).

My Australian colleague and I don't converse very often, and so we've unwittingly created two completely different objects with the same **ProgID** of **"CardServer.Hand"**. What happens now? Your machine doesn't know whether it can use the object it already has, or if it needs to go out and get a new one. There is no way it can tell whether the control it already has is different from the one on the page in Australia. Either way, whether it keeps the existing one, or goes and gets the new object, one of the pages that uses the **"CardServer.Hand"** object won't work properly, because we'll only have one of the objects on our machine.

CLSIDs solve this problem. A special algorithm generates each **CLSID** number when the object is developed. This algorithm guarantees that the **CLSID** won't be ever duplicated, on this world or in this galaxy, for thousands of years. So we can be sure that an object we design or use in our pages won't ever conflict with another object somewhere else on this planet (or off it!). On the other hand, we should be safe when using the **ProgID** on the server: we ought to know what objects we've got there, and so it should be easy to prevent conflicts.

Object Safety and Code Download

One topic that concerns everyone, especially with the increasing reports of rogue components circulating on the 'Net, is particularly important: how does someone viewing our pages know that the objects we've included will be safe to run on their machine? The code is actually running on their machine, and it's not just a scripting language with a few buttons anymore—it's very powerful. With that power comes the ability to do damage. There are two commonly used methods for providing object safety, **sandboxing** and **code signing**. We'll look at both of them before wrapping up this section, by talking briefly about the way that the objects get from the server to the client in the first place.

Sandboxing

The method of safety used by Java applets, and also by the VBScript and JavaScript scripting languages, is known as 'sandboxing'. This name refers to the practice of limiting the capabilities of these languages to actions that are defined to be safe to the machine. For example, since direct access to the hard drive of the machine could allow someone to erase files indiscriminately, sandboxed languages don't often support disk I/O. Disk access is 'outside the sandbox' and the language can't access it. While this method can ensure reasonably safe code, it can also be tremendously limiting to the developer. How many applications at our local software store don't use our hard drive? Instead, applets often save information back across the network to the server that's supplying the pages.

Code Signing

An alternative that preserves access to the full capabilities of the machine is called 'code signing'. With this method, the code can do whatever it wants, but–if it does something bad–the user knows who caused the problem and can take appropriate actions. A digitally signed piece of software identifies the person who created and signed it, and guarantees that the code hasn't changed since it was signed. One common way to describe code signing has been to think of it as 'shrink-wrapping for the Internet.' The box of software you pick up at the local store isn't guaranteed to be safe to your computer–it could reformat your hard drive just as easily as it displays graphics on your screen. However, since you bought it in a box at the store, you know that whatever company distributed it vouches for its safety, and (in most cases!) feel confident enough to install and run it on your computer.

The mechanics of code signing are based on publicly known algorithms and cryptographic techniques, and are not owned by any company or organization. If you've used the PGP (Pretty Good Privacy) encryption system, you've used some of the same techniques that code signing does. We'll be covering code signing, cryptography, and digital certificates in more details in the next couple of chapters.

Finally, it's important to note that code signing is complementary to sandboxing, and not used in competition with it. Any string of 1's and 0's, including Java applets, can be digitally signed to provide authentication. In fact, both Microsoft and Netscape support, or have announced support for digitally signed Java applets. If the applet is signed, the browser can relax the security restrictions and let the code move outside of the 'sandbox' and do more with the computer.

Code Download

On the server the objects we use are usually installed in the conventional way by a setup program. Imagine if we had to manually install each object that a certain web page used before we could view the page. We would probably be reticent about using objects unless we could be sure our users had already installed them, or they would be willing to go through the annoying process of location, download, and installation.

Not surprisingly, today's Java- and ActiveX-enabled web browsers have automatic methods for downloading and installing code. With Java applets, the only files that are needed are the `.class` file for the given applet and any dependent `.class` files it uses. When the browser sees an `<APPLET>` tag in the HTML, it knows to go to the server and retrieve these files in addition to any graphics or other objects embedded on a page. Both Netscape and Microsoft have different methods of packaging more than one class file into a compressed archive for quicker transmission over the network. Netscape uses `ZIP` files while Microsoft uses the same `CAB` and `INF` file formats that are used to distribute other applications.

The **CAB** file format is another compressed file format that has been used for some time by Microsoft to reduce file sizes. The part of Internet Explorer that performs the download and authentication process for software is called the **Component Download Service**. This element can use installation scripts to download one or more files depending on various factors, such as if the file is already installed on the machine, or if the version number of a currently present file is older than may be needed. Internet Explorer can also recognize another file with the `.inf` syntax used by some Windows setup programs. With files of this type, we specify a list of files and locations, and Internet Explorer downloads only those files it needs. This method can even be used to download different versions of controls for different operating systems or processor types.

If you are developing components for use with Navigator or Internet Explorer, you'll surely need to become more familiar with these issues. However, this introduction is appropriate for a book of this scope, and should be enough to give you an understanding of what actually happens when the browser sees an `<OBJECT>` or `<APPLET>` tag in our page.

To learn about creating ActiveX controls, look out for the Wrox Press book Instant VB5 ActiveX Control Creation.

An <OBJECT> Example - Using a Spin Button

Let's see an example to demonstrate what we're talking about. Open a new file in NotePad and enter this:

```
<HTML>
<HEAD>
<TITLE> Objects </TITLE>
</HEAD>

<BODY>
<CENTER>
<H1> Objects </H1>

<FORM NAME="frmTest">
  Spin Value: <INPUT TYPE="TEXT" NAME="txtSpinValue"><P>
</FORM>

<OBJECT CLASSID="clsid:79176FB0-B7F2-11CE-97EF-00AA006D2776" ID="spnTest"
  CODEBASE="http://activex.microsoft.com/controls/mspert10.cab">
</OBJECT>

<SCRIPT LANGUAGE="VBScript">
Sub spnTest_Change
  Document.frmTest.txtSpinValue.Value = spnTest.Value
End Sub
</SCRIPT>

</CENTER>
</BODY>
</HTML>
```

If you load this page into Internet Explorer, you'll notice that it contains a text box and a **spin button**. You've probably seen these in other Windows applications, but perhaps not in an HTML page.

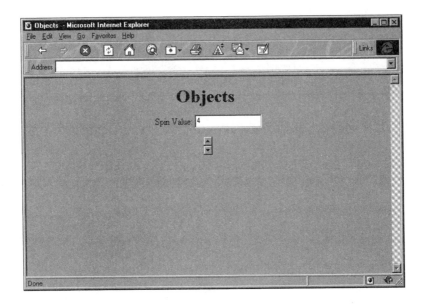

Spin buttons aren't one of the standard HTML form control elements, so we've created one ourselves with an <OBJECT> tag. Click on the up and down buttons and notice how the value in the text box changes—the code in our page connects the spin button's **Change** event with the text box, so the text box is updated each time the spin button is clicked.

The spin button control we're using here is from the Forms 2.0 Object Library. If you've installed the ActiveX Control Pad, Visual InterDev, the HTML Layout Control, or Internet Explorer 3.01 or 3.02, you'll have this file installed and registered on your system. However, with the additional **CODEBASE** attribute we've added, the file will be automatically downloaded from the Microsoft site if it's not already present on the machine you use to view this page.

Displaying the Spin Button's Value Property

We'll now briefly go over the code that causes the text box to interact with the spin button control. With the background we acquired from the last chapter, it's easy to understand what the script code on this page is doing.

We're using the **ObjectName_EventName** method of connecting code to an object's event. The spin button control fires an event called **Change** whenever its value changes. It also supports events called **SpinUp** and **SpinDown** that are only fired on an up or down click, respectively. For our purposes **Change** is fine, so that's the only event we'll handle.

```
<SCRIPT LANGUAGE="VBScript">
Sub spnTest_Change
    Document.frmTest.txtSpinValue.Value = spnTest.Value
End Sub
</SCRIPT>
```

The code that we execute when the value changes is simple. The spin button object's current value is stored in a property called **Value**. Because we've named the object **spnTest**, we can access this number with the code **spnTest.Value**. The rest of the code on this line is just performing an assignment to the

Value property of the text box (named **txtSpinValue**) on our form (named **frmTest**). We see the results of this assignment on the HTML page when the value displayed by the text box changes as we click the spin button.

Presetting the Value with a Parameter Tag

Now imagine that the page is not an **.htm** file, but an Active Server Page on our Intranet server. The spin button and text box display the number of items on a customer's order. If they are reviewing an existing order, it needs to be set to the value of the current order, ready for the customer to hopefully increase the quantity.

The **<OBJECT>** tag we used earlier sets the value of the spin button when it's created in the page to the default of zero. How do we go about setting it to a different 'default' value? The answer is to add a **<PARAM>** tag to the code. This example sets the value to **10**:

```
<OBJECT CLASSID="clsid:79176FB0-B7F2-11CE-97EF-00AA006D2776" ID="spnTest"
  CODEBASE="http://activex.microsoft.com/controls/mspert10.cab">
  <PARAM NAME="Position" VALUE="10">
</OBJECT>
```

In effect, all it's doing is setting a property to a default value. In fact, the code uses **Position** rather than **Value**, but the result is the same. When the object is created, its value will be **10**.

> *The only real way to work with objects like this is to use Microsoft's* ActiveX Control Pad, *or an equivalent such as* Visual InterDev, *which understands how to insert objects and set the properties.*

Doing It From a Database

This still doesn't answer the whole question, though. The value won't be a static number, it will be a value in a database. No problem, because the page is an **.asp** file rather than a normal **.htm** page. It can get the value and insert it into the **<PARAM>** tag, as well as into the text box:

```
...
<%
  Set oConn = Server.CreateObject("ADODB.Connection")
  oConn.Open "Contacts"
  Set oRs = oConn.Execute("SELECT * FROM Orders WHERE OrderNo = 'PR0172'")
  strExistingQty = CStr(oRs.Fields("Quantity"))
  oRs.Close
%>
...
<FORM NAME="frmTest" ACTION="AmendOrder.asp>
  Spin Value:
  <INPUT TYPE="TEXT" NAME="txtSpinValue" VALUE="<% = strExistingQty %>">
  <P>
</FORM>
...
<OBJECT CLASSID="clsid:79176FB0-B7F2-11CE-97EF-00AA006D2776" ID="spnTest"
  CODEBASE="http://activex.microsoft.com/controls/mspert10.cab">
  <PARAM NAME="Position" VALUE="<% = strExistingQty %>">
</OBJECT>
...
```

When it arrives at the client, ready to be displayed in the browser, the values have been filled in, and of course the ASP code is not sent anyway:

```
...
<FORM NAME="frmTest" ACTION="AmendOrder.asp>
  Spin Value:
  <INPUT TYPE="TEXT" NAME="txtSpinValue" VALUE="10">
  <P>
</FORM>
...
<OBJECT CLASSID="clsid:79176FB0-B7F2-11CE-97EF-00AA006D2776" ID="spnTest"
  CODEBASE="http://activex.microsoft.com/controls/mspert10.cab">
  <PARAM NAME="Position" VALUE="10">
</OBJECT>
...
```

This is just a simple example. There are many other things we could do; for example, we should be more thorough when querying the database. However, it's enough to illustrate the point that we are now firmly into client/server territory. The server creates the page containing the existing values, but the client is 'active' in the sense that it can handle all the work of setting the text box value without needing further involvement from the server.

Beyond Properties: Calling Methods

Like we've said, dealing with objects on the client is very similar to working with objects on the server. Where the **methods** of an object are concerned, they're actually exactly the same. Suppose we've already created an object, and assigned it's reference to a variable named **objVar**. Further, suppose that this object has a method called **myMethod**. Whether we're executing code in the browser or on the server, the way we call this method is identical:

```
objVar.myMethod
```

The syntax is also the same regardless of whether we're using JavaScript or VBScript, although it will differ slightly if the method accepts parameters. Method calls in VBScript do not use parentheses, while JavaScript method calls do.

Beyond Properties: Handling Events

While intrinsic ASP objects like **Application** have **events**, objects we create and use on the server don't generally fire events. Our exposure to these objects is limited to method calls and property access. As you've seen in the previous chapter, many objects on the client-side **do** fire events—it's one of the most commonly used ways to execute code.

The syntax to connect code to an object's event is exactly the same for user-created objects as it is for objects in the browser object model, and depends on the style we choose to connect our code to the event. Different methods of hooking up event code were discussed at length at the beginning of the last chapter. Our choice may depend on the scripting language. In VBScript, we can use:

```
<SCRIPT LANGUAGE="VBScript">
Sub ObjectName_Event1Name
    ...
End Sub
```

```
Sub ObjectName_Event2Name
   ...
End Sub
</SCRIPT>
```

JavaScript doesn't support the Visual Basic system of multiple event handlers in one `<SCRIPT>` block. Also since adding the event name to the `<INPUT>` tag is only supported for intrinsic elements that can be created with HTML, this leaves only one style for the combination of user-created objects and JavaScript:

```
<SCRIPT LANGUAGE="JavaScript" FOR="ObjectName" EVENT="Event1Name">
...
</SCRIPT>

<SCRIPT LANGUAGE="JavaScript" FOR="ObjectName" EVENT="Event2Name">
...
</SCRIPT>
```

This style can also be used with VBScript code if you wish.

Getting into Client/Server

For the rest of the chapter we'll focus on four separate examples that illustrate what we can do with a combination of client-side and server-side scripting, with a few objects thrown in to improve our pages. In the first example we'll show an extremely simple way in which we can improve the friendliness of forms on our web page, and then in the second we'll look at an extensible block of code we can use to prevalidate form input on the client instead of the server. These first two examples show some common things to make our pages better, and which can't actually be done with ASP at all.

The last two examples continue to demonstrate some neat client-side features, but use ASP as an integral part, generating different client-side code depending on settings on the server. The third example explains some different methods to control and synchronize frames. The final example uses a homegrown control created with Visual Basic 5.0 to give a taste of how powerful objects can be on the client and how ASP can be used to generate dynamic scripts and object insertion. Again, we're using VBScript code. However, as long as you understand the concepts behind the examples, there's nothing stopping you from rewriting them in any language supported by the browsers that your clients or customers will be using.

> **As with all of the sample code in the book, the code from this chapter is available from our web site:`http://www.rapid.wrox.com/books/0723/`**

Setting the Focus

Users of Windows applications are fickle: they actually expect the user interface to be easy to understand, straightforward, and logical. This means anything from menus that are ordered so they can easily find program options, to text boxes that automatically start with the text most commonly entered. It used to be difficult to achieve this friendliness with HTML. Only a few input elements were available to request data from the user, and fine layout of these elements was often hard to manage. Fortunately, HTML has advanced substantially over the last few years, and, with objects and script code, many previously impossible things can now be accomplished.

The ChangeFocus Example

The first example involves setting the input focus to the text box the user is most likely to want to enter data into on the 'Login' page. We'll be able to do this with only one line of script code. In Windows 95, Windows NT, and a number of other operating systems, the system's logon dialog includes user ID and password text boxes.

In most cases just one person uses a machine most of the time, so the logon dialog automatically presets the user ID text box to the ID of the last person who logged on, and puts the cursor in the password text box. All we have to do is sit down, enter our password, and press *Return* (assuming we were the last person to use the machine). This is a lot better than having to manually enter our ID, press *Tab* to move to the password field, enter our password, and, finally, press *Return*.

Our example page (**changefocus.htm**) shows a hypothetical logon screen with user ID and password fields:

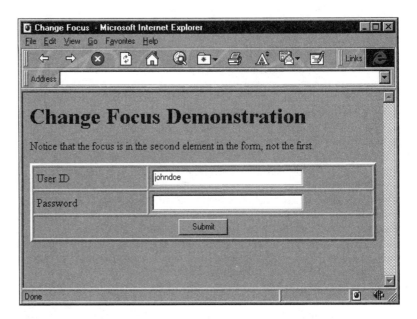

If you load this page into the browser and then look at the cursor, you'll find that it's in the password field, not the user ID text box. Normally, when an HTML page loads, the input focus is automatically positioned on the first form element that can take input. This isn't what we want because it requires the user to manually tab to the password text box every time they logon. Fortunately, the little bit of script code we've added to the file takes care of this problem.

> *The page in this example always shows the same user ID, johndoe, and doesn't do anything when the Submit button is clicked (take a look at the source and see that the **ACTION** attribute of the form is set to a non-existent file called **DeadLink.asp**). We'll see what we could do about this in a while, and for a more complete example of a logon page look back at Chapter 6, or the bug report case study in Chapter 12.*

The ChangeFocus Code

The HTML file for this sample, **ChangeFocus.htm**, contains only normal HTML, except for one small script block. The HTML creates a form called **myForm**, with a text box called **txtUserID**, a password text box called **pwdPassword**, and a single Submit button.

But the script block is where the action occurs:

```
<SCRIPT LANGUAGE="VBScript">
Sub Window_onLoad
   Document.myForm.pwdPassword.Focus
End Sub
</SCRIPT>
```

The `<SCRIPT>` tag tells the browser that the following lines are code. The next line, `Window_onLoad`, says that the code inside this subroutine (that is, everything until the `End Sub`) should be executed immediately after the page is loaded. Everything up until now has been just plumbing, the next line does our work by calling the `Focus` method of the `pwdPassword` password text box.

To call the `Focus` method, we first need to get a reference to the password text box. That's what everything on this line (except for the `.Focus`) is for. Think back to the last chapter and remember that the `Document` object represents the current document in the browser. Each `Document` object has a collection of `Form` objects, one for each form. In the same way, each `Form` object has its own collection of `Element` objects that represent each input element or object in a form.

The `Form` collection can be accessed by the numerical index of the form, or by its name as we've done here. Similarly, `Elements` can be accessed by an index or by the individual element name. In our example, we've used the name of the form and the name of the password text box instead of their indices, but this line of code would accomplish the same thing:

```
Document.Forms(0).Elements(1).Focus
```

Once we have a reference to the password text box, all that remains is to call the method we want, which in this case is `Focus`.

So, the page loads, the `Window_onLoad` event is called, and the focus is set to the password text box, ready for input. Our users are happy they don't have to press Tab many times every day, we get a huge raise, and retire. Sound far fetched? OK, maybe... but keep reading, we still have more interesting things to talk about in this chapter.

Using ASP to Create the Page

From the earlier spin button example, and the examples in Chapter 6, it's easy to see how we could set the user ID text box in an ASP file and send that to the browser instead of an `.htm` page. If it was part of an application, we might already have it stored elsewhere, so we would just use it in the `VALUE` attribute of the `<INPUT>` tag:

```
<INPUT TYPE="TEXT" NAME="txtUserID" VALUE="<% = strStoredUserID %>">
```

And of course, we could then emulate the behavior of the standard Windows logon dialog more closely, by checking if we'd actually got a user ID before we set the focus:

```
<SCRIPT LANGUAGE="VBScript">
Sub Window_onLoad
   If Document.myForm.txtUserID <> "" Then
      Document.myForm.pwdPassword.Focus
   End If
End Sub
</SCRIPT>
```

Client-Side Form Validation

One of the easiest and most practical applications of client-side code is input validation. When Microsoft and Netscape first started talking about adding scripting to HTML people asked why, and this was one of the first responses the marketing people gave. The horizons have expanded greatly with objects, but this remains one of the most beneficial uses of script code.

The Form Validation Example

The code for this example (**validation.htm**) is a bit more complex than the last one, but it should be accordingly more useful. The screenshot below shows a form with four fields called, in turn, Name, Age, Email Address, and Next Birthday. Each field (with the exception of Age—we don't want to offend anyone!) must have a certain type of input before the form can be submitted.

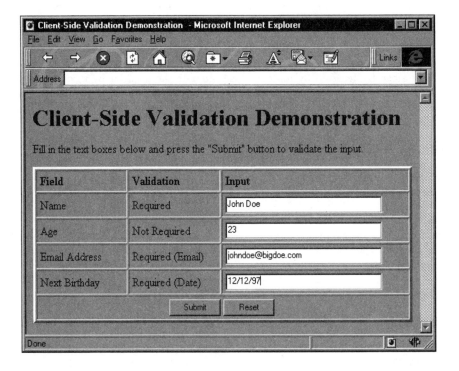

What is Valid Input?

So how do we determine what constitutes a valid input? The Name field is easy—it just requires some text. We're not going to try to make any judgements about whether or not a name is really a name. Email is similar—we couldn't expect to know if the user name or domain name was real. However, we do know that every valid email address always contains the @ character. Our validation criteria for the Email will just be that—we'll accept the input if we see a @.

How about the Next Birthday field? A date is more likely to follow a recognizable pattern, so we'll accept the input if it follows any date format our computer understands. With VBScript, it's taken care of easily in just a single line. In addition, we'll add one more parameter. Since we asked for the date of the user's *next* birthday, we'll need to check that the date hasn't already occurred.

Now load up the page **validation.htm** and enter some different combinations of input. If you enter everything it's asking for, you'll be rewarded by a 404—Object Not Found reply. We don't want to do anything real with the data at the moment, so–again–the **ACTION** attribute in our form points to **DeadLink.asp**. In a real application we would take the validated data and insert it into a database or perform other processing. If you try to sneak some bad data to the server you'll see dialogs like these:

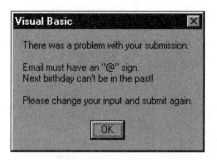 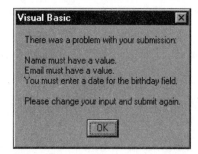

With invalid input, after pressing OK to dismiss the message box, you'll see the same page as before pressing Submit. The form data hasn't been sent to the server, and the page is still waiting patiently for input it can accept.

The Validation Code

We could come up with additional data types ad infinitum, but these will get us started. Requiring some input, an email address, and a date (in a certain range) are some of the most common requests made on HTML forms. In addition, as you'll see when we look at the code, it can be easily extended to incorporate validation for any type of data.

The non-script HTML for this page isn't anything we haven't seen before. After printing a header, it creates a six-element form with these elements:

Name	INPUT Type
txtName	TEXT
txtAge	TEXT
txtEmail	TEXT
txtBirthday	TEXT
sbmMyForm	SUBMIT
rstMyForm	RESET

As always, the action occurs in between the **<SCRIPT>** and **</SCRIPT>** tags. All of our code for this example is in one routine, the **onSubmit** handler for our form object.

```
Function myForm_onSubmit
   ...
   ...
End Function
```

This is different to the other event handlers we often see. Remember that **myForm_onSubmit** is a **Function**, not a **Sub**. Functions return a value, and subroutines don't. With a form, we might want to cancel the form submission. Remember our discussion about this in the last chapter—the browser is set up to pay attention to the return value of this handler. If we return **True**, the form is submitted; if we send back **False**, nothing happens—it's like the user never pressed Submit in the first place. An alternative method is to create a normal button with an **<INPUT TYPE="BUTTON">** tag and submit it using the **Submit** method of the **Form** object.

With **onSubmit** out of the way, we can focus on the code that does the validation. Since we might want to use this code with a wide variety of different forms, it's been set up so that adding and removing validation for various form fields is easy. The function itself can be subdivided into two parts: the validation code that may change for each form, and the supporting code that prints the error message.

Supporting the Validation Code

Take a look at the all of the code outside of the specific validation sections. This is the code we're talking about:

```
Function myForm_onSubmit
    Dim msgError
    Dim fRef
    Set fRef = Document.myForm     'get myForm reference

    '... VALIDATION CODE GOES HERE ...

    If msgError <> "" Then    'print error message if validation failure
        MsgBox "There was a problem with your submission:" _
               & Chr(13) & msgError & Chr(13) & Chr(13) _
               & "Please change your input and submit again."
        myForm_onSubmit = False
    Else
        myForm_onSubmit = True
    End If
End Function
```

This code first prepares for the validation. Then, if a problem with the user's input has been detected, it displays a message box explaining the problem and cancels the form submission. If the input is OK, the form is submitted.

We first declare two variables, **msgError** and **fRef**. Like we've said, declaring variables isn't absolutely necessary, but it's good practice and makes our code easier to read. The **msgError** variable is what we'll use to store a string describing the problem(s) with the input. We'll write to it in the validation code, and display it if we decide to cancel the form submission. After we declare **fRef**, we initialize it with this line of code:

```
Set fRef = Document.myForm     'get myForm reference
```

The variable **fRef** isn't absolutely necessary, but it simplifies our repeated references to the **myForm** object. This allows us to use refer to the form in our validation sections with the code:

```
fRef.txtName.Value
```

instead of:

```
Document.myForm.txtName.Value
```

In addition to simplifying our code, this technique makes it run faster. The script engine takes time to resolve each reference, so we shortcut this process by only performing the `Document.myForm` resolution once, and saving the result in a variable for later use.

After these initialization steps the validation code is allowed to do its work. We'll talk about these routines in a second, just understand for now that whenever the code detects a problem with the input it adds some text describing the problem to the string variable `msgError`. This is the basis for the code at the end of the routine. Since `msgError` starts as an empty string, we know that if it's still an empty string when the validation code is complete then there were no problems with the user's input, and we can submit the form by setting the return value of the `myForm_onSubmit` function to `True`.

If `msgError` holds anything other than the empty string, then we've found a problem. In this case we display a message box, wrapping the strings There was a problem with your submission: and Please change your input and submit again around the text in `msgError` describing the problem. We also set `myForm_onSubmit` to `False` to cancel the submission. The newline character, `Chr(13)`, is used to separate the lines in the message box.

Validating the Fields

The only thing left is to understand how each field is validated. Of course this depends on exactly what constitutes a valid input. Take a look at the code for the Name field, where we just want to make sure the user has entered some text:

```
If fRef.txtName.Value = "" Then
    msgError = msgError & Chr(13) & "Name must have a value."
End If
```

We first test to see if the value of the `txtName` text box is equal to the empty string. If it is we append a newline character and the error string Name must have a value to the `msgError` variable and store it back into `msgError`. We need to keep any previous contents of `msgError` intact, so we can't just assign our error string to the variable—if we did this anything that was there previously it would be overwritten. Name is the first field, so we can be sure there won't ever be anything in `msgError` yet, but it's a good practice to stay consistent between validation steps and we *will* need to append in all the code after this. Plus, it gives us a space between the default error text, and makes our message box look nicer.

If the user has entered something into the `txtName` text box, everything is cool and we can move on to the next field without doing anything to `msgError`. All of the validation code follows this pattern: 1—test the input and, 2a—write `msgError` if there's problem, or, 2b—don't write `msgError` if things are OK.

The only additional wrinkles are how we handle different kinds of validation, and how we deal with fields that must meet multiple criteria. Fortunately, the validation code for the Email field demonstrates both of these tasks.

When checking Email, we need to make sure it not an empty string, and that there is a @ character somewhere in it. We could check both of these in a single statement, but then our error message wouldn't give the user any clue about the specific thing that was wrong with their input. Instead we'll use an additional `ElseIf` clause in our code:

```
If fRef.txtEmail.Value = "" Then
    msgError = msgError & Chr(13) & "Email must have a value."
ElseIf InStr(fRef.txtEmail.Value, "@") = 0 Then
    msgError = msgError & Chr(13) & "Email must have an ""@"" sign."
End If
```

We first check to see if anything exists in the text box, because we can't possibly find an @ if the text box is empty. If the user hasn't entered anything in `txtEmail` the validation for this field fails and we write the same error string as above into `msgError`.

A Valid Email Address

If something does exist, we can use the VBScript `InStr()` function to see if the string includes an @. In its simplest form, `InStr()` (short for In String) takes two strings, one string to look in, and one string to look for. If it finds the second string in the first string it returns an integer specifying the location in the first string where the second string begins. If it doesn't find the string, it returns 0.

It's easy to understand how this code works then. If `Instr` doesn't find an @ in the value the user has entered it returns 0, and we know to write the message `Email must have an ""@"" sign` to the error string. We want the string displayed in the message box to include double quotation signs around the @, so we use the VBScript convention of specifying two double quotes when inside a string.

A Valid Date Value

Finally, we need to cover the validation of the Birthday field. In this we need to check three things: that `txtBirthday` has a value, that the value is a date, and that the date isn't in the past (since we asked for the user's next birthday). There are a lot of things to check, but they're actually very easy to do using the date manipulation ability of VBScript. The whole of the validation code is only five lines long:

```
If Not IsDate(fRef.txtBirthday.Value) Then
    msgError = msgError & Chr(13) & "You must enter a date for the birthday field."
ElseIf CDate(fRef.txtBirthday.Value) < Now Then
    msgError = msgError & Chr(13) & "Next birthday can't be in the past!"
End If
```

We wrap our first two criteria into one test using the `IsDate` function. `IsDate` takes a variable and returns `True` if the value in the variable can be converted into a date, or `False` if it can't. Fortunately, the empty string can't be converted into a date, so `IsDate` returns `False` both when nothing has been entered in the `txtBirthday` text box, and when the value entered can't be converted to a date. We can give a meaningful error message for both cases (and avoid using an additional `ElseIf` clause) by saying You must enter a date for the birthday field.

Once we're sure we have a valid date, we can compare it to the current date to make sure the user hasn't tried to sneak in with a date that has already gone. We can easily accomplish this by first converting the value in the text box to a date using the `CDate` function and then comparing our date value with the current date returned by the `Now` function. Since we're comparing two dates we just need to use the < (less than) operator to determine if our user's next birthday has already occurred. If it has then we write an appropriate error message to `msgError` and we are done.

From this discussion you can see how easy it is to add your own tests to the framework. All you need to do is plug in an `If...Then` block containing your validation test, and write to `msgError` if you detect a problem.

Adding ASP to the Validation Example

Again, there are plenty of ways that we could integrate this example with ASP. In fact it's likely that the results from a form like this will ultimately be stored in a database, so ASP would be an obvious way to manipulate the information after it has been submitted. You'll see some excellent examples of how this can be done in Chapter 12.

So, like the previous example, you could allow users to edit their details, by fetching them from the database with ASP, and building a page that contained the current values as the defaults. And, again as featured in the Chapter 12 example, we could quite easily add features such as sending a confirmation message to the user by email, using the address they had just entered.

Client-side vs Server-side Validation

One point to remember, and something we discussed in Chapter 6, is that you need to be aware of the limitations of client-side data validation. It is a great way of reducing server load and network traffic, because you can ensure that only data of the appropriate type is submitted from the form. However, there are a couple of problems.

What you can't do with just client-side validation, is be absolutely sure that the data is valid when it gets to your server. Unscrupulous users could send data from their own forms to your application—remember that the URL of the page that handles the data is freely visible in the original form page. In the next chapter, you'll see how we can reduce this risk, by using digital certificates and secure channels to communicate the results.

This also leads to the other concern we expressed in Chapter 6. If the method of validating the data requires some 'secret formula', it's not a good idea to do it in a scripting language on the client, where everyone can view the source of the page and see the code. Instead, you might want to use a custom control on the client, which hides the formula inside the control, or validate this data once you get it back at your server.

Manipulating Frames with VBScript and ASP

The first two examples in this chapter showed some things that can be done easily with client-side scripting. However, they didn't actually incorporate any of the features of ASP, we only suggested ways that this could be done. In this and the next examples, we'll be using ASP in conjunction with script code on the client.

While ASP is great at building the individual pages for a web application dynamically, its features are rather limited when it comes to handling the frameset pages that are so common to today's sites. Using the **Redirect** method of the **Response** object we can redirect to a single page, but we can't target it to a specific frame—only the browser can do that. The combination of client and server code in this example shows how scripting languages on both sides of the Web connection can, together, manage framesets and the pages inside the frames.

The Frames Example

This is more complicated than the first two examples we looked at. Before we launch into an explanation of what this example does, you might like to bring up **frameset.asp** in your browser and see for yourself. Experiment by clicking on a few of the links in the left hand pane. We'll spend some time discussing the code that makes this sample work, and you'll understand it better if we're familiar with the samples behavior in the browser. Since this is now an ASP file, you also need to be sure that it comes from your server and is loaded via HTTP.

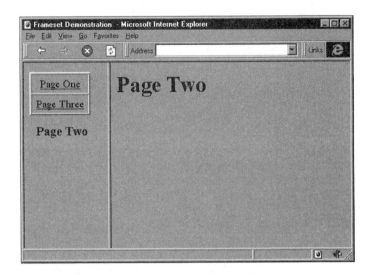

You'll notice that clicking on a page link on the left hand side loads that page into the right hand frame, and also updates the left frame itself so that only links to the pages not currently shown are available. This makes sense—if we're already viewing the second page we shouldn't be able to jump to it again.

Since we're viewing page two in the right hand frame, it's not visible in the list in the left hand frame.

Now click over to the third page, and you'll see a list of options in the main frame. If you choose one of the Option links, rather than a Page link, you'll see the left frame refresh with a list of the remaining options, and the right frame with the actual page you selected. If you watch closely, you'll see that the left frame is refreshed a split second *before* the right frame is updated. We'll talk about why this happens later in this section.

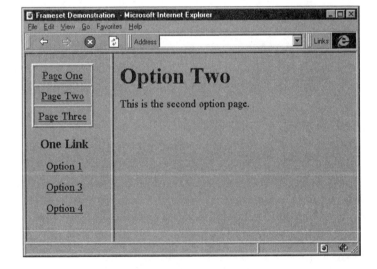

So that's what this example does: it displays a variety of pages in the main section of a two-pane frameset and keeps the left-hand pane in sync—and it uses both client and server-side scripting to accomplish this.

If you've designed a site with frames before, you know that creating a two-pane frameset with a navigation frame and contents frame isn't too difficult. The frameset HTML file contains the size and URL information for the frames, so that they can be created and laid out. Each of the pages is a separate file, as specified in the frameset file, and these are loaded into the frames just created.

Once the pages have been rendered, new pages are targeted to a specific frame by adding the **TARGET** attribute to the links that modify the other frame. For example, our frameset has two frames called **NavBar** and **MainFrame**. To change the contents of **MainFrame** from a click on a link in **NavBar**, we'd just use:

```
<A HREF="mypage.htm" TARGET="MainFrame">Go To My Page</A>
```

However, with this method, the left-hand frame doesn't change to reflect what is shown in the main frame. Our example does allow this, and this significant improvement comes from the combination of ASP and client-side code.

Where would we use something like this? The answer is any place that we currently use (or could use) frames, but want to give the viewer of our site more feedback as to what is happening. Or perhaps we'd like to customize the available options based on which user is accessing our site, or what part of the site they're viewing. We can easily extend this example to the specific needs of our site, but first we should understand how the code works.

How It Works

In contrast to the first two examples (and the next one), this sample consists of more than a few files, although the interesting work takes place primarily in two files: **frameset.asp** and **navbar.asp**. It's no coincidence that these files are the only Active Server pages of the whole lot. The rest of the pages are simple HTML files—that in the real, non-book-example, world would hold the site's content. So we can keep things straight, all of the files are listed below:

Filename	Purpose
frameset.asp	The top-level frameset page
navbar.asp	Navigation bar (left-hand pane) page
pageone.htm	Page one
pagetwo.htm	Page two
pagethree.htm	Page three (with option links)
option1.htm	Option page one
option2.htm	Option page two
option3.htm	Option page three
option4.htm	Option page four

Creating the Frameset with ASP

We first need to understand how the **frameset.asp** page works. This is the page you loaded into your browser earlier, and it's where everything starts. The ASP code in the page sets the values of two variables, **NavBarPage** and **MainFramePage**, depending on the value passed to the page in the URL. We'll see this in a while—just accept for now that they are set up correctly. So, **frameset.asp** sets up the frameset with different pages:

```
... the ASP code that sets NavBarPage and MainFramePage goes here ...
<HTML>
<HEAD>
<TITLE> Frameset Demonstration </TITLE>
</HEAD>

<BODY>
<FRAMESET COLS="150,*">
   <FRAME NAME="NavBar" SRC="<%= NavBarPage %>" SCROLLING="AUTO">
   <FRAME NAME="MainFrame" SRC="<%= MainFramePage %>" SCROLLING="AUTO">
</FRAMESET>

</BODY>
</HTML>
```

The **<FRAMESET COLS="150,*">** line creates a frameset consisting of two columns. The width of the left-hand column is **150** pixels, and the right hand column takes up the remainder. The two **<FRAME>** tags provide the information about each frame. The **NAME** attribute defines the frame's name, and is important because it's what we use in our links and script code to refer to the frame. The **SCROLLING** attribute turns scrolling on if needed. But what of the **SRC** attribute with that familiar ASP code string **<%= ... %>**?

Selecting the Pages to Display

We're telling ASP to insert whatever is in the variables **NavBarPage** and **MainFramePage** into the **<FRAME>** tags. The important thing is how these variables are set, and to understand this we need to look at the code we didn't show in the listing above. The page expects to find an argument in the query string, containing a parameter called **Nav**. In other words, it expects to be called with a URL like this:

```
http://www.yoursite.com/frameset.asp?Nav=all
```

Here's the code itself:

```
<%  'get Nav and use it to determine which frames to display
    'and which parameter to call navbar.asp with

NavChoice = Request.QueryString("Nav")

Select Case NavChoice
   Case "pageone"
      NavBarPage = "navbar.asp?BarChoice=pageone"
      MainFramePage = "pageone.htm"

   Case "pagetwo"
      NavBarPage = "navbar.asp?BarChoice=pagetwo"
      MainFramePage = "pagetwo.htm"

   Case "pagethree"
      NavBarPage = "navbar.asp?BarChoice=pagethree"
      MainFramePage = "pagethree.htm"

   Case "all"
      NavBarPage = "navbar.asp?BarChoice=all"
      MainFramePage = "main.htm"

   Case Else    'choose all
      Response.Redirect "frameset.asp?nav=all"

End Select  %>
... HTML code is here ...
```

The first line of real code uses the **QueryString** collection of the **Request** object to get the value of the **Nav** parameter, if it exists, from the URL. We store that value in the variable called **NavChoice**. With this information the code uses a **Select Case** statement to set the variables depending on what was specified in the URL. By using **all**, we can ask for the main content page (**main.htm**) to be displayed in the main frame, and the navigation bar to show links to all three pages.

If there is no value for **Nav** in the query string, as when we first loaded the page, the **Else** part of the **Select Case** construct is executed. This uses the **Response** object's **Redirect** method to refresh the page, showing the main content page and all of the links. Of course, we could have copied the code down from the **all** clause immediately above it–it has exactly the same effect. However, this is better style because it means we only have to change our code in one place if we decide to modify the default action.

Looking at the clauses themselves, it's easy to understand what they are doing. They put the name of the file that should be loaded into the main frame into **MainFramePage**. When our **Nav** option is **pageone** it's logical to think that **pageone.htm** should be the page we see, and so on. However, notice that setting the **NavBarPage** variable is a little different–we're loading the same file **navbar.asp** in each case. What our code does, however, is add a different parameter to the query string each time.

The Dynamic Navigation Bar

This is because the **navbar.asp** file changes its behavior, depending on the **BarChoice** value included in the URL. The part of **navbar.asp** that we're interested in is this:

```
<% BarChoice = Request.QueryString("BarChoice")

Select Case BarChoice
   Case "pageone" %>
      <TABLE WIDTH="100%" BORDER="2" CELLPADDING="5" CELLSPACING="2">
         <TR>
            <TD ALIGN="CENTER"><A HREF="javascript:GoPageTwo()">
            Page Two</A></TD>
         </TR>
         <TR>
            <TD ALIGN="CENTER"><A HREF="javascript:GoPageThree()">
            Page Three</A></TD>
         </TR>
      </TABLE>
      <P><CENTER><H3> Page One </H3></CENTER>

... similar code for "pagetwo", "pagethree" and "all" goes here ...
```

This works almost identically to the code in **frameset.asp**. First it stores the value of the **BarChoice** part of the URL in a variable of the same name, and then uses this variable in a **Select Case** construct to output the appropriate set of **<TABLE>** and **<A>** tags. When **BarChoice** equals **pageone**, the code only outputs links to **pagetwo.htm** and **pagethree.htm**. The code for the **pagetwo**, **pagethree**, and **all** options is nearly identical to the code here, so we haven't listed it. You can check it out in the **navbar.asp** source.

Changing Both Frames with Client-Side Code: Method One

Now that we've talked about how the two most important pages are created, we can discuss that new enigma we've unearthed: the use of **javascript:function-name()** in the anchor tags in **navbar.asp**. As we said earlier, it's possible to change the contents of one frame, when a link in another is clicked, by using the **TARGET** attribute in normal HTML. However, in our case, what we want to do is update *both* of the frames in our frameset, and HTML doesn't provide a way to do this. Fortunately, our task can be accomplished with a little client-side code. We show two different methods to accomplish this in the sample, and we're ready to discuss the first now.

If you remember back to the object model discussion in the last chapter, you'll recall the **Frames** collection of the **Document** object, and the **Location** object. **Frames** provides an interface to each frame in a frameset, while the **Location** object gives information about the current page displayed in the frame. Each frame and window has a **Location** object. It's no surprise, then that two lines of code can change the contents of both of our frames:

```
parent.frames("NavBar").location.href = "navbar.asp?BarChoice=pageone"
parent.frames("MainFrame").location.href = "pageone.htm"
```

We need to remember that, to access the **Location** objects of the frames in our frameset, we need to go back one step to the top-level frame. The **Frames** collection of the **NavBar** and **MainFrame** frames are both empty because these frames don't have any subframes. However, the parent frame of **NavBar** and **MainFrame** includes both **NavBar** and **MainFrame**. In the code above we use the **Parent** property of the (default) **Window** object to access the correct collection. Once we have the reference to the correct frame, setting the **HRef** property of the **Location** object causes the current window to display whatever URL is specified.

The only thing we haven't talked about is how the code above actually gets executed. Normally we connect client-side code to an event raised by an object. For example, we might execute code when form button is clicked, i.e. the **onClick** event is fired. In this case we'd like to execute the code when a link is clicked. Link objects do have an event called **onClick**, and we could specify that our relocation code be executed in response to this event. We're not going to use it in this case, because then we'd have to follow the unsightly practice of specifying an **HREF** attribute whose value is the empty string (because our code would be doing all the work). Holding the mouse over a link with no value can confuse viewers who depend on the status bar to see where they're going. In addition, in a more graphical site we might want to do the same thing but with an image map, and these don't have **onClick** events like **Link** objects do. Instead we'll directly specify the code to executed in the **HREF** attribute. This is where the **javascript:function-name()** syntax comes into our lives.

Using javascript:function-name() with VBScript

We've been using VBScript in the last few chapters, but Internet Explorer doesn't support the **vbscript:subroutine-name** syntax. It does support the equivalent **javascript:function-name()**. The clever part if that, if we specify the name of a VBScript subroutine instead of a JavaScript function it still works. The VBScript routine is executed correctly, and this is exactly what we do in on this page of the sample. The parts of **navbar.asp** we haven't see yet contain these routines:

```
<SCRIPT LANGUAGE="VBScript">
<!--
Sub GoPageOne()
    parent.frames("NavBar").location.href = "navbar.asp?BarChoice=pageone"
    parent.frames("MainFrame").location.href = "pageone.htm"
End Sub
... more similar routines here ...
-->
</SCRIPT>
...
<TD ALIGN="CENTER"><A HREF="javascript:GoPageOne()">Page One</A></TD>
```

Putting this all together, we can see that clicking the Page One link causes the browser to execute the code in the **GoPageOne** subroutine, and this code loads **pageone.htm** into the main frame and reloads **navbar.asp** with **BarChoice** equal to **pageone**. The rest of the Page links follow the same format. They call a VBScript function that changes the **HRef** properties of both frames to the correct URLs. When **navbar.asp** reloads, it changes the page links displayed, and everything is ready to go again.

The Option Links on Page Three

The last major feature of this example, which we haven't talked about yet, is the set of option links on page three. If you haven't already seen these, open up page three by clicking on the appropriate link.

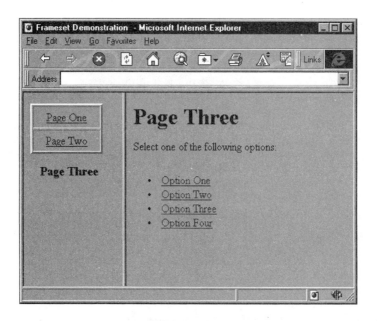

Click on one of the option links in the main frame. The **NavBar** frame reloads, displaying links to all three pages and to the options that weren't selected. The page for the option we clicked is displayed in the main frame.

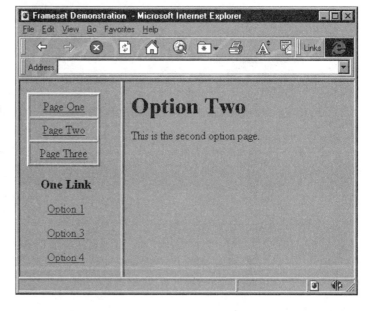

We could have implemented this in the same way we did the page navigation, but we've chosen an alternative method so that we can keep all of the navigation code in **navbar.asp**. If we used the first method, we would have to add many additional functions to the third page, making the content more difficult to modify independently of the script code, and further melding the site's logic and content–not a good thing.

In addition, suppose we had option arrays like this on each of our three pages. All of a sudden we need to maintain navigation code in four documents instead of one. Finally, as you'll see when we look at the code that implements this in **navbar.asp**, we are able to use the similarities between the text strings to move most of the code into a loop, further simplifying our design. In a real world situation we'd be far more likely to use entries from a database to populate this list, but even then the same code can apply—using the unique identifier for each database record instead of our arbitrary series of options from 1 to 4.

Changing Both Frames with Client-Side Code: Method Two

Those are the benefits, but how exactly does this second scheme work? Our first clue is the **HREF** attribute of each of the links on page three. Here's the code for the first link:

```
<LI><A TARGET="NavBar" HREF="navbar.asp?BarChoice=onelink&id=1">Option One</A>
```

We're using the **TARGET** attribute, which is the good old HTML-only way of targeting a page to a different frame from the one containing the link. The HTML here changes the contents of **NavBar** (which, since this code is in **MainFrame**, is in the other frame) to the URL **"navbar.asp?BarChoice=onelink&id=1"**. This code doesn't do anything about changing the page loaded into **MainFrame**, yet the page itself does indeed change.

It's only possible to directly change one frame or window with the **TARGET** attribute of the anchor tag. However, with some strategically placed client-side code, we can change more than that. In our example, code in **navbar.asp** is changing the contents of **MainFrame**, using the value of the **BarChoice** parameter—**onelink** in this case—to determine which block of code to execute. The value **id** parameter that follows it is used by the **onelink** code, as we'll see in a moment. Think about that for a second. The sequence is:

- ▲ Click on a link in frame **MainFrame** that points to **NavFrame** and **navbar.asp**,
- ▲ The **navbar.asp** page reloads and **NavFrame** is updated,
- ▲ Code in **navbar.asp** reloads **MainFrame**.

For example, the first link on page three passes the query string **BarChoice=onelink&id=1** to the navigation bar file **navbar.asp**. We've already looked at the **pagexxx** values of the **BarChoice** parameter that this code can handle, so let's look now at the final choice, **onelink**. The **Select Case** clauses for the other pages consisted of a block of HTML. The clause for **onelink** is a little more complicated, including two sets of ASP script in addition to the same HTML. We'll start with the familiar and move quickly into new territory.

The Navigation Bar 'onelink' Code

We see the same old table listing page options at the top of the finished **onelink** frame, and it's no surprise—the first visible HTML generated by **navbar.asp** for this option is the same as we've seen before in the other categories. After this table we display the list of options that aren't currently displayed. If we're currently showing **Option3.htm** in the main frame, we'd like to display links to options one, two, and four in the navigation bar. Our ASP code for this looks like:

```
<% For i = 1 to 4
       If CInt(CurrOption) <> i Then   'print link %>
           <A HREF="navbar.asp?barchoice=onelink&id=<%= i %>">
           Option <%= i %></a><p>
<%     End If
   Next %>
```

And it generates this HTML:

```
<A HREF="navbar.asp?barchoice=onelink&id=1">Option 1</a><p>
<A HREF="navbar.asp?barchoice=onelink&id=2">Option 2</a><p>
<A HREF="navbar.asp?barchoice=onelink&id=4">Option 4</a><p>
```

The code loops once for each element in our array of options, printing out a link every time, except for when the value stored in `CurrOption` is the same as our loop index. At the top of the `onelink` code we set a local variable called `CurrOption` to the value of the id portion of the query string. So calling `onelink` with an additional `&id=3` causes `CurrOption` to be set to `3`. This is the first use of the `id` parameter we've talked about–the second is in the code that loads the main frame.

Creating VBScript Code Dynamically

If you've looked at the entire code for the `onelink` clause you noticed this somewhat nasty looking section right at the beginning of the block:

```
Response.Write "<SCRIPT LANGUAGE=" & Chr(34) & "VBScript" & Chr(34) & ">" _
               & Chr(13) & Chr(10)
Response.Write "<!--" & Chr(13) & Chr(10)
Response.Write "Sub Window_OnLoad()" & Chr(13) & Chr(10)
Response.Write "On Error Resume Next" & Chr(13) & Chr(10)
strTemp = "Parent.frames(" & Chr(34) & "MainFrame" & Chr(34) _
         & ").location.href = " & Chr(34) & "Option" & CurrOption _
         & ".htm" & Chr(34)
Response.Write strTemp
Response.Write Chr(13) & Chr(10)
Response.Write "End Sub" & Chr(13) & Chr(10)
Response.Write "-->" & Chr(13) & Chr(10)
Response.Write "</SCRIPT>" & Chr(13) & Chr(10)
```

But, before we let ourselves be scared away by this mess, take a look at the nice and simple HTML code it generates for the browser:

```
<SCRIPT LANGUAGE="VBScript">
<!--
Sub Window_OnLoad()
   On Error Resume Next
   Parent.frames("MainFrame").location.href = "Option3.htm"
End Sub
-->
</SCRIPT>
```

What we have here is a block of ASP code on the server that generates a block of code that is to be executed on the client. This is very powerful–we're actually creating our client-side code 'on the fly' to suit our purposes.

Let's first understand how **navbar.asp** is using this code to reload **MainFrame**, and then we'll talk a little more about the ASP code that generated the code in the first place. The client-side code we end up with is relatively simple. Immediately after the HTML page has finished loading, the **Window_onLoad** event fires. In the code that is executed, we're using the **Frames** collection and **Location** object to load the contents of **Option3.htm** into our main frame. The only wrinkle is the handy placement of **On Error Resume Next** to avoid any unsightly errors in the navigation frame if a non-existent URL is accidentally specified in the next line.

All the ASP code does is to generate this small four-line subroutine by using a series of **Response.Write** calls. It uses **Chr(34)** to generate double quotes that can't be specified directly in the code because they will be interpreted as server-side code, and the line feeds and carriage returns so the final output is neatly placed on separate lines—a requirement for VBScript code.

Moving the Code to Our Own Site

That's all for this sample. We've covered a lot in the last few pages, and really showed how ASP can be used with client-side code to generate pages that weren't possible with just HTML or client-side code alone.

In moving the concepts in this example to your own site, you would keep much of the existing **frameset.asp** and **navbar.asp** code, modifying it to point to the actual files in your site. The rest of the files (**page*** and **option***) would be replaced by your content.

User Interface Improvements with Objects

We can wrap literally any code we might be able to execute in an application, inside an object for use on the World Wide Web. The last of our examples shows one of the many ways that objects can be used in HTML pages to better our user's perception our site. The object in this example, and correspondingly the sample itself, are both simple—but they'll give you an idea of what is possible.

This example uses a homemade ActiveX control object, created in Visual Basic 5. While we will be examining how we can build our own server components in this book, we won't even begin to get into creating client-side controls or objects. Rest assured it can be done, easily, with version 5.0 of Visual Basic.

> *For a detailed look at ActiveX control creation, see the Wrox Press publication* Instant VB 5.0 ActiveX Control Creation.

The User Interface Example

The single ASP page in this example asks first for a number in a single text box on a form:

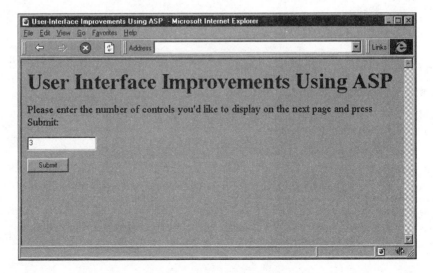

Clicking Submit returns a page, generated on the fly, containing as many objects as were specified on the first page. The object itself is an *extremely* simple bar graph control. This sample uses an ActiveX control created with Visual Basic 5.0, although we could use a Java applet if we had one available–the code would be the same.

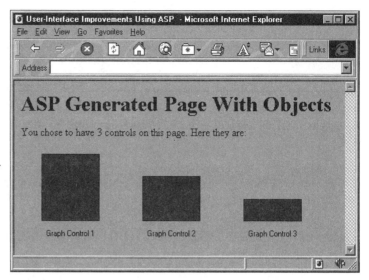

This example demonstrates the basic principles behind using the client-side **<OBJECT>** and **<APPLET>** tags to improve our ASP pages, and it does something that would be impossible with straight HTML–it displays data in a graphical format.

The UIImprovement Code

For the last time, let's dig into the code and see what's going on. One trick we use here, which you've seen earlier, is to have a single ASP page that both prompts for the initial input, and displays the page with the results on it.

Producing Two HTML Pages from One ASP File

Although we're generating two distinctly different pages in this example, all of our code resides in one **.asp** file. Our input form contains a hidden field named **hdnSecond**. When the page is first loaded, the value of this parameter in the **Request.Form** collection is an empty string, because we've never set it to anything. This makes the first **If ... Then** clause **True**, displaying the form and not the results. The entire page then, is dictated by this **If...Then...Else...End If** block:

```
<%
If Request.Form("hdnSecond") = "" Then
   'show input form with that includes this line:
   <INPUT TYPE="HIDDEN" NAME="hdnSecond" VALUE="Go">
   ...
Else
   'show result page with <OBJECT> tags
   ...
End If
%>
```

When the user presses the Submit button, the form is submitted to the same page because we used the **Request** object's **ServerVariables** collection, with the **SCRIPT_NAME** parameter, as the **ACTION** parameter of the new **<FORM>**. The **SCRIPT_NAME** member of the collection returns the name of the currently executing script page–which is where we want to send our data for processing again. However, this time the test on **hdnSecond** returns **False** because **hdnSecond** has been set to 'Go' in the input form.

The Results Page with <OBJECT> Tags

The second block of code generates the HTML for a page that contains a number of <OBJECT> tags– depending on how many the user originally specified:

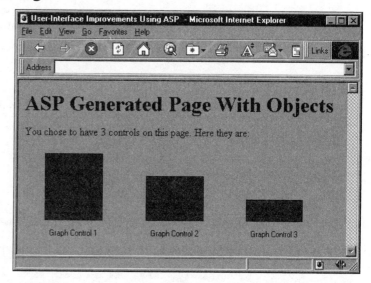

If they have accepted the default choice of three controls, we get a page with this HTML:

```
<HTML>
<HEAD>
<TITLE> User-Interface Improvements Using ASP </TITLE>
</HEAD>
<BODY>
<H1>ASP Generated Page With Objects</H1>
You chose to have 3 controls on this page. Here they are:<p>

<OBJECT ID="SimpleGraph1"
   WIDTH=155 HEIGHT=143 CODEBASE="control/graph.cab"
   CLASSID="CLSID:BD374B2A-8155-11D0-9472-9498CA000000">
   <PARAM NAME="Size" VALUE="100">
   <PARAM NAME="Caption" VALUE="Graph Control 1">
</OBJECT>

<OBJECT ID="SimpleGraph2"
   WIDTH=155 HEIGHT=143 CODEBASE="control/graph.cab"
   CLASSID="CLSID:BD374B2A-8155-11D0-9472-9498CA000000">
   <PARAM NAME="Size" VALUE="66.6666666666667">
   <PARAM NAME="Caption" VALUE="Graph Control 2">
</OBJECT>

<OBJECT ID="SimpleGraph3"
   WIDTH=155 HEIGHT=143 CODEBASE="control/graph.cab"
   CLASSID="CLSID:BD374B2A-8155-11D0-9472-9498CA000000">
   <PARAM NAME="Size" VALUE="33.3333333333333">
```

```
          <PARAM NAME="Caption" VALUE="Graph Control 3">
     </OBJECT>

     </BODY>
     </HTML>
```

Each of the three object tags is identical, except for the values of the **ID**, **NAME** and **SIZE** attributes in the **<PARAM>** tags. To differentiate the controls, and show how powerful ASP can be, we've modified these properties as we generated the page on the server. All that the requesting browser sees is the final HTML file; it doesn't know where or why the values are set as they are, it just does its job and renders the page.

The Magic within the Page

The great thing is how little server-side code really needs to be used to generate this HTML:

```
...
Else
    'show result page with <OBJECT> tags
     ...
    <% NumControls = Request.Form("txtNumControls") %>
    <H1>ASP Generated Page With Objects</H1>
    You chose to have <%= NumControls %> controls on this page.
    Here they are:<P>

<% For i = 1 to NumControls %>
    <OBJECT ID="SimpleGraph<%= i %>"
      WIDTH=155 HEIGHT=143 CODEBASE="control/graph.cab"
      CLASSID="CLSID:BD374B2A-8155-11D0-9472-9498CA000000">
        <PARAM NAME="Size" VALUE="<%= 100-((i-1) * (100 / NumControls)) %>">
        <PARAM NAME="Caption" VALUE="Graph Control <%= i %>">
    </OBJECT>
<% Next %>
...
End If
```

We first store the number of controls requested by the user in a variable called **NumControls**, then print out a string confirming this number. After this, all we have is a simple **For ... Next** loop that iterates **NumControls** times, printing a complete **<OBJECT>** tag each time. We append the loop index variable, **i**, to the string when producing the **ID** and **PARAM NAME** values. We also use **i** and some mathematics to generate a different **SIZE** value for each control.

The Control Directory

These **<OBJECT>** tags assume that the **CAB** file holding the VB 5.0 control is in a directory named **control**, beneath the current directory (i.e. in the **control** subdirectory of the directory where **uiimprovement.asp** lives). If the file **graph.cab** is in another location, and the control isn't already installed on your system, the graphs won't be displayed. You can fix this problem by moving the **CAB** file to the correct directory and refreshing the page.

And that's it. Again, our code in a real world situation with a more powerful control would likely be more complex, but the basic idea is the same. With ASP we generate dynamic **<OBJECT>** and **<APPLET>** tags on the fly, as we need them, even to the point of specifying different initialization parameters for each control.

Summary

We've covered a lot of ground over the last two chapters. You should now be able to judge when adding some client-side code or objects could improve your pages, both by adding responsiveness and reducing the workload placed on the server. And of course, the examples demonstrate ways that you can achieve tasks that just aren't possible using only server-side code.

The one big problem with client-side coding is the uncertainty about the environment of the browser. However, the two market leaders are tending to standardize on the features they support, while squeezing other browsers out altogether. As long as you ultimately design for these, you can be sure that the majority of viewers will benefit from your pages.

The main points in this chapter have been:

▲ There are often tasks we can't accomplish using just server-side code, and ASP. For this reason, client-side scripting, and objects like Java applets and ActiveX controls, can come in very useful.

▲ Client-side programming can also reduce network load and server processing requirements, especially with verification of information before submission.

▲ Spreading the processing load between server and client means that careful design is required, otherwise the application becomes almost impossible to maintain.

▲ Remember that client-side users can't be sure, with the examples we've see so far, that information submitted from form is not being intercepted or used improperly. At the same time, the server can never be really sure that the information they are receiving in genuine.

This last point is very important, and is the one thing likely to prevent the increasing spread of electronic commerce. In the next chapter, we change tack to look at this subject in a lot more detail.

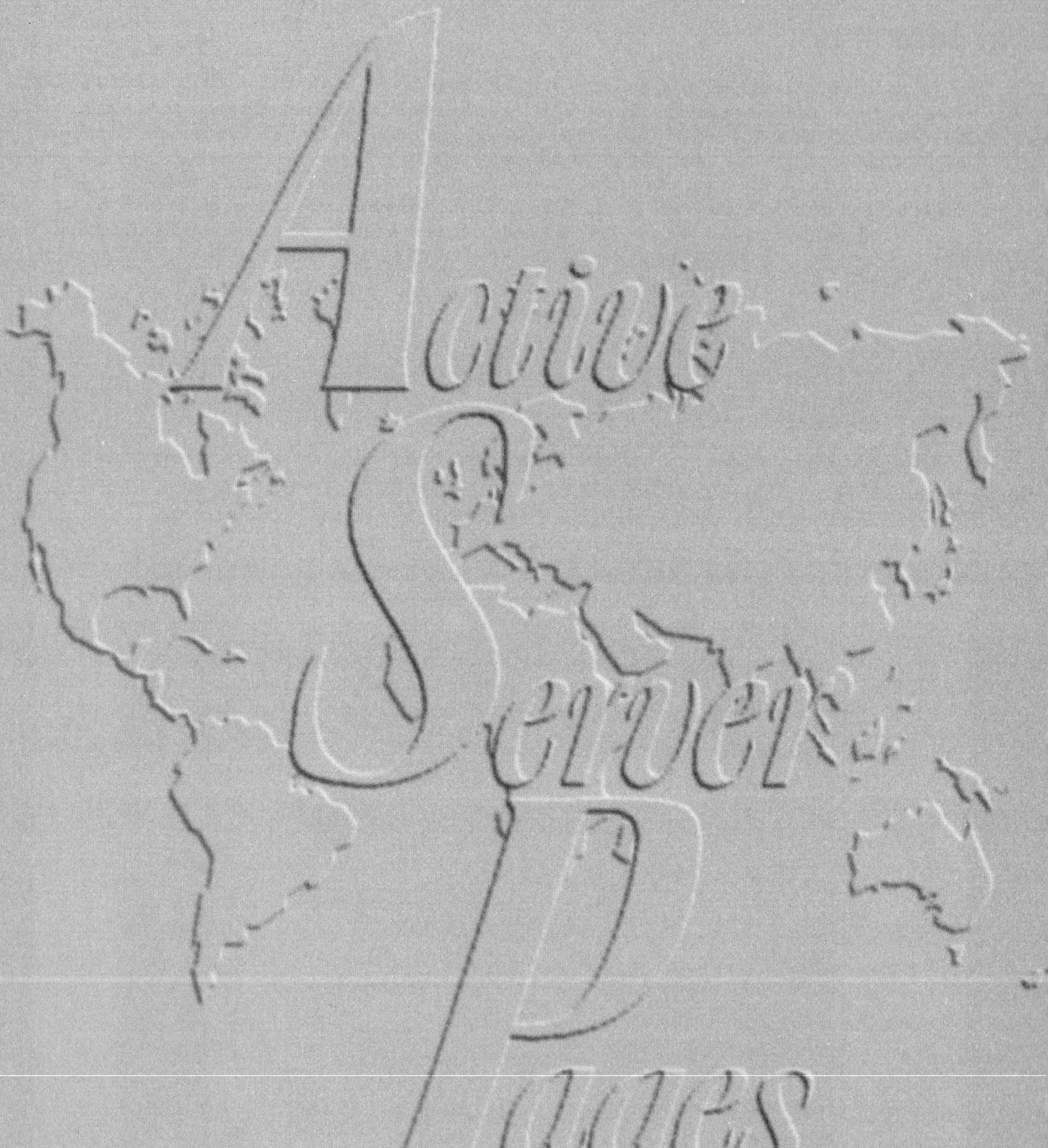
Active
Server
Pages

Implementing Server Security

CHAPTER 9

Many commercial organizations may regard the risks of doing business in cyberspace as unacceptable–but the rapid expansion of this powerful delivery channel means they make such decisions at their peril. Any hesitation means that their rivals will gain considerable momentum in using this potent technology.

There's also a lot of unfortunate and ignorant hype over Internet security. Scare stories are often generated by the same people who are quite happy to hand over a credit card to complete strangers in a shop and allow them to swipe, and potentially copy, their credit card. Like any commercial activity, the risks of using the Internet should be put in perspective. There now exists a comprehensive set of technologies enabling companies to build secure business applications for deployment over the Internet. To perform accurate risk analysis, it's important to understand what levels of protection each one provides.

In this chapter we shall address in depth the fundamental security technologies that are relevant to the Internet Information Server with Active Server Pages, and show how the Windows NT Active Server Framework provides the foundations of a bulletproof Web solution.

We'll be covering security issues in four different but related areas:

- Understanding and assessing the risks we face on the Internet
- The security features available from the NT operating system and IIS
- How we can use Secure Channel Services for our transactions
- The effect Active Server Pages has on the security of our site

But first, a little history....

Stand and Deliver!

In days gone by, evil highwayman, like the infamous Dick Turpin, patrolled the rough dirt tracks of Old England. They preyed on wayfarers and their possessions, and caused fear throughout the land. Only when the protection of the travelers and their cargo could be assured, were these rough tracks able to evolve into sensible highways, and provide the essential communications infrastructure for modern business and human lifestyle.

Today's so-called information superhighways are now going through a similar inaugural phase. Only when business has confidence that the systems can't be infiltrated, and network information can pass unimpeded will, electronic commerce–on a worldwide scale–intensify. We're on the way there, but there's still a long road lying out there in front of us.

Problems on the Internet

The security needs of Internet-based systems are very different from traditional networking. For example, there's no centralized infrastructure providing responsibility for network security. It's also on a huge global scale, with connected systems being open to a user base of potentially many millions. The initial conception and implementation of the Internet was to provide openness and robustness, and ensure the network was always available for all computers to connect to it. Even though the Internet was originally a defense network, the security of confidential information was considered secondary, because only trusted users had access to it.

In order for a business to access the full potential of the Internet and the huge user base, it must open its network and provide a shop window to promote its affairs. Whilst most visitors will be happy to look through this window, there will always be a few 'Peeping Toms' who will attempt to see things never intended for public scrutiny. Worst still, a small number of resourceful people will go one step further–and attempt to break the window, climb through, and without a doubt cause concern and damage.

The bandits of today's superhighway can be classified into three groups:

▲ **The Charlatans**–those who impersonate either an existing or a false person/organization. For example, consider the purchase of a book from a web site. How can you be confident that the vendor is really a legitimate business? Could your credit details have been sent to some imposter? Alternatively, how can the vendor be confident they are dealing with a legitimate customer?

▲ **The Spies**–those who access confidential information. For example, consider the transfer of some business plans via electronic mail. How can you be confident that these details are not being intercepted? Could they get passed on to your direct competitors?

▲ **The Vandals**–those who tamper with data. For example, consider the payment of your electricity bill via an Internet home banking service. How can you be confident that the instructions haven't been interfered with? Could the target account get altered, and the payment get directed to someone else's account?

Of course, some of these loathsome rogues, or 'hackers', will be resident in more than one of these groups. As Internet technology expands, these people are always finding new and ingenious mechanisms for their attacks. Unfortunately, the severe damage they can cause is often not discovered until it's too late.

If Internet communications are to become a key component in an organization's IT strategy, a set of technologies and standards to outmaneuver these people is required. The technologies that we'll discuss first in this chapter, in order to provide secure Active Server Pages solutions, are Windows NT Security and Secure Channel Services.

Windows NT Security Systems

The starting point for strong Internet security is the operating system of any machine connected to it. Fortunately for ASP users, strong levels of security were built into the core of Windows NT in order to meet and exceed certifiable security standards, i.e. the C2 security guidelines required by the U.S. Department of Defense's evaluation criteria. Windows NT security contrasts sharply with the thin and weak security layers that are often bolted on to the top of other operating systems.

Compliance with the C2 security standard was originally only required for government organizations. However, many commercial organizations are demanding the same level of security, and they recognize the value that such systems offer. The main requirements for C2 compliance are:

- ▲ **User identification and authentication**. Before gaining access to the systems, a user must prove their identity. This is typically done by providing a user-ID/password combination, for example by entering the details via a keyboard or by the presentation of a device such as a smart card which stores such information.

- ▲ **Discretionary access control**. Each object within the system, for example files, printers and processes, must have an owner—who can grant or restrict access to the resources at various degrees of granularity.

- ▲ **Auditing Capabilities**. The system must provide the ability to log all user actions and object access, and include enough information to identify the user that performed any operation. Such information must only be accessible by system administrators.

- ▲ **Safe Object reuse**. The system must guarantee that any discarded or deleted object can't be accessed, either accidentally or deliberately, by other entities.

- ▲ **System integrity**. The system must protect resources belonging to one entity, from being interfered with by another entity.

The C2 guidelines are applicable to standalone systems, and are specified in the document Trusted Computer System Evaluation Criteria (TCSEC). Fortunately, to make life simpler, this is often referred to as the **Orange Book**, thanks to the color of its cover. Other specifications that expand on the Orange Book include the Red Book for networking, and the Blue Book for subsystems.

Obtaining C2 certification is a long and complex task, and Microsoft are pushing hard for complete certification. Windows NT 3.51 has passed the Orange Book certification process and is on the DOD's official list of evaluated products. At the time of writing, Windows NT 4.0 is undergoing Orange Book re-certification, and Red and Blue book evaluations.

NT Directory Services

The following section is a crash course in **NT Directory Services** (NTDS). It's not intended to compete with the numerous books that are dedicated to NT administration, but is included to define various concepts that are used in the remainder of this chapter.

Directory Services is one of the services provided by NT. It enables a user to be identified, and provides access to the various resources throughout the systems and networks. In addition, it allows a system administrator to manage the users and the network, from any system on that network.

Understanding User Accounts

Everyone who has access to an NT system is identified by a **user account**, which comprises a user name, a password, and a number of logon parameters that are applied to that user; for example, the location of a script file that is automatically invoked at logon. A special NT user account is that of the **administrator**. Initially it is actually called Administrator, but really should be renamed: there's no point in giving a potential hacker half the account details for free!

The administrator has full control over the system, including the ability to create, amend and delete user accounts. The management of user accounts is done using the User Manager utility that is usually found by selecting the Start | Programs | Administrative Tools menus.

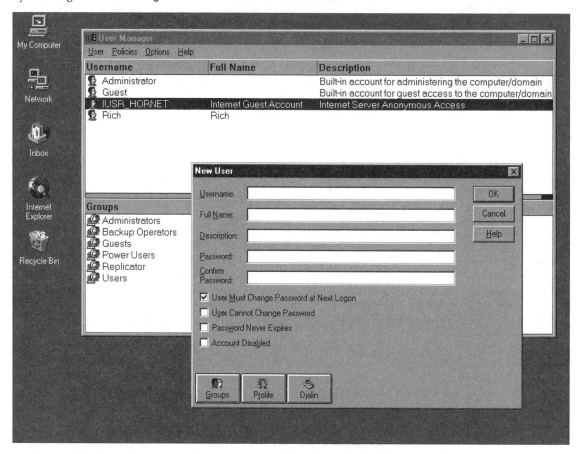

Another special user account created during NT installation is the guest account—initially called Guest and disabled. This is designed for people who require temporary access to the system.

Hopefully, the administrators will assign meaningful names to the user accounts, however these names are only used externally. Internally, NT handles user account names by using a one-to-one mapping with a unique identifier called the **Security ID** (SID). Even if a user account is deleted and then recreated with identical name, password, and logon parameters, it will be assigned a new SID. The internal SID value is never exposed to any users—including administrators.

Understanding User Groups

A group is a collection of user accounts, and is a powerful mechanism for granting common capabilities to a number of accounts in one operation. This is extremely useful when administrating systems with a large number of accounts. Groups are created, and users added into the groups, with the same User Manager utility as manages user accounts.

There are a number of predefined groups, including:

Administrators	users having full system control.
Users	users that can perform tasks for which they have been granted rights.
Guests	users requiring temporary access to the system.
Server Operators	users that can manage server resources
Account Operators	users that can manage user accounts.
Backup Operators	users that can back up and restore files.
Print Operators	users that can manage printers.

Understanding Domains

A **domain** is a logical group of computers that share a set of common user accounts and security information–this is stored in the NT Domain Services database. A version of the User Manager, called the User Manager for Domains, is used to maintain information in the NTDS database.

A domain includes one NT server designated as the **Primary Domain Controller** (PDC) that is responsible for storing the master NTDS database. In addition, one or more **Backup Domain Controllers** (BDC) may exist, which maintain a copy of the master NTDS database.

A user may logon to a domain, using any connected computer, and is validated by either a PDC or a BDC. The BDCs can share the workload in a heavily used network, and provide redundancy in case a PDC becomes unavailable. A PDC and BDC can also be an application server; for example, it can also host the Internet Information Server. In large enterprises, multiple domains may exist to reflect the business or territorial structure of the organization. It's possible to share resources across domains by setting up **Trust Relationships**.

However, the whole process of designing and setting up domains is outside the scope and concept of this book–we're assuming that you already have your internal network up and running, and you want to know more about how an Internet connection, and Active Server Pages, will affect it.

Understanding Access Rights

Once a user has successfully logged on to the domain, the NT security system dictates what resources that user may access. Different resources have different levels of access, and it's up to the users in the administrators and operators groups to define what level of access each user may have.

The User Rights Policy dialog within the User Manager utility can help to manage the rights granted to groups and user accounts. The security system will block any action by a user that doesn't have the appropriate rights.

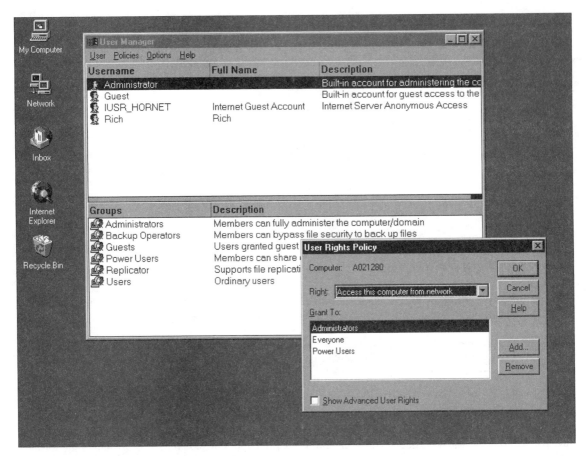

User rights are applicable to the system functions and differ from permissions that regulate to what level a user can access an individual object (such as a file or printer).

The following permissions can be assigned to a user for accessing a particular directory or file:

Read (R)   Allows viewing the names of files and subdirectories/file data.
Write (W)   Allows adding files and subdirectories/changing the file data.
Execute (X)   Allows running the file if it is a program file.
Delete (D)   Allows the deleting of a directory/file.
Change Permissions (P)   Allows changing the directory/file permissions.
Take Ownership (O)   Allows taking ownership of the directory/file.

Windows NT disks are either formatted as FAT (File Allocation Table) or NTFS (NT File System). Individual files resident on disks that are formatted as FAT don't have any security, and can only take the permissions of their parent directory. NTFS offers a greater level of security, since individual files can have their own specific permissions assigned.

Windows Explorer is used to apply or change the permissions of files and directories for individual users and groups. This is done by right-clicking on the appropriate directories, or files, and selecting the Properties option. In the Properties dialog, select the Security tab, followed by the Permissions button.

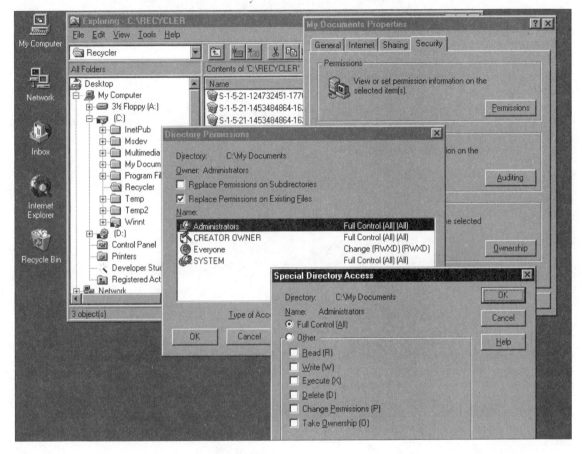

The security information of an object is stored in a **Security Descriptor**. This includes the name of the object owner, and something called an **Access Control List** (ACL). The ACL is a list of user accounts and groups (i.e. SIDs), and their associated access permissions. Each entry in the ACL is called an **Access Control Entry** (ACE).

Once a user's logon as been successfully validated, the system produces a **Security Access Token** (SAT), which is attached to any process invoked by that user. This SAT identifies the user, and is applied during all interactions with secured objects to determine the level of access allowed. All these terms are clarified in this diagram:

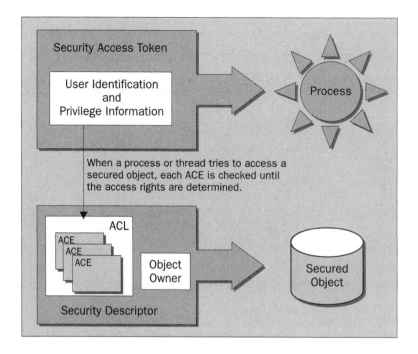

Internet Server Security

We shall now discuss how security is applied to users accessing our web site. The previous sections of this chapter have been a necessarily brief tour of the security features of Windows NT Server. This is intentional, because the subject that most concerns us is how we need to change our view of network security when we come to connect to the Internet.

To use Active Server Pages we have to be running a Microsoft Internet Server. For a 'real' web site, this will be Internet Information Server(IIS). In this section, we move on to see how security issues apply to this.

Aliased or Virtual Directories

The IIS and ASP services are built upon the NTDS security model. This means that all files and directories are protected by ACL permissions, applied as described above. All users accessing the IIS WWW service are either given guest access or authenticated (as we'll see shortly), and then given appropriate access to the various objects.

The WWW service restricts the files on the server that can be accessed to those that are resident in the WWWROOT directory created during installation. Access to additional directories, called **virtual directories**, can be configured using the Internet Service Manager utility. This is usually found by selecting the Start | Programs | Internet Information Server menus. These virtual directories can be created and deleted, and their attributes amended, by selecting the Directories tab of the WWW Properties page. As we saw back in Chapter 1, a virtual directory is a mapping between an **alias name** that is used as part of the URL, and a physical directory name–which could even be located on another machine. The Properties dialog allows Read and Executable permissions to be applied to IIS virtual directories.

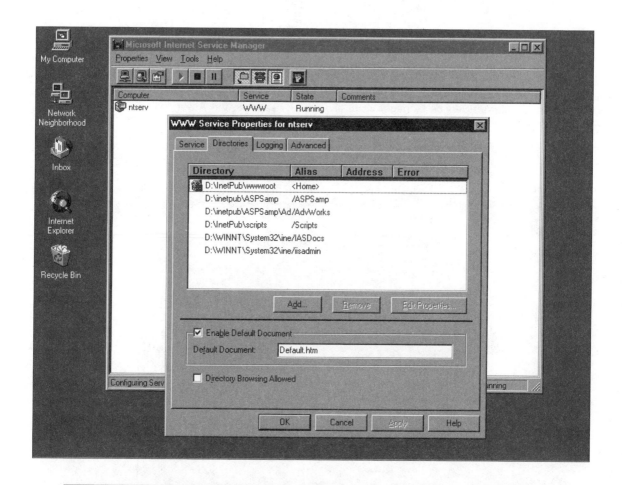

Shortly before publication of this book, Microsoft issued a security alert about a problem in IIS which affects any script files that are requested from a virtual directory that has both **Read** and **Execute** permissions set. Adding one or more extra periods (or full stops) on to the end of the URL will cause the file to be displayed in the browser instead of executed on the server, potentially allowing end-users to see information that may be confidential. Microsoft recommends that customers avoid this problem by putting script files in a separate virtual directory and disabling **Read** permission for that directory. A bug fix will be released in a future service pack.

IP Access Security Issues

This section describes some of the security options available for TCP/IP (Transmission Control Protocol/Internet Protocol). This is the communications protocol used by the Internet or an intranet. Most of the protocol's configuration is difficult, and well beyond the scope of this book. This chapter's focus is intended to highlight the security options available, and not get sucked into any low-level complexities–there are numerous books available dedicated exclusively to TCP/IP. What we're interested in, is what we need to do to ensure secure operation.

All machines on the Internet (or an intranet) are uniquely identified by four 8-bit numbers known as an **IP address**. IIS can be configured to either allow or deny access from any particular IP addresses. At first glance, you might think that this would provide a good mechanism for providing access control. However, the lack of available IP addresses has meant that many networks use techniques for randomly allocating IP addresses from an available pool, when the client first starts. The configuration of such IP addresses is done using the Internet Service Manager again–this time by selecting the Advanced tab of the WWW Properties page.

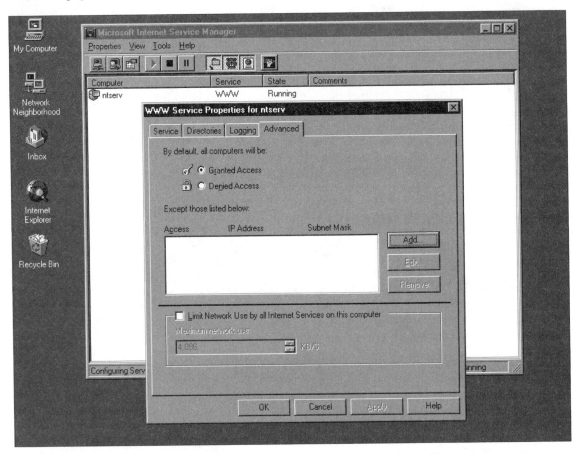

In addition to IP addresses, all communication channels over the Internet/intranet are identified by a number called a **port**. The value of the port number identifies the type of service operating on the channel. Some port numbers are reserved for common Internet services, for example:

21	**FTP**–File Transfer Protocol
23	**Telnet**–Terminal Emulation
25	**SMTP**—Simple Mail Transfer Protocol (email)

70	**Gopher**–navigation and file transfer of internet resources
80	**HTTP**—Hypertext Transfer Protocol (WWW)
119	**NNTP**–Network News Transfer Protocol (newsgroups)
194	**IRC**—Internet Relay Chat (conferencing)

Beginning with version 4.0, NT has the ability to filter IP protocol packets–allowing Internet services on particular ports to be either allowed or denied. Since you can use this to disable superfluous Internet services, NT can act in a similar way to a simple **firewall**. For example, you could configure NT with two network cards: one used to connect to the Internet, and the other to your LAN. Internet services on the Internet network card could be restricted to port **80** (HTTP) and port **21** (FTP). External access to any other services would be denied. To allow ASP full access to resources on the corporate LAN, all ports on the LAN network card would be enabled. This is shown here:

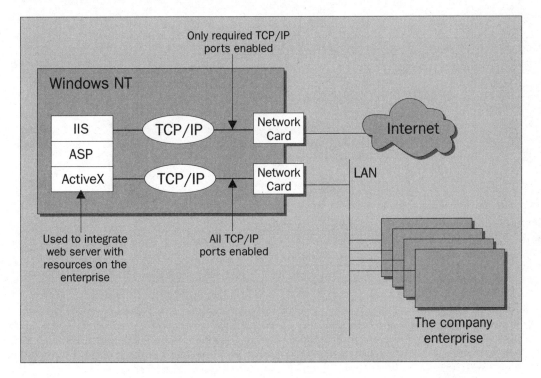

IP port filtering is enabled by means of the Network Control Panel. Select TCP/IP Properties on the Protocols tab. This provides an Advanced button, which displays a dialog including the Enable Security checkbox and a Configure button. This button finally produces another dialog where you can specify the filtering of ports.

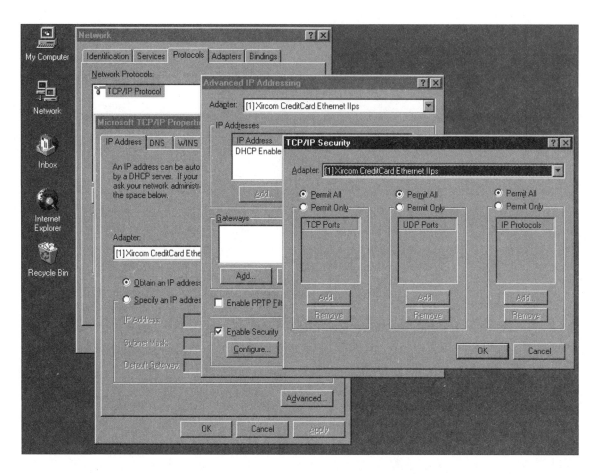

If the clients accessing our site are within a known set of approved users, or a closed user group, we can make life awkward for casual surfers by changing the port number of our WWW service. The port number is configured using the Internet Service Manager once more–this time by selecting the Service tab of the WWW Properties page. Users can access the HTTP service on a different port by specifying the port number as part of the URL. For example, `http://www.cyberdude.com:8989/` would be a web HTTP request on port `8989`. Conventional requests, which didn't include the port number, would fail.

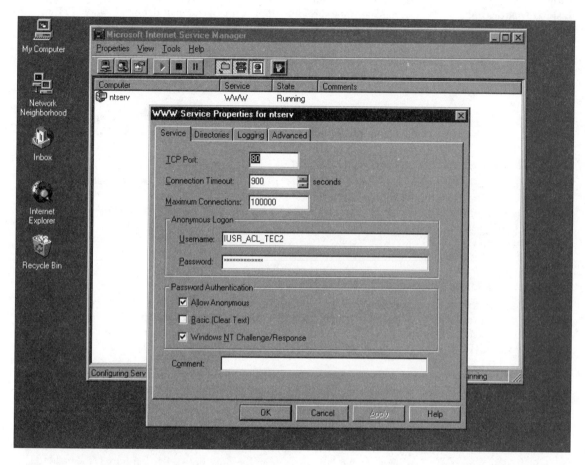

User Authentication by the Web Server

In order to apply NT security to the access of HTML, Active Server Pages, and other files, every user accessing the web site must be associated with an NT user account. This includes the web server itself, which is treated (almost) as just another user. The process of determining the user's identity, and having confidence that it really is that person, is known as **authentication**. Looking back at the previous screenshot, you can see that the WWW Properties page allows the following different authentication mechanisms to be configured:

Anonymous	A mechanism to allow access by a guest account user.
Basic Authentication	A mechanism to provide simple authentication as defined in the HTTP specifications by the World Wide Web Consortium (W3C), and the Organisation Européenne pour la Recherche Nucléaire (CERN–where the WWW was originally conceived).
Windows NT Challenge/Response	A mechanism developed by Microsoft to securely authenticate users.

The checkboxes for all of these methods work independently, meaning that it's possible to enable multiple authentication mechanisms, and the appropriate one is then automatically used for a request.

The IUSR Account—Anonymous Authentication

When IIS is installed, it creates an account called IUSR_*sysname* where *sysname* is the computer name of the NT system, as specified in the Identification tab of the Network Control Panel. This account is assigned to the Guests account group, allocated a random password, and given the user right to Log On Locally–which is a prerequisite to access the IIS WWW services. Provided that Anonymous authentication has been enabled, users accessing WWW services are allowed access to those resources with the permissions allocated to the IUSR_*sysname* account.

Basic and Challenge/Response Authentication

Both the Basic Authentication and the Windows NT Challenge/Response mechanism work in a similar fashion. If the user requests a resource for which the IUSR_*sysname* user account doesn't have the appropriate permissions, the request is rejected with a 401 Access Denied message, and the browser is informed through HTTP what authentication methods the server *will* support.

Provided that a suitable method has been enabled, most modern browsers will then prompt the user for a user name and password, and submit this with another request for the same resource. IIS will then validate the user account details supplied, and if successful invoke the request under the identity of this user rather than the IUSR_*sysname* account–thus having access to those resources for which the user account has permissions assigned. The difference between Basic Authentication and Windows NT Challenge/Response is that the latter provides encryption of the user name and password, whereas Basic Authentication sends this information as normal 'clear' text. At the time of writing, the only browser to support NT Challenge/ Response is Microsoft's Internet Explorer, although this is expected to change soon.

> *The undesirable transmission of user names and passwords as clear text can be overcome using Secure Channel encryption–which we'll meet shortly.*

The big advantage of using NT Challenge/Response methods and Internet Explorer in an intranet environment is that, should the user be currently logged on to an NT domain, their user account name and password will automatically be used–so avoiding the need to duplicate any logon process when retrieving files. Hence, access by different users to different sets of files and information can be secured– transparently and automatically in a normal LAN-like manner.

Authentication in Action

The following HTTP trace files show this WWW authentication in action. Firstly, **Anonymous Authentication**, where IUSR_*sysname* has Read permission for the file /rich/rhnav.htm:

29/01/97
23:40:23
Sent

```
GET /rich/rhnav.htm HTTP/1.0
Accept: image/gif, image/x-xbitmap, image/jpeg,
image/pjpeg, application/vnd.ms-excel, application/
msword, application/vnd.ms-powerpoint, */*

Accept-Language: en
UA-pixels: 800x600
UA-color: color8
UA-OS: Windows NT
UA-CPU: x86
User-Agent: Mozilla/2.0 (compatible; MSIE 3.0B; Win32)
Host: 194.1.1.32
Connection: Keep-Alive
-----------------------------------------------
```

This is the request message sent from the browser to the web server, to request the resource.

29/01/97
23:40:23
Received

```
HTTP/1.0 200 OK
Server: Microsoft-IIS/3.0
Connection: keep-alive
Date: Wed, 29 Jan 1997 23:40:23 GMT
Content-Type: text/html
Accept-Ranges: bytes
Last-Modified: Sat, 11 Jan 1997 19:34:16 GMT
Content-Length: 1653
<html>
.... etc ....
</html>
-----------------------------------------------
```

This is the response message, including the contents of the requested HTML file.

Here, the request contains no account information about the user, just the usual HTTP Host IP address. The server logs on to NT using the IUSR_*sysname* account, and finds that it can access and retrieve the file—so it can return it to the requestor.

Next, we'll see how **Basic Authentication** works. Both Anonymous Authentication and Basic Authentication have been enabled in the **WWW Properties** dialog. The difference this time is that the IUSR_*sysname* account does *not* have **Read** permission for the file:

30/01/97
14:52:49
Sent

```
GET /rich/rhnav.htm HTTP/1.0
Accept: image/gif, image/x-xbitmap, image/jpeg,
image/pjpeg,application/vnd.ms-excel,
application/msword, application/vnd.ms-powerpoint, */*

Accept-Language: en
UA-pixels: 800x600
UA-color: color8
UA-OS: Windows NT
UA-CPU: x86
User-Agent: Mozilla/2.0 (compatible; MSIE 3.0B; Win32)
Host: 194.1.1.32
Connection: Keep-Alive
-----------------------------------------------
```

This is the request message sent from the browser to the web server, to request the file. It's the same as the last time, of course, with no user account information.

30/01/97 14:52:49 Received	HTTP/1.0 401 Access Denied WWW-Authenticate: Basic realm="194.1.1.32" Content-Length: 24 Content-Type: text/html Error: Access is Denied.	*This is the response rejecting access, as the* IUSR *account doesn't have appropriate permissions. In the second line it informs the browser that that* Basic Authentication *is enabled.*

30/01/97 14:53:23 Sent	GET /rich/rhnav.htm HTTP/1.0 Accept: image/gif, image/x-xbitmap, image/jpeg, image/pjpeg, application/vnd.ms-excel, application/msword, application/vnd.ms-powerpoint, */* Accept-Language: en UA-pixels: 800x600 UA-color: color8 UA-OS: Windows NT UA-CPU: x86 User-Agent: Mozilla/2.0 (compatible; MSIE 3.0B; Win32) Host: 194.1.1.32 Connection: Keep-Alive Authorization: Basic YWRtaW5pc3RyYXRvcjpob3JuZXQ=	*The browser then prompts for the user name and password.* *This is the new request message (now including the account information) sent from the browser to the web server to request the resource.* *Though the account information looks encrypted it is in fact only Base64 encoded. The account name and password can easily be identified.*

30/01/97 14:53:23 Received	HTTP/1.0 200 OK Server: Microsoft-IIS/3.0 Connection: keep-alive Date: Thu, 30 Jan 1997 14:53:23 GMT Content-Type: text/html Accept-Ranges: bytes Last-Modified: Wed, 22 Jan 1997 09:18:08 GMT Content-Length: 909 <html> ...... etc ...... </html>	*The account details sent from the browser have been successfully validated. This is the response message including the contents of the file.*

So this process allows the web server to access files for which it doesn't have permissions, by simply passing on the user's ID and password. Providing that user has the correct permissions, NT then allows the web server, which is acting on behalf of that user, to access that file.

Lastly, let's look at the most complex of the three methods, **Windows NT Challenge/Response**. This time, all three types of authentication have been enabled in the **WWW Properties** dialog, and again the IUSR_*sysname* doesn't have **Read** permission for the file:

30/01/97 11:28:50 Sent	GET /rich/innav.htm HTTP/1.0 Accept: image/gif, image/x-xbitmap, image/jpeg, image/pjpeg, application/vnd.ms-excel, application/ msword, application/vnd.ms-powerpoint, */* Accept-Language: en UA-pixels: 800x600 UA-color: color8 UA-OS: Windows NT	*This is the request message sent from the browser to the web server, to request the resource.*

UA-CPU: x86
User-Agent: Mozilla/2.0 (compatible; MSIE 3.0B; Win32)
Host: 194.1.1.32
Connection: Keep-Alive

30/01/97 11:28:50 Received	HTTP/1.0 401 Access Denied WWW-Authenticate: NTLM WWW-Authenticate: Basic realm="194.1.1.32" Content-Length: 24 Content-Type: text/html Error: Access is Denied. ---	*This is the response rejecting access, as the* IUSR *account doesn't have appropriate permissions. This time it informs the browser that both* Basic Authentication *and* Challenge/ Response (NTLM) *are enabled.*
30/01/97 11:28:51 Sent	GET /rich/innav.htm HTTP/1.0 Accept: image/gif, image/x-xbitmap, image/jpeg, image/pjpeg, application/vnd.ms-excel, application/msword, application/vnd.ms-powerpoint, */* Accept-Language: en UA-pixels: 800x600 UA-color: color8 UA-OS: Windows NT UA-CPU: x86 User-Agent: Mozilla/2.0 (compatible; MSIE 3.0B; Win32) Host: 194.1.1.32 Connection: Keep-Alive Authorization: NTLM TlRMTVNTUAABAAAAA7IAAAMAAwAnAAAABwAHACAA AABBMDIxMjgwQUNMAAAAQAAAAAAAAABAAAAAcIA AA== ---	*The browser will now attempt authentication using the same account information that the user is currently logged onto the network with.* *This is the new request (now including the encrypted account information) sent from the browser to the web server to request the resource. The browser will automatically choose Challenge/Response if this is available.*
30/01/97 11:28:51 Received	HTTP/1.0 401 Access Denied WWW-Authenticate: NTLM TlRMTVNTUAACAAAAAAAAACgAAAABwgAAFoycWyKa YbMAAAAAkJMVAE== Connection: keep-alive Content-Length: 24 Content-Type: text/html Error: Access is Denied. ---	*This response message is sent back from the server. It's part of the NT Challenge/Response negotiation, and contains further authentication details.*
30/01/97 11:28:51 Sent	GET /rich/innav.htm HTTP/1.0 Accept: image/gif, image/x-xbitmap, image/jpeg, image/pjpeg, application/vnd.ms-excel, application/msword, application/vnd.ms-powerpoint, */* Accept-Language: en UA-pixels: 800x600 UA-color: color8 UA-OS: Windows NT UA-CPU: x86	*The browser automatically sends this request message back, again as part of the NT Challenge/Response negotiation.*

```
User-Agent: Mozilla/2.0 (compatible; MSIE 3.0B; Win32)
Host: 194.1.1.32
Connection: Keep-Alive
Authorization: NTLM
TlRMTVNTUAADAAAAAAAAAEAAAAAAAAAAQAAAAAAAAB
AAAAAAAAAEAAAAAAAAAAQAAAAAAAABAAAAAAclAAA==
-------------------------------------------------
```

At this point, the user ID and password that user logged into their workstation, LAN or domain with, is used by the web server to access the file, instead of the IUSR_*systemname* account information. If the user has permission for the file, it will now be returned–just like **Basic Authentication**. In our example, however, things aren't that simple. Let's assume that the user doesn't have permission for the file with the details they logged on to the LAN with. NT, and therefore the web server, will again deny the request:

30/01/97 11:28:51 Received	HTTP/1.0 401 Access Denied WWW-Authenticate: NTLM WWW-Authenticate: Basic realm="194.1.1.32" Content-Length: 24 Content-Type: text/html Error: Access is Denied. ---	*This is the response message that rejects access, because the user account currently logged on doesn't have the appropriate permissions. The browser automatically prompts for another user name and password.*
30/01/97 11:29:38 Sent	GET /rich/innav.htm HTTP/1.0 Accept: image/gif, image/x-xbitmap, image/jpeg, image/pjpeg, application/vnd.ms-excel, application/msword, application/vnd.ms-powerpoint, */* Accept-Language: en UA-pixels: 800x600 UA-color: color8 UA-OS: Windows NT UA-CPU: x86 User-Agent: Mozilla/2.0 (compatible; MSIE 3.0B; Win32) Host: 194.1.1.32 Connection: Keep-Alive Authorization: NTLM TlRMTVNTUAABAAAAA5IAAAMAAwAgAAAAAAAAAA AAAABBQ0wAAAAAAAAAAAAQAAAAAAAABAAAA AAclAAA== ---	*This is the new request message, which now includes account information entered by the user for this particular request. It's sent from the browser to the web server to request the resource again.*
30/01/97 11:29:38 Received	HTTP/1.0 401 Access Denied WWW-Authenticate: NTLM TlRMTVNTUAACAAAAAAAACgAAAABggAA5oKRq7F IM0QAAAAAAAAAA== Connection: keep-alive Content-Length: 24 Content-Type: text/html Error: Access is Denied. ---	*This response message is sent back from the server. It's part of the NT Challenge/Response negotiation.*

30/01/97	GET /rich/innav.htm HTTP/1.0	*The browser automatically sends this*
11:29:38	Accept: image/gif, image/x-xbitmap, image/jpeg,	*request message back, again as part of*
Sent	image/pjpeg, application/vnd.ms-excel,	*the NT Challenge/Response*
	application/msword, application/vnd.ms-powerpoint, */*	*negotiation.*

Accept-Language: en
UA-pixels: 800x600
UA-color: color8
UA-OS: Windows NT
UA-CPU: x86
User-Agent: Mozilla/2.0 (compatible; MSIE 3.0B; Win32)
Host: 194.1.1.32
Connection: Keep-Alive
Authorization: NTLM

TIRMTVNTUAADAAAAGAAYAHYAAAAYABgAjgAAAA4
ADgBAAAAAGgAaAE4AAAAOAA4AaAAAAAAAACm
AAAAAYIAAEEAMAAyADEAMgA4ADAAYQBkAG0AaQ
BuAGkAcwB0AHIAYQB0AG8AcgBBADAAMgAxADIAO
AAwAByc4FDb+4fwflx6Qtntd5lrkgegMrMWjacvu349PY
kEavY87CleD/lbMq4KSTedMg==

30/01/97	HTTP/1.0 200 OK	*The entered account details have been*
11:29:38	Server: Microsoft-IIS/3.0	*successfully validated. This is the*
Received	Connection: keep-alive	*response message that includes the*
	Date: Thu, 30 Jan 1997 11:29:38 GMT	*contents of the requested HTML file.*

Content-Type: text/html
Accept-Ranges: bytes
Last-Modified: Wed, 22 Jan 1997 09:18:08 GMT
Content-Length: 909
<html>
..... etc .....
</html>

The file is retrieved and returned to them only after the user has entered details of a different user account, that *does* have permission for the file. This allows the administrator to effectively divide up the resources on the site. Some can be available to individual users, who have to supply the relevant passwords before they can access them, while others will be freely available to everyone.

Secure Channel Services

We'll now move on to look at a software technology that provides a higher level of security than those we've just seen. It enables additional endpoint authentication, message encryption, and message authentication to be used–in fact, all the weapons we need to defeat the charlatans, spies and vandals we met earlier. This software is called **Secure Channel Services** (SCS).

As we all know, the Internet or an intranet is a network of many machines, all communicating using the **TCP/IP protocol** standards. A protocol is a set of rules and procedures that define how two entities communicate. A **protocol stack** is a combination of several protocols, where each layer is responsible for handling a specific function. The TCP/IP protocol stack is shown here:

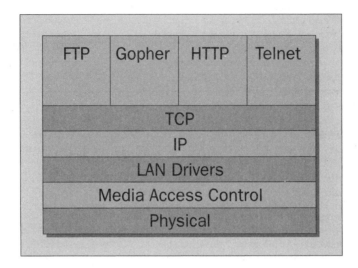

Transmission Control Protocol (the TCP part) is sometimes referred to as a transport protocol—it guarantees that packets of data are sent and received without error. It also ensures that received packets are ordered into the same sequence that they were transmitted.

Internet Protocol (the IP part) is sometimes referred to as a network protocol—it is responsible for addressing and routing packets over the network.

Application protocols (such as HTTP and FTP) provide the specific application data transfer logic using the lower levels for the actual delivery. Secure Channel Services transparently slots into the TCP/IP protocol stack, as shown here:

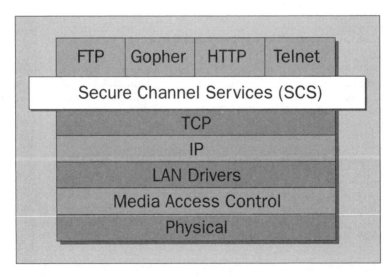

SCS is shipped with IE3.0 and NT4.0 as a dynamic-link library (`schannel.dll`) and provides the following features:

▲ **Privacy**–packets can't be examined

▲ **Integrity**–packets can't be tampered with

▲ **Authentication**–enables either the client or server to request identification of the other

SCS actually provides support for several standard security protocols:

SSL 2.0 / SSL 3.0	**Secure Socket Layer** developed by Netscape
PCT 1.0	**Private Communications Technology** developed by Microsoft
TLS (future release)	**Transport Layer Security** which is intended to provide a simpler and more robust solution by using the best parts of SSL and PCT

Before we can understand how SCS works, we need to investigate the cryptography it uses, and then see how to implement it on our systems.

Low-level discussions on cryptography are normally reserved for those with brains the size of a planet– since this book is supposed to be about Active Server Pages, we'll keep things simple and dive in just deep enough to get a basic understanding of how it all works.

A Simple Guide to Cryptography

Cryptography is an ancient mathematical science that was originally used for military communications, and designed to conceal the contents of a message should it fall into the hands of the enemy. Recent developments in cryptography have added additional uses, including mechanisms for authenticating users on a network, ensuring the integrity of transmitted information and preventing users from repudiating (i.e. rejecting ownership of) their transmitted messages.

In today's world of electronic commerce on the Internet, the need for secure communications is obviously crucial. Cryptographic technologies provide enterprises with the best mechanisms of protecting their information, without putting the business at risk by exposing it on the Net.

What is Encryption?

Encryption is the name given to the process of applying an algorithm to a message, which scrambles the data in it–making it very difficult and time consuming, if not practically impossible, to deduce the original given only the encoded data. Inputs to the algorithm typically involve additional secret data called **keys**, which prevents the message from being decoded–even if the algorithm is publicly known.

The safekeeping of keys, in other words their generation, storage and exchange, is of paramount importance to ensure the security of the data. There's no point applying the strongest levels of cryptographic algorithms, if your keys are stored on a scrap of paper in your in-tray.

The strength of the encryption is dependent on two basic items: the nature of the mathematical algorithm and the size of the keys involved. Under US arms regulations, the length of the key that can be used in exported software is limited. However, there's no limitation on the level of encryption used *within* the US, or sold in Canada.

Unfortunately the 40-bit encryption limit, which has been in force up until recently, has been proven to provide little security from attack. Today's powerful processors, costing just a few hundred dollars, can crack such a message in a few hours by using brute force– that is, by trying every possible key until the decrypted message has been found. More expensive supercomputers can crack such messages in sub-second times! Each extra bit in the key doubles the time needed for the brute force attack, and most experts now claim that 128-bit keys are required to ensure complete confidence, and are vital for markets such as electronic commerce.

Many non-US companies have now developed add-on cryptographic products, using 128-bit key technology, to fill the vacuum left by the US software industry's inability to compete in this market. Naturally, there's a lot of discussion between concerned parties, and the future of these export restrictions is unclear.

Symmetric Cryptography—Secret Keys

In **symmetric cryptography**, the encryption algorithm requires the same secret key to be used for both encryption and decryption. Because of the type of key, this is sometimes called **secret key encryption**. This diagram shows how it works:

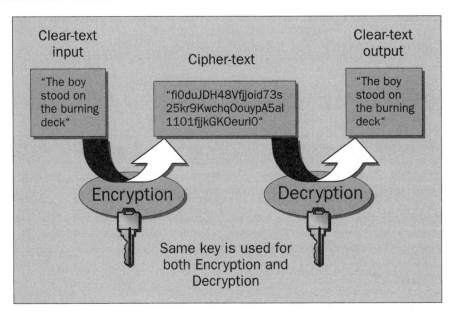

The advantage of these algorithms is that they are fast and efficient. However, the problem is that of key exchange–that is, the mechanism for safely ensuring both parties, the sender and the receiver, have the secret key. This is one of the weakest areas of symmetric cryptography. How do you send the key to your partners? You can't just send it in an email message, because it could be intercepted and, possibly unknowingly, compromise your security. Furthermore, how can you be sure that your partners will keep your key secure?

Asymmetric Cryptography—Public/Private Keys

One solution to the problem of key security is **asymmetric cryptography**. This uses two keys that are mathematically related. One key is called the **private key** and is never revealed, and the other is called the **public key** and is freely given out to all potential corespondents. The complexity of the relationship between the public key and the private key means that, provided the keys are long enough, it's practically impossible to determine one from the other. The one problem with asymmetric cryptography is that the processing required is very CPU intensive.

The almost universal public/private key algorithm is named **RSA** after its creators (Ron Rivest, Adi Shamir, and Len Adleman), and patented by RSA Data Security Inc. in 1977. A sender uses the receiver's public key to encrypt the message. Only the receiver has the related private key to decrypt the message. This is shown here:

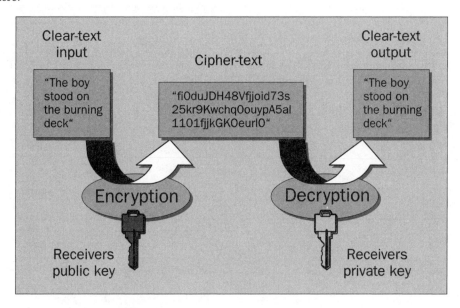

Digital Signature Encryption

An additional use of RSA is in **digital signatures**, which involves swapping the role of the private and public keys. If a sender encrypts a message using their private key, everyone can decrypt the message using the sender's public key. A successful decryption implies that the sender, who is the only person in possession of their private key, must have sent the message.

This also prevents repudiation, that is, the sender can't claim that they didn't actually send the message. A piece of data encrypted with a private key is called a digital signature. Common practice is to use a message digest as the item of data to be encrypted.

Using a Message Digest

A **message digest** is a digital fingerprint of a message, derived by applying a mathematical algorithm on a variable-length message. There are a number of suitable algorithms, called **hash functions**, each having the following special properties:

- The original message (the input) is of variable-length.

- The message digest (the output) is of a fixed-length.

- It's practically impossible to determine the original message (the input) from just the message digest (the output). This is known as being a **one-way hash function**.

▲ It's practically impossible to find two different messages (the inputs) that derive to the same message digest (the output) – this is known as being a **collision-free hash function**.

▲ The algorithm is relatively simple, so when computerized it isn't CPU-intensive.

▲ The calculated digest is (often considerably) smaller than the item it represents.

You can use message digests to guarantee that no one has tampered with a message during its transit over a network. Any amendment to the message will mean that the message and digest will not correlate. Also, message digests can also be used to supply proof that an item of information, such as a password, is known—without actually sending the password or information in the clear.

The most common message digest algorithms designed for 32-bit computer systems are **MD4**, **MD5** and **Secure Hash Algorithm** (SHA), which offer—in that order—increasing levels of security, and therefore CPU usage. The next diagram illustrates how a message digest is used to digitally sign a document:

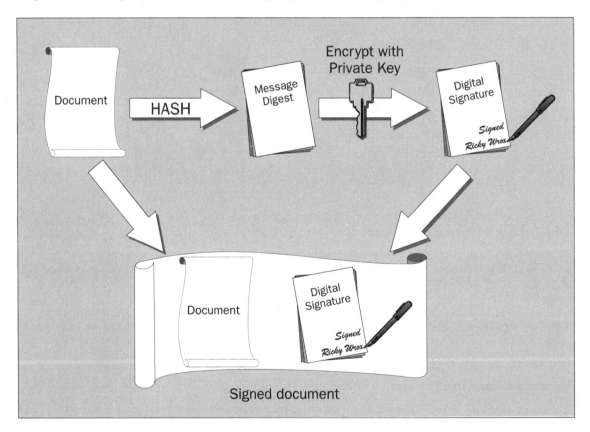

Note that this document is **signed** (its integrity and origin are assured) but it isn't **encrypted**—anyone could look at the original document included with the signed digest. This doesn't imply that the document can't be encrypted as well, however. This diagram shows how the same document is validated:

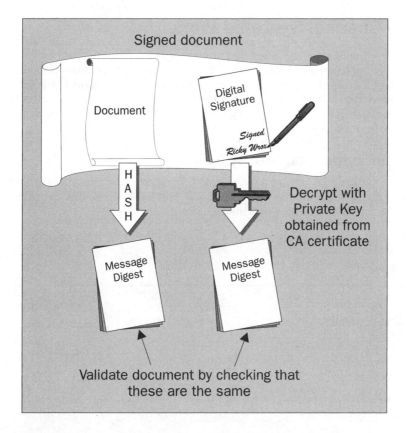

Digital Certificates and Certificate Authorities

A digital certificate is an item of information that binds the details of an individual or organization to their public key. The most widely accepted format for digital certificates is the X.509 standard, and is relevant to both clients and servers. If we can obtain access to someone's certificate we have their public key, and can therefore get involved in the secure communications already discussed.

But what is there to stop anybody just creating a false certificate, and pretending that they are someone else? The solution is **Certificate Authorities** (CAs), who are responsible for the issuing of digital certificates. A CA is a commonly trusted third party, responsible for verifying both the contents and ownership of a certificate.

There is an ever-increasing number of CAs. Different CAs will employ different amounts of effort in their verification processes, and they must publicly divulge what checks they perform. Then users can apply the appropriate levels of trust for each CA they encounter. Also, different classes of certificates are available, which reflect the level of assurance given by the CA–a certificate for users who just surf the web requires less verification than a certificate for a business server. If two entities trust the same CA, they can swap digital certificates to obtain access to each other's public key, and from then onwards they can undertake secure transmissions between themselves.

Digital certificates include the CA's digital signature (i.e. information encrypted with the CA's private key). This means that no one can create a false certificate. The public keys of trusted CA's are stored for use by applications like Internet Explorer as we'll see in a while.

How Secure Channel Systems Work

Now that we have a good understanding of some basic cryptographic concepts, we'll move on and see how they are actually put into practice. We learned earlier that SCS provides support for a number of security protocols. Each of these has their own specific low-level operation and complexities that we don't intend to cover. Instead we'll investigate how all such protocols solve the general problem of connection, negotiation, and key exchange; and how this software technology protects us against the spies, vandals and charlatans out there in the big wide world beyond our Internet connection.

Client-server Authentication with SCS

We'll first look at how a client called C and a server called S negotiate a secure communications link. The following table shows the messages that pass between C and S. S has to prove that its certificate is valid by showing that it has the private key to encrypt a message digest:

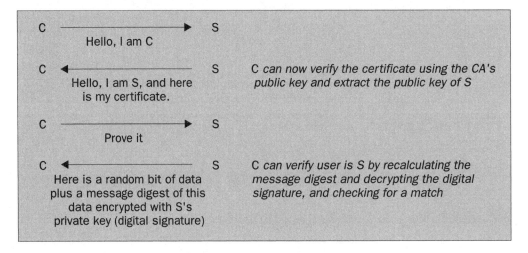

But what if there was an imposter called I, who was trying to impersonate S?

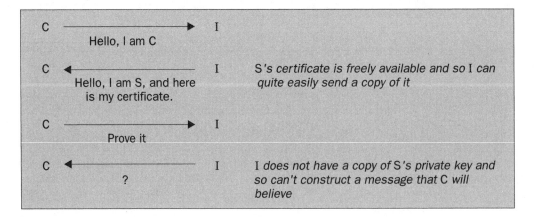

From this we can see how a user can be confident that remote server is who it claims to be. It also highlights the importance of the protection of private keys.

Encrypting and Sending Messages

Now that c has s's public key, it can send a message to s that only s can decrypt—because this task requires s's private key. However, we learned earlier that asymmetric cryptography is much more CPU-intensive than symmetric cryptography. Thus c generates a random secret key and informs s of its value using asymmetric cryptography. From then onwards, encryption is done by symmetric cryptography with only c and s knowing the secret key.

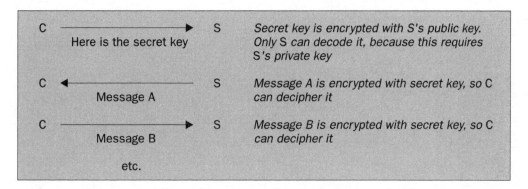

Authenticating Messages against Tampering

Now let's consider another bad guy called E who eavesdrops on the network, and could intercept and tamper with a messages en route to their destinations.

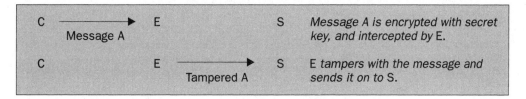

Because the message is encrypted, it is unlikely that tampering with it will create a valid message—but who knows, he might get lucky?

The solution is to attach a **message authentication code** (MAC) to each message. The MAC is a message digest value, calculated using a hash algorithm on the message contents and the secret key. The message receiver calculates the MAC value for the message and checks for a match with the attached MAC value. Since E doesn't know the secret key, it is unlikely that they could evaluate the correct MAC for his new tampered message.

Implementing Secure Channels

So now we know what Secure Channel Services is, and how it works in outline. The next step is to see how we configure IIS web services and Internet Explorer to use Secure Channels.

Configuring Internet Information Server

Enabling SSL security on IIS requires us to first obtain a digital certificate that contains our details, and is verified by a CA. The configuration of keys is handled by the Key Manager utility, which can be found by selecting the Start | Programs | Internet Information Server menus, or alternatively from the Tools menu options of the Internet Service Manager.

To create a new public/private key pair, select the Create New Key option from the Key menu and the dialog requests the following items:

- **Key Name**–name given to key

- **Password**–used to protect the private key

- **Bits**–key size: 512, 768, 1024–large keys are more secure. Export versions are restricted to 512.

- **User details**, comprising:

    organization–company name *e.g. Wrox Press Inc.*

    organization Unit–unit name within company *e.g. Richard Harrison*

    common Name–TCP/IP domain name of server *e.g. www.wrox.com*

    country–two character ISO code *e.g. US*

    state/Province–state name of address *e.g. Illinois*

    locality–city name of address *e.g. Chicago*

- **Request File**–name of a file to be generated by the Key Manager, and used to store the information that is sent to the CA for the certificate to be generated.

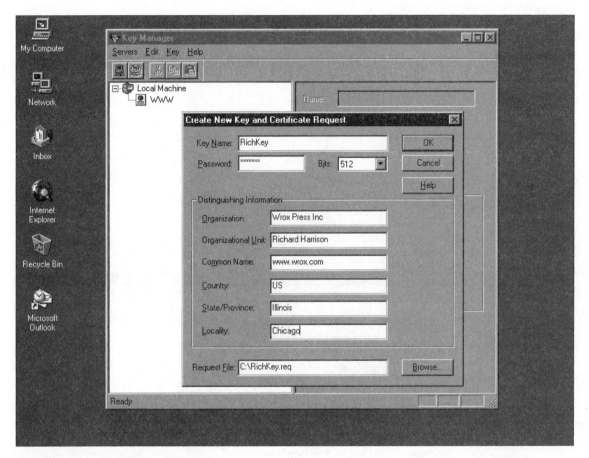

Sending the Certificate Request

After selecting OK and confirming the password, a dialog is displayed requesting the email address and telephone number of the administrator. Once these details have been entered, a dialog is displayed confirming that the keys have been created, and explaining that you must send the details to your CA for the certificate to be generated. These are the contents of the request file generated for the details shown in the previous screen shot:

```
Webmaster: rich@cyberdude.com
Phone: +44 1111 22222
Server: Microsoft Key Manager for IIS 2.0
```

```
Common-name: www.wrox.com
Organization Unit: Richard Harrison
Organization: Wrox Press Inc
Locality: Chicago
State: Illinois
Country: US

-----BEGIN NEW CERTIFICATE REQUEST-----
MIIBNzCB4gIBADB9MQswCQYDVQQGEwJVUzERMA8GA1UECBMISWxsaW5vaXMxEDAO
BgNVBAcTB0NoaWNhZ28xFzAVBgNVBAoTDldyb3ggUHJlc3MgSW5jMRkwFwYDVQQL
ExBSaWNoYXJkIEhhcnJpc29uMRUwEwYDVQQDFAx3d3cud3JveC5jb20wXDANBgkq
hkiG9w0BAQEFAANLADBIAkEAiBCE3Zen2P3b+0KPtlQ8xKkDbZanYxOgAfsA9Lk+
QP41UKjx2WvDCmBSUUgjn9sIcXZ2i4bt/g/Eo7RHvUCaWwIDAQABoAAwDQYJKoZI
hvcNAQEEBQADQQB2Smx2Ne1s7/wcOfrbhMXmBVPVzwWui99cGVlLW05ZA2LPLqlr
vAS8xZOYuWWzrPfJ+kie/hTNpPytDJHRTfrd
-----END NEW CERTIFICATE REQUEST-----
```

A useful CA for the creation of certificates that can be used for demonstration and testing purposes is Entrust (`http://www.entrust.com/`) who, at the time of writing, provide the service free of charge.

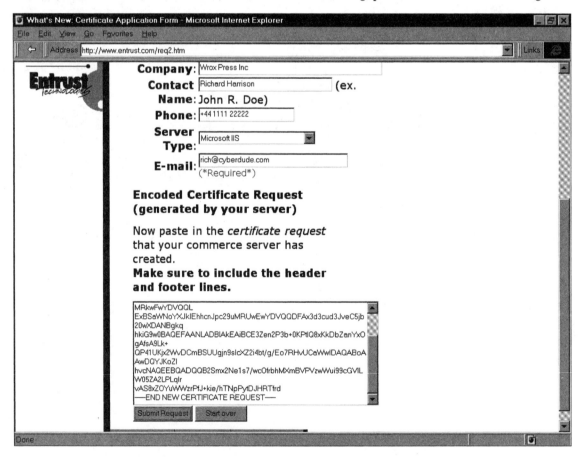

Installing the New Certificate

The response from Entrust for the above request is this:

```
Certificate request was received for:
cn=www.wrox.com, ou=Richard Harrison, o=Wrox Press Inc, l=Chicago,
st=Illinois, c=US

Your demo server certificate has been successfully signed by our Test
CA. The next step is to install the certificate on your server, and then
activate security. Each Server has a different procedure for this, so
consult your server documentation. Once the certificate is installed,
users will then be able to take advantage of certificate-based security.

** NOTE: We did not perform any background checks on you or your server,
so our test certificates should only be used for demonstration and
evaluation purposes.

Visit Entrust's homepage at http://www.nortel.com/entrust/ periodically
for updates and more information on network security and products.

By using this certificate, you agree that there is no liability assumed
in the identity created by Nortel.

Install the following certificate into your web server:

-----BEGIN CERTIFICATE-----
MIICKDCCAZECBDL02SEwDQYJKoZIhvcNAQEEBQAwfTELMAkGA1UEBhMCQ2ExDzAN
BgNVBAcTBk5lcGVhbjEeMBwGA1UECxMVTm8gTGlhYmlsaXR5IEFjY2VwdGVkMR8w
HQYDVQQKExZGb3IgRGVtbyBQdXJwb3NlcyBPbmx5MRwwGgYDVQQDExNFbnRydXN0
IER1bW8gV2ViIENBMB4XDTk3MDIwMjE4MTI0OVoXDTk3MDUwMjE4MTI0OVowfTEL
MAkGA1UEBhMCVVMxETAPBgNVBAgTCElsbGlub2lzMRAwDgYDVQQHEwdDaGljYWdv
MRcwFQYDVQQKEw5Xcm94IFByZXNzIEluYzEZMBcGA1UECxMQUmljaGFyZCBIYXJy
aXNvbjEVMBMGA1UEAxMMd3d3Lndyb3guY29tMFwwDQYJKoZIhvcNAQEBBQADSwAw
SAJBAIgQhN2Xp9j92/tCj7ZUPMSpA22Wp2MToAH7APS5PkD+NVCo8dlrwwpgUlFI
I5/bCHF2douG7f4PxKO0R71AmlsCAwEAATANBgkqhkiG9w0BAQQFAAOBgQBjfS5z
wXHLrPsWTuqPGuDa5nyDcUsU+9ZKVPivuTyU3t2B53HmwD8saTeqS0TlAs731kQx
achMN8dvszpylCwv4SXpMnJjE0ZWb6XTXXeaYjTozSMvBSa8caVCGik4pHLHrrXi
CgqqmmvMxPvb0BzYImqmLOR3DgAd6NAJqvY10A==
-----END CERTIFICATE-----
```

We just copy the section between, and including the -----BEGIN CERTIFICATE----- and -----END CERTIFICATE----- lines from the email message, paste it into a standard text file using, for example, NotePad, and save it on the server's hard disk.

To install the key certificate, right-click on it in **Key Manager** and select the **Install Key Certificate** menu option. A standard **File Open** dialog will now request the name of the file that we've just created and it will then request the key's password. We must then enforce the changes by selecting the **Commit Changes Now** option from the **Servers** menu. If the key installation has completed successfully, **Key Manager** will show the key as being installed, and display the certificate details.

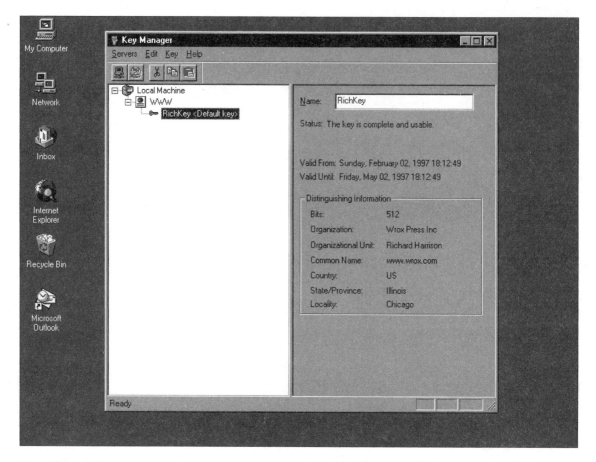

Once the certificate has been installed, we can enable SSL (one of the security protocols within SCS) on any virtual root using Internet Service Manager–just select the Directories tab in the WWW Properties dialog, and check Enable SSL. In addition, this dialog provides the Require Client Certificates check box. When this is set, IIS will instruct the browser to send a copy of its client certificate. We'll see later how ASP can utilize the details in this certificate.

Configuring and Using Certificates in Internet Explorer

All we've done so far is just install the Entrust certificate on our server. We'll next see how to install a certificate on our browser which gives us the Entrust public key, so that we can handle digital certificates generated by them–including our own, which we've just created.

Then we'll look at how we install a client certificate. Earlier we've set our server up so that it will require client browsers to supply a certificate–i.e. the details of the client browser user–when they request files from our server.

Installing Site Certificates from Entrust

The Entrust **site certificate** is installed on the browser by accessing their web site at `http://www.entrust.com/`, and following the instructions to the Client Certificate Demo page.

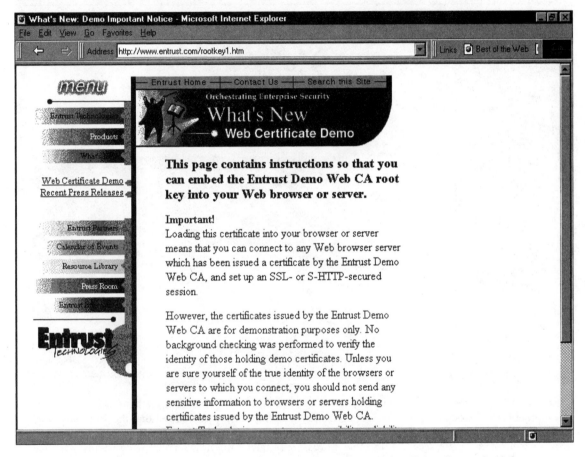

This page directs the browser we download to an ActiveX control, which will handle much of the installation. Once the process is complete, we get a confirmation message and can choose to accept and enable the site certificate.

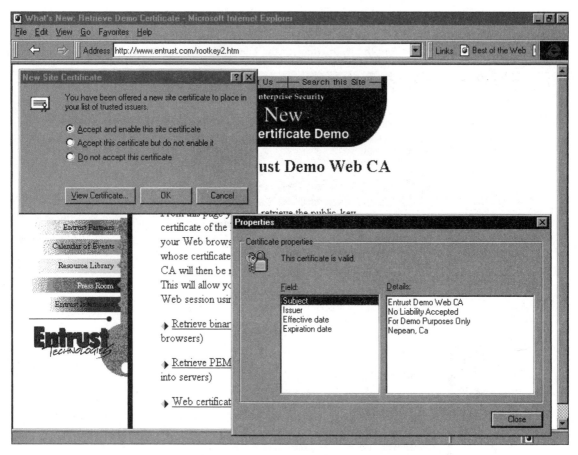

We can also inspect the browser's currently installed site certificates by selecting Options from the View menu, opening the Security tab, and clicking the Sites button. Here, we can see that the Entrust CA site certificate has been successfully installed. Now, when we log on to a site that uses this certificate, our browser will automatically accept it. In other words, we're telling the browser that we trust any sites that have this certificate.

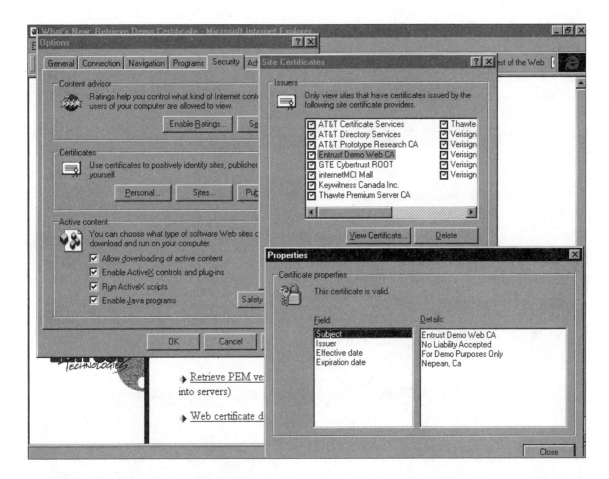

Installing a VeriSign Client Certificate

The next task is to install a **client certificate**, which will be used when we access a site that requires them, i.e. has the Require Client Certificates checkbox set, like we did on our server earlier. At the time of writing, VeriSign are providing client certificates free of charge for Internet Explorer users. These can be obtained from the VeriSign web site at `http://digitalid.verisign.com/id_pick.htm`.

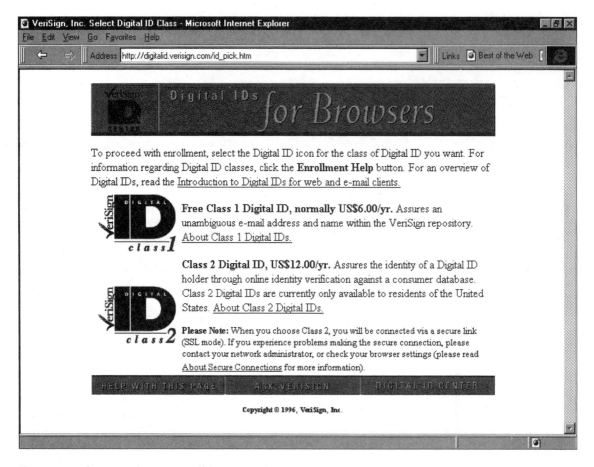

To create a client certificate, we will be required to provide our:

- ▲ First Name
- ▲ Last Name
- ▲ Email address
- ▲ Option to include or omit our email address in the certificate
- ▲ Password, this can be later used to revoke the certificate

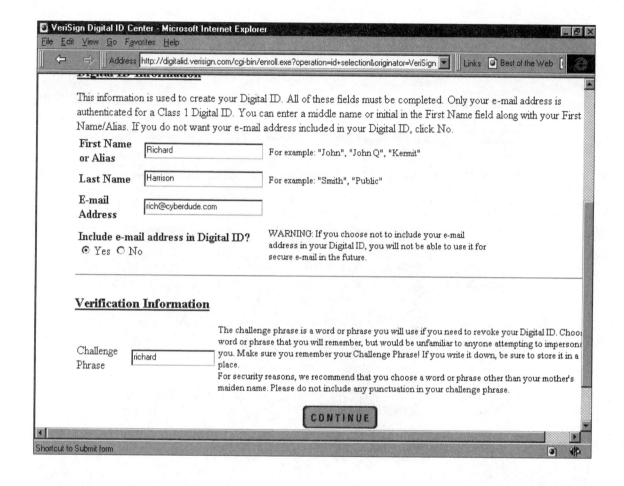

As before, these pages will download a wizard-like ActiveX control to handle the installation:

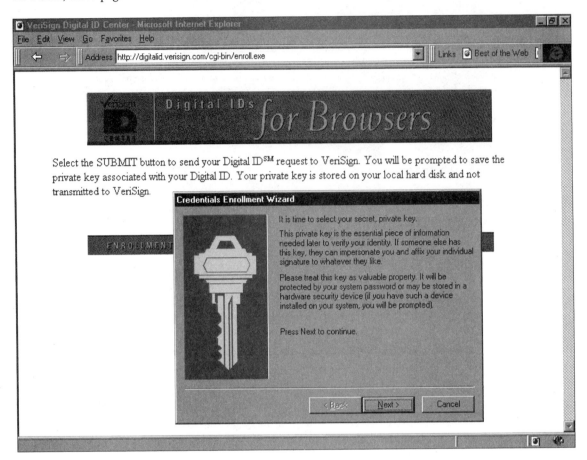

The first page in the wizard describes what the process involves. Then it asks for a name by which we want to refer to this certificate later:

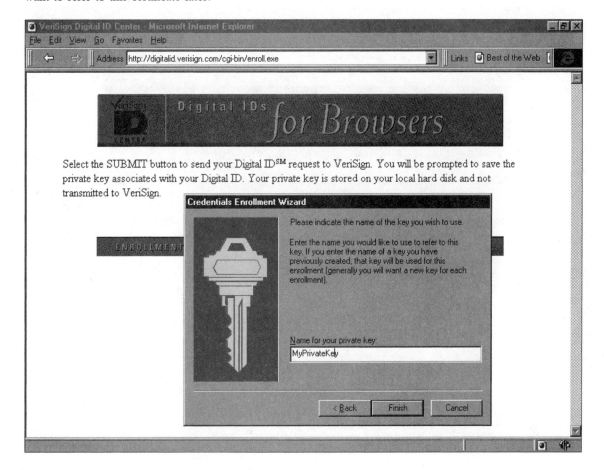

Click Finish, and after a short wait the web page tells us that we should have received an email message confirming either acceptance of our details, or the reason for the decline. You can see that we've been lucky.

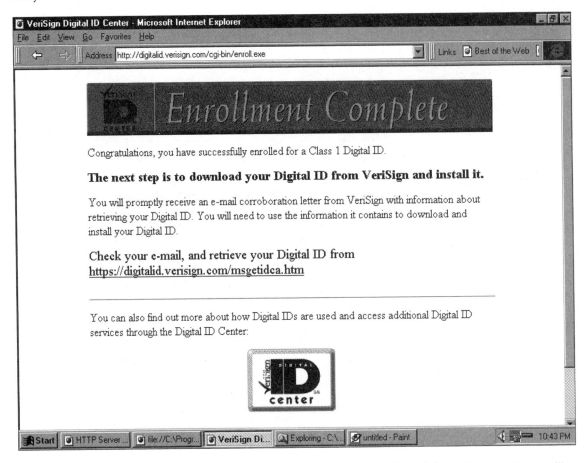

Here are the contents of the email message, containing the Digital ID PIN, and the web page where we'll need to go to collect our certificate:

```
Thank you for selecting VeriSign as your certification authority.

To assure that someone else cannot obtain a Digital ID that contains your
name and e-mail address, you must obtain your Digital ID from
VeriSign's secure web site using a unique Personal Identification
Number (PIN).

Your Digital ID PIN is: abbd70f4f2512345
```

```
You can get your Digital ID at this site:
https://digitalid.verisign.com/msgetidca.htm

Your Digital ID will contain the following information:
Name or Alias: RICHARD HARRISON
E-mail Address: rich@cyberdude.com

Thank you for using VeriSign's Digital ID Center.
```

So now, we can go to the page shown in the email message, and we just have to enter the Digital ID number, and click Submit:

The wizard and the ActiveX control will then complete the installation. A message box confirms that all went well:

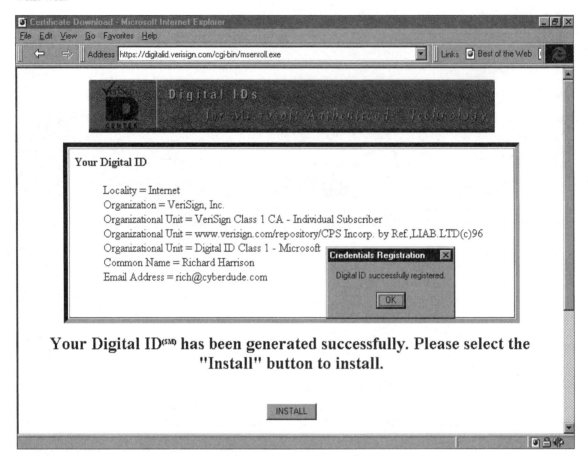

Now we can inspect the browser's personal certificates by selecting Options from the View menu, opening the Security tab, and clicking the Personal button. Here we can see that the client certificate has been successfully installed. When we access a site that requires client certificates, it will automatically be submitted.

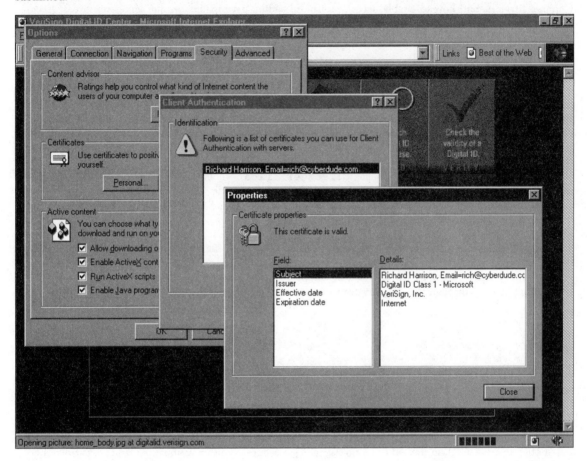

Security in Active Server Pages

Up to now, we've seen how to implement private information transfer and data integrity using Secure Channel Services, and how to enable access control by setting permissions on our server resources. All of this has been achieved by means of configuration of our NT system. There is one more area in which ASP scripting can add value.

Checking Client Certificates

In the previous section, we saw how to set up the server so that it would request a client certificate to be supplied by visitors. Active Server Pages code can help us to interrogate the contents of these client certificates, and act upon them accordingly. This might include additional verification, or personalization of page content.

We looked briefly at the **Request** object's **ClientCertificate** collection back in Chapter 2, without really letting on where the information in it actually came from. Well, now you know. The values for the certification fields are sent by the web browser, as long as a certificate has been installed and the server has been configured to request certificates.

The **Key** parameter to the collection is the name of the certification field to retrieve. A list of all possible values for the client certificate we created is shown in the example, and the corresponding screen dump given below. We saw how they can be used in Chapter 2–look back at it for more details. The following code simply iterates through the **ClientCertificate** collection, placing the contents into the page:

```
<HTML>
<BODY>
<H3>Client certificate</H3>
<% For Each key in Request.ClientCertificate
    Response.Write(key & " = " & Request.ClientCertificate(key) & "<BR>")
  Next %>
</BODY>
</HTML>
```

When we access the page from the browser where we installed the VeriSign client certificate earlier, we get this–notice that the URL in the Address box specifies a secure communications link using **https** rather than **http**.

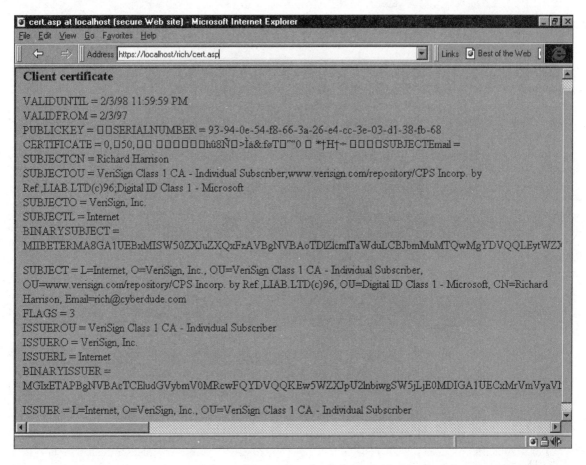

We can also inspect the certificate while we have a page loaded. Right-click on it, select Properties, and open the Security tab:

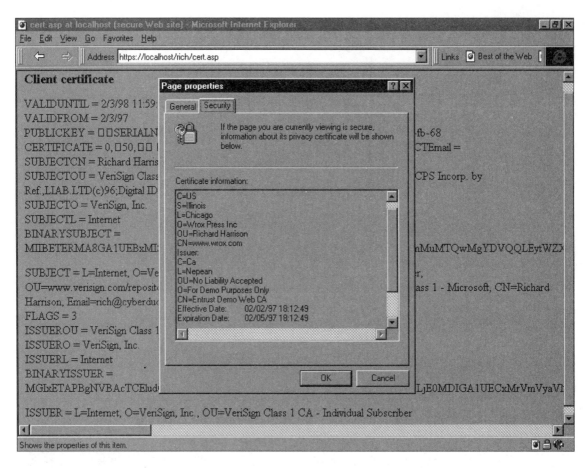

A list of the main key values for this collection is given in Chapter 3, and a complete list can be found in the Microsoft documentation. However, the most interesting ones are:

SUBJECT	A comma-separated list of fields within the certificate
SUBJECTCN	The Common name (i.e. users name)
SUBJECTOU	The Organization Unit (i.e. certificate authority)
VALIDUNTIL	The expiry date of certificate
VALIDFROM	The start date of certificate

So we could welcome someone to our site using the following code:

```
<HTML>
<BODY>
Hello <% = Request.ClientCertificate("SubjectCN") %>,
Welcome to our site <P>
</BODY>
</HTML>
```

If the browser doesn't present a certificate, all the members of the collection are `Empty`. The usual way to test for the presence of a certificate, as we saw in Chapter 2, is to check for a `Subject`. If all the collection fields are empty, we get an empty string:

```
<% If Len(Request.ClientCertificate("Subject")) = 0 %>
    You did not present a client certificate.
<% End if %>
```

Summary

That concludes our discussion on security. We have seen how Windows NT, IIS and ASP cooperate together to provide us with a comprehensive set of key software technologies enabling:

- ▲ Secure exchange of information over public networks

- ▲ Access control to server resources

- ▲ Confident identification of client and server

The Microsoft Active Server Framework forms a good secure foundation, and a flexible architecture, allowing the new emerging security standards to be easily incorporated into our web sites later—with minimum investment impact. This is vital, as there are likely to be many future changes in this area. Just on the horizon (expected sometime late 1997), the following are known to be on the way:

- ▲ **NT Directory Services**–the next version of NTDS is expected to provide user identification for NT logon simply by the presentation of a digital certificate.

- ▲ **Secure Electronic Transactions** (SET)–a set of standards designed to handle secure payment over the Internet, using cryptography and digital certificates. Information is only made available on a need-to-know basis, e.g. user's details aren't exposed to the goods vendor.

- ▲ **Microsoft Wallet**–a digital version of a wallet or purse, storing all our personal information for payment (i.e. credit and debit card details) and access control and identification (i.e. digital certificates). This information will be portable by means of floppy disks or smartcards.

- ▲ **Secure Channel Services**–support for a new protocol Transport Layer Security (TLS) that is the unification of Microsoft's PCT and Netscape's SSL.

Finally, remember that the weakest link is usually the administrator. These security technologies will only work if they have been configured correctly and *all* security holes are filled. If not there is always one smart person who will find a way to get through.

Active Server Pages

Creating Server Components with VB

Up until now we've just considered the different ways in which Server Components can be used within Active Server Pages. These components are provided ready made, either packaged with ASP or obtained from a third party. The power and flexibility of Active Server Pages really begins to show itself though when these built-in components are combined with custom Server Components that solve a particular programming challenge. This is the main focus of this chapter.

Server Components are really nothing more than ActiveX Controls that have some ability to interact with Active Server Pages code. Any tool that can be used to create ActiveX controls, can be used to create Server Components. Until recently, this meant a tool such as Visual C++ or Delphi. Earlier versions of Visual Basic had some ability to create OLE DLLs, which are very similar to ActiveX controls. However, these still required the overhead of the Visual Basic runtime DLLs, which were interpreted rather than compiled.

Now, with the advent of Visual Basic 5.0, we have a development tool that allows us to quickly and easily create the type of ActiveX object that can be used with Active Server Pages. We'll still provide tips for those of you still working in VB4, but of course you won't be able to create compiled components there.

So, in this chapter, we'll cover:

- An overview of some of the new features in Visual Basic 5.0, as well as the new-look user interface

- Creating a simple component, and identifying some of the features that make custom Server Components so powerful.

- An overview of the **ScriptingContext** object, which provides access to the ASP interface from within a Server Component

- A demonstration of creating a Server Component that provides support for reading directory information from the Web Server.

Let's first take a short look at some of the new features of Visual Basic 5.0.

What's New in Visual Basic 5.0

If you've used Visual Basic before, you'll quickly recognize how the improvements in version 5 have greatly enhanced its performance and usability. However, if you have never used Visual Basic, you may not be able to follow all of the examples in this chapter very easily–but hopefully you'll use this introduction to the power of VB as an impetus to start learning it.

Performance

First and foremost, the performance of Visual Basic 5.0 has been greatly increased. Two techniques have been employed, which have both contributed to this. After years of begging and pleading by millions of Visual Basic developers for the creation of compiled applications, VB 5.0 now includes a native code compiler. But all is not lost for those who enjoyed the simplicity of using interpreted application development. VB 5.0 also has an enhanced P-code interpreter. These changes finally give developers a choice: fast compiled code, or small interpreted code. Either way, VB 5.0 is a leap forward in terms of performance.

ActiveX Controls and Server Components

If the addition of a native code compiler to VB 5.0 is its number one enhancement, then the ability to create stand-alone ActiveX controls has to rank as a very close second. These controls will run on any ActiveX host, including VB, Visual C++, and Internet Explorer, or as Server Components inside of IIS 3. The Wizards included in VB 5.0 assist in the creation of ActiveX Controls.

The New User Interface

Previous versions of VB used an interface that sometimes left our development environment with a jumble of windows all floating above the desktop. It was difficult to see which windows belonged to VB itself, which were our Forms and Code Modules, and which were windows from other applications that happened to be running at the same time.

VB5 now has one main application window that holds all the windows a developer could need or want. It looks a bit like the other Visual tools from Microsoft, although it still retains a slightly different look from Visual C++ and Visual InterDev. If you long for the old style of interface, with all of its little windows, then buried deep in Tools | Options | Advanced dialog lies a little check box entitled SDI Development Environment. Check this, and VB will revert to its old familiar self.

New Tools and Tool Palettes

One of the greatest advantages of the new MDI environment is the new dockable tool palette. No more hunting around for that missing Project window, it will now stay docked and always on top, wherever you leave it. Another good feature, which we won't be using here, is the Form Layout palette. It allows us to accurately place our forms on the screen, and even lets us see how our forms will be arranged on different resolution screens.

Some of the new tools that VB 5 brings along really help to enhance the whole development process. No more having to remember the members of a user-defined data type. Just type the variable name and when you press the period, you get a list of all of the members and just need to pick the one you want:

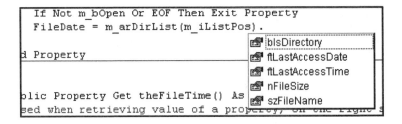

```
If Not m_bOpen Or EOF Then Exit Property
FileDate = m_arDirList(m_iListPos).
                                        bIsDirectory
                                        ftLastAccessDate
d Property                              ftLastAccessTime
                                        nFileSize
                                        szFileName
blic Property Get theFileTime() As
sed when retrieving value of a pro
```

The same thing happens when we call a function. No more having to press *F1* if you can't remember the parameters–VB5 brings up the list, and even follows along as you type:

```
szFileName = Left$ (|
If Left$ (find Left$(String As String, Length As Long) As String i
```

These have already proven to be the biggest time savers of all of the new features in VB5. And they don't only work with Visual Basic functions and objects. As soon as we add a reference to our project, as we'll do in a minute, all of the methods and parameters of that object are available through this instantaneous help.

The Object Browser

VB5 has a greatly enhanced Object Browser, making it very easy to look at the methods, parameters, and events of all the objects in our project. And since VB5 is still interpreted during design time, we aren't forced to follow the C++ method of compiling (*successfully that is!*) before browsing. As soon as we add a reference to another object or DLL, or declare a user-defined type and all of the information about it becomes available in the Object Browser:

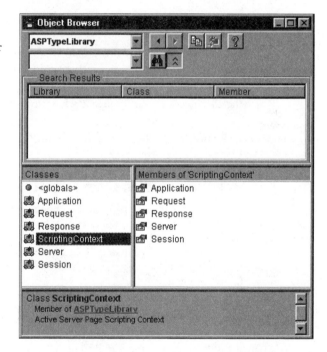

So, let's get on and do something with it. Creating Server Components is so easy now, that before long you'll have a whole library of your own home-brewed ones. We'll tackle two in this chapter. The first is a very basic example of the whole process, walked through at a brisk pace so that you get a feel for the complete cycle. The second is a real-world example that does accomplish a useful task, and we'll go through that one in a lot more detail.

Simple Server Components

A Server Component can be used for a variety of tasks, and Active Server Pages ships with several different server components. These allow us to do various things, such as determine the capabilities of the browser requesting the page, or select an image for a page with rotating display advertisements. A component can just encapsulate functionality that we *could* code directly using VBScript in our pages, or it might be able to do things that aren't possible with VBScript at all.

Encapsulating Scripting Language Functionality

By creating a server component to encapsulate script functionality, we can achieve a number of improvements in our application architecture:

▲ Our code is encapsulated in an object, and doesn't need to be replicated as script in a page each time it is used.

▲ Our actual source code is not visible when using the object, allowing us to keep proprietary code private, yet allowing its functionality to be used by all.

▲ We can modify the behavior of an application in future by changing the component, without having to change all the instances where that behavior occurs.

Let's look at an example of the type of simple server object that can be created, and how it shows all of the improvements specified above.

An Imaginary Commission Component

Imagine we are building an Intranet site for a company that has commissioned sales people. The commission schedule is reasonably straightforward, however it isn't static. The head of the sales department is constantly changing the schedule by which the commissions are calculated. Also, the company wants to make sure that the commission calculation is being done correctly, so only we are trusted to write the code. Let's look at how encapsulating the computation of the commission can increase the efficiency of the program and the programmer.

Improvement	Results in Commission Application
Code Encapsulation	We have stored all of the critical commission code in one place. Each page that needs to use the code now calls the same function.
Hidden Source Code	When the completed commission object is distributed for use, none of the source code is delivered with it. Only the object interface needs to be specified.
Ease of Change	Since all of the commission calculation is encapsulated in the object, and we are the sole owner of that source code, it becomes very easy to make changes to the commission calculation, and then distribute the updated object. And since there is only one place where the code is deployed, on the server, all changes become immediately available to all users.

To begin to create this simple Server Component, let's look first at the tools that we will be using. The ideal tool for creating most Server Components is Microsoft Visual Basic 5.0. VB5 has the ability to create both in-process and out-of-process ActiveX Servers, which can be accessed by Active Server Pages. The only restriction that exists right now is the inability to create session-scope or application-scope objects. These objects require a **both** threading model, and VB 5.0 only supports the **apartment** model.

Visual Basic 4.0 will also allow us to create an OLE server that can be accessed by Active Server Pages. As this example progresses, we'll point out where the differences between VB4 and VB5 come into play.

Create the Project

When we start VB5, we're asked what kind of project we want to create. For this example, as for the majority of Server Components, select ActiveX DLL.

> In VB4, we will need to modify the default project created at startup to build our Server Component. Because VB4 is tailored to creating application with user interfaces, the default project contains a form, and we need to remove this form to continue with the Server Component.

Name the Project

In the Project window, select the first line Project1 (Project1). The Properties window will now display the properties for the project, which in this case is only the name. Change it to Sales.

> In VB4, to name the project, select the **Tools** menu and choose **Options**. In the tabbed dialog box that appears, click on the **Project** tab. Erase the **Project1** in the **Project Name** text box and type in **Sales**.

Create the Commission Class

When we selected ActiveX DLL as the type of project we wanted to create, VB5 created a default class for us. For this component, we'll name this class Commission. In the Properties window, change the **(Name)** property to **Commission**. By default, VB5 sets the class's **Instancing** property to **MultiUse**, which is required for a server component.

> In VB4, we need to add a class module to the project and name the class Commission. Then select the property entry for `Instancing`. A Server Component needs to be `Createable MultiUse`, so select this from the drop down list. The new component also needs to have its `Public` property set to `True`, so that it can be instantiated by other applications.
>
> We also need to create a default entry point for the component. When it is first instantiated by the server, this code will be executed in the component. This is accomplished by adding a normal code module (not a class module) to the project, and adding a `Sub Main()` procedure to it. Since this component needs no special start up processing, we can just leave the body of the procedure blank.

Create the Commission Calculation Function

Now comes the time to calculate the commission. In this example, we'll be using a very simple formula. The commission will be based on the total *value* and *number* of sales made. These two values will be the input parameters to the commission calculation function. In a real-world application, the calculation would probably be quite a bit more involved, and require more input parameters.

In the `Commission` class module, create the following function:

```
Public Function CalcComm (totalSales As Single, salesEvents As Integer) As Single
    CalcComm = totalSales * 0.025 + (totalSales / salesEvents) * 0.05
End Function
```

The function is created as `Public` so that is can be called by applications instantiating this object. It calculates the commission by using the two parameters, and then returns the result to the calling application.

Save the Project

Now we save our project. Visual Basic will generate a default file name for our class module called `Commission.cls`, and a default for the project of `Sales.vbp`. Accept both of these defaults.

> In VB4, since we also created a code module to hold the `Sub Main()` function, we need to save this file as well.

Create the Server Component

When we started VB5, we selected an ActiveX DLL as the type of project that we wanted to create. VB5 set up all of the project parameters to make our life easy. From the File menu, select Make Sales.dll... and save the new component to a directory on the server so that it can be accessed in ASP.

> In VB4, we need to select Make OLE DLL File from the File menu, and select the directory to save the component.

A good place to store components is to the **\INETSRV\ASP\CMPNTS** directory. However, Windows uses the registry to locate the control, so using this location is not essential. It just makes managing all of our components easier if they are in one directory—with the components that ship with Active Server Pages.

After the component is created, it automatically notifies the operating system that it is available for use. This process is called **registering the control**, and VB5 and VB4 take care of it automatically. However, if we need to move the component to a different directory afterwards, we will need to manually re-register the control.

To do this, open a DOS Command Prompt window, and change to the directory where the component has been placed. Type **RegSvr32 Sales.DLL** and press *Return*. A dialog box will either confirm that the DLLRegisterServer in Sales.DLL succeeded, or will indicate any problems.

Test the Server Component

Now that we've created our new Server Component, we can begin to use it from in our Active Server Pages. This control was designed to be part of an Intranet application. For testing purposes, however, we'll just create a simple form that submits values to an Active Server Page, which will use these values to calculate the amount of commission due.

The Submission Form

Here is the HTML file, **testComm.html** that will be used to gather the data to pass to the ASP that contains the new object:

```
<HTML>
<HEAD>
    <TITLE> ASP Simple Component Test </TITLE>
</HEAD>
<BODY>
<FORM ACTION="testComm.asp" METHOD=POST>
  <BR>Total Sales: <INPUT TYPE="TEXT" NAME="TotalSales" VALUE="" SIZE=40>
  <BR>Number of Sales: <INPUT TYPE="TEXT" NAME="NumSales" VALUE="" SIZE=33>
  <P><INPUT TYPE="SUBMIT" NAME="" VALUE="Calculate Commission">
  <INPUT TYPE="RESET" NAME="" VALUE="Clear Values">
</FORM>
</BODY>
</HTML>
```

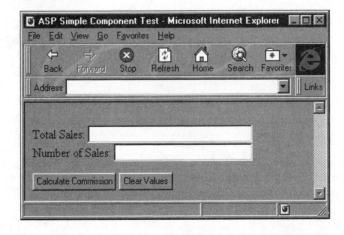

The Results Form

Now, let's create the ASP file **testcomm.asp** that will accept the values from this page, calculate the commission, and display the value to the user:

```
<HTML>
<HEAD> <TITLE> ASP Simple Component Test </TITLE> </HEAD>
<BODY>

<% 'get the values from the form
totalSales = Request.Form("TotalSales")
numberSales = Request.Form("NumSales") %>

Total Sales: <% = FormatCurrency(totalSales) %> <BR>
Number of Sales: <% = numberSales %> <P>

<% 'create an instance of our new component
Set tstComm = Server.CreateObject("Sales.Commission") %>

<% 'calculate the result and print it in the page
commAmt = tstComm.CalcComm(csng(totalSales), cint(numberSales))
Response.Write("The commission payable is : " + FormatCurrency(commAmt)) %>

</BODY>
</HTML>
```

> The `totalSales` and `numberSales` variants have to be converted into Single and Integer types, as when they are taken from the form, they are brought in effectively as strings.

If everything goes well, we should get back a valid response showing the amount of the commission for the amounts entered in the text boxes:

If It Doesn't Work...

If we don't get a value returned for some reason, or even an error message, then one of a few things may have gone wrong. Check back over our steps to make sure you didn't miss anything.

Make sure that all of the VB runtime DLLs are available on the machine where the Web server is running. The easiest way to achieve this is to install a minimal version of Visual Basic. This will also allow you to perform debugging easier, and to quickly make changes to the components.

And when it does work, well, wasn't that easy! Of course, this object doesn't do very much. But we have now seen the basics to creating real Server Components. Next, we will be adding more functionality to them, and allowing them to have a more involved interaction with the Active Server Page being processed. Before we can add more functionality, we need to look at an object that allows our components to get into deeper into Active Server Pages.

The ScriptingContext Object

Active Server Pages implements an object that allows our component to access the very heart of Active Server Pages, it's own object structure and the objects that make it up. These are the **Application**, **Request**, **Response**, **Server**, and **Session** objects. The **ScriptingContext** object contains methods that return a reference to each of these built-in objects. We can then use these references to access the objects' methods and properties. This allows us to implement a much more robust interface between our component and the rest of the ASP system, than we could get from passing parameters to functions.

ASP allows us to access the **ScriptingContext** object from an **OnStartPage** method within our component. When a user requests an ASP file, this method is called in each object which is instantiated on that page. The parameter is a reference to the **ScriptingContext** object. All Server Components need to handle this method, and save the reference to the **ScriptingContext** object for later use:

```
Dim m_ScriptingContext As ScriptingContext
Public Sub OnStartPage(theScriptingContext As ScriptingContext)
    Set m_ScriptingContext = theScriptingContext
End Sub
```

Alternatively, if we will only be using one or two of the built-in objects in our Server Component, we can just save direct references to them when the **OnStartPage** method is called:

```
Dim m_Request As Request
Dim m_Response As Response
Public Sub OnStartPage(theScriptingContext As ScriptingContext)
    Set m_Request = theScriptingContext.Request
    Set m_Response = theScriptingContext.Response
End Sub
```

Setting the Project References

You may have noticed that there are references to a number of objects that are not native to VB. In order to use these in VB, we will need to add a reference to the **ASP.DLL**, which is installed by default on the server in the **INETSRV** folder. Select Project | References in VB5 menu, or the Tools | References in VB4, followed by the Browse... button. Find the file **ASP.DLL** and add it as a reference. Now, our References dialog looks like this:

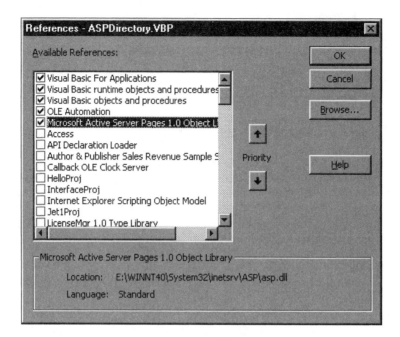

Now that we've learned how to create a simple control, and how to access the built-in ASP object from within a Server Component, we can move on to our demonstration component for this chapter. If you have used a Web server other than Internet Information Server before, and liked the flexibility of being able to allow directory browsing on a directory-by-directory basis, then you will find a great deal of use for the control we are about to build.

A Sample Directory Listing Component

There are numerous great features that Microsoft Internet Information Server 3.0 provides:

- Easy Installation
- Easy Administration
- Integrated Security Model
- Performance and Scalability
- And of course—Active Server Pages!

But there is one drawback that really annoys many users. Web servers such as O'Reilly's WebSite brought many innovations, such as WinCGI. Once nice feature it has is the ability to selectively determine which directories allowed Directory Browsing. Many people are disappointed to find that in IIS, the Allow Directory Browsing option applies to the entire site, even across multiple virtual servers. This is, to say the least, a major omission. But now, with the addition of Active Server Pages, we have a solution. A custom Server Component that allows us to display the contents of the current directory on the server!

But why stop there? Why not add other functions to the simple directory-listing object. Maybe we only want to see the **GIF** files in a directory—easy, add a filter property to the component. What if we want to display the files in a different way from the default, which usually uses an ugly Courier font and **<PRE>** formatting? How can we provide access to each of the files individually, so that we can format them the way we want?

The Concept

Well, we can think of the results of a directory listing as being like a database Recordset. So, we'll replicate the interface of a Recordset object, but instead of providing data from database records, it will be presenting files from a directory listing. Then we can format the listing any way we want afterwards.

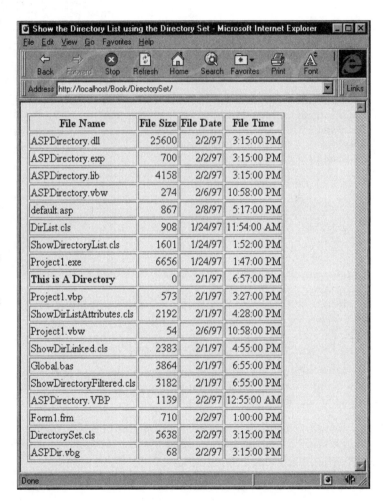

Here's the kind of thing what we're aiming to end up with. It's a directory listing formatted as a table, and each entry is a hyperlink that either opens that directory, or downloads or executes the file.

For the rest of this chapter, we will cover step-by-step the way to create an object that provides all of this functionality for we to use in our own web pages. So, let's get started!

You can download the files from this example, and the complete component, from our Web site at:
http://www.rapid.wrox.com/books/0723/

Creating the Project

The new version of Visual Basic allows us to create a number of different types of applications. In previous versions, the choice was between a Standard EXE file, an OLE Server DLL, and an OLE Server EXE. Even these weren't 'true' executables, as they were simply compiled p-code, which was run through a runtime engine known as VBRUNx00.DLL.

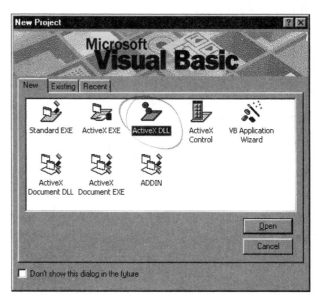

Version 5 changes all that. We can now create true Windows executables, and even ActiveX DLLs and OCXs. The VB5 New Project dialog has a number of different types of applications that it can create:

To create a Server Component, we have a choice of two of these types. ActiveX EXE and ActiveX DLL. Let's review the two types, and choose which one we want to build.

The Project Type—In and Out of Process

An ActiveX DLL is also known as an **in-process server**, which means that the code is executed in the same Win32 process space that is owned by the calling application. In the case of a Server Component, the calling application is Internet Information Server.

An ActiveX EXE is also known as an **out-of-process server**, meaning that the code it executed in its *own* process space. These differences can have serious performance considerations for an application like Internet Information Server. Most of the performance penalties are paid when using this ActiveX EXE type of server, because any information that needs to be transferred from the calling application to the server has to cross the Win32 process boundary.

ActiveX EXE objects cannot be created and used efficiently in an ASP Application or a Session object, because IIS will be limited to one single thread of operation and this places severe limits on performance. Given all the drawbacks of an EXE type server, all Server Components should be created as ActiveX DLLs.

Opening the Project

So, begin our project, select ActiveX DLL and click Open. VB 5 creates a new project entitled Project1, and we get a look at the new development environment. There are a few things that we have to do with our new project to make it work as a Server Component. First, we need to create a name for the project. This will also be the name placed in the Windows Registry as the package that holds all of the components we'll be creating. For this example, we're using the name ASPDirectory.

Use the Project menu to select Project1 Properties... and change the name of the project to **ASPDirectory**. Click OK and take a look at the project window (if this is not in view press *Ctrl-R*). Notice that the name of the project has been updated.

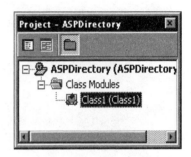

The other things we must do before continuing is add a reference to the Active Server Pages DLL to our project. As we noted earlier, we need to get a reference to the **ScriptingContext** object in order to access all of the information on an Active Server Page. By adding the file **ASP.DLL** as a reference to our project, we can easily access all of the properties of the **ScriptingContext** object when it is passed to the **OnStartPage()** method of our component.

Determining the File System Path

Now we can start the real development work. The first step in creating our directory listing object is to determine the relationship between where the ASP file resides in the virtual web server file system, with where it physically resides on the server's hard drive. For this Server Component, we are making the assumption that the directory list we will create is the directory in which the ASP file is stored. (If you don't like this idea, bring it up later when we talk about opportunities for enhancement.)

The PATH_TRANSLATED Variable

When a Web Browser makes an HTTP request to a Web server, the URL of the request is stored with all the other server variables. The server then translates this URL, which is a virtual web path, to a physical file path containing the actual location of the file on the Web server. This value is stored in the **ServerVariables** collection as **PATH_TRANSLATED**.

For example:

URL Request	`http://MyServer/Files/ShowDir.ASP`
PATH_INFO	`/Files/ShowDir.ASP`
PATH_TRANSLATED	`c:\inetpub\wwwroot\testserver\files\ShowDir.ASP`

So we need to retrieve this information from the Web Server, and write it to the response. To be able to access the server variables, we first need to be able to reference the **Request** object. Once we have determined the value of **PATH_TRANSLATED**, we can output that information to the response. In order to do this, we need to also be able to reference the **Response** object.

Getting a Reference to the ScriptingContext Object

As we talked about earlier, the way to reference these objects is through the **ScriptingContext** object. The interface between Active Server Pages and our Server Component makes this reference available when ASP executes the **OnStartPage** method for all of the components on the page. Let's add some code to our control's class file that will be executed when this method is called by ASP, and store the reference to the **ScriptingContext** object for use later:

```
Option Explicit
Private m_ScriptingContext As ScriptingContext

Public Sub OnStartPage(theScriptingContext As ScriptingContext)
   Set m_ScriptingContext = theScriptingContext
End Sub
```

> Notice that we've used Option Explicit in the module. Being forced to declare all of the variables before use is a good way to minimize errors, as we saw in earlier chapters.

We've created a **Private** class-level variable called **m_ScriptingContext** of type **ScriptingContext**. If you are wondering what data type **ScriptingContext** is, remember that when we added **ASP.DLL** as a reference, we got definitions for all of the classes and their properties and methods. **ScriptingContext** is just one of these classes.

Creating the Display Method

So now we have a class variable that contains a reference to the **ScriptingContext** object. The next step is to add a method to our class that we can call from the ASP file when we want to display the physical path to the file. Let's call this method **Display**.

```
Public Sub Display()
   Dim myRequest As Request
   Dim myResponse As Response

   'Make a reference to the Request object
   Set myRequest = m_ScriptingContext.Request

   'Make a reference to the Response object
   Set myResponse = m_ScriptingContext.Response

   'Print the value of PATH_TRANSLATED from the ServerVariables collection
   'This will show us the Server File system path to the file

   myResponse.Write myRequest.ServerVariables("PATH_TRANSLATED")
End Sub
```

We've declared a **Public** method of our new class called **Display**. The first step is allocate two local variables to hold the references to the **Request** object and the **Response** object, determined from methods of the **ScriptingContext** object which we saved a reference to earlier.

Getting the File Path

Next we need to retrieve the path of the ASP file, and we simply call the `Write` method of the `Response` object and pass as a parameter the value returned by the `ServerVariables` collection of the `Request` object. If you look closely at this code, you'll see it looks strangely like the VBScript code that we can use directly in an ASP file. In fact, to perform this simple function of determining the file path, we don't even need a Server Component. We could simply write the code directly in the ASP file using VBScript, but this wouldn't serve as a good starting point for building the rest of our control.

Before we go any further with compiling and testing the new class, we need to name it. In the Project window, select the class module currently named Class1 and the Properties window changes to display the properties of this module (click *F4* if it is not visible). Change the name from Class1 to ShowFileName. Now we will be able to reference this class by name when we instantiate it into an object.

Testing the Component

So now it's time to test the component as it stands. VB 5 takes care of registering it on our server when we compile it. Simply select File | Make ASPDirectory.dll from the menu, and select a directory *on the server* for the compiled DLL.

Now we are ready to build an ASP file to use our new Server Component. Here is a simple page that will test the methods of the `ASPDirectory` class:

```
<HTML>
<HEAD> <TITLE>Show the File Path</TITLE> </HEAD>
<BODY BGCOLOR="White">
The File System Path to this file is : <BR> <B>
<%
   Set theList = Server.CreateObject("ASPDirectory.ShowFileName")
   theList.Display    'call the Display method
%>
</B>
</BODY>
</HTML>
```

One of the nice features of IIS 3.0 is the ability to have multiple default documents for a server. Now, instead of requiring each default document per directory to have the same name, we can specify a list of valid default document file names. What this means is that we can still have our old `Default.htm` act as the default document in a directory, as well as a smart new `Default.asp`. For all examples in this chapter, we will be using `Default.asp` as the file name for each test ASP document, with each example being stored in a separated subdirectory. When we save this file on our web server and then access it, here is what we see:

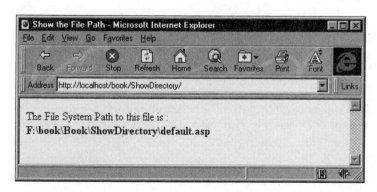

> Remember that you can't just double-click on the file to load it, you have to access it through HTTP, by typing the virtual path to it (and the name if you haven't set up the server with Default.asp as a default file).

So we haven't quite got a directory listing, but we do know that our component is properly registered and working OK. This is a good way to find the bugs as we go along, rather than writing the whole thing and then trying to debug it afterwards.

Stripping Off the Filename

Now, let's modify the code a little to strip off the name of the file, so that we are left with just the file path.

> *A procedural note here as we progress through the case study. Each time that we add a feature to our Server Component, we will be creating a new class to support it. Each new class will be started generally by copying all of the code from the previous class, and then giving it a new name. The existing class will be left intact. In a real world component, we probably would not choose to incur this overhead, but it makes it clearer as to what each successive step in the case study adds to the component.*

To create the new class, select Project | Add Class Module... and VB will present us with a dialog box asking what type of module we want to create. For our Server Component to be able to execute on a server, it can have no GUI component, so we will *never* add a VB Form. We could use the Class Builder to create our new class, but since we will be copying all of the code from the ASPDirectory class, we'll just choose the Class Module option:

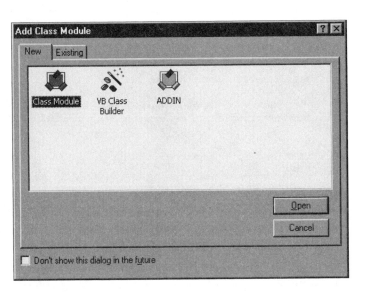

VB inserts a blank class module named Class1 into our project. We will need to rename this class module to ShowFilePath. Double-click on the ShowFileName class in the Project window to display its Code window. Now press *Ctrl-A*, or select Edit | Select All from the menu. When all of the code in the active code window is selected, copy it to the clipboard. Then double-click on the newly created ShowFilePath class, and paste the code from the clipboard into the Code window.

If you have VB5 set to require variable declaration (which all respectable programmers should do), you'll see that the **Option Explicit** line is in there twice. Just select one instance and delete it.

Now we are ready to modify the **Display** method to strip the file name from the path:

```
Public Sub Display()
    Dim myRequest As Request
    Dim myResponse As Response
    Dim szPath As String
    Dim iBSPosition As Integer

    'Create a copy of the Request object
    Set myRequest = m_ScriptingContext.Request

    'Create a copy of the Response object
    Set myResponse = m_ScriptingContext.Response

    'Store the value of PATH_TRANSLATED from the ServerVariables collection
    szPath = myRequest.ServerVariables("PATH_TRANSLATED")

    'Find the last backslash in the szPath variable
    iBSPosition = Len(szPath)
    Do While Mid(szPath, iBSPosition, 1) <> "\"
        iBSPosition = iBSPosition - 1
    Loop
    szPath = Left(szPath, iBSPosition)
    myResponse.Write(szPath)
End Sub
```

In this version of the **Display** method, we are storing the value of **PATH_TRANSLATED** in a local variable. Then we can determine the path by finding the last \ character in the string, and truncating it at the next character. The **Do While** loop starts at the rightmost character in the string and then backs up the character pointer until it finds a \. That position becomes the length of our new string, which we create using the **Left** function. Finally we use the **Write** method of the **Response** object to output the value of this new string to the client.

Before going any further, we ought to think about compiling and testing the component again to make sure everything is still OK. The output should be similar to the last time, but only show the path, with the filename of the ASP file removed. However, this isn't quite as easy as it sounds. Hang on until the end of the next step to see why. We'll compile and test the component again there.

Displaying the Files in the Current Directory

In the previous step, we created a Server Component that determines the path of the ASP file that invoked the object. With this information, we can look at how to use the Win32 functions for retrieving file and directory information. While VB5 has a native **Dir()** function, this only returns the filename. The eventual goal of this object is to replicate the IIS 3.0 directory listing display, which also displays the file date and time, and the file size. The Win32 functions **FindFirstFile**, **FindNextFile**, and **FindClose** allow us to retrieve that information. The two data structures that we need to support these functions are **WIN32_FIND_DATA** and **FILETIME**.

Using API Text Viewer

So where do we get this information from? VB5 ships with the same API Text Viewer application (located in the **VB\Winapi** directory) as prior versions, and this is an indispensable tool for adding Win32 API calls to your application. We'll be using it to retrieve the function prototypes for the three functions we need, as well as the two data structures that these functions require to deliver the information.

> Note that when you first load VB that the Win32API database has to be loaded as a text file **Win32API.txt** in the API viewer and converted to **.mdb** format.

Here, we've found and selected the three function definitions we need, and just need to click Copy to put them onto the clipboard:

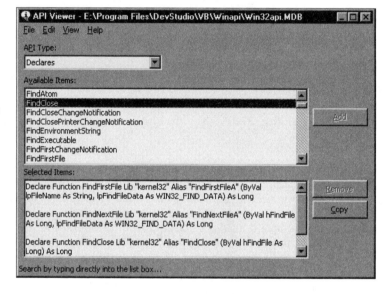

We want to add these definitions to a separate code module in our VB project. Select Project | Add Module from the menu, and we'll see the new Module file added to the Project window. Double-click on it to bring up the Code window, and copy the code from the API Text Viewer into it.

Now, go back to the API Text Viewer, select Types from the API Type: listbox and copy the data structure definitions for **WIN32_FIND_DATA** and **FILETIME**. Notice that when we paste the data structures into the Code module that in the **WIN32_FIND_DATA** definition, there is a constant called **MAX _PATH** that is being used as a string length definition.

```
.
cFileName As String * MAX_PATH
.
```

VB does not support constants here, so we will need to replace it with a value of **255**. Also, make sure that you place the **FILETIME** definition before the **WIN32_FIND_DATA** definition, or you'll get a forward declaration error.

Finally, we need to include the line that defines a constant that we'll be using in the Declarations section:

```
Public Const INVALID_HANDLE_VALUE = -1
```

Now that we have the API function definitions in place, we are ready to look at the contents of the directory. Our first task will be to simply list the files in the directory.

Modifying the Display Method

As we did before, create a new class module in the VB project. This time, let's name it ShowDirectoryList. Copy the code from the ShowFilePath module into this new class. Now we can begin to modify the code in the **Display** method to allow us to display the directory list:

```
Public Sub Display()
    Dim myRequest As Request
    Dim myResponse As Response
    Dim szPath As String
    Dim iBSPosition As Integer
    Dim findData As WIN32_FIND_DATA
    Dim hFindFile As Long

    'Create a copy of the Request object
    Set myRequest = m_ScriptingContext.Request

    'Create a copy of the Response object
    Set myResponse = m_ScriptingContext.Response

    'Store the value of PATH_TRANSLATED in the ServerVariables collection
    szPath = myRequest.ServerVariables("PATH_TRANSLATED")

    'Find the last \ in the szPath variable
    iBSPosition = Len(szPath)
    Do While Mid$(szPath, iBSPosition, 1) <> "\"
        iBSPosition = iBSPosition - 1
    Loop
    szPath = Left$(szPath, iBSPosition)
    szPath = szPath + "*.*"

    hFindFile = FindFirstFile(szPath, findData)
    If hFindFile = INVALID_HANDLE_VALUE Then
        'the value passed was invalid
        Exit Sub
    Else
        Do
            myResponse.Write("<BR>" + findData.cFileName)
        Loop While FindNextFile(hFindFile, findData)
        FindClose(hFindFile)
    End If
End Sub
```

We've added the file wildcard specifier ***.*** to the end of the string. This will instruct the API functions to return all of the files in that directory. We then call the API function **FindFirstFile** and pass as parameters the path that we have created and stored in **szPath** and a data structure called **findData**, declared at the top of the routine as of type **WIN32_FIND_DATA**.

The WIN32_FIND_DATA Structure

Windows will execute the **FindFirstFile** function and populate the **findData** structure's data members. This is the **WIN32_FIND_DATA** structure, of which **findData** is composed. For the class that we are creating at the moment, we're only be concerned with the value returned in the **cFileName** data member:

```
Type WIN32_FIND_DATA
    dwFileAttributes As Long
    ftCreationTime As FILETIME
    ftLastAccessTime As FILETIME
    ftLastWriteTime As FILETIME
    nFileSizeHigh As Long
    nFileSizeLow As Long
    dwReserved0 As Long
    dwReserved1 As Long
    cFileName As String * 255
    cAlternate As String * 14
End Type
```

But first, before we can read the file name from the structure, we need to check the value returned in **hFindFile**. If the function returned a value of **INVALID_HANDLE_VALUE** (**-1**), we have encountered an error, and exit the **Display** method. (In a more robust object, we should probably handle the error checking a bit more gracefully).

Using the Win32 Directory Functions

The 'directory' APIs in Win32 operate on an iterative basis. The call to **FindFirstFile** returns a populated data structure and a handle. That handle is used in subsequent calls to **FindNextFile**, to retrieve the information about the next file in the directory. When there are no more files in the directory, **FindNextFile** returns **False**.

We've created a **Do While** loop that will continue to run until **FindNextFile** returns **False**. Each time through the loop, we output the value in **findData.cFileName** to the client using the **Response.Write** method. After we have reached the end of the file list, we call **FindClose** to clean up the memory associated with the file retrieval functions.

Compiling and Testing the Component

When we go to compile this new component as a DLL, we may find that VB5 is unable to do so. This will happen if we are running IIS server on the same machine we are developing on. When the component is first loaded by IIS, it is kept in memory to speed up execution for later calls. This means that VB5 will be unable to write over the control's code file. We need to stop and restart the IIS Web Service, to remove it from memory. Then we can compile the new component.

So save the new modules you've created and then modify the test ASP file from the previous section to create a new object, and call its display method. The only change that needs to be made to the ASP file is to replace the old **Set theList** line with this line:

```
Set theList = Server.CreateObject("ASPDirectory.ShowDirectoryList")
```

When this page is loaded from the Web Server, the output looks like this:

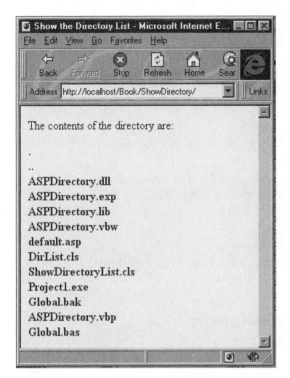

So now we have an object that displays the list of file names in the directory. Next we are going to use some of the other fields in the **findData** structure to display additional file information.

Displaying Additional File Information

In the previous step, we modified our Server Component to display a list of the file names in the current directory. Now we'll add the ability to display additional file information for each file, using the other fields in the **findData** structure. The challenge comes in translating the data stored in this structure to something that is more usable.

We will need to do two things to the data in **findData** to make it more usable. The value stored in **ftLastAccessTime** will need to be converted to a VB **Date** type so that we can display it. The values stored in **nFileSizeHigh** and **nFileSizeLow** will also need to be combined and presented for display. Finally, we'll need to handle the case where we have a subdirectory in our file list, and display **<dir>** instead of the file size.

The FileTime API Functions

We'll be adding the majority of the code that supports the time conversions to our common Code module, rather than putting them in a class module. To perform the conversion from the **FILETIME** structure to VB time, we will use two Win32 API functions and a new data structure. You can find and copy these from the API Text Viewer.

```
Declare Function FileTimeToLocalFileTime Lib "kernel32" (lpFileTime As _
                      FILETIME, lpLocalFileTime As FILETIME) As Long
Declare Function FileTimeToSystemTime Lib "kernel32" (lpFileTime As _
                      FILETIME, lpSystemTime As SYSTEMTIME) As Long
```

```
Type SYSTEMTIME
    wYear As Integer
    wMonth As Integer
    wDayOfWeek As Integer
    wDay As Integer
    wHour As Integer
    wMinute As Integer
    wSecond As Integer
    wMilliseconds As Integer
End Type
```

The first function `FileTimeToLocalFileTime` converts the file time, which is stored in Universal Coordinated Time (UCT) (i.e. Greenwich Mean Time) into the local file time. The second function, `FileTimeToSystemTime`, converts this local time structure into a data structure that we can use to build the 'real' date and time in VB.

Converting the File Date and Time

We've created two separate functions–one to convert the time and another to convert the date. This is for display purposes later on, where we may want to display the date and time in different formats or different places.

```
Public Function FileTimeToString(ft As FILETIME) As String
    Dim lft As FILETIME
    Dim st As SYSTEMTIME
    FileTimeToString = "INVALID"
    If FileTimeToLocalFileTime(ft, lft) = 0 Then Exit Function
    If FileTimeToSystemTime(lft, st) = 0 Then Exit Function
    Dim szAMPM As String
    If st.wHour > 12 Then
        szAMPM = "PM"
        st.wHour = st.wHour - 12
    Else
        szAMPM = "AM"
    End If
    If st.wHour < 10 Then FileTimeToString = " " Else FileTimeToString = ""
    FileTimeToString = FileTimeToString & CStr(st.wHour) & ":" _
                    & Format$(st.wMinute, "00") + " " + szAMPM
End Function
```

```
Public Function FileDateToString(ft As FILETIME) As String
    Dim lft As FILETIME
    Dim st As SYSTEMTIME
    FileDateToString = "INVALID"
    If FileTimeToLocalFileTime(ft, lft) = 0 Then Exit Function
    If FileTimeToSystemTime(lft, st) = 0 Then Exit Function
    FileDateToString = "/" + Right$(CStr(st.wYear), 2)
    FileDateToString = "/" + CStr(st.wDay) + FileDateToString
    FileDateToString = CStr(st.wMonth) + FileDateToString
    If st.wDay < 10 Then FileDateToString = " " + FileDateToString
    If st.wMonth < 10 Then FileDateToString = " " + FileDateToString
End Function
```

These functions display the date and time in the US format of **MM/DD/YY**. An opportunity for enhancement would be to examine the registry and determine the local time format of the server, then use that as a guideline to the format. The generated date would then be localized to the server, and all clients—regardless of their local time setting of the client's computer—would still see this format. These functions are also generating right justified strings for consistent listing. This will be used in a later section, when we will replicate the Directory Browsing function of IIS.

Converting the File Size to a String

Next, we need to create the function that converts the two file size fields into a string for display. This function is using the two fields in the **WIN32_FIND_DATA** structure, converting them to a numeric value, and then returning a string. We are also handling the case of the subdirectory in this function:

```
Public Const MAXDWORD = &HFFFF

Public Function GetFileSize(fd As WIN32_FIND_DATA) as String
    Dim szTmp As String
    If fd.dwFileAttributes = 16 Then       'a directory
        szTmp = "&lt;dir&gt;"
        GetFileSize = Space$(4) + szTmp
    Else
        Dim lFileSize As Double
        lFileSize = fd.nFileSizeHigh * MAXDWORD + fd.nFileSizeLow
        szTmp = CStr(lFileSize)
        GetFileSize = Space$(9 - Len(szTmp)) + szTmp
    End If
End Function
```

We look at the value in **dwFileAttributes**. If it's **16**, this identifies a directory entry, so we return the value **<dir>** in the string, rather than returning the calculated file size—which will be undefined.

Updating the Display Method

Our new class will be called ShowDirListAttributes. As before, create a new class and copy the source code from the previous class into it. The changes required to our new **Display** method for the ShowDirListAttributes class are shown below:

```
    ...
    hFindFile = FindFirstFile(szPath, findData)
    If hFindFile = INVALID_HANDLE_VALUE Then
        'the value passed was invalid
        Exit Sub
    Else
        myResponse.Write ("</B><HR><PRE>")
        Dim szDate As String
        Dim szTime As String
        Dim szFileSize As String
    Do
        If Left$(findData.cFileName, 1) <> "." Then
            szDate = FileDateToString(findData.ftLastWriteTime)
            szTime = FileTimeToString(findData.ftLastWriteTime)
            szFileSize = GetFileSize(findData)
            myResponse.Write(" " & szDate & " " & szTime & "   " _
                    & szFileSize & " " & Trim$(findData.cFileName))
```

```
            myResponse.Write("<BR>")
        End If
    Loop While FindNextFile(hFindFile, findData)
    myResponse.Write ("</PRE><HR>")
    FindClose (hFindFile)
End If
```

We're displaying the data using the **<PRE>** tag to make the display formatting easier. As we loop through all of the files, the first thing is to check if the first character in the file name is a period. This allows us to filter out the two directory entries (**..** and **.**) that we saw at the top of the previous example. Next we calculate values for the file date, file time, and file size, and output the concatenated strings using the **Response.Write** method. When we view this page it looks like this:

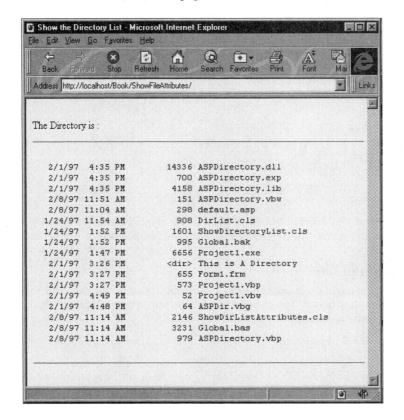

Now we finally have something that looks a bit more like the directory listing we are used to. In the next step, we'll add the final feature to completely replicate the IIS Directory Browsing function.

Replicating IIS Directory Browsing

We've got a nicely formatted directory listing, but we need to add one more feature to replicate the normal Directory Browsing function. To make the listing functional, we'll add hyperlinks to each of the files, so that clicking on any file will allow us to access it. The code to support this is very simple. But, as before, we'll create a new class, name it ShowDirLinked, copy the **Display** method from the ShowDirListAttributes class, and then make these few changes

```
...
Do
   If Left$(findData.cFileName, 1) <> "." Then
      szDate = FileDateToString(findData.ftLastWriteTime)
      szTime = FileTimeToString(findData.ftLastWriteTime)
      szFileSize = GetFileSize(findData)
      szFileName = Left$(findData.cFileName, InStr(findData.cFileName, _
                           Chr$(0))-1)
      myResponse.Write(" " & szDate & " " & szTime & "  " & szFileSize & _
                  " ")
      myResponse.Write("<A HREF=""" & szFileName & """>" & szFileName & _
                  "</A>")
      myResponse.Write ("<BR>")
   End If
Loop While FindNextFile(hFindFile, findData)
...
```

This new class will very closely replicate the directory browsing function of IIS. Each of the files and subdirectories now has a hyperlink allowing us to access it. When we click on a subdirectory, the default file for that directory is processed.

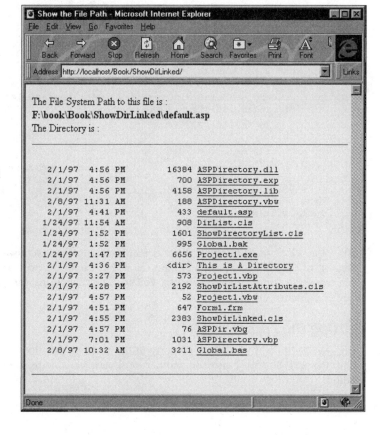

Filtering the File Types

Now, let's look at ways that the component can be enhanced to make it even more useful to a developer. Let's say, for instance, that we only want to display the HTML files in a directory that contains many different types of files. Our next step will be to create a filter to limit the files that are displayed.

The PassFilter Function

We'll add a property to our class to hold a string of valid file extensions that we want to be displayed. Let's call our new class ShowDirFiltered, and we'll add a function to the Code module that takes the file name and a filter string, and determines if that file should be displayed. For this example, we are assuming that the filter values can be found anywhere in the file extension. For example, if we set a filter value of .htm, then a file with the extension .html will also match. As well, this will filter based on file extension only, and not the file name–and it's not going to support wildcards either. These would all be valid enhancements to add to the code later.

```
Public Function PassFilter(szFile As String, vFilter As Variant) As Boolean
    Dim szType As String
    Dim szFilter As String
    Dim iCnt As Integer

    szFilter = UCase$(CStr(vFilter))
    If szFilter = "" Then
        PassFilter = True
        Exit Function
    End If

    For iCnt = Len(szFile) To 1 Step -1
        If Mid$(szFile, iCnt, 1) = "." Then
            szType = UCase$(Mid$(szFile, iCnt, Len(szFile) - iCnt + 1))
            If InStr(szFilter, szType) Then
                PassFilter = True
            Else
                PassFilter = False
            End If
            Exit Function
        End If
    Next iCnt
    PassFilter = False
End Function
```

First, we check to see if the filter string is empty. If it is, then we always return **True**. Next, we find the extension of the file being passed in, and see if that extension exists in the filter string. If it does, then again we return **True**. If not, we return **False**. The filter string can either be a single extension, or a string of delimited extensions.

Setting the Filter Property

Next, we need to add a **Public** property to the class, so that the developer can set the desired filter from within the ASP file. We'll also add another local class variable to store this value for use in the **Display** method:

```
Private mvar_Filter As Variant       ' a local copy of the value

Public Property Let Filter(vData As Variant)
    If vData = "*.*" Then vData = ""
    mvar_Filter = vData
End Property
```

We check if the filter string that is passed in is **.***, meaning the user wants to see all files. If it is we set it to an empty string, which is what the **PassFilter** function expects to see.

Modifying the Display Method

Finally, we need to modify the **Display** method, to check each file name against the filter:

```
Do
    szFileName = Left$(findData.cFileName, InStr(findData.cFileName, _
                                            Chr$(0))-1)
    If Left$(findData.cFileName, 1) <> "." _
            And PassFilter(szFileName, mvar_Filter) Then
        szDate = FileDateToString(findData.ftLastWriteTime)
        szTime = FileTimeToString(findData.ftLastWriteTime)
        szFileSize = GetFileSize(findData)
        myResponse.Write(" " & szDate & " " & szTime & "  " & szFileSize & _
                            " ")
        myResponse.Write("<A HREF = """ & szFileName & """>" & szFileName & _
                            "</A>")
        myResponse.Write("<BR>")
    End If
Loop While FindNextFile(hFindFile, findData)
```

Testing the New Component

Now that we have created a class that can display a filtered directory list, we need to modify the ASP file to pass a value to the **Filter** property for the files that we wish to display:

```
<HTML>
<HEAD>
    <TITLE> Show the Directory List - Filtered </TITLE>
</HEAD>
<BODY BGCOLOR="White">
<%
    Set theList = Server.CreateObject("ASPDirectory.ShowDirFiltered")
    theList.Filter = "*.cls"
    theList.Display
    theList.Filter = "*.vbg"
    theList.Display
%>
</BODY>
</HTML>
```

This ASP file produces the following output:

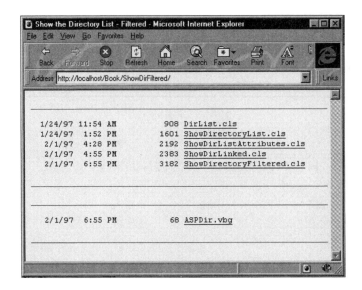

Creating a DirectorySet File List

Up to this point, we have been handling all of the output formatting within the object itself. While this has the advantage of making the object very easy to use, it also makes it very inflexible. To allow the developer more flexibility in the output, we'll create a method for the retrieval of all of the file information, so that it can be formatted at the script developer's discretion.

So, in this step, we'll be creating new class called **DirectorySet**. The design guidelines for this new class are based on the **Recordset** class from the VB Active Data Component or the Data Access Objects library. If we look at the type of information that we will be returning, and what the best method for retrieving that information is, a **Recordset**-type of object gives the script developer a great deal of flexibility. While we will not be replicating all the methods and properties of the **Recordset**, the basic functionality of the **DirectorySet** will be very similar.

The DirectorySet Interface

Let's take a look at the proposed interface specification for our **DirectorySet** object.

Methods	Properties
OpenSet	BOF
CloseSet	EOF
MoveFirst	
MoveLast	
MoveNext	
MovePrevious	

These properties and methods will have very similar functionality to their named counterparts in the **Recordset** class. We begin as usual by creating a new class module called DirectorySet, and then copying all of the code from the ShowDirFiltered class to this new class. Now we need to create some additional data structures to maintain the file information in the class.

Developing the DirectorySet Class

There are two possible ways that we can proceed with the development of this class. The primary requirement is to be able to iterate through the directory entries, either forwards or backwards, and to jump to either the first entry or last entry directly. We can access the data directly when it is needed, by using the **FindNextFile** function. However, two of our requirements, getting the last entry and the previous entry are quite difficult using this method.

The method we will use stores information about each file in an array of data structures, so that moving through the array is as simple as incrementing or decrementing the array index. Rather than store an array of **WIN32_FIND_DATA** records, we'll create a user-defined structure that will contain the information that we need for each file, in the format that suits Visual Basic best.

The MY_FIND_DATA Type and Private Variables

This is how we define the structure, which needs to into the **DirectorySet** class source file itself. We also need some **Private** class variables to help us maintain the array:

```
Private Type MY_FIND_DATA
    bIsDirectory As Boolean
    ftLastAccessTime As Date
    ftLastAccessDate As Date
    nFileSize As Double
    szFileName As String * 255
End Type
Private m_arDirList() As MY_FIND_DATA
Private m_iListCnt As Integer
Private m_iListPos As Integer
Private m_bOpen As Boolean
```

The dynamically sized array **m_arDirList()** will hold the records for each directory entry, each one being a **MY_FIND_DATA** structure holding the bits of information that are important for each entry. We also have **Private** variables that store the number of items in the array, the current record position, and a flag as to whether or not the set is 'open'. We'll see what an 'open' set is later on.

The Accessor Properties

We need to add a series of accessor methods that will allow we to retrieve the information for each record. Rather than return the entire data structure, which means that the calling application (the ASP script in this case) would have to know the structure, we will allow the ASP script to access each field individually.

```
Public Property Get FileSize() As Variant
    If Not m_bOpen Or EOF Then Exit Property
    FileSize = m_arDirList(m_iListPos).nFileSize
End Property
```

```
Public Property Get FileDate() As Date
    If Not m_bOpen Or EOF Then Exit Property
    FileDate = m_arDirList(m_iListPos).ftLastAccessDate
End Property
```

```
Public Property Get FILETIME() As Date
    If Not m_bOpen Or EOF Then Exit Property
    FILETIME = m_arDirList(m_iListPos).ftLastAccessTime
End Property
```

```
Public Property Get FileName() As String
    If Not m_bOpen Or EOF Then Exit Property
    FileName = Trim$(m_arDirList(m_iListPos).szFileName)
End Property
```

```
Public Property Get IsDirectory() As Boolean
    If Not m_bOpen Or EOF Then Exit Property
    IsDirectory = m_arDirList(m_iListPos).bIsDirectory
End Property
```

The Accessor Methods

For each accessor method, we check to see that the set has been opened, and also make sure that the current record pointer has not moved to the end of file. We obtain the current record from the array of records by using the **m_iListPos** variable, which identifies the current record. This value is manipulated using the following functions:

```
Public Sub MovePrevious()
    If Not m_bOpen Then Exit Sub
    If m_iListPos > 0 Then m_iListPos = m_iListPos - 1
End Sub
```

```
Public Sub MoveNext()
    If Not m_bOpen Or EOF Then Exit Sub
    If m_iListPos < (m_iListCnt) Then m_iListPos = m_iListPos + 1
End Sub
```

```
Public Sub MoveLast()
    If Not m_bOpen Then Exit Sub
    m_iListPos = m_iListCnt - 1
End Sub
```

```
Public Sub MoveFirst()
    If Not m_bOpen Then Exit Sub
    m_iListPos = 0
End Sub
```

Again, we check to see if the **DirectorySet** has been opened. We move through the array by incrementing or decrementing the record pointer **m_iListPos**, but make sure we will end up on a valid record before changing.

Retrieving the EOF and BOF Properties

In the accessor functions, we check the value of **EOF** to see if we have moved the record pointer past the last record, before accessing the array at that pointer. The functions to retrieve **EOF** and **BOF** are shown next:

```
Public Property Get EOF() As Boolean
    If Not m_bOpen Then Exit Property
    EOF = (m_iListPos = (m_iListCnt))
End Property
```

```
Public Property Get BOF() As Boolean
    If Not m_bOpen Then Exit Property
    BOF = (m_iListPos = 0)
End Property
```

The variable **m_iListCnt** represents the number of records in the array, or the number of directory entries in the set. Since we are using a zero-based array, the last valid array position is **m_iListCnt-1**. As in a normal **Recordset**, **EOF** becomes true when we move *past* the last record. The **EOF** for the **DirectorySet** class is implemented in the same way.

Opening a DirectorySet

In the property accessor function, we have checked if **m_bOpen** is **True**. This indicates that the **DirectorySet** has been opened. The **OpenSet** method is very similar to the **Display** method of previous classes. Its main difference is that instead of outputting the directory entries to the **Response** object as each entry is read, the **OpenSet** method stores the directory entry information in the **m_arDirList** array.

```
Public Sub OpenSet()
  ...
  'this is the same as the Display function we saw earlier
  ...
      Do
          szFileName = Left$(findData.cFileName, InStr(findData.cFileName, _
                           Chr$(0))-1)
          If Left$(findData.cFileName, 1) <> "." _
                 And PassFilter(szFileName, mvar_Filter) Then
              szDate = FileDateToString(findData.ftLastWriteTime)
              szTime = FileTimeToString(findData.ftLastWriteTime)
              szFileSize = GetFileSize(findData)
              ftData.bIsDirectory = (findData.dwFileAttributes = 16)
              ftData.ftLastAccessDate = DateValue(szDate)
              ftData.ftLastAccessTime = TimeValue(szTime)
              If Not ftData.bIsDirectory Then
                 ftData.nFileSize = CDbl(szFileSize)
              Else
                 ftData.nFileSize = 0
              End If
              ftData.szFileName = szFileName
              AddToDirList ftData
          End If
      Loop While FindNextFile(hFindFile, findData)
      FindClose (hFindFile)
      m_bOpen = True
    End If
End Sub
```

As you can see, the **OpenSet** function is very similar to the **Display** method. Each time through the **Do While** loop, we fill up a data structure called **ftData** with the values from that directory entry. After the data is stored in this record, it is passed to the **AddToDirList** subroutine to add it to the array:

```
Private Sub AddToDirList(fd As MY_FIND_DATA)
   If (m_iListCnt Mod 10) = 0 Then ReDim Preserve m_arDirList(m_iListCnt _
                                              + 10)
   m_arDirList(m_iListCnt) = fd
   m_iListCnt = m_iListCnt + 1
End Sub
```

This subroutine is declared as **Private**, because it should only be called from within the class. The current size of the array is checked, and if it has reached the upper dimension of the array, the array is resized with **10** additional elements.

Closing a DirectorySet

After the set has been opened, or if the developer wishes to use the set for a different directory list, the `CloseSet` method resets all of the array pointers to 0, and sets the open flag to **False**.

```
Public Sub CloseSet()
   ReDim m_arDirList(0)
   m_iListCnt = 0
   m_iListPos = 0
   m_bOpen = False
End Sub
```

Testing the New Component

Now that we have created our `DirectorySet` class, we need to create an ASP file that uses it. Since we have decided to move the display functionality from the object to the ASP file, the code needed to display a directory is a bit more involved than the code that was needed to invoke the original **Display** method from the previous classes:

```
<HTML>
<HEAD>
   <TITLE>Show the Directory List using the Directory Set</TITLE>
</HEAD>
<BODY BGCOLOR="White">
<TABLE BORDER=1>
<TR>
   <TH> File Name </TH><TH> File Size </TH>
   <TH> File Date </TH><TH> File Time </TH>
</TR>
<% Set theList = Server.CreateObject("ASPDirectory.DirectorySet")
   theList.OpenSet
   Do While Not theList.EOF
      Response.Write("<TR><TD>")
      If theList.IsDirectory then
         Response.Write("<B>")
      End If
      Response.Write(theList.FileName)
      Response.Write("</TD><TD ALIGN=RIGHT>")
      Response.Write(theList.FileSize)
      Response.Write("</TD><TD ALIGN=RIGHT>")
      Response.Write(theList.FileDate)
      Response.Write("</TD><TD ALIGN=RIGHT>")
      Response.Write(theList.FileTime)
      Response.Write("</TD></TR>")
      theList.MoveNext
   Loop
   theList.CloseSet %>
</TABLE>
</BODY>
</HTML>
```

In this ASP file, we create an instance of the `DirectorySet` class, call its `OpenSet` method, and then loop through each of the records using the **MoveNext** method. For each record in the set, we output the information to the **Response** object, this time adding table formatting tags as we go. After the **EOF** method returns **True**, we close the set using the **CloseSet** method, and then finish off the table. The results of this ASP file is:

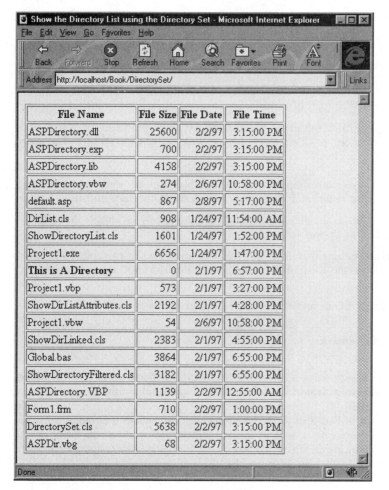

So we have created a versatile object for retrieving file information from a directory on our Web server as Server Component, developed in Visual Basic. The data that it provides can either be displayed to the user directly, or be used for many types of processing on the server-side within an ASP file. But, it's not the be-all end-all control to solve all of our directory and file access problems. Let's just go over a few of the places that we can enhance this control to make it even more effective.

Opportunities for Enhancement

This exercise was meant to show how the development of a Server Component is possible in Visual Basic. There are many other features that could be added to the control:

- The directory information is retrieved only for the directory that the ASP is physically in. It should be relatively easy to add a property that holds either a virtual or a physical path, and have the class generate a directory listing for that path.

- The function to convert from the **FILETIME** structure to a string for display will only display the date and time in the U.S. **MM/DD/YY** format. An enhancement would read the proper time format string from the server's registry, and display the date and time in that format.

- The filter function is very rudimentary, and presents a number of possible areas for enhancement.

- The **DirectorySet** only returns the file name, date/time, and file size. This class could be enhanced to return other entries in the **WIN32_FIND_DATA** structure, such as attributes or calculated short names.

Feel free to experiment with our component. And remember; by combining the power of Server Components developed in Visual Basic with the scripting capabilities of Active Server Pages, we have a very powerful development environment.

Summary

In this chapter we've seen an overview of Microsoft's new Visual Basic 5.0 development environment, and shown you how it can be used to develop Server Components for use with Active Server Pages. The main points of the chapter are:

- We can very quickly and easily create simple components, which can be used to hide source code, encapsulate code for easy reuse, and centralize code elements for easy update.

- Remember to include `ASP.DLL` as a reference, so that we have access to objects that allow us to interact with Active Server Pages.

- Add a method called `OnStartPage` that ASP will call whenever a page containing our class is loaded. In this method, store the copy of the reference to `ScriptingContext` for use in later functions.

- Use the methods in the `ScriptingContext` object to obtain references to the ASP built-in objects.

- Use these built-in objects the same way you would in an ASP script.

Following these simple steps will make it very quick and easy for we to create effective and efficient Server Components, and greatly enhance the performance of we Active Server Pages applications.

With this chapter, we've reached the end of Part 2 of the book–and with it the end of the traditional topic by topic chapter structure. In Part 3, we move on to look at some complete, real-world examples of client/ server applications–built with Active Server Pages, client-side scripting and objects, and custom Server Components. You'll see all the techniques we've been learning about so far used to great effect.

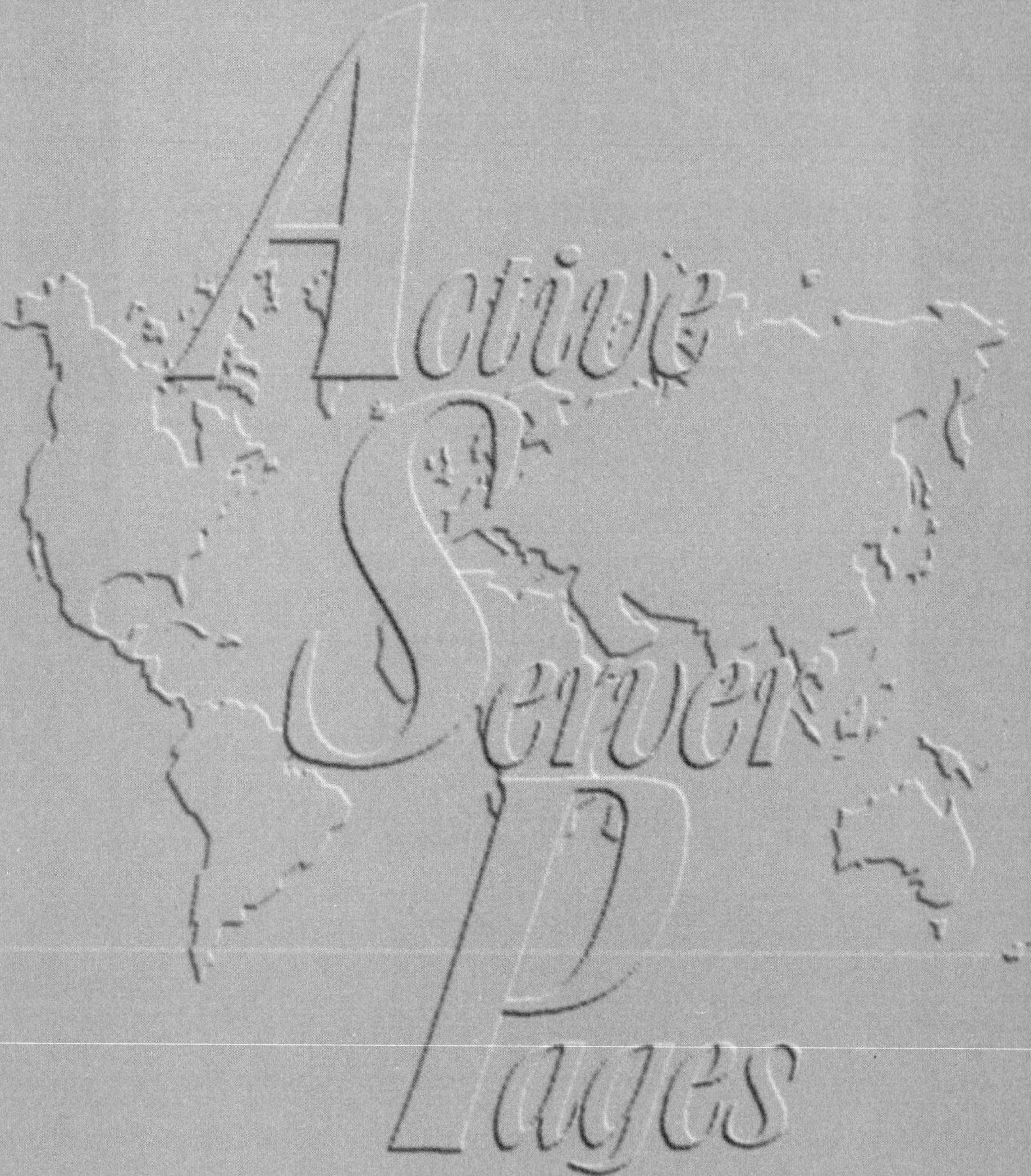
Active
Server
Pages

PART

3

Case Studies

By now, you will be very familiar with the background and working of Active Server Pages. In Part 1 of the book, we studied the basics that we need to know to get started using it, and then in Part 2 we moved on to look at how we go about implementing real solutions with it. This covered programming on both the server and client (browser).

In this, the final part of the book, we're taking a different approach to Active Server Pages. Three of the book's authors have put together real working applications as case studies. These are based around Active Server Pages, and in three of the four cases also combine this with some client-side programming as well. The case studies cover a range of the techniques we've seen so far, and blend them together to show you just what is possible.

We asked the authors to provide, in their own words, some background to the design of each application, as well as how the relevant parts are implemented. The four case studies are:

Chapter 11—The Wrox Forum

This case study, by Stephen Jakab, shows how ASP server-side programming can be used to create an application which is common on the Web, but could equally well form an on-line discussion tool in an intranet environment. It requires no browser-specific programming, and is based on an Access database.

Chapter 12—A Help Desk Application

Automating bug reporting is a task that can bring huge benefits and cost saving in both the corporate and Internet-wide environment. This case study, by Andy Enfield, looks at an application built for just that purpose. Again, this is designed to use an Access database, but could easily be upsized to SQL Server if required.

Chapter 13—Integrating Index Server and Legacy Applications

Index Server, Microsoft's search engine for IIS, is a very useful tool. It can make finding relevant pages on Web sites a great deal easier, and it really comes into its own on an intranet—where thousands of reference documents may be available. This case study, by Christian Gross, looks at Index Server in general, and examines some of the ways it can be integrated with Active Server Pages. It also shows some useful techniques for re-using your existing CGI-based programs.

Chapter 14—Client/Server Card Game

The second case study by Christian Gross uses a custom client application with an embedded browser, and some special custom controls and components, to build and interactive card game called '500'. It shows some of the surprising ways that ASP can be combined with other technologies.

Active Server Pages

Case Study 1— The Wrox Forum

Forums have just started appearing on the Web. They're a bit like Usenet groups, but are available for viewing and posting messages by anyone who visits the site. The idea is that it brings lots of people together who want to talk around certain topics which may range from general interest on personal home sites, to technical activities.

In the latter case, a forum can actually save you money when providing technical support. If a lot of people have a particular query, you soon get to know the shortcomings of your software. It's possible to post you own message in answer, and you know you are on to a good thing when other people who have had similar problems submit their own replies or suggestions–saving you the work of doing it yourself!

And of course, on your company intranet, they are a great way of promoting discussion and collecting opinions. Best of all, they are very easy to implement using Active Server Pages in its simplest form.

An Overview of the Forum Model

First, we'll cover the structure of our approach to the problem. There are several different parts to our Forum–the Message Thread view, the Message view, the Post view and the Confirmation view. The first diagram shows how users can navigate between them, and the files used at each stage:

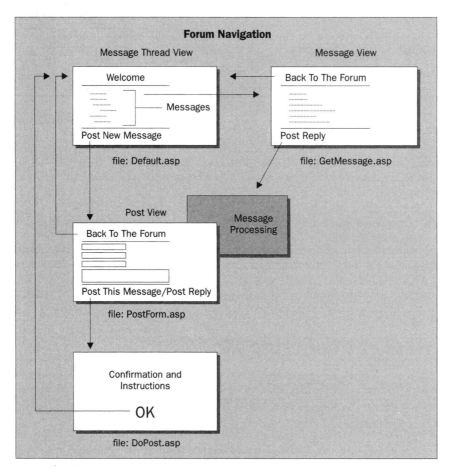

You'll notice that we've provided a way to get back to the **Message Thread** view at each stage, and that we've used some of the files twice—such as **PostForm.asp**, which is used for both posting new messages and replying to previously posted ones. We'll look at each of the areas in some detail, starting with the **Message Thread** view. But first, you need to install the files on your server.

Installing the Forum Application

To run the Forum application on your own server, you must follow these steps:

- Create a single directory somewhere on one of the server's disks—and copy all of the **Forum** project files into it.

- Create a virtual root, or alias, called **/Forum** and be sure to give it **Executable** access. We showed how to do this in Chapter 1.

- Create an ODBC data source for the **Forum.mdb** database, with the System Data Source Name of **Forum**. If you need help to do this, read Appendix G.

- Open and edit the **global.asa** file in the new application directory you created. Find the **Session_OnStart** event and change the 'DBQ=..." line to the full path of the **Form.mdb** database file on *your* server.

```
Sub Session_OnStart
    Set DBConn = Server.CreateObject("ADODB.Connection")
    DBConn.Open "DSN=Forum;" _
          & "DBQ=C:\INetPub\wwwroot\books\0723\Forum\Database\Forum.mdb;" _
          & "DriverId=25;FIL=MS Access;MaxBufferSize=512;PageTimeout=5;"
    Set Session("DBConn") = DBConn
End Sub
```

That's it. The application is now set up and should run without problem on your server. The next step is to see how it works.

The Message Thread View

When we connect to the Forum, we're presented with a list of the messages currently available. Here's how it looks:

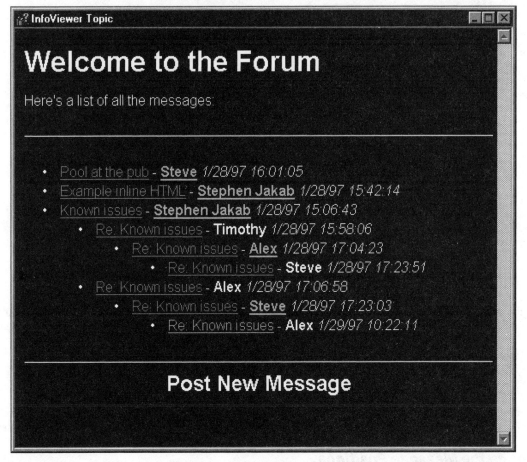

You can see that it presents a set of messages, including the sender's name, the subject and the time of the posting. The subjects of the messages are themselves hyperlinks, and when followed will retrieve that particular message. From a retrieved message, users have the option to post a reply to it if they wish.

New top-level messages can be posted by selecting the Post New Message link. Some of the sender's names are also hyperlinks that allow users to email them directly. In the screen shot, the message at the bottom of the list hasn't been read yet, and it appears in a brighter color to show this.

Managing the Message Threads

The way we've actually designed it to display the messages is for all the top-level items to be shown in reverse chronological order–that is, with the newest items appearing at the top. All sub-messages then appear in the order that they were posted, below the parent message. Consider the following diagram, which shows an extract from some of the existing messages in the database:

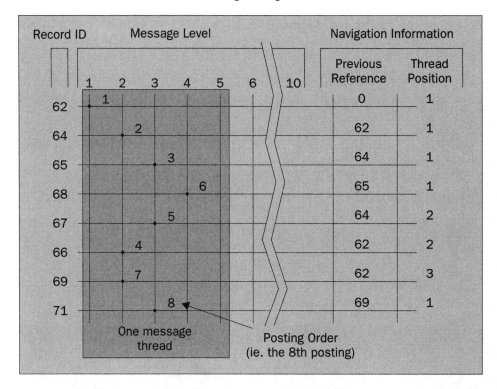

On the left, we have the record ID, which is an Access AutoNumber field. Next comes the message depth. In the Forum application, we've set the message depth limit to **10** to ensure that the message threads still look tidy in the browser. The short lines represent a message, with the 'blob' indicating the message level. The number above the line represents the order in which they were posted. As you can see from the previous picture of the Forum application, the layout of the messages is as shown in this diagram.

Now we can turn our attention to just what information we need to reconstruct the message order, assuming that we've got the necessary data available in our database. Of course, we'll need to get that data into the database, but that happens during the posting process, and you'll see how that's done a little later.

Storing the Message Positions

We've decided to use the simplest approach to solving the problem. We clearly need to know to which thread a message belongs. Glance back at the diagram. The message labeled **1** is a first-level message, and the remainder are replies to that **thread**. Now, let's assume someone read message **1** and posted a reply. This new message is message **2**. Another user then reads *this* message and posts a reply, which becomes message number **3**. Now, imagine that someone replies directly to message **1** and someone else then replies to message **2**. Messages **4** and **5** are thus created. At this stage, message **5** is directly above message **4** with no intervening messages between them. Another user posts a reply to message **3**—which becomes message number **6**. Both message **5** and **6** are placed as close to the messages they answer as possible, taking into account any interim postings. Lastly, in response to message **1**, someone posts message **7**, and another visitor responds to this with message **8**.

Storing the Parent Message Reference

This is all very well and good for seeing how the Forum works, but we need to capture the messages in a way that will let an algorithm reconstruct the threads again afterwards. We can easily find out which message was the parent for the reply by having a **PrevRef** field in our database to hold the ID of the previous branch message. This is also shown in the diagram above.

Storing the Thread Position

Even with this information available, we still need to know the order in which the messages were posted at each level—it is not merely enough to know which messages are dependent on a particular message. This is the **thread level**, and again is shown the diagram. We can see that there are three messages posted in response to the first one, the second, fourth and seventh. The second message was the first message posted in response, and so has the **ThreadPos** value of **1**. The others have a **ThreadPos** of **2** and **3**.

The message with **ID** of **66** is the fourth message posted against this thread. It has a **ThreadPos** value of **2**, however, because it's the second in the list of messages at this level. Even though some messages were posted in response to the earlier new messages, we are only currently concerned with the message level immediately running off the current (i.e. the first) message. Both the **PrevRef** and **ThreadPos** field values for the messages have been filled out in the diagram, and provide all the information we need to reconstruct the required message lists.

From all this, we can gather that displaying the messages is a process of retrieving the top-level messages (with message level of **1**) sorted in descending date order, and then looking up messages in each of these threads by using the unique combination of their **PrevRef** and **ThreadPos** values.

The Messages Table

Here's a definition for our **Message** table. We've partly populated the table so that you'll be able to see how the data produces the output represented by the diagram above. The **Subject, From, Email, Body** and **When** fields would obviously contain the data from the messages themselves, and we've omitted the data in the records that are not part of this thread for clarity:

ID	MsgLevel	PrevRef	ThreadPos	Subject	From	Email	Body	When
62	1	0	1	...	...	...	...	...
63	...	...	...	...	...	...	...	...
64	2	62	1	...	...	...	...	...
65	3	64	1	...	...	...	...	...
66	2	62	2	...	...	...	...	...

Table Continued on Following Page

ID	MsgLevel	PrevRef	ThreadPos	Subject	From	Email	Body	When
67	3	64	2	...	...	...	...	...
68	4	65	1	...	...	...	...	...
69	2	62	3	...	...	...	...	...
70	...	...	...	...	...	...	...	...
71	3	69	1	...	...	...	...	...

The `ID` field is an Access AutoNumber field, with values automatically generated by the database as new records are added. We've also included the `MsgLevel` field to allow us to determine the top-level messages (`MsgLevel = 1`) and the messages that appear below them (`MsgLevel > 1`). We can also use data from this field to facilitate easy formatting when we output the messages.

Managing the Message View

We'll now take you through the process of how the HTML and VBScript code that generates the Message view works. First off, we need to establish a connection to a data source. In this chapter, we store a connection to the database in the `Session` object. Here's how it's done:

```
Sub Session_OnStart   'in the Global.asa file
    Set oConn = Server.CreateObject("ADODB.Connection")
    oConn.Open "DSN=Forum;DBQ=C:\My Documents\Projects\Forum\Database\" _
             & "Forum.mdb;DriverId=25;FIL=MS Access;MaxBufferSize=512;" _
             & "PageTimeout=5;"
    Set Session("DBConn") = oConn
End Sub

Sub Session_OnEnd
    Session("DBConn").Close
    Set Session("DBConn") = Nothing
End Sub
```

This technique opens a connection to the data source for each current user. While this practice is simple, we could also use a global connection available to all users, as described in Chapter 6. Alternatively, we could take advantage of connection pooling with certain database systems, as described in Chapter 5.

Retrieving the Current Messages

Now we'll look at the file `Default.asp`, which displays the current messages. It starts off with some simple HTML:

```
<H1> Welcome to the Forum </H1>
Here's a list of all the messages: <HR>
...
```

After outputting the usual title, we then write code that will select all messages from the database. For our Forum, we've done this in two stages: we retrieve all the top-level messages and have them readily available in the right order within a recordset.

```
...
'get the top level items, and sort in decending chronological order
SQLQuery = "SELECT ID, Subject, Message.From, Email, Message.When, " _
        & "MsgLevel, PrevRef, ThreadPos FROM Message " _
        & "WHERE (MsgLevel=1) ORDER BY Message.When DESC;"
Set oConn = Session("DBConn")
Set oRS = oConn.Execute(SQLQuery)
...
```

Ultimately, we'll have to be able to process all the stored messages, and so we'll need to use some technique of walking down the message thread tree. We'll come back to this topic in a while.

Using the GetRows Method

If there is one record within the recordset object, then we know that at least one top-level message exists. For speed reasons, we've decided to put all the top-level message items into an array for quick access. This is significantly faster than scanning a recordset, or executing multiple SQL statements, and we've used the **GetRows** method of the recordset to achieve this easily:

```
...
If Not oRS.EOF Then
    arrRecTop = oRS.GetRows(cMaxTopLevel)
    ...
```

GetRows takes an optional argument specifying the number of records to be copied into the array (here it's named **arrRecTop**). We've decided to show just the **20** most recent messages, including all the messages posted in response these. We've included a constant at the top of our page to indicate this:

```
Const cMaxTopLevel = 20
```

> One thing we should mention about GetRows **is the way it organizes the array. The array becomes a transposed version of the recordset where the records and fields have been swapped over. This means that** arrRecTop(x,y) **refers to the xth field, and the** y**th row.**

Retrieving the Message Replies

Now that we've got the twenty most recent top-level messages, we can bring in all the other messages as well:

```
...
SQLQuery = "SELECT ID, Subject, Message.From, Email, Message.When, " _
        & "MsgLevel, PrevRef, ThreadPos " _
        & "FROM Message WHERE (MsgLevel>1);"
Set oRS = oConn.Execute(SQLQuery)
...
```

It may be possible that there are no responses to any of the top-level messages. We have to test for this; otherwise **GetRows** will generate an error. Our recordset has the first record as the current record when opened, so the recordset's **EOF** property will automatically provide the value **True** when there are no more records available at, or after, the current record position. In this case we can set the `arrRecRest` variable to `Empty` like this:

```
...
If Not oRS.EOF Then
  arrRecRest = oRS.GetRows()
Else
  Dim arrRecRest
  arrRecRest = Empty
End If
...
```

This makes it easy to test if there's any data in the array later, without using the `UBound` function and error handling.

Processing the Messages

Now, we'll look at how we get the message information into our page. We iterate through all of the top-level messages, outputting the top-level message first and then outputting all messages in the thread leading from that message. The global variable `gLastMsgLevel` refers to the current level of the last message processed. It's used when we're generating the HTML for the unordered lists that will display the results in the browser. Here's the next part of the page `Default.asp`:

```
...
gLastMsgLevel = 0

'now loop through all the top-level messages only
For intTopLevelRow = 0 To UBound(arrRecTop, 2)
   GenList arrRecTop(cMsgLevel, intTopLevelRow), arrRecTop, intTopLevelRow
   If Not IsEmpty(arrRecRest) Then
      ExpandFrom arrRecTop(cID, intTopLevelRow), 1
   End If
Next
GenList 0, Null, Null
Else
   Response.Write "<B>No messages<B>"
End If
...
```

Within the loop, we output the current message using the routine `GenList`. This routine takes three parameters—the message level of the array record, the array itself and the number of the element of the array that's to be displayed. We can then expand any message branches from the current message. That's the job of `ExpandFrom`, which takes two parameters; the ID of the message record we want to expand, and the position of the current message within the thread. Because we're only expanding top-level messages here, the `ThreadPos` parameter will always have the value 1 within this loop.

In the last call to `GenList`, we pass 0 for the current message level, and null values for the array and array index. This is because all we want the `GenList` routine to do here is output the appropriate number of `</UL>` tags to ensure the list is properly completed. With the message level set to 0, the other two parameters won't be used anyway, and we make this clear in our code by using `Null`s.

We've used some constants to make our algorithm clearer when referring to fields within the array. These are the constants as they appear in the constants section above this code block.

```
Const cMaxTopLevel = 20
Const cID = 0
Const cSubject = 1
Const cFrom = 2
Const cEmail = 3
Const cWhen = 4
Const cMsgLevel = 5
Const cPrevRef = 6
Const cThreadPos = 7
strQuote = Chr(34)
```

Remember that the array indices start from zero. We've also included **strQuote**, a constant which will make our code for outputting the list items a little clearer.

Processing the Message Replies

Having covered the top-level loop, we'll talk first about the **GenList** routine. We'll discuss the **ExpandFrom** routine a little later.

The idea behind the **GenList** routine is to generate the HTML for the unordered lists, complete with the details of the message that is to be output. Imagine that we wanted to output two lists of items, the second being a sublist of the first. This is what the HTML would look like:

```
<UL>
    <LI> Level 1
    <LI> Level 1
    <UL>
        <LI> Level 2
        <LI> Level 2
    </UL>
    <LI> Level 1
</UL>
```

This is the purpose of the code **GenList** routine. We need to remember the level of the last message, and generate the HTML to output another **<UL>** tag to start an unordered sub-list if the current message level is greater. But if the level of the current message is less than that of the previous message, then we need to output the appropriate number of **</UL>** tags instead. Within the **<UL>** and **</UL>** tags, the list of items is generated and output. The previous message level is finally set to the current message level, ready for the next iteration. Here's the code that does it:

```
Function GenList(intNewMsgLevel, arrSourceArray, intRow)
    Dim intIndex

    'Going up the list levels in the iterations
    For intIndex = gLastMsgLevel To intNewMsgLevel - 1
        Response.Write "<UL>" & vbCrlf
    Next

    'Going down the list levels in the iterations
    For intIndex = intNewMsgLevel To gLastMsgLevel - 1
        Response.Write "</UL>"
    Next
```

```
      'Process the message item in the list
      If intNewMsgLevel > 0 Then
         Response.Write ListItem(arrSourceArray, intRow)
      End If

      'And set the new message level
      gLastMsgLevel = intNewMsgLevel
   End Function
```

The ListItem Function

The code uses another function, `ListItem`, which warrants some explanation. We actually make the subject of the message a link to the source record in the database. The way we achieve this is by passing the record `ID` as a parameter using the query string, as part of the anchor. We know that we're going to use the `GetMessage.asp` file to retrieve the message being sought, and we just include the record ID after it:

```
   Function ListItem(arrSourceArray, intRow)
      ListItem = "<LI>" & vbCrlf & "<A HREF=" & strQuote _
              & "GetMessage.asp?ID=" & arrSourceArray(cID, intRow) _
              & strQuote & "> " & arrSourceArray(cSubject, intRow) _
              & "</A> - <B>" & From(arrSourceArray,intRow) & "</B> <I>" _
              & arrSourceArray(cWhen, intRow) & "</I>" & strEnd & vbCrlf
   End Function
```

The `ListItem` function uses another function named `From`:

```
   Function From(arrSourceArray, intRow)
      strName = arrSourceArray(cFrom, intRow)
      strEmail = arrSourceArray(cEmail, intRow)
      If InStr(strEmail, "@") > 0 Then          'email supplied and is OK
         From = "<A HREF=" & strQuote & "mailto:" & strEmail & strQuote _
              & ">" & strName & "</A>"
      Else
         From = strName
      End If
   End Function
```

We're now in a position to understand the real heart of the Message view. It revolves around the `ExpandFrom` routine, and brings us back to the discussion of how we are going to walk through the messages in each thread in the correct order, and display the contents.

Displaying the Message Tree

There is no doubt that many alternative algorithms can be used for a 'tree walking' task similar to the one we face, of displaying all the messages in a thread. Probably the simplest to build and understand is a **recursive** solution, because recursion is inherent in the structure of the message threads.

Using Recursion to Expand and Output the Messages

The solution to this tree-walking problem is best followed as a high-level pseudocode algorithm:

```
   Loop through all the rows in the messages table
      If we find a message leading off the message we've just encountered Then
         Output that message
```

```
    Expand and Output all messages leading from this new message
  End If
  Try to Expand and Output the next message below the current message
End Loop
```

In reading this, you may notice that there are two statements that seem to require the operation that is being performed by the entire algorithm! This naturally leads to recursion, that is, where the subroutine calls itself. Without going into a full lesson in recursion here, we must also be careful to ensure that the recursion eventually stops. This is known as the **base case** for our recursion, and all recursive algorithms must contain at least one base case.

We are now in a position to explain the coded algorithm. Recall how, in the loop that iterates around all the top-level messages, we call the **ExpandFrom** routine using:

```
ExpandFrom arrRecTop(cID, intTopLevelRow), 1
```

Let's have a look at how message 1 would be expanded. Here are the relevant records that will be used in constructing the message thread.

ID	MsgLevel	PrevRef	ThreadPos	Subject	From	Email	Body	When
62	1	0	1	...	...	...	...	...
64	2	62	1	...	...	...	...	...
65	3	64	1	...	...	...	...	...
66	2	62	2	...	...	...	...	...
67	3	64	2	...	...	...	...	...
68	4	65	1	...	...	...	...	...
69	2	62	3	...	...	...	...	...
71	3	69	1	...	...	...	...	...

The routine would be called like this:

```
ExpandFrom 62, 1
```

Tracing the Recursion

So we want to expand the message thread starting with the ID = 62, and we're looking for the first thread leading from it. Remember that the top-level message has already been output from the main loop that was shown earlier.

```
Call: ExpandFrom 62,1
Is there a message with PrevRef=62 and ThreadPos=1? Yes, message ID=64
  Output message with ID of 64
  ExpandFrom 64,1 'Because we're starting a new thread, ThreadPos = 1
ExpandFrom 62,2   'Output and expand any messages below the current one
```

Note that because **ExpandFrom 64,1** is called first, **ExpandFrom 62,2** won't be called until the previous call returns. This is the basis for recursion. Here's what happens with **ExpandFrom 64,1**:

```
Call: ExpandFrom 64,1
Is there a message with PrevRef=64 and ThreadPos=1? Yes, message ID=65
  Output message with ID of 65
  ExpandFrom 65,1 'Because we're starting a new thread, ThreadPos = 1
  ...

Call: ExpandFrom 65,1
Is there a message with PrevRef=65 and ThreadPos=1? Yes, message ID=68
  Output message with ID of 68
  ExpandFrom 68,1 'Because we're starting a new thread, ThreadPos = 1
  ...

Call: ExpandFrom 68,1
Is there a message with PrevRef=68 and ThreadPos=1? No, so drop back to:
ExpandFrom 65,2   'Output and expand any messages below the current one

Call: ExpandFrom 65,2
Is there a message with PrevRef=65 and ThreadPos=2? No, so drop back to:
ExpandFrom 65,3   'Output and expand any messages below the current one
```

You can see that infinite recursion would now occur because we're trying to find the next message in the current thread where there isn't one. We need a base case here. For now, though, we'll assume that our algorithm has stopped recursing from this call, and will 'wind back' executing the last line of the pseudo code for each message—finally stopping when all the calls have terminated.

Stopping the Recursion

You can see why we need that base case to stop infinite recursion! In this simple strategy, we call the **ExpandFrom** routine no matter whether a branch is found or not. This is fine as long as we can stop trying to find a message under a thread after we've determined that one doesn't exist.

This naturally leads to the following algorithm:

```
Sub ExpandFrom(lngID, intThreadPos)
    If intThreadPos <= 10 Then            'OK to continue processing
       For lngRow = 0 To UBound(arrRecRest, 2)
          If (arrRecRest(cPrevRef, lngRow) = lngID) And _
             (arrRecRest(cThreadPos, lngRow) = intThreadPos) Then
             'a child message was found so output a row
             GenList arrRecRest(cMsgLevel, lngRow), arrRecRest, lngRow
             ExpandFrom arrRecRest(cID, lngRow), 1
             'and expand ones below this
             Exit For
          End If
       Next
       ExpandFrom lngID, intThreadPos + 1  'expand branches below this one
    End If
End Sub
```

Of course, we also need to allow the users of the Forum to post new messages from this form in the first place. To achieve this, we've used a 'Post New Message' graphic as a hyperlink to open the **PostForm.asp** page. We'll be looking at this a little later.

```
<CENTER>
<A HREF="PostForm.asp"><IMG BORDER=0 SRC="Images/PostNewMessage.gif"></A>
</CENTER>
</BODY>
</HTML>
```

*By using a graphic rather than real text, the anchor won't turn the color of the **VLINK** attribute when we post a message.*

Generating the Message View

When an interesting subject is found in the Message Thread view, the user can simply click on the subject to view the entire message. It looks like this:

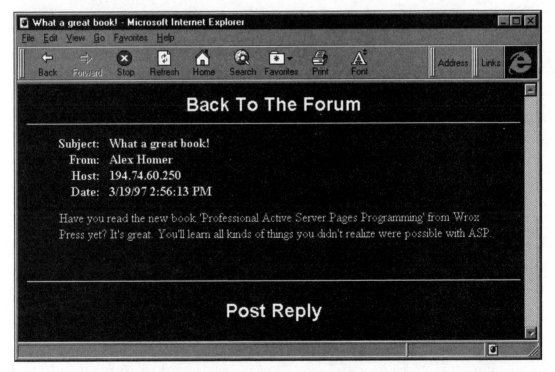

Here, any text in the message is visible. Users can even include HTML code in the message, and it will be interpreted. To go back to the list of messages, the user can select the 'Back To The Forum' link, and to post a reply to this message, they can click the 'Post Reply' link. If they create a message, it will appear at the appropriate place within that message thread. For the moment, we'll just concern ourselves with retrieving the message that they chose, and displaying it.

Retrieving a Message

In the last section, we mentioned that the ID of the selected message was passed as a parameter in the link to `GetMessage.asp`. We need to retrieve this ID in order to get the correct record from the database, and hence the message body. It's easy to get at the ID using the **Request** object. Combining it into an SQL query and executing it gives us the record we're after:

```
...
intID = Request.QueryString ("ID")
If intID > 0 Then              'there is an ID in the Request
   SQLQuery = "SELECT ID, Subject, Message.From, Email, " _
           & "Body, Message.When, MsgLevel FROM Message " _
           & "WHERE (Message.ID=" & intID & ");"
   Set oConn = Session("DBConn")
   Set oRS = oConn.Execute(SQLQuery)
End If %>
```

We also provide a route back to the Messages view for convenience:

```
<CENTER>
<A HREF="default.asp"><IMG BORDER=0 SRC="Images/BackToTheForum.gif"></A>
</CENTER><HR>
```

Displaying the Message

The next step is to output the details from the message record we've found. We know such a record will exist, as it has been displayed in the Messages view.

```
<%
strHostName = Request("REMOTE_HOST")     'the host address
strUserName = Request("REMOTE_USER")
If Len(strUserName) Then strHostName = strUsername & "@" & strHostName
<TABLE WIDTH=640 BORDER=0 CELLPADDING=0 CELLSPACING=0 VALIGN=TOP>
<TR>
   <TD ALIGN=RIGHT VALIGN=TOP WIDTH=95>
      <B>Subject:</B><BR> <B>From:</B><BR> <B>Host:</B><BR> <B>Date:</B>
   </TD>
   <TD VALIGN=TOP WIDTH=12>
   </TD>
   <TD VALIGN=TOP WIDTH=533>
      <B><% = oRS.Fields("Subject") %> </B><BR>
      <B><% = oRS.Fields("From") %> </B><BR>
      <B><% = strHostName %> </B><BR>
      <B><% = oRS.Fields("When") %> </B></TD>
</TR>
</TABLE>
<TABLE WIDTH=640 BORDER=0 CELLPADDING=0 CELLSPACING=0 VALIGN=TOP>
<TR><TD>
<BLOCKQUOTE>
<% = oRS.Fields("Body") %>
</BLOCKQUOTE>
</TD></TR>
</TABLE><HR>
<CENTER>
```

```
<A HREF="PostForm.asp?ID=<% = intID %>">
  <IMG BORDER=0 SRC="Images/PostReply.gif">
</A>
</CENTER>
</BODY>
</HTML>
```

Submitting a Message

Next, we'll have a look at the different ways in which messages can be posted to the Forum. All messages in the Forum fall into two broad categories. They are either new top-level messages, or replies to previous messages. The only real difference is that processing has to be performed on the previous message.

Retrieving and Replying to a Message

We start the page `PostForm.asp` with a link that provides a way back to the Message view:

```
<HTML>
<HEAD>
<TITLE>Post Message</TITLE>
</HEAD>
<BODY TEXT="#ffffff" BGCOLOR="#000000" LINK="#ffff00" VLINK="#c0c0c0">
<CENTER>
<A HREF="default.asp"><IMG BORDER=0 SRC="Images/BackToTheForum.gif"></A>
</CENTER>
<HR>
...
```

Because we're using this file to submit both new top-level messages and replies to other messages, we need to find out which area of the Forum was last visited. This is easily accomplished because if the user came from the Message view, then an ID of the message they were viewing is included in the query string. However, if a new top-level message is being posted, no ID is sent.

Retrieving the Original Message

So, if an ID has been sent, we can retrieve the message ready for processing. We're going to include information in the reply about when the message was submitted, and we're also going to indent it in the usual fashion. But more on that later. Here's the part that retrieves the original message:

```
...
<%
   intID = Request.QueryString ("ID")
   If intID > 0 Then              'we got a message ID
     SQLQuery = "SELECT ID, Subject, Message.From, " _
             & "Email, Body, Message.When, MsgLevel, PrevRef " _
             & "FROM Message WHERE (ID=" & intID & ");"
     Set oConn = Session("DBConn")
     Set oRS = oConn.Execute(SQLQuery)
     strSubjectText = oRS.Fields("Subject")
     If UCase(Left(strSubjectText,3)) <> "RE:" Then 'add reply indicator
        strSubjectText = "Re: " & strSubjectText
     End If
```

```
        lngID = oRS.Fields("ID")
        intMsgLevel = oRS.Fields("MsgLevel")
        lngPrevRef = oRS.Fields("PrevRef")
    End If %>
    ...
```

Linking the Message Details

Now, we're going to use another file called **DoPost.asp** to actually update the database. We're doing that to keep the structure of the application logical and consistent, and also because it's a good place to put some instructions on viewing the updated messages. In order to make the information available to the **DoPost.asp** file, we need to keep the pertinent details ready for the database update. We use hidden controls for this, because they'll be available in the **Form** collection in the next page:

```
...
<FORM NAME="frmMessage" METHOD=POST ACTION="DoPost.asp">
<INPUT TYPE=HIDDEN NAME="hidID" VALUE=<%= lngID %>>
<INPUT TYPE=HIDDEN NAME="hidMsgLevel" VALUE=<%= intMsgLevel %>>
<INPUT TYPE=HIDDEN NAME="hidPrevRef"  VALUE=<%= lngPrevRef %>>
...
```

Collecting the User's Input

Now, we need to lay out the rest of the form with the controls for a new message:

```
...
<TABLE WIDTH=590 BORDER=0 CELLSPACING=0 CELLPADDING=4>
<TR>
   <TD ALIGN=RIGHT VALIGN=TOP>
      <FONT FACE=ARIAL><B> Name: <BR>
   </TD>
   <TD ALIGN=LEFT VALIGN=TOP>
      <INPUT TYPE="TEXT" NAME="txtName" VALUE="" SIZE=50><BR>
   </TD>
</TR>
<TR>
   <TD ALIGN=RIGHT VALIGN=TOP>
      <FONT FACE=ARIAL><B> Email: <BR>
   </TD>
   <TD ALIGN=LEFT VALIGN=TOP>
      <INPUT TYPE="TEXT" NAME="txtEmail" VALUE="" SIZE=50><BR>
   </TD>
</TR>
<TR>
    <TD ALIGN=RIGHT VALIGN=TOP>
       <FONT FACE=ARIAL><B> Subject: <BR>
    </TD>
    <TD ALIGN=LEFT VALIGN=TOP>
       <INPUT TYPE="TEXT" NAME="txtSubject" VALUE="<% = strSubjectText %>" SIZE=50><BR>
    </TD>
</TR>
<TR>
   <TD COLSPAN=2 ALIGN=CENTER VALIGN=TOP>
      <FONT FACE=ARIAL><B><P> Message Text <BR>
      ...
```

Including the Original Message Details

The interesting part of this page, however, occurs when we wish to include the previous message body–if appropriate. If the user is replying to a message, then we'll retrieve the date, the sender's name and the message body from the recordset, and use these items as parameters to a routine `GenerateBody`. This creates the default return message, and the user can then cut out the parts of the included message as required, or just write underneath it:

```
   ...
<%
   If intID > 0 Then
   datWhen = ORS.Fields("When")
   strFrom = ORS.Fields("From")
   strBodyIn = ORS.Fields("Body") 'need to process it for reply format
   strBody = GenerateBody(datWhen, strFrom, strBodyIn, 78)
   End If %>
   ...
```

We assign the processed message body to a variable `strBody` for including in the HTML. If we include entire subroutines and functions that return strings within parts of the body, then we can wind up getting extra characters in our rendered document that we didn't want. To get over this problem, we just use the contents of a variable instead. Here's the `<TEXTAREA>` control where the user edits the new message:

```
   ...
   <TEXTAREA NAME="txtBody" ROWS=15 COLS=78><% = strBody ></TEXTAREA><BR>
   </TD>
</TR>
```

The GenerateBody Routine

We've talked quite a lot about generating the default, indented message, but we haven't covered how to do this yet. The routine `GenerateBody` we've written takes four arguments. The parameters `datWhen` and `strFrom` are just used to generate the first line of the reply, which is of the form:

```
On date and time, name wrote:
> Rest of indented message...
Reply to message...
```

The processing that the routine performs ensures that all of the indented lines starts with the `>` character followed by a space. In addition, all lines are to be no longer than the value defined by `intWidth`, the final parameter. Of course, we don't want words split in the middle just to satisfy these criteria, so we need to consider how to split up the text sensibly.

The approach we've taken is to look for the space before our selected cut-off point. This would be the most appropriate for lines of text that do contains spaces, but for others we have no choice but to take the exact number of characters.

Naturally, if we use a space before the end of the line, we'll have some characters that are left over. These cannot be forgotten, and so they become the start of the next line of included message. These characters are taken into account when getting the next lot of characters from the previous message body. Here's the entire routine:

```
Function GenerateBody(datWhen, strFrom, strOrigBody, intWidth)
   Dim strCopy, strCarryOver, strOutput, strProposedBodyLine
   Dim intCopyLength, intLastSpace, intCharPos, intLenProposed

   strCopy = strOrigBody
   intCopyLength = Len(strCopy)
   intLastSpace = -1 'No last space (yet).
   intCharPos = 1
   strCarryOver = ""
   strOutput = ""
   While intCopyLength > intWidth + 2     'add 2 because of the '> '
      strProposedBodyLine = strCarryOver _
                       & Left(strCopy, intWidth - Len(strCarryOver) - 2)
      intLenProposed = Len(strProposedBodyLine)
      strCopy = Right(strCopy, _
                 Len(strCopy) - intLenProposed + Len(strCarryOver))
      intCopyLength = Len(strCopy)
      intLastSpace = LastPositionIn(strProposedBodyLine, " ")
      If intLastSpace > 0 Then          'space found in body line
         strCarryOver = Right(strProposedBodyLine, _
                          intLenProposed - intLastSpace)
         strProposedBodyLine = "> " & Left(strProposedBodyLine, _
                          intLastSpace) & vbCrLf
      Else
         strCarryOver = ""                  'reset carry over
         strProposedBodyLine = "> " & strProposedBodyLine & vbCrLf
      End If
      strOutput = strOutput & strProposedBodyLine
   Wend
   strOutput = strOutput & "> " & strCarryOver & strCopy
   GenerateBody = "On " & datWhen & ", " & strFrom & " wrote: " & vbCrLf _
              & strOutput
End Function
```

We've used the function `LastPositionIn` (not shown here) which simply finds the starting position of the last character string specified.

Adding the Final Post Message Link

The last thing we need to do for this view is to display the appropriate hyperlink image, depending on whether the user is posting a new top-level message or replying to an existing message:

```
<TR>
<TD COLSPAN=2 ALIGN=CENTER>
<% If intID > 0 Then 'post reply %>
   <INPUT TYPE=IMAGE VALUE="Submit Post Reply" SRC="Images/PostReply.gif">
<% Else 'post new message %>
   <INPUT TYPE=IMAGE VALUE="Post Message" SRC="Images/PostMessage.gif">
<% End If %>
</TD></TR>
</TABLE>
</FORM>
</BODY>
</HTML>
```

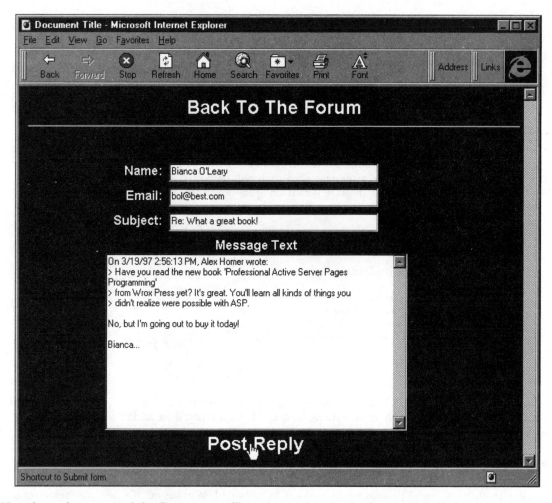

Now that we've generated the Post view, we'll need to update the database to include this new information.

Updating the Database

We've come to a critical part of the Forum application. We can enter dummy data into the database by hand in order to test the earlier parts of the system, but our Forum is not of much use if users cannot post new messages. In this section, we'll be covering how we can use the contents of the form controls of the Post Message view to update the database.

Collecting the New Message Details

The message details are submitted from the **PostForm.asp** page to the page **DoPost.asp**, which processes the message and updates the database. Here's the start of that page. Notice it uses the **#include** statement to include the ADO constants, as we saw in Chapter 4:

```
<!-- #include file="adovbs.inc" -->
<HTML>
<HEAD>
<TITLE>Confirmation</TITLE>
</HEAD>
<BODY>
...
```

Reading the Form Collection

We have defined a constant **cMaxMessageLevel** that determines the maximum message levels that we'll allow. We don't want to provide for infinite levels of messages, so we've decided to make a cut-off at level **10**. Any messages posted in reply to a message above this will be posted with a message level of **10**. Then, we can go on and retrieve the message details using the **Request.Form** collection:

```
...
<%
   Const cMaxMessageLevel = 10
   Dim rsAddMessage
   lngID = Request.Form("hidID")

   'first get the common data
   strFrom = Request.Form("txtName")
   strEmail = Request.Form("txtEmail")
   strSubject = Request.Form("txtSubject")
   strBody = Request.Form("txtBody")
   lngPrevRef = Request.Form("hidID")
...
```

However, we must still distinguish whether the message being posted is a new thread (i.e. a new top level message), or whether it is in reply to an existing message. If it's a reply, then **hidID** will have a non-empty value.

Setting the New Message Level

So, for a reply, we must increment the message level (if the previous message was at level **9** or below), and calculate the new thread position of the message to be posted. Working out the new message level is simple:

```
...
   Set oConn = Session("DBConn")
   If lngPrevRef <> "" Then                        'post reply
      intMsgLevel = Request.Form("hidMsgLevel")
      If intMsgLevel = cMaxMessageLevel Then       'max message level reached
         intNewMsgLevel = cMaxMessageLevel
      Else
         intNewMsgLevel = intMsgLevel + 1
      End If
   ...
```

Calculating the Thread Position

But how are we going to work out the new thread position of the message? Well, it's not as difficult as it may seem. We know the **ID** of the message to which we're replying, and so it's easy to retrieve all the messages that were posted as replies to it (i.e. their **PrevRef** values equal the **ID** of the parent message).

We've already worked out the message level of the reply, and we can use this in an SQL query to find the highest thread position from all of the records matching that criterion.

The SQL **Max** function, when applied to the **ThreadPos** field, comes up with the maximum thread position currently used, and we only need to increment this value to get the new thread position for our current reply. This works fine apart from in one case–when the message we're posting is the first reply. In this case, the **Max** function would return a record which has a **Null** value–not what we're after. It's simple enough to get around this problem in the database itself by using the **IIf** function. This function takes the form:

```
Result = IIf(Boolean condition, Value if True, Value if False)
```

So here's the SQL query:

```
...
SQLQuery = "SELECT IIf(Max([ThreadPos])=NULL,1,Max([ThreadPos])+1) " _
        & "AS NewThreadPos FROM Message " _
        & "WHERE (PrevRef=" & lngID & ");"
Set rsThreadPos = oConn.Execute(SQLQuery)
intNewThreadPos = rsThreadPos.Fields("NewThreadPos")
...
```

If we're posting a new top-level message, however, we already know what the message level, the previous record reference, and the thread position should be:

```
...
Else      'post new message
   intNewMsgLevel = 1
   lngPrevRef = 0
   intNewThreadPos = 1
End If
...
```

Adding the Message Details to the Database

Now we can go about adding the content of this new message to the database:

```
Set rsAddMessage = Server.CreateObject("ADODB.Recordset")
Application.Lock
rsAddMessage.Open "Message", oConn, 1, 4
rsAddMessage.AddNew
rsAddMessage.Fields("From") = strFrom
rsAddMessage.Fields("Email") = strEmail
rsAddMessage.Fields("Subject") = strSubject
rsAddMessage.Fields("Body") = strBody
rsAddMessage.Fields("When") = CStr(Now())
rsAddMessage.Fields("MsgLevel") = intNewMsgLevel
rsAddMessage.Fields("PrevRef") = lngPrevRef
rsAddMessage.Fields("ThreadPos") = intNewThreadPos
rsAddMessage.UpdateBatch
Application.Unlock
rsAddMessage.Close
Set rsAddMessage = Nothing %>
...
```

The page also displays some details for the user to read while the new message is added. Once they've read these, they'll want to go back to the Message Thread view to see their new message in place. As before, we provide a link to achieve this.

```
<HR>
<CENTER>
<H1> Message Received </H1>
<A HREF="default.asp"> OK </A>
</CENTER>
</BODY>
</HTML>
```

Summary

In this case study, we've used Active Server Pages and the Active Data Objects together to give you an indication of their power and flexibility, and a glimpse of what can be achieved with little code and effort. You are welcome to edit and adapt it as you see fit, and use it on your own web site.

Active Server Pages

# Case Study 2—A Help Desk Application

Help desks are sometimes described as the crisis center of the modern computing world. Often it's not because they assist in a crisis, but because they seem to be at the center of a crisis. Getting a sensible response within a sensible period can often be difficult. A good bug reporting application can make the help desk staff's job a lot easier, and in this chapter we'll see an example.

The application is designed to help keep track all of these issues of supporting a computerized environment. Because we're involved in book publishing, it seemed a good idea to focus our bug reporting application on books themselves. It allows our readers to easily provide feedback—either positive appreciation or complaints.

Specifically, we'll be looking at:

- ▲ Where to get the sample files for this application, and how to install them on your server
- ▲ How the Bug Report application works, and what it can do
- ▲ The design of the database for the application, and how it affects the design of the application itself
- ▲ An in-depth example of using frames in an ASP application
- ▲ Many examples of code to manipulate an ODBC data source in all kinds of ways
- ▲ Code that uses a mail component to automatically send email when certain actions occur in the application

So what of the application that does all of this? Let's talk about that now.

About the Application

In any environment where a team has to provide technical support, it's inevitable that issues will arise that need to be looked at by the software author or a technician—and with technical or programming books that contains code examples, this is equally true. All authors dream of the perfect book but, like everything to do with computers, it's hard not to find occasional problems when meeting the needs of all the diverse systems that are available today. Conversely, users may find that a book has been such an invaluable resource that they want to let the publishing company know—so that they keep producing similar kinds of books. Or maybe they've thought of a great way that the book could be improved. The editor wants to produce the best books possible, and is always interested in other peoples' comments.

We'll give an introduction to the application here, and explore it in detail before we look at the code. The first part we'll see is a portion of the program that allows any web surfer to submit problems (or compliments) on a given book. These comments are added to a database, which also includes editor information for each book. The submission pages also allow the submitter to check the status of any previous issues they have created.

The second main part of this application is the interface that the editor sees. Once a comment is submitted about a given book, the editor of that book needs to investigate the comment and act appropriately. Perhaps it's a compliment—the editor can forward these to the author. If it's an error, it should be checked and—when confirmed—added to the errata list for that title, so the next version of the book can be updated. People with the current version of the book can also benefit from these corrections: the application generates a list of confirmed errors so anyone can visit a web site and check the current list of problems with the book.

Editors see a list of the open issues with the books they're responsible for, and can add new comments to any of these. The senior editors should also be able to administrate the database: add new titles, delete old titles, and modify information about current ones—as well as change information about the editors of each book. These same senior editors should also have access to reports detailing issues for each book and the performance of each editor. The backend portion of this application handles all of these tasks.

Now that you have at least a preliminary indication of what the application does, the next step is to install the application files on a server machine and get some hands-on experience with the application before we dig into the code. The next part of this chapter covers this topic.

Using the Application

This section of the chapter walks you through each part of the application. First we'll test the submission side of things by submitting an example comment about a book, then we'll assume an editorial role, so that we can see what happens to the comment once it has been submitted.

Downloading and Installing the Application Files

Before we can do any of this we need to set the application files up on our server. To perform this task, just follow these simple steps:

- **Download** the compressed ZIP file for this book from our Web site (if you haven't already done so) at `http://www.rapid.wrox.com/books/0723/`

- **Unzip it** onto your machine. You'll find a `BugReport` directory containing the application.

- **Create a single directory** somewhere on one of the server's disks–and copy all of the project files into it.

- **Create a virtual root**, or alias, called `/BugReport` and be sure to give it `Executable` access. We showed how to do this in Chapter 1–look back there if you need help with this step.

- **Create an ODBC data source** for the `BugReport.mdb` database, with the System Data Source Name of `BugReport`. If you need help to do this read Appendix G.

- **Open and edit** the `global.asa` file in the new application directory you created. Find the `Application_OnStart` event that looks like this:

```
Sub Application_OnStart
  Application("SERVER_PATH") = "http://bossman/bugreport/"
  Application("FROM_MAIL_ADDRESS") = "bugreport@mycompany.com"
End Sub
```

and change the **SERVER_PATH** line from `http://bossman/bugreport/` to `http://`*yourserver*`/`**bugreport/** where *yourserver* is the name of the server you're running the application on. Change the email address on the next line to your own email address (for testing purposes only–we'll talk about this later in the chapter).

That's it. The application is now set up and should run without problem on your server. Let's take advantage of our hard work installing the app and see how it works.

Submitting and Checking Comments

All we need to do to start the application is to bring up our browser and enter the URL: `http://`*yourserver*`/`**bugreport/**–replacing *yourserver* with the name of your server.

You might find it handy to save this location as a Favorite (or bookmark) as it's the starting point for everything we'll do with the application. Even though we didn't enter anything but the two-word URL, the listing in the Address box says `http://`*yourserver*`/`**bugreport/navmain.asp**. You've been redirected without knowing it! We'll talk about this when we look at the code later in the chapter.

The Start Page

This is the first page we see when we start the application:

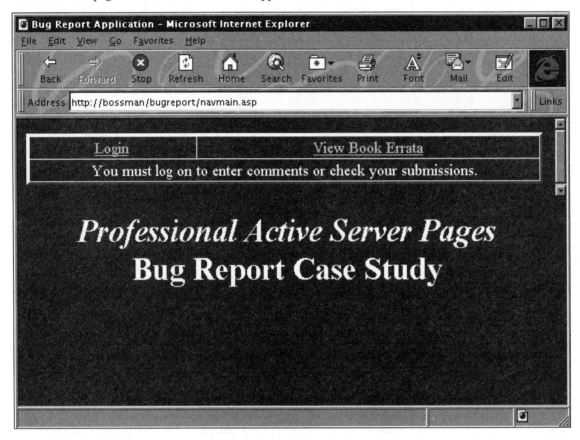

From this start page we can logon or check the errors for each book. For now, click on the Login link to log onto the application.

Submitter Login

The Submitter Login screen is the next one to be displayed. If we were deploying an application like this, the submitter logon page would be a prime target for beautification–this is one of the first pages someone from the external world would see, and it's not very pretty. Add a graphic or two, change the font ... you get the idea.

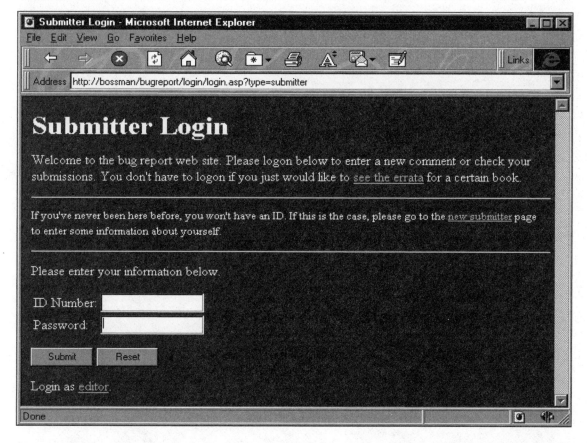

Since you've never visited this site, you won't have anything to enter in the ID and Password text boxes. Fortunately the text between the two horizontal rules explains that we need to submit some information about ourselves before we'll be able to say anything about the books we're reading. If we like, we could check book errata by clicking the first link on the page. Since we're going to look at that page a bit later, we'll skip it for now. Click the **new submitter** link.

Submitter Information

The submitter information page is a data entry person's dream come true—a form and whole slew of text boxes. Enter your relevant information and press the Submit button.

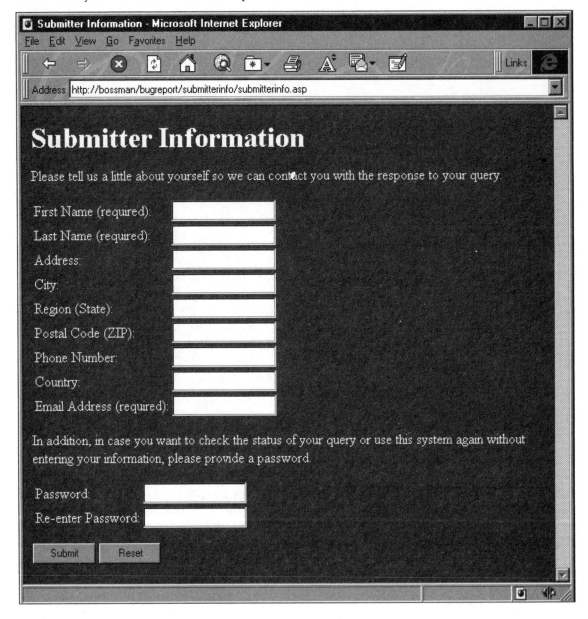

If you accidentally mess up, say you forget to enter either your first or last name, your email address, or enter two different passwords, you'll receive a helpful error screen telling you what you didn't enter correctly–together with a link back to the form page.

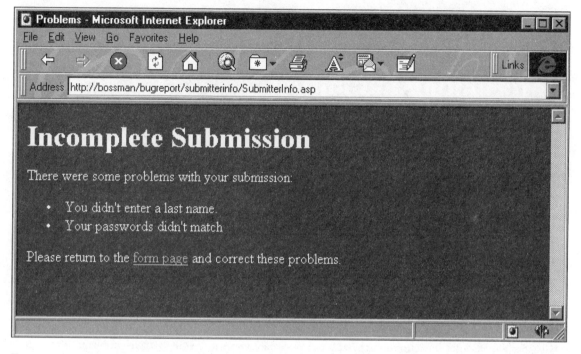

Try as you might, it won't let you pass without the required fields. The code doing the validation here is on the server, and is reasonably modular–we use nearly identical code on some of the other pages in the application.

> *In this application we've done our validation with code on the server. Chapter 8 has an example that shows how to do the same sort of data validation on the client side.*

Enter all of the required fields, though, and you'll get a more positive reply. As it says, be sure to remember your user ID and password so that you can log back on later to check your submissions (and to submit new issues without having to enter your contact information again).

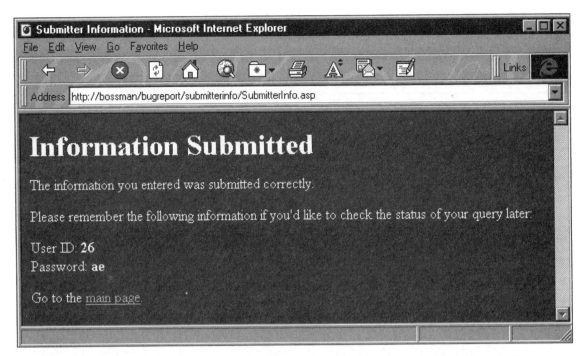

Alternatively, but hopefully not, you may have received a nasty looking error message instead of a confirmation page. Most likely this error is because the `bugreport.mdb` database wasn't correctly set up as an ODBC data source when you followed the steps to install the application. If you haven't set up an ODBC System DSN for the `bugreport.mdb` database then you will definitely have problems. The page doesn't include error checking to see if the data source is valid–it just goes ahead and uses it, and if it hasn't been set up properly data access won't work. In a real world situation we'd probably want to add code to give the user a nice message saying the database is offline or not available, but we haven't bothered here.

The Main Page

Now that we've identified ourselves, the system will finally let us log on and submit the comment we've been dying to get off our chests! Keeping the ID and password information in mind, click the main page link.

> Keep in mind that the Session object's Timeout property hasn't been changed from its default of 20 minutes. This means that if we leave our computer to go for a drink and come back more than twenty minutes later, we'll have to log back on with the ID number and password we chose. Something to keep in mind...

There, arrayed before us, is our list of options. We can:

- Report a problem or comment
- Check submissions
- View book errata
- Logout

We're seeing two frames here. The top frame is (always) controlled by a file called **navbar.asp**, while the bottom one changes depending on our selection. By default, when we first enter the application as a submitter, the bottom frame shows us the status of any of our previous comments. Since we're bug report virgins and this is the first time we've seen the page, it's no surprise that we have no submissions on record.

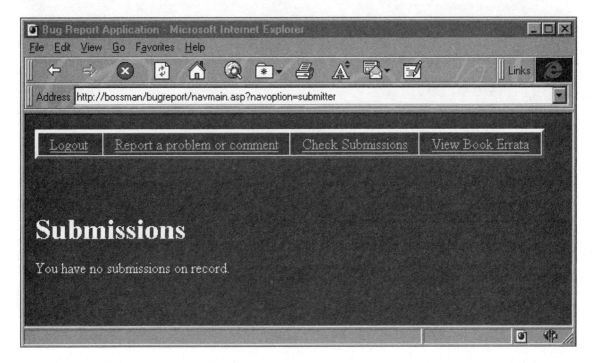

Entering a New Issue

We know what we're aiming for. Click the <u>Report a problem or comment link</u> and watch as the bottom frame changes to one titled New Issue with a variety of text boxes just begging for our input.

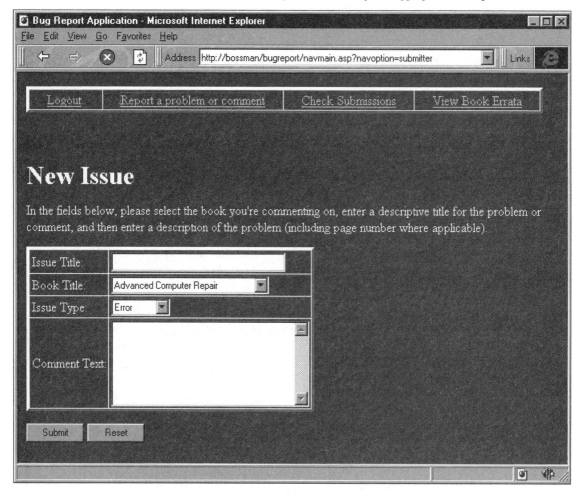

Let your imagination run wild. Pick a title for your issue, choose whether you're going to provide critique, a complaint or a compliment, and enter some text in the comment text area. One thing you need to be sure of, so that the rest of the application walk-through makes sense, is that the Book Title field is set to Advanced Computer Repair before submitting your comment. That's because we're going to log on later as the editor in charge of this title and we want to be sure to see our issue.

If we've set up the Data Source Name (DSN) for the `bugreport.mdb` database correctly, we'll receive a confirmation page in return for our submission.

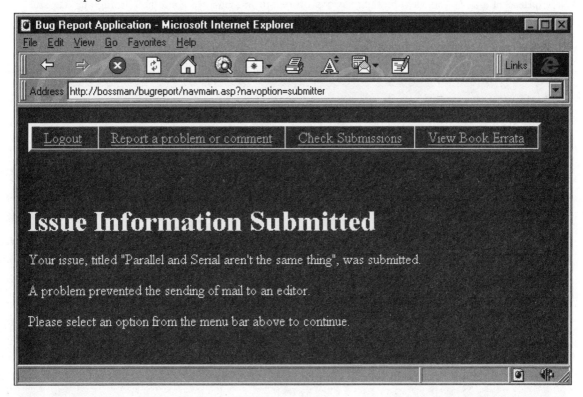

The second line of the confirmation page says, ominously, **A problem prevented the sending of mail to an editor.** Don't worry about this right now. This page has code that automatically sends an email to the editor of the book we've submitted a comment on. This very general code which uses one particular mail component that you may or may not have. It's commented out right now so that you don't receive errors about not having the object. Instead you receive a more general message that just says no mail was sent. Later on when we talk about this feature we can uncomment the line sending the mail or modify the code (probably only one line) to use a particular mail component you might have.

If our comment was actually submitted without problem, it should be visible on our list of submissions. Let's find out by following the page's instructions and clicking the <u>Check Submissions</u> link in the top menu bar.

Checking Submissions

Now instead of a terse You have no submissions on record message, we get a table listing our one and only issue, and its current status: New. This means that the editor hasn't had a chance to make any additions to the issue yet (although he may have received email about it—if our email component is working).

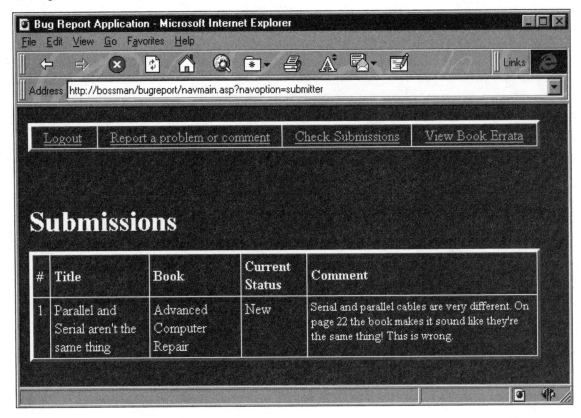

Viewing Book Errata

The issue is out of our hands now, and we need to give the editor time to do his or her job. Before we go, we'll use the last untouched option to see if the title has any other known problems. Click the View Book Errata link. When the page appears, showing a combo box with all of the titles, select Advanced Computer Repair and press Submit to check the errata.

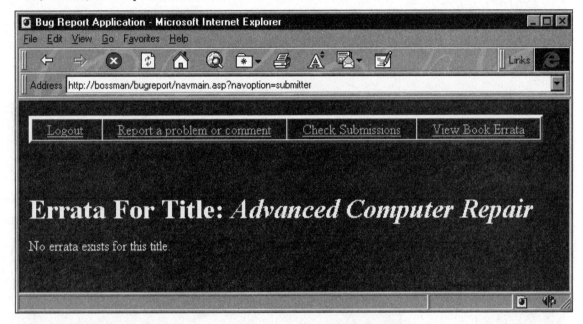

Well, as you can see, nothing exists for this title yet so we'll have to check back later after the editor has had a chance to look at our comment. If you like, you can go back and view errata for some of the other books—I know for a fact that Inside Computer Architecture has at least one known problem on its errata list.

We've exhausted the options as a submitter. Go ahead and log out so we can log back in as an editor and see about the comment we just entered.

The Internal Interface: Editor Pages

We've covered everything we can do as a submitter, and now we're ready to talk about what we can do as an editor.

The Editor Login Page

After logging out and clicking the <u>Login</u> link to log back in, scroll to the bottom of the page and click the link that says we'd like to log on as an editor. The application automatically detects who we last logged on as, and displays that page–since we logged on as a submitter we have to manually change to this page to the editor page, at least for the first time. The page shows the editor ID and password fields and also includes a link at the bottom so that we can switch back to the submitter page if we like.

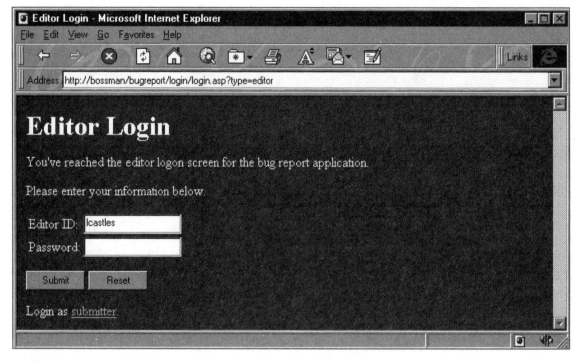

As we've seen, there's a corresponding link like this on the submitter page that displays the editor login. What about the safety of this link? We've protected the site with the logon screen as well as with more security mechanisms that we'll talk about later, but it still doesn't seem like a good idea to give anyone access to the editor logon screen. If this application was deployed in the real world we might want to add some code to only display this link in certain cases, like if the requesting browser is inside our organization. Alternatively, we might want to give our editors a special URL that they could enter from any machine on the Internet, to access the editor logon page. With this method we might be able to coerce work out of our employees no matter where they happen to be located in the world! All kidding aside, it's good to remember that ASP gives us the ability to finely tune our pages to the audience, and this ability can be used (in many ways) to restrict certain pages to certain users.

The editor logon screen looks similar to the submitter logon—which isn't surprising as they're both generated from the same ASP file. You'll notice there's no option to add yourself as an editor, like there is on the submitter page. Only editors with administrative privileges can add other editors. We'll talk about the different security levels later on in the chapter. For now, log on as an editor that already exists in the database using this information:

Editor ID: ejohns
Password: ej

Edith Johns happens to be the editor in charge of the title Inside Computer Architecture, and—surprise, surprise—there's our comment!

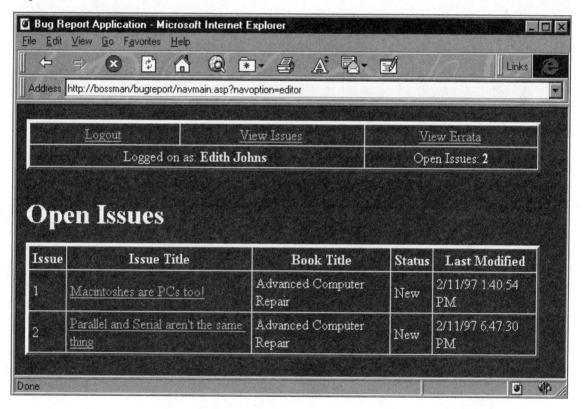

The Editor Access Level

This is our first experience with the editor side of the application and, although things look similar, you'll notice that the options in the menu bar are different. Our friend Edith is just an editor; she doesn't have administrative access. This limits her abilities in this application to checking and responding to her own issues, besides being able to view errata for all books (just like she could as a submitter). The menu bar also confirms that she is logged in as herself, and that she has two open issues.

Open Issues

The issues themselves are displayed in the lower frame. We see the first issue, Macintoshes are PCs too!, in the first location since it's been unmodified for a longer period of time, and the new issue we just added in the second location.

Seeing our comment, Edith might be curious as to its nature. Do what she would, and click the link pointing to the issue. After a brief pause, the list of issues is replaced by information specific to our issue.

Individual Issue Information

The table at the top of the individual issue page shows the issue number, issue title, book title, issue status, and issue type, as well as our name. An editor might want to get hold of the submitter of an issue, so all contact information is easily available from this page. Go ahead and see, click on your name and check out the information you originally submitted before entering your comment. When you're satisfied that it's the same, press the back arrow to return to the Issue Information page. Click the Enter a new comment link at the bottom of the page.

Entering a New Comment

The resulting New Comment page includes the same issue information, in addition to a table with fields to enter the text of the new comment, and whether or not it should be released and made part of the external errata list. Fields also exist to change the issue's type, title, or current status. Click the New Issue Status combo box and see that the New option doesn't exist here. Once we've added a comment, the issue is no longer new—it's either open pending research or a response from someone else, or closed.

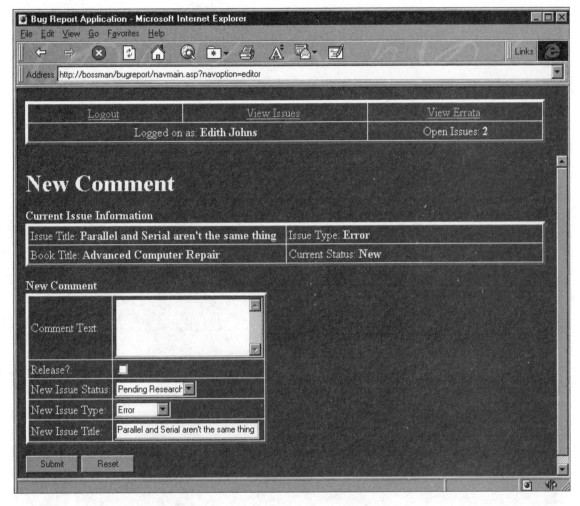

Let's suppose that Edith takes some time to investigate our comment, and decides it makes sense and should be added to the errata list for the book. First, check the Release? check box and then choose the Closed entry from the New Issue Status drop down. Then enter some text in the Comment Text area and press Submit to update the database. Since we checked Release?, whatever we enter for this comment will become part of the errata list.

When the confirmation page is displayed, click the link to refresh both frames. We're using a bit of client-side code here to do the simultaneous refreshes—using solely ASP the only way to refresh both pages is to refresh the top-level frameset. This is OK, but it means that the browser clears the screen before redrawing both frames, and it doesn't look as snazzy as doing it this way.

Viewing Errata as an Editor

When the pages are finished reloading, we'll see that Edith now has only one open issue, and that our issue is no longer listed in her list. Let's be sure we've achieved world-wide immortality with our entry on the errata list. Click the View Errata link in the top menu bar and select Advanced Computer Repair from the resulting page's drop down combo. After pressing Submit, you'll see that the errata list, which was empty before, now has one entry.

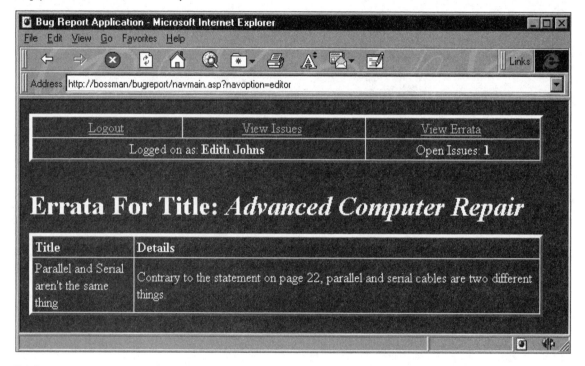

Edith needs to get back to work and resolve the other issue that has been there for a while. Stop peering over her shoulder and log out so we can explore the rest of the functionality available to editors with administrative privileges.

The Administrator Access Level

To check out the additional Administrator options, logon to the system with a new ID/password combination. The editor ID you need is lcastles, and the password is lc.

After we've been authenticated with our second editor identity of the day, Laticia Castles, look at the resulting menu bar on the generated menu. Instead of a View Errata option, administrators can View Reports (which includes the errata lists). The other additional entry is, appropriately enough for the Administrator access level, just called Administration. As we'll see in a moment, this option lets the user change information about titles and editors. We won't talk about the View Issues option again, or how the application handles open issues, because this doesn't change at all from the Editor to Administrator access level.

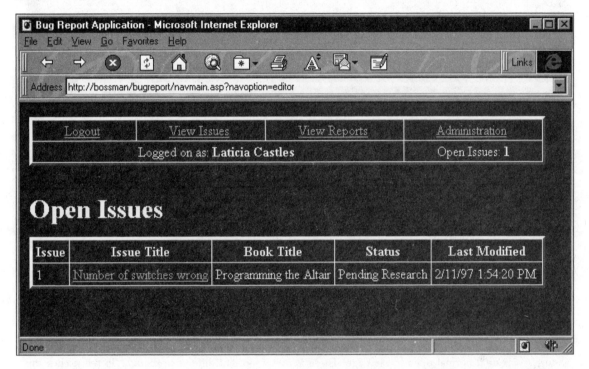

Let's see what other reports are available to us now that we're an administrator. Click the View Reports link.

Administrator Reports

What? Only one other report? As this is an example application, I spent my time doing different things with the code, instead of generating a lot of pages that differ only in format and what SQL statement is used to access the database. You have the best idea of what reports are useful in your application, and creating the individual pages often requires very little complex code.

Book Errata by Title is the same old errata lists that we've seen before, but Open Editor Issues by Editor is new. Don't wait, go ahead and click it.

Open Editor Issues

The resulting page shows a single combo box listing every editor in our database. Using this list, we can view any editor's current list of issues, and see how they're doing. We know our friend Laticia is sitting on one issue, but choose her name from the list to confirm it.

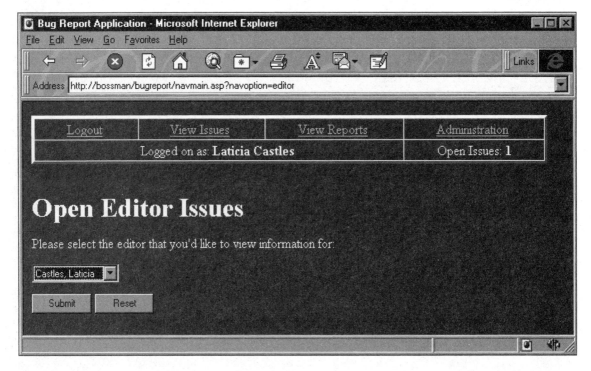

The resulting page of open issues looks similar, and it should—it's generated from the same ASP code that we use to create a normal open issues page. There is one important difference though. To see it click the Macintoshes are PCs too! link. Again, the generated page looks the same as before, but look below the list of comments. Where there was once a link to add a new comment, now there is nothing. This makes sense: although it's fine to let any administrator view open issues, only the person that owns an issue should be able to add new comments and change its properties.

Now that the reports are out of the way, let's cover the other new feature, the administration item. Click Administration in the top-level menu.

Administering the Database

This final option contains six links that allow administration of the database over the Web. Using these links we can add, modify, or remove both titles and editors from the database. We won't cover each of these in detail in this section, because their functions are reasonably self-explanatory. We will, however, cover the code in more depth when we dig into how they operate. At any rate, these pages are helpful to look at because there's a good chance that you'll be implementing some administration functionality in your own application, and that it will be at least somewhat similar to this.

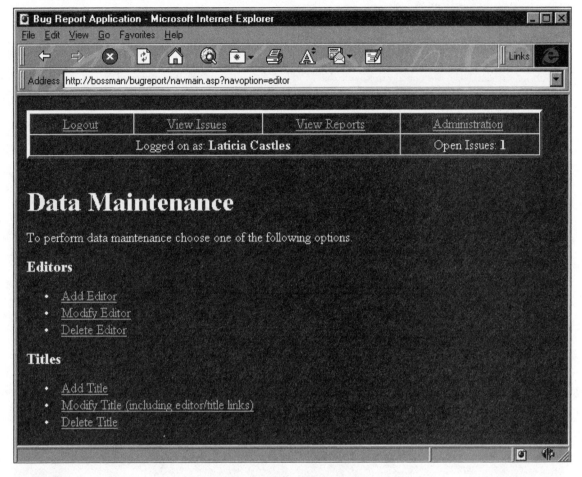

The functions of all of these links are detailed in the table below:

Link	Action
Add Editor	Add an editor to the Editors table (we'll detail the database in the next section)
Modify Editor	Modify the properties of a currently listed editor
Delete Editor	Delete an editor from the Editors table
Add Title	Add a new title information (including the editor owning the book)
Modify Title	Modify existing title information (including editor ownership)
Delete Title	Delete a title from the database

While we're not going to go into each of these options, let's look at a few interesting things that these pages do. First, suppose we decide that Edith needs a break (that PC/Mac issue has been around a while). To give her the time off, we'd like to transfer ownership of the Advanced Computer Repair title to another editor. Because the editor information for each title is stored in the `Titles` table (as we'll see when we talk about the database) we can do this with the <u>Modify Title</u> option—click it to proceed.

Modify Title Information

The first screen allows us to choose which title to modify. Make sure that Advanced Computer Repair is selected in the drop down combo box, and press Submit to continue.

We haven't covered the design of the database in detail yet. However, the fact that the only things we can modify about our title are the title itself, and the editor that owns the title, is a good clue that the `Titles` table includes only these two fields (in addition to a primary key column). As you'll see, this is indeed the case. However, the `Editors` table includes many more fields, and the Modify Editor page is correspondingly more complex.

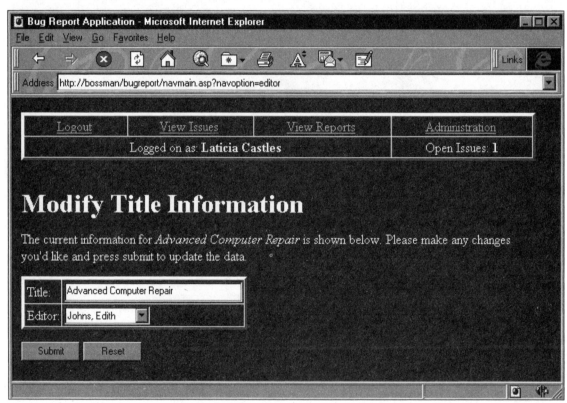

Ben Smith is idle, so let's give him ownership of Advanced Computer Repair. Choose the value Smith, Benjamin from the drop down combo box, and press Submit to continue. The next screen confirms our modification of the database. As we'll see in a second, if there was a problem the error information would be displayed here. If we want to be sure that things happened as we planned, feel free to log out, log on as the editor Ben Smith (uid: bsmith and password: bs) and check that he now has the issue Edith didn't work on.

Removing an Editor

To demonstrate some of the cool error handling abilities of these pages, let's try to remove an editor who is currently responsible for at least one title. If we could succeed at this, we'd really screw up our database–there would be title records without corresponding links to editors, our queries wouldn't know what to do. Fortunately, our database enforces referential integrity and won't let us do something like this. The code for these pages takes this into account and is ready to grab any errors, and produce a decent looking page that gives the user who made this terrible decision a chance to reconsider.

From the Data Maintenance page, click the Delete Editor link. Since we just transferred ownership of a title to Benjamin Smith, we know he has at least one title he's in charge of. Let's try to delete him from our database. Choose Smith, Benjamin from the drop down combo and press Submit to proceed.

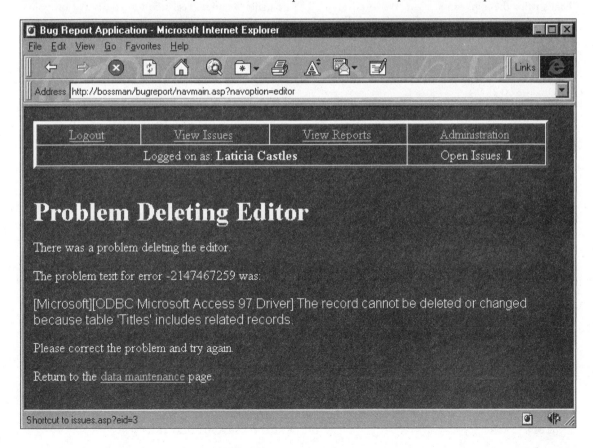

The database did indeed raise an error, and our script caught it and generated a nice looking page with the error number (-2147467259) and the error text:

> [Microsoft][ODBC Microsoft Access 97 Driver] The record cannot be deleted or changed because table 'Titles' includes related records.

If it wasn't for the error-handling code in the ASP file, we'd still get the error message–but it would be on a normal gray background, wouldn't have text explaining what had happened, and wouldn't possess a link to redirect the errant user. Since we're in control of what we output, we can do anything we like with the error text. For example, in this case, we might not want to display the reference to the ODBC driver. It would look like something had happened that the application didn't expect or know what to do with–a bad sign to users. To fix this we'd just remove this portion of the text from the string we display on the screen.

In this sample application, we haven't implemented it in every case where it could be, but it is *always* a great idea to add error handling code wherever there is even a small chance of an error. Users are much more forgiving of polite messages than they are of the abrupt default errors generated by the ASP engine.

That's it for the application itself. We've covered all of its major features. Feel free to experiment on your own, and become even more familiar with how it works.

Explaining the Application Database and Code

Now is the time to see some code–understanding how this application works will give you a distinct 'leg up' when you come to designing your own application.

The bug report application uses no less than 29 individual source files, but we won't need to cover each and every one of these in depth. Many of the files are organized in the same way, and contain similar code. After examining one or two in detail, you'll be able to understand the general flow of the code, and we'll only need to cover the new and different features of each subsequent file (trust me!).

We've listed all of the files, with a brief description of what each one does, in the table below:

File Name	Directory	Purpose
abandon.asp	<root>	Logout and abandon the current session
adovbs.inc	<root>	Included file for VBScript ADO constants
auth2.inc	<root>	Level 2 (*editor*) authentication included file
auth3.inc	<root>	Level 3 (*administrator*) authentication included file
authent.inc	<root>	Simple (*submitter*) authentication included file
checkstring.inc	<root>	Included file with **checkstring** function
default.htm	<root>	Redirect to **navmain.asp**
global.asa	<root>	**Session** and **Application** event code
navbar.asp	<root>	Content file for navigation top frame

File Name	Directory	Purpose
navmain.asp	<root>	Top-level frameset page
start.asp	<root>	Default main frame page
addeditor.asp	admin	Add editor to database
addtitle.asp	admin	Add title to database
adminstart.asp	admin	Administration options start page
deleteeditor.asp	admin	Delete editor from database
deletetitle.asp	admin	Delete title from database
modifyeditor.asp	admin	Modify editor information in database
modifytitle.asp	admin	Modify title information in database
checksubmission.asp	checksubmission	List all submissions and current status (*submitter use*)
issues.asp	issues	List open editor issues
newcomment.asp	issues	Add a new comment to an issue (*editor use*)
newissue.asp	issues	Add a new issue to the database (*submitter use*)
viewissue.asp	issues	Display individual issue information
login.asp	login	Login page (*editor and submitter use*)
errata.asp	reports	Display errata for a given title
openissues.asp	reports	Allow choice of which editor to view open issues
reports.asp	reports	Administration reports start page
submitterinfo.asp	submitterinfo	Add a new submitter to the database
viewinfo.asp	submitterinfo	View submitter information

These files can be broken down into four categories by their purpose:

Include files aren't self-contained blocks of HTML or script code. Instead they are individual pieces of code or HTML designed to be included in other pages. The files with an `.inc` extension (`auth2.inc`, `auth3.inc`, `authent.inc`, `adovbs.inc`, and `checkstring.inc`) are all include files.

Navigation files are responsible for the layout of the browser window and the menu bar in the top frame. The top-level frameset page, `navmain.asp`, and the menu bar, `navbar.asp`, are navigation files.

Content files perform some functionality, and generate HTML for the entire browser window or just the main frame (depending on the individual file). They include everything not mentioned above in the include or navigation categories.

Other files encompass all of the other functionality needed by the application. `Global.asa` holds the code for the `Application` and `Session` object's events, and `default.htm` redirects browsers to the top-level frameset page that resides in the navigation file section.

The content files constitute the majority of the application, and we'll spend most of our time talking about them. The navigation files provide the foundation that the content files use, and are also interesting. Finally, we'll be using code in the include files in many of the pages, for authentication and string manipulation, and we'll cover these files too.

The BugReport Database

A lot of the code we'll look at accesses our database using ADO. So, before we dig into the code, it's important to have some idea how the database we're using is organized.

Access is a great tool for prototyping database applications quickly, but isn't designed to function as the engine for an application that might have tens or hundreds of simultaneous users. Applications that are to be deployed on the World Wide Web, or on a high-volume Intranet, should use a more robust backend like an SQL Server or Oracle database.

To get a graphical overview right from the beginning, here is the relationships dialog for our database showing each table and how they are linked together:

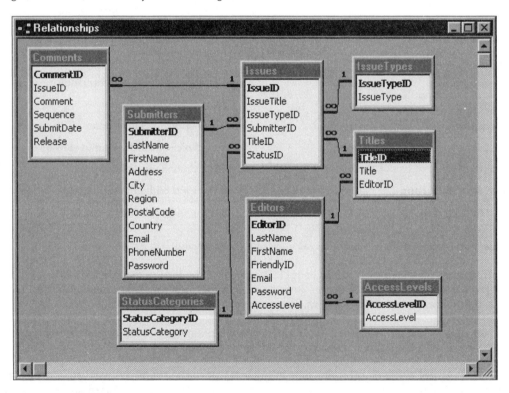

The Issues Table

From the diagram, you can see that the central table in our database is **Issues**, although most of its fields are links to other tables. This table includes one record for each issue submitted by an external source. The only non-linked field in this table is **IssueTitle**, which holds the title of the issue as entered by the submitter, and possibly modified by the editor. All of the other fields are keys to related records in other tables. Each record in **Issues** relates to one title (**Titles**), one submitter (**Submitters**), and has an **IssueType** (error, complaint, accolade, or other) and a **StatusLevel** (new, pending research, waiting on other, or closed). In addition, each issue can have one to any number of related records in the **Comments** table.

Issue Comments

The **Comments** table holds one record for each comment ever made about any issue. When a submitter creates a new issue by filling out a form on the Web, the code in the ASP file creates a new record in the **Issues** table, and also creates the first **Comment** record that relates to this issue.

Each record in **Comments** includes the following fields:

Field Name	Data Type	Purpose
CommentID	Integer	Primary key
IssueID	Integer	Link to the record in the **Issues** table that this comment relates to
Comment	Memo	The actual text of the comment
Sequence	Integer	Number in comment sequence (from **1** to **n** where **n** is the total number of comments)
SubmitDate	Date/Time	Time and date the comment was added to the database
Release	Boolean	Whether or not the comment should be released to the errata list

Tracking Book Titles

Where would we be in an application that tracks problems with books if we didn't have a table that held the title of each book we were interested in? The **Titles** table fulfills this function and has these elements:

Field Name	Data Type	Purpose
TitleID	Integer	Primary key
Title	String	The title of the book
EditorID	Integer	Link to the related editor record in the **Editors** table

User Information: Editors and Submitters

Each issue has a record in the **Submitters** table corresponding to the person that submitted the initial comment. A record in this table is created when someone fills out and submits the new submitter information form. This information can be used to respond to the submitter, or track what kind of people are sending comments. In addition to acting as the table's primary key, **SubmitterID** is also returned to the user for use (with the **Password** field) when logging on to the system later to check the status of their comments or submit new issues.

Field Name	Data Type	Purpose
SubmitterID	Integer	Primary key
LastName	Text	The submitter's last (family) name
FirstName	Text	First name
Address	Text	Street address
City	Text	City of residence
Region	Text	Region of residence (state, county, or other)
PostalCode	Text	Postal code (possibly ZIP)
Country	Text	Country of residence
Email	Text	Submitter's email address
PhoneNumber	Text	Phone number
Password	Text	Password to access submissions

The **Editors** table is similar to **Submitters**, although it doesn't hold as much information. All we care about in this application is the editor's name, their email address (so we can send them mail), and their access level (editor or administrator). For authentication purposes, we also need to track their 'friendly ID' (note the difference—editors log on with a string instead of a number) and the password.

Field Name	Data Type	Purpose
SubmitterID	Integer	Primary key
LastName	Text	The editor's last (family) name
FirstName	Text	First name
FriendlyID	Text	Friendly identifier (for logon purposes)
Email	Text	Editor's work email address
Password	Text	Logon password
AccessLevel	Text	Link to a record in the **AccessLevels** table

AccessLevels, IssueTypes and StatusCategories

These three tables are used simply to hold the text strings for the relevant category. Each table has two fields: one primary key to link to another table, and a field to hold the string. The table below shows the values for each one:

(Index)	AccessLevels	IssueTypes	StatusCategories
1	Submitter (not used)	Error	New
2	Editor	Complaint	Pending Research
3	Administrator	Accolade	Waiting For Other
4		Other	Closed

The `Issues` table includes links to `IssueTypes` and `StatusCategories`. The `Editors` table links to `AccessLevels`.

Database Wrapup

That completes our description of the database, arguably one of the most important parts of this application. Understanding how the database is laid out will help greatly when we start looking at the ADO and SQL code that's so prevalent in our pages. Whether we're designing our own applications from scratch, or interfacing to an already existing data source, the organization of the databases we're talking to will usually play a large role in our design.

The Navigation Pages: NavMain and NavBar

Our application revolves around the upper and lower frames in the browser window. Accordingly, we'll jump into our discussion of the code with the pages that implement this functionality. After we've talked about these pages, we'll move on to cover the individual content pages in more depth. Like we said before, we often use the same techniques in different pages. Since we'll try to explain these methods as they come up, it will take us longer to cover the first pages we talk about, because we'll be explaining nearly all the code. As we move through the application, we'll be able to omit discussion of more and more sections, and our descriptions will grow correspondingly smaller.

We've seen the basic operation of the application: click on a link in the top frame and see the resulting page in the bottom frame. The two files responsible for this behavior are `navmain.asp` and `navbar.asp`. `Navmain.asp` creates two frames, named `navframe` and `mainframe`. It calls `navbar.asp` to load the upper frame, `navframe`, while loading the lower frame, `mainframe`, with a given content file. We've seen a wide combination of different pages and formats over the course of using the application, so how do these two files work together to do so much?

NavMain.asp

Let's take a look at the `navmain.asp` code first. Not only does it generate the top-level frameset page, it's also a lot simpler than `navbar.asp`. In fact, it's a lot simpler than most of our pages, but it is important—without it we wouldn't have an application!

This page includes a script block first, and then a very small HTML section that uses the value of this script block. Here's the code:

```
<%
NavOption = Request.QueryString("NavOption")
Select Case NavOption
  Case "editor"
    MainFramePage = "issues/issues.asp?eid=" & Session("EditorID")
  Case "submitter"
    MainFramePage = "checksubmission/checksubmission.asp"
  Case Else
    MainFramePage = "start.asp"
End Select %>

<html>
<head>
  <meta http-equiv="Expires" content="0">
  <title>Bug Report Application</title>
</head>
<frameset rows="90, *" frameborder="0" framespacing="0">
  <frame name="navframe" src="navbar.asp" scrolling="auto">
  <frame name="mainframe" src="<%= MainFramePage %>" scrolling="auto">
</frameset>
</html>
```

You can see at a glance what this page does. The first line of code checks the query string for a parameter named **NavOption**, storing its value (if any) in the variable of the same name. It then runs through a **Select Case** statement to set the page to display in the content frame. If **NavOption** is **submitter** then we know that a submitter, not an editor, is using the application. In this case, we want to display a list of any previous issues that have been submitted. To do this the script sets **MainFramePage** to the **checksubmission.asp** file. If an editor is using the application, we set **MainFramePage** to the **issues.asp** file to load the editor's open issues into the content frame. **Issues.asp** expects that the editor ID of the issues to display is appended to the query string, so we make sure we do this in our code. Finally, if neither the submitter or editor option was chosen, the script just sets **MainFramePage** to our default **start.asp** file–which is what we see in the lower frame when we first start the application.

After the **MainFramePage** variable has been set, the script outputs a simple HTML frameset page, sizing and selecting the number of rows (**2**) and columns (**0**) before setting the bottom frame to whatever the script has stored in **MainFramePage**.

In this implementation of the application, **navbar.asp** changes its outcome based on the current values of some **Session** variables we've already set, so we don't need to call it with any special parameters. There are two general ways a page can modify its output based on circumstances: through parameters passed to the page as part of the **Request** object, or through **Session** or **Application** variables set on other pages. Even in this example, we see that **checksubmission.asp** performs its tasks using the **Session** object while **issues.asp** uses the value in the query string (although we set it in this code with the **Session** object's value). Many tasks can be performed with both methods.

NavBar.asp

Navbar.asp is a bit more complicated than **navmain.asp**–it generates a wide variety of different menu bars and generally does a lot more than **navmain.asp**. What are its primary concerns? Its actions depend on:

> ▲ Whether it's generating the menu bar for an editor or a submitter.

> ▲ If it's an editor, what access level does the editor have (i.e. an administrator or just an editor?)

> ▲ Whether the user has logged on and been authenticated.

The **navbar** code will generate a different set of options for each combination of the above parameters. Go ahead, take a look and see. The code is a set of **If...Then** statements that rely on the **Session** variables **UserType** and **Authenticated** to add the appropriate table cell. For example, the code below is executed when **UserType** is **submitter**. If the user has been authenticated (that is, they've logged on successfully), then the code adds a <u>Logout</u> option to the menu bar. If they haven't logged on, it displays the converse: a link to the Login page.

```
<% If Session("UserType") = "submitter" Then %>
  <td align="center"><% cols = cols + 1 %>
<% if Session("Authenticated") <> -1 Then %>
     <a href="login/login.asp" target="_top">Login</a>
     <% msg = "You must log on to enter comments or check your submissions."
   else %>
     <a href="abandon.asp" target="_top">Logout</a>
     <% msg = ""
   end if %>
  </td>
...
<% End If %>
```

The remainder of the script works the same way. Different elements are added to the menu bar at the top of the page, depending on the value of **UserType**, **Authenticated**, and (later in the page) the individual access level of the editor (stored in **AccessLevel**. Check it out. You should be able to find every option we've ever seen in the menu bar in this script.

Displaying Arbitrary Messages to the User

OK, but what's the deal with the **msg** variable that we seem to set at certain times? Well, sometimes we'd like to display an informative message within the table displayed in the navigation frame. For example, in the above code when the submitter hasn't logged on, we show the text You must logon to enter comments or check your submissions. This text shows up in a second row of the menu bar that covers the entire width of the browser. At other times (like when the submitter or editor has logged on) we don't show any message at all.

After we've evaluated the code for the editor or submitter options, and generated our menu bar in the process, we check the contents of the **msg** variable. If it's empty we don't need to add anything to the table. If it's holding a value, however, we should display it–and that's what our code does.

```
<% 'show message if msg <> ""
  If msg <> "" Then %>
    <tr>
      <td align="center" colspan="<%= cols %>"><%= msg %></td>
    </tr>
<% End If %>
```

The only wrinkle to smooth out is making sure that this second row of the table meshes well with the first row. If we've added four items to the menu, we don't want our message row to have one column the same width as a quarter of the first row–it would look bad. To fix this problem we use the **COLSPAN** attribute of the **<TD>** tag. **COLSPAN** takes the number of columns in the current table to span, so we just want to give it the number of columns in the menu bar.

However, since the menu bar is generated dynamically each time the page is loaded, we won't know when we're creating the page how many columns to use. To fix this problem, we've added code so that each time a cell is added to the menu bar, a variable named **cols** is incremented–check out the first bit of code on the last page–there's a **<% cols = cols + 1 %>** line after **<td align="center">**. After the menu bar is completely generated and the **cols** variable has been set, the **msg** code generates a table cell using **cols** with **COLSPAN**, displaying the value of the **msg** variable in the very wide cell.

Using ADO in a Real Application

The last interesting part of this page is our first touch of database access using ADO. We've already covered this topic in depth earlier in this book, but here's a practical example (in a sample application at least) of how it can be used. If an editor is logged on, we'd like to display the number of open issues in the navigation frame so the editor can see easily how much work he or she needs to do. To find this out, we need to perform a query that counts the number of open issues for the current editor. Given an SQL statement that performs this query, our task is just a matter of using ADO to run the query and then formatting the HTML to display the results.

The SQL statement for this query (generated by the Access Query Builder and completely unoptimized, as are all the queries in this book) is displayed in the code below.

```
<% 'get count of open issues
  sql = "SELECT Count(Issues.IssueID) AS CountOfIssueID, " _
      & "Editors.EditorID FROM (Editors INNER JOIN " _
      & "Titles ON Editors.EditorID = Titles.EditorID) " _
      & "INNER JOIN Issues ON Titles.TitleID = Issues.TitleID " _
      & "WHERE (Issues.StatusID<>4) GROUP BY Editors.EditorID " _
      & "HAVING (Editors.EditorID=" & Session("EditorID") &");"
  Set RS = DBConn.Execute(sql)
  If RS.EOF Then
    IssueCount = 0    'empty recordset, no issues
  Else
    IssueCount = RS("CountOfIssueID")
  End If %>
```

We're using the database connection called **DBConn**, which we opened at the start of the page. If the recordset is empty, we know that we have no open issues. But if we get something back, we can read the count of issues in the **CountOfIssueID** field of our recordset.

The global.asa File and Session Variables

You've already seen our use of the **Session** object to save information about the current user's session. In **navbar.asp** we used the **UserType** element to determine whether to display the editor or submitter menu options. In fact, even before we log on, the **navbar.asp** code displays a menu. If you play around with both the editor and submitter parts of the application for any length of time you'll see that whether this screen displays the editor or submitter pre-login options depends on what you last used the application for. To put it another way, if you last logged in as an editor, you'll see the editor option–<u>Login</u>. If you were a submitter the last time you used the application, the menu bar will display the submitter options: <u>Login</u> and <u>View Book Errata</u>. The first time you use the application, the submitter options are displayed– people accessing the site to submit a problem shouldn't see editor options.

To determine which set of options to display, the **navbar** code tests the **Session("UserType")** element. If this equals **submitter**, the submitter options are displayed. Putting two and two together, we can see that in order for new users to receive the submitter options, they must have had their **UserType** value set to **submitter** somewhere before **navbar.asp** does its job. We know this assignment doesn't happen in **navmain** or **navbar**, so where could it be?

The Session_onStart Event

The only code that executes before these pages load is in the **Session_onStart** and **Application_onStart** events of the **global.asa** file. Our application sets **UserType** in the **Session** object's **onStart** event, so it has a valid value when the first page loads. The way we set **UserType** is also interesting. As you'll see in a moment, when we log on to the application we save the type of login (editor or submitter) in a cookie on the client machine.

```
Session("UserType") = Request.Cookies("UserType")
If Session("UserType") = "" Then         'no usertype cookie available
    Session("UserType") = "submitter"    'so assume user is a submitter
End If
```

Our **Session_onStart** event simply checks this cookie to see if the user has previously visited the application and, if so, whether they were using the editor or submitter part of it last time. If the **UserType** element of the **Cookies** collection is empty it means it's never been set, so we assume the visitor is here for the first time and wants to submit a comment. Other important **Session** variables, like **Authenticated**, are set during the login process and elsewhere in the application.

The remainder of the executing code in the **onStart** event sets other variables that we save in the cookie collection, if they exist in the user's cookie. These are used simply to make the interface tailored to the user, by automatically opening the correct login page based on the last use they made of the application.

Lastly, the first line of the event code sets the string we use when connecting to our data source. Since we're using automatic connection pooling (see Chapter 4 for more details) we don't bother to open a connection and store it in the **Session** object too–the code to do this is at the bottom of the page, but it's commented out.

Application_onStart

In **Application_onStart** we're setting the values of two global variables to use elsewhere in the application. **SERVER_PATH** is the full URL to the root of our application. By default it's set to **http:// bossman/bugreport**–the URL on my machine. You should have changed this to the name of your server when you installed the application back at the beginning of this chapter. The other variable is used when we send mail in response to a new submission. **FROM_MAIL_ADDRESS** is the address that the mail is actually sent *from*.

The onEnd Events

In our application we don't execute any code when the session or application ends, so we don't have any code in these events.

The Login Screen

While this is still fresh in our minds, let's take a look at the login page and see how user authentication is handled, and how most of the other **Session** variables are set.

The One-page Processing Method

In our application we have many pages that need to follow a two-step process:

- Display a page with a form asking for user input
- Process the results after the form is submitted

One way to implement this is to create two separate files: one that shows the initial form and one that is called by the initial form page called to process the results. Alternatively, we can combine the two steps into a single page, keeping our code together and the number of files down. This is the technique we'll use for most of our input.

How do we tell if we should be displaying the original form page or processing the input? We add a hidden field to the form on the first page that is displayed, and then check the value of this field to determine whether data exists to be processed. You've seen some examples of this earlier in the book, and we'll show you another in a moment with the **login.asp** page.

So, this makes the general form for an input page:

```
<% If Request.Form ("HiddenFieldName") <> "" Then
        'process the results
    Else
        'create a page with a form that includes this tag:
        '<INPUT TYPE="HIDDEN" NAME="HiddenFieldName" VALUE="Go">
    End If %>
```

Not surprisingly, the login page uses this method, as we'll see in a moment.

Displaying the Login Form

When we walked through the application, we pointed out how the editor and submitter login pages looked different. The Submitter Login page included more instructions, a link to create a new submitter record, User ID and password fields, and a link to display the editor login screen.

The Editor Login page includes a password field, but everything else about it has changed. The title says "Editor", there's no new editor link, the Submitter ID field has been replaced by a text box asking for an Editor ID, and the link now allows the submitter login page to be displayed.

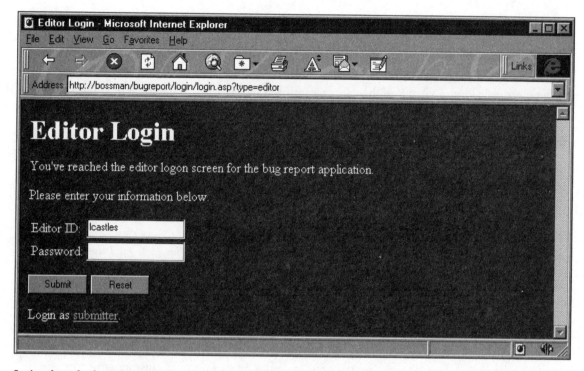

Let's take a look at the second part of `login.asp` and see exactly how this we achieve this. First, we check to see if an editor (someone with `Session("UserType")` set to `"editor"`) is accessing the page for the first time. If so, we redirect them to the same page, using a URL that contains a name/value pair called `LoginType` within the query string. We need to do this so that we can support the submitter/editor link at the bottom of the page.

After `LoginType` has been set successfully, we use this variable to determine what to display in the rest of the page. The title, instructions, ID field, and link at the bottom page are all dependent on this variable and will change when it does.

Why do we use `LoginType` instead of just using the `UserType` value we've stored in the `Session` object? Our code in this page sets `UserType` based on what flavor of the form is displayed–if we show the editor form, `UserType` is set to `editor`, and likewise for the submitter form.

Notice also that the `<INPUT>` tags displayed for the Submitter ID or Editor ID are automatically filled with the relevant variable from the `Session` object, if it exists. In this way we can avoid making the user enter their ID every single time they use the application–the text box automatically displays the last ID, just like it does when you log onto Windows 95 or Windows NT.

We're also using a bit of client-side code to make the form work a little better. The single line of code `Document.loginform.txtPassword.Focus` executes immediately after the page loads. It moves the cursor to the password text box, readying the form for input. Several techniques like this were discussed in Chapter 8.

Finally, it's true that we're submitting the user's password in the clear across the network to our server. To be exceptionally safe, it would be a good idea to encrypt this password before form submission.

Processing the Login Form

The other part of `login.asp` is the code that processes the form we displayed in the first step. It determines whether the user ID is present in our database, and if the matching password in the database is the same as the one entered on the form. If all is OK, we can display a response form giving the results of the authentication, and set any additional variables we're interested in.

Validating the ID / Password Combination

The `Editors` and `Submitters` tables hold ID and password information for each valid user. What we need to do is to find the record in the database that corresponds to the ID entered (if it exists) and then check to see that the password entered matches the one that's in the database. After opening a database connection in our code, we form an SQL statement to retrieve the correct record from the appropriate table. We need different SQL statements for editors and submitters, so we use `UserType` to select the correct statement.

Our routine for submitters checks that a numerical input has been entered in the `txtSID` text box before executing a query. If this wasn't done the `DBConn.Execute` statement would cause an error when `txtSID` was empty or holding a text value. Since our SQL statement for the editors assumes a string (remember we're checking the `FriendlyID` value, not the `EditorID`) we don't have to worry about this same problem.

The next step is to check the results. If we didn't execute the statement, our `RS` variable won't point at a valid recordset and `IsEmpty(RS)` will return true. If the ID wasn't found, then we'll have an empty recordset, and both the `BOF` and `EOF` properties of the recordset will be true at the same time. Either of these conditions means that the given ID/password combination isn't valid, and we won't authenticate the user.

```
If IsEmpty(RS) Then
  Session("Authenticated") = 0
ElseIf (RS.EOF and RS.BOF) Then
  Session("Authenticated") = 0
Else
  'at least we found the editor or submitter, so check we the password
  DBPwd = RS("Password")
  EnteredPwd = Request.Form("txtPassword")
  'take care of null value in DB during comparison
  If (DBPwd = EnteredPwd) Or (IsNull(DBPwd) And (EnteredPwd = "")) Then
    Session("Authenticated") = -1     'ok, we'll let them in...
  Else
    'this is not absolutely necessary, should already be 0
    Session("Authenticated") = 0
  End If
End If
```

If we've found the right record, we can check to see that the password entered matches the password field in the database. If the database's password field is null and **txtPassword** is empty, we should accept that combination also, so we actually have two tests in our **If...Then** statement. A match results in **Session("Authenticated")** being set to **True** (-1).

Displaying Authentication Feedback

After we've set **Authentication**, our page displays HTML informing the user of the success or failure of their logon attempt. The failed authentication page includes a link back to the login form so that the user can try again. If authentication was successful, the confirmation page links to the start page of the application.

The only part of this code that we haven't covered so far is the extra code we execute when we authenticate someone. This is the code that follows immediately after the **If Session("Authenticated") Then** line, about a third of the way down the page. We're doing two things in this code: setting **Session** variables based on the values in the database, and setting a cookie on the client with the same values so we'll be able to access them when the user returns to our site some time in the future.

LastName, **FirstName**, and **Email** are common to both editors and submitters, so we set these values before a test for editor or submitter. The following code just sets these variables from the first (**LastName**), second (**FirstName**), and third (**Email**) elements in our returned recordset.

```
Session("LastName") = RS(1)
Session("FirstName") = RS(2)
Session("Email") = RS(3)
```

What about the line after line of **Response.Cookie** manipulation? It's really quite simple. This is the code for the **FirstName** property:

```
Response.Cookies("FirstName") = RS(2)
Response.Cookies("FirstName").Expires = Date + 365
Response.Cookies("FirstName").Path = "/BugReport"
```

The first line sets the value for the **FirstName** element of the cookie to whatever the database returned for a first name. **Expires** sets the expiration date (when the cookie will be removed from the user's machine) to one year from today's date, and the **Path** property sets the URL path that this cookie applies too. Each element we save in the cookie uses three lines of code just like these.

After we've set the common properties, we can set editor- and submitter-specific properties in their own dedicated blocks of code. The most important of these properties is the **Session("AccessLevel")** property–it's used by the authentication system to limit the accessing of certain pages to those with appropriate rights. So, let's talk about how we control who can see which pages in our application.

The Authentication System

We've implement a page-level security system in this application using the **Session("Authenticated")** and **Session("AccessLevel")** elements, and a series of three include files. Our system demonstrates an interesting and extensible way to limit access entirely using ASP.

For a discussion of other security methods, see Chapter 9.

How Authentication Works

There are three access levels in our application: level 1 (submitter), level 2 (normal editor), and level 3 (administrator). For our purposes we can also consider a fourth level we might euphemistically call level 0– when the user hasn't logged on. In our system, we require a way to limit access to a given page, to everyone of a certain access level or above.

So how does the system work? To implement this we use three include files, one for each level after level 0. Each of these files has a bit of code that checks that the current **AccessLevel** is equal to or greater than the required level, and that the user is authenticated. By using a Server-Side Include directive, we can automatically add this checking code to any page that requires it.

The Auth2 Include File

To demonstrate what we're talking about, let's see the include file that limits access to editors or administrators (users with an **AccessLevel** of **2** or **3**). This file is **auth2.inc**. The companions of this file limit the users to administrators only (**auth3.inc**), and to anyone who is authenticated (**authent.inc**).

```
<html>
<head>
<% If Not Session("Authenticated") OR Session("AccessLevel") < 2 Then %>
  <!-- Redirect them to the login page -->
  <title>Not Authenticated</title>
  </head>
  <body background="/bugreport/images/blue_roc.gif"
   TEXT="white" BGCOLOR="black" LINK="#FFFF00" VLINK="#FFFF00">
  <h1>Not Authenticated</h1>
  To view the contents of this page, you must be authenticated and
  have an access level of 2 or higher.<p>
  Please go to the
  <a href="/bugreport/login/login.asp" target="_top">login page</a>
    to log on as a user with correct rights. <p>
  </body>
  </html>
<% else
   'user is authenticated %>
```

This is the entire text of the **auth2.inc** file. It simply checks that **Session("Authenticated")** is **True** and **Session("AccessLevel")** is not less than **2**. If either of these tests fail it displays a message denying access to the current page.

You might be a bit confused by the fact that we're starting an **If...Then** construct and using an **Else** statement, but not closing the statement with an **End If**. We can do this because we know that any of the authentication include files will only be used in conjunction with another page that will include an appropriate **End If**. Making the **Else** statement the last line of code in the include file is our way of ensuring that the entire text of the page using this include file will only be displayed or executed if the current user has access rights and is logged on.

> *Notice that, while a code construct like our* **If...Then...Else...End If** *can span the two files, a <SCRIPT>...</SCRIPT> or <%...%> block cannot. You must enclose the code in the two files in their own separate <SCRIPT>...</SCRIPT> or <%...%> tags.*

Using Auth2.inc To Limit Page Access

To limit access to logged in editors or administrators, we only need to add two lines to the page we want to protect. The first line, the include directive for the `auth2.inc` file, should be placed at the very beginning of the document. The second bit of code, an **End If** statement to close the **If...Then** block started in `auth2.inc`, should be placed at the end of the file, after the text of the page, but before the closing **</BODY>** and **</HTML>** tags.

Each page safeguarded by the security system looks like this:

```
<!-- #include virtual="/bugreport/auth2.inc" -->

... All normal page code and HTML here ...

<% End If %>
</html>
</body>
```

That's all that it takes to protect a page—we just add these two lines and we're done.

Extending the Authentication System

In addition to being easy to use with current pages, it's easy to expand this system to include more than the three access levels we're using. To do this we'd just create new include files–which would be exactly the same as the current ones except for the access level checked–and update the database and login routines to take into account these new levels.

Displaying Issues

So far we have been explaining each page we've talked about at a reasonably deep level of detail. In doing this we've been able to explain many of the foundations and fundamentals of the application. These basic blocks repeat themselves over and over in the rest of the files that we haven't talked about yet. Rather than waste space detailing things repeatedly, We're going to begin to move faster now. We'll only talk about the new things that each page does–you'll be able to understand the rest of the code because we've talked about it already.

One more comment: almost all of the pages we're going to look at are usually displayed in the main frame of our two-pane frameset. This doesn't mean that they can't be displayed in isolation, just that they're usually not.

The first page displayed in the main frame of the browser when we log on as either a submitter or editor is the list of issues we've submitted, or the ones we own, respectively. The code for these tasks is similar, differing only in the SQL statement and the formatting of the data returned.

User Submissions

The file **checksubmission.asp** is used to display all of the issues that a given submitter has created. The code for this file is simple: after the page header, a database connection is opened and used to retrieve information about every issue that particular user has created. The SQL statement uses the **SubmitterID** value of the **Session** object to limit the query in this manner. The query itself is complicated because we're retrieving information from **Issues** (the issue title), **Titles** (the book title), **Comments** (the first comment–the one submitted), and **StatusCategories** (the current status of the issue).

After we execute the query we either display the string We have no submissions on record if the recordset is empty, or we print a header row and then use a loop to display each element in our recordset.

```
<% Do While Not RSIssues.EOF
    Issues = Issues + 1 %>
    <tr>
      <td valign="top"><% = Issues %>.</td>
      <td valign="top"><% = RSIssues("IssueTitle") %></td>
      <td valign="top"><% = RSIssues("Title") %></td>
      <td valign="top"><% = RSIssues("StatusCategory") %></td>
      <td valign="top">
        <font size="2"><% = RSIssues("Comment") %></font>
      </td>
    </tr>
<% RSIssues.MoveNext
Loop %>
```

This code prints out a series of **<TD>** and **</TD>** tags enclosing the values from the database fields. In this case we're printing, in order, the issue number (which we calculate as we loop), the issue title, the book title, the current status, and the comment the user first submitted. The **Do While Not RSIssues.EOF** test returns **True** until we reach the end of the recordset.

Open Editor Issues

The code in the **issues.asp** file, which displays open issues for an editor, works exactly the same way as the file used to view user submissions. The SQL statement is different because we're pulling out all open issues that correspond to a given **EditorID**. We'll talk more about where this **EditorID** value comes from in a second–we don't use the **Session** object here, at least not directly. Our SQL also uses the **Max** function to pull out the time of the last comment–that is, the time the issue was last modified. We order our records by this value so that the issue that hasn't been touched for the longest amount of time appears first in the list (get to work!).

The only other difference is where the value that we use to decide what editor to pull issues for comes from. In **checksubmission.asp** we just used the current **SubmitterID** (stored in **Session("SubmitterID")**). Here we pull **EditorID** from the **Request** object instead. Why? Well, we want to use this page for more than just the current editor who might be logged on. Later, when we talk about the reports this application can generate, we'll see that administrators can check the open issues of any editor. We'd like to use the same code, so we require that the **EditorID** parameter be specified in the **Request** object with the name **eid**. Since we're not specifically using the **Form** or **QueryString** objects, **eid** can be present in either of them. We'll see that in every place we call **issues.asp** from, we either append a value for **eid** to the reference, or make sure it's an element in a form that is submitted to the page.

Working with Issues

Seeing a list of the issues we care about is cool, but it wouldn't be much use by itself–as an editor we need to be able to view details of each issue, and add new comments. Submitters need to be able to add a new issue and comment itself. We'll talk about the pages that implement all three of these functions in this section.

Submitting A New Issue

After we've logged on as a submitter, we can send a new comment to the editors by clicking the <u>Report a problem or comment</u> link in the menu bar. This link points to the `newissue.asp` file, which contains code to add a new record to the `Issues` and `Comments` tables.

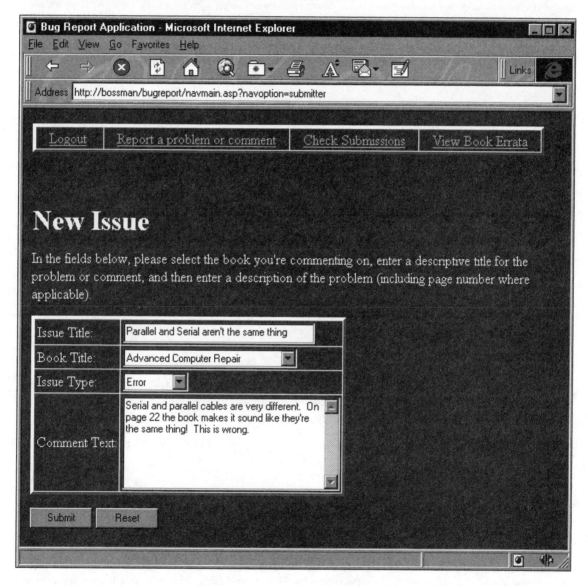

This file includes a few interesting things that we'll cover in more detail here.

The New Issue Form

When we first see the HTML generated by the **newissue.asp** file, we're looking at a form that includes two text elements and two combo boxes. The combo boxes are filled with all of the book titles and issue types in our database. Combo boxes work well for this type of input—since we can only accept issues relating to our books, we don't want to give the submitter a choice of entering any arbitrary text. Plus, we don't want to make them type the entire title, and neither do we want to attempt to figure out which title they're talking about from an incomplete string. Instead, we'll use some ASP code to dynamically fill the combo boxes with the information the user is allowed to choose.

The code for both combo boxes is similar, differing only in the SQL statement and resulting formatting. Let's take a look at the script for the list of book titles:

```
<td>Book Title:</td>
<td>
<select name="cboTitles" size="1">
<% sql = "SELECT Titles.TitleID, Titles.Title FROM Titles ORDER BY Title"
   Set RSCategories = DBConn.Execute(sql)
   Do While Not RSCategories.EOF %>
     <option value="<%= RSCategories(0) %>">
       <% = RSCategories(1) %>
     </option>
     <% RSCategories.MoveNext
   Loop %>
</select>
</td>
```

First, a row is added to the HTML table and the combo box is given a descriptive title (which is Book Title: in this case). An HTML **<SELECT>** element is created, and then our script code goes to work. We execute a query on the database to return a recordset listing just the text and unique index of the information we're interested in. When we have this recordset, we loop until we've covered each record, adding an **<OPTION>** tag to the **<SELECT>** list for each element in the recordset. We display the text of the record in the combo box and set the **VALUE** attribute of the **<OPTION>** tags to the index of the record—this is what will be submitted to the form processing code.

This is a common loop construct that we can use whenever we want to fill a combo box with a predefined set of data from the database.

Inserting the Information into the Database

Now it's time you had the privilege of looking at some code that inserts records into our database. We could do this using specific parts of the ADO object model, but here we will just use a standard SQL **INSERT** statement.

The code on this page needs to insert a record into the **Issues** table first, and then insert a record into the **Comments** table that relates to the new record in the **Issues** table. This is a straight forward exercise: pull the information we need out of the form, prepare an SQL statement incorporating this information, and use the **DBConn** object to execute the SQL statement.

Our code that accomplishes this for the new **Issues** record is:

```
SubmitterID = Session("SubmitterID")
IssueTitle = Request.Form("txtIssueName")
IssueTypeID = Request.Form("cboIssueType")
BookTitleID = Request.Form("cboTitles")

sql = "INSERT INTO Issues (IssueTitle, IssueTypeID, SubmitterID, " _
    & "TitleID, StatusID) VALUES(" & CheckString(IssueTitle,",") _
    & IssueTypeID & "," & SubmitterID & "," & BookTitleID & ",1);"
DBConn.Execute (sql)
```

This produces an SQL statement like the following (where the parts of the **VALUES** clause are determined by the information entered in the HTML form that has just been submitted):

```
INSERT INTO Issues (IssueTitle, IssueTypeID, SubmitterID, TitleID, StatusID)
VALUES('This is the new title',1,2,3,1);
```

All this is good, except for that **CheckString** function. It's not part of the VBScript language so where did it come from? Actually, we've inserted **CheckString** (which, by the way, came from the Adventure Works sample that ships with IIS) into this page using a Server-Side Include directive. When working with text and SQL statements, **CheckString** is a handy little function. It checks to make sure that any embedded single quotes in the string we're adding are read correctly by adding another single quote in front of them. In addition it adds single quotes around each side of the string (which is what SQL expects) and appends whatever character is passed as the second parameter to the end of the string. For more information on how this function works take a look at the file **checkstring.inc**.

Our **StatusID** field is always set to **1** when we insert a new issue because **1** is the index corresponding to the **New** status category.

After the SQL statement has been executed and the record submitted, we use another query to the database to determine the index value for the new record—we need this index to be able to insert a related record into the **Comments** table.

The SQL for this task (listed below) selects the maximum **IssueID** value from the **Issues** table and returns that in the recordset. We store this value into the variable **CurrentIssueID** for later use when inserting our new **Comments** record.

```
sql = "SELECT MAX(IssueID) FROM Issues"
Set RS = DBConn.Execute(sql)
CurrentIssueID = RS(0)
```

After we have this index value, the code to insert our comment is just another **INSERT** statement, and is similar to the code we used to insert the new **Issues** record.

Emailing A Notice to the Editor

Remember way back, when we walked through the application and we got that funky error about a problem preventing the sending of mail to an editor? We now have a chance to fix it—and provide an example of how easy it is to add powerful functionality like email to an application with just a component and a few lines of code.

ASP doesn't ship with a built-in component that sends email, but we can add one of any number of available components to perform our task. The mail component we'll be using is the SendMail component from the Microsoft Personalization System (we looked at this component briefly in Chapter 3). If you don't have a copy of MPS, you can find other mail components on the Internet, often free or at a small charge. As you'll see, the code that actually sends the mail is only one line, and most components work in a similar kind of way. In addition most of the code we'll talk about, like the database queries and message formulation, stays constant–it won't change when mail components do.

We'd like to send an email message to the appropriate editor, whenever someone submits a comment about a book the editor is in charge of. To do this, our code queries the database for the relevant editor and submitter information, and then generates a message that is sent to the editor automatically by using the `SendMail` method of the SendMail component. For example, the following was automatically generated when we submitted a comment about the book <u>FPGA Programming for Geeks</u>:

```
From:  bugreport@mycompany.com
To:    jeditora@company.com


Hi John Editora -

This is an automated message from the book error site.
Tom Mot (bigman@cs.washington.edu) has submitted a comment about FPGA
Programming For Geeks.

Issue Title: No Chapter Five
Issue Type: Error

The comment is:
Chapter five is missing, wassup?
```

We placed additional code after the `SendMail` call to handle any errors that occurred while trying to send the mail. This code will change depending on how our mail component handles errors, but should be comparable to ours.

If you have the SendMail component, you can try this out for yourself. Uncomment the line in `newissue.asp` that calls the `SendMail` method, make sure at least one entry in the editors table has your email as its email value, and then submit a comment about a book that editor is in charge of.

And that's everything (a lot!) that we're interested in talking about for the `newissue.asp` file.

Viewing Issue Details

As an editor, when we click on the link for a particular issue in our open issues list, we'll see the issues list replaced by the Issue Information page, which is created by the `viewissue.asp` file.

`Viewissue.asp` doesn't hold many surprises. We pass the index of the current issue from the open issues page as part of the query string, and `viewissue` reads `QueryString("IssueID")` to retrieve this value. Then the code queries the database once to retrieve general information about the issue, so it can display an informative table before the list of comments. This code automatically generates a link to the page for viewing the contact information of the person who submitted the comment.

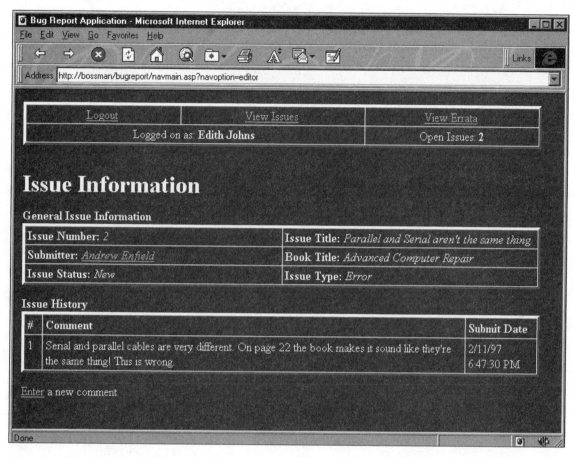

After the general information has been output we again query the database, this time for all of the comments related to the issue we're dealing with. We use a standard `Do While Not RS.EOF` loop to add each comment to the page.

Finally, we hit the database one more time to retrieve the editor ID of the editor who owns the issue we're looking at. If this value is the same as the editor ID of the logged on editor, we display a link that allows the user to add a new comment. If it isn't, that means we're viewing this issue as an administrator, so we can't add comments. Remember that only the editor that owns the issue can submit comments. Also, take notice of the **href** attribute of this link–it's extremely long because we're submitting the pertinent issue information to the new comment page as part of the URL. To encode our information so it's passed correctly to the new page we use the **Server.URLEncode** method repeatedly. For example, the following URL was generated by this code for a sample I was working with:

```
newcomment.asp?id=38&ititle=Xilinx+FPGAs+Not+Covered&btitle=FPGA+
Programming+For+Geeks&itype=Complaint&istatus=New
```

Using the **URLEncode** method ensures that our information will be fully transmitted to the next page without losing or mangling any characters.

Adding A Comment

So, if we are the owning editor, we can click on the <u>Enter new comment</u> link to load the new comment page. `Newcomment.asp` is interesting because, in contrast to the database access we've seen up until now, it uses actual ADO methods to do some of its data manipulation rather than SQL statements.

Generating the New Comment Input Form

The code first retrieves the information it needs from the query string, and generates a small general information table and a form. This has fields for the new comment text, whether the comment should be released to the errata list and three places to modify current issue information–an issue status combo box, an issue type combo box, and an issue title text box.

We use the same old `Do...While` loop construct to fill the combo boxes, but with an extra twist. The `SELECTED` attribute of the `<OPTION>` tag can be used to indicate that an element other than the first option should be the default selection. Normally we haven't used this attribute, because it's just fine for us to assume that the first element in the option list will be the default selection. In this case, with the issue status and issue type fields, we have to be a little more selective. For example, if the current status is Waiting On Other we should make sure that Waiting On Other is the default selection, otherwise an editor would find it easy to accidentally change the status to something they didn't intend.

Let's see what we're talking about with the `IssueType` code. We've added a few lines of code to our loop:

```
If RSCategories("IssueType") = IssueType Then
  stext = "selected"      'set selection text for this one
End If %>
<option <%= stext %> value="<%= RSCategories(0) %>">
  <%= RSCategories(1) %>
</option><%
RSCategories.MoveNext
stext = ""                'reset stext
```

We use an `If...Then` statement to test the value of the `IssueType` during each iteration of the loop. If we find that the value from our recordset is the same as the value for the current issue, then we set `stext` to `"selected"` and generate an `<OPTION>` tag with the `SELECTED` attribute. The code for the Issue Status field works exactly the same except that we automatically exclude the `New` status category. By definition, if we're adding a comment to an issue, it's no longer `New`.

Adding the Comment to the Database

Once we've generated the input form, and our user has made their selections and submitted it, then our processing code can go to work.

After opening a database connection we query the `Comments` table to find the maximum value of the `Sequence` field for the current issue. To this value we add one, so that our new comment will be the next in sequence for this issue. We set the `Release` variable to `True` or `False`, based on the value of the `chkRelease` form element, and then form an SQL `INSERT` statement that inserts the new comment into the `Comments` table.

This is where we see the new code. If the user has modified the `IssueType`, `IssueStatus`, and / or `IssueTitle` fields, we need to update the corresponding fields within this issue record in the `Issues` table. We could do this with SQL code, but we're going to use ADO methods instead:

```
Set rsTemp = Server.CreateObject("ADODB.Recordset")
sql = "SELECT Issues.IssueTypeID, Issues.StatusID, Issues.IssueTitle " _
    & "FROM Issues WHERE Issues.IssueID = " & IssueID & ";"

'use Open method of Recordset object to a open an updateable recordset
rsTemp.Open sql, DBConn, adOpenKeyset, adLockOptimistic, adCmdText

'we now have the record and can modify it. We could optimize the code by
'only modifying it if the values have changed.
rsTemp("IssueTypeID") = Request.Form("cboNewType")
rsTemp("StatusID") = Request.Form("cboNewStatus")
rsTemp("IssueTitle") = Request.Form("txtNewTitle")
On Error Resume Next
rsTemp.Update
```

We first create an additional database object of type **ADODB.Recordset**. Then we use the **Open** method of this **Recordset** object to create a recordset that we can modify. We pass our SQL statement, the current database connection (held in the **DBConn** variable), as well as three additional parameters that control what kind of recordset is returned. We can use named constants like **adOpenKeyset**, **adLockOptimistic**, and **adCmdText** here because we've included the **adovbs.inc** file at the top of this page.

> *For more information about the* **Open** *method and its constants, check out Chapter 4, and the ADO documentation that ships with IIS.*

After we get our recordset, we modify the three fields we're concerned with, and write the changes back to the database with the recordset's **Update** method. The **On Error Resume Next** statement is there in case the **Update** method fails for some reason. If we detect an error we write one message to the page; if we succeed we write another (more positive) reply.

In either case we print one final line of text with a link that calls a client-side JavaScript function to update both the upper and lower frames. If we've closed an issue then the information in the upper frame needs to be updated as well. Refreshing two pages simultaneously isn't possible directly with this version of ASP, but with a little client-side code we can get around the problem. This technique is discussed in greater detail in Chapter 8, where we looked at integrating client-side code with ASP.

Submitter Information

Before anyone can submit anything, they need to fill out the new submitter form and provide information so that the editors can contact them with questions (or other, more sales-oriented issues!). We provide a simple page that displays this information.

Adding A New Submitter

This page holds one new feature: a flexible system for validating the input in a form. When first loaded, **submitterinfo.asp** checks to make sure we haven't inadvertently gotten to this page while already logged on. It displays a message and stops the form generation if we have. After this check, **submitterinfo** creates a rather large table with input fields for each field in the **Submitters** table. The only thing a little out of place here is how we set the **VALUE** attributes of each text field. Instead of omitting this attribute as we usually do when we want the text box to be blank, we're using **Request.QueryString("txtFieldName")** where **txtFieldName** is the name of the field in question. We'll see why we did this in a second, when we talk about the validation system. When the user presses Submit the form data is sent to **submitterinfo.asp** for processing.

Input Validation with SubmitterInfo

We'd like to insist that any person who submits a comment provide at least their first and last names, and an email address. To avoid later problems, we should also check that the password and password confirmation the user entered match. In **submitterinfo.asp** we show a somewhat general routine that we can use to check the validity of the fields we require.

The first part of this validation methodology is a series of **If...Then** statements that explicitly test each criteria. For example, we use this code to make sure the user has entered a value for the **LastName** field:

```
If Request.Form("txtLastName") = "" Then
   Invalid = True
   itxt = itxt & "<LI> You didn't enter a last name."
End If
```

Our criteria can be anything that we can formulate into a comparison (for an example of a different test, see the line comparing passwords). If the test fails, we set the **Invalid** flag to **True** to indicate that we have invalid data, and write a descriptive message explaining what the problem was to the variable **itxt**. Because other tests may write to this variable as well, we need to make sure we append our data to the variable's contents instead of overwriting them.

After we've tested all the criteria we care about, we check to see if **Invalid** is **True** or **False**. If it's **False**, then all the tests were passed and we can proceed as normal—we'll cover what happens in this file when it passes the validation tests in a moment, but for now let's keep our focus on the validation routine. If **Invalid** is **True**, we need to stop processing, inform the user that their data didn't pass muster, and allow them to try again. That's what the HTML generation in this part of the **submitterinfo** file does. The value of **itxt** is used to display all of the problems that occurred with the submission.

Preserving Entered Data

Suppose the user has spent five minutes or so entering a value into every single one of our fields, but they accidentally hit a wrong key when entering their password. Of course, the validation routine will catch this problem. It would be nice, especially on a form as big as this one, if the user could return to the page with all of their previously entered data intact so they didn't have to re-enter anything except the field that caused the validation to fail in the first place. Remember those **Request.QueryString** lines in the original form generation? We added them so we could save the user's already entered data.

We're going to reload this page, but we need to transmit each and every one of the values in the form along with our request for the new page, so the form can display these values when it is rendered. The following slick little function accomplishes exactly this in only four lines of code. It first appends a **?** to the name of the current file (which is **submitterinfo.asp** in this case) and then loops through each element of the **Request.Form** collection, adding the element name and the contents of that element (in URL encoded form) to the query string.

```
'form a query string to reload entered data into fields
lnk = Request.ServerVariables("SCRIPT_NAME") & "?"
For Each e in Request.Form
   lnk = lnk & "&" & e & "=" & Server.URLEncode(Request.Form(e))
Next %>
```

This might seem too good to be true, so if you're skeptical, enter some bad input so that you fail the validation checks, and then do a view source on the Problems page that submitterinfo generates. You'll see an incredibly long link at the bottom of the page, and all of the values originally entered will be present in the query string portion of this URL. When the page reloads, the values are stripped from the URL and automatically re-inserted into the appropriate text box. Pretty cool, eh?

> *Note that it's possible for an extremely long comment to be truncated because only a finite number of characters can be submitted as part of the query string.*

As a final comment on the validation issue, note that we could also have implemented this same logic in client-side code, which would execute on the browser. With this method we only use network bandwidth to transmit a good set of data; everything that isn't acceptable is caught on the client before it's sent over the wire. One of the examples in Chapter 8 shows how to do this kind of validation in the browser.

Processing the SubmitterInfo Data

Once we're sure that the data is OK, we add it to the database with a giant INSERT statement that uses the CheckString function repeatedly. After we've added the new record to the Submitters table, we need to find the SubmitterID of the submitter as well as setting other appropriate Session variables and values in the user's cookie. The code in the page uses the SQL MAX function to get the SubmitterID, and writes it into the Session("SubmitterID") element. We also write other important information, like the name and email of the user, to the Session object at this time. Finally, we save these same bits of information to the user's cookie with the Response.Cookies collection. The Expires and Path properties of this collection work the same as they do with the Request.Cookies collection.

After we've done all this work on the server, we prepare a page that includes the user's submitter ID and password. The page instructs the user to remember both of these pieces of information, because they'll be needed to log back on to the system later.

Viewing Submitter Information

As far as complexity goes, submitterinfo.asp and viewinfo.asp are on opposite ends of the spectrum. We just spent two pages talking about submitterinfo and we can explain viewinfo.asp in a single paragraph.

This page displays the information from the Submitters table for a given submitter ID value, specified in the query string as ID. We open a database connection, send a query to retrieve the submitter's information, and display it in a table. That's all this page does.

Generating Reports

As we said before, if this was a real application we'd probably have access to many more reports than we've actually made available. But reports are easy to add. The code is simple and usually follows a reasonably regular pattern—create the SQL statement that returns the information we need, and then write some HTML to format the information and makes it look nice in the page.

The reports we have included in our sample allow us to view the errata for a given book title, and to select an editor and view all of their open issues.

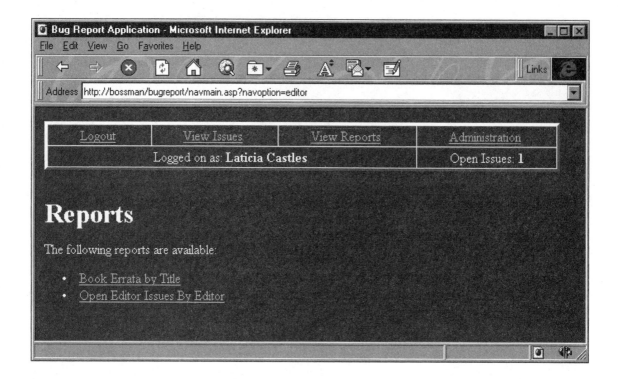

Errata Lists

Everyone, even a non-logged-in external user, has access to this report. The first time `errata.asp` is loaded it displays a header, one line of instructional text, and a combo box that has been filled with each book title in our database.

When the user selects a title and presses Submit, the other part of `errata.asp` generates the list of the comments that have previously been released to the world. The only information we have coming into this processing is the title ID value, so we need to do a query first to find the text title of the book (we could have passed this along from the form page to save time and resources, but we didn't bother). After retrieving this information we do another query to retrieve all of the comments where the `Release` field is `True`, and display them in a table on our page.

Viewing Other Editor's Open Issues

The other report, this time only accessible to administrators, allows us to view the issues each editor currently has open. We want to reuse as much code as possible, so we've designed the `issues.asp` and `viewissue.asp` code (as mentioned above) to be conducive to editors other than the owning editor viewing the issue contents.

Having said this, we can see why the code for this page is so minimal—all we're doing is loading a combo box with the names of the editors and then calling `issues.asp` with the index value of the editor that the user chooses.

Database Administration

The last major category we haven't covered is database administration. While these pages are relatively complex, at this point there's virtually nothing new in them that we haven't already seen and talked about. However, we'll go over them briefly anyway. As you'll see, the code to execute a particular task (whether it be adding, modifying, or deleting data) is very similar. Because of this we'll cover the following files together: `addeditor.asp` and `addtitle.asp`, `modifyeditor.asp` and `modifytitle.asp`, and `deleteeditor.asp` and `deletetitle.asp`.

Adding Records

The `addeditor.asp` and `addtitle.asp` pages facilitate adding editors and titles respectively to the database. Both pages create an input form first, generating text boxes and combo boxes with data from the database.

After the data is submitted we use the same validation method that we outlined when talking about `submitterinfo` to make sure each element has some data. Finally, assuming we pass the validation tests, we add the information to the database with our old friend the SQL `INSERT` statement.

Modifying Records

The `modifyeditor.asp` and `modifytitle.asp` pages work in pretty much the same way as the code we've seen before, but with one added element. Instead of using a two pass system, as normal with a form and processing code in the same document, we do three tasks—so each page has three, rather than one or two, main sections.

The first section displays a form that allows us to choose the editor or title we want to modify information for. When we submit this form, the value of the hidden field named `hdnProcess` is `modify`. The top-level `If...Then` statement sees this value and knows that we've picked an editor or title that we want to modify. It shows another form containing the results of a database query, to show the current values for the editor or title we've picked to change. When this second form is submitted, `hdnProcess` holds the value `update`. The last section of these pages handles the update task by opening a recordset object, modifying the fields in question and using the recordset's `Update` method to propagate the changes back to the database.

Again, this is a reasonably complex example, but, aside from the three pass method of form processing, it doesn't show anything we haven't discussed in detail already.

Deleting Records

The last task an administrator can perform with the database maintenance pages is the deletion of an editor or title from the database.

The first form page for `deleteeditor.asp` and `deletetitle.asp` is nearly identical to the first form for the modify pages—it just shows a combo box to allow the user to choose an editor or title to delete. The processing code creates an SQL `DELETE` statement, and executes it after turning error handling on. If the delete doesn't succeed for some reason—maybe there are related records in another table in the database—a page is generated explaining the error, and giving the user an opportunity to retry after they've fixed the problem that caused the error.

Other Files

These last files perform very small tasks, and we're including them here for the sake of completeness (or in case you really wanted to know what the **start.asp** page does!).

default.htm

The default IIS setup automatically returns the page titled **default.htm** if a user enters a directory name in a URL without a file name. Since we want the first page our user sees to be **navmain.asp**, **default.htm** uses the following HTML to redirect the browser to **navmain.asp** immediately (i.e., after 0 seconds):

```
<meta http-equiv="Refresh" content="0;URL=navmain.asp">
```

We could have used the **Response** object's **Redirect** method–it serves our purposes equally as well in this case.

abandon.asp

When a user clicks the <u>Logout</u> link, we want to kill their session immediately. The **Session.Abandon** method can do this. **Abandon.asp** includes one line of ASP code that calls this method, and a few lines of HTML to display a page telling the user they've truly logged out.

start.asp

When **navmain.asp** first loads (for example, when **default.htm** redirects the browser to it) there is no query string specifying whether **navmain** should load the editor or submitter menu bar. So, with nothing specified, **navmain.asp** loads **start.asp** into the bottom frame. **Start.asp** could equally as well be an HTML file–it includes no script code, just HTML to display the a title for the application.

Summary

We designed this application around a specific task, that of allowing readers to communicate directly with the editors of our books. However, the concept is much more general, and it could easily find a home on almost any Web site or corporate Intranet where a help-desk style of application is required. It shows a lot of the general methods that are used when interacting with users, and storing and retrieving their submissions. You are, of course, free to use and adapt the application to suit your own particular needs.

As much as this application does, there are a number of improvements that could make it more useful to the submitters and editors, and more attractive. The following ideas are just a start. Perhaps you have some of our own.

- Upgrade the backend database to a more robust multi-user system like SQL Server, Oracle, or Informix. Access isn't too good at handling a lot of simultaneous users.

- Improve the appearance of all of the pages–especially the ones that external submitters will see. We didn't spend too much time making this application look nice because we wanted to focus on making the code do interesting things. However, our users won't know that–they'll want to look at a pretty set of pages with graphics, style, and everything this application doesn't have in the way of looks.

- Expand the automatic notification functions to do more than send an email when a new issue has been submitted. Maybe we'd like to send emails to editors if they let an issue sit idle for too long–or maybe we want to send mail to the editor's boss!

- Add more reports to give administrators and managers a better idea of how the process of tracking problems and comments is going.

Like we said, these are just a few suggestions to get you started. In implementing your own applications you can never do quite everything you'd like to, so it's always good to have a list of improvements in case you actually get the time to make them.

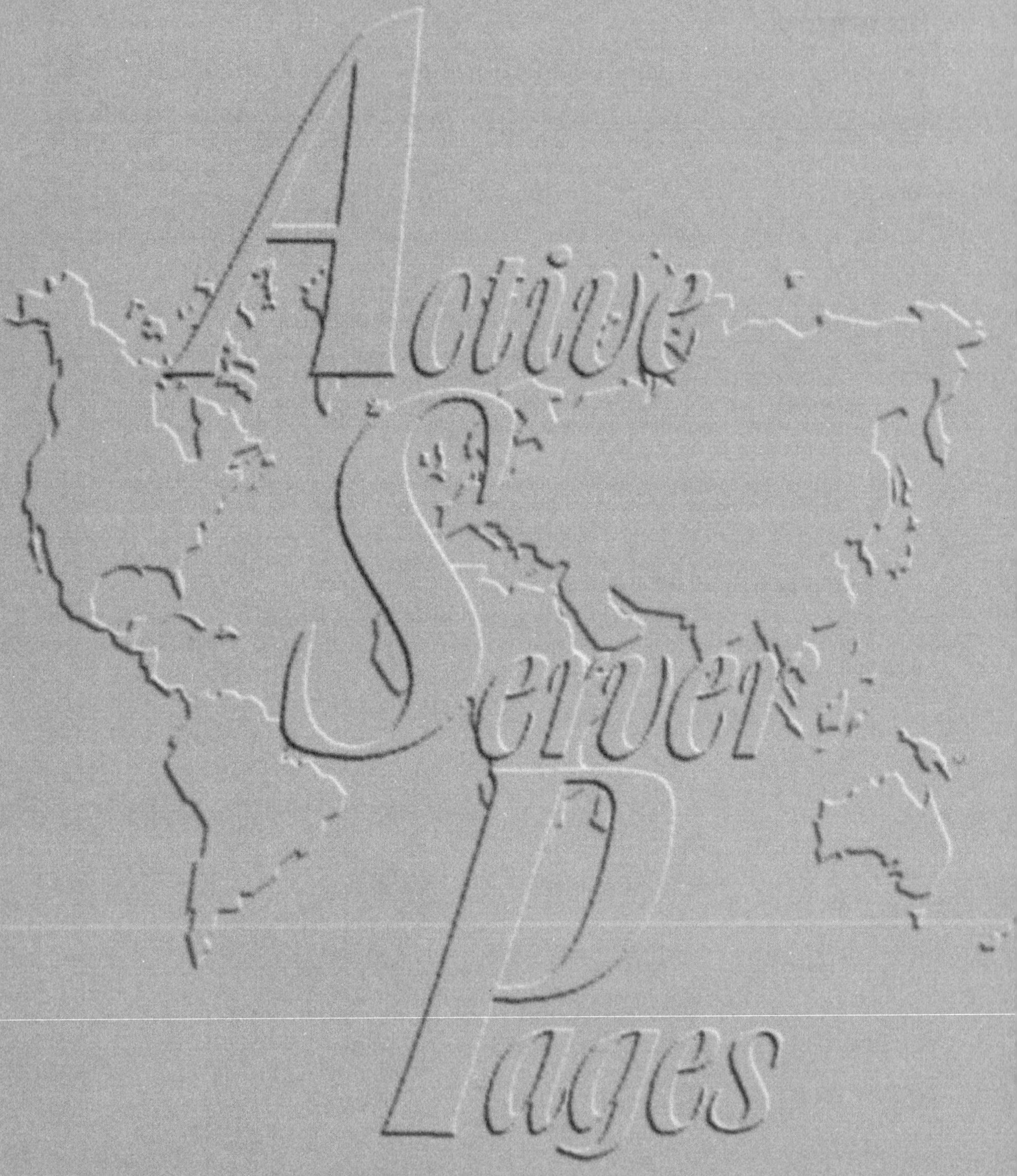
Active
Server
Pages

Case Study 3— Integrating Index Server

As with a book, indexing is a very important function. If your web site contains more than a handful of pages, it can be difficult for visitors to find information about particular topics quickly. For example, on a software support site, visitors may need help installing a particular component. Instead of looking for menu hyperlinks that lead to the relevant page, they would probably find it easier to enter details of their query and get a list of matching pages.

Microsoft Index Server allows you to make your site available to web searches with very little effort. And on the company intranet easy search access is just as important, if not more so. With hundreds or even thousands of company documents available, being able to find the right one while the customer is hanging on the phone is vital. Index Server uses a background application that maintains an on-disk catalog, or index, of the content of specified documents stored on your system. To search the catalog to get information about the indexed documents, you just use a query page containing some fairly simple HTML code.

In this case study, we're going to look specifically at Index Server, simply because it is now an integrated part of IIS version 3.0 (although you still need to install it yourself in IIS 2.0). But the method we use to integrate it with Active Server Pages, as you'll see, opens up a whole new window of opportunities. It provides a neat way to carry on using all kinds of existing server-based applications and scripts within the ASP environment.

So, in this chapter you'll see:

- ▲ How we can integrate other server applications with ASP
- ▲ What Index Server is, and how we use it
- ▲ How we capture output from Index Server in Active Server Pages
- ▲ The Billboard method of executing other applications

First we'll install the sample files, then have a look at the problems you'll probably have to face if you're upgrading an existing web site to Active Server Pages.

Installing the Sample Files

To run the sample applications on your own server, you must follow these steps:

- ▲ Create a single directory somewhere on one of the server's disks, and copy all the **IndxServ** project files into it.
- ▲ Create a virtual root, or alias, called **/IDXSRV** and be sure to give it **Executable** access. We showed how to do this in Chapter 1, look back there if you need help with this step.

> Open and edit the following files in the new application directory you created: **Billboard.asp**, **SearchComponents.asp** and **GetPartDetail.asp**. In each one, find the line near the start that reads:

```
strServerPath = "http://yourserver"
```

and change *yourserver* to the name or IP address of your own server. This is necessary because, at present, the component we are using can't accept virtual or relative paths.

Integrating ASP with Existing Applications

Before we can even think about integrating something like Index Server into our Active Server Pages, we need to step back a little and consider the whole concept of the problem. To do this, we'll look at an example that uses something a little more 'down-to-earth'.

Traditional CGI Applications and Scripts

Before the advent of the newer technologies like the Internet Database Connector, and of course Active Server Pages, most dynamic web pages were produced by either a CGI-based application, or a traditional server-scripting language like Perl or Awk. The overall principle is the same as we've seen with ASP throughout this book—a **<FORM>** on a web page submits the values in the controls to the application or script, which then creates the new page dynamically and sends it back to the browser:

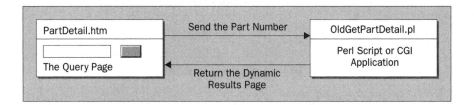

Displaying Part Details

Let's assume we have a similar arrangement, which supplies details of a stock part from our vast range of grommets. We have a page with a text box where the user fills in the part number, and a Submit button that references the script to create the results page. As we redesign our site with ASP, we'll update the form page to make it match the new corporate scheme:

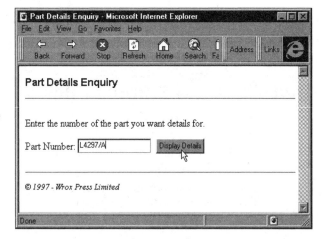

Redesigning this page is easy enough to do. This is only a static `.htm` page, so we can build it using any of our usual design tools:

```html
<html>
<head>
<title>Part Details Enquiry</title>
</head>
<body bgcolor="#FFFFFF">
<B><font face="Arial">Part Details Enquiry</font></B><HR>
<form method="GET" action="OldGetPartDetail.pl">
   Enter the number of the part you want details for.<P>
   Part Number:
   <input type="text" size="20" maxlength="255" name="txtPartNumber">
   <input type="submit" value="Display Details"><p>
</form>
<HR>
<FONT SIZE=2><CITE>&copy; 1997 - Wrox Press Limited</CITE>
</body>
</html>
```

The Legacy Application

However, in the middle of switching our site to Active Server Pages, we discover that the code which retrieves the part details is horrendously complex. There's no chance of switching it over to ASP quickly or easily—it means a visit from the technician who looks after our database system. In the meantime, the results of running the Perl script look decidedly out of place:

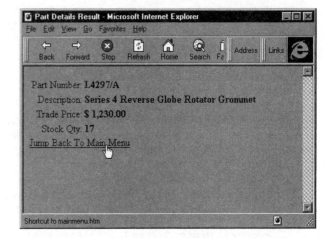

Worse than that, the hyperlink points to a nonexistent page. When we redesigned our site, the parts list page became **newmenu.asp** instead of **mainmenu.htm**, and that's where we want to return. This means that we have to create a dummy page that redirects the browser to the correct one.

Wrapping up the Legacy Page

There's a way of handling all of these problems, using a simple Server Component. The source of our difficulty is that, when we reference an old script or application, the HTML and text stream it produces is sent straight back to the browser. What we need to do is be able to capture the output from the script or application, and then process it to meet our new requirements. To do this, we use a component that can retrieve the page for us.

The ASP HTTP Server Component

There are several components available that can satisfy our need to capture the HTTP stream created by an application, a script or even a static page. We've used one called **Asphttp.dll**, from Steve Genusa. Steve has kindly allowed us to include the component with our sample files. Before you use it in your own applications, be sure to read the terms and conditions in the file **License.txt**.

ASP HTTP is a new component that is very simple to use, although currently poorly documented. This will improve once it is actually released as Version 1.0. However, Steve answered within two hours of our inquiry, and even in its current version it will easily meet our needs. The URL for the site that hosts this component, and many other samples, is **http://www.genusa.com/asp***.*

What the Component Does

The purpose of the ASP HTTP component is to allow the developer to **GET** documents via the HTTP protocol, without the documents being sent back to the browser. It returns the entire text of the document as a string. To use it, we just declare it like any other component, and use its methods and properties:

```
Set HttpObj = Server.CreateObject("ASPsvg.HTTP")
HttpObj.Url = "http://www.genusa.com/asp/"
HttpObj.Port = 80        'this is the default value if not set otherwise
HttpObj.TimeOut = 80     'this is the default value if not set otherwise
strResult = HttpObj.GetURL
```

One point to note is that the URL has to be well-formed, that is, it has to include the full URL string in the form **http://**servername/document. The **http://** part must always be present, otherwise an error will occur.

The other two properties specify the **Port** to which the connection should be made, and the **Timeout**. By default, both are set to **80** unless we set them otherwise. To receive the contents of the document, we just call the **GetURL** method, and assign the results to a string variable ready for processing.

You will have to install the component yourself on your server—there's no setup program with it. To do this, place the **Asphttp.dll** *file in an appropriate directory, such as* **Winnt/System32/ InetSrv/ASP/Cmpnts***. Then in a* **DOS** *Command Window, enter:*

regsvr32 **Winnt/System32/InetSrv/ASP/Cmpnts/Asphttp.dll**

substituting the path where you placed the component.

Using the ASP HTTP Component

While the principle of the component seems simple enough, the extra processing abilities it makes available to us are really quite dramatic. Now, we can get the entire content of any page, static or dynamic, and play around with it within our ASP code—without the browser being aware that anything is happening.

Coming back to our earlier Part Description example, you can see how we can use it to get round the problems we met. All we have to do is use the component to get the contents of the page, modify it as required to match our new site layout and appearance, and send it off to the browser. In outline, the plan is:

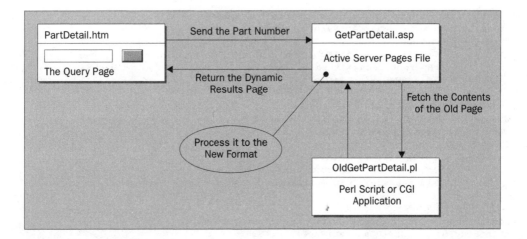

Getting the Page Contents

Here's the code to do it. The first section sets the URL of the old page in a string **strURL**, adds the entire query string being sent from the **<FORM>**, creates the component instance, and then fetches the result into a string **strPage**.

> *Notice the first line, where you must change the code to your own server name or IP address—remember, the ASP HTTP component doesn't support virtual or relative addresses at present:*

```
<% strServerName = "http://yourserver"
   strURL = strServerName & "/IDXSRV/OldGetPartDetail.pl?" & Request.QueryString

'Create the HTTP object and retrieve the page
Set objHttp = Server.CreateObject("ASPsvg.HTTP")
objHttp.Url = strURL
strPage = objHttp.GetURL
...
```

Changing the Contents

Having got the contents of the page as a string, we can now play around with it. We want to change the background color, add a new heading in the correct font, change the **HREF** in the hyperlink to point to our new menu page and add our company's standard copyright text at the foot of the page. And if you've got this far through the book, you won't need us to explain how the code actually works–it's remarkably simple:

```
...
'Set the background color to white in the opening BODY tag
intBodyPos = InStr(UCase(strPage), "<BODY")
If intBodyPos Then
   strPage = Left(strPage, intBodyPos + 4 ) _
          & " BGCOLOR=""#FFFFFF""" & Mid(strPage, intBodyPos + 5)
End If
```

```
'Add the new heading in the page, before the table
intTablePos = InStr(UCase(strPage), "<TABLE")
If intTablePos Then
   strPage = Left(strPage, intTablePos - 1 ) _
           & "<B><font face=""Arial"">Part Details Result</font></B><HR>" _
           & Mid(strPage, intTablePos)
End If

'Change the link at the end of the table to point to our new menu page
intHrefPos = InStr(UCase(strPage), "<A HREF=")
If intHRefPos Then
   strPage = Left(strPage, intHrefPos + 8 ) _
           & "newmenu.asp"">Return to Main Part List" _
           & Mid(strPage, InStr(strPage, "</A>"))
End If

'Add the new copyright text before the closing BODY tag
intEndBodyPos = InStr(UCase(strPage), "</BODY>")
If intEndBodyPos Then
   strPage = Left(strPage, intEndBodyPos - 1 ) _
           & "<HR><FONT SIZE =2><CITE>&copy; 1997 - Wrox Press Limited" _
           & "</CITE>" & Mid(strPage, intEndBodyPos)
End If

'And finally send the new page to the browser
Response.Write strPage %>
```

So, we can pull existing dynamic pages apart, add and remove things, and put them back together any way we like—all without changing the original application that created the page. Here's the result of our efforts:

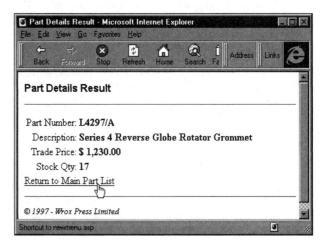

The pages for this example are included in the samples available for this book from http:// *www.rapid.wrox.com/books/0723. Notice that, in the code we supply, the application that produces the legacy results page is actually an ASP file, not a Perl script that queries a database. However, the results are the same as far as this example is concerned.*

Working with Other Pages

The principle we've just shown is simple enough, though we have to be aware of the contents of the original page, so that we know where to add and remove parts. In general, this isn't a problem. We can load the dynamic page in the browser in the normal way, and select View Source to see what it actually contains.

The trick is to change those parts of the page that are constant each time it is created, rather than looking for the dynamic content. That's why we focussed on the **<BODY>** and **<TABLE>** tags, because they don't change. Of course, there's no reason why we shouldn't modify dynamic content if it's *really* necessary:

```
...
'don't show the details of green grommets
intGreenPos = InStr(UCase(strPage), "<TR><TD>GREEN GROMMETS")
If intGreenPos Then
   intGreenEnd = InStr(intGreenPos, strPage, "</TR>")
   strPage = Left(strPage, intGreenPos - 1 ) & Mid(strPage, intGreenEnd + 5)
End If
...
```

This code looks for **<TR><TD>GREEN GROMMETS** in the page, knowing that it contains a table holding a list of our range of grommets. If the listing does happen to contain any green ones, it removes the whole table row, between **<TR>** and **</TR>**. The viewer never gets to see them.

> *This code uses the extended version of the **InStr** function, which accepts a starting position for the search as the first parameter. In other words, in our example, it looks for the first occurrence of* **</TR>** *from the position referenced by* **intGreenPos**.

Introducing Index Server

Before we go on to look at how we can integrate Index Server into our shiny new Active Server Pages site, we'll have a look at what Index Server actually is, and how it works. It's a surprisingly powerful search engine package, and can quite easily perform the most complex kinds of query and search tasks.

Once installed, Index Server is, to a large extent, self-maintaining. During periods of little or no system activity, it trawls round the folders in the selected areas of your system, building and maintaining a catalog of information about each document stored there. When you perform a search in the catalog, it uses the contents of the index to build the HTML results page and returns it to the client. The whole cataloging and indexing system is practically transparent as far as the user is concerned. It is also very fast, because only the index file needs to be searched each time.

> *Note that the index file can be up to 40% of the total size of the documents on your system, if you have full indexing features in use.*

The Types of Information Index Server Stores

Index Server doesn't just keep a list of file names (if we wanted to do this, we could use the Windows Find dialog), it also stores a multitude of document details. These include many of the stored document's properties, the time and date it was created and last updated, the size, the file attribute status, etc. Plus, and here's the clever bit, it keeps an **abstract** of the contents.

This abstract is a selection of the text in the document, irrespective of what type of document it actually is. And Index Server contains natural language processing systems, dedicated to your own particular spoken language, so it really 'understands', as far as computers can understand, the file contents.

This means that we can search for a word, or group of words, as well as specifying the type of the file and other properties such as the author. The language engine can match words literally, so that `catch*` will include `catcher` and `catching`, and also grammatically, where `catch**` will include `catching` and `caught`. As well as this, there is a 'noise' list file, which we can edit, that prevents words such as **and**, **or**, **the**, etc. from being included in the index. This makes it a very powerful way of finding information stored anywhere on our system.

Types of Documents that can be Catalogued

Index Server will catalog, by default, all the documents stored in the virtual paths set up in Internet Information Server. These can be HTML files, documents created in Microsoft Word, Excel or PowerPoint, or plain text files. Index Server even maintains a list of non-document files in the catalog, such as executables, but, of course, it can't perform searches for meaningful information within these.

You'll find that many document types aren't directly supported by Index Server. At the moment only the Microsoft formats are supported. However, Index Server has a **filter interface** which enables third party software vendors to provide the logic to enable Index Server to support their own application file formats. This means that other suppliers can, potentially, allow any file type to be fully cataloged.

Index Server in Action

To show you what Index Server can do with very little effort here's some examples of it in use. You'll see how easy it is, both from a developer's and an end-user's point of view.

All we need is a `<FORM>` section in the page, with a single text box and a Submit button. Here, we've also included a standard Reset button to clear the text box as well. We use the text box to enter a search criterion for which matching files will be listed. In this case, we've entered the criteria `zip*` to find any documents containing words that start with `zip`:

Enter the contents of a document to find:

| zip* | | Search Now | Clear |

Clicking Search sends Index Server off to look in its catalog, and after a short while a list of matching documents appears. Here, we've found 15 that match, and the list shows details of the first 10 of these:

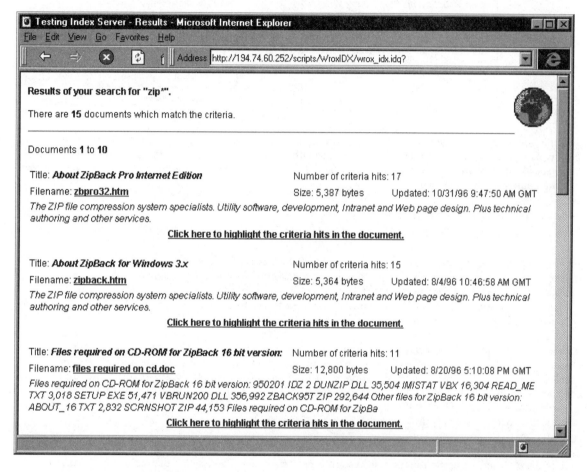

For each one, there's the document title, filename, and some of the abstract information. The page also shows the number of 'criteria hits'–the number of times the keyword is found in the document. However, the documents are actually listed in descending order based on their **ranking** by the search engine, and not just the number of keyword hits.

> *The **ranking** is generated automatically and reflects how well the document matches the query, so that the most appropriate ones can be listed first; for example, when doing a **NEAR** search, the ranking is affected by the proximity of the keywords, and not just their frequency.*

There's also the size in bytes, and the date and time it was last updated. At the bottom of the page is a button where we can show the next page of results. Notice that it 'knows' there are only five more to look at. Clicking it displays the next page with the title Documents 11 to 15.

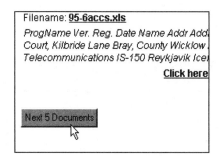

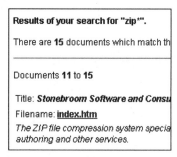

At the bottom of this page is a message confirming that there are no more matches, and some controls that allow us to perform a new search. One of the strengths of Index Server is that there are several ways we can specify the documents we want to find. The default, as we've been using here, is to search for the text in the content of the document.

Index Server's Query Language

When composing a query, we need to bear in mind a few simple rules:

Words separated by spaces or ordinary punctuation (which is not listed as a special character in the tables later in this section) are treated as a **phrase**. The search will only return documents which contain this phrase. However, words within the phrase which are listed in the **noise list** (such as `a`, `as`, `and`, `but`, `for`, etc.) are ignored completely. Matching is also **case-insensitive**. So searching for `the State; and the County` will also match `the state of a county`.

To search for a phrase that contains quotation marks, or one of the special characters such as an exclamation mark, we have to enclose the whole phrase in quotation marks and then place double quotation marks where we want a quotation mark to appear. For example `"he yelled ""Hello!"" from across the street"`. To search for several individual words in a document, we separate the words with a comma. The result will be documents that contain all, or only *some*, of the words listed. The more that match, however, the better the ranking of the result.

Other than that, we can use the normal wildcards and Boolean operators. An asterisk matches any number of characters, and a question mark matches any single character. There's also the option of a `fuzzy search`. Adding two asterisks to the end of a word will match 'stem words' with the same meaning. A search for `catch**`, for instance, will include `catching` and `caught`.

To combine words in the search string, we use Boolean operators like this:

Boolean Keywords	Shorthand	Meaning
Apples **AND** Pears	Apples **&** Pears	**Both** must exist in the document.
Apples **OR** Pears	Apples **|** Pears	**Either** must exist in the document.
Apples **AND NOT** Pears	Apples **&** ! Pears	The first word **must** exist in the document, but **not** the second.

Boolean Keywords	Shorthand	Meaning
Apples **NEAR** Pears	Apples ~ Pears	**Both** must exist in the document, and be **within 50 words** of each other. The closer they are, the higher the ranking in the results.
NOT @size < 2049	! @size < 2049	Document must be larger than 2KB

As you can see from the last entry, we can also search by any other of the attributes or properties of the documents that Index Server stores in its catalog, for example:

Attribute or Property	Meaning
Contents	Words and phrases in the document. This is the default if no other attribute or property is specified.
Filename	The name of the file.
Size	The size of the file in bytes.
Path	The actual path and file name of the document.
VPath	The server's virtual path and file name for the document.
HitCount	The number of hits for the content search in the document.
Rank	The relative matching score for the query, from 0 to 1000.
Create	The date and time that the file was originally created.
Write	The date and time that the file was last updated.
DocTitle	The `Title` property for that document.
DocSubject	The `Subject` property for that document.
DocPageCount	The number of pages in the document.
DocAuthor	The `Author` property for that document.
DocKeywords	The keywords specified for that document.
DocComments	The value of the `Comments` property for that document.

The properties starting with Doc are only available for documents created by applications which can store these document properties in their files. In the case of an executable file, for example, there will be no DocPageCount or DocKeywords properties available.

We can search for the value of a property, or the attributes of a file, using the @ or # prefixes. In a relational expression, like the expression ! @size < 2049 we used in the table above, the prefix is @. For a normal expression-based search, we use #. For example, #filename *.xlw will only match Microsoft Excel workbook files.

There's one other prefix that you'll find useful, **$contents**. This tells Index Server to treat the query as a 'free text meaning' search. In other words, it will try to interpret the *meaning* of the query string and find documents that best provide a match—even if they don't contain the actual phrase. For example, **$contents tell me how to create a query** will provide a match to any document which covers creating queries.

Index Server on your Intranet

Generally, Index Server will only catalog documents that we specifically place in virtual paths—such as the Internet **WWWroot** and **FTProot** folders and all their sub-folders. However, we can create virtual paths to other directories—Active Server Pages creates one to its own **samples** directory, so these files will be included in the catalog.

We can also select which virtual paths to use when we actually create the query file, and add new ones to point to our existing file resources—such as a **My Documents** folder. These can even be on another machine on the network, so long as we can supply the domain or computer name.

> *There are a series of administrative pages supplied with Index Server that can be used to set all such options. You can also create your own admin pages, using an* **.ida** *script file. Check out the Index Server Help pages for more details.*

So, on a company intranet, we can set up information repositories and point Index Server at them as required. And remember that the files can be of almost any type that filters are available for. Word processor documents and spreadsheets are likely to be a popular choice in this situation, so let's have a look at some of the other features of Index Server that are appropriate to these. For example, this time we're just looking for documents which have the single word **sales** in them:

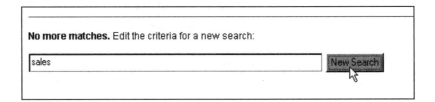

Among the list of hits, we've found a Word document file (called **lynne_cv.doc**) which we'd forgotten was still lurking in a dark and dusty corner of the disk. Underneath the abstract listing is a hyperlink: Click here to highlight the criteria hits in the document. This doesn't open the document directly, but sends it to a separate routine which is part of Index Server. It shows an HTML page made up of extracts of the document, with the hits highlighted:

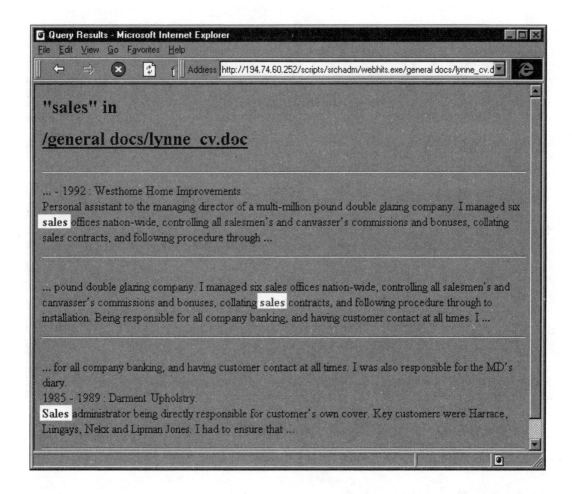

Back in the list of matching files, we've come across the spreadsheet file `excelsample.xls`. Clicking on this filename in the list opens it within a copy of Excel, and inside the Internet Explorer window. We can edit it here and save the changes when we move to another page. How's that for information at your fingertips?

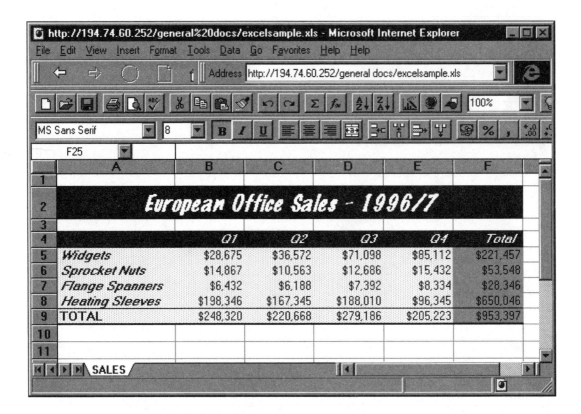

Browsers other than Internet Explorer will not open the file inside the browser window like this. You'll find that a copy of the original application is opened separately, containing the document.

How Index Server Works

Having seen just a few examples of what Index Server can do, we'll take an equally brief look at how it works. It is a highly complex query development environment, so we can only hope to cover the basics in this chapter. However, we'll walk through the methods we used to create the query system you've just seen at work.

Index Server Overview

Well, it's a small world. Index Server, like Active Server Pages, is really just a development of the techniques used in the Internet Database Connector. The next diagram shows the principle components, which are an Internet Data Query (**IDQ**) script and an Extended HTML Template (**HTX**) file.

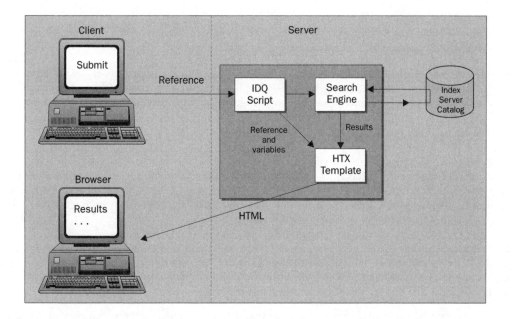

Basically, we reference the IDQ script from the browser, and this controls the whole operation. It instructs the search engine to retrieve the matching document details from the catalog stored on disk, sort them, insert them into the HTX template, then return this as HTML to the browser. Because it only has to search this catalog, and not the whole disk each time, the process is very quick.

Referencing the IDQ Script

We can use a **<FORM>** section in the browser's HTML page to send the contents of the controls in the form to the IDQ script, or we can supply them as parameters in the **HREF** argument of an **<A>** tag. In the example you've just seen, we used this code to create the text box and buttons (we've omitted the server address from the **ACTION** argument for clarity):

```
<FORM ACTION="http://..../scripts/WroxIDX/wrox_idx.idq?" METHOD="POST">
    Enter the contents of a document to find:<P>
    <INPUT TYPE="TEXT" SIZE="70" MAXLENGTH="70" NAME="CiRestriction">
    <INPUT TYPE="SUBMIT" VALUE="Search Now">
    <INPUT TYPE="RESET" VALUE="Clear">
</FORM>
```

Inside the IDQ Script

When the form is submitted, the script **wrox_idx.idq** is referenced. This contains the following code:

```
[Query]
CiColumns=filename,size,characterization,rank,path,hitcount,vpath,DocTitle,write
CiCatalog=c:\IndexServer
CiScope=/
CiFlags=DEEP
CiRestriction=%CiRestriction%
CiMaxRecordsInResultSet=1000
```

```
CiMaxRecordsPerPage=10
CiTemplate=/WroxTest/wrox_idx.htx
CiSort=rank[d]
```

`CiColumns` acts rather like an **SQL Statement**. It defines which columns (or properties and attributes of the indexed files) are returned from the catalog. With the exception of **characterization**, we've already looked at the selection above–when we talked about the query language of Index Server. **characterization** is the **abstract** that Index Server automatically builds from the document, and is intended to indicate its broad contents. We can't actually query this property from the browser, though.

Having specified which properties we want, we have to tell Index Server where to search for the documents. `CiCatalog` is the location of the catalog storing the document details (it's possible to create different ones), and `CiScope` is the virtual root from where we want to include documents. We can select any physical or mapped virtual folder here. In our case, we're starting at the main Internet Server root. To include all the subfolders below it, we've included `CiFlags=DEEP`.

The `CiRestriction` line in the script defines the query we want to use, and because it's sent from the browser as the value of the text box named `CiRestriction`, we use this value in our script by enclosing it in percent signs, as `%CiRestriction%`. We can either send the values of these variables from the controls on the form like this, or preset them directly as text values within the `.idq` file.

The next two lines then set the maximum number of documents to return, and the number we want to display in each page of the resulting HTML code that is sent back to the browser. Lastly, we specify the location of the HTX template file, and how the matching document details are to be sorted. In this case, we've chosen the usual: descending order by rank.

As a summary, the next table shows a list of the common variables that are set in an `.idq` script–either directly, or as a variable from a control in the `<FORM>` section of a page:

Variable	Meaning
`CiCatalog`	Location of the catalog, if not using the default.
`CiForceUseCi`	**TRUE** to use the current index, even if out of date.
`CiScope`	Start directory for the search.
`CiFlags`	**DEEP** to include all subdirectories below `CiScope`, or **SHALLOW** for only the directory in `CiScope`.
`CiColumns`	List of all the indexed values to be returned, i.e. the columns for the results set, separated by commas.
`CiRestriction`	The query to be executed, i.e. what to search for.
`CiMaxRecordsInResultsSet`	Maximum number of documents to be retrieved.
`CiMaxRecordsPerPage`	Maximum number of documents to be returned on each page.
`CiSort`	Order of the returned records, using the column names separated by commas. **[d]** indicates descending order. For example: **State, Size [d], Name**
`CiTemplate`	Full virtual path to the `.htx` template file.

Inside the HTX Template

All the work of formatting the information that is to be returned to the browser is done in the HTX template. Like Active Server Pages, it uses the `<%...%>` tags to delineate code or values. However, we don't have to include an equals sign, as we do in ASP, when placing the value of a variable in the page. The two special tags `<%BeginDetail%>` and `<%EndDetail%>` denote a section that is repeated for each 'record' returned by the Index Server engine. We also have options for displaying the information as separate pages, rather than as a single long page. The IDQ variable `CiMaxRecordsPerPage` tells Index Server how many records to retrieve each time.

Index Server HTX templates also support `<%If...%>` `<%Else%>` `<%EndIf%>`, and in a template we can retrieve the value of any of the controls on the form which originally referenced the IDQ script, or which are listed in the `CiColumns` line of the script. We can also use the regular HTTP variables, such as `SCRIPT_NAME` or `SERVER_NAME`, as we did with ASP in earlier chapters.

After running the IDQ script, Index Server sets the values of various built-in variables, which indicate the results of the query:

Variable	Meaning
CiMatchedRecordCount	Total number of documents which match the query.
CiTotalNumberPages	Total number of pages used to contain query results.
CiCurrentRecordNumber	Number of current documents in the total matched.
CiCurrentPageNumber	Current page number of query results.
CiFirstRecordNumber	Number of the first document on the current page.
CiLastRecordNumber	Number of the last document on the current page. May not be correct until after the `<%EndDetail%>` section.
CiContainsFirstRecord	Set to 1 if the current page contains the first document in the query results, or 0 otherwise.
CiContainsLastRecord	Set to 1 if the current page contains the last document in the query results, or 0 otherwise. May not be correct until after the `<%EndDetail%>` section.
CiBookmark	Reference to the first document on the current page.
CiOutOfDate	Set to 1 if the content index is out of date, or 0 if OK.
CiQueryIncomplete	Set to 1 if the query could not be completed using the current content index, or 0 if completed.
CiQueryTimedOut	Set to 1 if the query exceeded the time limit for query execution, or 0 if completed.

Here's the 'working parts' of the template file we used to create the query results pages you saw earlier. We've omitted the code which just creates the header and footer:

```
. . .
<B>Results of your search for "<%CiRestriction%>".</B><P>
There are <%CiMatchedRecordCount%> documents which match the criteria.
```

```
<HR>
<%If CiMatchedRecordCount NE 0%>
   Documents <%CiFirstRecordNumber%> to <%CiLastRecordNumber%><P>
<%EndIf%>
<TABLE WIDTH=100%>
   <%BeginDetail%>
      <TR>
      <%If DocTitle ISEMPTY%>
         <TD>Untitled document</TD>
      <%Else%>
         <TD>Title: <I><B><%DocTitle%></B></I></TD>
      <%EndIf%>
         <TD COLSPAN="2">Number of criteria hits: <%HitCount%></TD>
      <TR>
      </TR>
         <TD>Filename: <A HREF="<%EscapeURL vpath%>"><%filename%></A></TD>
         <TD>Size: <%size%> bytes</TD>
         <TD>Updated: <%write%> GMT</TD>
      </TR>
      <TR>
         <TD COLSPAN="3"><I><%characterization%></I></TD>
      </TR>
      <TR>
         <TD COLSPAN="3" ALIGN="CENTER">
         <!-- following must be all on one line -->
         <A HREF="http://<%SERVER_NAME%>/scripts/srchadm/webhits.exe
               <%EscapeURL vpath%>?CiRestriction=<%EscapeURL
               CiRestriction%>&CiBold=YES">
         Click to highlight the criteria hits in the document.</A>
         </TD>
      </TR>
      <TR>
         <TD COLSPAN="3" ALIGN="RIGHT">.</TD>
      </TR>
   <%EndDetail%>
</TABLE>
<FORM ACTION="<%EscapeURL SCRIPT_NAME%>?" METHOD="POST">
   <%If CiMatchedRecordCount EQ 0%>
      Enter the criteria for a new search:<P>
      <INPUT TYPE="TEXT" SIZE="70" MAXLENGTH="70" NAME="CiRestriction">
      <INPUT TYPE="SUBMIT" VALUE="New Search">
      <INPUT TYPE="RESET" VALUE="Clear">
   <%Else%>
     <%If CiRecordsNextPage EQ 0%>
      <HR><B>No more matches.</B> Edit the criteria for a new search:<P>
      <INPUT TYPE="TEXT" SIZE="70" MAXLENGTH="70" NAME="CiRestriction"
                                          VALUE="<%CiRestriction%>">
      <INPUT TYPE="SUBMIT" VALUE="New Search">
     <%Else%>
      <INPUT TYPE="HIDDEN" NAME="CiBookmark" VALUE="<%CiBookmark%>">
      <INPUT TYPE="HIDDEN" NAME="CiBookmarkSkipCount"
                                    VALUE="<%CiMaxRecordsPerPage%>">
      <INPUT TYPE="HIDDEN" NAME="CiMaxRecordsPerPage"
                                    VALUE="<%CiMaxRecordsPerPage%>">
      <INPUT TYPE="HIDDEN" NAME="CiRestriction" VALUE="<%CiRestriction%>">
      <INPUT TYPE="HIDDEN" NAME="CiScope" VALUE="<%CiScope%>">
```

```
        <INPUT TYPE="SUBMIT" VALUE="Next <%CiRecordsNextPage%> Documents">
      <%EndIf%>
    <%EndIf%>
  </FORM>
  ...
```

From your knowledge of Active Server Pages, it should be obvious how the IDQ variables (such as `<%CiRestriction%>`) and the values obtained from the search (such as `<%DocTitle%>`) are used. We create a table to hold the results and, within the `<%BeginDetail%>` `<%EndDetail%>` section, create a table row containing the document title, size, last update time, filename, hit count and abstract. Because some documents do not have a title, we use an `<%If..%>` `<%Else%>` `<%EndIf%>` construct to display Untitled document in this case:

```
  ...
      <%If DocTitle ISEMPTY%>
        <TD>Untitled document</TD>
      <%Else%>
        <TD>Title: <I><B><%DocTitle%></B></I></TD>
      <%EndIf%>
  ...
```

> *Note that we can't put a `<%BeginDetail%>` `<%EndDetail%>` section inside an `<%If..%>` `<%Else%>` `<%EndIf%>` construct. If we do, we get an error message saying that an `<%Else%>` or `<%EndIf%>` can't be found.*

Opening a Matching Document

To allow the user to open a matching document, we make the filename a hyperlink using the normal `<A>` tag. However, we have to refer to the virtual path and not the actual physical path, if we want it to be loaded using HTTP rather than as a file. And to make sure that any spaces or other characters that aren't recognized by HTTP are properly encoded, we **escape** the string by prefixing the variable name with `EscapeURL`:

```
  <TD>Filename: <A HREF="<%EscapeURL vpath%>"><%filename%></A></TD>
```

> *The `EscapeURL` keyword works like ASP's `Server.URLEncode` method. It converts the string following it into a fully URL-encoded version so that it can be used in the `HREF` or `SRC` argument of an `<A>`, `<FORM>`, `<IMG>` or `<FRAME>` tag, for example. There are two similar keywords, `EscapeHTML` and `EscapeRAW`. `EscapeHTML` converts the string into HTML format, for example replacing '>' with '>'. In some cases, Index Server executes a conversion automatically, for example in the arguments sent from a form. The `EscapeRAW` keyword can be used to prevent any automatic conversion.*

Displaying Another Page of Documents

Once we've displayed all the documents, we can provide controls so that the user can navigate to the next (or previous) page. In our case, we're just allowing them to display the next page, but we can use the various HTX variables we looked at earlier to control whether a Previous Page button is included as well.

There are two possibilities where there are no documents on the next page–if there were no matches at all (`CiMatchedRecordCount EQ 0`), or if we have already displayed all the matching documents (`CiRecordsNextPage EQ 0`). In both these cases we just display a message and add the original query text box, Submit and Reset buttons again, so that the user can start a new search:

```
<FORM ACTION="<%EscapeURL SCRIPT_NAME%>?" METHOD="POST">
   <%If CiMatchedRecordCount EQ 0%>
      ...
      <!-- no documents found - controls to start a new search -->
      ...
   <%Else%>
     <%If CiRecordsNextPage EQ 0%>
       ...
       <!-- no documents on next page - controls to start a new search -->
       ...
     <%Else%>
     <!-- more documents on next page -->
     <INPUT TYPE="HIDDEN" NAME="CiBookmark" VALUE="<%CiBookmark%>">
     <INPUT TYPE="HIDDEN" NAME="CiBookmarkSkipCount"
                                  VALUE="<%CiMaxRecordsPerPage%>">
     <INPUT TYPE="HIDDEN" NAME="CiMaxRecordsPerPage"
                                  VALUE="<%CiMaxRecordsPerPage%>">
     <INPUT TYPE="HIDDEN" NAME="CiRestriction" VALUE="<%CiRestriction%>">
     <INPUT TYPE="HIDDEN" NAME="CiScope" VALUE="<%CiScope%>">
     <INPUT TYPE="SUBMIT" VALUE="Next <%CiRecordsNextPage%> Documents">
     <%EndIf%>
   <%EndIf%>
</FORM>
```

If there are more documents, however, we use the value of `CiRecordsNextPage` to set the proper caption of the Submit button. When the form is submitted, we run the same IDQ script, `<%EscapeURL SCRIPT_NAME%>`, again. However, this time we have to include the settings for the internal IDQ variables. We do this in hidden text boxes on the form, and to display the correct page we set the value of `CiBookmark` and `CiBookmarkSkipCount`.

We would usually set `CiBookmark` to the same value as last time, and specify the first document for the new page by setting `CiBookmarkSkipCount` to an appropriate value. To display the *next* page, we set the contents of the `CiBookmarkSkipCount` control to the value of `CiMaxRecordsPerPage`. To display the *previous* page we use `CiMaxRecordsPerPage`. To *jump* to a particular page we would use a positive or negative value which is a multiple of `CiMaxRecordsPerPage`.

Notice that we could also change the query in `CiRestriction`, or the Scope, if we wanted to. By creating a complex query results page, which changes these values, the user could easily tailor their search to find a specific document more quickly.

Coping with Errors

Although we haven't done so to keep our example code as simple as possible, you should consider including some error checking in your HTX results templates. Before or after displaying the matching documents, we can check the value of the error indicator variables and include appropriate messages:

```
<%If CiOutOfDate EQ 1%>
   <B>Warning: the document indexes are not fully up to date.</B>
<%Else%>
```

```
    <%If CiQueryTimeOut EQ 1%>
        <B>Warning: the query could not be completed.</B>
    <%EndIf%>
<%EndIf%>
```

Hit-highlighting the Matching Documents

The final feature we offered users in our earlier example was the ability to highlight the matching words within the documents that were found by the query (providing, of course, it was a **content**-based search). Below each document displayed on the returned page is a hyperlink that they can click to open a new page in the browser window. This page contains extracts from the document, with the matching words or phrases highlighted.

To do this, we use a separate program supplied with Index Server, called **Webhits.exe**. It's installed in the **/scripts/srchadmin** folder, which also contains a range of pages we can use to fine-tune the performance of Index Server. To use **Webhits**, we have to supply the virtual path to the file we want highlighted, and the query string that originally found it:

http://[path to webhits.exe]**/webhits.exe/**[document]**?**[parameters]

In our case, the path is **<%SERVER_NAME%>/scripts/srchadm** (we use the HTTP variable **SERVER_NAME** here), and the full path and filename of the document is the same URL-encoded string that we used earlier–**<%EscapeURL vpath%>**. We set the query string using the value of **CiRestriction**, and add a parameter **CiBold** to make the highlighted text, which is colored red by default, display in bold type as well:

```
<A HREF="http://<%SERVER_NAME%>/scripts/srchadm/webhits.exe
            <%EscapeURL vpath%>?CiRestriction=<%EscapeURL
            CiRestriction%>&CiBold=YES">
        Click to highlight the criteria hits in the document.</A>
```

Integrating Index Server with ASP

Now that we've seen what Index Server is all about, we can consider how we're going to integrate it with our ASP pages. Normally we would create an IDQ script and HTX template, then reference the script directly in a **<FORM>** or **<A>** tag, as we did in our earlier example. And there's no reason why we shouldn't do this in a page created with ASP.

However, there are two problems that arise when we come to use dynamic ASP pages on our site. Firstly, we can't add ASP code to an HTX template, because it won't be executed on the server like it is in an **.asp** file–it will just be sent to the browser. Secondly, Index Server only understands static pages. It's not able to catalog the other dynamic pages on our site, such as those we're creating with Active Server Pages. We'll look at solutions to both these problems in this chapter, starting with something I've called the **Billboard** method.

Index Server and the Billboard Method

We have a problem with Index Server. Like other CGI- or script-based dynamic page methods, it automatically returns the results to the browser when referenced. This is the same problem we found with our earlier Parts Description example. And we can use the same kinds of techniques to solve our Index Server problem.

The Billboard method attempts to answer this problem using standard Active Server Pages code and a single Server Component, without involving any special tricks—it's not an exotic solution. It also integrates with the standard development tools for creating HTML pages and Active Server Pages files.

What Does Billboard Actually Do?

What Billboard *does* do is allow us to tie together several applications, by streaming the output of each one to a single browser page. With it we can connect in turn to various search engines, without making our life difficult by needing to program in any other language than the one we use with ASP. Some search sites are already offering multi-engine searching, but using CGI scripts as the interface mechanism.

Of course, the method isn't limited to search engines. We already know how to capture the output of *any* web application, or even a static page, using the **Asphttp.dll** component. The Billboard method allows us to combine the outputs from any other applications that produce web pages.

A Billboard Overview

To help you understand the logic behind it, and see how the various parts fit together, here's an overview diagram. Notice that there's a page called **SearchComponent.asp** that is referenced by the Query page, **Billboard.htm**, and which is responsible for calling the other pages to produce the final results. Only when it has collected all the results are they passed back to the browser as a complete single page.

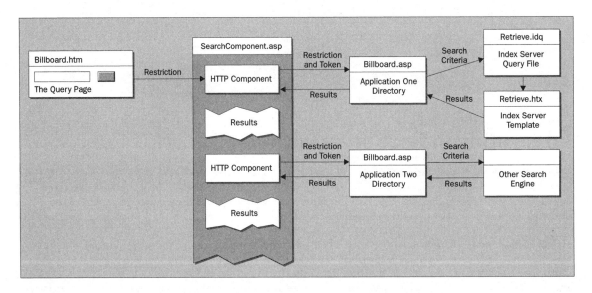

We'll look at each of the files in turn, starting with the Query page **Billboard.htm**. If you want to try this application, you'll find it in the samples available from our web site at **http://www.rapid.wrox.com/books/0723**. Installation instructions are given at the beginning of this chapter.

The Query Page—Billboard.htm

This page is extremely simple, consisting basically of just a form with a single text box named `txtExpression`, and a Submit button:

```
...
<form method="GET" action="SearchComponent.asp">
   Query:
   <input type="text" size="30" maxlength="255" name="txtExpression">
   <input type="submit" value="Submit"><p>
</form>
...
```

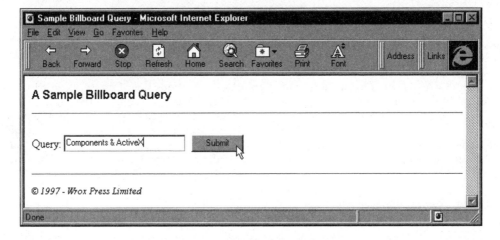

When the Submit button is clicked, the contents of the text box are sent to the page `SearchComponent.asp`. This is the page that does all the real work.

SearchComponent.asp

The `SearchComponent` page contains the ASP code that submits the query to all of the search engines, and is also responsible for combining all of the resulting pages into one single page for return to the browser. Let's look at the source code of this page:

```
<html>
<head>
<title>Search Results</title>
</head>
<body bgcolor="#FFFFFF">
<h3><font face="Arial">Results of your query:
'<% = Request.QueryString("txtExpression") %>'</font></h3><HR>

<%
strServerPath = "http://yourserver"  'edit to suit your server IP/name
strQueryString = Request.QueryString & "&token=codeword"

'Create the HTTP object and retrieve the search results from IDXSRV...
Set objHttp = Server.CreateObject("ASPsvg.HTTP")
```

```
objHttp.Url = strServerPath & "/IDXSRV/billboard.asp?" & strQueryString
strResult = objHttp.GetURL
Response.Write "<H3>Results from Index Server Search</H3>"
Response.Write strResult & "<HR>"

'Now retrieve the search results from another application directory...
objHttp.Url = strServerPath & "/SEARCH2/billboard.asp?" & strQueryString
strResult = objHttp.GetURL
Response.Write "<H2>Results from SEARCH2 Application</H2>"
Response.Write strResult & "<HR>

'And do it again with another search engine...
objHttp.Url = strServerPath & "/NEWSEARCH/billboard.asp?" & strQueryString
strResult = objHttp.GetURL
Response.Write "<H2>Results from NEWSEARCH Application</H2>"
Response.Write strResult  & "<HR> %>

</body>
</html>
```

You'll see that this ASP file has the usual **<html>**, **<title>** and **<body>** sections, so it can be returned to the browser like any other page containing ASP code. After placing a heading in the page, the remainder consists entirely of ASP code, divided into four sections. The first one is used to define the name of the server–as we're using the ASP HTTP component, we have to provide the full server address. Then the code just collects the original query string sent from the Query page, and adds another name/ value pair to it that defines **token** as **codeword**. The next three sections are the calls to each search application.

Defining the Search Applications

In the code above we're querying three applications, **IDXSRV**, **SEARCH2**, and **NEWSEARCH**. In the sample file, you'll find that the second two are actually commented out at present to make setting up easier. You'll see more when we come to look at **Billboard.asp** in a while. The definition of the word **application** is the same as that used throughout the book–a set of files within a single directory and its subdirectories on the server, and for which a **virtual root** (or **alias**) has been defined in IIS. **IDXSRV**, **SEARCH2**, and **NEWSEARCH** are these virtual roots. There can exist only one search mechanism per defined application.

Executing the Search Applications

The script first creates an instance of the ASP HTTP component we used at the start of this chapter, naming it **objHttp**. We can then use this component to fetch the results from the various search applications in turn by calling a **Billboard** for that application. We call them 'Billboards' because they are effectively all the same, and they simply pronounce their wares to the world with no concern about who or what that world might be. In our context, this means that they return the information we want from the search application, but in such a way that it's the same irrespective of the application involved.

In fact this is the whole methodology behind Billboard, and one that can be extended to other situations. It's the same principle as the software drivers used in Windows. The operating system places one of a whole library of printer-specific drivers between a program and the printer, so that any program can use that printer. However, the program/driver interface is a defined standard, so the program is the same irrespective of the actual driver, and hence printer, being used.

In our case, there is a `Billboard.asp` page in all the application directories. As far as `SearchComponent.asp` is concerned, they are all the same—it references them all in the same way, and the result is just a string that is added to the current page. So, for each application, it sets the URL in `objHttp`, and references `Billboard.asp`—adding the query string to the URL. The results are just dropped into the page:

```
...
Set objHttp = Server.CreateObject("ASPsvg.HTTP")
objHttp.Url = strServerPath & "/IDXSRV/billboard.asp?" & strQueryString
strResult = objHttp.GetURL
Response.Write "<H3>Results from Index Server Search</H3>"
Response.Write strResult & "<HR>"
...
```

So we've got a results page built up in `SearchComponent.asp`, which is just the strings returned from each application as they are executed in turn. This means that all the work of creating the string has been delegated to the `Billboard.asp` files in the respective application directories.

The Billboard.asp Files

Although the various `Billboard.asp` files all look the same to `SearchComponent.asp`, it doesn't mean that they are. This is the 'printer driver' technique we talked about earlier. As long as the parameters sent by `SearchComponent.asp` are enough to actually run the application, and the contents of the resulting page are acceptable to `SearchComponent.asp`, each Billboard file can do its own thing internally. We'll be looking at just one Billboard file, but you can create as many as you like, specific to any applications you want to use.

Running the IDXSRV application

The first application call our example makes is to the `IDXSRV` application, which is of course Index Server. To make setting up easier, we've only included this application in our sample files, and we've placed it in the same folder as the other files to avoid having to set up other System DSNs.

All `Billboard.asp` files referenced by `SearchComponent.asp` receive the same query string:

> `txtExpression=`*CriteriaFromQueryPage*`&token=codeword`

The first parameter, `txtExpression`, contains the query criteria. The second parameter, `token`, has the value of `codeword`. Why? Well it gives us a chance to protect the page from being referenced directly, rather than as part of the application:

```
...
<% If Request.QueryString("token") = "codeword" Then   'OK to continue
       ... 'run the application and return the results
   Else %>
       <H4>This page was not called from a proper index form.</H4>
<% End If %>
```

Because all of the processing occurs on the server side, the name/value key can be anything—we could just as well have used `doitnow=noproblem`. The only prerequisite is that the caller key and billboard key must match. With this kind of security, it's more or less impossible for the user to figure out the key without guessing randomly.

To see how the Billboard runs the Index Server query script, here's the complete code for this particular `Billboard.asp` page. Note that this page isn't a valid HTML page–there are no `<HEAD>` and `<BODY>` tags. This is because the page is being called by the ASP HTTP component from another page and, since we only want to manipulate the resulting text, tags like these would only confuse the issue.

```
<% strServerPath = "http://yourserver"

If Request.QueryString("token") = "codeword" Then    'OK to do the search
    strQueryString = "txtExpression=" _
                & Server.URLEncode(Request.QueryString("txtExpression")) _
                & "&CiMaxRecordsInResultSet=300&CiMaxRecordsPerPage=300" _
                & "&CiSort=rank[d]&CiScope=/&CiFlags=DEEP"
    strURL = strServerPath & "/IDXSRV/Retrieve.idq?" & strQueryString

    'Create the HTTP object and open the URL
    Set objHttp = Server.CreateObject("ASPsvg.HTTP")
    objHttp.Url = strURL
    strResult = objHttp.GetURL

    'Process the output from this URL
    iStartLoc = 1
    iCount = 0
    Do
        iStartLoc = InStr(iStartLoc, strResult, "**[")
        If iStartLoc = 0 Then Exit Do       'no matches found
        iEndLoc = InStr(iStartLoc, strResult, "]**")
        strFile = Mid(strResult, iStartLoc + 3, iEndLoc - iStartLoc - 3)
        iStartLoc = iEndLoc
        iCount = iCount + 1
        Response.Write "<H4>File number:" & iCount & "</H4>" & strFile & _
                    "<HR>"
    Loop %>
    <HR>
    <H4>Found <% = iCount %> matching files.</H4>
<% Else %>
    <H4>This page was not called from a proper index form.</H4>
<% End If %>
```

Building the URL and Query String

The first task for the Billboard is to create the query string that we're going to send to the IDQ file. When we collected the original query string in `SearchComponent.asp`, to pass on to `Billboard.asp`, we just used `Request.QueryString`. You'll recall from Chapter 2 that this returns the entire query string in URL-encoded form, so it's safe to pass it on knowing that any non-URL characters such as spaces will already be encoded properly.

Now, however, we need to extract individual parts of the query string. We use the syntax `Request.QueryString("txtExpression")` to get the value of the criteria that were entered in the `txtExpression` control on the original Query page. However, before we include it in the new query string, we have to URL-encode it again using the `Server` object's `URLEncode` method.

Next, we add the other name/value pairs we need for the IDQ script. We've chosen to put them here rather than setting them directly in the IDQ file–as you'll see when we come to look at this file, you could do either.

```
<% strServerPath = "http://yourserver"

If Request.QueryString("token") = "codeword" Then    'OK to do the search
    strQueryString = "txtExpression=" _
              & Server.URLEncode(Request.QueryString("txtExpression")) _
              & "&CiMaxRecordsInResultSet=300&CiMaxRecordsPerPage=300" _
              & "&CiSort=rank[d]&CiScope=/&CiFlags=DEEP"
    strURL = strServerPath & "/IDXSRV/Retrieve.idq?" & strQueryString

    'Create the HTTP object and open the URL
    Set objHttp = Server.CreateObject("ASPsvg.HTTP")
    objHttp.Url = strURL
    strResult = objHttp.GetURL
    ...
```

Finally, we can add the complete query string to the URL of the Index Server application, create the ASP HTTP object instance **objHttp**, set its **URL** property, and get the results into **strResult**. There's no reason why we couldn't just dump this back into the **SearchComponent** page as it stands, but we want to do more than that. We've constructed the Index Server IDQ and HTX files to return the results in a particular format, and we'll process them in the Billboard file.

> *You may be tempted to store the **txtExpression** value in a **Session** variable in the page* **SearchComponent.asp**, *and retrieve it in this file using **Session('txtExpression')**. There's a problem with this strategy, however, in that when the page is called, ASP attempts to start a new session. The **ASPHttp** component makes a valid HTTP request and therefore is not within the same* **Session** *as* **SearchComponent.asp**.

Processing the Search Results

We'll look at the IDQ and HTX files in a moment. In the meantime, just appreciate that they produce a set of matches for our search criteria which is formatted like this:

```
Documents
**[ Filename: <A HREF="/pets/alligator.htm">alligator.htm</A></B><BR>
Title: Breeding Alligators     File date: 11/3/96<BR>
When it comes to breeding alligators, you'll find that you need some quite thick
gloves ... ]**
**[ Filename: <A HREF="/food/jello.html">jello.html</A></B><BR>
Title: Fossilized Jello     File date: 5/7/96<BR>
Return to story Office of Research Publications Editorial comments about ASU Research
should be sent to James Dean at jd@appluvm.com... ]**
 ...
```

Notice that each matching file is delimited by the markers ****[** and **]****. This means that we can easily extract them individually from the text stream using ASP code, and put them into the page that we return to **SearchComponent.asp**:

```
    ...
    'Process the output from this URL
    iStartLoc = 1
    iCount = 0
    Do
        iStartLoc = InStr(iStartLoc, strResult, "**[")
```

```
        If iStartLoc = 0 Then Exit Do        'no matches found
        iEndLoc = InStr(iStartLoc, strResult, "]**")
        strFile = Mid(strResult, iStartLoc + 3, iEndLoc - iStartLoc - 3)
        iStartLoc = iEndLoc
        iCount = iCount + 1
        Response.Write "<H4>File number:" & iCount & "</H4>" & strFile & _
                       "<HR>"
    Loop %>
    <HR>
    <H4>Found <% = iCount %> matching files.</H4>
    ...
```

The 'boundary' markers can be anything, except that some choices are better than others. For example, using just alphabetic characters as boundary markers would not be a good idea, because they could occur within the text we return. The key in choosing good boundary markers is to make sure that combination can't occur within the data they delineate, and it simplifies the parsing process if we use different markers to indicate the start and end.

So, the `Billboard.asp` page serves only one purpose—that of executing the Index Server search and returning the results in a format suitable for inclusion in the page created by `SearchComponent.asp`. It must be stressed that, though our example only uses Index Server, database-searching features, or the output from any other application, can also be included.

The Index Server Files

Our `Billboard.asp` file references the Index Server script, and this is what does all the work of creating the list of matching files. Remember, the returned page is made up of the details from each 'hit', delimited with the `**[` and `]**` markers, so that Billboard can split it up into sections as required. In our example, we've returned a block of text formatted with HTML tags for each hit, but it could just as easily be a simple list of filenames.

The Retrieve.idq Script File

The first step is to define the IDQ script. What we get from the Billboard file is a list of parameters:

```
...
'this is in Billboard.asp
strQueryString = "txtExpression=" _
            & Server.URLEncode(Request.QueryString("txtExpression")) _
            & "&CiMaxRecordsInResultSet=300&CiMaxRecordsPerPage=300" _
            & "&CiSort=rank[d]&CiScope=/&CiFlags=DEEP"
...
```

So, we can use these parameters in our query script. We set `CiColumns` to define the information we want to retrieve from the catalog, and set `CiTemplate` to the virtual path of the template file we intend to use:

```
[Query]
CiColumns=filename,rank,characterization,vpath,DocTitle,write
CiFlags=%CiFlags%
CiRestriction=%txtExpression%
CiMaxRecordsPerPage=%CiMaxRecordsPerPage%
CiMaxRecordsInResultSet=%CiMaxRecordsPerPage%
CiScope=%CiScope%
```

```
CiSort=%CiSort%
CiForceUseCi=TRUE
CiTemplate=/IDXSRV\Retrieve.htx
```

The result we'll get is up to 300 matching files, and for each one we'll be able to use the `filename`, the `rank` (i.e. how well it matches the criteria), an extract or abstract of the document in `characterization`, the virtual path to the document in `vpath`, the document title (`DocTitle`) and the date it was last updated in `write`.

The Retrieve.htx Template File

So, let's see what the template that uses these values looks like. We include a simple introduction to identify the text, then a `<%begindetail%>...<%enddetail%>` section to loop for each matching file. Within the loop, we just create the formatted text we want to send back:

```
Documents
<%begindetail%>
**[
<B>Filename: <A HREF="<%EscapeURL vpath%>"><%filename%></A></B><BR>
Title: <%DocTitle%>     File date: <%write%><BR>
<%characterization%>
]**
<%enddetail%>
```

Returning the Results to the Browser

So, the HTX template creates the text string that includes a section for each matching file, delimited with `**[` and `]**`, and sends it back to `Billboard.asp`. There, we use the extended version of the `InStr` function to find the start and end markers, and extract the text for each file. This is an excerpt from `Billboard.asp` that carries out this task for each file:

```
...
iStartLoc = 1
Do
    iStartLoc = InStr(iStartLoc, strResult, "**[")
    iEndLoc = InStr(iStartLoc, strResult, "]**")
    strFile = Mid(strResult, iStartLoc + 3, iEndLoc - iStartLoc - 3)
    ...
    iStartLoc = iEndLoc
Loop
...
```

Each file's details are written to the Billboard page in turn, with extra information added such as the file number and a horizontal rule. Once the Billboard page has collected all the files, it sends the whole block back to `SearchComponent.asp`, which dumps it into the page sent back to the browser:

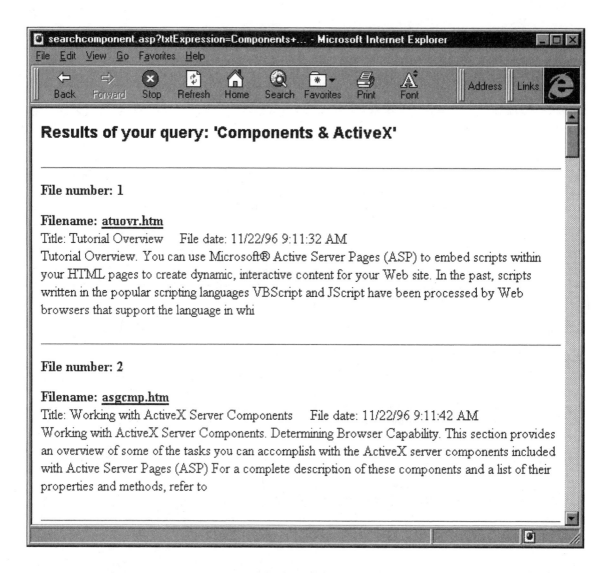

searchcomponent.asp?txtExpression=Components+... - Microsoft Internet Explorer

Extending the Billboard Method

The techniques we've shown you for combining the results from several search engines or other applications into one page really only scratch the surface. Recall that in Chapter 3 we looked at how we could write text files to the server's disk from within an Active Server Pages file. We could quite easily use this method to create the IDQ scripts or HTX templates for Index Server on the fly. However, this is an extreme solution. It's probably easier to use several different script and template files, and just select the appropriate one at runtime within the ASP code.

In our example, we provided a very simple query page, containing just a text box to enter the criteria for the query. There's no reason why the form couldn't be expanded to offer the user more control over the Billboard process. For example, we could allow them to select which applications or search engines to include in the process each time, and which query script and/or template to use with each one.

By combining these techniques, we can produce all kinds of Billboard applications. These might be very finely tuned to the particular task in hand, making them especially useful for the Internet as a whole. Alternatively, we can offer a range of different options—something probably better suited to use on the corporate intranet.

Using Single File Retrievals

Although we returned a full block of formatted text for each matching file we found with Index Server, including a hyperlink to that file, we could use a process which added another layer. For example, we could retrieve just the virtual path and filename for the matching files with a simpler HTX template:

```
Documents
<%begindetail%>
**[<%EscapeURL vpath%>">]**
<%enddetail%>
```

Then, in `Billboard.asp`, we could use the virtual path to retrieve each matching page in turn through the ASP HTTP component. This would allow us to extract the sections containing the reference ourselves, in the same way as the `Webhits` program we used earlier in the chapter. However, the process would be considerably slower than our sample. And in our case, the user can select which page to view themselves, using the hyperlinks we've provided.

Indexing Dynamic Pages

While we've found various ways to search for and retrieve pages using Index Server, there's a deeper problem which none of these methods addresses. Dynamic pages have little or no actual **content** while sitting on the server's disk. For example, a page that retrieves the stock of grommets from a database will not contain a list of grommet types—just some code that queries the database, builds the list dynamically, and inserts it into the returned page.

Solving the Problem

This means that Index Server, or any other search engine for that matter, will not see anything in the dynamic list, because it only indexes the files as they reside on the disk. We have to make sure we include some static text in the page that will identify it to Index Server. One way is obviously through a heading such as `<H2>Listing of Grommet Part Descriptions</H2>` or in the title, i.e. within the `<TITLE>...</TITLE>` tags. Another way is to include `<META>` tags with keywords—and some search engines depend on these to index the files anyway.

Hiding Keywords in Code

However, another possibility, where the text is not intended for display in the final page, is to insert it in a code section that is never executed—but which will still be read by Index Server as the file is sitting on the server:

```
<html>
<head>
<title>Document Title</title>
</head>
```

```
<body>
Residing in this page, but out of sight, are the keywords that caused this page to be
included in your search results. <p>
<% If 1 = 0 Then %>
   Keywords: grommets rotator "series 4"
<%End If%>
</body>
</html>
```

The trick is to create a comparison that never returns **True**—here we've used **If 1 = 0**. Therefore any information that's stored within this section of the code will never be sent to the client. However, Index Server will still index the document with the keywords defined, because it believes this information is part of the document.

The only difficulty now is knowing what to put in the code section. It's no good using specific items unless they are always included in the results page. And if it's a dynamic page, we don't want to have to keep updating it to match the data in our database—this defeats the whole object of a dynamic page. At best, it needs to be something generic that will be in every dynamic page.

Pointing to a Query Page

Alternatively, we can create a query page that has plenty of references to the types of information it can be used to locate. For example, look back at our dynamic page that lists our stocks of grommets. We could hide a generic listing of all the types in a similar Query page, and the search engine would find this page for every grommet inquiry.

Then, the user can specify the grommet they want information on, and submit the query to the dynamic page. Of course, it would be better to use a description of the part as the criteria, rather than asking them for the part number this time!

Summary

In this case study, we've focussed on several interlinked subjects, and combined them to give you some idea of how powerful the overall techniques used in our sample application can be. Much of the focus of this example revolves around a special server component called 'ASPHTTP', which can retrieve a web page as a string, without actually sending it to the browser. We first demonstrated how useful this technique can be by showing how it can integrate an old CGI-based legacy application with our shiny-new ASP site.

Then we changed direction to look at Microsoft Index Server. We saw how to write queries and templates, and how to specify the criteria for a search using it. Remember, the quality of the results is directly related to the criteria we use. We also created the 'Billboard' method to use with Index Server, and indicated how it could be used with several other search engines or applications. It provides a framework that is flexible, simple, and easy to extend as the requirements change.

The final subject we briefly mentioned is the difficulty of indexing dynamic pages. There is no complete solution to this problem, but we provided some simple techniques that can help.

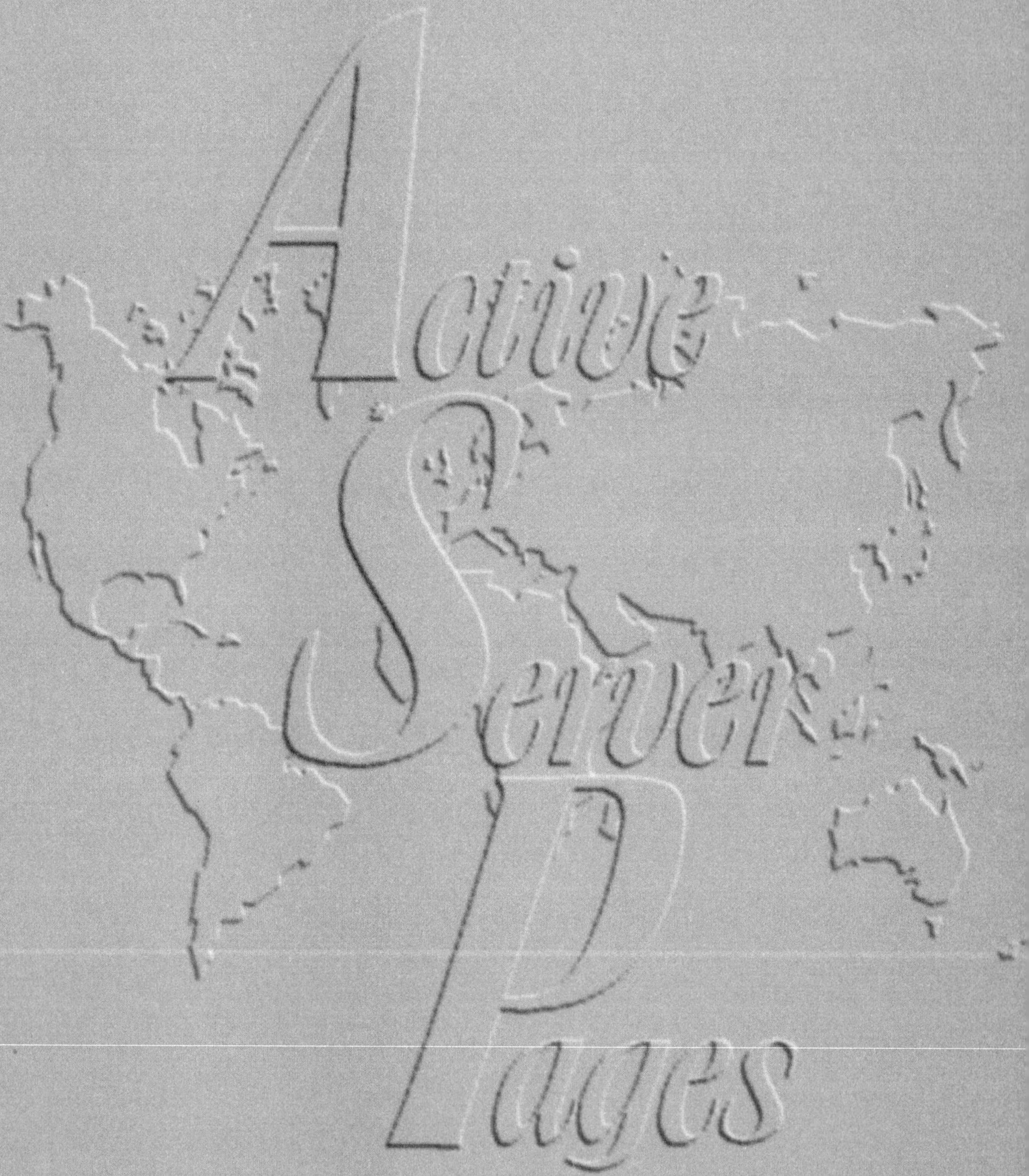
Active
Server
Pages

Case Study 4—A Client-server Card Game

To finish up this book, we'll look at a client server application that embodies the typical problems that programmers face everyday. Of course, as players, we think a card game example is interesting in itself!

The card game called 500 is an excellent example of a web-based client-server application. It requires client interaction, past-action information, and it has business rules. There's also a small amount of database work to keep the purists happy. All in all, the card game server is an example of an application that uses all of the capabilities of ASP. Without the **Session** object and **Application** object this task would be that much more complicated.

In this chapter, you'll see:

▲ The background to the game called 500

▲ The different components used to create it

▲ An overview of how the various parts work

About the Card Game Application

We're not going to give you an exhaustive description of each part of the application. It's implemented using many of the techniques we've already seen in earlier chapters, but underneath employs some very specialized components. For example, the client isn't an ordinary web browser, but an application written in Visual Basic that has a web browser embedded within it. At the server end, most of the work of controlling the game is carried out by a server component, again written in Visual Basic. It provides a global object that manages the entire game, and subsidiary objects for each player.

So, overall, it's a complex piece of work, and would take a whole book to explain in detail. However, we've included the source files for the Visual Basic client application and the sever component in the samples available from our web site at: **http://www.rapid.wrox.com/books/0723/**. You'll also find all the Active Server Pages files that are used in the application there as well.

> *You can run the application yourself from the author's web site. Point your browser at:* **http://www.eusoft.com** *and follow the* Game *link.*

Creating a game that is multi-user, and that can be played in real time with other people, isn't a simple task. The major problems are connected with state and concurrency—two topics we looked at in depth in Chapter 6. Our real-time game must be able to handle 1-2 second delays due to network transfers, and be asynchronous. The ability to handle bursts of data that aren't synchronized is required, because it can't be guaranteed that the player will still be accessible or can react within a specified time frame.

About the Game

The card game called 500 is something that the author Christian Gross was introduced to when living in Quebec, Canada. It's also known as Bridge or Euchre in other places. As he had very limited French linguistic skills, learning the game became ever more complicated. The only thing this linguistic deficiency achieved was the inability to cheat successfully.

The Rules of the Game

The game is played with a deck of cards that has the cards of rank 2 and 3 removed and the jokers added. The jokers must have different appearances, and all players must know which joker has the higher value–the higher value joker is the right and the lower value joker is the left. Four players play in pairs: each pair being a team. The team members sit opposite each other. For each turn, one of the players becomes the dealer, who shuffles the deck and asks a member of the other team to cut it. This ensures that the dealer doesn't cheat by shuffling the cards in a controlled manner. Once the cut has been made, the deck is put back together again with the top part of the split deck placed underneath the rest.

Dealing the Cards

The next step is to deal the cards. The dealing order is three cards to each player in a clockwise fashion, with the player on the dealer's left being given the first three. Once each player including the dealer has three cards, another hand is dealt to the kitty. This is a 'pot' of cards on the center of the table, which can't be picked up until someone wins them–as will be explained later. After the first round of dealing, each player gets four more cards, and this time the kitty gets none. Next another three cards are dealt to each player, this time including the kitty.

Once all of the cards have been dealt, the person on the dealer's left starts the bidding. Then the next person in a clockwise direction can bid, but it must be higher. The last person to bid is the dealer. Whoever has the highest bid wins the round, and can take the kitty. They then choose the cards they want for their hand. Because the kitty contains six cards, the bid winner must, before starting the game, remove face down six cards from his hand of sixteen.

The Bidding Explained

A **trick** is a round in which the players play a card from their hand, and **bidding** is the process of predicting how many tricks that team will win. The prediction is affected by which suit is **trumps**. Trumps is defined as one suit being more powerful than any of the cards in other suits, regardless of their rank. For example a 4 of a trumps suit beats all non-trump cards, including an Ace. The only exception is the joker, which is considered to be a trump card at all times.

The trumps bidding rank, from lowest to highest, is clubs, spades, diamonds, hearts and no trump. This means that if someone bids 8 of clubs, a bid of 8 of spades is higher. A 'no trump' bid means that, other than the jokers, there is no suit that is trump. Playing a game without trumps is more difficult, because if another player plays a card of a suit that the player doesn't have, they can't win by using a trump card instead.

How the Game Starts

The game starts once the bid winner drops the first card into the kitty face up. Then, in a clockwise fashion, each player drops a card. This must be the same suit as the original, unless the player doesn't have any cards of that suit—in which case he or she can play a trump card or joker if they have one to win the trick. In a no trump situation the joker can only be played if the player can't follow suit, or if the player that is dropping the joker is the first player. After one round the card that is highest wins the trick, and a point is awarded to that team.

The highest card is based on which suit is trumps. It is determined as follows:

- ▲ Jokers are the highest in a trump and no trump situation.

- ▲ If there is no trump then the Ace of the suit is highest.

- ▲ If there is a trump suit then the highest card is the Jack of that suit, followed by the Jack of the opposing same color suit, and finally the Ace of the trump suit.

If the team that did the bidding wins, then they score. If the team that wins beats the other team and prevents them winning the number of tricks they originally bid, then that score becomes theirs. For example if a team bid 8 and the opposing team won 3 tricks then the bidding team lost because it is impossible for them to still get 8 tricks. This means the opposing team gets the score of 8.

How the Game Ends

Finally, the rounds stop with the first team that has won 1000 points. There are more detailed rules to the game, but you now have enough to get started. You can find out more as you go along.

The Technologies and Components

The game could have been programmed totally within Active Server Pages. While this would have been an interesting exercise, it's probably not advisable. The information we need to manipulate is very complex. Cards need to be shuffled, dealt, and traded; tricks need to be counted; the trump suit needs to be determined, etc. The end result is that we need to develop the game using a language that supports complex structures. Our choice is Visual Basic 5.0, and the interface from the ASP page to the Visual Basic language is COM. We'll be defining the game server class structures, and then implementing them using Visual Basic classes.

The Building Blocks of the Application

Just to indicate how different this application is from the ones we've seen previously in this book, here's how the player sees the game from his end:

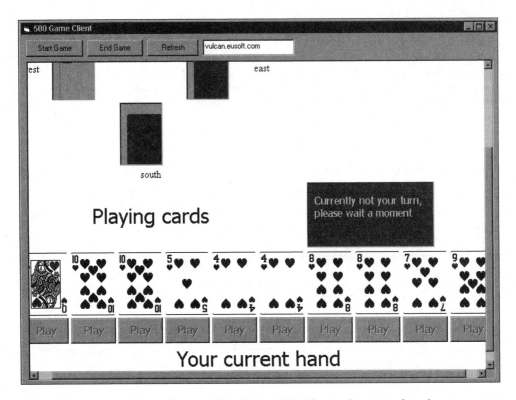

As you can see, this is no ordinary browser. The client end of the application is based on a custom program written in Visual Basic, which has a web browser window embedded. And while this may look like one window, there is in fact a separate frame which holds the status messages. We'll look at the whole thing in detail in a moment.

There are other components used in the application as a whole. For example, to make the client interactive and reduce processing load on the server, there's some client-side scripting using both VBScript and JScript. The pages also make use of FrontPage Web Bots and ActiveX controls, and the server hosts a custom component that controls the entire game.

The Requirements for the Client

So, let's first look in more detail at the client. The browser application is written using Visual Basic 5.0 and it hosts an embedded web browser. The advantage of using this approach is simplicity. The player doesn't need to know anything about web technology–they only need to know how to operate the program. And since it is Web based, the application content can be updated without having to update the client.

At the top of the client application window are three buttons:

- ▲ **Start Game**: Causes the client to retrieve the root application document and load it into the browser control.

- ▲ **End Game**: Causes the client to retrieve the application end document. Note that this document doesn't end the entire **Application**, just that player's **Session**

- ▲ **Refresh**: Causes the client to refresh whichever document is currently loaded.

As far as the user is concerned, this is really all that's involved in controlling their part in the game. The client application wraps the browser interface up in an easy to use program. The big window in the middle of the client application is the main browser interface, and the darker colored window above the player's own cards is the status window—which replaces the usual built-in status bar.

How the Status Window Works

The main browser window loads a required document in response to a button-click. This is simple, and avoids explanations and instructions. However, the status window is a little more complex. The code in the custom browser application that loads the HTML page is:

```
Private lastString As String

Private Sub conTimerStatus_Timer()
  'Call the server and retrieve the status
  Dim currentString As String
  currentString = ConTransfer.OpenURL _
              ("mercury.eusoft.com/game500/status.asp", icString)
  If currentString <> lastString Then
    conBrowserStatus.Refresh       'refresh the status bar page
    lastString = currentString
  End If
End Sub
```

There is a **Timer** control and an **Internet Transfer** control on the client form. The timer is set to trigger every five seconds, and when this happens the **Internet Transfer** control retrieves the HTML text for the current status using the **OpenURL** method. The return from this function is stored in **currentString**. This is compared to the **lastString** that was loaded, and if they are different the browser status window (named **conBrowserStatus**) is refreshed. Then the value of **currentString** is assigned to **lastString**, ready for the next **OpenURL** call. You may be wondering why we don't just call **conBrowserStatus.Refresh** directly every time the timer fires. The answer is because it takes time to do a GUI refresh, and this can also produce an annoying flicker if there are no changes to take account of.

Sending Commands to the Client

The other function of the status window is to provide a callback mechanism. We need this so that the client performs certain actions without the intervention of the user. Going back to the previous status refresh example, the status window is only actually refreshed when there's new data coming from the **OpenURL** method. This is important, because when the status window *does* refresh, it triggers an event that tells the application that a new HTML page has been loaded. This event is trapped in the client application's code:

```
Private Sub conBrowserStatus_NavigateComplete(ByVal URL As String)
  'check if we need to refresh the main window
  On Error Resume Next
  Select Case conBrowserStatus.Document.Script.Document.frmStatus _
          .txtStatusCode.Value
    Case 1, 2
      conBrowser.Refresh   'refresh the main page
  End Select
End Sub
```

The purpose of this event is to tell the client program to do something. We've kept the example simple, because we just need it to refresh the main browser window. But take a closer look at how the status code is found. The code:

```
conBrowserStatus.Document.Script.Document.frmStatus.txtStatusCode.Value
```

is interesting, because it goes from inside the client program to an ActiveX control named **txtStatusCode** on the HTML page itself. To fully understand the object relationship to this control, here's the **status.asp** file that creates the status window page:

```
<html><head><title>StatusWindow</title></head>
<body bgcolor="#FFFFFF">
<form method="POST" name="frmStatus">
<% If IsEmpty(Session("PlayerObject")) Then %>
    <font face="Tahoma"> Status: You have not started the game </font>:
    <input type="text" size="4" name="txtStatusCode" value="0"> <p>
<% Else %>
    <font face="Tahoma"> <B>Status</B>:
    <% = Session("PlayerObject").GameServer.CurrentStateString %> </font>:
    <input type="text" size="4" name="txtStatusCode"
    value="<% = Session("PlayerObject").GameServer.CurrentStateCode%>">
<% End If %>
</form>
</body>
</html>
```

The Requirements for the Server

On the server side, things are more complicated. There are more parts that need to communicate with each other. First, the machine used should be a minimum of P133 with at least 64MB of RAM. The operating system should be Windows NT 4.0 with service pack 2 installed. On top of Windows NT Server, there are two main services that need to be installed.

The first is Microsoft Internet Information Server, or IIS. The version that we used comes with Windows NT 4.0 Server, together with the IIS 3.0 update already installed.

> The only difference between IIS 2.0 and 3.0 is the number of added tools. The IIS administration remains identical, as does any public interface definition.

The other service is the Microsoft Chat Server or Microsoft Conference Server. At the time of writing there was no released version and we continued to use Beta 2. And while a full version of Access isn't actually required, it does make it easier to edit the database that stores the player's details.

COM and the Threading Object

Before we look at the source code of the server objects, we should step back and look at what they are doing, and why. The concept of threading is difficult to get to grips with as a newcomer to Visual Basic, and you can easily incorporate it incorrectly–because you don't know what's going on. The problem is compounded by the fact that Visual Basic 5.0 'hides' many of the nasties connected with this topic.

What we need is a global object that manages the deck of cards, the player's actions, and other global events. We also need a player-specific, or local, object that contains the player's hand of cards and other local attributes. Visual Basic and COM can do this, but there's a trick to it. To show how it's done, let's move away from our complex current example and replace it with a simple example. This contains two classes, and one module.

The Main Module (simple version)

```
Name: modmain (modMain.bas) [module]
Public globalGame As GameServer
Public globalReferenceCount As Integer
```

The purpose of **modMain** is to store the instance reference of the **GameServer** object. This is very important, because all references to the global object must be identical—otherwise there will data consistency problems. Also in this module is the **globalReferenceCount** counter, which indicates the number of objects that are currently referencing the **GameServer** object.

The GameServer Class (simple version)

```
Name: GameServer (gameserver.cls) [class]
Instancing: PublicNotCreatable
```

```
Private localPlayerCount As Integer

Public Sub AddPlayer()
  localPlayerCount = localPlayerCount + 1
End Sub

Public Function GetPlayerCount() As Integer
  GetPlayerCount = localPlayerCount
End Function
```

The **GameServer** class is the global class, meaning only one instance of it can exist, regardless of the number of players that are present. The **Private** variable **localPlayerCount** keeps track of the number of players that are currently active, and is incremented using the **AddPlayer** method. Because the **GameServer** object isn't directly instantiated or released, and it can't be guaranteed that the **AddPlayer** method is ever called, an interrelationship must exist between the creator of the **GameServer** and the **GameServer** itself. The rule is simple: whoever creates the object, or makes a reference to it in a method call, must increment the **GlobalReferenceCount** counter. It is also assumed that the creator of the object will also check that the creation was successful.

You may wonder why there are two reference counters, because the private player count is itself a sort of reference counter. The answer is that the player counter isn't a reference counter. The player counter is an abstraction of our business rule that requires we keep track of the number of active players—a player is considered active if they call the **AddPlayer** method. If, however, there was an object such as a status indicator, it would still access the **GameServer** without actually becoming a player. That simple reference requires a valid **GameServer** instance. If the instance is invalid, an error will occur unless the **GlobalReferenceCount** counter is incremented.

The Player Class (simple version)

```
Name: player (player.cls) [class]
Instancing: MultiUse
```

```
Private localCardCount As Integer

Private Sub Class_Initialize()
  If globalGame Is Nothing Then
    Set globalGame = New GameServer
  End If
```

```
      globalReferenceCount = globalReferenceCount + 1
      globalGame.AddPlayer
    End Sub

    Private Sub Class_Terminate()
      globalReferenceCount = globalReferenceCount - 1
      If globalReferenceCount = 0 Then
        Set globalGame = Nothing
      End If
    End Sub

    Public Function GetPlayerCount() As Integer
      GetPlayerCount = globalGame.GetPlayerCount
    End Function

    Public Sub AddCard()
      localCardCount = localCardCount + 1
    End Sub

    Public Function GetCardCount() As Integer
      GetCardCount = localCardCount
    End Function
```

The **Player** class can be considered as the creator class, and with it comes the responsibility of creating the **GameServer** object correctly. The only logical place to add the interrelationship code is in the **Class_Initialize** and **Class_Terminate** events. The **Class_Initialize** event is called when the object instance is created, and the **Class_Terminate** event is called when the object is destroyed. Looking at the **Class_Initialize** event, the code first checks if **globalGame** is a valid object with **Is Nothing**. If it returns **True** the object can be created. Every time the object is created the **globalReferenceCount** count is incremented. The last step, which isn't actually required but added for convenience, is the call to the **AddPlayer** method. It's there because of the business rule that all players must register themselves to the **GameServer**.

The **Class_Terminate** code decrements the **globalReferenceCount** count, and once the count reaches zero the **globalServer** object is destroyed by assigning the value **Nothing** to it. While this assignment doesn't directly destroy the instance of the object, it tells the Visual Basic garbage collector that this object isn't referenced any more. This in turn marks the instance as removable.

The other functions within the **Player** class can be used to retrieve information about the number of current players, and cards that each player holds. **GetPlayerCount** references the global object and then retrieves the number of active players. **AddCard** adds a card to the local hand, and **GetCardCount** retrieves the number of cards the player is currently holding.

Project Settings, and How Synchronization Works

With the structure we've just described, it's possible to create a **Player** object, and then directly access the global **GameServer** object. The last step is to properly define the properties of this program. The definition is absolutely critical because of the way the COM library works.

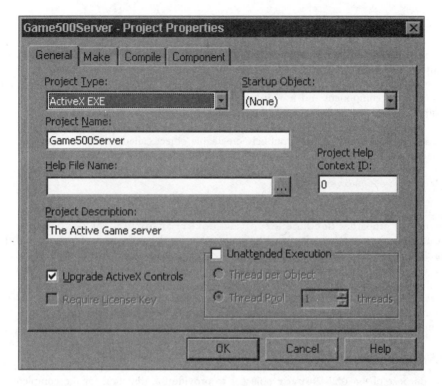

The project type is ActiveX DLL, which is an in-process server. This declaration is fine, because the shared information is only required within the same process. If the information were required within various processes, the server would have to be declared as an ActiveX Executable. This is an out-of-process executable. The major disadvantage with the ActiveX Executable is that it isn't as fast as an ActiveX DLL. This is because the COM layer needs to work across process boundaries, something that is computationally more time consuming.

Our program will work under all circumstances because there's only one thread allocated for the **Player** and **GameServer** object. The class instancing setting of **MultiUse** does this, and means that all requests to these objects will be automatically queued. This is a good thing, because we don't have to worry about one player writing a variable and another player overwriting it at the same time. However, notice that this does have a performance hit, and should only be considered for objects that do not take a long time to process.

So now we've seen how to develop a global object from local objects. It's always advisable to create a local object. It may be possible to create the global object directly, but we wouldn't recommend it. Visual Basic is a great language for developing objects and applications but, unlike C++, doesn't provide absolute control over the individual objects.

The Game Server Component

The `GameServer` component is the heart of the entire game. It controls the moves every person makes, and without it the system wouldn't work at all. Unlike the previous section, we won't go into the internal details of the component–our focus in this book is on Active Server Pages itself. However, we'll outline the exact functionality of the component and how to use it properly. The Visual Basic source code for the component is supplied, and you can expand its functionality yourself.

The `GameServer` component exposes one publicly createable object called the `Player` object, which can be created directly using the syntax:

```
CreateObject("Game500Server.Player")
```

The other objects that `Player` exposes can't under any circumstance be publicly created. They can only be referenced using the properties `GetGameServer` and `GetErrorServer`. The `GetGameServer` property returns the `GameServer` object, which is responsible for the main game functions and the coordination of the players. The `GetErrorServer` property retrieves an error object. If any action or function returns an error then more details regarding that fault can be retrieved from this object.

The `GameServer` object doesn't perform any security. It assumes that any players who are added to the game have already been verified. Also note that error handling in our sample game is minimal, and is left as a continuation project for the developer.

The GameServer Object

So to recap, the purpose of the `GameServer` object is to provide the direction for the complete game. Most of the properties and methods are read-only, including the state of the game, what the winning bid was, how many tricks have been won, and various other global items. The following table lists the publicly available properties:

Property and Return Type	Description
CurrentCount (Integer)	Retrieves the current number of references to the main `GameServer` object. This property isn't directly related to the number of active players, but is purely a software count.
GetGameState (Integer)	Retrieves the state of the game. The states can be: **NOT_START** (0): The game hasn't yet started, and there aren't yet enough players for a full game.
	BIDDING (1): The game has begun, and currently players are bidding the number of tricks they will win.
	CENTER_DECIDING (2): One of the players has won the kitty and is deciding which cards to keep.
	PLAYING (3): The game is currently being played.
CurrentPlayerCount (Integer)	The number of players that have decided to join the game. The highest that this number can be is **4**.
GetBidTrickCount (Integer)	The number of tricks that the bid winner team will take. When `GetGameState = BIDDING` this number changes to reflect who has currently bid highest.

Property and Return Type	Description
GetBidSuit (String)	Retrieves the suit of the winning bid. Can be: **HEART, DIAMOND, SPADE, CLUB, NO TRUMP**.
	When GetGameState = BIDDING this reflects the suit of the currently highest bid.
GetBidder (String)	Retrieves the name of the winner of the bidding when **GetGameState = BIDDING**.
GetKittySuit (cardNum As Integer) (String)	Retrieves the suit of a card in the kitty depending on the index supplied, which is in the range **1** to **6**. Also sets GetGameState to CENTER_DECIDING.
GetKittyRank (cardNum As Integer) (String)	Retrieves the rank of a card in the kitty depending on the index supplied, which is in the range **1** to **6**. Also sets GetGameState to CENTER_DECIDING.
DealtCardRank (location As String) (String)	Retrieves the rank of the card that has been played. The location is one of the four directions (**North, East, South, West**). If the card hasn't been played the return string is "**cardempty**".
DealtCardSuit (location As String) (String)	Retrieves the suit of the card that has been played. The location is one of the four directions (**North, East, South, West**). If the card hasn't been played the return string is "".
TricksWon (Integer)	Retrieves the number of tricks that the winning bidder has won. If the number they lost exceeds **10** minus their bid, the round is over.

All of the exposed items are properties, so the player can only retrieve global statistics about the game. There's no way to influence the results of the game from the **GameServer** object. One critical reason why the object is read-only is the simplicity in controlling synchronization–if the player can only read the data it simplifies the process dramatically. In the sections to come, you'll see how this read-only data is used to inform the player of what is going on.

The Player Object

The purpose of the player object is to provide an interface to the game through the moves that player can make. If we compare the objects to reality, players can only play a card and make a decision. The global context of the game can't be changed directly. For example, if one player wins the kitty, another player can't look at it.

The player object has the following methods and properties:

Type	Name and Return Data Type	Description
Variable	WonHand (Boolean)	A flag specifying whether the player has won the hand in the bidding round.
Property	Name (String)	Read/write property holding the person's name–it doesn't need to be anything specific. For the purpose of this game, it is the logon user name

Table Continued on Following Page

Type	Name and Return Data Type	Description
Function	`AddPlayer (Boolean)`	Adds the current player to the game.
Function	`Bid(count As Integer, suit As String) (Boolean)`	Adds a bid for the player. The function is turn-synchronized and will not allow a bid unless it is that player's turn.
Function	`PassBid (Boolean)`	If the player does not want to bid, they can pass by calling this function.
Function	`GetCard(index As Integer, retSuit As String, retRank As String) (String)`	Retrieves the suit and rank of a card based on the index, which refers to the location of the card in their hand. Can be in the range 1 to 10.
Function	`PlayCard(index As Integer) (Boolean)`	Plays a card when it's that player's turn. The card is defined by the index, which refers to the location of the card in the hand. Can be in the range 1 to 10.
Property	`GetGameServer (Object)`	Retrieves the `GameServer` global object.
Property	`GetErrorServer (Object)`	Retrieves the `ErrorServer` global object.
Property	`IsMyTurn (Boolean)`	Indicates if it is the player's turn.
Property	`WonKitty (Boolean)`	Indicates if the player has won the kitty.
Property	`GetCardSuit(cardNum As Integer) (String)`	Retrieves the suit of the card in the player's hand based on the index or location. The range can be from 1 to 10.
Property	`GetCardRank(cardNum As Integer) (String)`	Retrieves the rank of the card in the player's hand based on the index or location. The range can be from 1 to 10.
Function	`Start (Boolean)`	Called if the player has won the kitty and is ready to discard some cards.
Function	`KeepHandCard(cardNum As Integer) (Boolean)`	If the player has won the kitty and called the `Start` function, this keeps a card from the player's dealt cards.
Function	`KeepKittyCard(cardNum As Integer) (Boolean)`	If the player has won the kitty and called the `Start` function, this keeps a card from the kitty.
Function	`Finished`	Called after the final `KeepHandCard` and `KeepKittyCard` to move all of the 'kept' cards to the player's new hand.
Property	`SeatingPosition (String)`	Retrieves the player's current seating position: `North`, `East`, `South`, or `West`.
Property	`IsCardValid(cardIndex As Integer) (Boolean)`	Checks to see whether a card has been played. If the card is playable then the value will be `False` otherwise it is `True`.

Starting a Game

We've looked at the client application, and defined the server component. Now we have to actually play the game. This is interesting, because we now have to string together the component and the ASP pages to produce a client-server game that will make sense.

GameBoard.asp

The first page that the user sees is **GameBoard.asp**, so we'll look at that now:

```
<% If Session("bLogged") <> True Then
    Response.Redirect "loguser.asp"
  Else
    If Session("PlayerObject").GetGameServer.GetGameState = 1 Then
      'The game is active and we are bidding
      Response.Redirect "GameBoardBidding.asp"
    ElseIf Session("PlayerObject").GetGameServer.GetGameState = 2 Then
      'The kitty is being decided
      If Session("PlayerObject").WonKitty = True Then
        'The player has won the kitty
        Response.Redirect "GameBoardKitty.asp"
      End If
    ElseIf Session("PlayerObject").GetGameServer.GetGameState = 3 Then
      'The game is active and we are playing
      Response.Redirect "GameBoardPlaying.asp"
    End If
  End If %>
<html>
<head>
<META HTTP-EQUIV="REFRESH" CONTENT="5">
<title>GameBoard</title>
</head>
<body bgcolor="#008000">
<font color="#FFFF00" face="Tahoma">
<% If Session("playerObject").GetGameServer.GetGameState = 2 Then %>
<H1>Please wait a moment until the kitty has been decided</H1>
    <% Else %>
<H1>The game is not yet active</H1> Please wait until it is active
There are currently
<% = Session("playerObject").GetGameServer.CurrentPlayerCount %>
players. You need 4 players to start a game.
<% End If %>
</font><p>
</body>
</html>
```

You will probably notice that this page uses the techniques outlined in Chapter 6 to redirect a user to the appropriate page in an application. It demonstrates the 'business rules' we must follow. The first step is to check whether the player has logged in yet. If they have, the **bLogged** session variable will be set. If not, we just redirect them to a login page.

You are not registered in the database, please fill out the following form

Name (First, last) [   ]

Nickname [maperry   ]

Email [   ]

Password [   ]

Password (again) [   ]

[Submit]

The login page uses some more of the techniques you saw in Chapter 6 to ensure that the player is unique. A list of all players, past and present, is stored in a database, and when the login is complete a **Player** object is created for them in their **Session** and the **bLogged** value is set. They are then redirected back to the **GameBoard.asp** page.

The purpose of the **GameBoard.asp** page is to provide a central point where all the other pages or actions are referenced. This is very important because it gives us the ability to move easily from one page to another, without resorting to hyperlinks and large complicated pages. So what are the options available once the player has logged in? We'll look at these now.

Once the user has been verified, we need to determine the state of the game using **GetGameServer.GetGameState**. If **GameState** is 1 then we are at the bidding stage, and the player is redirected to **GameBoardBidding.asp**.

If **GameState** is 2 it means that we are at the kitty decision stage. A check must then be made to see if this player is the one who won the kitty, by examining the **WonKitty** property. If it's **True** the player is redirected to the **GameBoardKitty.asp** page.

If **GameState** is 3 it means we are at the playing stage, and we redirect the player to the **GameBoardPlaying.asp** page.

We checked whether a player had won the kitty when **GameState** is 2. If they hadn't won, we continue with the HTML code in the page, which displays a message telling the player to wait.

The steps above outline the entire game, and all of its possibilities. If no redirection occurs, the main part of the page is displayed, which contains a refresh tag:

```
<META HTTP-EQUIV="REFRESH" CONTENT="5">
```

So, the page is automatically reloaded every five seconds until a redirection does occur. The reload is required because without it the player would be stuck in this page.

So now we have three options for the game to continue:

> `GameBoardBidding.asp`–bidding is taking place
>
> `GameBoardKitty.asp`–the kitty is being decided
>
> `GameBoardPlaying.asp`–the rest of the game is being played

In the remainder of this chapter, we'll look at each of these pages in turn.

GameBoardBidding.asp

The `GameServer` object changes the game state from **WAITING** to **BIDDING** when enough players have been added. You will recall that the exact method that triggers the state change is
`Session("PlayerObject").AddPlayer` and the player count must reach four. Once this has been achieved, the players are redirected to the `GameBoardBidding` page so that they can submit a bid. They get the following page:

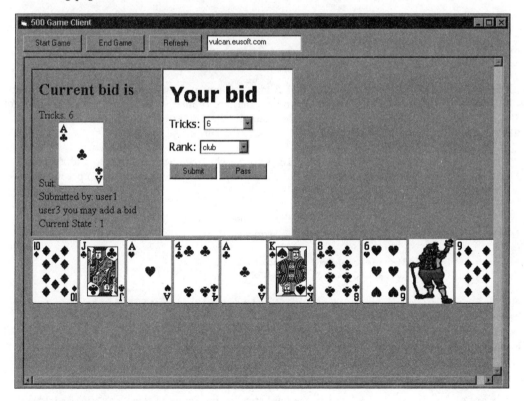

The code behind this page is:

```
<HTML>
<HEAD><TITLE>Bidding</TITLE></HEAD>
<BODY>
```

```
<IFRAME FRAMEBORDER="1" SCROLLING="NO" HEIGHT="250" WIDTH="200"
  SRC="CurrentBid.asp">
</IFRAME>
<IFRAME FRAMEBORDER="1"SCROLLING="NO" HEIGHT="250" WIDTH="200"
  SRC="AddBid.asp">
</IFRAME>
<table border="0" width="100%">
<tr>
  <td><p align="center">
    <img src="images/<% = Session("PlayerObject").GetCardSuit(1)%>
    <% = Session("PlayerObject").GetCardRank(1)%>.gif"
    width="68" height="96"></p>
  </td>
  <!--The rest of the fields 2-9 have been removed for simplicity-->
  <td><p align="center">
    <img src="images/<% = Session("PlayerObject").GetCardSuit(10)%>
    <% = Session("PlayerObject").GetCardRank(10)%>.gif"
    width="68" height="96"></p>
  </td>
</tr>
</table>
</BODY>
</HTML>
```

Notice that we've omitted the code for image tags 2 to 9, because it's just a replication of the ones you see here. Looking at the screenshot, there are two windows that are of interest to us: Current bid is and Your bid. Both of these windows are floating frames; for example, the Current bid is frame is the HTML `<IFRAME...SRC="CurrentBid.asp">`, and it displays the current highest bid.

The Your bid frame is `<IFRAME...SRC="AddBid.asp">`, which allows the player to add their bid. Floating frames are an incredibly useful feature, and allow dynamic content to be built up without affecting the main page.

Located on the main page is the player's current hand. These cards are images that are stored on the server. The naming of these images follows a strict sequence:

```
[suit=heart|diamond|spade|club|white|black]
[rank=4|5|6|7|8|9|10|Jack|Queen|King|Ace|Joker].gif
```

Looking at the naming convention, you'll see that it matches what the **Game500Server** component returns as text. The key is to concatenate the strings in the **GameServer.GetCardSuit** and **GamerServer.GetCardRank** properties to form a valid image name. For example, we can display a five of Hearts by using **heart5.gif**.

CurrentBid.asp

The **CurrentBid.asp** page is displayed in the left-hand floating frame of the **GameBoardBidding** page. This is what the code looks like:

```
<HTML>
<HEAD>
<META HTTP-EQUIV="REFRESH" CONTENT="5">
<TITLE>CurrentBid</TITLE>
</HEAD>
```

```
<BODY>
<% If Session("PlayerObject").GetGameServer.GetBidTrickCount <> 0 Then %>
    <H2>Current bid is</H2> Tricks:
    <% = Session("PlayerObject").GetGameServer.GetBidTrickCount%>
    <BR>Suit: <img src="images/
    <% = Session("PlayerObject").GetGameServer.GetBidSuit%>
    ace.gif" width="68" height="96"> <BR>Submitted by:
    <% = Session("PlayerObject").GetGameServer.GetBidder
  Else %>
    <H2>There is no bid</H2><BR>
<% End If
  If Session("PlayerObject").IsMyTurn = True Then %>
    <%=session("PlayerObject").Name%> you may add a bid
<% Else %>
    <BR>Please wait!!!
<% End If %>
</BODY>
</HTML>
```

This page is complicated by the data it displays. It prompts the player on what they can or can't do at this point. For example, we saw in the definition of the **Player** object that they can only add a bid if it is their turn. If it's not, an error message is returned. Therefore, to keep the player from guessing when they can submit a bid, a visual cue is given by the **CurrentBid** page. Implementing this only requires us to test the **Player** object to see if it is this player's turn:

```
If Session("PlayerObject").IsMyTurn = True Then ...
```

Notice how we 'talk' directly to the player, using their name:

```
<% = Session("PlayerObject").Name%> you may add a bid.
```

This is a simple little feature, but it makes the page appear friendlier. If it's not this player's turn, a warning message is displayed instead. This doesn't stop the player from submitting a bid, but it gives them an idea of when it's actually their turn.

However, the main purpose of this page is to tell all the players what the current highest bid is. If we go back to our **GameServer** object definition, there are a series of properties that allow us to retrieve the characteristics of the highest bid. By default the bid count starts at zero. It would make sense to display a message like There is no bid yet rather than current bid: 0. Our page uses this approach by testing whether the bid count is zero:

```
If Session("PlayerObject").GetGameServer.GetBidTrickCount <> 0 Then ...
```

If the count is not zero, meaning that there is a bid, the parameters are output by using the properties **GetBidTrickCount, GetBidSuit, GetBidder**. Otherwise, a simple message **<H2>There is no bid</H2>** is used.

The final thing that this page does is reload itself every five seconds, again using the HTTP refresh tag **<META HTTP-EQUIV="REFRESH" CONTENT="5">**. The page appears dynamic, and any changes in the bid or whose turn it is are reflected in the next update.

AddBid.asp

The `AddBid.asp` page is displayed in the right-hand floating frame of the `GameBoardBidding` page. In this frame, the player can submit their bid, as long as it's their turn. Looking at our screenshot, the message states that, yes, it is this player's turn.

The game requires the player to either submit a bid or pass. Both of these actions have the same result, passing on the turn to the next player. Submitting a successful bid requires that it be higher than the current highest bid. However, this isn't our concern as the player object takes care of this detail. Let's look a bit closer at the `addbid.asp` page:

```html
<html>
<head> <title>AddBid</title> </head>
<body bgcolor="#FFFFFF">
<h1><font face="Tahoma">Your bid</font></h1>
<form method="GET" action="ProcessBid.asp">
  <font face="Tahoma"> Tricks:
  <select name="cmbTrickCount" size="1">
    <option selected>6</option>
    <option>7</option>
    <option>8</option>
    <option>9</option>
    <option>10</option>
  </select></font><p>
  <font face="Tahoma">Rank: </font>
  <select name="cmbSuit" size="1">
    <option selected>club</option>
    <option>spade</option>
    <option>diamond</option>
    <option>heart</option>
    <option>no trump</option>
  </select><p>
  <input type="submit" name="cmdBidAction" value="Submit">
  <input type="submit" name="cmdBidAction" value="Pass">
</form>
</body>
</html>
```

The page is a normal form, which references the page `ProcessBid.asp` in the `ACTION` attribute of the `<FORM>` tag. One difference between this and normal forms is that there are two Submit buttons—one for submitting a bid and one for just passing. Note that both buttons have the same **name**, but different **value** attributes. If a Submit button on a form is given a name, its **value** attribute is sent to the server with the values of the other controls. With one button on a form this is superfluous information, but with two it allows us to distinguish which one was clicked.

ProcessBid.asp

When either of the buttons is pressed, the form is submitted to the `ProcessBid.asp` page, which looks like this:

```asp
<% Response.Buffer = True %>
<HTML>
<HEAD>
<% If Session("PlayerObject").IsMyTurn = False Then %>
    <!--META HTTP-EQUIV="REFRESH" CONTENT="5; URL=AddBid.asp"-->
```

```
<% End If %>
<TITLE>ProcessBid</TITLE>
</HEAD>
<BODY>
Trick Count: <% = Request.QueryString("cmbTrickCount")%>
Suit: <% = Request.QueryString("cmbSuit")%>
<% 'Check to see if it's your turn to play
If Session("PlayerObject").IsMyTurn = True Then
    'Now the bid can be added
    If Request.QueryString("cmdBidAction") = "Pass" Then
     'The bid is a pass so ignore
     Session("PlayerObject").PassBid %>
     <BR>Bid was successfully passed
<% Else
     If Session("PlayerObject").Bid(Request.QueryString("cmbTrickCount"), _
        Request.QueryString("cmbSuit")) = True Then %>
          <BR>Bid was successfully added
   <% Else %>
     <% Response.Clear
        Response.Redirect "AddBid.asp"
        End If
   End If
Else %>
   <BR>It's not your turn
<%
End If %>
</BODY>
</HTML>
<% Response.End %>
```

Processing the bid is easy. The hard part is ensuring that this bid is valid, but this is handled by the **GameServer** component itself. We check to make sure that the player can submit a bid by checking the **IsMyTurn** property. If it's the player's turn, a check is made on which button was pressed using:

```
If Request.QueryString("cmdBidAction") = "Pass" Then ...
```

This will return **True** if the player passed, and the **Player.Pass** method is then called to register the pass and give the next player a turn. If the player is submitting a bid, however, the comparison will return **False** and a bid is made using the **Bid** method:

```
Session("PlayerObject").Bid(Request.QueryString("cmbTrickCount"), _
        Request.QueryString("cmbSuit"))
```

This function call does quite a bit of work. If the bid is valid, the page is returned with the confirmation **
Bid was successfully added**. However, if the bid wasn't valid, we just redirect the user back to the same page–thereby reloading it.

However, as you'll recall from Chapter 6, this produces a problem. When the page **ProcessBid.asp** is first referenced, ASP starts processing the page with the first line of HTML and scripting code. Once HTML code is written to the page, either directly from HTML tags, or with the **Write** and **WriteLn** methods, it's impossible to redirect the user to another page. If you look at our page, you can see that half of the HTML tags have already been sent to the browser before our bid is submitted, and at this stage it is too late to redirect the page.

Our only solution is the technique we saw in Chapter 6, and which we have included in this page. We store the HTML in a temporary buffer by setting `Response.Buffer = True` in the first line. If the bid request fails, the buffer is cleared using `Response.Clear` and the page is redirected with `Response.Redirect "AddBid.asp"`. If all is OK, however, we use `Response.End` to return the completed page to the player.

GameBoardKitty.asp

The second main page is `GameBoardKitty.asp`, which is referenced from `GameBoard.asp` when the game state is 2. In other words, the bidding has stopped and someone has won the kitty. At this stage, the winner needs to select which cards they want to keep and which cards to discard. With the kitty, the player has sixteen cards to choose from. The page looks like this:

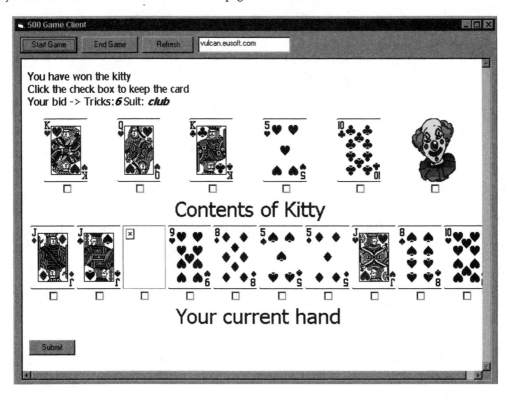

The code behind this page is:

```
<html>
<head> <title>Kitty</title> </head>
<body bgcolor="#FFFFFF">
<font face="Tahoma">You have won the kitty</font>
<font face="Tahoma"><BR>Click the check box to keep the card
<BR>Your bid -> Tricks:<I><B>
<% = Session("PlayerObject").GetGameServer.GetBidTrickCount %>
</B></I> Suit: <I><B>
<% = Session("PlayerObject").GetGameServer.GetBidSuit %>
</B></I></font>
```

```
<form method="Get" action="ProcessKitty.asp">
  <table border="0" width="100%">
    <tr>
      <% Dim i
        For i = 1 To 6 %>
          <td><p align="center">
            <img src="images/<% = Session("PlayerObject").GetGameServer._
            GetKittySuit(CInt(i)) %>
            <% = Session("playerObject").GetGameServer. _
            GetKittyRank(CInt(i)) %>
            .gif" width="68" height="96"></p>
          </td>
      <% Next %>
    </tr>
    <tr>
      <% For i = 1 To 6 %>
          <td><p align="center">
            <input type="checkbox" name="Kitty<% = i %>" value="Keep"></p>
          </td>
      <% Next %>
    </tr>
    <tr>
      <td colspan="6"><p align="center">
        <font size="6" face="Tahoma">Contents of Kitty</font></p>
      </td>
    </tr>
  </table>
  <table border="0" width="100%">
    <tr>
      <% For i = 1 To 10 %>
          <td><p align="center">
            <img src="images/<% = Session("PlayerObject"). _
            GetCardSuit(CInt(i)) %>
            <% = Session("PlayerObject").GetCardRank(CInt(i)) %>
            .gif" width="68" height="96"></p>
          </td>
      <% Next %>
    </tr>
    <tr>
      <% For i = 1 To 10 %>
          <td><p align="center">
            <input type="checkbox" name="Card<% = i %>" value="Keep"></p>
          </td>
      <% Next %>
    </tr>
    <tr>
      <td colspan="10"><p align="center">
        <font size="6" face="Tahoma">Your current hand</font></p>
      </td>
    </tr>
  </table>
  <input type="submit" name="B1" value="Submit"><p>
</form>
</body>
</html>
```

Let's compare this page to the `GameBoardBidding.asp` page. In that page, we cut out some repeated code to save space. That code retrieved our cards and displayed them on the page. Moving through the code blocks, the only difference from one block to another was the card index, and by using a modern editor such as Visual InterDev these code blocks could be easily copied and pasted into the page.

However, this method is not maintainable, and so we've used a different strategy this time. A `For...Next` loop, with a loop variable `i`, is used to generate the code that will retrieve the images. This method is more maintainable, because if we make any changes inside the loop it will automatically affect all the elements. With the other page, the changes need to be made to each code section separately.

> *Look closely at the previous HTML. The variable i is declared with no type—the only type that VBScript supports is* `Variant`. *This isn't a problem until a property or method from our* `GameServer` *component is called, such as the property* `GetKittySuit` *that requires an* `Integer` *as the index. If we call the function as* `GetKittySuit(i)`, *a type mismatch error will occur. The only way to circumvent this is to use the calling convention* `GetKittySuit(CInt(i))`.

Moving back to how the page actually works, we can again see that it is a simple form, whose purpose is to allow the player to choose which cards they want by clicking the checkboxes for the cards to be kept. The form `ACTION` argument references the `ProcessKitty.asp` page. This provides a challenge because, if the user decides to keep the first and third card from their original hand, the HTTP query string will be:

```
ProcessKitty.asp?card1=Keep&card3=Keep&...etc.
```

Notice that there isn't a checkbox item for `card2`, because of the way that the `GET` and `POST` methods work—we saw this in Chapter 2. We can't change this behavior, so we need to consider how this will affect the page `ProcessKitty.asp`.

ProcessKitty.asp

The `ProcessKitty.asp` page is called by the `GameBoardKitty.asp` page that we've just looked at. It processes the player's decision on which cards to keep. Remember we also have the extra problem of trying to deal with missing fields in the query string. The source code for this page is:

```
<HTML>
<HEAD> <TITLE>Process Kitty</TITLE>
<META HTTP-EQUIV="REFRESH" CONTENT="8; URL=GameBoard.asp">
</HEAD>
<BODY>
<% Dim cardName
   Dim i
   Dim totalCount

   totalCount = 0
   For i = 1 To 6
     cardName = "kitty" & i
     If Request.QueryString(cardName) = "Keep" Then
       totalCount = totalCount + 1
     End If
   Next
   For i = 1 To 10
     cardName = "card" & i
     If Request.QueryString(cardName) = "Keep" Then
       totalCount = totalCount + 1
```

```
      End If
   Next
   If totalCount <> 10 Then %>
     <BR>Please select 10 cards to keep
<% Else
     Session("PlayerObject").Start
     For i = 1 To 10
       cardName = "card" & i
       If Request.QueryString(cardName) = "Keep" Then
         Session("PlayerObject").KeepHandCard(CInt(i))
       End If
     Next
     For i = 1 To 6
       cardName = "kitty" & i
       If Request.QueryString(cardName) = "Keep" Then
         Session("PlayerObject").KeepKittyCard(CInt(i))
       End If
     Next
     Session("PlayerObject").Finished %>
     <BR>Thanks, the game is about to start
<% End If %>
</BODY>
</HTML>
```

The approach we've used is to check the query string for every possible value it can hold, to see if there's a variable associated with that value. ASP allows the **Request.QueryString("**_VariableName_**")** syntax to query a variable that isn't present without producing any error–if it doesn't exist we just get an empty value returned. Therefore we can check the query string for all the known values of **Keep**, and see which cards should kept and which should be discarded:

```
For i = 1 To 6
  cardName = "kitty" & i
  If Request.QueryString(kitty) = "Keep" Then
  ...
Next

For i = 1 To 10
  cardName = "card" & i
  If Request.QueryString(cardName) = "Keep" Then
  ...
Next
```

But before we can actually remove the unwanted cards, we need to make sure that the player actually selected ten cards. The first two **For...Next** loops simply count the number of checkboxes that are set. If there are ten, the cards can be moved. Otherwise the page informs the player that they did not choose ten cards.

If they have selected ten cards then the remainder can be removed. The first thing is to prepare the **Player** object for the card movements by calling the **Start** method. We then repeat the loops for each checkbox, but this time we call methods of the **GameServer** object for each one. In the first loop, going through the player's original hand the call is:

```
Session("PlayerObject").KeepHandCard(CInt(i))
```

In the second loop, for the kitty, the call is:

```
Session("PlayerObject").KeepKittyCard(CInt(i))
```

Once both loops have finished, a call to the **Finished** method is made. This moves the game state to the **PLAYING** stage. From this moment on, the page `GameBoardPlaying.asp` is loaded into all the players' client applications

Gameboardplaying.asp

This is the final page that we'll be discussing. It's the most important one and it's the one that the players will see the most often. It looks like this:

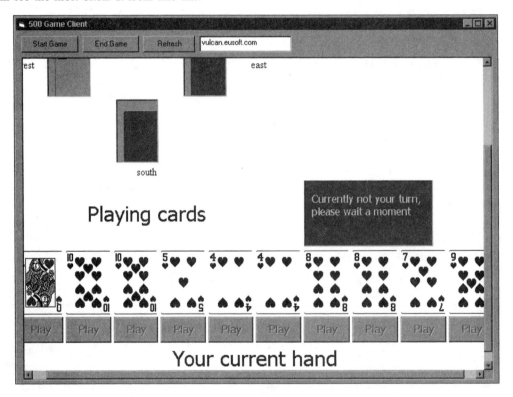

This time, because of the length, we won't print all the code in one go. Instead, we'll discuss the page using a piecemeal approach. Notice that in the screenshot, some of the page has been scrolled out of sight–namely a card is missing at the top of the page. This represents the **North** player. The dark colored frame to the right is our local status window. This is very important, and does a neat trick–but more about that later. The cards at the bottom have been generated using the same process we discussed earlier of looping through the player's current hand.

Dealt Cards

The cards visible at the top of the picture are the dealt cards, and are in floating frames. Each frame is a position: **North**, **East**, **South**, and **West**. Within each frame, a correspondingly named ASP page is loaded. So if we were looking at the **North** frame, the ASP card page is named **DealtCardNorth.asp.** An example of the code in the main frame that creates this floating frame is:

```
...
<table border="0" width="100%">
  <tr>
    <td> </td>
    <td> </td>
    <td>
      <IFRAME FRAMEBORDER="1" SCROLLING="NO" HEIGHT="96" WIDTH="68"
        SRC="DealtCardNorth.asp">
      </IFRAME>
    </td>
    <td> </td>
    <td> </td>
    <td width="40%"> </td>
  </tr>
</table>
...
```

The content of the **DealtCard** frame is a very simple page, which loads an image representing the card played at that position. In our example, **DealtCardNorth.asp** looks like this:

```
<HTML>
<HEAD>
<META HTTP-EQUIV="REFRESH" CONTENT="5">
<TITLE>DealtCardNorth</TITLE>
</HEAD>
<BODY>
<img src="images/
<% = Session("PlayerObject").GetGameServer.DealtCardSuit("North") %>
<% = Session("PlayerObject").GetGameServer.DealtCardRank("North") %>
  .gif" width="68" height="96"></p>
</BODY>
</HTML>
```

This code uses the **GameServer** properties **DealtCardSuit("North")** and **DealtCardRank("North")**, which return the suit and rank of the card that has been played. In our reference to the property, if a card hasn't been played, the string 'cardempty' is returned.

The Status Frame

The status frame is very important because it controls the player's main frame. We saw how this is done when we looked at the Visual Basic code for the **GameServer** object earlier in the chapter. This frame enables and disables the buttons below the playing cards.

You may ask why we would want to do this. Let's go back to the bidding stage. There we had two frames. The current bid frame contained a visual cue that would tell the players when they could bid. However, this cue couldn't control the Your bid window, which results in this problem: if the person really wanted to submit a bid, the system would say OK, but its not your turn. This process is wasteful and not error proof, so a more sophisticated method has been developed here. This is possible because we know a bit about the environment we're dealing with. Look at the source code of the status frame ASP page:

```
<HTML>
<HEAD>
<SCRIPT LANGUAGE="VBScript">
Sub window_onLoad()
<% Dim i
   If Session("PlayerObject").IsMyTurn = True then
     For i = 1 To 10
       If Session("PlayerObject").IsCardValid(CInt(i)) = True Then %>
           Parent.frmGlobal.cmdPlayCard<% = i %>.Enabled = True
     <% Else %>
           Parent.frmGlobal.cmdPlayCard<% = i %>.Enabled = False
     <% End If
     Next
   Else
     For i = 1 To 10 %>
         Parent.frmGlobal.cmdPlayCard<% = i %>.Enabled = False
   <% Next
   End If %>
End Sub
</SCRIPT>
<% If Session("PlayerObject").IsMyTurn <> True Then %>
<META HTTP-EQUIV="REFRESH" CONTENT="5">
<% End If %>
<TITLE>Playing</TITLE>
</HEAD>
<BODY bgcolor="#008000">
<font color="#FFFF00" face="Tahoma">
<% If Session("PlayerObject").IsMyTurn <> True Then %>
    Currently not your turn, please wait a moment
<% Else %>
    It's your turn
<% End If %>
</font>
</BODY>
</HTML>
```

There's a block of code within **Sub window_onLoad()** and **End Sub**, and the **<SCRIPT>** tag doesn't contain the **RUNAT=SERVER** argument. Therefore this code will be executed on the client, rather than on the server. Now look at the ASP code embedded within this section. This is server-based code, but it generates client-side script. What is this code doing? Simply, it enables or disables the buttons that play each card.

So why do we want to do this? It prevents 'click-happy' players from clicking buttons more than once, while they are waiting for the server's response–the buttons are enabled again once it is their turn.

So the first thing the code does is check the **IsMyTurn** property to see if it is this player's turn. If not, all buttons are disabled with the client script:

```
Parent.frmGlobal.cmdPlayCard<% = i%>.Enabled = False
```

The player then has to wait for their turn. Once it arrives, however, things become a bit more complicated–all of the buttons can't be blindly enabled because with each round that they play, a card will disappear from their hand. Therefore a previously played card must not have an enabled Play button. The **GameServer**'s **IsCardValid** property tells us if the card is valid, and the Play button can be enabled or disabled as appropriate.

And because we placed this code in the status frame's **window_OnLoad** function, we know that the routine will be executed automatically whenever the frame is loaded. If we periodically reload the frame, we can control the entire main frame without having to reload the main frame's state every time–the real hidden purpose of the status frame window.

The HTTP refresh **<META HTTP-EQUIV="REFRESH" CONTENT="5">** is an interesting feature, but if it this player's turn it would be annoying if every 5 seconds a flicker went across the buttons. Therefore we don't carry out the refresh in this case, because we know that nothing else can happen until this player has played a card.

Playing a Card

When the status frame enables the Play buttons, the player is free to choose a card to play. At this stage, there's no restriction on the card that is played. If the player presses button 1, the **cmdPlayCard1_Click()** event is fired. The code for this event looks like this:

```
Sub cmdPlayCard1_Click()
  frmGlobal.cmdPlayCard1.Enabled = False
  Parent.Frames(4).location.href = "ProcessPlay.asp?card=1"
End Sub
```

The first thing this code does is to disable the Play button. The next step is to reference the page **ProcessPlay.asp** with the variable **card=1**. The code **Parent.Frames(4)** refers to the status frame.

Now, if we combine a few of the things we've seen, you should begin to see how the system works. When it is this player's turn, the status window isn't updating itself periodically. This forces the player to play some card, and the status window will now be updated with the page **ProcessPlay.asp**.

ProcessPlay.asp

So, next we need to see what the **ProcessPlay.asp** page does. Here's the code:

```
<HTML>
<HEAD>
<META HTTP-EQUIV="REFRESH" CONTENT="15; URL=PlayStatus.asp">
<TITLE>ProcessPlay</TITLE>
</HEAD>
<BODY>
<% If Session("PlayerObject").IsMyTurn = True Then
    If Session("PlayerObject").PlayCard(Request.QueryString("card")) _
    = True Then %>
    Thanks, for playing
  <% Else %>
    Card could not be played
  <% End If
  Else %>
    It is not your turn, please wait

</BODY>
</HTML>
```

This page is automatically refreshed after 15 seconds, regardless of the results, and loads the status frame again. But before this page is finished executing, it calls the **Player.PlayCard** function with the index of the card that is being played. If that card can be played successfully the page will return the message Thanks, for playing. If not, the message Card could not be played is returned.

Either way the state of the **GameServer** object is changed. When the page is refreshed and the status frame is loaded again, the player's status will be updated. If they played a card that wasn't valid, the status frame will re-enable the Play buttons and wait until the player chooses another card. If the card could be successfully played, the status window will disable all of the buttons and pass the turn to next player. At this point the events are simply repeated for the next player, and so it continues.

To finish up, here's a diagram that shows how the main pages of the application link together. Remember, it's the regular refreshes of the pages, combined with the changes to the **GameState** made automatically by the **GameServer** object as each action–like playing a card–takes place, which controls the pages that are displayed at each stage.

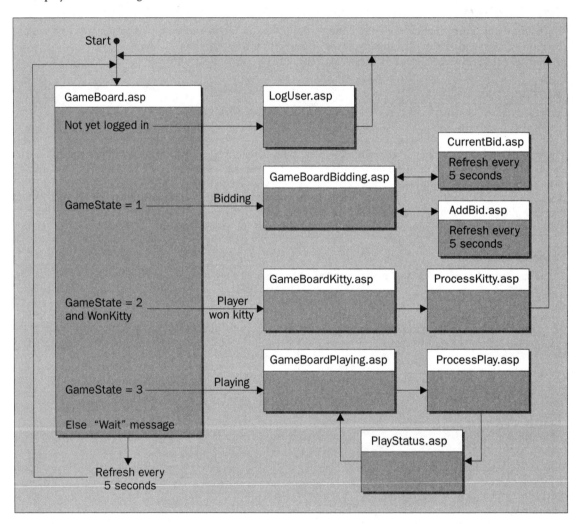

Summary

In this case study, we've taken a lightning tour around what is a very complex client-server application. It's implemented using many of the techniques we've described in previous chapters, and the result is a complex multi-user game.

We've used a custom client application and a server component written in Visual Basic, and a selection of Active Server Pages to link it all together. It's worthwhile, once you are familiar with ASP generally, to go through the source code yourself, and play the game to see it working. Remember you can play it now from the author's own web site by going to `http://www.eusoft.com` and following the Game link.

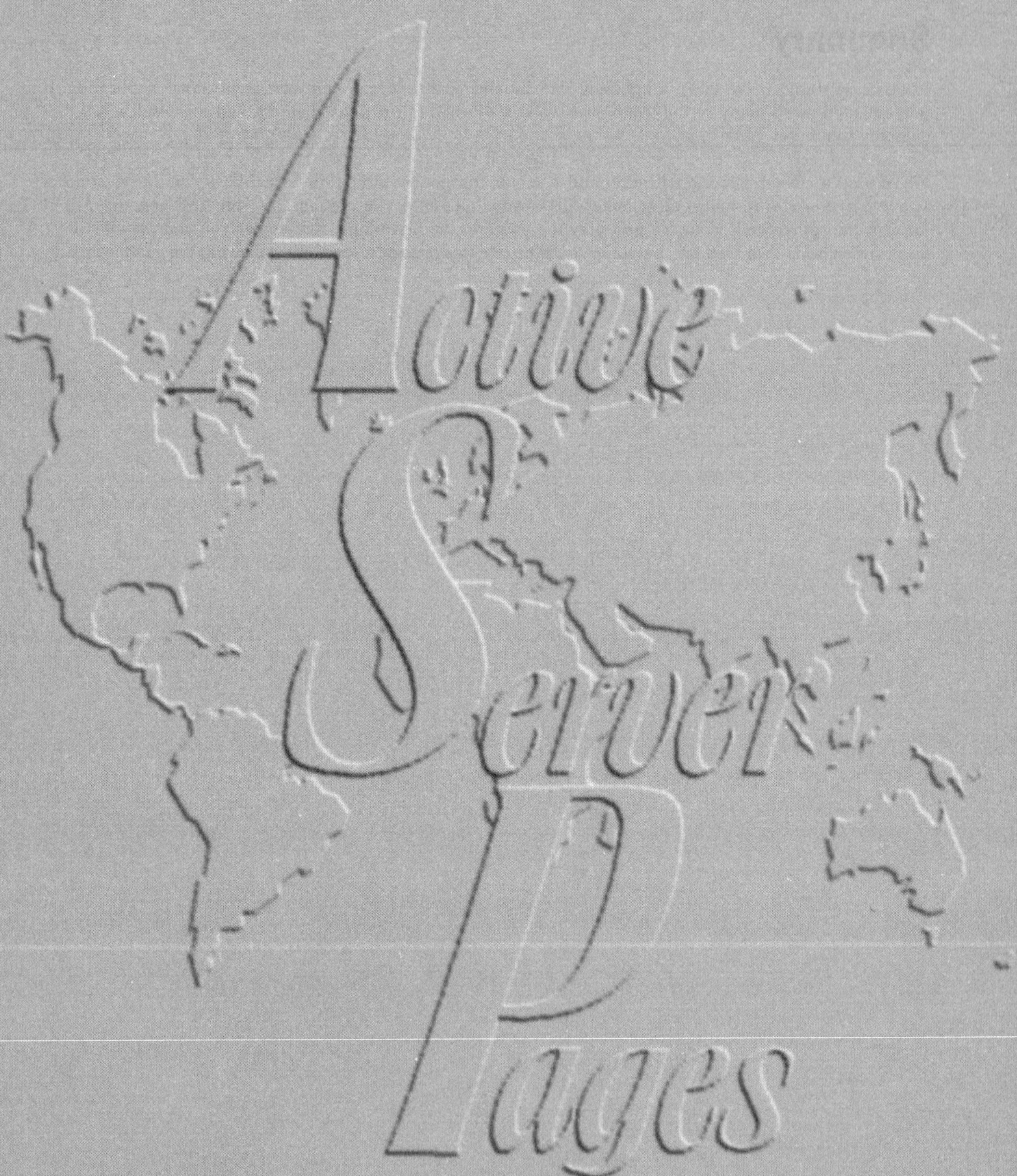
Active
Server
Pages

Reference Section

PART 4

To finish off the book, we've included a large amount of reference material, which you'll find invaluable when you start to develop using Active Server Pages. It contains not only details of the ASP objects and methods themselves, but all kinds of other practical help on client-side issues, Server-side Includes, and how to set up a System Data Source Name.

Reference Contents

Active Server Pages

VBScript Reference

Array Handling

Dim–declares an array variable. This can be static with a defined number of elements or dynamic and can have up to 60 dimensions.

ReDim–used to change the size of an array variable which has been declared as dynamic.

Preserve–keyword used to preserve the contents of an array being resized. If you need to use this then you can only re-dimension the rightmost index of the array.

```
Dim strEmployees ()
ReDim strEmployees (9,1)

strEmployees (9,1) = "Phil"

ReDim strEmployees (9,2)              'loses the contents of element (9,1)
strEmployees (9,2) = "Paul"

ReDim Preserve strEmployees (9,3)    'preserves the contents of (9,2)
strEmployees (9,3) = "Smith"
```

LBound– returns the smallest subscript for the dimension of an array. Note that arrays always start from the subscript zero so this function will always return the value zero.

UBound–used to determine the size of an array.

```
Dim strCustomers (10, 5)
intSizeFirst = UBound (strCustomers, 1)      'returns SizeFirst = 10
intSizeSecond = UBound (strCustomers, 2)     'returns SizeSecond = 5
```

> **The actual number of elements is always one greater than the value returned by UBound because the array starts from zero.**

Assignments

Let–used to assign values to variables (optional).

Set–used to assign an object reference to a variable.

```
Let intNumberOfDays = 365

Set txtMyTextBox = txtcontrol
txtMyTextBox.Value = "Hello World"
```

Constants

Empty—an empty variable is one that has been created but not yet assigned a value.
Nothing—used to remove an object reference.

```
Set txtMyTextBox = txtATextBox        'assigns object reference
Set txtMyTextBox = Nothing            'removes object reference
```

Null—indicates that a variable is not valid. Note that this isn't the same as Empty.
True—indicates that an expression is true. Has numerical value –1.
False—indicates that an expression is false. Has numerical value 0.

Error constant:

Constant	Value
vbObjectError	&h80040000

System Color constants:

Constant	Value	Description
vbBlack	&h00	Black
vbRed	&hFF	Red
vbGreen	&hFF00	Green
vbYellow	&hFFFF	Yellow
vbBlue	&hFF0000	Blue
vbMagenta	&hFF00FF	Magenta
vbCyan	&hFFFF00	Cyan
vbWhite	&hFFFFFF	White

Comparison constants:

Constant	Value	Description
vbBinaryCompare	0	Perform a binary comparison.
vbTextCompare	1	Perform a textual comparison.
vbDatabaseCompare	2	Perform a comparison based upon information in the database where the comparison is to be performed.

Date and Time constants:

Constant	Value	Description
VbSunday	1	Sunday
vbMonday	2	Monday
vbTuesday	3	Tuesday
vbWednesday	4	Wednesday
vbThursday	5	Thursday
vbFriday	6	Friday
vbSaturday	7	Saturday
vbFirstJan1	1	Use the week in which January 1 occurs (default).
vbFirstFourDays	2	Use the first week that has at least four days in the new year.
vbFirstFullWeek	3	Use the first full week of the year.
vbUseSystem	0	Use the format in the regional settings for the computer.
vbUseSystemDayOfWeek	0	Use the day in the system settings for the first weekday.

Date Format constants:

Constant	Value	Description
vbGeneralDate	0	Display a date and/or time in the format set in the system settings. For real numbers display a date and time. For integer numbers display only a date. For numbers less than 1, display time only.
vbLongDate	1	Display a date using the long date format specified in the computers regional settings.
vbShortDate	2	Display a date using the short date format specified in the computers regional settings.
vbLongTime	3	Display a time using the long time format specified in the computers regional settings.
vbShortTime	4	Display a time using the short time format specified in the computers regional settings.

File Input/Output constants:

Constant	Value	Description
ForReading	1	Open a file for reading only.
ForWriting	2	Open a file for writing. If a file with the same name exists, its previous one is overwritten.
ForAppending	8	Open a file and write at the end of the file.

String constants:

Constant	Value	Description
vbCr	Chr(13)	Carriage return only
vbCrLf	Chr(13) & Chr(10)	Carriage return and linefeed (Newline)
vbLf	Chr(10)	Line feed only
vbNewLine	-	Newline character as appropriate to a specific platform
vbNullChar	Chr(0)	Character having the value 0
vbNullString	-	String having the value zero (not just an empty string)
vbTab	Chr(9)	Horizontal tab

Tristate constants:

Constant	Value	Description
TristateTrue	-1	True
TristateFalse	0	False
TristateUseDefault	-2	Use default setting

VarType constants:

Constant	Value	Description
vbEmpty	0	Un-initialized (default)
vbNull	1	Contains no valid data
vbInteger	2	Integer subtype

Constant	Value	Description
vbLong	3	Long subtype
vbSingle	4	Single subtype
vbDouble	5	Double subtype
vbCurrency	6	Currency subtype
vbDate	7	Date subtype
vbString	8	String subtype
vbObject	9	Object
vbError	10	Error subtype
vbBoolean	11	Boolean subtype
vbVariant	12	Variant (used only for arrays of variants)
vbDataObject	13	Data access object
vbDecimal	14	Decimal subtype
vbByte	17	Byte subtype
vbArray	8192	Array

Control Flow

For...Next—executes a block of code a specified number of times.

```
Dim intSalary (10)
For intCounter = 0 to 10
   intSalary (intCounter) = 20000
Next
```

For Each...Next Statement—repeats a block of code for each element in an array or collection.

```
For Each Item In Request.QueryString("MyControl")
   Response.Write Item & "<BR>"
Next
```

Do...Loop—executes a block of code while a condition is true or until a condition becomes true.

```
Do While strDayOfWeek <> "Saturday" And strDayOfWeek <> "Sunday"
   MsgBox ("Get Up! Time for work")
   ...
Loop
```

```
Do
   MsgBox ("Get Up! Time for work")
   ...
Loop Until strDayOfWeek = "Saturday" Or strDayOfWeek = "Sunday"
```

`If...Then...Else`—used to run various blocks of code depending on conditions.

```
If intAge < 20 Then
   MsgBox ("You're just a slip of a thing!")
ElseIf intAge < 40 Then
   MsgBox ("You're in your prime!")
Else
   MsgBox ("You're older and wiser")
End If
```

`Select Case`—used to replace `If...Then...Else` statements where there are many conditions.

```
Select Case intAge
Case 21,22,23,24,25,26
   MsgBox ("You're in your prime")
Case 40
   MsgBox ("You're fulfilling your dreams")
Case 65
   MsgBox ("Time for a new challenge")
End Select
```

Note that `Select Case` can only be used with precise conditions and not with a range of conditions.

`While...Wend`—executes a block of code while a condition is true.

```
While strDayOfWeek <> "Saturday" AND strDayOfWeek <> "Sunday"
   MsgBox ("Get Up! Time for work")
   ...
Wend
```

Functions

VBScript contains several functions that can be used to manipulate and examine variables. These have been subdivided into the general categories of:

- Conversion Functions
- Date/Time Functions
- Math Functions
- Object Management Functions
- Script Engine Identification Functions
- String Functions
- Variable Testing Functions

For a full description of each function, and the parameters it requires, see the VBScript Help file. This is installed by default in the **Docs/ASPDocs/VBS/VBScript** subfolder of your IIS installation directory.

Conversion Functions

These functions are used to convert values in variables between different types:

Function	Description
Asc	Returns the numeric ANSI code number of the first character in a string.
AscB	As above, but provided for use with byte data contained in a string. Returns result from the first byte only.
AscW	As above, but provided for Unicode characters. Returns the **Wide** character code, avoiding the conversion from Unicode to ANSI.
Chr	Returns a string made up of the ANSI character matching the number supplied.
ChrB	As above, but provided for use with byte data contained in a string. Always returns a single byte.
ChrW	As above, but provided for Unicode characters. Its argument is a **Wide** character code, thereby avoiding the conversion from ANSI to Unicode.
CBool	Returns the argument value converted to a **Variant** of subtype **Boolean**.
CByte	Returns the argument value converted to a **Variant** of subtype **Byte**.
CDate	Returns the argument value converted to a **Variant** of subtype **Date**.
CDbl	Returns the argument value converted to a **Variant** of subtype **Double**.
CInt	Returns the argument value converted to a **Variant** of subtype **Integer**.
CLng	Returns the argument value converted to a **Variant** of subtype **Long**.
CSng	Returns the argument value converted to a **Variant** of subtype **Single**
CStr	Returns the argument value converted to a **Variant** of subtype **String**.
Fix	Returns the integer (whole) part of a number.
Hex	Returns a string representing the hexadecimal value of a number.
Int	Returns the integer (whole) portion of a number.
Oct	Returns a string representing the octal value of a number.
Round	Returns a number rounded to a specified number of decimal places.
Sgn	Returns an integer indicating the sign of a number.

Date/Time Functions

These functions return date or time values from the computer's system clock, or manipulate existing values:

Function	Description
Date	Returns the current system date.
DateAdd	Returns a date to which a specified time interval has been added.
DateDiff	Returns the number of days, weeks, or years between two dates.
DatePart	Returns just the day, month or year of a given date.
DateSerial	Returns a **Variant** of subtype **Date** for a specified year, month, and day.
DateValue	Returns a **Variant** of subtype **Date**.
Day	Returns a number between **1** and **31** representing the day of the month.
Hour	Returns a number between **0** and **23** representing the hour of the day.
Minute	Returns a number between **0** and **59** representing the minute of the hour.
Month	Returns a number between **1** and **12** representing the month of the year.
MonthName	Returns the name of the specified month as a string.
Now	Returns the current date and time.
Second	Returns a number between **0** and **59** representing the second of the minute.
Time	Returns a **Variant** of subtype **Date** indicating the current system time.
TimeSerial	Returns a **Variant** of subtype **Date** for a specific hour, minute, and second.
TimeValue	Returns a **Variant** of subtype **Date** containing the time.
Weekday	Returns a number representing the day of the week.
WeekdayName	Returns the name of the specified day of the week as a string.
Year	Returns a number representing the year.

Math Functions

These functions perform mathematical operations on variables containing numerical values:

Function	Description
Atn	Returns the arctangent of a number.
Cos	Returns the cosine of an angle.
Exp	Returns **e** (the base of natural logarithms) raised to a power.

Function	Description
Log	Returns the natural logarithm of a number.
Randomize	Initializes the random-number generator.
Rnd	Returns a random number.
Sin	Returns the sine of an angle.
Sqr	Returns the square root of a number.
Tan	Returns the tangent of an angle.

Object Management Functions

These functions are used to manipulate objects, where applicable:

Function	Description
CreateObject	Creates and returns a reference to an ActiveX or OLE Automation object.
GetObject	Returns a reference to an ActiveX or OLE Automation object.
LoadPicture	Returns a picture object.

Script Engine Identification

These functions return the version of the scripting engine:

Function	Description
ScriptEngine	A string containing the major, minor, and build version numbers of the scripting engine.
ScriptEngineMajorVersion	The major version of the scripting engine, as a number.
ScriptEngineMinorVersion	The minor version of the scripting engine, as a number.
ScriptEngineBuildVersion	The build version of the scripting engine, as a number.

String Functions

These functions are used to manipulate string values in variables:

Function	Description
Filter	Returns an array from a string array, based on specified filter criteria.
FormatCurrency	Returns a string formatted as currency value.
FormatDateTime	Returns a string formatted as a date or time.
FormatNumber	Returns a string formatted as a number.
FormatPercent	Returns a string formatted as a percentage.
InStr	Returns the position of the first occurrence of one string within another.
InStrB	As above, but provided for use with byte data contained in a string. Returns the byte position instead of the character position.
InstrRev	As InStr, but starts from the end of the string.
Join	Returns a string created by joining the strings contained in an array.
LCase	Returns a string that has been converted to lowercase.
Left	Returns a specified number of characters from the left end of a string.
LeftB	As above, but provided for use with byte data contained in a string. Uses that number of bytes instead of that number of characters.
Len	Returns the length of a string or the number of bytes needed for a variable.
LenB	As above, but is provided for use with byte data contained in a string. Returns the number of bytes in the string instead of characters.
LTrim	Returns a copy of a string without leading spaces.
Mid	Returns a specified number of characters from a string.
MidB	As above, but provided for use with byte data contained in a string. Uses that numbers of bytes instead of that number of characters.
Replace	Returns a string in which a specified substring has been replaced with another substring a specified number of times.
Right	Returns a specified number of characters from the right end of a string.
RightB	As above, but provided for use with byte data contained in a string. Uses that number of bytes instead of that number of characters.
RTrim	Returns a copy of a string without trailing spaces.
Space	Returns a string consisting of the specified number of spaces.
Split	Returns a one-dimensional array of a specified number of substrings.
StrComp	Returns a value indicating the result of a string comparison.

Function	Description
`String`	Returns a string of the length specified made up of a repeating character.
`StrReverse`	Returns a string in which the character order of a string is reversed.
`Trim`	Returns a copy of a string without leading or trailing spaces.
`UCase`	Returns a string that has been converted to uppercase.

Variable Testing Functions

These functions are used to determine the type of information stored in a variable:

Function	Description
`IsArray`	Returns a **Boolean** value indicating whether a variable is an array.
`IsDate`	Returns a **Boolean** value indicating whether an expression can be converted to a date.
`IsEmpty`	Returns a **Boolean** value indicating whether a variable has been initialized.
`IsNull`	Returns a **Boolean** value indicating whether an expression contains no valid data
`IsNumeric`	Returns a **Boolean** value indicating whether an expression can be evaluated as a number.
`IsObject`	Returns a **Boolean** value indicating whether an expression references a valid ActiveX or OLE Automation object.
`VarType`	Returns a number indicating the subtype of a variable.

Variable Declarations

Dim–declares a variable.

Error Handling

On Error Resume Next–indicates that if an error occurs, control should continue at the next statement.
Err–this is the error object that provides information about run-time errors.

Error handling is very limited in VBScript and the **Err** object must be tested explicitly to determine if an error has occurred.

Input/Output

This consists of **Msgbox** for output and **InputBox** for input:

MsgBox

This displays a message, and can return a value indicating which button was clicked.

```
MsgBox "Hello There",20,"Hello Message","c:\windows\MyHelp.hlp",123
```

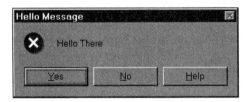

The parameters are:
"Hello There"—this contains the text of the message and is obligatory.
20— this determines which icon and buttons appear on the message box.
"Hello Message"—this contains the text that will appear as the title of the message box.
"c:\windows\MyHelp.hlp"—this adds a Help button to the message box and determines the help file that is opened if the button is clicked.
123—this is a reference to the particular help topic that will be displayed if the Help button is clicked.

The value of the icon and buttons parameter is determined using the following tables:

Constant	Value	Buttons
vbOKOnly	0	OK
vbOKCancel	1	OK Cancel
vbAbortRetryIngnore	2	Abort Retry Ignore
vbYesNoCancel	3	Yes No Cancel
vbYesNo	4	Yes No
vbRetryCancel	5	Retry Cancel

Constant	Value	Buttons
vbDefaultButton1	0	The first button from the left is the default.
vbDefaultButton2	256	The second button from the left is the default.
vbDefaultButton3	512	The third button from the left is the default.
vbDefaultButton4	768	The fourth button from the left is the default.

Constant	Value	Description	Icon
vbCritical	16	Critical Message	
vbQuestion	32	Questioning Message	
vbExclamation	48	Warning Message	
vbInformation	64	Informational Message	

Constant	Value	Description
vbApplicationModal	0	Just the application stops until user clicks a button.
vbSystemModal	4096	Whole system stops until user clicks a button.

To specify which buttons and icon are displayed you simply add the relevant values. So, in our example we add together 4 + 256 + 16 + 4096 to display the Yes and No buttons, with No as the default, with the Critical icon, and the user being unable to use any application, besides this one, when the message box is displayed.

You can determine which button the user clicked by assigning the return code of the MsgBox function to a variable:

```
intButtonClicked = MsgBox ("Hello There",35,"Hello Message")
```

Notice that brackets enclose the MsgBox parameters when used in this format. The following table determines the value assigned to the variable intButtonClicked:

Constant	Value	Button Clicked
vbOK	1	OK
vbCancel	2	Cancel

Table Continued on Following Page

Constant	Value	Button Clicked
vbAbort	3	Abort
vbRetry	4	Retry
vbIgnore	5	Ignore
vbYes	6	Yes
vbNo	7	No

InputBox

This accepts text entry from the user and returns it as a string.

```
strTextEntered = InputBox ("Please enter your name","Login","John Smith",500,500)
```

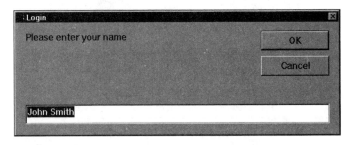

"Please enter your name"—this is the prompt displayed in the input box.
"Login"— this is the text displayed as the title of the input box.
"John Smith"— this is the default value displayed in the input box.
500—specifies the x position of the input box.
500—specifies the y position of the input box.

As with the **MsgBox** function, you can also specify a help file and topic to add a Help button to the input box.

Procedures

Call—optional method of calling a subroutine.
Function—used to declare a function.
Sub—used to declare a subroutine.

Other Keywords

Rem—old style method of adding comments to code.
Option Explicit—forces you to declare a variable before it can be used.

Visual Basic Run-time Error Codes

The following error codes also apply to VBA code and many will not be appropriate to an application built completely around VBScript. However, if you have built your own components then these error codes may well be brought up when such components are used.

Code	Description	Code	Description
3	Return without GoSub	62	Input past end of file
5	Invalid procedure call	63	Bad record number
6	Overflow	67	Too many files
7	Out of memory	68	Device unavailable
9	Subscript out of range	70	Permission denied
10	This array is fixed or temporarily locked	71	Disk not ready
		74	Can't rename with different drive
11	Division by zero	75	Path/File access error
13	Type mismatch	76	Path not found
14	Out of string space	322	Can't create necessary temporary file
16	Expression too complex		
17	Can't perform requested operation	325	Invalid format in resource file
18	User interrupt occurred	380	Invalid property value
20	Resume without error	423	Property or method not found
28	Out of stack space	424	Object required
35	Sub or Function not defined	429	OLE Automation server can't create object
47	Too many DLL application clients		
48	Error in loading DLL	430	Class doesn't support OLE Automation
49	Bad DLL calling convention	432	File name or class name not found during OLE Automation operation
51	Internal error		
52	Bad file name or number	438	Object doesn't support this property or method
53	File not found		
54	Bad file mode	440	OLE Automation error
55	File already open	442	Connection to type library or object library for remote process has been lost. Press OK for dialog to remove reference.
57	Device I/O error		
58	File already exists		
59	Bad record length	443	OLE Automation object does not have a default value
61	Disk full		
		445	Object doesn't support this action

Table Continued on Following Page

553

Code	Description	Code	Description
446	Object doesn't support named arguments	1015	Expected 'Function'
447	Object doesn't support current locale setting	1016	Expected 'Sub'
448	Named argument not found	1017	Expected 'Then'
449	Argument not optional	1018	Expected 'Wend'
450	Wrong number of arguments or invalid property assignment	1019	Expected 'Loop'
		1020	Expected 'Next'
451	Object not a collection	1021	Expected 'Case'
452	Invalid ordinal	1022	Expected 'Select'
453	Specified DLL function not found	1023	Expected expression
454	Code resource not found	1024	Expected statement
455	Code resource lock error	1025	Expected end of statement
457	This key is already associated with an element of this collection	1026	Expected integer constant
		1027	Expected 'While' or 'Until'
458	Variable uses an OLE Automation type not supported in Visual Basic	1028	Expected 'While', 'Until' or end of statement
481	Invalid picture	1029	Too many locals or arguments
500	Variable is undefined	1030	Identifier too long
501	Cannot assign to variable	1031	Invalid number
1001	Out of memory	1032	Invalid character
1002	Syntax error	1033	Unterminated string constant
1003	Expected ':'	1034	Unterminated comment
1004	Expected ';'	1035	Nested comment
1005	Expected '('	1036	'Me' cannot be used outside of a procedure
1006	Expected ')'	1037	Invalid use of 'Me' keyword
1007	Expected ']'	1038	'loop' without 'do'
1008	Expected '{'	1039	Invalid 'exit' statement
1009	Expected '}'	1040	Invalid 'for' loop control variable
1010	Expected identifier	1041	Variable redefinition
1011	Expected '='	1042	Must be first statement on the line
1012	Expected 'If'	1043	Cannot assign to non-ByVal argument
1013	Expected 'To'		
1014	Expected 'End'		

Active Server Pages

Variable Naming Conventions

In VBScript, the only variable type available is the **Variant**. However, in most cases, you will want to store a specific data type in a variable. To help to avoid errors, make your code easier to read, and easier to debug when things aren't working correctly, it's good practice to use a naming convention for all your variables. There are other conventions around, but we use the following:

Variables

Data Type	Prefix	Example	VarType()
Boolean	bln	blnAccepted	11
Byte	byt	bytPixelValue	17
Date or Time	dtm or dat	dtmFirstTime	7
Double	dbl	dblTotalDistance	5
Error	err	errOverflow	10
Integer	int	intCount	2
Long	lng	lngFreeSpace	3
Object	obj	objListBox	9 or 13
Single	sng	sngLength	4
String	str	strAddress	8

The **VarType** function can be used to discover how a value is stored in a **Variant**. The results are shown in the table above for each of the variable types.

Controls

Control Type	Prefix	Example
Check Box	chk	chkFullPacksOnly
Combo List Box	cbo	cboThickness
Command Button	cmd or btn	cmdCalculate
Horizontal Scroll Bar	hsb	hsbWidth

Table Continued on Following Page

Control Type	Prefix	Example
Image Control	img	imgDisplayPicture
Label	lbl	lblDescription
List Box	lst	lstBrickTypes
Pop-up Menu	mnu	mnuSelection
Radio/Option Button	opt	optIncludeCement
Spin Button	spn	spnVolume
Tab Strip	tab	tabOptionPages
Text Box	txt	txtCustomer
Vertical Scroll Bar	vsb	vsbHeight

Active Server Pages

Active Server Pages Object Model

Request Object

ClientCertificate collection   Client certificate values sent from the browser.
Cookies collection   Values of cookies sent from the browser.
Form collection   Values of form elements sent from the browser.
QueryString collection   Values of variables in the HTTP query string.
ServerVariables collection   Values of the HTTP and environment variables.

Response Object

Cookies collection   Values of all the cookies to send to the browser.
Buffer property   Indicates whether to buffer the page until complete.
ContentType property   HTTP content type (i.e. **"Text/HTML"**) for the response.
Expires property   Length of time before a page cached on a browser expires.
ExpiresAbsolute property   Date and time when a page cached on a browser expires.
Status property   Value of the HTTP status line returned by the server.
AddHeader method   Adds or changes a value in the HTML header.
AppendToLog method   Adds text to the web server log entry for this request.
BinaryWrite method   Sends text to the browser without character-set conversion.
Clear method   Erases any buffered HTML output.
End method   Stops processing the page and returns the current result.
Flush method   Sends buffered output immediately.
Redirect method   Instructs the browser to connect to a different URL.
Write method   Writes a variable to the current page as a string.

Server Object

ScriptTimeout property   Amount of time a script can run before an error occurs.
CreateObject method   Creates an instance of an object or server component.
HTMLEncode method   Applies HTML encoding to the specified string.
MapPath method   Converts a virtual path into a physical path.
URLEncode method   Applies URL encoding including escape chars to a string.

Session Object

SessionID property	Returns the session identification for this user.
Timeout property	The timeout period (mins) for sessions in this application.
Abandon method	Destroys a **Session** object and releases its resources.
OnStart event	Occurs when a user first requests a page in the application.
OnEnd event	Occurs when the session ends, i.e. when no requests have been received for the timeout period (default 20 mins).

Application Object

Lock method	Prevents other clients from modifying application properties.
Unlock method	Allows other clients to modify application properties.
OnStart event	Occurs when a page in the application is first referenced.
OnEnd event	Occurs when the application ends, i.e. when the web server is stopped.

Active Server Pages

Scripting Object and Server Component Methods and Properties

The Scripting.Dictionary Object

Method / Property	Description
Add method	Adds the key/item pair to the **Dictionary**.
Exists method	**True** if the specified key exists, **False** if it not.
Items method	Returns an array containing all the items in a **Dictionary** object.
Keys method	Returns an array containing all the keys in a **Dictionary** object.
Remove method	Removes a single key/item pair.
RemoveAll method	Removes all the key/item pairs.
CompareMode property	Sets or returns the string comparison mode for the keys.
Count property	Read-only. Returns the number of key/item pairs in the **Dictionary**.
Item property	Sets or returns the value of the item for the specified key.
Key property	Sets or returns the value of a key.

The Scripting.FileSystemObject Object

Method	Description
CreateTextFile method	Creates a file and returns a **TextStream** object to access the file.
OpenTextFile method	Opens a file and returns a **TextStream** object to access the file.

The Scripting.TextStream Object

Method / Property	Description
Close method	Closes an open file.
Read method	Reads characters from a file.
ReadAll method	Reads an entire file as a single string.

Table Continued on Following Page

Method / Property	Description
`ReadLine` method	Reads a line from a file as a string.
`Skip` method	Skips and discards characters when reading a file.
`SkipLine` method	Skips and discards the next line when reading a file.
`Write` method	Writes a string to a file.
`WriteLine` method	Writes a string (optional) and a newline character to a file.
`WriteBlankLines` method	Writes newline characters to a file.
`AtEndOfLine` property	**True** if the file pointer is at the end of a line in a file.
`AtEndOfStream` property	**True** if the file pointer is at the end of a file.
`Column` property	Returns the column number of the current character in a file.
`Line` property	Returns the current line number in a file. Both start at **1**.

The Err Object

Method / Property	Description
`Clear` method	Clears all current settings of the **Err** object.
`Raise` method	Generates a run-time error.
`Description` property	Sets or returns a string describing an error.
`Number` property	(Default) Sets or returns a numeric value specifying an error.
`Source` property	Sets or returns the name of the object that generated the error.

The Content Linking Component

Method	Description
`GetListCount` method	Number of items in the file *list*.
`GetListIndex` method	Index of the current page in the file *list*.
`GetNextURL` method	URL of the next page in the file *list*.
`GetNextDescription` method	Description of the next page in file *list*.
`GetPreviousURL` method	URL of the previous page in the file *list*.
`GetPreviousDescription` method	Description of previous page in file *list*.
`GetNthURL` method	URL of the *n*th page in the file *list*.
`GetNthDescription` method	Description of the *n*th page in the file *list*.

The Ad Rotator Component

Method / Property	Description
GetAdvertisement method	Gets details of the next advertisement and formats it as HTML.
Border property	Size of the border around the advertisement.
Clickable property	Defines whether the advertisement is a hyperlink.
TargetFrame property	Name of the frame in which to display the advertisement.

The User Property Database Component

Method/Property	Description
Item method	(Default) Reads or writes user properties to the database.
Append method	Adds items to multivalue user properties.
LoadFromString method	Writes properties direct from the browser's query string.
Remove method	Removes items from multivalue properties in the database.
Defaults property	Sets default user properties in the database.
ID property	Sets or returns the user's **ID** in the database.
ReadOnly property	Sets the database to read-only mode for the page.
PropertyString property	Returns all the user properties as a complete query string.
Count property	The number of items in a multivalue user property.

The Voting Component

Method	Description
Open method	Opens a connection to the vote database.
SetBallotName method	Specifies the ballot on which the vote should be counted.
Submit method	Processes the user's vote.
GetVote method	Returns the results of the votes as a table.
GetVoteCount method	Returns a count of the votes as a table.

The SendMail Component

Method	Description
`SendMail` method	Sends a message using an SMTP mail server.

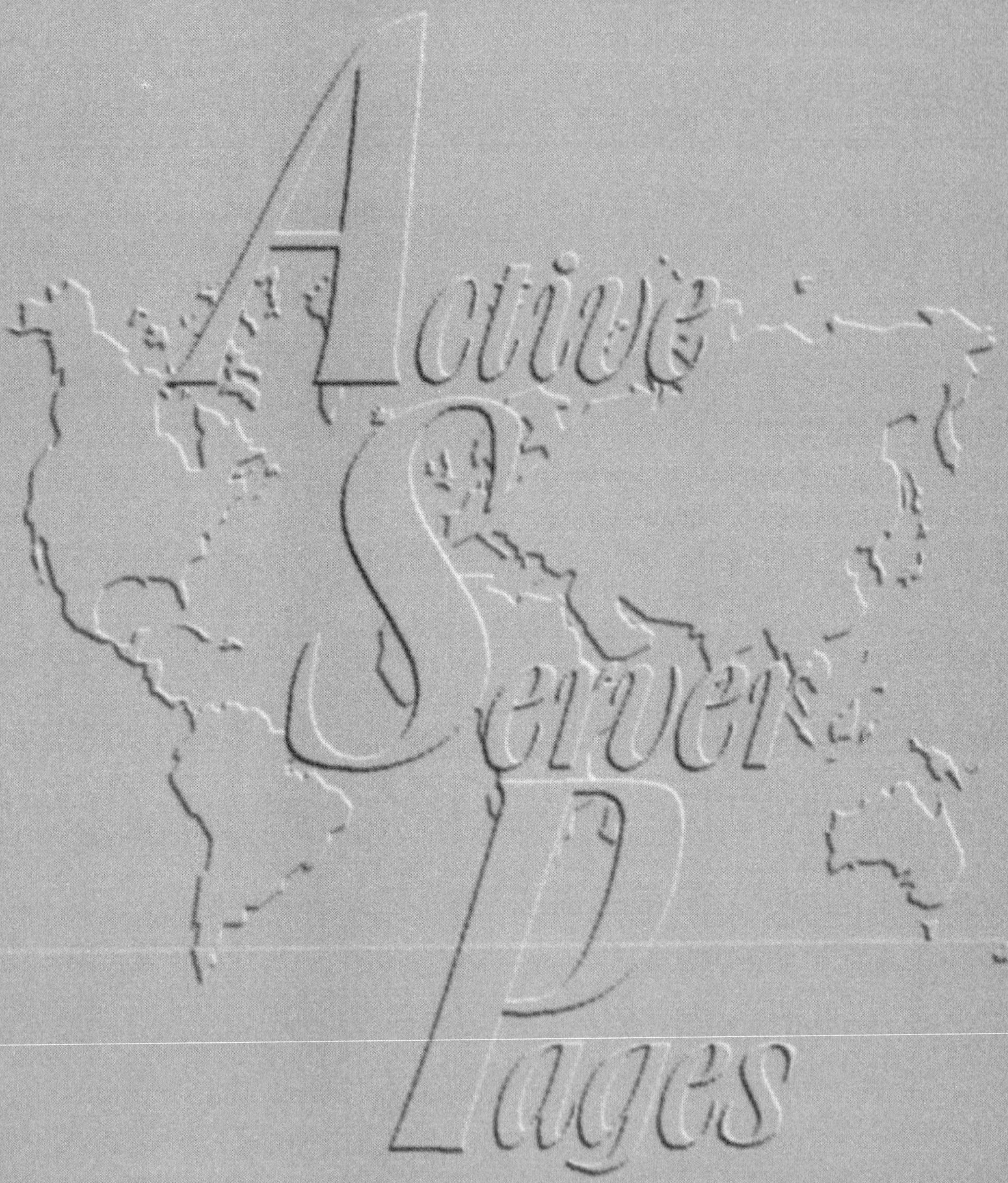
Active
Server
Pages

Active Database Component Methods and Properties

The Connection Object

Method	Description
Open	Opens a new connection to a data source.
Close	Closes an existing open connection.
Execute	Executes a query, SQL statement, or stored procedure.
BeginTrans	Begins a new transaction.
CommitTrans	Saves any changes made and ends the transaction. May also start a new transaction.
RollbackTrans	Cancels any changes made and ends the transaction. May also start a new transaction.

Property	Description
Attributes	Controls whether to begin a new transaction when an existing one ends.
CommandTimeout	Number of seconds to wait when executing a command before terminating the attempt and returning an error.
ConnectionString	The information used to create a connection to a data source.
ConnectionTimeout	Number of seconds to wait when creating a connection before terminating the attempt and returning an error.
DefaultDatabase	Sets or returns the default database to use for this connection.
IsolationLevel	Sets or returns the level of isolation within transactions.
Mode	Sets or returns the provider's access permissions.
Provider	Sets or returns the name of the provider.
Version	Returns the ADO version number.

The Command Object

Method	Description
CreateParameter	Creates a new **Parameter** object in the **Parameters** collection.
Execute	Executes the SQL statement or stored procedure specified in the **CommandText** property.

Property	Description
ActiveConnection	The **Connection** object to be used with this **Command** object.
CommandText	The text of a command to be executed.
CommandTimeout	Number of seconds to wait when executing a command before terminating the attempt and returning an error.
CommandType	Type of query set in the **CommandText** property.
Prepared	Whether to create a prepared statement before execution.

The Parameters Collection

Method	Description
Append	Adds a parameter to the collection.
Delete	Deletes a parameter from the collection.
Refresh	Updates the collection to reflect changes to the parameters.

Property	Description
Count	Returns the number of parameters in the collection.
Item	Used to retrieve the contents of a parameter from the collection.

The Parameter Object

Property	Description
Attributes	The type of data that the parameter accepts.

Property	Description
Direction	Whether the parameter is for input, output or both, or if it is the return value from a stored procedure.
Name	The name of the parameter.
NumericScale	The number of decimal places in a numeric parameter.
Precision	The number of digits in a numeric parameter.
Size	The maximum size, in bytes, of the parameter value.
Type	The data type of the parameter.
Value	The value assigned to the parameter.

The Recordset Object

Method	Description
AddNew	Creates a new record in an updatable recordset.
CancelBatch	Cancels a pending batch update.
CancelUpdate	Cancels any changes made to the current or a new record.
Clone	Creates a duplicate copy of the recordset.
Close	Closes an open recordset and any dependent objects.
Delete	Deletes the current record in an open recordset.
GetRows	Retrieves multiple records into an array.
Move	Moves the position of the current record.
MoveFirst, MoveLast, MoveNext, MovePrevious	Moves to the first, last, next or previous record in the recordset, and makes that the current record.
NextRecordset	Returns the next recordset by advancing through a set of commands.
Open	Opens a cursor on a recordset.
Requery	Updates the data by re-executing the original query.
Resync	Refreshes the data from the underlying database.
Supports	Determines whether the recordset supports certain functions.
Update	Saves any changes made to the current record.
UpdateBatch	Writes all pending batch updates to disk.

Table Continued on Following Page

Property	Description
AbsolutePage	The absolute 'page' on which the current record is located, or specifies the 'page' to move to.
AbsolutePosition	The ordinal position of the current record.
ActiveConnection	The **Connection** object that the recordset currently belongs to.
BOF	True if the current record position is before the first record.
Bookmark	Returns a bookmark that uniquely identifies the current record, or sets the current record to the record identified by a valid bookmark.
CacheSize	The number of records that are cached locally in memory.
CursorType	The type of cursor used in the recordset.
EditMode	The editing status of the current record.
EOF	True if the current record position is after the last record.
Filter	Indicates whether a filter is in use.
LockType	The type of locks placed on records during editing.
MaxRecords	The maximum number of records to return from a query.
PageCount	The number of 'pages' of data that the recordset contains.
PageSize	The number of records constituting one 'page'.
RecordCount	The number of records currently in the recordset.
Source	The source for the data in the recordset, i.e. **Command** object, SQL statement, table name, or stored procedure.
Status	Status of the current record with respect to batch updates or other bulk operations.

The Fields Collection

Method	Description
Refresh	Updates the collection to reflect changes to the field values.

Property	Description
Count	Returns the number of fields in the collection.
Item	Used to retrieve the contents of the fields in the collection.

The Field Object

Property	Description
ActualSize	The actual length of the field's current value.
Attributes	The kinds of data that the field can hold.
DefinedSize	The size or length of the field as defined in the data source.
Name	The name of the field.
NumericScale	The number of decimal places in a numeric field.
OriginalValue	The value of the field, before any unsaved changes were made.
Precision	The number of digits in a numeric field.
Type	The data type of the field.
UnderlyingValue	The field's current value within the database.
Value	The value currently assigned to the field, even if unsaved.

The Properties Collection

Method	Description
Refresh	Updates the collection to reflect changes to the property values.

Property	Description
Count	Returns the number of properties in the collection.
Item	Used to retrieve the values of the properties in the collection.

The Property Object

Property	Description
Attributes	Indicates when and how the value of the property can be set.
Name	The name of the property.
Type	The data type of the property.
Value	The value of the property.

The Errors Collection

Method	Description
Clear	Removes all of the errors in the collection.

Property	Description
Count	Returns the number of errors objects in the collection.
Item	Used to retrieve the contents of the error objects in the collection.

The Error Object

Property	Description
Description	A description of the error.
HelpContextID	Context ID, as a **Long** value, for the matching help file topic.
HelpFile	The path to the help file for this topic.
NativeError	The provider-specific error code number.
Number	The ADO error code number.
Source	Name of the object or application that generated the error.
SQLState	The SQL execution state for this error.

Active Data Object Constants

To use the constant names in your code, instead of specifying the actual values, you need to include a constants definition file in the page using a Server-side Include (SSI). These files are supplied with ASP, and installed by default in the **ASPSamp/Samples** directory on the server. For VBScript you use **Adovbs.inc**. For JScript, use **Adojavas.inc**. For example, usingVBScript:

```
<!-- #include virtual="/Aspsamp/Samples/Adovbs.inc" -->
```

You can copy the file into the application directory instead, and include it using:

```
<!-- #include file="Adovbs.inc" -->
```

See Chapter 1 for more information about using the **#include** SSI statement.

CursorTypeEnum Values

Constant	Value	Description
adOpenForwardOnly	0	**Forward-only cursor** (*Default*). Identical to a static cursor except that you can only scroll forward through records. This improves performance in situations when you only need to make a single pass through a recordset. Supports **adAddNew, adDelete, adUpdate, adUpdateBatch**
adOpenKeyset	1	**Keyset cursor**. Like a dynamic cursor, except that you can't see records that other users add, although records that other users delete are inaccessible from your recordset. Data changes by other users are still visible. Supports **adAddNew, adDelete, adMovePrevious, adUpdate, adUpdateBatch**
adOpenDynamic	2	**Dynamic cursor**. Additions, changes, and deletions by other users are visible, and all types of movement through the recordset are allowed, except for bookmarks if the provider doesn't support them. Supports **adAddNew, adBookmark, adDelete, adHoldRecords, adMovePrevious, adResync, adUpdate, adUpdateBatch**
adOpenStatic	3	**Static cursor**. A static copy of a set of records that you can use to find data or generate reports. Additions, changes, or deletions by other users are not visible. Supports **adAddNew, adBookmark, adDelete, adHoldRecords, adMovePrevious, adResync, adUpdate, adUpdateBatch**

CursorOptionEnum Values

Constant	Value	Description
adHoldRecords	&H00000100 (256)	You can retrieve more records or change the next retrieve position without committing all pending changes and releasing all currently held records.
adMovePrevious	&H00000200 (512)	You can use the **MovePrevious** or **Move** methods to move the current record position backward without requiring bookmarks.
adBookmark	&H00002000 (8192)	You can use the **Bookmark** property to access specific records.
adApproxPosition	&H00004000 (16384)	You can read and set the **AbsolutePosition** and **AbsolutePage** properties.

Table Continued on Following Page

Constant	Value	Description
adUpdateBatch	&H00010000 (65536)	You can use batch updating to transmit changes to the provider in groups.
adResync	&H00020000 (131072)	You can update the cursor with the data visible in the underlying database.
adAddNew	&H01000400 (16778240)	You can use the **AddNew** method to add new records.
adDelete	&H01000800 (16779264)	You can use the **Delete** method to delete records.
adUpdate	&H01008000 (16809984)	You can use the **Update** method to modify existing data.

LockTypeEnum Values

Constant	Value	Description
adLockReadOnly	1	**Read-only**. You cannot alter the data.
adLockPessimistic	2	**Pessimistic locking**, record by record. The provider does what is necessary to ensure successful editing of the records, usually by locking records at the data source immediately upon editing.
adLockOptimistic	3	**Optimistic locking**, record by record. The provider uses optimistic locking, locking records only when you call the **Update** method.
adLockBatchOptimistic	4	**Optimistic batch updates**. Required for batch update mode as opposed to immediate update mode.

DataTypeEnum Values

Constant	Value	Description
adEmpty	0	No value was specified.
adSmallInt	2	A 2-byte signed integer.
adInteger	3	A 4-byte signed integer.
adSingle	4	A single-precision floating point value.
adDouble	5	A double-precision floating point value.
adCurrency	6	A currency value (8-byte signed integer scaled by 10,000).

Constant	Value	Description
adDate	7	A Date value.
adBSTR	8	A null-terminated character string (Unicode).
adIDispatch	9	A pointer to an IDispatch interface on an OLE object.
adError	10	A 32-bit error code.
adBoolean	11	A Boolean value.
adVariant	12	An OLE Automation Variant.
adIUnknown	13	A pointer to an IUnknown interface on an OLE object.
adDecimal	14	An exact numeric value with a fixed precision and scale.
adTinyInt	16	A 1-byte signed integer.
adUnsignedTinyInt	17	A 1-byte unsigned integer.
adUnsignedSmallInt	18	A 2-byte unsigned integer.
adUnsignedInt	19	A 4-byte unsigned integer.
adBigInt	20	An 8-byte signed integer.
adUnsignedBigInt	21	An 8-byte unsigned integer.
adGUID	72	A globally unique identifier (GUID).
adBinary	128	A binary value.
adChar	129	A String value.
adWChar	130	A null-terminated Unicode character string.
adNumeric	131	An exact numeric value with a fixed precision and scale.
adUserDefined	132	A user-defined variable.
adDBDate	133	A date value (*yyyymmdd*).
adDBTime	134	A time value (*hhmmss*).
adDBTimeStamp	135	A date-time stamp (*yyyymmddhhmmss* plus a fraction in billionths).
adVarChar	200	A String value. (Parameter object only).
adLongVarChar	201	A long String value. (Parameter object only).
adVarWChar	202	A null-terminated Unicode character string. (Parameter object only).
adLongVarWChar	203	A long null-terminated string value. (Parameter object only).
adVarBinary	204	A binary value. (Parameter object only).
adLongVarBinary	205	A long binary value. (Parameter object only).

ConnectPromptEnum Values

Constant	Value	Description
adPromptAlways	1	...
adPromptComplete	2	These values are set by the **Provider**.
adPromptCompleteRequired	3	If it supports the **Prompt** property.
adPromptNever	4	...

ConnectModeEnum Values

Constant	Value	Description
adModeUnknown	0	The permissions have not yet been set or cannot be determined.
adModeRead	1	Read-only permissions.
adModeWrite	2	Write-only permissions.
adModeReadWrite	3	Read/write permissions.
adModeShareDenyRead	4	Prevents others from opening connection with read permissions.
adModeShareDenyWrite	8	Prevents others from opening connection with write permissions.
adModeShareExclusive	&HC (12)	Prevents others from opening connection with read/write permissions.
adModeShareDenyNone	&H10 (16)	Prevents others from opening connection with any permissions.

IsolationLevelEnum Values

Constant	Value	Description
adXactChaos	&H00000010 (16)	Indicates that you cannot overwrite pending changes from more highly isolated transactions.
adXactBrowse	&H00000100 (256)	Indicates that from one transaction you can view uncommitted changes in other transactions.
adXactReadUncommitted	&H00000100 (256)	Same as **adXactBrowse**.

Constant	Value	Description
adXactCursorStability	&H00001000 (4096)	Indicates that from one transaction you can view changes in other transactions only after they've been committed. (*Default*)
adXactReadCommitted	&H00001000 (4096)	Same as **adXactCursorStability**.
adXactRepeatableRead	&H00010000 (65536)	Indicates that from one transaction you cannot see changes made in other transactions, but that requerying can bring new recordset.
adXactIsolated	&H00100000 (1048576)	Indicates that transactions are conducted in isolation of other transactions.
adXactSerializable	&H00100000 (1048576)	Same as **adXactIsolated**.
adXactUnspecified	&HFFFFFFFF (-1)	If the provider is using a different **IslationLevel** than specified, but which one cannot be determined, the property returns this value.

XactAttributeEnum Values

Constant	Value	Description
adXactPollAsync	2	Performs asynchronous commits. You'll not be able to confirm the outcome of transactions you commit.
adXactPollSyncPhaseOne	4	Calls commits after phase one of the two-phase commit protocol.
adXactAbortRetaining	&H00040000 (262144)	Performs retaining aborts. Calling **RollBack** automatically starts a new transaction. Not all providers will support this.
adXactAbortAsync	&H00080000 (524288)	Performs asynchronous aborts. You will not be able to confirm the outcome of transactions you rollback.
adXactCommitRetaining	&H00020000 (131072)	Performs retaining commits. Calling **CommitTrans** automatically starts a new transaction. Not all providers will support this.

FieldAttributeEnum Values

Constant	Value	Description
adFldMayDefer	&H00000002 (2)	Indicates that the field is deferred, that is, the field values are not retrieved from the data source with the whole record, but only when you explicitly access them.
adFldUpdatable	&H00000004 (4)	Indicates that you can write to the field.
adFldUnknownUpdatable	&H00000008 (8)	Indicates that the provider cannot determine if you can write to the field.
adFldFixed	&H00000010 (16)	Indicates that the field contains fixed-length data.
adFldIsNullable	&H00000020 (32)	Indicates that the field accepts **Null** values.
adFldMayBeNull	&H00000040 (64)	Indicates that you can read **Null** values from the field.
adFldLong	&H00000080 (128)	Indicates that the field is a long binary field. Also indicates that you can use the **AppendChunk** and **GetChunk** methods.
adFldRowID	&H00000100 (256)	Indicates that the field contains some kind of record ID (record number, unique identifier, etc.).
adFldRowVersion	&H00000200 (512)	Indicates that the field contains some kind of time or date stamp used to track updates.
adFldCacheDeferred	&H00001000 (4096)	Indicates that the provider caches field values and that subsequent reads are done from the cache.

EditModeEnum Values

Constant	Value	Description
adEditNone	&H0000 (0)	No editing operation is in progress.
adEditInProgress	&H0001 (1)	Data in the current record has been modified but not yet saved.
adEditAdd	&H0002 (2)	The **AddNew** method has been invoked, and the current record in the copy buffer is a new record that hasn't been saved in the database.

RecordStatusEnum Values

Constant	Value	Description
adRecOK	&H0000000 (0)	The record was successfully updated.
adRecNew	&H0000001 (1)	The record is new.
adRecModified	&H0000002 (2)	The record was modified.
adRecDeleted	&H0000004 (4)	The record was deleted.
adRecUnmodified	&H0000008 (8)	The record was unmodified.
adRecInvalid	&H0000010 (16)	The record was not saved because its bookmark is invalid.
adRecMultipleChanges	&H0000040 (64)	The record was not saved because it would have affected multiple records.
adRecPendingChanges	&H0000080 (128)	The record was not saved because it refers to a pending insert.
adRecCanceled	&H0000100 (256)	The record was not saved because the operation was canceled.
adRecCantRelease	&H0000400 (1024)	The new record was not saved because of existing record locks.
adRecConcurrencyViolation	&H0000800 (2048)	The record was not saved because optimistic concurrency was in use.
adRecIntegrityViolation	&H0001000 (4096)	The record was not saved because the user violated integrity constraints.
adRecMaxChangesExceeded	&H0002000 (8192)	The record was not saved because there were too many pending changes.
adRecObjectOpen	&H0004000 (16384)	The record was not saved because of a conflict with an open storage object.
adRecOutOfMemory	&H0008000 (32768)	The record was not saved because the computer has run out of memory.
adRecPermissionDenied	&H0010000 (65536)	The record was not saved because the user has insufficient permissions.
adRecSchemaViolation	&H0020000 (131072)	The record was not saved because it violates the structure of the underlying database.
adRecDBDeleted	&H0040000 (262144)	The record has already been deleted from the data source.

GetRowsOptionEnum Values

Constant	Value	Description
adGetRowsRest	-1	In GetRows call, get all remaining records

PositionEnum Values

Constant	Value	Description
adPosUnknown	-1	No current record
adPosBOF	-2	Before the first record
adPosEOF	-3	After the last record

AffectEnum Values

Constant	Value	Description
adAffectCurrent	1	Cancel pending transactions only for the current record.
adAffectGroup	2	Cancel pending transactions for records that satisfy the current Filter property setting.
adAffectAll	3	Cancel pending updates for all the records in the Recordset object, including any hidden by the current Filter property setting.

FilterGroupEnum Values

Constant	Value	Description
adFilterNone	0	Removes the current filter and restores all records to view.
adFilterPendingRecords	1	Allows you to view only records that have changed but not yet sent to the server. Only applicable for batch update mode.
adFilterAffectedRecords	2	Allows you to view only records affected by the last Delete, Resync, UpdateBatch, or CancelBatch call.
adFilterFetchedRecords	3	Allows you to view records in the current cache, that is, the results of the last fetch from the database.

PropertyAttributesEnum Values

Constant	Value	Description
adPropNotSupported	&H0000 (0)	Indicates that the provider does not support the property.
adPropRequired	&H0001 (1)	Indicates that the user must specify a value for this property before the data source is initialized.
adPropOptional	&H0002 (2)	Indicates that the user does not need to specify a value for this property before the data source is initialized.
adPropRead	&H0200 (512)	Indicates that the user can read the property.
adPropWrite	&H0400 (1024)	Indicates that the user can set the property.

ErrorValueEnum Values

Constant	Value	Description
adErrInvalidArgument	&HBB9	Invalid argument.
adErrNoCurrentRecord	&HBCD	No current record.
adErrIllegalOperation	&HC93	Invalid operation.
adErrInTransaction	&HCAE	Operation not supported in transactions.
adErrFeatureNotAvailable	&HCB3	Operation is not supported for this type of object.
adErrItemNotFound	&HCC1	Item not found in this collection.
adErrObjectNotSet	&HD5C	Object is invalid or not set.
adErrDataConversion	&HD5D	Data type conversion error.
adErrObjectClosed	&HE78	Invalid operation on closed object.
adErrObjectOpen	&HE79	Invalid operation on opened object.
adErrProviderNotFound	&HE7A	Provider not found.
adErrBoundToCommand	&HE7B	Invalid operation. The recordset source property is currently set to a command object.
adErrInvalidConnection	&HE7D	Invalid operation on object with a closed connection reference.
adErrInvalidParamInfo	&HE7C	Invalid parameter definition.

ParameterAttributesEnum Values

Constant	Value	Description
adParamSigned	&H0010 (16)	Indicates that the parameter accepts signed values (*Default*)
adParamNullable	&H0040 (64)	Indicates that the parameter accepts **Null** values.
adParamLong	&H0080 (128)	Indicates that the parameter accepts long binary data.

ParameterDirectionEnum Values

Constant	Value	Description
adParamUnknown	&H0000 (0)	Unknown Type
adParamInput	&H0001 (1)	Input parameter (*Default*)
adParamOutput	&H0002 (2)	Output parameter.
adParamInputOutput	&H0003 (3)	Input and output parameter.
adParamReturnValue	&H0004 (4)	Return value.

CommandTypeEnum Values

Constant	Value	Description
adCmdUnknown	0	The type of command in the **CommandText** property is not known. (*Default*)
adCmdText	1	Evaluates the **CommandText** as a textual definition of a command.
adCmdTable	2	Evaluates **CommandText** as a table name.
adCmdStoredProc	4	Evaluates **CommandText** as a stored procedure.

Active Server Pages

The Browser Object Model, Properties, Methods and Events

The History Object

Property	Description
Length	Returns the length of the history list.

Methods	Description
Back *n*	Jumps back in the history *n* steps, like clicking back button *n* times.
Forward *n*	Jumps forward in the history *n* steps, like clicking forward *n* times.
Go *n*	Goes to the *n*th item in the history list.

The Navigator Object

Property	Description
AppCodeName	Returns the code name of the application.
AppName	Returns the actual name of the application.
AppVersion	Returns the version of the application.
UserAgent	Returns the user agent of the application (a combination of the above three properties).

The Location Object

Property	Description
Href	Gets or sets the compete URL for the location.
Protocol	Gets or sets the protocol portion of the URL.

Table Continued on Following Page

Property	Description
Host	Gets or sets the host and port portion of the URL (hostname:port).
Hostname	Gets or sets just the host portion of the URL.
Port	Gets or sets just the port portion of the URL.
Pathname	Gets or sets the path name in the URL.
Search	Gets or sets the search portion of the URL, if specified.
Hash	Gets or sets the hash portion of the URL, if specified.

The Window Object

Property	Description
Name	Returns the name of the current window.
Parent	Returns the window object of the window's parent.
Self	Returns the window object of the current window.
Top	Returns the window object of the topmost window.
Opener	Returns the window object of the window that opened the current window.
Location	Returns the location object for the current window.
DefaultStatus	Gets or sets the default text for the left portion of the status bar.
Status	Gets or sets the status text in the left portion of the status bar.
Frames	Returns the collection of frames for the current window.
History	Returns the history object of the current window.
Navigator	Returns the navigator object of the current window.
Document	Returns the document object of the current window.

Method	Description
Alert	Displays an alert message box.
Confirm	Displays a message box with OK and Cancel buttons, returns TRUE or FALSE.
Prompt	Displays a dialog box prompting the user for input.

Method	Description
Open	Creates a new window.
Close	Closes the window.
SetTimeout	Sets a timer to call a function after a specific number of milliseconds.
ClearTimeout	Clears the timer having a particular ID.
Navigate	Navigates the window to a new URL.

Events	Description.
onLoad	Fired when the contents of the window are loaded.
onUnload	Fired when the contents of the window are unloaded.

The Document Object

Property	Description
LinkColor	Gets or sets the color of the links in a document.
ALinkColor	Gets or sets the color of the active links in a document.
VLinkColor	Gets or sets the color of the visited links in a document.
BgColor	Gets or sets the background color of a document.
FgColor	Gets or sets the foreground color.
Anchors	Returns the collection of anchors in a document.
Links	Returns the collection of links for the current document.
Forms	Returns the collection of forms for the current document.
Location	Returns a read-only representation of the location object.
lastModified	Returns the last modified date of the current page.
Title	Returns a read-only representation of the document's title..
Cookie	Gets or sets the cookie for the current document.
Referrer	Gets the URL of the referring document.

Table Continued on Following Page

Method	Description
write	Places a string into the current document.
WriteLn	Places a string plus new-line character into the current document.
Open	Opens the document stream for output.
Close	Updates the screen showing the text written since last open call.
Clear	Closes the document output stream and clears the document.

The Form Object

Property	Description
Action	Gets or sets the address for the ACTION of the form.
Encoding	Gets or sets the encoding for the form.
Method	Gets or sets the METHOD for how the data should be sent to the server.
Target	Gets or sets the TARGET window name for displaying the form results.
Elements	Returns the collection of elements contained in the form.

Method	Description
Submit	Submits the form, just like clicking a SUBMIT button.

Event	Description
onSubmit	Fired when the form is submitted.

Link Object

Property	Description
Href	Returns the compete URL for the link.
Protocol	Returns the protocol portion of the URL.
Host	Returns both the host and port portion of the URL (hostname:port).
Hostname	Returns just the host portion of the URL.

Property	Description
Port	Returns just the port portion of the URL.
Pathname	Returns the path name in the URL.
Search	Returns the search portion of the URL, if specified.
Hash	Returns the hash portion of the URL, if specified.
Target	Returns the name of target window for the link, if specified.

Event	Description
mouseMove	Fires an event any time the pointer moves over a link.
OnMouseOver	Fires an event any time the pointer moves over a link.
OnClick	Fires an event any time you click on a link.

The Anchor Object

Property	Description
Name	Gets or sets the name of the anchor.

The Element Object

The element object can be a normal HTML control, an ActiveX control, or any other control object. The properties, methods, and events supported by the browser directly relate to the normal HTML controls:

HTML Controls

Element	Properties	Methods	Events
Button, Reset, Submit	form, name, value	click	onClick
Check box	form, name, value, checked, defaultChecked	click	onClick
Radio	form, name, value, checked	click, focus	onClick

Table Continued on Following Page

Element	Properties	Methods	Events
Password	form, name, value, defaultValue	focus, blur, select	
Text, Text Area	form, name, value, defaultValue	focus, blur, select	onFocus, onBlur, onChange, onSelect
Select	name, length, options, selectedIndex	focus, blur	onFocus, onBlur, onChange
Hidden	name, value	<none>	<none>

Property	Description
form	Gets the form object containing the element.
name	Gets or sets the name of the element.
value	Gets or sets the value of the element.
defaultValue	Gets or sets the default value of the element.
checked	Gets or sets the checked state of the check box or the radio button.
defaultChecked	Gets or sets the default checked property of the check box.
length	Gets the number of options in a select element.
selectedIndex	Gets the index of the selected option, or the first one selected when there is more than one object selected.
options	Gets the <options> tags for a select element, with these properties:

defaultSelected	The currently selected attribute.
index	The index of an option.
length	The number of options in the selected object.
name	The name attribute of the selected object.
selected	Used to programmatically select an option.
selectedIndex	The index of the selected option.
text	The text to be displayed.
value	The value attribute.

Method	Description
click	Clicks the element.
focus	Sets the focus to the element.

Method	Description
blur	Clears the focus from the element.
select	Selects the contents of the element.
removeItem	Removes the item at index from the element.
addItem	Adds the item to the element before the item at index.
clear	Clears the contents of the element.

Event	Description
onClick	Fired when the element is clicked.
onFocus	Fired when the element gets the focus.
onBlur	Fired when the element loses the focus.
onChange	Fired when the element has changed.
onSelect	Fired when the contents of the element are selected.

The InternetExplorer Object

Here's a few of the common properties and methods of the InternetExplorer object:

Property	Description
LocationName	Returns the short name of the current document.
LocationURL	Returns the URL of the current document.
MenuBar	Sets or returns the display state of the menu bar.
StatusBar	Sets or returns the display state of the window's status bar.
StatusText	Sets or returns the text content of the window's status bar.
ToolBar	Sets or returns the display state of the tool bar.
Visible	Displays or hides the application.
Left	Sets or returns the left position of the application window.
Top	Sets or returns the top position of the application window.
Width	Sets or returns the width of the application window.
Height	Sets or returns the height position of the application window.
FullScreen	Displays the application using the whole screen.

Table Continued on Following Page

Method	Description
GoBack	Equivalent to clicking the Back button.
GoForward	Equivalent to clicking the Forward button.
GoHome	Equivalent to clicking the Home button.
GoSearch	Equivalent to clicking the Search button.
Navigate	Sets the URL of the file to display..
Quit	Quits the application.
Refresh	Equivalent to clicking the Refresh button.
Stop	Equivalent to clicking the Stop button.

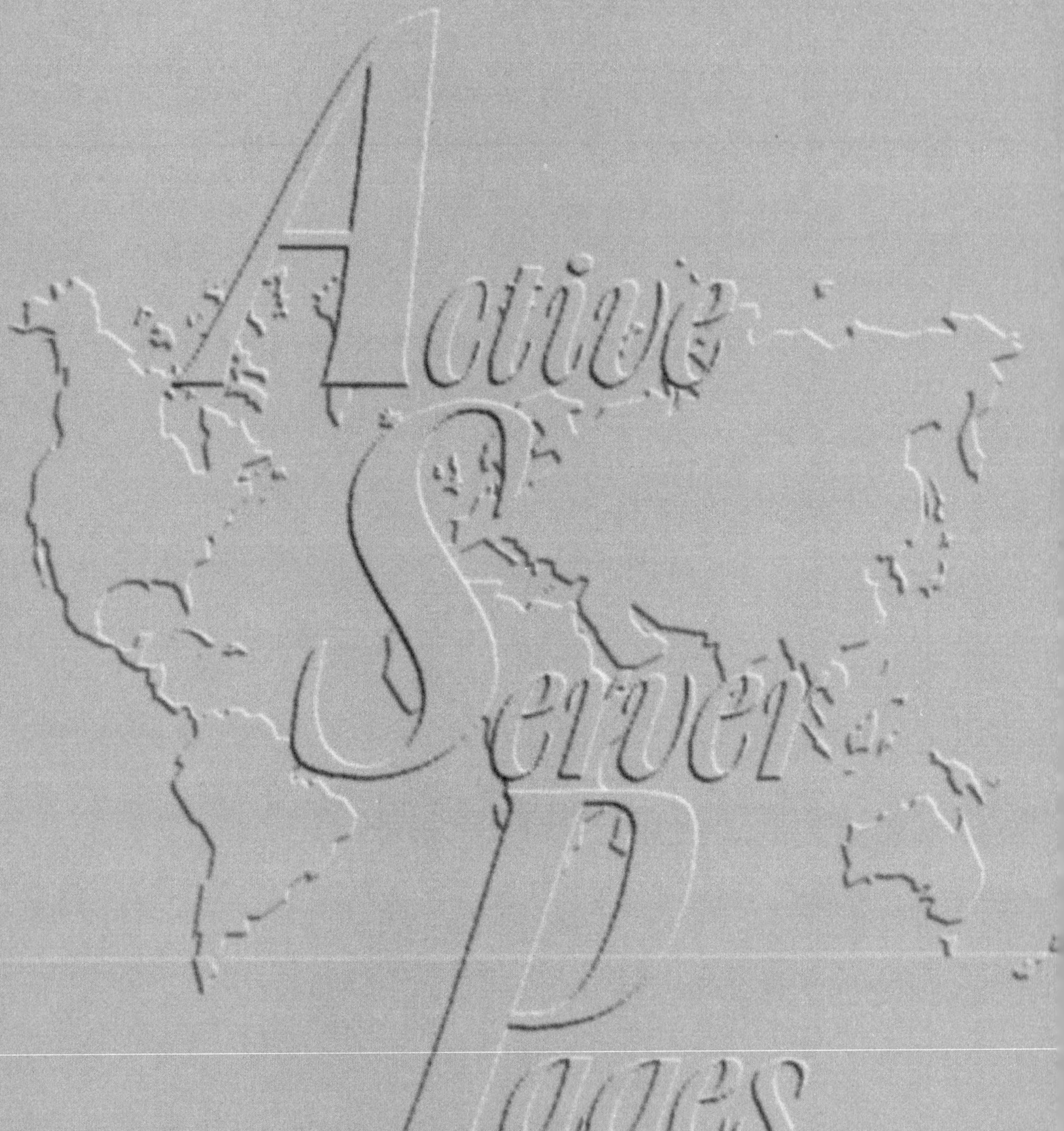
Active
Server
Pages

Creating a System Data Source Name

To use **Internet Database Connector** (IDC), **dbWeb**, or **ActiveX Server Scripts** on Internet Information Server (IIS), you need to set up access to the data source by providing the correct **System Data Source Name** (System DSN).

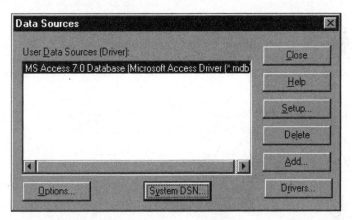

Launch the ODBC Administrator program by double-clicking on its icon in Window's Control Panel. The Data Sources dialog shows a list of the currently installed ODBC drivers. Here, we're using an Access database, so we select the Microsoft Access Driver (***.mdb**) entry from the list. If you're using a different database system, you'll need to select the appropriate ODBC driver. If an entry for it isn't present, you will need to install the driver from your original setup disk, or a disk provided by the database vendor.

We're going to set up a system **Data Source Name (DSN)** which will allow our database to be accessed by (potentially) all users on the network. Clicking on the System DSN button displays the System Data Sources window that lists all of the system DSNs that are currently installed.

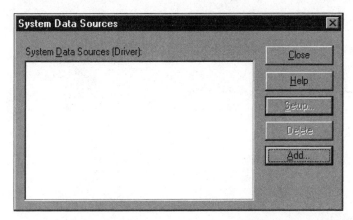

▲ To set up a new system DSN, click on the Add button to show the Add Data Source window. We want to create an Access system DSN, so we've selected the Microsoft Access driver from the list.

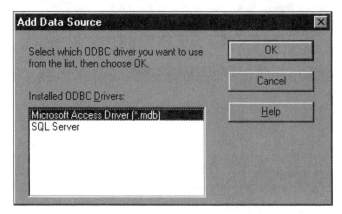

▲ Click OK to open the ODBC Microsoft Access 7.0 Setup dialog. We now have to enter the name of the data source. This will be the name that our ASP scripts will use as the **Datasource** parameter, and can also be used for ODBC connections in OLE Automation servers. We also select the path where our database resides—either by typing it in directly, or clicking the Select button. Because we're using an Access database, we have the opportunity to repair and compact the database as well. We can also specify a workgroup (**system.mdw**) database, to restrict user access if this is required.

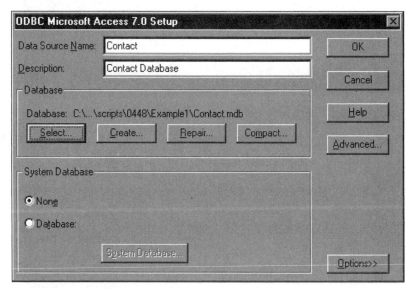

If you're using a different type of data source, such as SQL Server, you'll see a different Setup dialog. You'll need to supply extra details to access the database, such as the server name and network address.

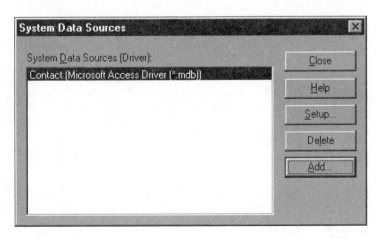

ODBC SQL Server Setup

Data Source Name:	Contact
Description:	Contacts Database
Server:	(local)
Network Address:	(Default)
Network Library:	(Default)

Login
Database Name: contact
Language Name: (Default)
☑ Generate Stored Procedure for Prepared Statement

Translation
☑ Convert OEM to ANSI characters

OK   Cancel   Help   Options >>   Select...

When you've entered all the details, click on OK to return to the System Data Sources screen again. The new System DSN will be shown, and is ready for use.

System Data Sources

System Data Sources (Driver):
Contact (Microsoft Access Driver (*.mdb))

Close
Help
Setup...
Delete
Add...

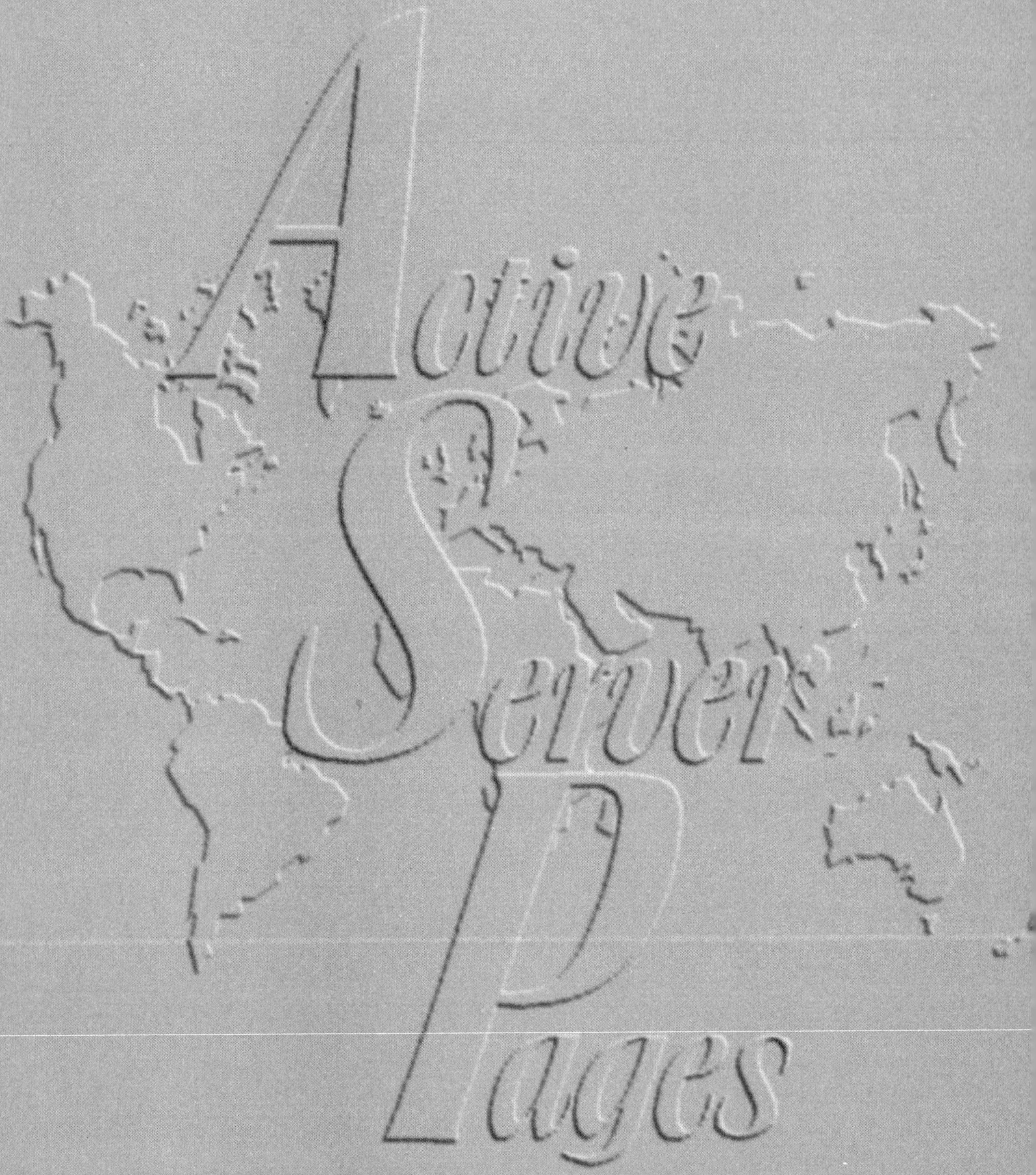
Active
Server
Pages

Variable	Meaning
AUTH_TYPE	User authorization type. **Basic** if the username is authenticated by the server, otherwise omitted.
CONTENT_LENGTH	Number of bytes being sent by the client.
CONTENT_TYPE	Content type when the request is of type **POST**.
DOCUMENT	Current document file name.
DOCUMENT_URI	Virtual path to the current document.
DATE_GMT	Current date, GMT. Can be formatted using **#CONFIG** directive.
DATE_LOCAL	Current date, local. Can be formatted using **#CONFIG** directive.
GATEWAY_INTERFACE	CGI specification of the gateway.
LAST_MODIFIED	Last edit date of the document.
LOGON_USER	Windows NT account details for the user.
PATH_INFO	Additional path information as supplied by client—i.e. the part of the URL after the script name but before any query string.
PATH_TRANSLATED	Value of **PATH_INFO** with any virtual path converted to a physical directory name.
QUERY_STRING	Information following the question mark (**?**) in the URL string.
QUERY_STRING_UNESCAPED	Un-escaped version of the query string.
REMOTE_ADDR	IP address of the client.
REMOTE_HOST	Hostname of the client.
REMOTE_IDENT	Hostname of the client if it supports RFC931 identification.
REMOTE_USER	Client's user name, as authenticated by the server.
SCRIPT_NAME	Name of the script or application to be executed.
SERVER_NAME	Hostname or IP address of server for self-referencing URLs.
SERVER_PORT	TCP/IP port which received the request.
SERVER_PORT_SECURE	Value of **1** indicates the request is on an encrypted port.
SERVER_PROTOCOL	Protocol name and version, usually **HTTP/1.0**.
SERVER_SOFTWARE	Name and version of the web server software.

Table Continued on Following Page

All other HTTP header information, which isn't parsed into one of the variables listed above, can be obtained using the form **HTTP_<*fieldname*>**, for example:

HTTP_ACCEPT	List of the **MIME** data types that the browser can accept. Values of the HTTP header **ACCEPT** fields are separated by commas in the **HTTP_ACCEPT** variable, i.e.:
	ACCEPT: */*; q=0.1
	ACCEPT: text/html
	ACCEPT: image/jpeg
	produces the value in **HTTP_ACCEPT** of:
	/; q=0.1, text/html, image/jpeg
HTTP_ACCEPT_LANGUAGE	List of the human languages that the client can accept.
HTTP_USER_AGENT	Product name of the client's browser software.
HTTP_REFERER	URL of the page containing the link used to get to this page.
HTTP_COOOKIE	Cookie sent from the client's browser.

#CONFIG Variable Formatting Tokens

Token	Description	Token	Description
%W	**Week** of the year (with Monday as first day of the week) as **00** to **51**.	%U	**Week** of the year (with Sunday as first day of the week) as **00** to **51**.
%a	**Weekday** name as **Mon**, **Tue**, etc.	%A	**Weekday** name in full.
%w	**Weekday** as **0** to **6**, **Sunday = 0**.	%m	**Month** as **01** to **12**.
%b	**Month** name as **Jan**, **Feb**, etc.	%B	**Month** name in full.
%j	**Day** of the year as **001** to **366**.	%d	**Day** of the month as **01** to **31**.
%y	**Year** as **00** to **99**.	%Y	**Year** as **1980** to **2099**.
%x	**Date** as appropriate for the locale.	%X	**Time** as appropriate for the locale.
%c	**Date/Time** appropriate for the locale.	%z,%Z	**Time-zone** name or abbreviation.
%H	**Hour** in 24-hour format **00** to **23**.	%I	**Hour** in 12-hour format **01** to **12**.
%M	**Minute** as **00** to **59**.	%S	**Second** as **00** to **59**.
%p	**A.M.** or **P.M.** indicator.	%%	**Percent** sign.

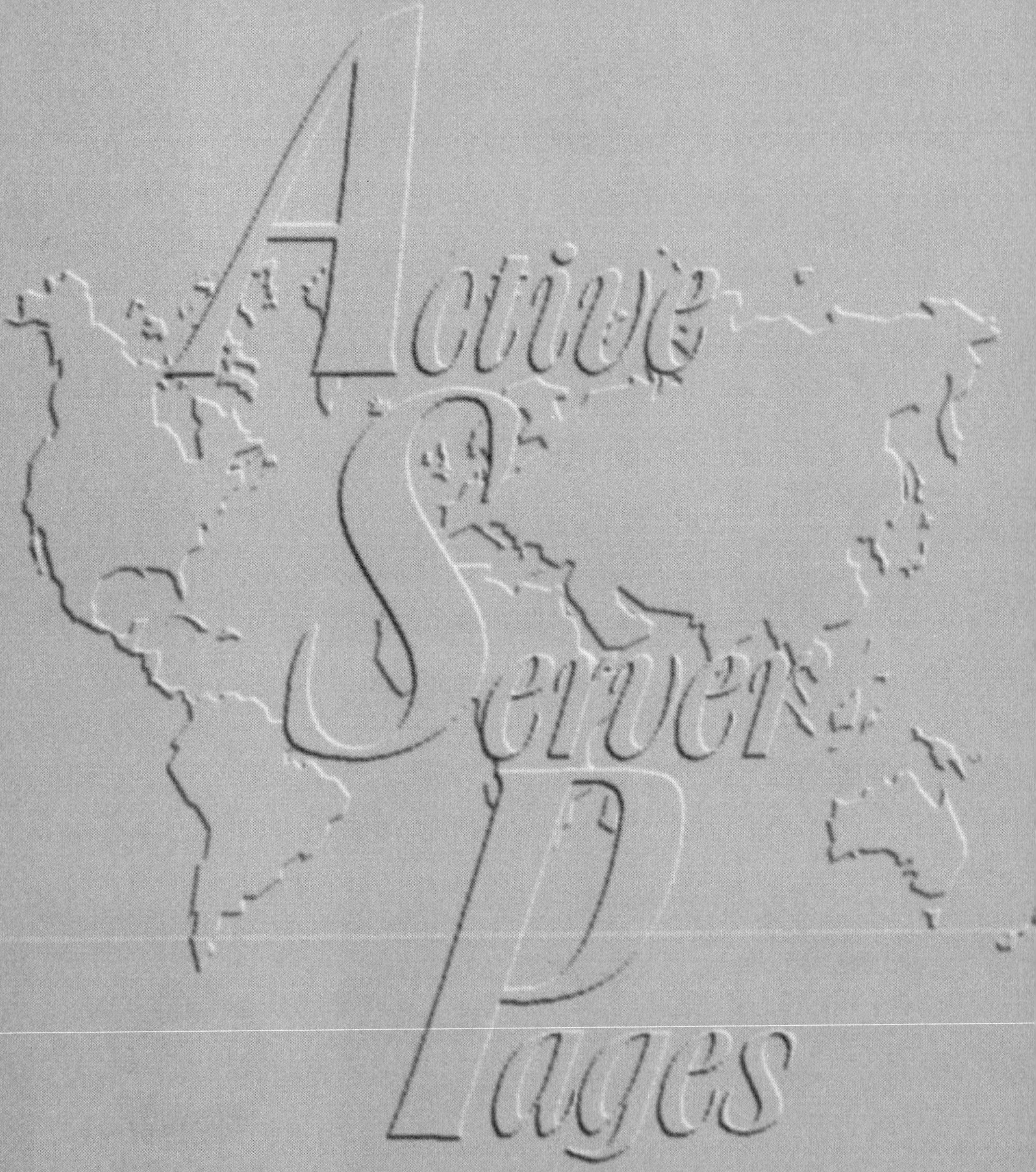
Active
Server
Pages

URL Encoding
Character Translations

Un-encoded character	URL-encoded equivalent
space	+
~	%7E
!	%21
#	%23
$	%24
%	%25
^	%5E
&	%26
(	%28
)	%29
+	%2B
=	%3D
[	%5B
{	%7B

Un-encoded character	URL-encoded equivalent
]	%5D
}	%7D
\	%5C
|	%7C
`	%60
'	%27
:	%3A
;	%3B
/	%2F
<	%3C
>	%3E
Chr(13)	%0D
Chr(10)	*ignored*

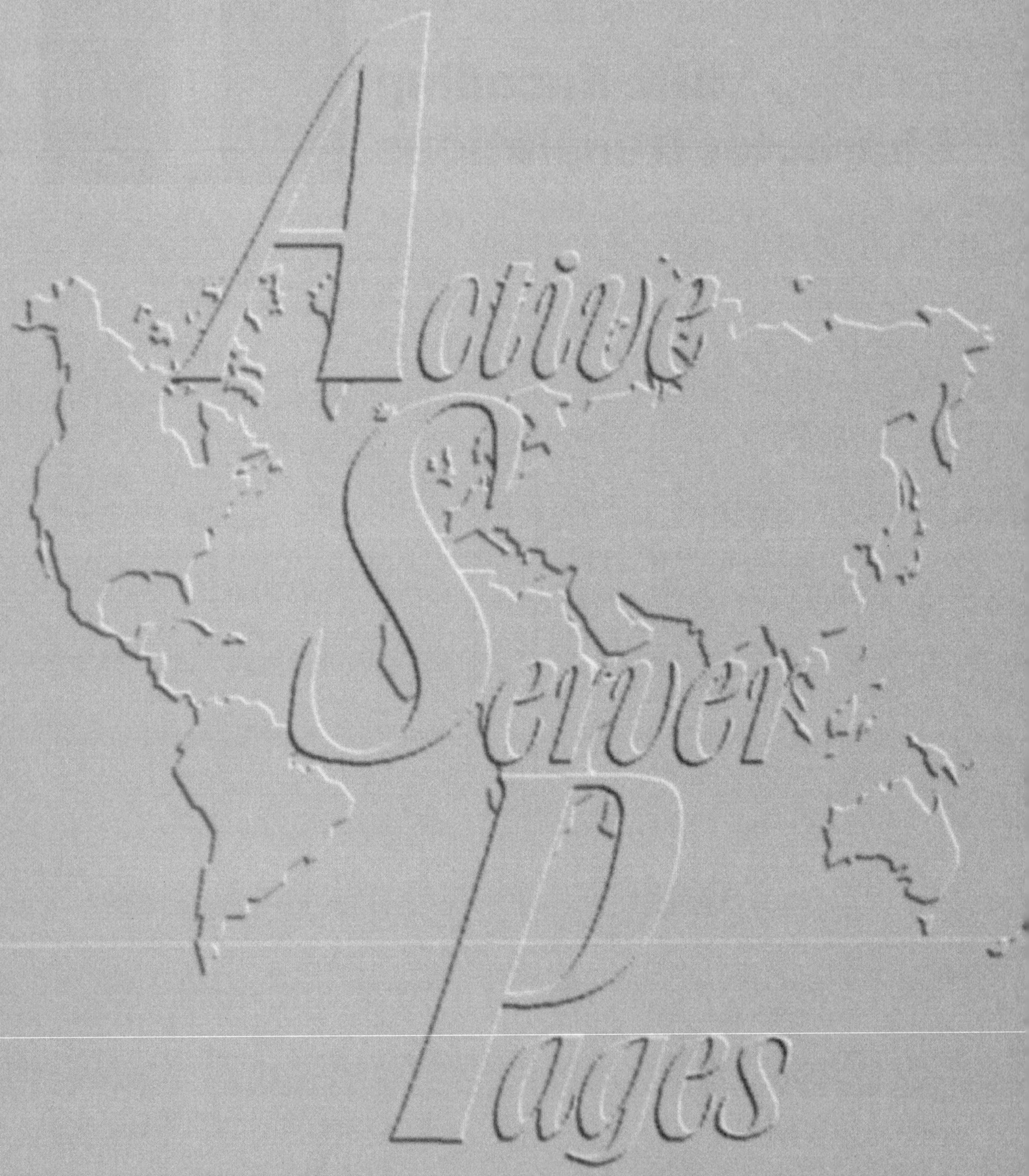
Active
Server
Pages

ADO and OLE-DB in the Real World

So far in this book we've been guilty of being more than a little Microsoft-centric. However we are the first to recognize that there are lot of data sources out there in the real world that are not conveniently contained in either Access or SQL Server. For ASP to be really useful as a universal data hub it needs to be able to access all the data available on a network.

OLE-DB is a new interface from Microsoft that provides the glue to connect a myriad of real world data formats to ADO, and from there making it easily accessible from ASP scripts. OLE-DB is a new beast, so we've asked one of the pioneers, ISG, to give us an overview of what OLE-DB is and how it works, and to explain how they themselves are using it.

OLE-DB is a very wide spectrum interface to databases that isn't restricted to the perceived database norm of Relational and SQL.

The OLE-DB Data Model

A **data model** reflects a world view of how data is used. It includes certain elements for representing data (such as databases, tables, records, indexes, fields, data types, etc.) plus an exhaustive list of the various methods for accessing or changing data. The OLE-DB model is meant to apply to a very wide variety of data sources, including many not commonly thought of as 'databases'.

The reason for including diverse data sources under a common umbrella is the possibility of defining common methods on them, and then plugging the different objects into a complex process (such as a query processor). This process can then transparently call the common methods recognized by each object. OLE-DB specifies the methods that a data source object can implement.

Objects, Interfaces and Methods

OLE-DB exposes object types to the client application—**Data Source** objects, **Rowset** objects, **Command** objects and others. All objects of the same type have the same defined interfaces. **Data Source** objects, for example, may represent data sources as diverse as relational and hierarchical database management systems, indexed and flat file systems, electronic mail systems, spreadsheets and many more. OLE-DB defines a set of uniform interfaces for all object types.

The implementation of a method may vary among objects of the same type. The execution of an SQL query, for example, may be different for Oracle and Sybase objects. Some objects might not support all the OLE-DB methods defined for a given type of object. For example, one interface deals with indexes. A particular data source object might not support indexes and therefore will not support this interface.

Methods Common to All Objects

All objects, regardless of their type, support common interfaces. These contain general object management methods such as `QueryInterface` (returns handles to other interfaces exposed by this object), `GetProperties` and `SetProperties` (properties are scalar-valued and identified by globally unique identifiers), and `GetErrorInfo` (returns extended error information for the last method on this object).

Data Source objects

A `Data Source` object (DSO) is a generalization of a database. This is the initial object you instantiate by calling `CoCreateInstance`, or binding to a moniker. Once you obtain a DSO you can create a `DBSession` object by calling `CreateSession`. You can only create and/or execute `Command` objects within a `DBSession` object, through which you execute queries to obtain result `Rowsets` with the data you want. Transactions similarly must occur within a single `DBSession` object.

In the OLE-DB model, any data provider whose data can be viewed as consisting of rows and columns can implement a `Data Source` object and participate to a greater or lesser extent in OLE-DB. More generally, a `Data Source` object is a container; it can store tables, views, procedure definitions, or even other `Data Source` objects. This would be the case, for instance, for a database server that contains a variety of databases.

Methods for Contained Data Source Objects

`GetSourcesRowset` returns a list of `Data Source` objects contained in a container object. Like all variable-length metadata in OLE-DB, this list is returned in the form of a `Rowset` object—an instantiated `Rowset` with one row of information per contained `Data Source` object. This information includes binding name, class information, a 'moniker' required for the connect handshaking process, etc.

`BindToMoniker` requests that a connection be established with a contained `Data Source`. The method returns a handle of the instantiated `Data Source` object.

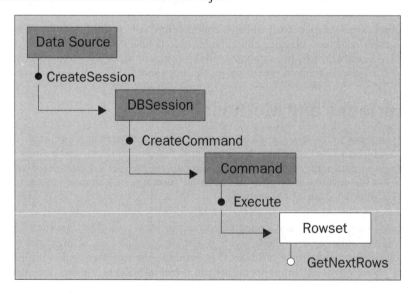

Note that data source objects (such as databases) which aren't containers for other Data Source objects will not implement this interface.

> *In ISG Navigator, the **Object Manager** implements these methods. Note that, although these are standard OLE methods, ISG Navigator implements them on non-OLE platforms as well. Other implementations may be based on various system services such as NT/OLE Registries.*

Methods For Working With Other Contained Objects

`OpenRowset` opens a table (i.e. a stored named `Rowset` object) and returns a `Rowset` object.

`CreateCommand` called on a `DBSession` object, instantiates a new `Command` object with an initially empty definition. This command can then be assigned a definition, saved, executed, etc.

`Load` activates a `Command` for a previously saved query definition (i.e. a stored procedure) for editing or execution

`Save` is an OLE method that makes it possible to persistently save a command's query definition, in its compiled and optimized form, and persistently save the `Rowset` resulting from executing a command. These saved objects can subsequently be referenced in other commands.

Rowset Objects

A `Rowset` is an abstraction of the use of a collection of data rows. Users can obtain a `Rowset`, for example, by opening a base table or executing a command. `Rowsets` are also used for collections of metadata. Thus a user can obtain a `Rowset` on the columns of a table or a query (one row of information for each column of the original table or query), or on the contents of a `Data Source` (one row of information per contained object). A particular table may have multiple `Rowsets` open on it. `Rowsets` are used primarily for reading or modifying data.

Mapping a Data Buffer, or 'Binding Columns'

When fetching data from a `Rowset`, all of the specified column values from a row are fetched at the same time. The mapping of desired columns into a buffer is specified via a template called a `ColumnBinding`. For each specified column a `ColumnBinding` (using a `DBBINDING` structure) describes:

- Displacement from the start of the buffer.
- Amount of space allocated for the value.
- Desired data type (which may be different from the 'native' data type within the storage medium).
- Displacement of this column's indicator field, used (among other things) to indicate a 'null' value.

You specify the `ColumnBindings` for a `Rowset` using an `Accessor`, which consists of one or more `ColumnBindings` for the columns you want to fetch to the buffer. `Accessors` are created with the `CreateAccessor` method, which takes as input the number of columns for the `Accessor`, an array of `DBBINDING` structures (one for each column), and various flags describing the properties of the `Accessor`. Subsequent fetch operations will return rows built according to the buffer template defined by `CreateAccessor`. The `GetBindings` method reads the current binding for this `Rowset`.

In addition to 'real' columns, some pseudocolumns may also be included in the binding. The most important pseudocolumn defined in OLE-DB is a bookmark: a unique row identifier which is at least as persistent as the **Rowset** object itself, and which allows efficient random access to this row. Bookmarks are implementor-defined, and not every **Rowset** needs to support this concept. Examples of bookmarks include: a database key, a relative record number, a primary key and a memory buffer address.

Fetching and Reading Data

After obtaining the **Rowset** object, you can fetch rows of data into a cache, which is internal to the data source implementation. For each row fetched, you get back a row handle. Rows are typically fetched to the buffer with the **GetNextRows** method, which takes as input the count of rows to fetch to the buffer and a pointer to memory for the array of row handles.

After you've created an **Accessor** and fetched rows from the provider, you can read the data for one row with the **GetData** method. As input to this method you specify the handle of the row to retrieve, the handle of the **Accessor** to use in retrieving the row, and the buffer where the data is returned. **GetData** casts the data to the data type specified by the binding.

Modifying Data

Rows which have been accessed, and therefore have a row handle, can be modified using the **SetData** method with an **Accessor** and a row handle. One or more rows can be deleted using the **DeleteRows** method and specifying the row handles. New rows can be inserted using **InsertRow** and specifying an **Accessor**; a row handle for the new row is returned.

OLE-DB has an optional three-tier 'deferred update' capability. The above operations operate only on the **Rowset** cache, and are not transferred, even temporarily, to the permanent storage. They also are not visible outside the updating context regardless of the 'isolation levels' of other concurrent users or tasks. The changes can still be canceled using the **Undo** method, without reference to transactions. The update can be transferred to permanent storage using the **Update** method, where it is potentially visible to other users. Finally, if there's a current transaction context, the entire transaction may be committed or aborted.

Releasing the Rows, Accessors, and Rowset

When an application is done reading a row, it should release it and so free resources from the **Rowset**'s data cache. The application can then resume its cycle of retrieving rows and accessing the data they contain. You release rows by calling **ReleaseRows**, which takes as input the number of rows to release and an array of handles to these rows. The **Accessors** must also be released, as well as (eventually) the **Rowset** object itself. Releasing the **Accessor** is done with the **ReleaseAccessor** method. To release the **Rowset** object you call **Release** on each of the interfaces that have been obtained on the **Rowset**.

Handling Metadata

As mentioned earlier in connection with the **GetSourcesRowset** method on **Data Source** objects, metadata, or information about data, is returned mostly in the form of **Rowsets**, each row containing information about the entity in question. Information from these **Rowsets** is read in the normal way: specifying an **Accessor** for the columns of interest, and then fetching the data into a buffer using **GetNextRows** and **GetData**.

The **GetSchemaRowset** method returns **Rowsets** of metadata about tables, columns, stored procedures, indexes and other entities. A subset of the same information about columns can be obtained more compactly and conveniently using the **GetColumnsInfo** method on **Rowsets** or **Command** objects.

Handling Indexes

An index is a special `Rowset` that defines a key-based ordering on another `Rowset`. An `Index` contains a set of columns that form the key, plus a column that contains the bookmark of the corresponding row in the main `Rowset`. The index is physically ordered on the key, so that main `Rowset` rows can be fetched in the desired order by fetching the index `Rowset` rows, accessing the bookmark, and then fetching the main row.

Index `Rowset`s support several additional methods in addition to those supported by every `Rowset`. `GetIndexInfo` returns information about the index key. `Seek` allows rapid positioning within the index `Rowset` based on a full or partial key value. `SetRange` sets lower and upper bounds for the values of the keys visible in the `Rowset` for the `Seek` and `GetNextRows` methods.

Refreshing Data

`ReQuery` requests the data provider to bring fresh data associated with this `Rowset`. This method has several effects:

- ▲ If any data had been cached, the caches are discarded.
- ▲ The `Rowset` is repositioned at the start of the `Rowset`.
- ▲ If the `Rowset` was the result of executing a command, the command is executed again—possibly producing a completely different result set this time. This may happen if the command is parameterized, and a different set of parameter values is now supplied to the `ReQuery` method.

Command Objects

A `Command` is an activation of a command specification, typically a query. A `Command` may be thought of as an SQL-like text string. OLE-DB also supports a tree form of specifying commands, which we won't discuss here. The semantics of what the text means are implementor-defined for each data provider.

A `Command` object is instantiated when `CreateCommand` is called on a data source object. A `Command` may be edited using the `SetCommandText` method.

Every `Command` object must support the `Execute` method. In the case of an SQL Select statement, or its equivalent, this method returns the result as a `Rowset`. A variety of execution modes for the command may be requested, such as updateable, scrollable result, dynaset and so on. An implicit part of the `Command` object is the executable form of the query, which may be reused at the discretion of the method implementor. `Execute` allows you to specify values for the `Command`'s parameters prior to execution. `GetParameterInfo` interrogates the `Command` object about its expected parameters and their current values.

When `Execute` returns a `Rowset` object, this `Rowset` is detached from the 'parent' `Command` and is unaffected by subsequent operations such as `SetCommandText`. If `ReQuery` is subsequently issued to the `Rowset` object, it is the original query specification that is executed again.

The Active Data Objects (ADO)

This new product by Microsoft simplifies the writing of applications that access and manipulate data through OLE-DB data sources. ADO has a simpler object model than OLE-DB. The primary types of ADO object are:

     `Connection` objects

     `Command` objects

    `Recordset` objects

ADO Connection Object

A `Connection` object represents a unique session with a data source. In OLE-DB terms, a `Connection` object is a `DBSession` obtained on an initialized DSO. A `Connection` object, like an OLE-DB `DBSession`, lets users manage transactions and execute commands.

ADO Command Object

A `Command` object is equivalent to an OLE-DB `Command`: both objects contain a specific definition of a command the user wants to execute.

ADO Recordset Object

A `Recordset` object represents the entire set of records from a base table or the results of an executed command. A `Recordset` object is equivalent to an OLE-DB `Rowset`.

Using ADO

ADO presents a higher-level view of data than does OLE-DB, and is therefore far easier for programmers to use. Many new Microsoft development tools use ADO for accessing data: Active Server Pages (ASP), Visual Basic, VBScript, Visual J++, JavaScript. ADO is not limited to Microsoft products; any development tool, (such as Borland's Delphi, for example) that can access Active X components can readily use ADO.

Embedded Rowsets and Arrays

Columns in a `Rowset` can contain other embedded `Rowset`s, called chapters. A `Rowset` with such columns is called a **chaptered `Rowset`**. To access rows in the child `Rowset`, a chapter identifier must be supplied; this identifier is obtained from the parent row as a 'value' for this column. A `Rowset` may have several different chapter-valued columns, and the embedded `Rowset`s may themselves have child `Rowset`s.

`Chaptered Rowset`s support 'drill-down' operations and are much more economical and convenient to use than equivalent relational 'normalized' flat files if the embedded `Rowset`s are accessed selectively. `Chaptered Rowset`s are obtained, for example, when the backend source data is already hierarchical, as may be the case for IMS child segments or Adabas repeating groups.

A column may also contain an array of scalars of any type. Such arrays are generally assumed to be small and to be physically stored with the rest of the row data. Large arrays are better modeled as embedded `Rowset`s with a single column.

BLOBs and Other OLE Objects as Column 'Values'

Column values may also consist of BLOBs (large binary byte streams) or of arbitrary OLE objects. The binding to such objects is deferred: when a row is fetched into a cache, the contained complex object is not yet accessed. When specifying an **Accessor** that includes such columns, the user also specifies the desired interface on this object. For example, for a BLOB object a user would request the **IStream** interface. **IStream** includes such methods as **Read** (get a specified number of bytes at the current byte position in the stream), **Write** (which rewrites part of the current stream or extends it) and **Seek** (positions at a specified byte offset from the start of the stream).

When the user accesses the row value (**GetData** method) using this **Accessor**, an interface pointer for this instance of the object is returned which they get as the column 'value'. The object data is first accessed only when the actual method of this interface (e.g. **Read**) is called.

Hierarchical Queries

A command that produces a **chaptered Rowset** is called **hierarchical**.

Assume, for example, a normal relational table **Emp** with columns **Name**, **Dept**, **Job**, **Salary** and **Manager**. The following hierarchical query returns a **Rowset,** one row per manager, with columns **Name**, **Dept** and a column called **Staff.** This 'contains' all of the people who directly report to this manager, with their names, salaries and job descriptions:

```
Select A.Name, A.Dept { Select B.Name, B.Salary, B.Job From Emp B
Where B.Manager = A.Name } AS Reports From Emp A
```

Note that unlike 'normalized' representations, we only have one main-table row per manager. When the complex object in **Staff** is opened for a particular manager, we get a **Rowset** that lists all of the employees who report to this manager together with their salaries and their job descriptions.

OLE-DB in Action - ISG Navigator

The introduction of the OLE-DB and ADO models by Microsoft has made possible the construction of an industry standard, universal data access middleware. One of the first to appear, ISG Navigator, makes it easy for the ASP programmer to access a huge variety of data sources on various platforms, with high performance, low communication cost and a high degree of operational simplicity. In addition to common relational databases, it provides access to, and integration with, data sources that were previously out of reach because of format or location:

- ▲ Data sources such as hierarchical databases, indexed sequential files, simple files, personal databases, spreadsheets, mail folders and more–all through a uniform OLE-DB interface.

- ▲ Local and remote data on different platforms and across the Internet.

What ISG Navigator Provides

ISG Navigator includes a sophisticated distributed query processor and optimizer to boost performance in heterogeneous and non-relational environments. The query processor not only enables you to join data from multiple, local and remote sources, but also compensates for functionality not available in the native data source, particularly through its support of SQL queries on data sources without query capabilities.

It allows applications to access and manipulate hierarchical and other non-flat-file data using extended SQL, while preserving the levels of detailed information needed for efficient drill-down operations.

ISG Navigator, itself playing the role of an OLE-DB provider, implements a Query Processor that supports and extends ANSI SQL 92. In addition, it extends standard SQL to enable users to generate chaptered **Rowsets**.

The components it uses are distributed across the enterprise network on multiple platforms and communicate with each other by efficient built-in, object-oriented communication links, allowing true enterprise deployment. Therefore, it's ideally suited for implementing multi-tier and Internet applications that require efficient access to heterogeneous data sources.

Technical Overview

ISG Navigator provides a data access tier that buffers the application from the native interface of the data source, the location of the data source, and the data model. To the client application, it presents a single consistent interface and data model, regardless of the type and number of data sources.

It contains a query processor and optimizer that, by virtue of its distributed architecture, performs joins and filtering as close as possible to the physical location of the data. ISG Navigator employs a cost-based optimization algorithm that is tuned to minimize network traffic and to use the processing power of database servers to optimize application performance.

The components can be installed on one machine (client or server) or can be distributed throughout the network in a multi-tier architecture. In the latter case, they interact to provide optimal performance and minimal communication traffic.

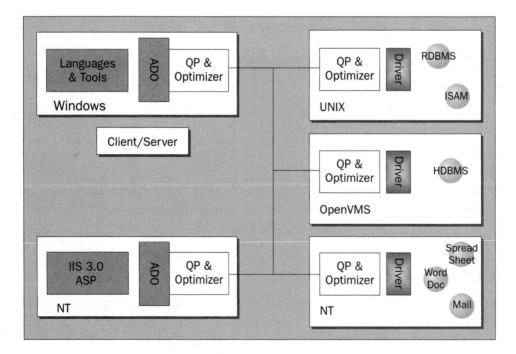

ISG Navigator is object-oriented. All data sources are objects that expose interfaces strictly defined by the OLE-DB model. The implementations of these interfaces may differ among the objects, but the user always sees a uniform and consistent interface. The objects are database information processing agents (for retrieval, update and analysis) which provide direct and easy access to their functions through operations called methods. These methods are logically grouped into interfaces. An ISG Navigator object can 'live' anywhere—within the same process space as a user application, in another process on the same machine, or as a server on another machine.

ISG Navigator's object orientation is based on Microsoft's Component Object Model. Where COM and Distributed COM aren't available on various platforms, a supplied object manager that provides DCOM-like connectivity services to objects can be used instead

The Environments Supported

ISG Navigator supports a broad base of platforms:

HP-UX	IBM-AIX	Alpha UNIX
SUN-Solaris	Alpha OpenVMS	IBM-MVS
DEC OpenVMS		

ISG Navigator supports a wide range of databases:

Oracle	RMS	IMS/DB*
Sybase	Rdb	VSAM*
Informix	Adabas*	C-ISAM
CA-Ingres	DB2	MUMPS*
SQL Server	DBMS	

* Planned

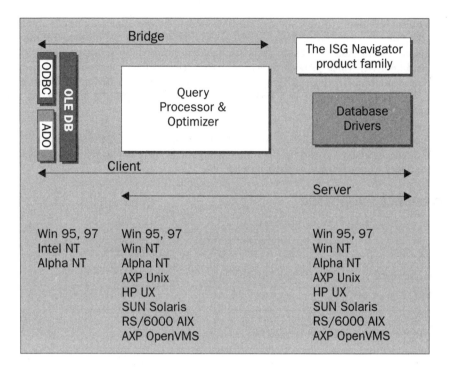

The ISG Navigator Architecture

In its fullest configuration, ISG Navigator includes the following components: an object manager, a query processor and optimizer, a local data store, database drivers, a client proxy and a server stub.

ISG Navigator components can be resident on a single system or distributed across a variety of platforms that operate as either clients or servers or a combination of the two.

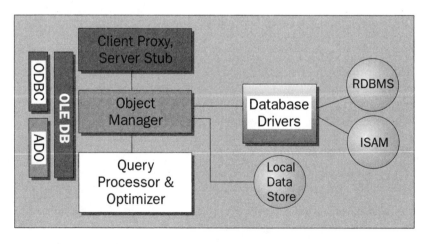

Object Manager

The object manager instantiates Data Source objects and (on non-OLE platforms) processes OLE-DB method calls. Hence it is a required component of every ISG Navigator site. Every object, once instantiated, comes equipped with arrays of pointers to its implementations of the supported methods. On any method call, the object manager invokes the implementation specified by the object. If the object and its implementations are remote or out-of-process, the object manager invokes a local proxy for this method which, using the server stub, eventually calls the object manager at the site local to the object. When the object is within the process address space, the subroutine jump to the method's implementation is very fast, involving overhead of at most a few instructions.

Interfaces

Applications interact with the object manager through interfaces. The native interface to ISG Navigator is OLE-DB. Applications can access it either directly with OLE-DB calls, or indirectly though Microsoft's ADO. The latter is simpler to use since ADO is a higher level interface than OLE-DB. Alternatively, applications can access ISG Navigator through ODBC calls, which are translated by the ODBC Interface to equivalent OLE-DB calls.

All three interfaces are available on Windows 95 and NT platforms. Support for OLE-DB and ADO interfaces on Unix, OpenVMS, and other server platforms will be available in the future.

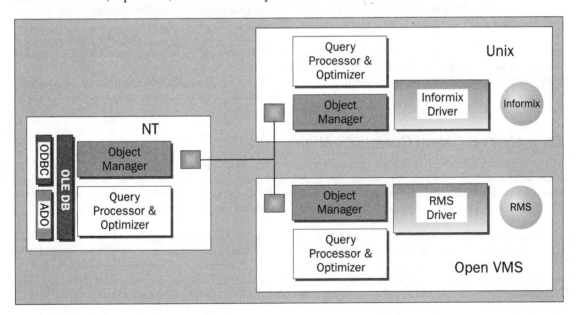

Query Processor and Optimizer

The query processor and optimizer are central to the efficient operation of ISG Navigator. Every query directed to the query processor object is parsed, analyzed and optimized, and an execution plan is initiated. If a query can be sent to a relational database system (local or remote) for execution, this is always the approach selected: the optimizer assumes it can't execute queries more efficiently than the native database system. If, however, tables from several RDBMSs or from non-relational systems are involved, the query processor decides which joins will be executed where and performs local joins and other operations accordingly.

The optimizer is cost-based. It uses statistics on table and index sizes and communications costs and is oriented toward minimizing network traffic; the optimizer utilizes a variety of access strategies making extensive use of locally caching remote data. The query processor also compensates for functionality not available in the native database systems, particularly in its ability to execute hierarchical queries and in rich rowset support.

Local Data Store

The local data store provides a conventional B-tree indexed-table capability, and important temporary-table support–which is used by the query processor to implement scrollable rowsets and data caching strategies. Temporary tables, when reasonably small, stay entirely memory-resident and are organized for efficient searches. If a table overflows its allocated buffer, it is written to the disk and accessed just like any other ISAM file. The local data store is also available to client application programs, since it implements OLE-DB interfaces, thus providing a complete development environment without the need for a back-end database.

Database Drivers

The database drivers map the particular data source functionality into OLE-DB. A typical driver may only need to implement a small subset of the defined OLE-DB methods. For example, a particular data source might not support indexes, and therefore its driver will not implement index-related methods. The client application can interrogate any object for its support of a specific interface. The ISG Navigator query processor and other components implement most of the defined OLE-DB interfaces.

Drivers are always local to the native data source. If ISG Navigator needs to access a data source on a remote computer, it does so through its local Client proxy, which, using the remote Server stub and the object manager on that computer, passes the request to the proper driver. Thus the architecture is always multi-tier. This enables it to optimize network data access and incidentally obviates the need for multiple database-specific network products provided by the vendors.

Client-Server Object Communication

The architecture described in this section applies to 'remote' objects, not accessed via OLE DCOM. When DCOM is used to access a remote object, this is entirely transparent to ISG Navigator, to whom the object seems local. The ISG Client-Server is used when either the Client or the Server is on a non-OLE platform. The two modes of remote object communication can coexist side by side on the same system.

ISG Navigator doesn't distinguish between 'client' and 'server' machines. This distinction is determined only by usage, and by which software components are present. A minimal configuration on a client machine might include only the object manager and the Client proxy. A minimal configuration on a 'data source' machine might include only one database driver, the object manager and the Server stub. Several full ISG Navigator servers, distinguished only by the data sources locally accessible from each, may be present in the network.

Summary

You can see ADO and Navigator at work at: `http://www.isgsoft.com/navdemo`. Here, full SQL queries can be created to access multiple data sources from multiple platforms, and you can view the query source code. This is an example of full ADO/ASP at work.

Alternatively, evaluation copies and other details are available from the ISG web site at `http://www.isgsoft.com`, or from the Microsoft and Digital's web sites.

Our thanks to ISG for supplying OLE-DB reference material for this appendix.

Active Server Pages

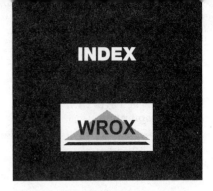
INDEX

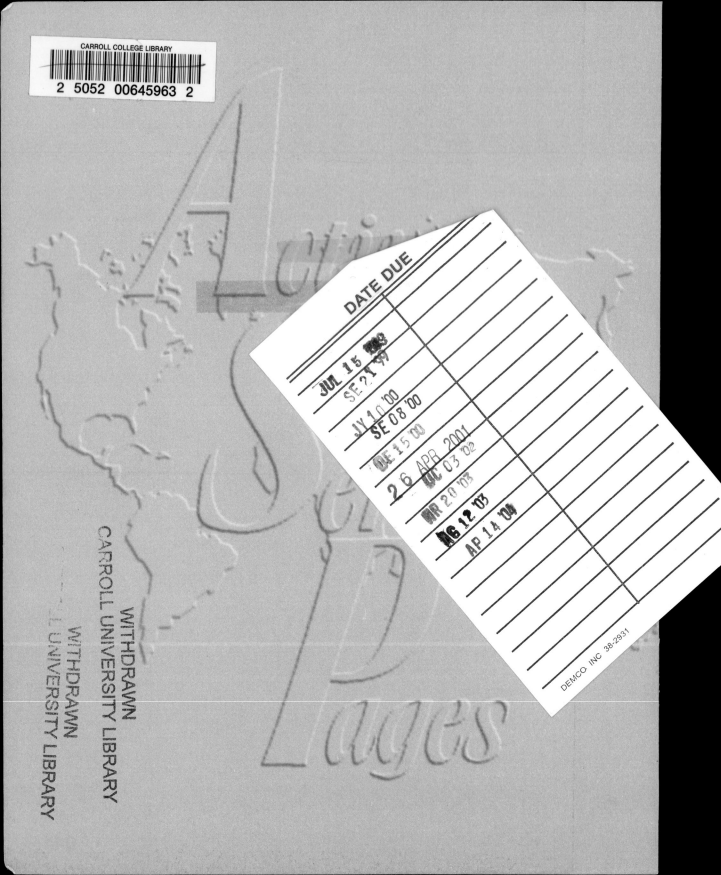

Register Professional Active Server Pages and sign up for a free subscription to The Developer's Journal.

A bi-monthly magazine for software developers, The Wrox Press Developer's Journal features in-depth articles, news and help for everyone in the software development industry. Each issue includes extracts from our latest titles and is crammed full of practical insights into coding techniques, tricks, and research.

Fill in and return the card below to receive a free subscription to the Wrox Press Developer's Journal.

Professional Active Server Pages Registration Card

Name _____

Address _____

_____

_____

City_____ State/Region _____

Country_____ Postcode/Zip _____

E-mail _____

Occupation _____

How did you hear about this book?_____

☐ Book review (name) _____

☐ Advertisement (name) _____

☐ Recommendation _____

☐ Catalog_____

☐ Other _____

Where did you buy this book?_____

☐ Bookstore (name)_____ City _____

☐ Computer Store (name)_____

☐ Mail Order_____

☐ Other_____

What influenced you in the purchase of this book?

☐ Cover Design

☐ Contents

☐ Other (please specify) _____

What did you find most useful about this book? _____

What did you find least useful about this book? _____

Please add any additional comments. _____

What other subjects will you buy a computer book on soon? _____

What is the best computer book you have used this year? _____

How did you rate the overall contents of this book?

☐ Excellent   ☐ Good

☐ Average   ☐ Poor

Note: This information will only be used to keep you updated about new Wrox Press titles and will not be used for any other purpose or passed to any other third party.

Check here if you DO NOT want a subscription to The Developer's Journal or further support for this book

WROX

WROX PRESS INC.

Wrox writes books for you. Any suggestions, or
ideas about how you want information given in
your ideal book will be studied by our team.
Your comments are always valued at Wrox.

Free phone in USA 800-USE-WROX
Fax (773) 465 4063

UK Tel. (0121) 706 6826   Fax   (0121) 706 2967

———— *Computer Book Publishers* ————

NB. If you post the bounce back card below in the UK, please send it to:
Wrox Press Ltd. 30 Lincoln Road, Birmingham, B27 6PA

NO POSTAGE
NECESSARY
IF MAILED
IN THE
UNITED STATES

BUSINESS REPLY MAIL
FIRST CLASS MAIL   PERMIT#64   LA VERGNE, TN

POSTAGE WILL BE PAID BY ADDRESSEE

**WROX PRESS
2710 WEST TOUHY AVE
CHICAGO IL 60645-9911**